AMNESTY INTERNATIONAL

Amnesty International is a global movement of more than 3 million supporters, members and activists who campaign for internationally recognized human rights to be respected and protected. Its vision is for every person to enjoy all of the human rights enshrined in the Universal Declaration of Human Rights and other international human rights standards.

Amnesty International's mission is to conduct research and take action to prevent and end grave abuses of all human rights – civil, political, social, cultural and economic. From freedom of expression and association to physical and mental integrity, from protection from discrimination to the right to housing – these rights are indivisible.

Amnesty International is funded mainly by its membership and public donations. No funds are sought or accepted from governments for investigating and campaigning against human rights abuses. Amnesty International is independent of any government, political ideology, economic interest or religion.

Amnesty International is a democratic movement whose major policy decisions are taken by representatives from all national sections at International Council meetings held every two years. The current members of the International Executive Committee, elected by the Council to carry out its decisions, are Bernard Sintobin (Belgium Flemish – International Treasurer), Guadalupe Rivas (Mexico – Vice-Chair), Julio Torales (Paraguay), Mwikali Nzioka Muthiani (Kenya), Nicole Bieske (Australia), Pietro Antonioli (Italy – Chair), Rune Arctander (Norway), Sandra S. Lutchman (Netherlands) and Zuzanna Kulinska (Poland).

United against injustice, we work together for human rights.

First published in 2013 by
Amnesty International Ltd
Peter Benenson House
1 Easton Street
London WC1X 0DW
United Kingdom

© Amnesty International 2013
Index: POL 10/001/2013

ISBN: 978-0-86210-480-1
ISSN: 0309-068X

A catalogue record for this book is available from the British Library.

Original language: English

Printed by
Artes Gráficas Enco S.L.
Calle de Luis I, 56 - 58
28031 Madrid
Spain

Printed on 100% recycled paper using vegetable-oil-based inks.

This report documents Amnesty International's work and concerns throughout the world during 2012. The absence of an entry in this report on a particular country or territory does not imply that no human rights violations of concern to Amnesty International have taken place there during the year. Nor is the length of a country entry any basis for a comparison of the extent and depth of Amnesty International's concerns in a country.

AMNESTY INTERNATIONAL REPORT 2013
THE STATE OF THE WORLD'S HUMAN RIGHTS

13

WITHDRAWN

This report covers the period
January to December 2012.

CONTENTS
ANNUAL REPORT
2013

ABBREVIATIONS

ASEAN	Association of Southeast Asian Nations
AU	African Union
CEDAW	UN Convention on the Elimination of All Forms of Discrimination against Women
CEDAW Committee	UN Committee on the Elimination of Discrimination against Women
CERD	International Convention on the Elimination of All Forms of Racial Discrimination
CERD Committee	UN Committee on the Elimination of Racial Discrimination
CIA	US Central Intelligence Agency
ECOWAS	Economic Community of West African States
EU	European Union
European Committee for the Prevention of Torture	European Committee for the Prevention of Torture and Inhuman or Degrading Treatment or Punishment
European Convention on Human Rights	(European) Convention for the Protection of Human Rights and Fundamental Freedoms
ICCPR	International Covenant on Civil and Political Rights
ICESCR	International Covenant on Economic, Social and Cultural Rights
ICRC	International Committee of the Red Cross
ILO	International Labour Organization
International Convention against enforced disappearance	International Convention for the Protection of All Persons from Enforced Disappearance
LGBTI	lesbian, gay, bisexual, transgender and intersex
NATO	North Atlantic Treaty Organization
NGO	non-governmental organization
OAS	Organization of American States
OSCE	Organization for Security and Co-operation in Europe
UK	United Kingdom
UN	United Nations
UN Convention against Torture	Convention against Torture and Other Cruel, Inhuman or Degrading Treatment or Punishment
UN Refugee Convention	Convention relating to the Status of Refugees
UN Special Rapporteur on freedom of expression	Special Rapporteur on the promotion and protection of the right to freedom of opinion and expression
UN Special Rapporteur on racism	Special Rapporteur on contemporary forms of racism, racial discrimination, xenophobia and related intolerance
UN Special Rapporteur on torture	Special Rapporteur on torture and other cruel, inhuman or degrading treatment or punishment
UN Special Rapporteur on violence against women	Special Rapporteur on violence against women, its causes and consequences
UNFPA	United Nations Population Fund
UNHCR, the UN refugee agency	Office of the United Nations High Commissioner for Refugees
UNICEF	United Nations Children's Fund
USA	United States of America
WHO	World Health Organization

PREFACE

"I NEVER IMAGINED THAT... TELLING THE TRUTH ABOUT WHAT WAS HAPPENING COULD MEAN WALKING THE LINE BETWEEN LIFE AND DEATH... MANY TIMES I'VE FELT AS THOUGH FEAR HAS SOAKED THROUGH TO MY BONES, BUT THE FEELING OF RESPONSIBILITY IS STRONGER"

Dina Meza, Honduran journalist, human rights defender and member of the Committee of Relatives of the Detained and Disappeared (COFADEH)

The *Amnesty International Report 2013* documents the state of human rights during 2012. The Foreword and the country-by-country survey of 159 individual countries and territories set out a global overview of human rights violations and abuses inflicted by those in power on those who stand in the way of their vested interests.

Human rights defenders, often themselves living in precarious situations, battled to break through the walls of silence and secrecy to challenge abusers. Through the courts, in the streets and online, they fought for their right to freedom of expression, their right to freedom from discrimination and their right to justice. Some paid a heavy price. In many countries, they faced vilification, imprisonment or violence. While governments paid lip service to their commitment to human rights, they continued to use national security and concerns about public security to justify violating those rights.

This report bears witness to the steadfast and rising clamour for justice. Regardless of frontiers and in defiance of the formidable forces ranged against them, women and men in every region stood up to demand respect for their rights and to proclaim their solidarity with fellow human beings facing repression, discrimination, violence and injustice. Their actions and words show that the human rights movement is growing ever strong and more deep-rooted, and that the hope it inspires in millions is a powerful force for change.

AMNESTY INTERNATIONAL REPORT 2013
PART ONE: FOREWORD

HUMAN RIGHTS KNOW NO BORDERS

Salil Shetty, Secretary General

"Injustice anywhere is a threat to justice everywhere. We are caught in an inescapable network of mutuality, tied in a single garment of destiny. Whatever affects one directly, affects all indirectly."

Martin Luther King Jr., "Letter from Birmingham Jail", 16 April 1963, USA

On 9 October 2012, 15-year-old Malala Yousafzai was shot in the head by Taliban gunmen in Pakistan. Her crime was to advocate the right to education for girls. Her medium was a blog. Like Mohamed Bouazizi, whose act in 2010 sparked widespread protests across the Middle East and North Africa, Malala's determination reached far beyond the borders of Pakistan. Human courage and suffering combined with the power of social media unbounded by borders has changed our understanding of the struggle for human rights, equality and justice, even as it has led to a perceptible shift in discourse around sovereignty and human rights.

People everywhere – at great personal risk – have taken to the streets as well as to the digital sphere to expose repression and violence by governments and other powerful actors. They have created a sense of international solidarity – through blogs, other social media and the traditional press to keep alive the memory of Mohamed and the dreams of Malala.

Such courage, coupled with the ability to communicate our profound hunger for freedom and justice and rights, has alarmed those in power. Soundbites of support for those protesting against oppression and discrimination stand in stark contrast to the actions of many governments cracking down on peaceful protests and trying desperately to control the digital sphere – not least by rebuilding their national borders in this sphere.

For what does it mean to those in power who hold tight to, and abuse the concept of, 'sovereignty', once they realize the potential power of the people to dismantle ruling structures, and to shine the spotlight on the tools of repression and disinformation they use to stay in power? The economic, political and trade system created by those in power often lead to human rights abuses. For example, the trade in arms destroys lives but is defended by governments who either use the arms to repress their own people or profit from the trade. Their justification is sovereignty.

Sovereignty and solidarity

In pursuit of freedoms, rights and equality, we need to rethink sovereignty. The power of sovereignty should – and can – arise through taking hold of one's own destiny, such as states that have emerged from colonialism or from overbearing neighbours or that have risen from the ashes of movements that have overthrown repressive and corrupt regimes. This is sovereignty's power for good. To keep that alive, and to contain its exploitative side, we need to redefine sovereignty and recognize both global solidarity and global responsibility. We are citizens of the world. We care because we have access to information and we can choose to be unbound.

States routinely claim sovereignty ... to hide or deny mass murder, genocide, oppression, corruption, starvation, or gender-based persecution.

States routinely claim sovereignty – equating it to control over internal affairs without external interference – so they can do what they want. They have made this claim to sovereignty – however specious – to hide or deny mass murder, genocide, oppression, corruption, starvation, or gender-based persecution.

But those who abuse their power and privilege can no longer easily hide that abuse. People with mobile phones record and upload videos that reveal the reality of human rights abuses in real time and expose the truth behind the hypocritical rhetoric and self-serving justifications. Likewise, corporates and other powerful private actors are more easily subjected to scrutiny because it is increasingly difficult to hide the consequences of their actions when they are devious or criminal.

We work in a human rights framework that assumes sovereignty but does not inherently defend it – not least following the establishment of the doctrine of Responsibility to Protect, agreed at a UN world summit in 2005, and repeatedly reaffirmed since then.

It is easy to see why; 2012 alone gives us ample evidence of governments violating the rights of the people they govern.

A key element of human rights protection is the right of all people to be free from violence. Another key element is the strong limits on the state's ability to interfere in our personal and family lives. This includes protecting our freedom of expression, of association and of conscience. It includes not interfering with our bodies and how we use them – the decisions we make over reproduction, the sexual and gender identities we embrace, how we choose to dress.

In the first few days of 2012, 300 families were left homeless in the Cambodian capital Phnom Penh, after being violently evicted from their neighbourhood. Just a few weeks later, 600 Brazilians met the same fate in Pinheirinho slum in São Paulo state. In March, 21 people were killed in Jamaica in a wave of police shootings, Azerbaijani musicians were beaten, arrested and tortured in detention, and Mali was plunged into crisis after a coup took place in the capital Bamako.

And so it continued: more forced evictions in Nigeria; journalists killed in Somalia and Mexico and elsewhere; women raped or sexually assaulted in the home, in the street, or as they exercised their right to protest; lesbian, gay, bisexual, transgender and intersex communities banned from holding Pride festivals and their members beaten up; human rights activists murdered or thrown in jail on trumped-up charges. In September, Japan executed a woman for the first time in more than 15 years. November saw a new escalation in the Israel/Gaza conflict, while tens of thousands of civilians fled their homes in the Democratic Republic of the Congo as the Rwandan-backed armed group March 23 Movement (M23) marched on the capital of North Kivu province.

And then there was Syria. At year-end, the death toll according to the UN had reached 60,000, and was still rising.

Failure to protect

Too often over the last few decades, state sovereignty – increasingly closely linked with the concept of national security – has been used to justify actions that are antithetical to human rights. Internally, those who are powerful claim that they and only they can make decisions regarding the lives of the people they govern.

Like his father before him, President Bashar al-Assad has stayed in power by turning the Syrian army and security forces against the people calling for him to step down.

But there is a key difference. At the time of the Hama massacre in 1982, Amnesty International and others highlighted what was happening and worked tirelessly to try to stop it. But the mass killings took place largely out of view of the rest of the world. In the past two years, by contrast, brave Syrian bloggers and activists have been able to tell the world directly about what is happening to them in their country, even as it happens.

Despite the mounting death toll – and despite the abundant evidence of crimes committed – the UN Security Council again failed to act to protect civilians. For nearly two years the Syrian military and security forces have launched indiscriminate attacks and detained, tortured and killed people they perceived to support the rebels. One Amnesty International report documented 31 different forms of torture and other ill-treatment. Armed opposition groups have also carried out summary killings and torture, albeit on a much smaller scale. The UN Security Council's failure to act is defended, particularly by Russia and China, as respecting the sovereignty of the state.

The idea that neither individual states nor the international community should act decisively to protect civilians when governments and their security forces target their own people – unless there is something in it for them – is unacceptable. Whether we are talking about the 1994 genocide in Rwanda, the corralling of Tamils into the lethal "no fire zone" in northern Sri Lanka, in which tens of thousands of civilians died in 2009, the ongoing starvation of people in North Korea or the Syrian conflict – inaction in the name of respect for state sovereignty is inexcusable.

Ultimately, states are responsible for upholding the rights of the people in their territory. But no one who believes in justice and human rights could argue that these concepts are currently served by sovereignty in any way but their lack of fulfilment.

Surely it is time to challenge this toxic mix of states' claims to absolute sovereignty and their focus on national security rather than human rights and human security. Let's have no more excuses. Now it is time for the international community to step up and reframe its duty to protect all global citizens.

Our countries have an obligation to respect, protect and fulfil our rights. And many have not done so. At best they have done so inconsistently. Despite all the successes of the human rights movement over the last few decades – from the prisoners of conscience released to the global prohibition of torture and the creation of an International Criminal Court – this distortion of sovereignty means billions are still left behind.

Guardianship or exploitation

One of the starkest examples of this over the last decades has been the treatment of the world's Indigenous Peoples. A key value that unites Indigenous communities around the world is their rejection of the concept of "owning" land. Instead, they have traditionally identified as guardians of the land on which they live. This rejection of the concept of owning real property has come at a huge price. Many of the lands on which Indigenous Peoples live have proven to be rich in resources. So the government that is meant to protect their rights appropriates the land for the 'sovereign state', then sells it, leases it or allows it to be plundered by others.

Instead of respecting the value of communities being guardians of the land and its resources, states and corporations have moved into these areas, forcibly displacing Indigenous communities and seizing ownership of the land or the mineral rights associated with it.

Governments should be learning from Indigenous communities in order to rethink the relationship with natural resources.

In Paraguay, the Sawhoyamaxa spent 2012 as they have spent the last 20 years; displaced from their traditional lands, despite a ruling by the Inter-American Court of Human Rights in 2006 recognizing their right to their lands. Further north, dozens of First Nations communities in Canada were continuing to oppose a proposal to build a pipeline connecting the Alberta oil sands to the British Columbia coast, crossing their traditional lands.

At a time when governments should be learning from Indigenous communities in order to rethink the relationship with natural resources, Indigenous communities the world over are under siege.

What makes this devastation particularly distressing is the extent to which states and corporate actors are ignoring the UN Declaration on the Rights of Indigenous Peoples, which explicitly requires states to ensure the full and effective participation of Indigenous Peoples in all matters that concern them. Indigenous rights activists face violence and even murder when they seek to defend their communities and their lands.

Such discrimination, marginalization and violence were not limited to the Americas, but took place across the globe – from the Philippines to Namibia, where 2012 saw the children of the San, Ovahimba people and other ethnic minorities facing numerous barriers preventing them from accessing education. This was particularly the case in Opuwo among the Ovahimba children who were forced to cut their hair and to not wear traditional dress to attend public schools.

The flow of money and people

The race for resources is just one element of our globalized world. Another is the flow of capital through borders, across oceans, and into the pockets of the powerful. Yes, globalization has brought economic growth and prosperity for some, but the Indigenous experience is playing out in other communities who watch governments and corporations benefiting from the land they are living, and starving, on.

In sub-Saharan Africa, for example, despite significant growth in many countries, untold millions continue to live in life-threatening poverty. Corruption and the flow of capital into tax havens outside Africa continue to be two key reasons. The region's mineral wealth continues to fuel deals between corporations and politicians in which both profit – but at a price. A lack of transparency about concession agreements and the utter lack of accountability mean that both the shareholders of the corporations and the politicians are unjustly enriched, while those whose labour is exploited, whose land is degraded and whose rights are violated, suffer. Justice is largely beyond their reach.

Another example of the free flow of capital is the remittances sent home by migrant workers around the world. According to the World Bank, remittances from migrant workers in developing countries are three times as much as official international development assistance. Yet those very same migrant workers were often left in 2012 with neither their home nor host states adequately protecting their rights.

Recruitment agencies in Nepal in 2012, for example, continued to traffic migrant workers for exploitation and forced labour, and charged fees above government-imposed limits, compelling workers to take large loans at high interest rates. Recruiters deceived many migrants on terms and conditions of work. Recruitment agencies that violated Nepalese law were rarely punished. In an example of a law that pays little more than lip service to women's rights, in August the government banned women under the age of 30 from migrating for domestic work to Kuwait, Qatar, Saudi Arabia and the United Arab Emirates due to complaints of sexual and other physical abuse in those countries. But the bans potentially increased risks to women now forced to seek work through informal routes. What the government should have done is fought to secure safe working environments for the women.

Once people have left, the sending states claim that since their migrant workers are no longer within their territory, they have no obligations and the host states claim that because they are not citizens they have no rights. In the meantime, the UN Convention on the Rights of Migrant Workers and Their Families, which was opened for signature in

1990, remains one of the least ratified human rights conventions. No migrant-receiving state in Western Europe has ratified the Convention. Nor have others with large migrant populations such as the USA, Australia, Canada, India, South Africa and states in the Gulf.

This vulnerability is even greater for refugees. The most vulnerable are the 12 million stateless people in the world, equivalent in numbers to the world's great agglomerations such as London, Lagos or Rio. And around 80% of them are women. Without the protection of their 'sovereign' state these people are true global citizens. And their protection falls to all of us. They are the purest argument for the fulfilment of the duty to protect there is. For human rights protections must be applied to all humans, whether at home or not.

The most vulnerable are the 12 million stateless people in the world, equivalent in numbers to the world's great agglomerations such as London, Lagos or Rio. And around 80% of them are women.

At the moment, this protection is seen as subservient to state sovereignty. Women are raped in camps across South Sudan, asylum-seekers from Australia to Kenya are locked up in detention centres or metal crates, hundreds die in leaky boats as they desperately search for safe harbour.

Boats of Africans floundering off the coast of Italy were turned away from the safety of European shores again in 2012, because states claimed that control of their borders was sacrosanct. The Australian government continued to interdict boats of refugees and migrants at sea. The US Coast Guard defended its practice: "Interdicting migrants at sea means they can be quickly returned to their countries of origin without the costly processes required if they successfully enter the United States." In each case – sovereignty trumped the right of individuals to seek asylum.

Around 200 people die every year trying to cross the desert into the US – a direct result of measures taken by the US government to make safer passages impassable for migrants. These numbers have remained steady even as immigration is declining.

These examples show the most heinous abnegation of the responsibility to promote human rights – including the right to life – and they stand in stark contrast to the free flow of capital detailed earlier.

Immigration controls also stand in stark contrast to the largely unimpeded flow of conventional weapons – including small arms and light weapons – across borders. Hundreds of thousands of people have been killed, injured, raped and forced to flee from their homes as a result of this trade. The arms trade also has direct links to discrimination and gender-based violence, disproportionately affecting women. This has far-reaching implications for efforts to consolidate peace, security, gender equality and secure development. The abuses are fuelled in part by the ease with which weapons are easily bought and sold, bartered and shipped around the world – too often ending up in the hands of abusive governments and their security forces, warlords and criminal gangs. It's a lucrative business – US$70 billion a year – and so those with entrenched interests try to protect the trade from regulation. As this report goes to print, the top arms-brokering governments are poised to enter negotiations for an arms trade treaty. Our demand is that where there is a substantial risk that these weapons will be used to commit violations of international humanitarian law or serious violations of human rights law – the transfer should be prohibited.

The arms trade also has direct links to discrimination and gender-based violence, disproportionately affecting women. This has far-reaching implications for efforts to consolidate peace, security, gender equality and secure development.

The flow of information

The crucial positive to take from these examples, however, is that we know about them. For half a century, Amnesty International has documented human rights violations around the world and uses every resource it has to try to halt and prevent abuses and protect our rights. Globalized communication is creating opportunities the founders of the modern human rights movement could never have imagined. Increasingly, there is very little that governments and corporations can do in hiding behind "sovereign" boundaries.

The speed with which new forms of communication have taken root in our lives is breathtaking. From 1985, when the dotcom domain name was created, to today, when 2.5 billion people can access the internet, the wheels of change have spun with extraordinary speed. 1989 saw Tim Berners Lee propose the document retrieval element of the internet, Hotmail was born in 1996, blogs in 1999, Wikipedia launched in 2001. In 2004 Facebook was born, followed by YouTube a year later – along with the internet's billionth user, said to be "statistically likely to be a 24-year-old woman in Shanghai". 2006 brought Twitter, and Google's censored Chinese site Gu Ge. By 2008 China had more people online than the USA. And in the same year, activists working with Kenyan citizen journalists developed a website called Ushahidi – the Swahili word for "testimony" – initially to map reports of violence in Kenya after the election, and since developed into a platform used around the world with the mission to "democratize information".

We live in an information-rich world. Activists have the tools to make sure violations are not hidden. Information creates an imperative to act. We face a crucial time: will we continue to have access to this information or will states in collusion with other powerful actors block that access? Amnesty International wants to make sure everyone has the tools to access and share information and to challenge power and sovereignty when it is abused. With the internet, we can build a model of global citizenship. The internet forms a counterpoint to the whole concept of sovereignty and citizenship-based rights.

What Martin Luther King Jr. phrased so eloquently around the "inescapable network of mutuality" and the "single garment of destiny", has been espoused and promoted by many great thinkers and defenders of rights before and after him. But now is the moment to seed it into the very "fabric" of our international model of citizenship. The African concept of 'Ubuntu' puts it most clearly: "I am because we are".

It is about connecting all of us, not allowing borders, walls, seas, portrayals of enemies as "the other" to pollute our natural sense of justice and human-hood. Now the digital world has truly connected us with information.

Agency and participation

It is simple. The openness of the digital world levels the playing field and allows many more people access to the information they need to challenge governments and corporations. It is a tool that encourages transparency and accountability. Information is power. The internet has the potential to significantly empower all 7 billion people living in the world today. It is a tool that allows us to see and document and challenge human rights abuses wherever they may be happening. It enables us to share information so that we can work together to solve problems, promote human security and human development and fulfil the promise of human rights.

The abuse of state sovereignty is the opposite. It is about walls and control of information and communication and hiding behind state secrecy laws and other claims of privilege. The narrative behind the claim of sovereignty is that what the government is doing is no one's business but its own, and as long it acts within its own borders, it cannot be challenged. It is about the powerful acting on the powerless.

The power and possibilities of the digital world are immense. And, as technology is value neutral, these possibilities can enable actions that are coherent with building rights respecting societies or enable actions that are antithetical to human rights.

It is interesting for Amnesty International, whose history is rooted in defending freedom of expression, to live again what governments do when unable to control it, and decide to manipulate access to information. Nowhere is this more apparent than in the prosecution or harassment of bloggers in countries from Azerbaijan to Tunisia, and from Cuba to the

Palestinian Authority. In Viet Nam, for example, popular bloggers Nguyen Van Hai, known as Dieu Cay, "Justice and Truth" blogger Ta Phong Tan, and Phan Thanh Hai, known as AnhBaSaiGon, were tried in September for "conducting propaganda" against the state. They were sentenced to 12, 10 and four years' imprisonment respectively, with three to five years' house arrest on release. The trial lasted only a few hours, and their families were harassed and detained to prevent them from attending. Their trial was postponed three times, the last time because the mother of Ta Phong Tan died after setting herself on fire outside government offices in protest at her daughter's treatment.

But imprisoning people for exercising their freedom of expression and challenging those in power using digital technology is only the first line of defence of governments. We increasingly see states trying to build firewalls around any digital communications or information systems. Iran, China and Viet Nam have all tried to build a system that allows them to regain control over both communications and access to information available in the digital sphere.

We can demand that states ensure that all the people they govern have meaningful access to the digital world.

What may be even more worrisome is the number of countries that are exploring less obvious means of control in this area through massive surveillance and more artful means of manipulating access to information. The USA, which continues to demonstrate a remarkable lack of respect for recognizing parameters – as evidenced by the drone strikes being carried out around the world – has recently proclaimed the right to conduct surveillance of any information kept in cloud storage systems – digital filing cabinets that are not bound to territorial domains. To be clear, this includes information owned by individuals and companies that are not based in or citizens of the USA.

This struggle over access to information and control of the means of communication is just beginning. So what can the international community do to show its respect for those who so bravely risked their lives and freedoms to mobilize during the uprisings in the Middle East and North Africa? What can all of us do to show solidarity with Malala Yousafzai and all the others who dare to stand up and say "Enough"?

We can demand that states ensure that all the people they govern have meaningful access to the digital world – preferably through high-speed and truly affordable internet access whether via a portable hand-held devise such as a mobile phone, or a desktop computer. In doing so they would be fulfilling one of the principles of human rights as articulated in Article 15 of the International Covenant on Economic, Social and Cultural Rights: "To enjoy the benefits of scientific progress and its applications." And Article 27 of the Universal Declaration of Human Rights says: "Everyone has the right freely to participate in the cultural life of the community, to enjoy the arts and to share in scientific advancement and its benefits."

Meaningful access to the internet surely qualifies as enjoying the benefit of scientific progress.

Many years ago, states created an international postal service that would be set up nationally but would interconnect with all other postal services creating a global mail system. Every person could write a letter, buy a stamp and send that letter to somewhere else, pretty much anywhere else, in the world. If there was no delivery to your doorstep – there was the system of poste restante or general delivery that designated a place where one could call for one's mail.

And that mail was considered private – no matter how many borders it crossed. This form of communications and information sharing, which can seem rather quaint in today's world, changed the way we communicated and was built on a presumption of the right to privacy of those communications. Most importantly, states undertook to ensure that all people had access to this service. And while many governments undoubtedly used their access to mail to read what was private, they did not challenge the principle of the right to privacy of these communications. In countless countries it opened people up to the sharing of information and family and community life.

Today, access to the internet is critical to ensure that people can communicate, and also to ensure people's access to information. Transparency, access to information and the ability to participate in political debates and decisions are critical to building a rights respecting society.

Few actions by governments can have such immediate, powerful and far-reaching positive consequences for human rights.

Each government of the world has a decision to make. Will it take this value-neutral technology and use it to reclaim its power over others – or will it use it to empower and promote the freedom of individuals?

The advent of the internet and its global penetration – via cellphones, internet cafés, and computers accessible at schools, public libraries, workplaces and homes – has created a huge opportunity for empowering people to claim their rights.

The choice for the future

States have an opportunity to seize this moment and ensure that all the people they govern have meaningful access to the internet. They can ensure that people have affordable access to the internet. States can also support the creation of many more venues such as libraries and cafés where people can access the internet for free or at affordable rates.

Crucially, states can ensure women – only 37% of whom currently access the internet – can actively participate in this information system and therefore in the actions and decisions being taken in the world they live in. As a new report by UN Women, Intel and the US State Department details, there is a the huge internet gender gap in countries such as India, Mexico and Uganda. This means states must create systems that enable access in homes, schools and workplaces, as places such as internet cafés are impractical for women who can't leave their homes for religious and cultural reasons.

Knowledge, information and the ability to speak are power. Rights respecting states do not fear that power.

States can also work to eradicate social discrimination against women and negative stereotyping. An Indian woman with an engineering degree told the report's authors that she was banned from the computer "for fear that if she touched it, something would go wrong". Other anecdotal evidence pointed to some husbands forbidding their wives to use the family computer in case they saw inappropriate sexual content. That is one reason cited for why only 14% of women in Azerbaijan have ever gone online, although 70% of men there have.

In recognizing the right of people to access the internet, states would be fulfilling their duties with respect to freedom of expression and the right to information. But they must do so in a manner that respects the right to privacy.

To fail to do so risks creating two tiers of people domestically and globally – in which some people have access to the tools they need to claim their rights while others are left behind.

Knowledge, information and the ability to speak are power. Rights respecting states do not fear that power. Rights respecting states promote empowerment. And the borderless nature of the digital sphere means that we can all engage in an exercise of global citizenship to use these tools to promote respect for human rights in small places close to home and in solidarity with people living far away.

Traditional forms of solidarity can have even greater impact as they go 'viral'. Take the 12 individuals that thousands of activists campaigned for as part of Amnesty

International's 10th global "Write for Rights" marathon in December 2012. This is the world's largest human rights event and in the last few years has embraced emails, digital petitions, SMS messages, faxes, tweets, leading to 2 million actions taken expressing solidarity, providing support and helping get those imprisoned for their beliefs released.

For Amnesty International we see in the internet the radical promise and possibilities that our founder Peter Benenson saw more than 50 years ago – the possibility of people working together across borders to demand freedom and rights for all. His dream was dismissed as one of the larger lunacies of our time. Many former prisoners of conscience owe their freedom and lives to that dream. We are on the cusp of creating and fulfilling another dream that some will dismiss as lunacy. But today, Amnesty International embraces the challenge and calls on states to recognize our changed world and create the tools of empowerment for all people.

"One thing that gives us hope is support and solidarity from regular people. People are the only impetus for change. Governments will not improve or do anything unless there is pressure from people... The amount of messages I received [from Amnesty activists] gives me a lot of hope, despite all the challenges."

Azza Hilal Ahmad Suleiman, who is still recovering from a vicious attack near Tahrir Square, Egypt, was one of the 12 cases featured in December 2012's Write for Rights campaign. She intervened after seeing a group of soldiers beating and removing a young woman's clothes, and was left with a fractured skull and memory problems. She is now suing the military.

AMNESTY INTERNATIONAL REPORT 2013
PART TWO: COUNTRY ENTRIES

AFGHANISTAN

ISLAMIC REPUBLIC OF AFGHANISTAN
Head of state and government: **Hamid Karzai**

**Thousands of civilians continued to suffer from
targeted and indiscriminate attacks by armed
opposition groups, with international and national
security forces also responsible for civilian deaths
and injuries. The UN Assistance Mission in
Afghanistan (UNAMA) reported more than 2,700
civilians killed and 4,805 injured, the vast majority
– 81% – by armed groups. Torture and other
ill-treatment were common in detention facilities
across the country, despite some government efforts
to reduce incidence. Violence and discrimination
against women and girls remained rife both
institutionally and within wider society. The
government sought to introduce tougher controls on
the media, prompting an outcry among media
workers, who continued to be threatened and
detained by the authorities and armed groups.
Persistent armed conflict prompted more families to
flee their homes, with 459,200 people still displaced
within Afghanistan by the conflict. Many lived in
informal settlements with inadequate shelter, access
to water, health care, and education. Some 2.7
million refugees remained outside the country.**

Background

In January the Taliban agreed to open a political office in
Qatar allowing for direct peace negotiations; efforts
faltered in March over requested exchanges of
prisoners. In early November, negotiations between
Pakistan and Afghanistan's High Peace Council
resulted in Pakistan releasing several detained Taliban
leaders. On 17 November, the head of the High
Peace Council, Salahuddin Rabbani, stated that
Taliban officials who joined the peace process would
receive immunity from prosecution despite the fact
that some of the detained Taliban were suspected
of war crimes. Women members of the High Peace
Council remained sidelined from the main peace
consultations.

States at NATO's biennial Summit in May stressed
the importance of women's participation in
Afghanistan's peace, political, reconciliation and
reconstruction processes, and the need to respect the
institutional arrangements protecting their rights. At
the same time, women's groups raised concern about
their effective exclusion from national consultations
over the transfer of security responsibility from
international to national security forces. Women
activists condemned President Karzai's "code of
conduct", proposed on 2 March, which stipulated
that women should only travel with a male guardian
and not mix with men in work or education.

In July, international donors met in Tokyo, Japan,
where they pledged US$16 billion in civilian aid to
Afghanistan until 2015, with sustained support until
2017. However, the UN reported in December that
humanitarian funding had decreased from 2011 by
nearly 50% to US$484 million in 2012. According
to the Afghanistan NGO Safety Office, threat levels
against NGOs and aid workers remained similar to
2011 with 111 security incidents caused by armed
groups and pro-government security forces, including
killing, injury and abduction.

In September, Parliament confirmed without debate
Assadulah Khalid as the new head of the National
Directorate of Security (Afghanistan's intelligence
services), despite reports of his alleged involvement in
acts of torture during his previous terms as Governor
of Ghazni and Kandahar provinces.

The work of the Afghanistan Independent
Human Rights Commission remained under-
resourced following the President's controversial
dismissal of three of its nine commissioners in
December 2011. Another post remained vacant since
January 2011 when a commissioner and her family
were killed in a bomb attack.

Violent protests broke out in February after charred
copies of the Qur'an were found on a military base
near Kabul; 30 people died in the violence.

Abuses by armed groups

Despite a 2010 Taliban code of conduct (*Layeha*)
ordering fighters to avoid targeting civilians, the
Taliban and other armed groups continued to breach
the laws of war by indiscriminately killing and
maiming civilians in suicide attacks. Improvised
explosive devices were the main cause of civilian
casualties. Armed groups targeted and attacked
public places; civilians, including officials, perceived
as supporting the government; and staff of
international organizations.

■ On 6 April, a suicide bomber killed the head of Kunar Provincial Peace Council Maulavi Mohammad Hashim Munib and his son, as they returned home from Friday prayers.

■ On 6 June, two suicide bombers killed at least 22 civilians and injured 24 others in a crowded market in Kandahar province. The Taliban claimed responsibility for the attack.

■ On 21 June, Taliban forces attacked the Spozhmay Hotel, a popular resort for locals, killing 12 civilians and injuring nine, in a siege that lasted 12 hours.

■ A boy was reportedly abducted and beheaded in August in Zherai district by the Taliban because his brother served in the Afghan Local Police (ALP); the Taliban denied responsibility.

■ On 19 October, 18 women were reported killed in Balkh province when a minibus hit a roadside bomb.

Children continued to be recruited by armed groups.

■ On 26 October, a suicide bomber, reportedly aged 15, killed 40 civilians, including six children, at a mosque during Eid prayers in Mainmana city, Faryab province.

Violations by Afghan and international forces

Pro-government security forces continued to cause civilian deaths and injury mainly by air strikes. According to UNAMA 8% of civilian deaths were caused by national and international forces.

■ On 8 February, eight boys were killed in NATO airstrikes in Kapisa province; the attack was condemned by President Karzai. NATO expressed regret but reportedly claimed the youths had been perceived as a threat.

■ On 11 March, a rogue US soldier killed civilians, including nine children, and injured others in a night-time shooting spree in two villages in the Panjwai district of Kandahar province. By December, the soldier was facing a court-martial for 16 counts of murder and six counts of attempted murder.

■ On 6 June, 18 civilians, including children, were reportedly killed in a NATO airstrike targeting Taliban fighters who had taken shelter in someone's home during a wedding in Logar province.

In September, the Afghan authorities assumed nominal control of the US detention facility at Bagram, north of Kabul. However, the degree of continued US influence over the cases of individual Bagram detainees remained unclear. The Afghan authorities were reported to have taken custody of approximately 3,100 Afghan nationals who were at the facility as of 9 March, when the transfer agreement was finalized. More than 600 detainees reported to have been taken to the base since March apparently remained under US military jurisdiction, as did the cases of at least 50 non-Afghan nationals currently held at the base, many of whom were rendered from third countries to Afghanistan and had been in US custody for a decade. An unknown number of Afghans, captured before the agreement, had not been transferred to Afghan custody.

According to UNAMA, there was a slight drop in incidence of torture and other ill-treatment as of October by the National Directorate of Security, but an increase in its use by national police and border police.

Allegations of human rights violations by members of ALP were widespread and human rights groups raised concern that members were not vetted. More than 100 ALP members were reportedly jailed for murder, rape, bombings, beatings and robbery.

■ In November, four members of the ALP unit in Kunduz were jailed for 16 years each for abducting, raping and beating 18-year-old Lal Bibi over five days in May.

Freedom of expression

A draft media law proposed greater government control over the media. It called for the creation of a 15-member High Media Council, headed by the Minister of Information and Culture and comprising other government officials, charged with checking and controlling press and broadcast media.

Journalists were threatened, arbitrarily arrested, beaten or killed during the year. Afghan media watchdog Nai recorded 69 attacks on journalists by security forces, armed groups and private individuals; this was 14% fewer attacks than in 2011. Prompted by the Ulema Council, the Attorney General threatened criminal proceedings against media organizations for writing or talking about matters deemed immoral or against Islam.

■ Afghan TV journalist Nasto Naderi was detained on 21 April for several days without charge or access to a lawyer.

Violence against women and girls

Despite the passage of the Elimination of Violence against Women Act in 2009, law enforcement and judicial officials failed to properly investigate violence against women and girls and bring perpetrators to justice.

Women and girls continued to be beaten, raped and killed. They were targeted and attacked by armed groups, and faced discrimination by the authorities and threats within their own communities and families. The Afghanistan Independent Human Rights Commission documented more than 4,000 cases of violence against women from 21 March to 21 October – a rise of 28% compared with the same period for 2011, reportedly due to increased public awareness. The actual number of incidents was likely to be still higher given the continuing stigma and risk of reprisal associated with reporting such violence.

■ In May, an appeals court in Kabul upheld prison sentences of 10 years each in the case against the in-laws of an Afghan girl. The girl had been severely abused by them after being forced to marry at the age of 13.

■ In July, an Afghan woman, named in media reports as 22-year-old Najiba, was shot dead on "charges" of adultery, reportedly by a Taliban insurgent.

■ On 16 September, a 16-year-old girl was publicly flogged in the southern province of Ghazni for an "illicit relationship". The girl had been sentenced to 100 lashes, following a verdict issued by three mullahs in Jaghori district.

■ On 10 December, Nadia Sidiqi, the acting head of the Department for Women's Affairs in Laghman province, was killed by unidentified gunmen while on her way to work. Her predecessor, Hanifa Safi, was killed and her family injured by a remote-controlled explosive device on 13 July. No one claimed responsibility for either incident.

Refugees and internally displaced people

By the end of October, about half a million people remained internally displaced as a result of the conflict and natural disaster. Many continued to seek refuge in city slums and other informal settlements, fashioning makeshift shelters from plastic sheeting, and living under the constant threat of forced and sometimes violent evictions. Poor sanitation and lack of access to education and health care coupled with bitter 2011/2012 weather conditions meant that scores died of illness, cold or both. Over 100, mainly children, reportedly died during this period amid criticism over the lack of timely humanitarian assistance provided. By March, the government had responded with an announcement that it was developing a comprehensive national policy on internal displacement.

In September, the Pakistan government agreed that Afghan refugees could remain in Pakistan for another three years, rescinding an order by officials in Khyber-Pakhtunkhwa province calling for all illegal Afghan immigrants to leave the country by 25 May, or face imprisonment and deportation.

Death penalty

On 20 and 21 November, the authorities executed 14 prisoners on death row, the first executions since June 2011, despite serious concerns about the lack of guarantee of a fair trial in the country. Thirty people had their death sentences confirmed by the Supreme Court; 10 people had their death sentences commuted to long prison terms. By the end of November more than 250 people remained on death row.

Amnesty International visits/reports

🚗 Amnesty International delegates visited Afghanistan in February, March, May, June, October and December.

📄 Fleeing war, finding misery: The plight of the internally displaced in Afghanistan (ASA 11/001/2012)

📄 Strengthening the rule of law and protection of human rights, including women's rights, is key to any development plan for Afghanistan (ASA 11/012/2012)

📄 Open letter to the Government of Afghanistan, the United Nations, other humanitarian organizations and international donors (ASA 11/019/2012)

ALBANIA

REPUBLIC OF ALBANIA
Head of state: **Bujar Nishani (replaced Bamir Topi in July)**
Head of government: **Sali Berisha**

The government adopted reforms which restricted the immunity of MPs and other public officials from prosecution and revised the Electoral Code, following previous allegations of fraud. In December, the European Council postponed the granting of EU candidate status to Albania, conditional on further reform.

Enforced disappearances

In November, proceedings before the Serious Crimes Court concerning the enforced disappearance in 1995 of Remzi Hoxha, an ethnic Albanian from Macedonia, and the torture of two other Albanian men, ended with the conviction of three former state security agents. One of them, Ilir Kumbaro, who fled extradition proceedings in the UK in 2011, was sentenced to 15 years' imprisonment in his absence. The charges against his two co-defendants were changed by the court to offences covered by a 1997 amnesty, resulting in them not being sentenced. In December, all three defendants appealed against their convictions.

Unlawful killings

In May, the trial opened of former Republican Guard commander, Ndrea Prendi, and former Guard officer, Agim Llupo, charged with killing four protesters, the injury of two others, and concealing evidence. The charges arose from violent clashes between police and protesters during anti-government demonstrations in January 2011 in Tirana.

Torture and other ill-treatment

In June, the UN Committee against Torture expressed concerns about the lack of effective and impartial investigations by the Ministry of Interior into alleged ill-treatment by law enforcement officers. The Committee also reported that basic safeguards against torture were not provided to people in detention, including timely access to lawyers and doctors, and noted the excessive length of pre-trial detention.

In July, four prison guards were each fined 3,100 leks (€22) by Tirana District Court for beating Sehat Doci in Prison 313 in August 2011.

■ In September, a group of former political prisoners went on hunger strike in protest against the government's prolonged failure to provide reparations for their imprisonment by the communist government between 1944 and 1991. Thousands were imprisoned or sent to labour camps during this period and subjected to degrading treatment and, often, torture. During the 31-day protest, two men set themselves on fire; one, Lirak Bejko, died of his injuries in November. The Ombudsperson considered the actions of the Tirana police in denying hunger strikers medicines and liquids to be an act of torture.

Violence in the family

There were 2,526 reported incidents of domestic violence, 345 more than in the previous year, and petitions by victims for court protection orders also increased. Most victims were women. An amendment to the Criminal Code making violence in the family an offence punishable by up to five years' imprisonment came into force in April. However, there was no minimum sentence for such offences, except when committed repeatedly and prosecutions could only be initiated on the basis of a victim's complaint.

The Director of the National Centre for Victims of Domestic Violence was dismissed in May, after the Ombudsperson investigated complaints by women at the Centre that they had been subjected to arbitrary punishments and restrictions.

Discrimination

Roma

Many Roma continued to be denied their right to adequate housing.

■ Some Roma, forced to move from their homes near Tirana railway station after a 2011 arson attack, were evicted from temporary tented accommodation. In February, lacking adequate alternative housing, eight families moved briefly into the premises of the Ombudsperson's Office. They were later transferred to disused military barracks. However, their very poor accommodation and inadequate police protection from threats and attacks by the neighbouring community obliged them to leave. By the end of the year, no permanent solution to their housing had been found.

■ In July, the livelihoods of an estimated 800 Romani families were affected when Tirana police implemented an administrative order prohibiting the collection of scrap and other recyclable materials by seizing their vehicles and other equipment. The Ombudsperson opened an inquiry into excessive use of force and ill-treatment by police during the operation.

Lesbian, gay, bisexual, transgender and intersex people

The first Tirana Pride took place in May. In July, Tirana Prosecutor's Office dismissed a criminal complaint by LGBTI organizations against Deputy Minister of Defence Ekrem Spahiu about his homophobic remarks concerning the Pride.

Housing rights – orphans

Young people leaving social care remained at risk of homelessness, despite legislation guaranteeing homeless registered orphans up to the age of 30 priority access to social housing. Many continued to live in dilapidated disused school dormitories or struggled to pay for low-grade private rented accommodation.

ALGERIA

PEOPLE'S DEMOCRATIC REPUBLIC OF ALGERIA
Head of state: **Abdelaziz Bouteflika**
Head of government: **Abdelmalek Sellal (replaced Ahmed Ouyahia in September)**

The authorities continued to restrict freedoms of expression, association and assembly, dispersing demonstrations and harassing human rights defenders. Women faced discrimination in law and practice. Perpetrators of gross human rights abuses during the 1990s, and torture and other ill-treatment against detainees in subsequent years, continued to benefit from impunity. Armed groups carried out lethal attacks. At least 153 death sentences were reported; there were no executions.

Background

The year saw protests and demonstrations by trade unionists and others against unemployment, poverty and corruption. These were dispersed by the security forces, which also thwarted planned demonstrations by blocking access or arresting protesters.

Algeria's human rights record was assessed under the UN Universal Periodic Review in May. The government failed to address recommendations to abolish laws originating under the state of emergency, in force from 1992 until 2011, to ease restrictions on freedoms of expression, association and assembly, and to recognize the right to truth of families of victims of enforced disappearances during the 1990s.

The UN High Commissioner for Human Rights visited Algeria in September, and discussed with the authorities a long-requested visit by the UN Working Group on Enforced or Involuntary Disappearances.

Freedoms of expression and association

New laws on information and associations adopted in December 2011 restricted media reporting of issues relevant to state security, national sovereignty and Algeria's economic interests, and tightened controls on NGOs, empowering the authorities to suspend or dissolve them and deny them registration or funding. Journalists faced prosecution for defamation under the Penal Code.

■ Manseur Si Mohamed, a journalist at *La Nouvelle République* newspaper in Mascara, was fined and sentenced to two months' imprisonment in June for making "defamatory comments" in reporting that a state official had failed to implement a judicial decision. He remained at liberty pending an appeal.

■ In October, the authorities rejected an application for registration from the National Association for the fight against corruption (ANLC), giving no specific reasons.

Freedom of assembly

Despite lifting the state of emergency in 2011, the authorities continued to prohibit demonstrations in Algiers under a 2001 decree. There and elsewhere, security forces either prevented demonstrations by blocking access and making arrests or dispersed them through actual or threatened force.

■ On 24 April, security forces were reported to have beaten up and arrested judicial clerks engaged in a sit-in protest over their working conditions.

Human rights defenders

The authorities continued to harass human rights defenders, including through the courts.

■ Abdelkader Kherba, a member of the Algerian League for the Defence of Human Rights (LADDH) and the National Committee for the Defence of the Rights of the Unemployed (CNDDC), was fined and received a suspended prison sentence of one year in May after a court convicted him of "direct incitement to a gathering" for joining and filming a sit-in protest by judicial clerks. He was held in custody from 19 April to 3 May. He was again arrested, detained and prosecuted after attempting to film a demonstration against water cuts at Ksar El Boukhari, Médéa, in August. Charged with insulting and committing violence against an official, he was acquitted and released on 11 September.

■ Yacine Zaïd, a trade union activist and president of the LADDH's Laghouat branch, was arrested and beaten by police in October. He received a suspended six-month prison term and was fined for "violence against a state agent". The court ignored his allegation of assault by police despite medical evidence.

■ Yacine Zaïd and three other human rights defenders who participated in a sit-in outside the court trying Abdelkader Kherba in April were charged with "inciting a non-armed gathering", which carries a punishment of up to one year's imprisonment. On 25 September, the court declared it was unable to try them; however, the charges were still pending at the end of the year.

Counter-terror and security

Armed groups, including Al-Qa'ida in the Islamic Maghreb (AQIM), carried out bombing and other attacks, mostly against military targets. The authorities reported killings of members of armed groups by the security forces but disclosed few details, prompting fears that some may have been extrajudicially executed. At least four civilians were reportedly killed by bombs or security forces' gunfire. The Department of Information and Security (DRS) retained wide powers of arrest and detention, including incommunicado detention of terrorism suspects, facilitating torture and other ill-treatment.

■ Abdelhakim Chenoui and Malik Medjnoun, who were jailed for 12 years in 2011 for the murder of Kabyle singer Lounès Matoub, were released in March and May 2012 respectively. Both had been detained continuously from 1999 until their trial in 2011. Abdelhakim Chenoui said he was forced to "confess" under duress and Malik Medjnoun alleged that he was tortured in security police detention in 1999.

Impunity for past abuses

The authorities took no steps to investigate thousands of enforced disappearances and other human rights abuses committed during the internal conflict of the 1990s. The Charter for Peace and National Reconciliation (Law 06-01), in force since 2006, gave immunity to the security forces and criminalized public criticism of their conduct. Families of those forcibly disappeared were required to accept death certificates in order to receive compensation but were denied information about the fate of their disappeared relatives. Those who continued to call for truth and justice faced harassment.

■ Mohamed Smaïn, former head of the LADDH in Relizane and an advocate of truth and justice for the families of the disappeared, was arrested in June when he failed to respond to a summons from the Relizane prosecutor. The summons was in connection with a two-month prison sentence and fines imposed on him after he criticized the authorities for moving corpses from a mass grave in Relizane in 2001. His sentence had been confirmed by the Supreme Court in 2011. He was released under a presidential pardon issued in July on health grounds.

Women's rights

Women continued to face discrimination in law and practice. However, following legislation in 2011 to increase women's representation in parliament, women won almost a third of the seats in national elections in May.

In March, the CEDAW Committee urged the government to reform the Family Code to give women equal rights with men in relation to marriage, divorce, child custody and inheritance. The Committee also urged the government to withdraw Algeria's reservations to CEDAW, ratify the Optional Protocol to CEDAW, enact laws to protect women against domestic and other violence, and address gender inequality in education and employment.

Death penalty

The courts handed down at least 153 death sentences, mostly to defendants who were sentenced in their absence after they were convicted on terrorism charges. There were no executions; the authorities maintained a de facto moratorium on executions in place since 1993.

■ Eight men were sentenced to death on 25 October after they were convicted of kidnapping and murder. At least two of the defendants alleged they had been tortured in pre-trial detention in 2011.

Amnesty International visits/reports

🗎 Algérie : La suspension d'un avocat stagiaire et militant des droits humains doit être immédiatement levée (MDE 28/001/2012)

🗎 Activists targeted in Algeria (MDE 28/002/2012)

ANGOLA

REPUBLIC OF ANGOLA
Head of state and government: José Eduardo dos Santos

Police and security forces continued to use excessive force, including against peaceful demonstrators, as well as to carry out arbitrary arrests and detentions. Freedom of assembly was suppressed throughout the country. Two people were feared to have been subjected to enforced disappearance. Freedom of expression was restricted and the press was censored. There were reports of forced evictions.

Background

In April Angola presented its human rights report to the African Commission on Human and Peoples' Rights.

A new political party, the Broad Convergence for the Salvation of Angola-Electoral Coalition (Convergência Ampla de Salvação de Angola-Coligação Eleitoral, CASA-CE), was registered by the Constitutional Court in April. CASA-CE took part in national elections on 31 August, which were the second elections since 1992 and the third since independence in 1975. Prior to the elections, there were reports of sporadic political violence by members of the ruling People's Movement for the Liberation of Angola (Movimento Popular de Libertação de Angola, MPLA) against the National Union for the Total Independence of Angola (União Nacional para a Independência Total de Angola, UNITA), CASA-CE and other political parties, as well as of UNITA against MPLA. The MPLA won with almost 72% of votes, with about 40% of the population abstaining from voting. Although a number of irregularities were registered prior to the elections, observers judged the elections as free and fair. The results were officially contested by UNITA, CASA-CE and the Social Renewal Party (PRS), but the challenges were rejected as unfounded by Angola's National Electoral Committee (CNE).

On 27 October, Media Investe, the company that owns the weekly newspaper *Semanário Angolense*, censored one edition reportedly because it contained a speech on the state of the nation by UNITA leader Isaías Samakuva which was critical of the government. Although printed versions of the newspaper were burned, an online version was circulated.

Police and security forces

There were reports of excessive use of force and arbitrary arrests and detentions by the police, including of peaceful demonstrators. Police also reportedly used excessive force against detainees, resulting in at least one death. There were also suspected cases of extrajudicial executions by police, including of seven young men found handcuffed and shot in Cacuaco municipality, Luanda. No further information was made publicly available regarding investigations into alleged past cases of human rights violations by police.

■ On 3 October Manuel "Laranjinha" Francisco was arrested by police officers, who reportedly beat him during arrest before taking him to the 17th Police Station, Cazenga Division, in the neighbourhood of Luanda known as Antenove. Witnesses said police beat him at the station. The following day the police told his family that he had been transferred to the Police Command of Cazenga. The family could not find him there; they reportedly received a call later that day informing them that Manuel Francisco's body was in a morgue in a Luanda hospital after having been found in Cacuaco municipality. His body reportedly bore signs of beatings, including a missing fingernail, missing tooth and a broken leg. Although the family filed a complaint at Cazenga Police Division, police authorities did not comment on allegations that Manuel Francisco had been killed while in custody, and nor did they state whether an investigation was being carried out into the circumstances surrounding his death. No further information was available by the end of the year.

Freedoms of assembly and association

Authorities continued to suppress freedom of assembly throughout the country. Anti-government demonstrations which started in March 2011 continued into 2012 and took place mainly in Luanda, Benguela and Cabinda. As in 2011, police not only failed to intervene to prevent violence against those peacefully demonstrating, but also reportedly used excessive force against demonstrators, some of whom were arbitrarily arrested and detained. Police further used excessive force during strikes, including by the Union of Health Workers in Cabinda, and

A

during a demonstration by the war veterans of the People's Armed Forces for the Liberation of Angola (FAPLA) in Luanda. No one was held responsible for excessive use of force and arbitrary arrests during demonstrations in 2011.

■ In March, state media aired threats against anti-government protesters by an individual claiming to represent an anonymous group calling themselves defenders of national peace, security and democracy. Throughout the year, a number of unidentified men suspected of being aligned with the police infiltrated peaceful demonstrations and attacked demonstrators. On 22 May, a group of people meeting to organize a demonstration were attacked and beaten by unidentified assailants in Bairro Nelito Soares in Luanda. Also in May, organizers of demonstrations identified four individuals linked to the police whom they said were involved in attacks against peaceful demonstrators. Although police authorities claimed that investigations were being carried out into the televised threats and attacks, no one had been held responsible by the end of the year.

■ Police in Cabinda used batons and water canon against members of the Union of Health Workers who had been picketing outside the provincial hospital between 30 January and 3 February. On 3 February police blocked access to the hospital for the strikers, who moved on 4 February to the offices of the Syndicate of Unions. Police beat strikers and used a water canon to disperse the crowd whom they said were unlawfully demonstrating in close proximity to a government building. Seventeen women and five men were detained and released the same day.

Freedom of association was restricted.

■ The trial of 15 Presidential Guards from the Central Protection and Security Unit in the Military Bureau of the Angolan Presidency started in the Luanda Regional Military Court on 15 September. The guards were charged with "making collective demands" on the grounds that they had signed a petition on 11 September calling for fairer salaries, challenging the application process for junior officers' posts and calling for improved social assistance in the event of death of immediate family. The trial continued at the end of the year.

Freedom of expression – journalists

Freedom of expression, particularly of the press, continued to be suppressed. Attempts were made to prevent publication of newspapers or articles which were seen as potentially anti-government. There were no further developments in the appeals by Armando Chicoca and William Tonet, convicted of defamation in 2011.

■ On 12 March, around 15 police officers from the National Directorate of Criminal Investigation (DNIC) entered the offices of the newspaper *Folha-8* and confiscated 20 computers as part of an investigation into the publication on 30 December 2011 of a satirical photo montage of the President, Vice-President and Head of the Military Bureau. In June, seven newspaper staff members were questioned by the DNIC.

Enforced disappearances

At least two cases of suspected enforced disappearances were reported during the year.

■ António Alves Kamulingue and Isaías Sebastião Cassule disappeared on 27 and 29 May respectively. They were involved in the organization of a demonstration planned for 27 May by war veterans and former Presidential Guards to demand payment for pensions and salaries owed to them.

Housing rights – forced evictions

Despite government talks to improve access to housing, small-scale forced evictions continued and thousands of people remained at risk. Thousands of families forcibly evicted in the past remained without compensation. The government undertook in June 2011 to rehouse by April 2012 over 450 families in Luanda whose homes were demolished between 2004 and 2006, but none had been rehoused by the end of the year. In September, UN Habitat announced that it was preparing to sign a co-operation agreement with Angola to send a representative to the country to provide technical advisory services for housing in Luanda from 2013.

Prisoners of conscience and possible prisoners of conscience

Two members of the Commission of the Legal Sociological Manifesto of the Lunda Tchokwe Protectorate, Mário Muamuene and Domingos Capenda, who remained in Kakanda prison despite the expiry of their sentence on 9 October 2011, were released on 17 January 2012.

Despite the November 2011 conclusion by the UN Working Group on Arbitrary Detention calling for the release of members of the Commission detained between 2009 and 2011, five members – Sérgio Augusto, Sebastião Lumani, José Muteba, António Malendeca and Domingos Henrique Samujaia – remained in prison. There were further reported arrests of Commission members during the year.

■ On 12 February Eugénio Mateus Sangoma Lopes and Alberto Mulozeno were arrested and charged with crimes against the security of the state after police in Lucapa reportedly went to their homes and told them to report to the police station to discuss the Commission. According to the written Court Mandate, they were convicted and sentenced in June to 18 months' imprisonment for rebellion.

Amnesty International visits/reports

🚗 Amnesty International delegates visited Angola in April.

📄 Angola: Submission to the African Commission on Human and Peoples' Rights, 51st Ordinary Session, April 2012 (AFR 12/001/2012)

📄 Angola: Open letter to Presidential candidates, candidates to the National Assembly and political party leaders – a human rights agenda for political parties and candidates in the general elections, 17 July 2012 (AFR 12/002/2012)

ARGENTINA

ARGENTINE REPUBLIC
Head of state and government: **Cristina Fernández de Kirchner**

Women pregnant as a result of rape continued to face obstacles in accessing legal abortions, despite a Supreme Court ruling affirming this right. Indigenous Peoples' land rights remained unfulfilled. Trials to end impunity for human rights violations committed during the military regime (1976-83) continued.

Background

In October, Argentina's human rights record was examined under the UN Universal Periodic Review. Recommendations were made on issues including sexual and reproductive rights, Indigenous Peoples' rights, freedom from torture and migrants' rights.

Investigations in Argentina based on universal jurisdiction continued during the year into crimes committed in Spain between 1936 and 1977 –

including the period of the Spanish Civil War and the Franco regime.

In May, a law was passed allowing people to change their names and sexes on official documents without the approval of a judge or doctor. This was an important step towards the recognition of the rights of transsexual people.

Indigenous Peoples' rights

In July, the UN Special Rapporteur on the rights of indigenous peoples published a report expressing concerns about issues including the lack of measures to protect Indigenous Peoples' rights to their lands and natural resources. The report also highlighted the failure to comply with Emergency Law 26.160 which prohibits the eviction of Indigenous communities pending a nationwide survey to define Indigenous territories.

A draft law to reform the Civil Code, which included measures that affect Indigenous Peoples' rights to their traditional lands, was before Parliament at the end of the year. Indigenous Peoples expressed concern that their views had not been sought while the law was being discussed.

■ In March, the Supreme Court of Justice held a public hearing about obstacles preventing the Toba Qom community of La Primavera, Formosa province, from claiming traditional lands. In November, a Federal Court dropped the charges against Indigenous leaders Félix Díaz and Amanda Asikak in connection with a roadblock erected in 2010. The judges argued that the roadblock was the only protest measure available to them. Threats and acts of intimidation against Félix Díaz and members of his family remained a concern. In August, Félix Díaz was hit by a truck while he was on his motorbike. Witnesses said the truck belonged to the family that owns the traditional land claimed by the community. The driver fled and the accident had not been investigated by the end of the year.

Women's rights

In March, a Supreme Court ruling established that any woman or girl pregnant as a result of rape should have access to safe abortion without the need for judicial authorization. However, lack of compliance with the ruling in several parts of the country remained a concern. Following the Supreme Court ruling, the Parliament of Buenos Aires City passed legislation to allow legal abortions, without the requirement for judicial involvement, for rape

A

survivors and in cases where carrying the pregnancy to term would place the woman's life at risk. However, the law was vetted by the governor leaving Buenos Aires under previous legislation that does not comply with the Supreme Court's decision.

■ In October, a Buenos Aires court prevented a 32-year-old woman from having an abortion. She was a victim of trafficking and her pregnancy was the result of rape. A public outcry followed and the Supreme Court overturned the lower court's decision. The woman was eventually able to access abortion services.

Concerns remained at the lack of full implementation of the legislation to prevent and punish violence against women passed in 2009, including the failure to collect reliable data.

Legislation was passed making gender-based motivation an aggravating factor in homicides.

Impunity

Progress continued in securing prosecutions and convictions of those responsible for grave human rights violations under military rule (1976-1983).

■ In June, former military officer Alfredo Omar Feito and former federal police officer Pedro Santiago Godoy were sentenced to 18 and 25 years' imprisonment respectively for the torture and unlawful detention of 181 people in the clandestine detention centres of Primer Cuerpo del Ejército Atlético, Banco and Olimpo.

■ Former Argentine Presidents Jorge Rafael Videla and Reynaldo Bignone were convicted in July of the systematic kidnapping of children and sentenced to 50 and 15 years' imprisonment respectively.

■ In October, three former marines were sentenced to life imprisonment in connection with the "Trelew massacre" in which 16 political prisoners were executed after an attempt to escape from a prison in Chubut province in 1972.

Torture and other ill-treatment and prison conditions

In November, the establishment of a national mechanism for the prevention of torture was approved.

In July, video footage appeared on the internet showing at least five police officers torturing two detainees in the police detention office of General Güemes, Salta province. The footage which was allegedly filmed in 2011 shows the detainees being beaten up and suffocated with a bag. Investigations into the torture remained open at the end of the year.

Amnesty International visits/reports

▣ Argentina: Amnesty International submission to the UN Universal Periodic Review: 14th session of the UPR working group (Index: AMR 13/003/2012)

ARMENIA

REPUBLIC OF ARMENIA
Head of state: Serzh Sargsyan
Head of government: Tigran Sargsyan

Public attitudes were hostile towards topics which were perceived as unpatriotic. Conditions in prisons were reported to amount to inhuman treatment.

Background

President Sargsyan's Republican Party won parliamentary elections on 6 May. While freedom of expression, assembly and movement were largely unrestricted around the election, monitors reported widespread vote buying as well as instances of pressure on voters.

Freedom of expression

Freedom of expression was largely unrestricted. However, those expressing opinions perceived as unpatriotic or anti-nationalist faced widespread public hostility and occasionally violence. Police and local authorities appeared at times to be colluding in the attacks. They also failed to properly investigate or to publicly and unequivocally denounce such acts.

■ Civil society activists attempting to hold a festival of Azerbaijani films in Armenia were subjected to violent attacks and forced to cancel the event on two occasions. On 12 April, dozens of protesters blocked the venue of the film festival, scheduled in Armenia's second city, Gumri. They physically assaulted Giorgi Vanyan, the organizer and chairman of the local Caucasus Centre for Peace-Making Initiatives, and forced him to publicly announce that the festival was cancelled. Festival organizers reported that the local authorities had harassed and used psychological pressure to dissuade them from holding the event.

On 16 April, another attempt to hold the film festival in the city of Vanadzor at the Helsinki Citizens

Assembly (HCA) office also prompted public protests and violence. Approximately 200 people – including students, political party members and veterans from the Nagorno-Karabakh war – gathered in front of the HCA office. They forced their way into the premises, vandalizing office equipment, throwing eggs and rocks and injuring one member of staff. Police officers present throughout failed to intervene to ensure the safety of the staff members or to stop the violence. Despite the HCA's requests, additional police did not arrive until after the incident. After an investigation, one woman was fined for throwing a stone at the building, but no thorough or impartial investigation took place. The authorities failed to condemn the violence.

■ On 8 May, a gay-friendly bar in the capital, Yerevan, was attacked. Two people were caught on a security camera throwing Molotov cocktails through the windows. However, police reportedly only arrived at the scene 12 hours later to investigate the attack. Two young men were arrested as part of the investigation, but were bailed shortly afterwards by two MPs for the nationalist Armenian Revolutionary Federation – Dashnaktsutyun party (ARF). They condoned the attack, saying it was in line with "the context of societal and national ideology". Eduard Sharmazanov, spokesperson for the ruling Republican Party and Parliamentary Deputy Speaker was quoted justifying the violent attack in local newspapers.

Torture and other ill-treatment

On 3 October, the European Committee for the Prevention of Torture published a report following their visit to Armenia in December 2011. It stated that "virtually none of the recommendations made after previous visits as regards the detention of lifers have been implemented". The report also noted that the poor conditions at Kentron Prison in Yerevan made it unsuitable for lengthy periods of detention. The Committee found that the detention conditions of life-sentenced prisoners held at Kentron amounted to inhuman treatment.

Conscientious objectors

By the end of the year, more than 30 men were serving prison sentences for refusing to perform military service on grounds of conscience. Alternative civilian service remained under military control. On 27 November, the European Court of Human Rights, in its fourth decision against Armenia on conscientious

objection, found that Armenia had violated the rights of 17 Jehovah's Witnesses in the case of *Khachatryan and Others v. Armenia*. The Court found that the rights of the Jehovah's Witnesses to liberty and security, as well as the right to compensation for unlawful detention, had been violated. They faced criminal charges and detention because they had left their alternative service when they realized that they were under military control.

Amnesty International visits/reports

🚍 Amnesty International delegates visited Armenia in June.
📄 Armenian authorities must protect free speech and ensure safety for Azerbaijani film festival organizers (EUR 54/001/2012)

A

AUSTRALIA

AUSTRALIA
Head of state: Queen Elizabeth II, represented by
                                                           Quentin Bryce
Head of government: Julia Gillard

Despite the establishment of a federal human rights committee to consider all new bills before Parliament, laws were passed restricting the rights of Indigenous Peoples in the Northern Territory and reintroducing a policy of offshore processing where asylum-seekers arriving by boat are sent to Nauru or Papua New Guinea.

Background

The government announced that it would ratify the Optional Protocol to the UN Convention against Torture in January 2011. However, it had not done so by the end of the year. A parliamentary human rights scrutiny committee was established in March to consider all new bills, and ensure that they included a statement of human rights compatibility.

Indigenous Peoples' rights

Aboriginal and Torres Strait Islander youth continued to be over-represented in Australia's criminal justice system. Indigenous youth accounted for 59% of the national juvenile detention rates while Indigenous Peoples as a whole only made up 2% of the total population. Australia maintained its reservation to the UN Convention on the Rights of the Child, allowing states and territories to detain children in adult prisons.

■ In Victoria, a 16-year-old Aboriginal boy was held in an adult prison in solitary confinement for up to 22 hours per day from August to November.

■ In April, police opened fire on a suspected stolen vehicle occupied by Aboriginal youths in Kings Cross, Sydney. Two Aboriginal boys, one aged 14, were shot. An independent Ombudsman's report into the incident had not been released by December.

In June, the Stronger Futures legislation, which extended laws contained in the controversial and discriminatory 2007 Northern Territory Intervention (a series of laws including welfare changes and law enforcement in Indigenous communities), was passed without genuine consultation or scrutiny by the Parliamentary Joint Committee on Human Rights. The legislation allows for far-reaching intervention into Indigenous Peoples' lives in the Northern Territory.

In September, the government deferred the referendum on constitutional recognition of Australia's Indigenous Peoples.

Refugees and asylum-seekers

In August, legislation was passed reintroducing offshore processing of asylum-seekers. Australia's annual humanitarian intake was increased to 20,000 places in October.

Under new legislation introduced in November, asylum-seekers who arrived by boat would either be processed offshore or have fewer rights in Australia; those arriving by plane would not face such restrictions. As of 30 October, there were 7,633 asylum-seekers and refugees detained in Australia, including 797 children. More than 7,000 of these asylum-seekers were designated for offshore processing and had not started the refugee status determination process. In November, 63 refugees with negative security assessments remained in indefinite detention, including one girl and five boys.

■ As of 15 December, Australia was detaining 385 asylum-seekers, all men, on Nauru, and 47 asylum-seekers on Manus Island, Papua New Guinea, including 16 children.

AUSTRIA

REPUBLIC OF AUSTRIA
Head of state: Heinz Fischer
Head of government: Werner Faymann

The Criminal Code was amended to introduce the crime of torture. Concerns about racism in the criminal justice system remained. Legal safeguards for asylum-seekers were reduced.

International justice

Criminal investigations against the former Guatemalan deputy-head of police, Javier Figueroa, suspected of involvement in extrajudicial executions in Guatemala, were pending. The Austrian authorities had arrested Javier Figueroa in May 2011, after they turned down an extradition request to Guatemala.

Torture and other ill-treatment

At the end of the year the Criminal Code was amended to introduce the crime of torture, to take effect from 1 January 2013.

While welcoming the broadening of the mandate of the Austrian Ombudsman Board to work as a national preventive mechanism under the Optional Protocol to the UN Convention against Torture in August, the CERD Committee remained concerned about the independence of the Board members and recommended that their appointment fully comply with international standards.

■ In May, an official of the Ministry of the Interior apologized to Gambian citizen Bakary J., who was tortured by four police officers in 2006 following an unsuccessful deportation attempt. His residence ban was lifted. Negotiations about compensation were ongoing.

Police and security forces

After a six-year trial period, the Ministry of the Interior authorized the regular use of electro-stun devices in police operations. The Ministry qualified the devices as in principle non-lethal. However, there were reports of human rights abuses carried out with electro-stun devices in several countries and the incidence of several hundred deaths following the use of such devices, which led to calls for electro-stun devices to be strictly limited to situations where they are necessary to avoid recourse to police firearms.

Racism

Reports of racially motivated police misconduct against foreign nationals and ethnic minorities continued.

In August, the CERD Committee criticized Austria's failure to provide statistical data on the ethnic composition of its population and expressed concern about reports of racial profiling and stop-and-search practices on people from ethnic minorities. It also criticized the failure to adequately prosecute and punish law enforcement officials for offences against people with migration backgrounds; to ensure equal protection under the law; and to prosecute all violations of the prohibition of racial discrimination.

Austria maintained its refusal to adopt a National Action Plan against Racism as required by the 2001 Durban Declaration and Programme of Action.

Migrants' and asylum-seekers' rights

In August, Austria adopted amendments to the Asylum and Aliens Laws, which reduced legal safeguards for people in need of international protection. The right of asylum-seekers and migrants to free legal counsel was restricted and, in some proceedings, denied.

Amnesty International visits/reports

Austria: Briefing to the UN Committee on the Elimination of Racial Discrimination (EUR 13/001/2012)

AZERBAIJAN

REPUBLIC OF AZERBAIJAN
Head of state: **Ilham Aliyev**
Head of government: **Artur Rasizade**

The government continued to intimidate and imprison people and groups who criticized the government. Peaceful protests in the centre of the city were banned and dispersed by the police with excessive use of force. Torture, especially in police custody, was frequently reported.

Prisoners of conscience

Four prisoners of conscience were released on 26 December by presidential pardon: activists Vidadi Iskandarov and Shahin Hasanli, arrested in connection with the 2011 protests; and Taleh Khasmammadov and Anar Bayramli, both convicted on fabricated charges in 2012. Human rights defender Taleh Khasmammadov was sentenced to four years' imprisonment for allegedly attacking police officers in a police station shortly after he had published several articles implicating the involvement of local police in organized criminal activities. Anar Bayramli, a journalist working for the Azeri language and Iranian-sponsored television station Sahar, was arrested on 17 February for drugs possession, shortly after relations between Azerbaijan and Iran deteriorated.

A

Freedom of expression

The government targeted human rights defenders and journalists for their work and subjected them to intimidation, harassment and arrest. The authorities used arrests and spurious charges to clamp down on activities and protests at the time of the Eurovision song contest in the capital Baku in May.

■ On 7 March, Khadija Ismayilova, a well-known investigative journalist with Radio Free Europe (Azadliq Radiosu), received a threatening letter containing intimate photos of her, after her apartment was broken into and a hidden camera installed in her room. The letter threatened to "shame" her if she did not abandon her work. After Khadija Ismayilova publicly exposed the blackmail attempt, a video showing her in an intimate relationship was published on the internet.

■ On 8 April, Ogtay Gulaliyev, a human rights defender with the Kur Civil Society Organization working on environmental issues was arrested on charges of hooliganism and "inciting violence". He was released on bail on 13 June and by the end of the year his trial had not begun, although the charges against him remained, carrying a sentence of three years' imprisonment. On 8 June Ilham Amiraslanov, another human rights activist with the Kur Civil Society Organization, was arrested on charges of illegal possession of a gun and ammunition, which he maintained were planted on him. On 12 September, he was sentenced to two years in prison after an unfair trial. Both Ogtay Gulaliyev and Ilham Amiraslanov had been helping flood victims and were vocal against the cases of aid embezzlement by the local authorities. Ilham Amiraslanov's arrest came a few days after he met with the Minister of Emergency Situations regarding the problems of the flood victims.

■ On 18 April, several journalists were violently assaulted when they tried to film illegal house demolitions on the outskirts of Baku. Among them, journalist Idrak Abbasov was beaten unconscious by police and state employees.

■ On 13 June, trumped-up charges of hooliganism were brought against pro-democracy activist Mehman Huseynov apparently in retaliation for his journalism and campaigning activities before the Eurovision song contest. He was later released from pre-trial detention, but remained under investigation.

■ On 21 June, Hilal Mamedov, editor of a minority language newspaper *Tolyshi sado* (*The Voice of Talysh*), was arrested on spurious drugs charges. The next day a Baku city court ordered him to spend three months in pre-trial detention. On 3 July, additional charges of treason and inciting religious and national hatred were also brought against him. The case did not reach court before the end of the year.

■ On 29 September, Zaur Gurbanli, pro-democracy campaign activist and chair of the opposition youth movement Nida, was imprisoned for 15 days after he posted an article criticizing the government for nepotism and a poem by the daughter of President Aliyev being mandatory reading in the school curriculum.

Freedom of association

NGOs working on human rights and democracy issues faced pressure and harassment and found it difficult to hold meetings or operate freely, especially outside Baku.

■ On 7 February, Democracy Development Resource Centre, an NGO operating in Nakhchivan Autonomous Republic, and the Institute for Reporters' Freedom and Safety received a letter from the Ministry of Foreign Affairs, which warned them against "spreading inflammatory information" through their websites Nakhchivan Human Rights and Media Monitor.

■ Aftandil Mammadov, co-ordinator of the Guba branch of Election Monitoring and Democracy Studies Centre, reported being summoned to the local police station on 27 July and again on 27 August, and warned against organizing any activities without the knowledge and permission of the local police. He previously reported being persistently followed by the police and prevented from holding group meetings.

■ The Baku branch of the Human Rights House, an international NGO, remained closed after authorities forcibly shut down the organization on 7 March 2011 on the grounds that they had failed to comply with registration requirements.

Freedom of assembly

Public protests continued to be banned in the centre of Baku. In November, amendments to the Criminal Code increased the maximum punishment for those organizing and participating in "unauthorized" or "banned" protests. The new sentence could be up to three years in prison and a fine of US$10,000.

Peaceful assemblies were regularly dispersed with excessive force by police and those who attempted to take part in peaceful rallies faced harassment, beatings and arrest.

■ In March and April, police violently broke up several peaceful protests by youth groups and opposition activists, beating and arresting participants. The youth groups had applied for but had been denied permission to hold a peaceful rally in areas officially designated for demonstrations.

■ On 20 October, police dispersed a peaceful rally of approximately 200 people. The protest called for the dissolution of parliament in response to video recordings published online which revealed the extent of political corruption and bribery in parliament. Over 100 people were arrested at the protest and 13 leading activists were jailed for periods ranging from seven to 10 days, on charges of "disobeying police orders" and for attending an "illegal protest".

■ On 17 November Dayanat Babayev, a former prisoner of conscience, was arrested for taking part in a protest in the centre of Baku that called for the President's resignation and the dissolution of parliament. He was sentenced to seven days of administrative detention for allegedly disobeying police. On 24 November, when his administrative detention expired, new criminal charges of hooliganism were brought against him and he was re-arrested as a suspect in a criminal case. On 26 November, the Nasimi district court released Dayanat Babayev, but the charges against him have not been dropped.

Torture and other ill-treatment

Torture and other ill-treatment remained widespread amid a prevailing climate of impunity.

■ On 17 March, activists Jamal Ali and Natig Kamilov alleged that they were beaten and otherwise ill-treated in police custody and later in detention.

■ On 6 March, activists Jabbar Savalan, Dayanat Babayev, Majid Marjanli and Abulfaz Gurbanly alleged that they were beaten and otherwise ill-treated in detention, after police broke up another peaceful protest in central Baku and arrested 16 participants.

■ Hilal Mamedov, the editor of newspaper *Tolyshi sado* alleged that he had been tortured while in police custody following his arrest on 21 June. The photo evidence of bruising on his feet and ankles was sent to the Nizami District Prosecutor, who initiated an investigation but there was no outcome published at the end of the year.

Amnesty International visits/reports

🚗 Amnesty International delegates visited Azerbaijan in May and November.

📄 Azerbaijan: No more running scared (EUR 55/001/2012)

📄 Azerbaijan: Authorities determined to silence dissent to ensure successful Eurovision (EUR 55/008/2012)

📄 Azerbaijan: Human rights abuses placed under the e-spotlight (EUR 55/018/2012)

BAHAMAS

COMMONWEALTH OF THE BAHAMAS
Head of state: **Queen Elizabeth II, represented by Sir Arthur Alexander Foulkes**
Head of government: **Perry Gladstone Christie (replaced Hubert Alexander Ingraham in May)**

At least six people were reportedly killed by police in disputed circumstances. Haitian migrants continued to face discrimination and forcible repatriation. One person remained on death row.

Background

In August, a Commission was established to review the Constitution and to address issues including strengthening fundamental rights and freedoms and the death penalty.

The Bahamas continued to face a worrying public security crisis. The homicide rate remained high, despite a 13% decrease in reported cases compared with 2011; 111 homicides were reported in 2012.

Death penalty

In August, the Inter-American Commission on Human Rights called on all states in the region to "impose a moratorium on executions as a step toward the gradual disappearance of this penalty". However, Prime Minister Christie reiterated his support for the death penalty and announced that a response would be submitted to the Commission.

■ One person, Mario Flower, was believed to remain on death row at the end of the year. He was sentenced to death in 2010 for the murder of a police officer.

Police and security forces

At least six people were reportedly killed by police in disputed circumstances and at least one man died in police custody. Reports of ill-treatment and excessive use of force by police continued. The conviction in June of a police officer for the death in custody of Desmond Key in 2007 was a rare instance of police being held to account for such abuses.

■ On 5 July, police shot Reno Rolle on New-Providence Island for no apparent reason in front of various witnesses. Reno Rolle, who reportedly has learning difficulties, sustained serious injuries to his kidney and pancreas.

Refugees and migrants

The Bahamas failed to comply with calls from the UN to stop all involuntary returns of Haitian nationals. In June, the Independent Expert on the situation of human rights in Haiti stated that "individuals returned to Haiti are vulnerable to human rights violations, especially the fundamental rights to life, health and family".

Use of violence during arrests of irregular migrants continued to be reported.

Rights of lesbian, gay, bisexual, transgender and intersex people

Discrimination against LGBTI people remained a concern. The government failed to establish a legal framework to protect LGBTI people from discrimination.

Violence against women and girls

In July, the CEDAW Committee expressed concern about the high prevalence of violence, including rape, and the persistence of domestic violence.

Amnesty International visits/reports

📖 Bahamas: Legislative challenges obstruct human rights progress: Amnesty International submission to the UN Universal Periodic Review (AMR 14/001/2012)

BAHRAIN

KINGDOM OF BAHRAIN
Head of state: **King Hamad bin 'Issa Al Khalifa**
Head of government: **Shaikh Khalifa bin Salman Al Khalifa**

The authorities continued to crack down on protests and dissent. The government made some reforms based on the recommendations of a major inquiry into human rights violations in 2011, but failed to implement some of the inquiry's main recommendations in relation to accountability. Scores of people remained in prison or were detained for opposing the government, including prisoners of conscience and people sentenced after unfair trials. Human rights defenders and other activists were harassed and imprisoned. The security forces continued to use excessive force against protesters, resulting in deaths, and allegedly tortured or otherwise ill-treated detainees. Only a few security officers were prosecuted for human rights violations committed in 2011, perpetuating a climate of impunity. One death sentence was imposed; there were no executions.

Background

There were further anti-government protests, mostly by members of the majority Shi'a community who complained of being politically marginalized by the ruling Sunni minority. There were reports of demonstrators throwing Molotov cocktails and blocking roads. Security forces used excessive force in dispersing some demonstrations. Political dialogue between the government and the opposition remained largely stalled.

In November, the government reported that "two Asians" had been killed and a third injured by bomb explosions in Manama. Days later, the authorities stripped 31 people of their Bahraini nationality saying they had damaged state security.

The government introduced several reforms recommended by the Bahrain Independent Commission of Inquiry (BICI) in 2011, including reinstating dismissed workers and establishing police reform mechanisms. In October, it amended some articles of the Penal Code and included a new definition of torture. However, the government failed to implement other key recommendations of the BICI, which was appointed by the King in 2011 to investigate human rights violations committed by government forces when suppressing popular protests in the early months of 2011. In particular, the authorities failed to release all prisoners of conscience and to independently investigate allegations of torture of detainees and bring all the perpetrators to justice. However, under the UN Universal Periodic Review in May, the government accepted over 140 recommendations, including calls to implement the BICI's recommendations. The government rejected other recommendations under the UN Universal Periodic Review concerning abolition of the death penalty. The government imposed tighter visa controls on foreign NGOs in March and, in October, banned all public rallies and gatherings. It lifted the ban in December. In November, the Ministry of Social Development overruled the election results for the board of the Bahrain Lawyers Society, and reinstated the previous board.

Impunity

There was a continuing climate of impunity, reflected by the low number of prosecutions of police officers and security forces members relative to the extent and gravity of human rights violations committed in 2011. The authorities failed to independently investigate all allegations of torture. Only a handful of low-ranking security officers and two senior officers were brought to trial in connection with killings of protesters or torture and other abuses against detainees in custody in 2011. Three were convicted and sentenced to seven years' imprisonment but at least one remained at liberty pending an appeal. Three others were acquitted, prompting a prosecution appeal.

■ In September, a court acquitted two security officers of killing two protesters at Manama's Pearl Roundabout on 17 February 2011. The officers' own statements were reported to be the only evidence presented and they did not attend court hearings. The prosecution lodged an appeal against the verdict in October.

Excessive use of force

The security forces continued to use excessive force, using shotguns and tear gas against protesters, sometimes in enclosed spaces. Two children were among four people reported to have died after being shot with firearms or by the impact of tear gas canisters. At least 20 other people were reported to have died as a result of tear gas. The authorities said in September that 1,500 security officers had been injured in protests since the beginning of the year. Two police officers were killed in the second half of the year.

■ Hussam al-Haddad, aged 16, died on 17 August after being shot by riot police in al-Muharraq. An inquiry by the Special Investigation Unit (SIU) concluded that the shooting was justifiable "to ward off imminent danger".

■ Ali Hussein Neama, aged 16, died on 28 September after riot police shot him in the back in Sadad village. His family said police threatened them and prevented them from approaching him as he lay on the ground. An investigation by the SIU dismissed the case, considering it an "act of self-defence" on the part of the security officer.

Torture and other ill-treatment

The government took steps to improve police behaviour, issuing new regulations for the police including a code of conduct and providing human rights training. However, the police continued to arrest people without warrants, detain them incommunicado for days or weeks, deny them access to lawyers, and allegedly subject them to torture or other ill-treatment, including beatings, kicking, verbal abuse and threats of rape.

■ Hussein Abdullah Ali Mahmood al-Ali was arrested without a warrant on 26 July in Salmabad village. He was allegedly beaten and taken to an undisclosed location. He reported being tortured while held incommunicado and forced to sign a "confession". His family did not know his whereabouts for three weeks, and for months after his arrest neither his family nor lawyers knew his exact location. He said he was given electric shocks and threatened with rape.

Tens of children aged 15 to 18, including those arrested at or during demonstrations, were held in adult prisons and detention centres; many were accused of "illegal gathering" or rioting. Some were beaten at or following arrest and denied access to their families or lawyers during the first hours of detention, during which time they alleged they were forced to sign "confessions". Some were sentenced to prison terms.

■ Salman Amir Abdullah al-Aradi, aged 16, was arrested in February and again in May when he was taken to Al Hidd police station and allegedly beaten and threatened with rape to make him sign a "confession" without the presence of his family or lawyer. He was then charged with "illegal gathering" and other offences, convicted and sentenced to one year's imprisonment in July, confirmed on appeal.

■ Mariam Hassan Abdali Al Khazaz, aged 17, said police beat and kicked her following her arrest in Manama after a protest on 21 September. She was made to sign a "confession" without the presence of a lawyer or her family and charged with "illegal gathering", assaulting a police officer and other offences. She was released on bail on 17 October and was awaiting trial at the end of the year.

Human rights defenders and other activists

Human rights defenders and other activists were harassed, detained and sentenced by the authorities, and vilified in the state media.

■ Nabeel Rajab, president of the Bahrain Centre for Human Rights, was particularly targeted, being repeatedly arrested and prosecuted. In May, he was charged with "insulting a national institution" through remarks made on Twitter about the Ministry of the Interior. On 9 July, he was sentenced to three months' imprisonment for criticizing the Prime Minister. On 16 August, he was convicted for participating in "illegal gatherings" and "disturbing public order" and sentenced to three years in prison, reduced to two years in December. He was a prisoner of conscience.

■ Zainab al-Khawaja was detained for six weeks from April for staging a sit-down protest against her father's detention and other human rights violations. She was arrested again in August and sentenced to two months in prison for tearing up a picture of the King. She was released on bail in October but re-arrested in December and sentenced to a month in prison while awaiting further charges. She was released at the end of the year.

In August, several UN Special Rapporteurs jointly urged the Bahraini government to cease harassing human rights defenders.

Prisoners of conscience

Prisoners of conscience, including those sentenced in connection with mass popular protests in 2011, remained in prison. They appeared to have been targeted for their anti-government views.

■ Ebrahim Sharif, 'Abdulhadi Al-Khawaja and 11 other leading critics of the government were serving prison terms ranging from five years to life. Their convictions and sentences were confirmed in September. They were convicted of establishing terrorist groups to overthrow the government and change the Constitution, and on other charges that they denied, despite a lack of evidence that they had used or advocated violence.

■ Mahdi 'Issa Mahdi Abu Dheeb, former president of the Bahrain Teachers' Association, had his conviction upheld but his sentence reduced from 10 to five years in prison by the High Criminal Court of Appeal in October. In September 2011, an unfair military court convicted him of calling a teachers' strike, inciting hatred and seeking to overthrow the government by force, despite a lack of evidence to support the charges. He said he was tortured following his arrest in 2011 while held incommunicado in pre-trial detention.

■ Six health professionals, including 'Ali 'Esa Mansoor al-'Ekri and Ghassan Ahmed 'Ali Dhaif, were arrested in October the day after the Court of Cassation confirmed their convictions and upheld reduced prison sentences of between one month and five years imposed on them in June. Originally, they were sentenced to between five and 15 years in prison after an unfair trial in September 2011. The appeal court quashed the convictions of several others. Two of the six were released at the end of their sentences, but the four others were held at al-Jaw prison at the end of the year.

Freedom of assembly

On 30 October the Interior Minister banned all rallies and gatherings alleging that they allowed people to express opposition to the government and led to rioting, violence and destruction of property. He said the ban would remain in place until "security is maintained" and that anyone breaching the ban would be prosecuted. The ban was lifted in December and the Ministry of the Interior announced a proposal to amend the Code on Public Meetings, Processions and Gatherings, which imposed restrictions on the right to freedom of assembly.

■ Sayed Yousif Almuhafdah, a human rights activist, was detained on 2 November for attending an unauthorized gathering to document police behaviour towards protesters. He was released two weeks later and the charges of "illegal gathering" were dropped. He was re-arrested in December and charged with "spreading false news".

Death penalty

One death sentence was reportedly imposed in March and upheld by the Court of Appeal in November. There were no executions. Two death sentences imposed in 2011 by a military court were quashed by the Court of Cassation and the two defendants were retried before a civilian court.

Amnesty International visits/reports

🚗 Amnesty International cancelled a planned visit to Bahrain in March when the government imposed new visa restrictions on international NGOs. Trial observers representing Amnesty International visited Bahrain in August and September.

📄 Flawed reforms: Bahrain fails to achieve justice for protesters (MDE 11/014/2012)

📄 Bahrain: Reform shelved, repression unleashed (MDE 11/062/2012)

BANGLADESH

PEOPLE'S REPUBLIC OF BANGLADESH

Head of state:	Zillur Rahman
Head of government:	Sheikh Hasina

Some 30 extrajudicial executions were reported. State security forces were implicated in torture and other ill-treatment and at least 10 enforced disappearances. Political violence resulted in the death of at least four men. Women continued to be subjected to various forms of violence. The government failed to protect Indigenous communities from attack by Bengali settlers. **At least 111 workers died in a factory fire, some allegedly because officials refused to let them leave the premises. More than 20 Buddhist temples and monasteries, one Hindu temple and scores of Buddhist homes and shops were set on fire during a communal attack. One person was executed and at least 45 people were sentenced to death.**

Background

In January, the Prime Minister stated that no human rights violations had been committed in the country.

Political violence escalated in December, when opposition parties tried to impose day-long general strikes. At least four people died and dozens of strikers and police sustained injuries. Jamaat-e-Islami demanded the release of their leaders currently being tried on war crimes charges. The Bangladesh Nationalist Party (BNP) demanded that the forthcoming general elections be held under a caretaker government. Members of a group affiliated with the governing party attacked opposition members, beating and stabbing one bystander to death.

National and international concern about allegedly high levels of corruption were echoed in June when the World Bank cancelled US$1.2 billion credit for the construction of Padma bridge in central Bangladesh, due to the government's insufficient response to allegations of corruption. An inquiry by the Anti-Corruption Commission remained open.

The authorities continued to raise concerns with India over killings of Bangladeshis by Indian border control forces. More than a dozen Bangladeshis were killed by Indian forces while crossing the border into India.

Extrajudicial executions

At least 30 people were victims of alleged extrajudicial executions. Police claimed they had been killed in gun battles with security forces. Families said they had been killed after being arrested by people in plain clothes identifying themselves as Rapid Action Battalion (RAB) personnel or other police. No one was brought to justice for these killings.

■ RAB personnel allegedly shot dead Mohammad Atear Rahman (also known as Tofa Molla), a farmer, in Kushtia district on 12 September. RAB said he was killed in "crossfire", although Atear Rahman's family and other witnesses said RAB had arrested him at his

home the previous evening. His body reportedly bore three gunshot wounds, two in the back.

Torture and other ill-treatment

Torture and other ill-treatment were widespread, committed with virtual impunity by the police, RAB, the army and intelligence agencies. Methods included beating, kicking, suspension from the ceiling, food and sleep deprivation, and electric shocks. Most detainees were allegedly tortured until they "confessed" to having committed a crime. Police and RAB allegedly distorted records to cover up the torture, including by misrepresenting arrest dates.

Enforced disappearances

At least 10 people went missing throughout the year. In most cases the victims were never traced. Those bodies that were recovered bore injuries, some caused by beatings.

■ Ilias Ali, Sylhet division secretary of the opposition BNP, disappeared together with his driver Ansar Ali on 17 April. The government promised to investigate the case but provided no information by the end of the year.

Violence against women and girls

Women continued to be subjected to various forms of violence. These included acid attacks, murder for failing to pay the requested dowry, flogging for religious offences by illegal arbitration committees, domestic violence, and sexual violence.

■ Aleya Begum and her daughter were arrested without a warrant on 9 September and were allegedly tortured at Khoksa police station in Kushtia district. After two days they were transferred to Kushtia city police station and kept in a dark room. The daughter, a college student, was separated from her mother at night and sexually abused by police officers. The two women were released on 18 September, after appearing in court. Aleya Begum and her daughter shared their story with the media, and were arrested and jailed again on 26 September.

Indigenous Peoples' rights

As in previous years, the authorities failed to settle Indigenous Peoples' claims to land that had been seized from them during the internal armed conflict (1975-1997), or recently occupied by increasing numbers of Bengali settlers. Tension between the two communities and the failure of the security forces to

B

protect local Indigenous people against attacks by Bengali settlers led to several clashes and injuries on both sides.

■ At least 20 people were injured in a clash between Indigenous people and Bengali settlers in Rangamati on 22 September. Local people said security forces came to the scene but failed to stop the violence.

Workers' rights

Trade union leaders supporting garment factory workers' rallies against low pay and poor working conditions were harassed and intimidated. One man was killed.

■ Trade union leader Aminul Islam went missing on 4 April. He was found dead a day later in Ghatail town, north of Dhaka. His family saw evidence of torture on his body and believed he had been abducted by security forces. He had previously been arrested and beaten by members of the National Security Intelligence for his trade union activities.

■ At least 111 workers died from burns and other injuries, some allegedly because factory officials refused to open the gates to let them escape a fire that broke out at Tazreen Fashion in Savar town, north of the capital Dhaka, in November.

Communal violence

Attacks against members of minority communities took a new turn in late September. Thousands of people protesting against an image posted on Facebook of the Qur'an, which they considered derogatory, set fire to more than 20 Buddhist temples and monasteries, one Hindu temple and scores of homes and shops in the southern cities of Cox's Bazar and Chittagong.

Death penalty

At least 45 people were sentenced to death. One man was executed in April.

BELARUS

REPUBLIC OF BELARUS
Head of state: Alyaksandr Lukashenka
Head of government: Mikhail Myasnikovich

Prisoners of conscience remained in detention; some were sentenced to increased prison terms for violating prison rules. Civil society activists, including human rights defenders and journalists, faced violations of their rights to freedom of expression, assembly and association. Three men were executed.

Background

On 5 July, the UN Human Rights Council voted to appoint a Special Rapporteur on Belarus, following the adoption of a report by the UN High Commissioner for Human Rights which documented a serious decline in the respect for human rights since December 2010.

Parliamentary elections on 23 September failed to return any opposition candidates. The OSCE election observation mission found violations of the rights to freedom of expression and association and concluded that the elections were not free or fair. On 27 August the Central Election Committee decreed that any candidates who called for an election boycott should be denied airtime, effectively depriving two opposition parties of any media coverage.

Prisoners of conscience

Six people remained in prison in connection with their participation in a demonstration on 19 December 2010, at least four of whom – Mykalaj Statkevich, Pavel Sevyarynets, Zmitser Dashkevich and Eduard Lobau – were prisoners of conscience.

■ On 24 January, Minsk City Court refused Ales Bialiatski's appeal against his four-and-a-half-year sentence for "concealment of income on a large scale", and in September the sentence was upheld by the Supreme Court. Ales Bialiatski, chairperson of Human Rights Centre Viasna, and Vice-President of the International Federation for Human Rights, was sentenced on 24 November 2011. The conviction was related to the use of personal bank accounts in Lithuania and Poland to support the work of Human Rights Centre Viasna in Belarus.

B

■ On 14 April, former opposition presidential candidate Andrei Sannikau was released following a presidential pardon. He was reportedly pressured into signing a request for a pardon, and was told that his criminal record would remain for eight years. He had served 16 months of his five-year sentence. Zmitser Bandarenka, a member of Andrei Sannikau's campaign team, was released on 15 April.

■ On 28 August, a court sitting in a closed session in Hlybokaye (Glubokoe) prison colony sentenced Zmitser Dashkevich to a further year in prison for allegedly violating prison rules. Zmitser Dashkevich had been repeatedly punished for various minor violations of prison rules; the prison authorities reportedly placed him in the punishment cell on some occasions to protect him from physical attacks by fellow prisoners.

Freedom of expression

The authorities continued to use the crimes of "libelling the President" and "insulting the President" against journalists to discourage legitimate criticism of government authorities.

■ On 21 June, Andrzej Poczobut, correspondent for the Polish daily newspaper *Gazeta Wyborcza* and a prominent Polish-Belarusian minority activist, was arrested in his apartment in Hrodna and charged with "libelling the President" for articles published in Belarusian independent media. He was released on bail on 30 June. Andrzej Poczobut was already serving a three-year suspended prison sentence on the same charge for other newspaper articles. If found guilty under the new charge, he would serve both sentences consecutively and could face imprisonment for over seven years. At the end of the year the investigation was ongoing.

Human rights defenders

Human rights defenders were subjected to various forms of harassment, including travel bans and prosecution for administrative offences such as swearing in public. Valiantsin Stefanovich, deputy chair of the Human Rights Centre Viasna, was turned back at the Lithuanian border on 11 March, allegedly in connection with his failure to appear for military reserve duties. Oleg Volchek, a human rights lawyer, was informed in March that his name had been put on a list of those forbidden to leave the country.

■ On 26 June, shortly after the NGO Platforma – which monitors prison conditions – called for a boycott of the 2014 hockey championships in Minsk, its chair Andrei Bondarenko was officially warned by the Minsk City Prosecutor that he could be prosecuted for "discrediting the Republic of Belarus and its state institutions". On 19 July, he was informed that he was on a list of people forbidden to leave the country because he was being investigated for tax evasion. The investigation against him was stopped and his name was removed from the list after he complained to the Ministry of Internal Affairs.

■ On 26 November, the staff of Human Rights Centre Viasna were evicted from their office when it was confiscated as part of the sentence against the chair of the organization, Ales Bialiatsky.

During 2012, at least 15 human rights activists, journalists and opposition activists were prosecuted under the administrative code for swearing in public.

Freedom of association

The Law on Public Associations continued to set out restrictive rules for the registration and functioning of organizations. All NGOs still required authorization from the state in order to function and it remained a criminal offence under Article 193 (1) of the Criminal Code to act in the name of an unregistered organization.

■ In January, the LGBTI organization Human Rights Project Gay Belarus was informed that its application for registration had been refused on the grounds that the names of two of the 61 founders were misspelled and that their dates of birth were incorrect.

■ On 9 October, Minsk Economic Court ruled that the prison-monitoring NGO Platforma should be liquidated. The organization was accused by Sovetskiy district tax authorities in Minsk of failing to present a declaration of income on time, or to inform the tax authorities of a change of address. Its chair, Andrei Bondarenko, insisted that he had presented the income declaration on time and the organization had not changed its legal address.

Freedom of assembly

The Law on Mass Events continued to impose unreasonable limits on assemblies. It required organizers of any pre-planned public gathering to report "financial sources" used and they were only allowed to publicize events after official permission was granted, which might not be until five days beforehand. Applications to hold public events were routinely denied for technical reasons.

B

■ Alexander Denisenko, a member of the independent trade union REP, was refused permission by the local authorities in Brest to hold a public event on 17 March to protest against the cost of housing. Refusal was made on the grounds that he did not have contracts with the police, the ambulance service and the local authorities regarding cleaning and hygiene facilities. Alexander Denisenko appealed against the decision of the local authorities to the court of first instance, the appeal court, the district court and the Supreme Court, all of which supported the decision of the local authorities.

Death penalty

Belarus continued to carry out executions in conditions of utmost secrecy. Neither the prisoners condemned to death, nor their relatives, are informed of the execution before it is carried out. The body is not returned to relatives and they are not informed of the burial site. They can be left waiting weeks or even months before they receive the official death notice.
■ Uladzslau Kavalyou and Dzmitry Kanavalau were executed in March in connection with a series of bomb attacks, most recently in a metro station in the capital Minsk on 11 April 2011. There were serious concerns over the fairness of the trial. As in the cases of Vasily Yuzepchuk and Andrei Zhuk (executed in March 2010), and Andrei Burdyko (executed in July 2011), the authorities ignored a request made by the UN Human Rights Committee not to execute Uladzslau Kavalyou and Dzmitry Kanavalau until it had considered their cases.

Amnesty International visits/reports

◰ Belarus: Continuing human rights concerns – submission to the 20th session of the United Nations Human Rights Council (EUR 49/006/2012)
◰ Still behind bars: The plight of long-term prisoners in Belarus (EUR 49/013/2012)
◰ Belarus must release bodies of convicts executed over Minsk metro bombing (PRE01/146/2012)

BELGIUM

KINGDOM OF BELGIUM
Head of state: King Albert II
Head of government: Elio Di Rupo

The European Court of Human Rights found that Belgium had violated the right to a fair trial. The authorities took the first steps towards the creation of a National Human Rights Institution.

Unfair trials

The government was found to have used evidence that may have been obtained by torture in a trial of a terrorism suspect.
■ On 25 September, the European Court of Human Rights ruled in El Haski v. Belgium that, by using evidence likely to have been obtained through torture in criminal proceedings, Belgium had violated Lahoucine El Haski's right to a fair trial. He had been convicted in 2006 of participating in the activities of a terrorist group on the basis of testimonies of witnesses interrogated in third countries, including Morocco. The Court found that there was a "real risk" that statements used against him from Morocco may have been obtained through torture or other ill-treatment, and that the Belgian courts should have excluded such evidence.

Prison conditions

Psychiatric facilities for prisoners with mental disabilities continued to be inadequate. On 2 October the European Court of Human Rights ruled that Belgium had violated the right to liberty and security of L.B., a man with mental health problems, by detaining him for over seven years in prison facilities which were inadequate for his condition.

In December, the European Committee for the Prevention of Torture expressed concerns over overcrowding and inadequate sanitary facilities in many Belgian prisons.

Discrimination

Discrimination on the grounds of religion or belief continued, especially against Muslims, in public education and in the workplace. The general prohibition on wearing religious and cultural symbols and dress remained in force in Flemish public education.

A law criminalizing the concealing of the face in public remained in force. On 6 December, the Constitutional Court ruled that the law was consistent with Belgium's constitution and obligations under international law.

Refugees, asylum-seekers and migrants

In January, the authorities increased the number of spaces in reception centres for asylum-seekers. However, places remained insufficient, and undocumented migrant families were still denied access. Some unaccompanied minors were housed in inadequate facilities, where they did not receive adequate legal, medical and social assistance.

Housing rights

On 21 March, the European Committee of Social Rights found that Belgium had violated the non-discrimination clause of the European Social Charter as well as the right of the family to social, legal and economic protection on account of the inadequate provision of temporary and permanent sites for Travellers.

Arms trade

In June, the Flemish and Walloon parliaments passed new regional legislation on the import, export and transfer of arms, imposing inadequate checks on the final destination of the weapons sold.

Legal, constitutional or institutional developments

In July, the authorities decided to establish a National Human Rights Institution.

On 11 September, Belgium signed the Council of Europe Convention on preventing and combating violence against women and domestic violence.

Amnesty International visits/reports

🚍 An Amnesty International delegate visited Belgium in April and June.

📗 Choice and prejudice – discrimination against Muslims in Europe (EUR 01/001/2012)

BENIN

REPUBLIC OF BENIN

Head of state: **Thomas Boni Yayi**
Head of government: **Pascal Koupaki**

Throughout the year, the government tried to repress dissenting voices amid disputes about governance and a project on revision of the Constitution. Benin ratified the Second Optional Protocol to the ICCPR, aiming at the abolition of the death penalty.

Freedom of expression

■ In September, a private television channel, Canal 3, was interrupted for a few days following statements by Lionel Agbo, a former adviser to President Boni Yayi, accusing the Head of State of corruption. The state television justified this cut by referring to non-compliance with transmission rules. Lionel Agbo was charged with offending the Head of State but had not been tried by the end of the year.

Prison conditions

Prisons remained overcrowded. The prison in Cotonou held six times its capacity, resulting in harsh conditions. Official figures showed that of the some 2,250 inmates held, 97% were in pre-trial detention.

Death penalty

In July, Benin ratified the Second Optional Protocol to the ICCPR, aiming at the abolition of the death penalty. By the end of the year the government had not yet adopted implementing laws to remove the death penalty from its national legislation.

Amnesty International visits/reports

📗 Benin ratifies key UN treaty aiming at the abolition of the death penalty (AFR 14/001/2012)

BOLIVIA

Plurinational State of Bolivia
Head of state and government: **Evo Morales Ayma**

Indigenous Peoples' rights to consultation and to free, prior and informed consent over developments affecting them remained unfulfilled. Victims of human rights violations committed during past military regimes continued to be denied full reparations. Delays in the administration of justice persisted. Violations of freedom of expression were reported.

Background

Protests in support of economic and social demands and Indigenous Peoples' rights were widespread. In some cases police responded with excessive use of force.

In September, following his visit to Bolivia, the UN Special Rapporteur on racism acknowledged some advances, but expressed concern at continuing persistent discrimination against Indigenous Peoples and other communities at risk.

Indigenous Peoples' rights

In February, a law was passed calling for consultation with Indigenous Peoples in the Isiboro-Sécure Indigenous Territory and National Park (Territorio Indígena y Parque Nacional Isiboro-Sécure, TIPNIS) over government plans to construct a road through the park. In April, Indigenous communities opposed to the road marched to La Paz arguing that the consultation was contrary to previous legislation passed to protect the TIPNIS and to international standards and the Constitution.

In June, the Plurinational Constitutional Court ruled that the consultation was constitutional, but that its parameters must first be agreed with all the Indigenous communities potentially affected. In July, the government decided to go ahead with the consultation after reaching agreements with only some of the Indigenous communities. In October, before the consultation was completed, construction began of the first stretch of the road outside the park and Indigenous territory. Official reports on the results of the consultation were still pending at the end of the year.

No police officers responsible for excessive use of force in 2011 during peaceful protests against the road in the TIPNIS had been brought to justice by the end of 2012.

Lack of prior consultation over mine exploration in Mallku Khota, Potosí Department by a Bolivian subsidiary of a Canadian mining company led to violent unrest between local communities and the police. In August, the government announced the nationalization of the mine to put an end to the protests by those opposed to the Canadian mining company. However, conflicts between supporters and opponents of the project continued in December.

Impunity and the justice system

Delays in bringing those responsible for human rights violations under military governments (1964-1982) persisted. Delays in the administration of justice led to impunity in other cases. Allegations of misuse of the judiciary against opponents or critics of the government were reported.

■ In April and May, legislation was passed modifying compensation payments for victims of political violence under military governments and providing for the publication of the names of people entitled to compensation. There were concerns about the lack of transparency and unfairness of the reparation process. Of 6,200 applicants, only around 1,700 qualified as beneficiaries. Victims and relatives of human rights violations maintained months-long protests in front of the Ministry of Justice to demand greater transparency, among other things.

■ In September, the US authorities refused a request to extradite former President Gonzalo Sánchez de Lozada to Bolivia. He faced charges in connection with "Black October", when 67 people were killed and more than 400 injured during protests in El Alto, near La Paz, in late 2003.

■ Trial proceedings connected to the 2008 Pando massacre in which 19 people, mostly peasant farmers, were killed and 53 others injured, continued but were subject to delays.

■ Hearings in the case of 39 people accused of involvement in an alleged plot in 2009 to kill President Evo Morales began in October. By the end of the year, there had been no investigations into allegations of lack of due process or into the killings of three men in 2009 in connection with the case.

Freedom of expression

In August, criminal complaints of inciting racism and discrimination were filed against two newspapers and a national news agency. The government argued that the three media outlets had misused President Evo Morales' comments about the behaviour of people in the east of the country and portrayed him as a racist. There was concern that this was a disproportionate restriction on freedom of expression.

The Plurinational Constitutional Court ruled in September that the crime of "contempt for public officials" was unconstitutional and a violation of freedom of expression.

In October, radio journalist Fernando Vidal was seriously injured when four masked men set him alight while he was on the air in Yacuiba, near the Argentine border. Fernando Vidal had publicly criticized local officials and reported on drug trafficking in the region. Four men were arrested in connection with the attack. Investigations were continuing at the end of the year.

Women's rights

In September, a law was passed punishing harassment and political violence against women. The law, which was welcomed by women's organizations, establishes preventive mechanisms and provides for sanctions for acts of harassment and violence against women who are electoral candidates, elected officials or who work in public institutions.

Amnesty International visits/reports

🚗 Amnesty International delegates visited Bolivia in March and June.

📄 Open letter to the authorities of the Plurinational State of Bolivia in the context of the dispute concerning the Isiboro Sécure Indigenous Territory and National Park (TIPNIS) (AMR 18/002/2012)

BOSNIA AND HERZEGOVINA

BOSNIA AND HERZEGOVINA
Head of state: **rotating presidency – Željko Komšić, Nebojša Radmanović, Bakir Izetbegović**
Head of government: **Vjekoslav Bevanda (replaced Nikola Špirić in January)**

Nationalist rhetoric by main political parties across the country increased. Challenges to the integrity of the state intensified. Institutions at the state level, including the judiciary, were weakened. Prosecution of crimes under international law continued before domestic courts, but progress remained slow and impunity persisted. Many civilian victims of war were still denied access to justice and reparations.

Background

The country faced a deteriorating economic situation, high unemployment and accompanying social problems. The Council of Ministers was formed in January, and the state budget was adopted in April, finally ending the stalemate that had continued since the 2010 general elections.

Nationalist rhetoric by leading political parties across both entities, including increasingly secessionist remarks by top politicians in the Republika Srpska (RS), weakened state-level institutions, particularly the judiciary. The Office of the High Representative (OHR) in Bosnia and Herzegovina (BiH), the body in charge of overseeing the implementation of the Dayton Peace Accord, reported in November that "Not only was there little progress towards closer integration with the European Union, but direct challenges to the General Framework Agreement for Peace, including to the sovereignty and territorial integrity of Bosnia and Herzegovina, intensified significantly." The lack of political will hampered the efficiency of the work of the Parliamentary Assembly. The leadership of RS intensified its policy of direct challenges to the Dayton Peace Agreement and use of separatist rhetoric. Local elections, held in October, were assessed as generally in line with democratic standards by election observers.

B

The international community maintained its presence in BiH. Both the EU Special Representative to BiH and the OHR continued their respective mandates. The decision to reduce the EU military mission from 1,300 to 600 personnel was partially offset by some EU member states stationing additional reserve forces in the country.

International justice

By the end of the year, five cases concerning BiH were pending before the Trial Chamber of the International Criminal Tribunal for the Former Yugoslavia (the Tribunal). Three other cases were on appeal.

■ Proceedings against former Bosnian Serb leader Radovan Karadžić continued. In June, the Trial Chamber of the Tribunal issued an oral decision dismissing the motion for acquittal on 10 counts of the indictment. However, it granted it in relation to count one, in which the accused was charged with genocide for crimes committed in several municipalities in BiH between March and December 1992. The Tribunal reported that the evidence "even if taken at its highest, did not reach the level from which a reasonable trier of fact could infer that genocide occurred in the municipalities".

■ Following his arrest in Serbia and his transfer to the Tribunal in 2011, the trial of Ratko Mladić, former commander of the main staff of the Army of Republika Srpska, commenced in May before the Trial Chamber. Ratko Mladić was charged on the basis of individual criminal responsibility and superior criminal responsibility with two counts of genocide, persecutions, extermination, murder, deportation, inhumane acts, terror and unlawful attacks on civilians, and the taking of hostages.

Justice system – crimes under international law

The justice system continued to work on the large backlog of war crimes cases.

In early 2012, the BiH Prosecutor's Office obtained an overview of cases investigated in all jurisdictions within BiH. It handed them over to the State Court of BiH to decide, in accordance with the criteria set in the National Strategy for Prosecution of War Crimes (Strategy), which cases should be prosecuted at the state or entity levels.

There were 1,271 cases reviewed in the process, 592 (47%) of which were transferred to the entity Prosecutors' Offices, and 679 (53%) were pending before the State Prosecutor's Office. This represented a positive development as the significant delay in establishing the exact number of criminal case files was holding up the implementation of the Strategy. The possibility of parallel investigations and prosecutions at state and entity levels was also greatly reduced.

However, around half of these case files had already been pending in entity Prosecutors' Offices for many years prior to the review and transfer process. The fact that an additional 120 case files were transferred to the entity Prosecutors' Offices did not automatically accelerate the investigations.

The War Crimes Chamber of the State Court of BiH continued to play a central role in prosecuting crimes under international law. However, verbal attacks on this and other judicial institutions dedicated to investigating and prosecuting those crimes, along with the denial of crimes under international law – such as the genocide in Srebrenica in July 1995 – by high-ranking politicians, undermined the state's efforts to prosecute them. In February, a coalition party from RS filed a motion to abolish the State Court of BiH and the Prosecutor's Office of BiH. The draft proposals were rejected by the BiH Parliament, but politicians continued to make public declarations undermining the work of the state judicial institutions.

Despite calls from various international human rights treaty bodies for the BiH authorities to amend its legislation to include a definition of sexual violence in line with international standards and jurisprudence, the 2003 Criminal Code was not changed. This Code required that the victim be subjected to force or threat of immediate attack on his or her life or body. It still did not take into account the circumstances of armed conflict, which could create a coercive context that would vitiate consent to sexual intercourse.

Moreover, the entity courts continued to apply the Criminal Code of the former Socialist Federal Republic of Yugoslavia in prosecuting crimes committed during the conflict. As noted in the concluding observations of the UN Human Rights Committee in November, this Code had serious gaps, including the absence of a definition of crimes against humanity and command responsibility.

Although witness support services at the state level were available, adequate witness support and protection measures in cases tried in entity courts were absent. This continued, despite the fact that half of all pending war crimes cases were due to be heard at this level.

The authorities failed to provide a comprehensive programme of reparations for victims of crimes under international law.

Women's rights
Survivors of war crimes of sexual violence
Between its creation in 2005 and the end of 2012, the State Court of BiH had issued final decisions in 29 cases involving crimes of sexual violence committed during the 1992-1995 war. Two additional cases were pending appeal. There were no reliable figures available of the total number of allegations of rape and other forms of wartime sexual violence under investigation at the state and entity level.

The state failed to adopt the draft Law on the Rights of Victims of Torture and Civilian War Victims, the Strategy on Transitional Justice, and the Programme for Victims of Sexual Violence in Conflict, all of which would have improved the ability of survivors of sexual violence to realize their right to reparation.

Many survivors continued to be denied their right to reparation and were stigmatized as rape victims. Female survivors were denied access to adequate health care services even when they suffered from medical conditions developed as a result of rape. Only a few of those who suffered from post-traumatic stress disorders were able to secure psychological assistance.

Enforced disappearances
Around 10,000 people who disappeared during the 1992-1995 war were still unaccounted for. The state's failure to implement the 2004 Law on Missing Persons led to problems for the families of the disappeared, including the denial of their rights to justice and reparation. The Fund for Providing Assistance to the Families of Missing Persons envisaged by the 2004 Law had still not been established. Many judgements of the Constitutional Court of BiH in cases involving enforced disappearances remained unimplemented.

Discrimination
Minority rights
The authorities failed to implement the December 2009 judgement of the European Court of Human Rights in the case brought by Dervo Sejdić (a Romani man) and Jakob Finci (a Jewish man). The European Court had ruled that the constitutional framework and the electoral system discriminated against the applicants as they did not belong to any of the three named constituent peoples (Bosniaks, Croats and Serbs).

Rights of lesbian, gay, bisexual, transgender and intersex people
Despite the Anti-discrimination Law prohibiting discrimination on the grounds of sexual orientation and gender identity, the authorities did not develop a system to register discrimination cases. The state failed to publicly condemn violent attacks against LGBTI people. No individuals responsible for the attacks on the organizers and the participants of the 2008 Sarajevo Queer Festival were investigated or prosecuted.

Amnesty International visits/reports
🚗 Amnesty International delegates visited Bosnia and Herzegovina between March and April and between October and November.

📋 The right to know: Families still left in the dark in the Balkans (EUR 05/001/2012)

📋 Bosnia and Herzegovina: Stanković arrest – victims of wartime rape must feel safe to testify (EUR 63/001/2012)

📋 Old crimes, same suffering: No justice for survivors of wartime rape in north-east Bosnia and Herzegovina (EUR 63/002/2012)

📋 BiH should allow individuals to petition the Committee on Enforced Disappearances (EUR 63/008/2012)

📋 Bosnia and Herzegovina: Families of the victims of genocide committed in Srebrenica 17 years ago are still waiting for truth, justice and reparation (EUR 63/010/2012)

📋 Bosnia and Herzegovina: Submission to the UN Human Rights Committee (EUR 63/011/2012)

📋 When everyone is silent: Reparation for survivors of wartime rape in Republika Srpska in Bosnia and Herzegovina (EUR 63/012/2012)

BRAZIL

FEDERATIVE REPUBLIC OF BRAZIL
Head of state and government: **Dilma Rousseff**

Levels of violent crime remained high. The authorities frequently responded with excessive force and torture. Young black men continued to make up a disproportionate number of homicide victims. Torture and other ill-treatment were reported in the detention system, which was characterized by cruel, inhuman and degrading conditions. Rural workers and Indigenous Peoples and *Quilombola* communities (descendants of runaway slaves) suffered intimidation and attacks. Forced evictions in both urban and rural settings remained a serious concern.

Background

The socio-economic situation continued to improve, with more people moving out of extreme poverty. Nevertheless, the homes and livelihoods of Indigenous Peoples, landless rural workers, fishermen and urban slum dwellers continued to be threatened by development projects.

In November, Brazil was re-elected to the UN Human Rights Council. Brazil criticized violations in the Syrian armed conflict, but abstained over a resolution in the General Assembly expressing concern over the human rights situation in Iran.

In May, the Chamber of Deputies passed a constitutional amendment that allows for the confiscation of lands where slave labour is found to be used. The reform was before the Senate awaiting approval at the end of the year.

Impunity

In May 2012, the National Truth Commission was established by President Dilma Rousseff. The Commission is mandated to investigate human rights violations from 1946 to 1988. The Commission began hearing testimonies and investigating records during the year, although some concern was expressed at the use of some *in camera* hearings. The establishment of the National Truth Commission led to the creation of several truth commissions at the state level, for example in the states of Pernambuco, Rio Grande do Sul and São Paulo. However, concerns remained about the ability to address impunity for crimes against humanity while the 1979 Amnesty Law remained in place; the Amnesty Law had been declared "null and void" by the Inter-American Court of Human Rights in 2010.

Federal prosecutors initiated criminal prosecutions of members of the security services accused of kidnappings during the military governments (1964-1985), arguing that it was a "continuous crime" and thus not covered by the Amnesty Law.

Public security

States continued to adopt repressive and discriminatory policing methods in the face of armed criminal violence. Tens of thousands of people were killed in criminal violence, with young black men disproportionately targeted, especially in the north and north-east of the country.

The number of killings fell in some states, often as a consequence of localized public security projects. For example, in Rio de Janeiro, the Police Pacification Units project expanded to new *favelas* and contributed to a reduction in homicide rates.

In January, the federal government cut by almost half the funding for its national public security project (Programa Nacional de Segurança Pública com Cidadania, PRONASCI). Although the government did promise some important projects to ensure greater protection, such as the plan to prevent violence against black youth (known as "Living Youth"), there were concerns that these were not effectively funded.

In Rio de Janeiro and São Paulo states, killings by police officers continued to be registered as "acts of resistance" or "resistance followed by death". Few, if any, such cases were effectively investigated despite evidence that they involved excessive use of force and possible extrajudicial executions. The National Human Rights Council passed a resolution in November calling on all states to stop registering police killings as "acts of resistance" or "resistance followed by death". The resolution further called for all killings by police to be investigated, for forensic evidence to be safeguarded and for the numbers of killings by police to be published regularly. The resolution was under consideration by the São Paulo state government at the end of the year, with a view to introducing changes to the designation of killings by police and measures to preserve crime scenes in 2013.

São Paulo state saw numbers of homicides increase dramatically, reversing the reductions achieved over the previous eight years. Between January and September there was a rise of 9.7% over the same period in 2011, with 3,539 killings registered. Killings of police officers also rose steeply: more than 90 were killed by November alone. The police, academics and the media reported this rise in the context of increased confrontations between police and the state's main criminal gang, the First Command of the Capital (Primeiro Comando da Capital, PCC). A joint federal-state initiative was announced to combat the violence, under the control of a newly appointed State Secretary for Public Security.

■ In May, three members of the Military Police's Shock Troop were arrested. They were accused of the extrajudicial execution of a suspected member of the PCC during a police operation in Penha, in the east of São Paulo, the same month. A witness described how the officers detained one of the suspects, beat him and shot him dead in a police vehicle.

Police involvement in corrupt and criminal activity persisted. In Rio de Janeiro, while there were some advances in the provision of public security, the milícias (groups made up of active or former law enforcement agents) continued to dominate many of the city's favelas.

■ In October, members of the League of Justice (Liga da Justiça) milícia reportedly issued death threats to the owners of one of the city's informal bus companies, warning them to stop working in four areas of the city. This effectively cut off transport links for up to 210,000 people. The threats occurred as the group attempted to wrest control of transport services in the west of the city.

Torture and cruel, inhuman and degrading conditions

In July, the UN Subcommittee on Prevention of Torture expressed concern at the widespread use of torture and the failure of the authorities to ensure effective investigations and prosecutions. Efforts by the federal authorities and some state authorities to combat and prevent torture were made within the Integrated Action Plan to Prevent and Combat Torture. Central to this was pending federal legislation for the creation of a National Preventative Mechanism, in line with the requirements of the Optional Protocol to the UN Convention against Torture. However, human rights groups were concerned by a change to the legislation that allowed the President alone to select the members of the National Committee to Prevent and Combat Torture. This was seen to violate the requirements of the UN Optional Protocol and the UN Principles relating to the Status and Functioning of National Institutions for the Protection and Promotion of Human Rights (the "Paris Principles").

The UN Subcommittee on Prevention of Torture praised Rio de Janeiro's state mechanism for the independence of its selection criteria and structure and the mandate it had been set. However, there were concerns that it was not receiving full funding.

The number of people detained continued to rise. A shortfall of over 200,000 places meant that cruel, inhuman and degrading conditions were commonplace. In Amazonas state, detainees were held in foetid, overcrowded, insecure cells. Women and minors were detained in the same units as men, and there were numerous reports of torture, including near-suffocation with a plastic bag, beatings and electric shocks. These reports mostly involved members of the state military police.

Land rights

Hundreds of communities were condemned to live in appalling conditions by the authorities' failure to fulfil their constitutional rights to land. Land activists and community leaders were threatened, attacked and killed. Indigenous and Quilombola communities were at particular risk, often as a consequence of development projects.

The publication by the Attorney General's Office of a controversial resolution (Portaria 303) in July prompted protests by Indigenous Peoples and NGOs across Brazil. The resolution would permit the establishment of mining, hydro-electric schemes and military installations on Indigenous lands, without the free, prior and informed consent of affected communities. At the end of the year, the resolution was suspended, pending a Supreme Court decision.

A constitutional amendment was before Congress at the end of the year that would pass responsibility for demarcating Indigenous and Quilombola land from official bodies to the National Congress. There were concerns that, if approved, the amendment would politicize the process and jeopardize constitutional protections.

Development projects continued to have a detrimental impact on Indigenous Peoples. Long-standing efforts to identify and demarcate Indigenous lands remained stalled.

■ Despite a series of legal challenges and protests, construction of the Belo Monte dam continued. In August, work was halted following a federal court ruling that Indigenous Peoples had not been adequately consulted, but the ruling was subsequently overturned by the Supreme Court.

In Mato Grosso do Sul state, Indigenous Guarani-Kaiowá communities continued to face intimidation, violence and the threat of forced eviction from their traditional lands.

■ In August, after staging a re-occupation of their traditional lands in Mato Grosso do Sul, the Guarani-Kaiowá community of Arroio-Korá was attacked by gunmen who burned crops, shouted abuse and fired shots. According to witnesses, the gunmen abducted Eduardo Pires. His whereabouts remained unknown at the end of the year.

■ In the face of an eviction order, the Pyelito Kue/Mbarakay community in Mato Grosso do Sul issued an Open Letter in October to the Brazilian government and the judiciary in which they complained that they were living under virtual siege, surrounded by gunmen and without adequate access to food and health care. In October, a woman from Pyelito Kue/Mbarakay was repeatedly raped by eight gunmen who then interrogated her about the community. The following week, a federal court suspended the eviction order, pending the completion of an anthropological report officially identifying their lands.

Quilombola communities fighting for their constitutional rights to land continued to suffer violence and threats of forced eviction at the hands of gunmen hired by landowners. The situation in Maranhão state remained critical, with at least nine communities suffering violent intimidation and scores of community leaders receiving death threats.

■ In November, the community of Santa Maria dos Moreiras, in the municipality of Codó, Maranhão state, was invaded by gunmen who fired shots over the settlement. The attack was part of a systematic attempt by local landowners to drive the community off the land, using methods such as the destruction of crops and death threats against community leaders.

Human rights defenders

Human rights defenders were subjected to threats and intimidation as a direct consequence of their work. Those challenging vested economic and political interests were particularly at risk. Protection for defenders was patchy because of the failure to implement the federal protection programme effectively.

■ Nilcilene Miguel de Lima, a rural activist in the municipality of Lábrea, Amazonas state, was threatened, beaten and driven from her home in May after she denounced illegal logging in the region. She was provided with armed protection through the National Protection Programme, but was withdrawn from the region after threats intensified. At least six rural workers have been killed in the region in land conflicts since 2007.

■ Environmental activist Laísa Santos Sampaio from the Praia Alta Piranheira settlement in Nova Ipixuna, Pará state, continued to receive death threats. The threats began following the killing of her sister, Maria do Espírito Santo da Silva, and brother-in-law, José Cláudio Ribeiro da Silva, by contract killers in May 2011. At the end of 2012, she had still not been provided with protection because of the failure to implement the National Protection Programme.

■ In Magé, Rio de Janeiro state, the president of the local fishing association (Associação de Homens e Mulheres do Mar, Ahomar), Alexandre Anderson de Souza, and his wife, Daize Menezes, received a series of death threats. Ahomar has campaigned against the building of a petrochemical refinery in Rio de Janeiro's Guanabara Bay. In late June 2012, the bodies of two fishermen and active members of Ahomar, Almir Nogueira de Amorim and João Luiz Telles Penetra, were found in Guanabara Bay. They had been tied up before being drowned.

Housing rights

Urban infrastructure projects, many in preparation for the World Cup in 2014 and the Rio Olympics in 2016, led to the forced eviction of families in several communities across Brazil during 2012. The evictions were carried out without giving residents full and timely information about government proposals affecting their communities. The authorities also failed to engage in genuine negotiation with communities to explore all alternatives to eviction, and, where necessary, to offer full compensation or alternative, adequate housing in the area. Instead, families were moved long distances into inadequate housing, often with limited access to basic services, and in areas with serious security problems.

■ In Providência, in the centre of Rio de Janeiro, 140 houses were demolished during the year as part of an urban revitalization project in the port area, where up to 800 houses had been slated for removal.

Some evicted communities were moved long distances into Rio de Janeiro's west zone, where many areas are dominated by *milícias*. Families living in housing estates in the neighbourhoods of Cosmos, Realengo and Campo Grande reported that they were threatened and harassed by members of the *milícia* and that some had been forced out of their apartments under duress.

■ In January, more than 6,000 people were removed from the site known as Pinheirinho in São José dos Campos, São Paulo state. Residents had been living at the site since 2004. During the eviction, police used dogs, tear gas and rubber bullets. The eviction came despite the suspension of the eviction order and amid negotiations with the federal government to find a solution that would enable residents to remain. The residents were not notified in advance, and were not given sufficient time to remove their belongings from homes. The authorities did not offer adequate alternative housing to the residents and at the end of the year most were living in degrading conditions in temporary shelters and other irregular settlements.

In the city of São Paulo, a parliamentary inquiry was launched to investigate the high incidence of fires that had destroyed a number of *favelas*, many of which were next to wealthy neighbourhoods. In September, 1,100 people were left homeless when the Morro do Piolho *favela* burned down. In November, 600 residents lost their homes in a fire that destroyed the Aracati *favela*. Some 400 people were left homeless by a fire in the Humaitá *favela* in July. Residents of the Moinho *favela* complained that they were prevented by police from reconstructing their houses, after a fire destroyed several houses in the community in September.

Women's rights

Women's sexual and reproductive rights continued to be under threat.

In March, the High Court of Justice acquitted a man of raping three 12-year-old girls on the grounds that they were allegedly "sex-workers". The decision, which sparked national and international condemnation, was annulled by the High Court in August.

Amnesty International visits/reports

🚍 Amnesty International delegates visited the State of Amazonas in March to carry out research on ill-treatment in detention.

BULGARIA

REPUBLIC OF BULGARIA
Head of state: Rosen Plevneliev (replaced Georgi Parvanov
in January)
Head of government: Boyko Borissov

Roma continued to face discrimination in areas such as education, employment, health care and housing. Conditions of detention fell short of international human rights standards. Homophobic violence persisted.

Discrimination – Roma

In January, the UN Independent Expert on minority issues expressed concerns that Roma remained at the bottom of the socio-economic ladder in key areas such as education, employment, health care and housing. Roma continued to be vulnerable to forced evictions.

■ On 24 April, the European Court of Human Rights ruled in the case *Yordanova and Others v. Bulgaria* that the planned eviction of a Romani community from informally occupied land in Batalova Vodenitsa would violate the rights to private and family life. The Court criticized legislation allowing summary arbitrary evictions.

■ On 26 July, in an interview in the *Standard* newspaper, the Mayor of Sofia, the capital, referring to Romani settlements, stated that "illegal dwellings must be pulled down, people who come from other parts of the country should be sent back because they have no homes here or they live in illegal constructions". The Mayor reportedly stated that similar measures had been followed in Lyulin and Vazrazhdane districts and the same approach would be used to deal with other settlements in Sofia.

■ In November, the UN Human Rights Committee, in the case *Liliana Naidenova et al v. Bulgaria*, issued a permanent injunction preventing the forced eviction of the Dobri Jeliazkov community, which had existed in the capital for 70 years and faced imminent forced eviction in July 2011. The Committee ordered the authorities not to evict the community until they had agreed upon alternative housing.

■ In October, the European Court of Human Rights ruled in the case *Yotova v. Bulgaria* that Bulgaria had violated the rights to life and to non-discrimination of a Romani woman by failing to conduct an effective investigation into her attempted murder in 1999, which left her severely disabled. The authorities also failed to consider whether the crime was racially and ethnically motivated, despite being aware of ethnic tensions in the applicant's village of Aglen.

Torture and other ill-treatment

In December, the European Committee for the Prevention of Torture criticized detention conditions and ill-treatment reported in Bulgarian prisons.

■ In January, in the case *Shahanov v. Bulgaria*, the European Court of Human Rights ruled that an inmate imprisoned for seven years in Varna was subjected to inhuman and degrading treatment due to inadequate sanitation facilities.

■ In January, in the case *Stanev v. Bulgaria*, the European Court of Human Rights held that Bulgaria had violated six Articles of the European Convention on Human Rights, including the rights to liberty and security, the prohibition of torture and inhuman and degrading treatment and the right to a fair trial in the case of a man forced to live since 2002 in inhuman conditions in a psychiatric institution.

Refugees and asylum-seekers

Asylum-seekers continued to face obstacles in accessing international protection.

■ In May, the European Court of Human Rights held that Bulgaria violated the right to effective remedy of Iranian citizen Mohammad Madah, and would violate his right to family life by deporting him to Iran. The European Court found that his 2005 expulsion order was based on a declaratory statement contained in a National Security Service internal document. The statement implicated Mohammad Madah in drug trafficking to finance a terrorist organization and described him as a national security threat. The European Court stated that the applicant and his family were not given the minimum protection against arbitrary deportation.

■ On 11 September, the Court of Appeal in Veliko Tarnovo authorized the extradition of Mukhad Gadamouri to the Russian Federation, where he is accused of terrorism, weapons trafficking and belonging to an armed group, despite his having been granted refugee status by another EU member state. At the end of the year, Mukhad Gadamouri was still awaiting extradition. He lodged an appeal with the European Court of Human Rights, which issued an interim measure against his extradition pending the ruling in the case.

Rights of lesbian, gay, bisexual, transgender and intersex people

Homophobic public discourse and acts of violence persisted. Bulgarian legislation does not currently criminalize hate crimes perpetrated on the basis of sexual orientation or gender identity.

■ On 30 June, the fifth Sofia Pride parade passed without incident despite calls by opponents for widespread violence against participants and supporters, and discriminatory remarks by the Bulgarian Orthodox Church and the Holy Synod. The far-right Bulgarian National Union held a counter-demonstration a few hours before the Pride march.

■ In December, four years after the murder of Mihail Stoyanov in Borisova Garden in Sofia, and several months after the end of the investigation, two suspects were charged with deliberately murdering the 25-year-old medical student. Allegedly, they belonged to a group claiming to be cleansing the park of gay men.

Amnesty International visits/reports

🚌 Amnesty International delegates visited Bulgaria in March and June.
📓 Changing laws, changing minds: Challenging homophobic and transphobic hate crimes in Bulgaria (EUR 15/001/2012)

BURKINA FASO

BURKINA FASO
Head of state: Blaise Compaoré
Head of government: Luc Adolphe Tiao

Demonstrations and clashes took place in the months before the December legislative and municipal elections against a background of attempts by the President's party to amend the Constitution in order to allow President Compaoré to run for another term. As a result of the crisis in Mali, up to 100,000 people sought refuge in the north of Burkina Faso. Camps lacked basic necessities and health care.

Torture and other ill-treatment

In January, Moumouni Isaac Zongo and Ousséni Compaoré, arrested on suspicion of theft, were ill-treated by members of the Anti-Crime Brigade of the National Police in Boulmiougou.

In February, bodyguards for the Minister of Justice and Promotion of Human Rights, Jérôme Traoré, ill-treated a mechanic following an altercation. A few days later, the Minister was dismissed.

Right to health – maternal mortality

Maternal and child health remained a priority for the authorities, who worked with civil society organizations on assessing the feasibility of policies to improve access to services for children aged under five, and to a certain extent for women. However, no real improvement was achieved either in the quality of maternal health services or increased access to family planning and reproductive health services.

Impunity

In June, Parliament passed an amnesty law for heads of state enshrining impunity.

Amnesty International visits/reports

📖 Burkina Faso: La compétence universelle pour mettre fin à l'impunité (AFR 60/001/2012)

BURUNDI

REPUBLIC OF BURUNDI
Head of state and government: Pierre Nkurunziza

The cycle of impunity remained unbroken and the government did not fully investigate and prosecute extrajudicial executions from previous years. Promising signs that the government would establish a Truth and Reconciliation Commission in 2012 faded progressively throughout the year. Human rights defenders and journalists faced repression because of their work.

B

Background

The ruling party, the National Council for Defence of Democracy-Forces for Defence of Democracy (CNDD-FDD), was able to govern without any effective opposition engagement. The ruling party and ADC-Ikibiri, the coalition of opposition parties which withdrew from the 2010 elections, did not engage in meaningful dialogue.

Following an increase in the cost of living, Burundian civil society organized a national campaign to call to account the economic practice of the government.

Impunity

UN human rights monitors recorded 30 extrajudicial executions during 2012. The figure was lower than in 2010 and 2011, when a total of 101 extrajudicial executions were recorded. Most of the 2012 killings seemed not to have been politically motivated; however, impunity persisted.

A Commission of Inquiry was established by the Public Prosecutor in June to investigate allegations of extrajudicial executions and torture reported by Burundian and international human rights organizations and the UN. The Commission's report, made public in August, accepted that killings had occurred but denied that they were extrajudicial. It stated that judicial case files had been opened for certain cases reported by human rights organizations. Following the report, two police officers, an army major, a local administrator and several *Imbonerakure* (youth members affiliated to the ruling party) were arrested; no trials took place, however. Concerns remained that not all perpetrators had been held to account.

Truth and reconciliation

No progress was made to investigate and establish the truth behind grave violations of human rights committed between 1962 and 2008. A revised draft law establishing a Truth and Reconciliation Commission (TRC) was submitted to parliament but was not discussed.

The draft law left open the possibility of amnesties, including for those accused of genocide, crimes against humanity, war crimes, torture, enforced disappearances and extrajudicial executions. It did not specify that the Special Tribunal, the judicial mechanism that will follow the TRC, should have an independent prosecutor who can investigate and prosecute cases referred by the TRC as well as new cases.

Justice system

The recruitment of judges through the Ministry of Justice was not conducted in a public and transparent way, leaving the process open to accusations of corruption and political bias. According to the law, the Minister of Justice must organize a competitive examination to decide on candidates.

The justice system remained weak and politicized and the authorities failed to bring perpetrators of human rights violations to justice.

■ The May verdict in the trial of those accused of killing anti-corruption activist Ernest Manirumva, murdered in 2009, failed to deliver justice. The prosecution did not consider recommendations from the US Federal Bureau of Investigations (FBI) to require high-ranking police and intelligence officers implicated by witnesses to be questioned and DNA tested. The decision of the Appeal Court of Bujumbura was pending at the year's end.

Freedom of expression – journalists and human rights defenders

Journalists and human rights defenders reported harassment and intimidation by the authorities.

■ In February, Faustin Ndikumana, President of the organization Words and Action for the Awakening of Conscience and the Evolution of Mindsets, spent two weeks in custody, solely for exercising his right to freedom of expression, before being released on bail. He had made public comments to the media after he wrote to the Minister of Justice asking him to investigate and halt corruption in the recruitment of judges. In July, the Anti-Corruption Court found him guilty of making false statements and sentenced him to five years' imprisonment and a fine of 500,000 Burundian francs (approx. US$333). The judgement had not been enforced by the end of the year.

Draft legislation, if enacted in its current form, could threaten freedom of expression and association. A draft law on demonstrations and public meetings would give the authorities disproportionate powers to close down public meetings. A draft of the revised press law included new provisions introducing circumstances in which journalists must disclose sources, an increased number of possible press-related crimes, excessive state regulation of the press, and exorbitant fines for journalists who violate provisions of the law and the Penal Code.

Prison conditions

Inmates were kept in extremely insanitary conditions and thousands were held in pre-trial detention.

President Nkurunziza passed a decree on 25 June granting pardon to prisoners serving a term of five years or less (excluding those sentenced for rape, armed robbery, armed robbery in organized gangs, illegal possession of firearms or threatening state security), pregnant or breastfeeding women, prisoners aged 60 and over, minors aged under 18 who have not been tried and prisoners suffering from terminal illness. All other sentences were reduced by half. In April, 10,567 prisoners were held in 11 prisons with a combined capacity of only 4,050. This number had decreased to 6,581 by the end of December.

Amnesty International visits/reports

🚍 Amnesty International delegates visited Burundi in May.

📄 Burundi: Free activist who spoke out – Faustin Ndikumana (AFR 16/001/2012) and further information (AFR 16/002/2012)

📄 Burundi: Time for change – a human rights review: Submission to the UN Universal Periodic Review (AFR 16/003/2012)

📄 Burundi: Verdict in activist's killing fails to deliver justice (PRE01/262/2012)

CAMBODIA

KINGDOM OF CAMBODIA
Head of state: **King Norodom Sihamoni**
Head of government: **Hun Sen**

Respect for freedom of expression, association and assembly deteriorated. The authorities increasingly used excessive force against peaceful protesters. Human rights defenders faced threats, harassment, legal action and violence. Forced evictions, land disputes and land grabbing continued to affect thousands of people. Impunity for perpetrators of human rights abuses and a non-independent judiciary remained major problems, with flawed or no investigations into killings and shootings. Judicial investigations at the Extraordinary Chambers in the Courts of Cambodia stalled as allegations of government interference persisted.

Background

The ruling Cambodian People's Party won the majority of seats in the commune elections held in June. Two opposition parties merged to form the Cambodian National Rescue Party ahead of national elections in July 2013, but its leader Sam Rainsy remained abroad to avoid serving a prison sentence for politically motivated convictions. The Special Rapporteur on the human rights situation in Cambodia issued two highly critical reports following his May visit: one on the electoral system, and the other on the impact of Economic Land Concessions on the human rights of affected communities. Cambodia chaired ASEAN, which in November adopted the ASEAN Human Rights Declaration, despite serious concerns that it fell short of international standards. King Father Norodom Sihanouk died in October, aged 89.

Excessive use of force

Protests by communities over land and housing rights and by trade union activists were met with increasing violence. In January, security guards opened fire on peaceful protesters in Kratie province, injuring four people. The governor of Bavet town in Svay Rieng province shot three women during a protest over working conditions in February. A 14-year-old girl was shot dead in Kratie in May as security forces entered her village to carry out a forced eviction of 600 families. A union activist was beaten and detained by police after a group of workers submitted a petition to the Prime Minister's office in July. No adequate investigation was carried out into any of these incidents.

Impunity for attacks against human rights defenders persisted.

■ In December, the Appeal Court upheld the 20-year sentences of Born Samnang and Sok Sam Oeun who were wrongly convicted for the killing of trade union leader Chea Vichea in 2004 despite lack of evidence and credible alibis. The killers of Chea Vichea remained free.

■ Chut Wutty, a well-known environment activist and Director of the Natural Resource Protection Group, a Cambodian NGO that campaigns against the destruction of the country's forests, was shot dead by a military police officer in Koh Kong province in April. The officer who reportedly shot him was also killed in the incident. The government investigation and subsequent court case were flawed and inadequate. In October, Koh Kong provincial court dropped the investigation into Wutty's death.

Freedom of expression – human rights defenders

The authorities harassed and threatened to arrest and take legal action against human rights workers and members of communities resisting forced eviction. Workers with the Cambodian Human Rights and Development Association and the Cambodian Center for Human Rights, and a Radio Free Asia reporter, were summoned for court questioning after carrying out their legitimate activities in different land-related cases. In March and November, the authorities used intimidation and harassment to disrupt and prevent civil society associations and grassroots networks, including local and regional NGOs, from holding workshops and events around the ASEAN summits on a range of human rights issues.

■ In May, 13 women from the Boeung Kak Lake community in Phnom Penh were arrested and sentenced to two and a half years in prison after a summary trial. The women had held a peaceful protest to support 18 local families whose homes were destroyed in forced evictions. They were charged with illegal occupancy of public property and obstruction of public officials with aggravating circumstances. They

C

were released on appeal in June, with their sentences suspended. Another woman activist, Yorm Bopha, was sentenced to three years' imprisonment on fabricated charges in December.

■ Prominent journalist and government critic Mam Sonando, aged 71, was sentenced to 20 years' imprisonment in October for anti-state offences, including instigating "insurrection" in Kratie province. The charges were believed to be politically motivated, and no evidence warranting a conviction was presented at the trial. He was a prisoner of conscience.

Forced evictions

The crisis over land continued, with forced evictions, land disputes and land-grabbing affecting thousands of people and resulting in a rise in protests. In May, the government announced a moratorium on granting Economic Land Concessions (ELCs), and a review of existing ELCs to ensure that they conformed with existing regulations. Several ELCs were granted after the moratorium. In June, the Prime Minister launched a project to allocate land titles to people living inside state forests, and economic and other land concessions. Thousands of student volunteers were tasked with mapping land and collecting information on occupancy.

■ In a violent forced eviction in January, the homes of around 300 families living in Borei Keila, central Phnom Penh, were destroyed by construction workers from a development company. Security forces used tear gas and rubber bullets against the residents, and rocks, logs and bottles were thrown during clashes. More than 64 people were reportedly injured, and eight people arrested. The evictees were taken to two relocation sites outside Phnom Penh with no adequate sanitation, housing or work opportunities. Some 125 families refused to go, and remained in squalid conditions near their former homes.

International justice

Investigations into Cases 003 and 004 were stalled amidst allegations of government interference in the Extraordinary Chambers in the Courts of Cambodia (ECCC). The Supreme Council of Magistracy rejected the appointment of reserve Judge Laurent Kasper-Ansermet as International Co-Investigating Judge in January, despite his nomination by the UN. He resigned, effective early May, citing obstruction by his Cambodian counterpart. US Judge Mark Harmon

replaced him in October, but no progress in the two cases was reported. Lack of funding resulted in the trial hearings in Case 002 being reduced to three days a week. Ieng Thirith, one of four alleged senior Khmer Rouge leaders on trial in Case 002, was declared unfit to stand trial and released into the care of her family in September. She was believed to have Alzheimer's disease.

■ In February, the Supreme Court Chamber at the ECCC upheld the conviction of prison chief Kaing Guek Euv, known as Duch, for war crimes and crimes against humanity, and increased his sentence from 35 years to life in prison. The Court also overturned an earlier decision to grant a legal remedy to Duch for his illegal detention for eight years by the Cambodian military court.

Amnesty International visits/reports

🚌 Amnesty International delegates visited Cambodia in February to April, August/September and November/December.

▤ Cambodia: Imprisoned for speaking out – update on Phnom Penh's Boeung Kak Lake (ASA 23/010/2012)

▤ Summit leaders should push Cambodia on human rights failures (ASA 23/019/2012)

▤ Cambodia: Convictions of activists demonstrate dire state of justice (PRE01/633/2012)

CAMEROON

REPUBLIC OF CAMEROON
Head of state: Paul Biya
Head of government: Philémon Yang

As in previous years, the authorities continued to restrict the activities of political opponents and journalists. People suspected of engaging in same-sex activities were detained and some were sentenced to prison terms. Those defending the rights of lesbian, gay, bisexual, transgender and intersex people were subjected to harassment and abuse. The authorities did not act to protect people from attacks. Conditions in some prisons were harsh and sometimes life-threatening.

Background

In November President Biya celebrated 30 years in power. Protest actions by opposition groups, linked to the anniversary, were dispersed by riot police.

Corruption remained pervasive, and government efforts to tackle the problem were limited in their effectiveness. In September a former government minister was jailed for 25 years for embezzling US$29 million of public funds.

In September, Amnesty International submitted a memorandum to the government highlighting numerous human rights concerns.

Harassment of political opponents

The authorities continued to use the criminal justice system to harass and silence political opposition groups.

■ The trial of several dozen members of the Southern Cameroons National Council (SCNC), arrested in 2008 and charged with holding illegal meetings and failing to produce identity cards, had not taken place by the end of the year. The accused had appeared in court on more than 30 occasions but the trial was adjourned each time because of the failure of the prosecution to present witnesses or the absence of court officials, including presiding judges.

■ Three members of the SCNC – Felix Ngalim, Ebeneza Akwanga and Makam Adamu – were arrested in April and charged with secession and revolution, offences under the Penal Code, in connection with their membership of and activities relating to the SCNC. During May members of the Territorial Surveillance police were alleged to have taken Felix Ngalim, detained at Kondengui prison in the capital, Yaoundé, to their offices in the city and beaten him with a truncheon, reportedly causing injuries to the soles of his feet, legs and other parts of the body. On 28 May, he was transferred to the central prison in Bamenda, capital of North West province. He appeared before the Bamenda High Court on 5 and 17 June and again on 3 July; each hearing was adjourned on the grounds that prosecution witnesses were unavailable to testify. Ebeneza Akwanga was reported to have escaped from Kondengui prison and fled Cameroon in May. Felix Ngalim was granted provisional release on 4 December and was awaiting trial at the end of the year.

■ In December, Dieudonné Enoh Meyomesse, an author critical of President Biya, was found guilty of armed robbery and sentenced to seven years'

imprisonment after an unfair trial by a military court in Yaoundé. He was considered a prisoner of conscience. He and several co-defendants, who were also sentenced to between two and nine years, had been arrested in November 2011.

Critics of the government expressed concern that some prosecutions for corruption targeted individuals who had disagreed with the government.

■ Titus Edzoa and Michel Thierry Atangana, who were due to complete their 15-year prison term for corruption, were tried on new charges and sentenced to 20 years' imprisonment in October. As in 1997, their trial in 2012 was unfair and appeared to be politically motivated.

■ Paul Eric Kingué, who had been imprisoned for alleged involvement in riots in February 2008 and for corruption, was sentenced to life imprisonment in February following further unfair trials on corruption charges. The Court of Appeal quashed the sentence but conducted a new trial and sentenced him in November to 10 years' imprisonment.

Human rights defenders

Human rights defenders and members of their families received death threats or were targeted by people they believed to be government agents or supporters.

■ On 27 March government officials prevented LGBTI activists in Yaoundé from holding an EU-financed workshop on the rights of sexual minorities. This action followed a violent disruption of the workshop by members of a self-confessed anti-LGBTI group known as the Rally for Cameroonian Youth. Members of the security forces had earlier arrested Stéphane Koche, the organizer of the workshop, and detained him for several hours.

■ In January, human rights defender Maximilienne Ngo Mbe was threatened with rape by men who claimed to be members of the security forces. Her niece was abducted and raped by men who told her that they were attacking her because of her aunt's activities against the government.

■ Lawyers Michel Togue and Alice Nkom were threatened with violence because they had represented people charged with homosexual acts. Family members were also threatened. The authorities failed to condemn the threats or to offer any protection.

Freedom of expression – journalists

Several journalists were prosecuted during the year.
■ Television journalists Alex Gustave Azebaze, Thierry Ngogang and Anani Rabier Bindji, who were arrested in June 2008 together with university lecturer Manassé Aboya, were still awaiting trial, charged with conspiracy to handle a confidential document without authorization, as well as conspiracy to make biased commentary. The charges were believed to be politically motivated. The four men had been arrested after they criticized a government anti-corruption initiative and the arrests of two newspaper journalists during a televised debate.

Rights of lesbian, gay, bisexual, transgender and intersex people

Violence, arbitrary arrests and detention, and other human rights violations targeting individuals because of their real or perceived sexual orientation, continued to occur. The authorities failed to protect people who were subjected to attacks and other abuse by non-state actors.
■ Franky Ndome Ndome who, together with Jonas Nsinga Kimie, was serving a five-year prison sentence for homosexual conduct, was beaten and otherwise ill-treated in June by guards at Kondengui prison. The two men were also repeatedly assaulted by fellow inmates. The authorities took no action against those responsible or to protect them from violence.
■ Three women – Martine Solange Abessolo, Esther Aboa Belinga and Léonie Marie Djula – were arrested on 14 February in Ambam, Southern province. They were accused of being lesbians after Léonie Djula's husband reportedly told the authorities that his wife had been enticed by the other two women into engaging in same-sex sexual relations. Martine Abessolo and Esther Belinga subsequently appeared before the Ambam Court of First Instance on charges of engaging in same-sex sexual relations and defaming Léonie Djula. They were granted provisional release on 20 February and appealed against irregularities in their arrest. The Ebolowa Court of Appeal had not delivered a verdict by the end of the year.
■ On 17 December the Court of Appeal upheld the 2011 conviction of Jean-Claude Roger Mbede for homosexual activity. He had been sentenced to three years' imprisonment.

Prison conditions

Conditions in Cameroon's two largest prisons, in Yaoundé and Douala, were harsh and constituted cruel, inhuman or degrading treatment, and in some cases were life-threatening. Prisoners suffering from mental illness did not have access to psychiatric care. At the end of the year both prisons were holding five times their intended capacity.

Death penalty

Government information indicated that 102 prisoners were on death row at the start of the year. The Cameroonian National Commission on Human Rights and Freedoms recommended that the government abolish the death penalty.

Amnesty International visits/reports

🚌 Amnesty International delegates visited Cameroon in December.

CANADA

CANADA
Head of state: Queen Elizabeth II, represented by
                                        Governor General David Johnston
Head of government: Stephen Harper

There were continuing systematic violations of the rights of Indigenous Peoples. Immigration and refugee law reforms violated international human rights norms.

Indigenous Peoples' rights

In January, hearings began before a government-appointed review panel to consider a proposal to build a pipeline connecting the Alberta oil sands and the British Columbia coast. The controversial Northern Gateway project would pass through or near the traditional lands of dozens of First Nations, many of whom have expressed public opposition.

In February, the federal government acknowledged before the CERD Committee that the UN Declaration on the Rights of Indigenous Peoples could be used when interpreting Canadian laws, but took no steps to work with Indigenous Peoples to implement the Declaration.

In February, the government introduced the Safe Drinking Water for First Nations Act but the Act's regulations provide no additional resources for water infrastructure in First Nations communities.

In April, the Federal Court overturned a 2011 Canadian Human Rights Tribunal ruling dismissing a discrimination complaint regarding public spending on child protection in First Nation communities as compared to predominantly non-Indigenous communities. The case was before the Federal Court of Appeal at the end of the year.

Legislative changes in 2012 dramatically restricted federal environmental impact assessments. The government had claimed that these assessments were crucial for fulfilling its constitutional obligations towards Indigenous Peoples.

Women's rights

In February and June the UN CERD Committee and Committee against Torture respectively called on Canada to develop a national action plan to address violence against Indigenous women. The federal government failed to do so.

In October, video footage was released of the ill-treatment in detention of 19-year-old Ashley Smith, who died in an Ontario provincial jail in 2007. A Coroner's inquest into her case was continuing at the end of the year.

The report of a British Columbia inquiry into the police response to cases of missing and murdered women, many of whom were Indigenous, was released in December. Amnesty International and other organizations were critical of the inquiry's failure to ensure the full and effective participation of affected communities.

Counter-terror and security

The Military Police Complaints Commission released a report in June clearing individual military police officers of fault, but pointing to systemic failings with respect to the transfer of prisoners in Afghanistan to the custody of Afghan officials.

In August, a Ministerial Direction from 2011 was made public instructing the Royal Canadian Mounted Police and the Canadian Border Services Agency, in cases involving a serious threat to public safety, to make use of foreign intelligence that may have been obtained through torture and to share information with foreign governments even if doing so would give rise to a substantial risk of torture.

In September, Omar Khadr, a Canadian citizen apprehended by US forces in Afghanistan in 2002 when he was 15 and detained at Guantánamo Bay since, was transferred to a Canadian prison. Further to a 2011 plea deal, he had been eligible for transfer for 11 months.

Refugees and asylum-seekers

In June, legislation was passed requiring mandatory detention of asylum-seekers arriving in Canada in an irregular manner. The legislation denied access to the Refugee Appeal Division to such individuals as well as to refugee claimants coming from designated safe countries of origin.

In June, the government introduced new legislation which would strip large numbers of permanent residents with criminal records of the ability to appeal or seek humanitarian relief from deportation orders.

Also in June, the government instituted drastic cuts to the Interim Federal Health Program for refugees. Among other restrictions, refugee claimants from designated safe countries of origin would only be eligible for health care if they posed a risk to the health of others.

■ In September, Kimberly Rivera, whose claim for refugee status based on her desertion from the US military for reasons of conscience was rejected, was deported to the USA where she was arrested. She was confined to Fort Carson Army Base awaiting court-martial at the end of the year.

Police and security forces

Emergency legislation limiting freedom of expression and assembly was enacted in the province of Quebec in May in response to mass student demonstrations. It was suspended in September following a change of government. The government did not respond to calls for a public inquiry into police abuses during the demonstrations.

In May, the Office of the Independent Police Review Director in the province of Ontario recommended disciplinary proceedings against 36 police officers for offences associated with the policing of demonstrations at the G20 Summit in Toronto in 2010. Disciplinary hearings and court challenges were continuing at the end of the year.

C

Corporate accountability

In May, a mandated report was released, assessing the human rights impacts of the Canada-Colombia Free Trade Agreement which had entered into force in August 2011. The government claimed it was too early to assess the impacts.

In November, the Supreme Court refused to hear an appeal in a case brought against a Canadian mining company for alleged responsibility for human rights abuses in the Democratic Republic of the Congo. Lower courts had ruled that Canada was not the appropriate jurisdiction in which to hear the case.

Amnesty International visits/reports

📄 Canada: Summary of recommendations from Amnesty International's briefing to the UN Committee on the Elimination of Racial Discrimination (AMR 20/003/2012)

📄 Canada: Briefing to the UN Committee against Torture, 48th Session (AMR 20/004/2012)

📄 Canada: Briefing to the UN Committee on the Rights of the Child: 61st Session (AMR 20/006/2012)

CENTRAL AFRICAN REPUBLIC

CENTRAL AFRICAN REPUBLIC
Head of state: François Bozizé
Head of government: Faustin Archange Touadéra

The people of the Central African Republic remained at grave risk of abuse and violence, as numerous armed groups continued to operate, despite several declaring they had ceased fighting. Many civilians were killed, abducted, ill-treated or subjected to rape and other forms of sexual violence. Most perpetrators enjoyed complete impunity.

Background

The Economic Community of Central African States (ECCAS) decided that MICOPAX (Mission for the consolidation of peace in Central African Republic) would end in December 2013. Several hundred French soldiers continued to be deployed in the Central African Republic (CAR), supporting and training government soldiers and supporting MICOPAX.

In September, the African Union took political responsibility for a regional force combating the Lord's Resistance Army (LRA). Peacekeepers in the CAR clashed several times with small contingents of the LRA, killing some and capturing others. In May, the Ugandan army announced it had captured senior LRA commander Caesar Achellam.

In early December, a coalition of armed groups known as Seleka launched a campaign to overthrow the government. By the end of December, it had captured large swathes of northern CAR, but was prevented from advancing on the capital, Bangui, by MICOPAX troops. At the end of the year, the two sides agreed to negotiate. Several hundred South African troops were deployed in Bangui at the request of the government.

Abuses by armed groups

Abuses by armed groups – including killings, torture and abductions – were reported throughout the year in the northern and eastern parts of the country.

Numerous abuses in northern CAR – including killings, abductions and looting – were attributed to remnants of the Popular Front for Recovery (FPR), which originated from Chad. In January, a combined force of the CAR and Chadian armies in northern CAR attacked bases of the FPR, scattering combatants. In September, FPR leader Baba Laddé returned to Chad. Hundreds of FPR combatants, and civilians who had been living with them, were repatriated a month later.

Although there were reportedly fewer killings by the LRA than in previous years, LRA combatants continued to kill unarmed civilians, loot property and use women and girls as sex slaves.

■ In March, 13 men working at a mine in a game reserve in Mbomou province were killed. Erik Mararv, a Swedish owner of the game reserve, and David Simpson, a UK pilot, were accused of killing the men but human rights groups and lawyers claimed the killings bore the hallmarks of the LRA. The charges against the two men were dropped in August after several months in detention.

Disarmament, demobilization and reintegration

Several armed groups announced an end to the conflict with the government and committed to disarmament, demobilization and reintegration (DDR). The Union of Republican Forces (Union des forces républicaines, UFR) announced in June that it had completed its disarmament and dissolution. The Popular Army for the Restoration of Democracy (Armée populaire pour la restauration de la démocratie, APRD) declared in July it had ceased to exist as an armed group. Its demobilization had been delayed in January after its leader (national vice-president of the DDR programme Jean-Jacques Demafouth) and two other politicians were accused of plotting against the government and detained. Opposition leaders said that the arrests were politically motivated to sabotage the DDR. The charges were dropped and the men released in May.

In August, the Convention of Patriots for Justice and Peace (CPJP) armed group and the CAR government signed an agreement to cease hostilities. Scores of CPJP child soldiers had been demobilized in the preceding months. A process to disarm CPJP fighters had not been completed by the end of the year, however, and a faction of the CPJP which did not support the agreement carried out attacks against government soldiers during the second half of the year.

Excessive use of force
CAR government soldiers ill-treated and killed civilians, largely with impunity. Many of the perpetrators were members of the presidential guard.
■ Mijora Delphine Dengwize died in August from injuries sustained when she was shot by an army captain. The captain had opened fire at a crowd protesting against his attempt to arrest civilians he accused of involvement in a violent incident in Bangui. The soldier had a long-standing reputation for committing human rights abuses with impunity.

Violence against women and girls
Chadian government soldiers who had participated in the January operation against the FPR raped more than a dozen women in the northern town of Ndele. Neither the CAR nor the Chadian authorities took action against the perpetrators.

Prisoners of conscience
Eleven prisoners of conscience who had been arrested in June 2010 for their links to a lawyer and a businessman sought by the authorities were granted provisional release in April after a judge ruled they

had no case to answer. However, the government appealed against the judge's decision and a charge of arson was still pending at the end of the year.

Detention without charge or trial
Several people associated with the Ministers of Finance and Justice (who had been dismissed in June and July respectively amid reports that President Bozizé suspected them of plotting to overthrow the government) were arrested in July and August. Those arrested were Laurent Feindiro, brother of the former Minister of Justice, Jean Bianga and Serge-Venant Magna, the driver and a civil servant of the former Minister of Finance respectively. They were still being held without charge or trial at the end of the year.

Amnesty International visits/reports
🚌 Amnesty International delegates visited the Central African Republic in May and June.

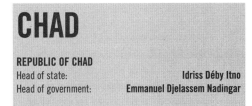

CHAD

REPUBLIC OF CHAD
Head of state: **Idriss Déby Itno**
Head of government: **Emmanuel Djelassem Nadingar**

Trade unionists, journalists and human rights defenders were intimidated and the criminal justice system was used to harass political opponents. People continued to be arbitrarily arrested and held in lengthy pre-trial detention. Many children were recruited as child soldiers. Prison conditions remained extremely harsh. Impunity for human rights violations and abuses continued.

Background
Chad continued to host a large number of refugees and internally displaced persons. According to the UN, as of 31 December, there were 281,000 Sudanese refugees in 12 refugee camps in eastern Chad and 79,000 refugees from the Central African Republic in the south, in addition to 120,000 internally displaced people in various sites on the border with Darfur, Sudan.

Rebel leader Abdel Kader Baba Laddé of the Popular Front for Redress (Front populaire pour le

C

redressement, FPR), who was based in northern Central African Republic, returned to Chad in September after negotiations between the FPR and the Chadian and Central African Republic governments. He was accused by human rights groups of recruiting child soldiers.

Cruel, inhuman or degrading punishment

Cruel, inhuman or degrading punishments, including beatings, continued to be widely practised by security forces and prison guards, with almost total impunity.

Detention without trial

Most prisoners were held in lengthy pre-trial detention. Several had spent years in detention without the authorities being aware of their presence. In March, a 17-year-old boy had spent more than 18 months in Doba prison without the knowledge of the local prosecutor.

Arbitrary arrests and detentions

People continued to be arrested and detained without charge. Detainees were routinely held in police cells as well as in secret detention facilities.

Prison conditions

Conditions remained harsh, amounting to cruel, inhuman and degrading treatment. Cells were severely overcrowded, and food and drinking water were inadequate. There was no health care in prisons, including for serious transmissible diseases such as tuberculosis. Men, women and children were held together indiscriminately in the majority of prisons. No mechanisms were in place to allow prisoners to complain about their treatment.
■ Inmates were often chained in the prisons in Abéché, Sarh and Doba. In March, at least 15 prisoners were chained by their legs day and night in Abéché prison.

Enforced disappearances

No effective action was taken to bring to justice those suspected in the disappearance of opposition leader Ibni Oumar Mahamat Saleh. His whereabouts remained unknown more than four years after his arrest in February 2008. A 2009 report of a national commission of inquiry had confirmed that he was arrested from his home by eight members of the security forces.

Harassment of political opponents

Chadian officials continued to use the criminal justice system to harass political opponents and influence the judiciary.
■ In March, opposition MP Gali Ngothé Gatta of the United Democratic Forces (Union des Forces Démocratiques) was arrested and sentenced to one year's imprisonment for attempted corruption and poaching by the Tribunal of first instance in Sahr, southern Chad. He was tried and sentenced three days after his arrest, despite his parliamentary immunity not being lifted. He was detained in Sahr prison and later transferred to Moundou prison following an appeal. On 24 April, the Moundou Court of Appeal annulled the proceedings due to "grave flaws" and ordered the release of Gali Ngothé Gatta. The Supreme Court later confirmed the Court of Appeal's ruling.
■ Emmanuel Dekeumbé, a judge at the Moundou Court of Appeal who refused to sentence Gali Ngothé Gatta and denounced the procedural irregularities, was dismissed by the Supreme Judicial Council (Conseil supérieur de la Magistrature). The decision was confirmed by a Presidential ordinance in July.

Freedom of expression
Church leaders
■ Monsignor Michele Russo, Catholic bishop of Doba, was expelled from Chad by the authorities on 14 October following an address he gave during a mass on 30 September. In his statement, broadcast by a Doba-based radio station, he denounced mismanagement by the authorities and unequal distribution of wealth from oil revenues of the region.
Journalists
The authorities continued to threaten media outlets and harass journalists.
■ On 18 September, Jean-Claude Nekim, chief editor of the bi-weekly newspaper N'Djamena Bi-Hebdo, was sentenced to one year's suspended imprisonment and fined CFA 1 million (US$2,000) after his newspaper printed extracts from a petition issued by the Union of Chad Trade Unions (Union des syndicats du Tchad, UST). He was charged with "incitement of racial hatred" and "defamation". The newspaper was also banned for three months. His appeal against the decision was still pending at the end of the year.

Human rights defenders

Human rights defenders, including trade union leaders, were attacked and continued to be subjected to intimidation and harassment by government officials. In some instances, the judiciary was used to silence them.

■ On 18 September, Michel Barka, Younous Mahadjir and François Djondang, all leading members of the UST, were sentenced to 18 months' suspended imprisonment and each fined CFA 1 million (US$2,000). The N'Djamena First Instance Tribunal found the three men guilty of "incitement to racial hatred" and "defamation" in relation to the UST's petition published earlier that month. Their appeal was pending at the end of the year.

■ On 19 October, Jacqueline Moudeina, a lawyer and president of the human rights organization Association tchadienne de promotion et de défense des droits de l'homme (ATPDH), was attacked by unidentified armed men in front of her house in N'Djamena. She was unharmed but her vehicle was taken by the men and found on 22 October in the village of Malo-Tama, 35km away. This incident occurred several days after Jacqueline Moudeina received the 2011 Right Livelihood Award for her human rights work. Arrests were made but by the end of the year it was not clear if anyone had been charged.

■ On 20 October, six men in the military uniform of the gendarmerie entered the compound of Dobian Assingar, a human rights activist and honorary president of the Chadian League of Human Rights (LTDH). They searched the house without a warrant and said they were looking for a stolen car. Dobian Assingar filed a complaint but no reply had been received by the end of the year.

Child soldiers

There were persistent reports during the year that children were recruited by the Chadian National Army, including massive numbers in February-March. The recruitment and use of children by Chadian and Sudanese armed groups also continued. Information collected by various sources between February and April reported that many children in the departments of Assoungha and Kimiti in eastern Chad, including already demobilized children who had been reunited with their families, regularly travelled to Sudan where they served in armed groups.

■ At least 24 children aged between 14 and 17 were found by social workers at the Mongo Military Training Center in June.

Housing rights – forced evictions

Forced evictions continued to take place throughout the year, even in cases where there was a court injunction against eviction. No alternative housing or compensation were offered to victims, even those who had won compensation before a court.

■ In January, more than 600 people were forcibly evicted and their homes destroyed in Sabangali, N'Djamena, to make way for the construction of a hotel. In April, some of those evicted were allocated plots of land, but only half of the former residents received compensation promised by an inter-ministerial commission.

International justice – Hissène Habré

On 22 August, an agreement was signed between Senegal and the African Union to establish a special court to try former President Hissène Habré. In September, Chadian authorities stated that they had confirmed their financial contribution of CFA 2 billion (around US$4 million) for the trial. In December, Senegal's national assembly adopted a law creating a special tribunal to try Hissène Habré.

Violence against women and girls

The authorities consistently failed to prevent and address sexual violence by both state and non-state agents.

■ On the night of 8 January, 13 women detainees were sexually assaulted by prison guards at Moussoro prison. All women detained in the prison were subsequently transferred to Amsinene prison in N'Djamena, on the orders of the Minister of Justice. No independent investigation had begun by the end of the year.

Amnesty International visits/reports

🚍 Amnesty International delegates visited Chad in March and September.

📄 Chad: 'We are all dying here' – human rights violations in prisons (AFR 20/007/2012)

📄 Chad: Judicial harassment of political opponents and journalists must stop (PRE01/455/2012)

CHILE

REPUBLIC OF CHILE
Head of state and government: Sebastián Piñera Echenique

Consultation with Indigenous Peoples on projects that affect them remained inadequate. A law to prevent and punish discrimination was passed. Police responded to a number of protests with excessive use of force. Legal proceedings regarding past human rights violations continued.

Background

There were demonstrations, at times violent, throughout the year over reforms of the public education system, Indigenous Peoples' rights and living costs.

A draft law on public order raised concerns at the possible criminalization of social protest. The legislation was before Congress at the end of the year.

Police and security forces

In February, residents from the Patagonian region of Aysen blocked roads and set up barricades in protest at the government's failure to address economic concerns. The police used tear gas, rubber bullets and water cannon to disperse protesters; several people were injured.

By the end of the year claims of abuses – including sexual violence against women and girls – by the police during student demonstrations across the country in 2011 and 2012 remained widely unpunished.

Discrimination

In July, the Anti-Discrimination Law came into force. The law prohibits discrimination on grounds of race, ethnicity, religion, sexual orientation, gender identity, age, appearance and disability. The law was finally passed following the brutal killing in March of Daniel Zamudio who was beaten to death allegedly for being homosexual. The investigation into his killing was continuing at the end of the year.

In February, the Inter-American Court of Human Rights issued a landmark ruling condemning the 2003 ruling of the Chilean Supreme Court that stripped a lesbian mother of custody of her three daughters on the basis of her sexual orientation.

Impunity

Following a visit to Chile in August, the UN Working Group on Enforced or Involuntary Disappearances welcomed progress in investigations of human rights violations during the government of General Augusto Pinochet (1973-1990). However, it expressed concern that few of the convicted perpetrators were in fact serving a sentence because of the short penalties imposed. The Working Group also called for the 1978 Amnesty Law to be repealed; for a national plan to search for the disappeared; and for the allocation of additional resources in order to expedite judicial proceedings.

In December a judge ordered the arrest of eight former military officers in connection with the murder of singer-songwriter Víctor Jara a few days after the military coup that brought General Pinochet to power in 1973.

According to official data, as of August 2012, court proceedings in 150 cases of past human rights violations had been completed since 2002; 133 of these had resulted in convictions.

Indigenous Peoples' rights

In April, the Supreme Court confirmed a decision by an appeal court suspending a mining project in the north of the country until the local Indigenous community had been consulted, in accordance with ILO Convention No. 169 on Indigenous and Tribal Peoples.

A government plan to replace the widely criticized 2009 decree governing consultation with Indigenous Peoples was rejected by a majority of Indigenous leaders in August. They argued that the new regulations did not comply with international standards on effective participation. In November, the UN Special Rapporteur on the rights of indigenous peoples also expressed concerns at the definition of consultation in the government proposal.

There were renewed allegations of excessive use of force and arbitrary arrests during police operations against Mapuche Indigenous communities. Unfair trials of community members were reported. Clashes with the security forces resulted in the killing of a police officer in April.

■ In July, several members of the Mapuche Temucuicui community, including children, were injured after police fired rubber bullets and used tear gas to evict them from land they had occupied in

Ercilla, Araucanía region, as part of their campaign for the return of their traditional territory.

■ In October, four Mapuche imprisoned in Angol prison called off their 60-day hunger strike after the Supreme Court granted a new trial for one of the men and imposed lesser charges on one other; his sentence was subsequently reduced from 10 years to prison to three years in parole. Both men had been initially convicted of the attempted murder of a policeman in 2011.

■ In August, a military court acquitted a policeman of the murder of Jaime Mendoza Collio, a 24-year-old Mapuche, in 2009. There were concerns about the impartiality of investigations into this case and about the use of military courts to deal with crimes committed by members of the police and military against civilians.

Sexual and reproductive rights

Abortion remained a criminal offence in all circumstances. In October, the CEDAW Committee called on Chile to review its legislation and to decriminalize abortion in cases of rape, incest or threats to the health or life of the woman.

Amnesty International visits/reports

Chile: Carta abierta al Presidente de la República de Chile al cumplir dos años de su mandato (AMR 22/001/2012)

CHINA

PEOPLE'S REPUBLIC OF CHINA
Head of state: Hu Jintao
Head of government: Wen Jiabao

The authorities maintained a stranglehold on political activists, human rights defenders and online activists, subjecting many to harassment, intimidation, arbitrary detention and enforced disappearance. At least 130 people were detained or otherwise restricted to stifle criticism and prevent protests ahead of the leadership transition initiated at the 18th Chinese Communist Party Congress in November. Access to justice remained elusive for many, resulting in millions of people petitioning the government to complain of injustices and seek redress outside the formal legal system. Muslims,

Buddhists and Christians, who practised their religion outside officially sanctioned channels, and Falun Gong practitioners, were tortured, harassed, arbitrarily detained, imprisoned and faced other serious restrictions on their right to freedom of religion. Local governments continued to rely on land sales to fund stimulus projects that resulted in the forced eviction of thousands of people from their homes or land throughout the country. The authorities reported that they would further tighten the judicial process in death penalty cases; however thousands were executed.

Background

The Chinese Communist Party made its first official top leadership change in 10 years at the 18th Chinese Communist Party Congress (CCPC) in November. Xi Jinping was promoted to party leader and Li Keqiang to the second ranked member of the Communist Party Politburo Standing Committee. The two were expected to replace, respectively, President Hu Jintao and Premier Wen Jiabao, in March 2013.

Justice system

The state continued to use the criminal justice system to punish its critics. Hundreds of individuals and groups were sentenced to long prison terms or sent to Re-education Through Labour (RTL) camps for peacefully exercising their rights to freedom of expression and freedom of belief. People were frequently charged with "endangering state security", "inciting subversion of state power" and "leaking state secrets", and were sentenced to long prison terms, in many cases, for posting blogs online or communicating information overseas that was deemed sensitive.

Lawyers who took on controversial cases faced harassment and threats from the authorities and, in some cases, the loss of professional licences, severely curtailing people's access to justice.

Criminal defendants faced routine violations of the right to a fair trial and other rights, including denial of access to their lawyers and family, detention beyond legally allowed time frames, and torture and other ill-treatment in detention. The use of torture to extract confessions remained widespread.

Revisions to the Criminal Procedure Law, adopted in March to be effective 1 January 2013, introduced strengthened protections for juvenile criminal

C

suspects and defendants, and those with mental disabilities. However, for the first time, the revisions authorized police to detain suspects for up to six months for certain types of crimes, including "endangering state security", without notifying the suspect's family of the location or reasons for detention. The revisions therefore potentially legalized enforced disappearance.

Arbitrary arrests and detentions

Police arbitrarily deprived hundreds of thousands of people of their liberty by placing them in administrative detention, including RTL camps, without recourse to independent courts.

The authorities operated hundreds of places of detention, including "black jails" and Legal Education Training Centres where they held thousands arbitrarily, and where torture, sometimes leading to death, was an established method of "correction" or deterrence.

■ Blind Shandong legal activist Chen Guangcheng, and members of his family, were tortured and held under illegal house arrest for a year and a half before they escaped to the US embassy in April 2012. After a diplomatic stand-off, they were permitted to leave for the USA in May.

■ Human rights and environmental activist Hu Jia remained under house arrest and monitoring since his release in June 2011. Prior to the CCPC in November 2012, he was forced out of his Beijing home by the internal security police and kept in a hotel until 16 November.

Human rights defenders

Tension between civil society and the government remained acute. Academics and activists issued several public letters to the government and incoming leaders, calling for elimination of RTL and other arbitrary detention systems such as "black jails" and psychiatric detention.

The authorities budgeted over 701 billion yuan (approximately US$112 billion) to maintain public security, an increase of over 30 billion from 2011. Provincial governments called on lower level authorities to "strengthen community works" in the run-up to the Chinese Communist Party leadership transition. This included collecting information from community monitors, frequently warning dissidents and their families, and imprisoning government critics

or placing them under house arrest all as a means to silence dissent.

At the end of 2011 and beginning of 2012, several human rights defenders who consistently called for political reform were sentenced to long jail terms for "inciting subversion of state power" through articles and poems they wrote and distributed. Sentences included 10 years for Guizhou human rights forum leader Chen Xi and activist Li Tie, nine years for Sichuan human rights activist Chen Wei, seven years for Zhejiang Democratic Party member Zhu Yufu and, at the end of 2012, eight years for Jiangsu internet activist Cao Haibo, who set up an online group to discuss constitutional law and democracy.

Human rights defenders working on economic, social and cultural rights were also targeted. They were either placed under surveillance, harassed, or charged with vaguely worded offences.

■ Shanghai housing rights activist Feng Zhenghu was put under house arrest at the end of February and remained so throughout the year.

■ Women's rights and housing activist Mao Hengfeng was again detained for "disturbing public order" one month before the 18th CCPC and eventually ordered to serve 18 months of RTL.

■ Human rights lawyer Ni Yulan and her husband, both housing rights activists, were sentenced in July to 30 months and 24 months respectively for "picking quarrels and causing trouble", after a second trial.

■ On 6 June, veteran dissident and labour rights activist Li Wangyang was found dead in hospital just days after an interview, in which he spoke about being tortured, aired in Hong Kong. The authorities claimed he committed suicide by hanging himself; however many questioned the likelihood of this. Li Wangyang was blind, deaf and unable to walk without assistance as a result of being tortured when he was jailed after the 1989 crackdown. He had been jailed twice for a total of more than 21 years.

Death penalty

Death sentences continued to be imposed after unfair trials. More people were executed in China than in the rest of the world put together. Statistics on death sentences and executions remained classified. Under current Chinese laws, there were no procedures for death row prisoners to seek pardon or commutation of their sentence.

■ In May, the authorities rescinded the death sentence imposed on business woman Wu Ying for "fraudulently raising funds", adding to debates about the abolition of capital punishment for economic crimes.

Amendments to the Criminal Procedure Law would allow the Supreme People's Court to amend death sentences in all cases. These would make it mandatory to record or videotape interrogations of suspects potentially facing the death penalty or life imprisonment. The amendments would require the courts, prosecutors and the police to notify legal aid offices to assign a defence lawyer to all criminal suspects and defendants who face potential death sentences or life imprisonment and who have not yet appointed legal counsel. Chinese legal scholars called for legal aid to be assured at all stages of a criminal process which may lead to the death penalty.

In November, the authorities announced that a voluntary organ donation system would be launched nationwide in early 2013 to phase out reliance on organs removed from executed prisoners.

Housing rights – forced evictions

Sudden and violent evictions were widespread, and were typically preceded by threats and harassment. Consultation with affected residents was rare. Compensation, adequate alternative housing and the ability to access legal remedies were severely limited. In many cases, corrupt village leaders signed deals with private developers, handing over land without residents knowing. Those who peacefully resisted forced eviction or sought to protect their rights through legal channels risked detention, imprisonment and RTL. Some resorted to drastic measures, setting themselves on fire or resorting to violent forms of protest.

Enforcement of the 2011 Regulations on the Expropriation of Houses on State-owned Land and Compensation remained weak. The Regulations outlawed the use of violence in urban evictions and granted urban home-owners facing eviction limited protections. In November, the State Council put forward to the National People's Congress proposed draft amendments to the 1986 Land Administration Law. Revisions to the law were expected to provide legal protections against forced eviction and increased compensation to rural residents.

■ The authorities continued to demolish houses in Shiliuzhuang village, Beijing, between April and August. Some demolitions took place at 5am and without advance notice. The residents were not offered alternative housing and some received no compensation for their loss. The residents said they were not genuinely consulted, and some said they had been beaten and briefly detained in the run-up to the eviction.

Tibet Autonomous Region

The authorities continued to repress Tibetans' right to enjoy and promote their own culture as well as their rights to freedom of religion, expression, peaceful association and assembly. Socioeconomic discrimination against ethnic Tibetans persisted unchecked. During the year, at least 83 ethnic Tibetan monks, nuns and lay people set themselves on fire, bringing the total number of self-immolations in Tibetan populated areas in China to at least 95 since February 2009.

■ At least three men were sentenced to up to seven and a half years in prison in separate cases for passing on information about cases of self-immolation to overseas organizations and media.

Numerous people allegedly involved in anti-government protests were beaten, detained, subjected to enforced disappearance or sentenced following unfair trials. At least two people were believed to have died because of injuries sustained from police beatings.

■ In January, security forces reportedly shot at Tibetan protesters in three different incidents in Sichuan province, killing at least one and injuring many others.

The authorities used "patriotic" and "legal education" campaigns to force Tibetans to denounce the Dalai Lama. Officials increased their interference in management of monasteries and expelled monks.

Xinjiang Uighur Autonomous Region (XUAR)

The authorities maintained their "strike hard" campaign, criminalizing what they labelled "illegal religious" and "separatist" activities, and clamping down on peaceful expressions of cultural identity.

■ In January, media reports stated that 16 of 20 Uighurs who were forcibly returned from Cambodia in December 2009 were sentenced to prison terms ranging from 16 years to life.

■ In May, nine Uighurs were sentenced to prison terms ranging from six to 15 years for participating in alleged "illegal religious activities". In June, an 11-year-old boy, Mirzahid, died in custody after being detained for studying in an "illegal religious school".

C

■ In July, several dozen families revealed to overseas groups their ongoing search for relatives missing since the crackdown that followed the July 2009 unrest. The youngest person missing was aged 16 when he disappeared.

■ Patigul, mother of Imammet Eli, aged 25 when detained, revealed to overseas media that she had searched for her son since his detention on 14 July 2009. She said that former inmates told her Imammet had been tortured in detention, and was taken to a hospital in August 2009. Since then she had no further news of him.

Hong Kong Special Administrative Region
Legal and institutional developments

In March, Leung Chun-ying was selected as Hong Kong's next Chief Executive not directly by the people but by a 1,193-strong Election Committee. Just days before the election, 220,000 people cast ballots in a straw poll in protest against the "small circle election", the outcome of which was widely perceived to have been determined by the Beijing government.

Fears for the independence of the judiciary and other government bodies were raised when in September the Chief Secretary remarked that the Ombudsman's Office and the Independent Commission Against Corruption were a major hurdle against policy implementation. In October, the former Secretary of Justice criticized Hong Kong judges for a lack of understanding of the relationship between Beijing and Hong Kong.

The government planned to introduce Moral and National Education in primary schools, starting from 2012. Many perceived the subject as political propaganda and students were reportedly to be graded not only on their knowledge of the subject matter, but also on their emotional identification with the state. On 29 July, more than 90,000 people rallied against the curriculum. After the government initially ignored protesters' demands, in late August protesters gathered outside government headquarters, and some went on hunger strike. At the height of the campaign, a reported 100,000 people joined a week-long protest. On 8 September, the government announced that the subject would be suspended indefinitely.

In November, Cyd Ho Sau-lan, a legislator, made a non-binding motion calling for a public consultation on a new law to protect people from discrimination on the basis of sexual orientation. The motion was defeated.

Migrant workers' rights

There were approximately 300,000 migrant domestic workers in Hong Kong, all of whom were excluded from the minimum wage law. Migrant domestic workers regularly paid the equivalent of three to six months of their salary in fees to recruitment agencies, despite Hong Kong law limiting the amount an agency can charge to 10 per cent of the workers' first month's salary. In September, the separate minimum allowable wage for migrant domestic workers increased from HK$3,740 (US$483) to HK$3,920 (US$506) per month, but many workers did not receive this minimum.

■ On 28 March, the Court of Appeal overturned an earlier ruling by the Court of First Instance in favour of Filipino national Vallejos Evangeline Baneo. She was employed as a domestic worker in Hong Kong since 1986, and was seeking the right for migrant domestic workers to apply for permanent residency and the right of abode. The case was admitted by the Court of Final Appeal and was likely to be heard in early 2013.

Macau Special Administrative Region

On 29 February, the Standing Committee of China's National People's Congress decided that there would be no direct election of the Chief Executive in 2014. The job of selecting the Chief Executive would continue to be performed by the Election Committee which in the last election had 300 members, only six of whom were directly elected. Pro-democracy politicians urged the government to reform the existing electoral system, including by increasing the ratio of directly elected seats in the legislature. In an online public opinion poll conducted in April the majority of respondents supported electoral reform.

■ On 1 May, police interfered with a peaceful demonstration which included dozens of reporters wearing black T-shirts, protesting against self-censorship in Macao's mainstream media.

Amnesty International visits/reports

Standing their ground: Thousands face violent eviction in China (ASA 17/001/2012)

COLOMBIA

REPUBLIC OF COLOMBIA
Head of state and government: **Juan Manuel Santos Calderón**

Formal peace talks between the government and the Revolutionary Armed Forces of Colombia (FARC) began in Norway in October, the first such talks in a decade. Concerns remained that a stable peace would not be possible without a verifiable commitment from the two sides to put an end to human rights abuses and a commitment by the authorities to bring abusers to justice.

Congress approved a law in December that gave the military justice system greater control over investigations into human rights violations, thereby threatening to undermine the rights of victims to truth, justice and reparation.

All the parties to the long-running conflict – the security forces, either acting alone or in collusion with paramilitaries, and guerrilla groups – continued to be responsible for serious human rights abuses and violations of international humanitarian law, including unlawful killings, forced displacement, torture, abductions or forced disappearances, and sexual violence. The main victims were Indigenous Peoples, Afro-descendent and peasant farmer communities, human rights defenders and trade unionists.

The Victims and Land Restitution Law, designed to return to the rightful owners some of the millions of hectares of land misappropriated, often through violence, during the course of the conflict, came into force on 1 January. However, a backlash from those who benefited from misappropriated lands led to threats against and killings of those campaigning for land restitution as well as of those seeking to return to their lands.

Internal armed conflict

Civilians continued to bear the brunt of conflict-related human rights abuses and violations of international humanitarian law. Although precise figures were not available, tens of thousands of people were known to have been forced from their homes in 2012 as a direct result of the conflict. Most were members of Indigenous Peoples and Afro-descendent and peasant farmer communities in rural areas.

- In June, over 130 people from El Tarra, Norte de Santander Department, and around 400 from Leiva, Nariño Department, were forced to flee their homes.

Civilian communities, such as the Peace Community of San José de Apartadó in Antioquia Department, campaigning to ensure the warring parties did not drag them into the conflict, continued to be subjected to serious human rights abuses.

- On 28 June, two members of the Peace Community were followed by 50 armed paramilitaries of the "Gaitanista Forces of Colombia" who threatened to kill peasant farmer Fabio Graciano.
- On 4 February, two paramilitaries on a motorbike shot at Jesús Emilio Tuberquia, the legal representative of the Peace Community. The attack, in the town of Apartadó, took place only about 100m from a police control post.

Bomb attacks in urban areas led to the loss of civilian lives.

- On 15 May, a car bomb injured more than 50 people, including former Interior Minister Fernando Londoño, in the capital Bogotá. His driver and bodyguard were killed. No group claimed responsibility, although the authorities blamed the FARC.

In July, Colombia ratified the International Convention for the Protection of All Persons from Enforced Disappearance. However, it did not recognize the competence of the UN Committee on Enforced Disappearances, thereby denying victims and their families an important recourse to justice. Although accurate numbers were hard to establish, at least 30,000 people were thought to have been forcibly disappeared during the conflict.

- Hernán Henry Díaz, spokesperson for the Departmental Roundtable of Social Organizations in Putumayo Department and member of the National United Trade Union of Agricultural Workers, was last seen on 18 April. At the time of his enforced disappearance, he was co-ordinating the participation of delegates from Putumayo in a national political demonstration due to take place later that month in Bogotá.

Indigenous Peoples' rights

The impact of the conflict on Indigenous Peoples intensified as hostilities raged in their territories, especially in Cauca and Valle del Cauca departments. According to the National Indigenous Organization of Colombia, at least 84 Indigenous people were killed in 2012, including 21 leaders.

C

■ On 12 August, Lisandro Tenorio, a spiritual leader for the Nasa Indigenous People, was shot dead, reportedly by FARC guerrillas, outside his home in Caloto, Cauca Department.

Thousands of Indigenous people were forced from their homes as a result of the hostilities. In July, more than 1,500 Indigenous people were forcibly displaced from their lands in Bagadó, Chocó Department.

High-ranking officials made statements linking Indigenous leaders and communities with guerrilla groups. For example, in August, the Defence Minister accused the FARC of infiltrating the Indigenous movement. Such statements encouraged a climate in which abuses against Indigenous Peoples were tolerated, encouraged or facilitated.

Land restitution

The Victims and Land Restitution Law provoked a backlash from some of those who benefited from misappropriated lands. Those campaigning for land restitution were killed or threatened and concerns remained about the authorities' ability to protect them. Paramilitaries calling themselves "anti restitution armies" were reported in several parts of Colombia. Several death threats were issued by these groups to human rights organizations and land activists during the year.

The law excluded many victims of abuses by paramilitary groups, which the government no longer acknowledged as a party to the conflict. It also included provisions that undermined efforts to return land and the right of victims to truth, justice and reparation. On 12 September, the Constitutional Court ruled that parts of the law were unconstitutional. These included measures that exempted from prosecution "strawmen" who surrendered misappropriated lands. The Court also declared unconstitutional wording that would have denied land restitution to victims deemed to have taken "illegal" action to campaign for the return of occupied lands that had been misappropriated from them.

Security forces

The security forces were responsible for serious human rights abuses and violations of international humanitarian law, sometimes in collusion with paramilitary groups. Extrajudicial executions carried out directly by the security forces continued to be reported, although not on the scale of previous years.

■ On 2 October, the body of 15-year-old Norbey Martínez Bonilla was handed over to the civilian authorities in the city of Cali by the security forces who claimed he was a guerrilla killed in combat. He had disappeared from his home in Caloto, Cauca Department, on 28 September during fighting between the security forces and guerrilla groups. Norbey Martínez Bonilla lived in El Pedregal, a hamlet which in 2010 was granted protection measures by the Inter-American Commission on Human Rights.

Scant progress was made in bringing perpetrators to justice. The military justice system regularly closed investigations into human rights violations in which members of the security forces were implicated. A report by the UN Special Rapporteur on extrajudicial, summary or arbitrary executions published in May noted that: "the continuous attempts by the military justice system to claim jurisdiction over cases are of great concern."

Paramilitaries

Despite their supposed demobilization, paramilitary groups, labelled "criminal gangs" (*Bacrim*) by the government, were responsible for serious human rights violations, including killings, enforced disappearances and "social cleansing" operations in poor urban neighbourhoods. Some were committed with the collusion or acquiescence of the security forces. The victims were mainly trade unionists and human rights defenders, as well as representatives of Indigenous Peoples and Afro-descendent and peasant farmer communities.

■ On 23 March, paramilitaries forcibly disappeared Manuel Ruíz and his 15-year-old son Samir de Jesús Ruíz, members of the Afro-descendant and Afro-mestizo community of Apartadocito in the Curvaradó River Basin, Chocó Department. On 24 March a paramilitary informed their family that they had been killed. Manuel Ruíz' body was found on 27 March and that of his son, who had been tortured, the following day. The killings occurred just before a government inspection to determine ownership of land in Los Piscingos, from where Manuel Ruíz' family and others had been displaced by paramilitaries and the security forces in 1996.

The Justice and Peace process, which began in 2005, continued to deny victims of paramilitary abuses their right to truth, justice and reparation. According to the Office of the Attorney General, by

1 December only 14 paramilitaries had been convicted of human rights violations under the Justice and Peace process.

In December, Congress approved a reform of the Justice and Peace Law that allowed illegal combatants who had not demobilized when the law came into force to benefit from its provisions.

The guerrilla

The FARC and the National Liberation Army (Ejército de Liberación Nacional, ELN) committed serious human rights abuses and violations of international humanitarian law, including killings, hostage-taking, forced displacement, recruitment of children, and the use of indiscriminate weapons. In the first seven months of 2012, landmines, laid mostly by guerrilla groups, killed 25 civilians and 22 members of the security forces.

In February, the FARC announced it would end the kidnapping of civilians for ransom, but failed to make a commitment to end all abuses. More than 305 people were kidnapped in 2012, mainly by criminal groups but also by guerrilla groups.

■ On 24 July, journalist Élida Parra Alfonso and engineer Gina Paola Uribe Villamizar were kidnapped by the ELN in Saravena, Arauca Department. Both women were released a few weeks later.

■ In April, the FARC released six police officers and four soldiers the group had held captive since the 1990s.

The FARC were responsible for indiscriminate attacks that placed civilians at risk.

■ In July, the FARC attacked an oil field in Putumayo Department, killing five civilians.

Impunity

There were some successes in holding to account perpetrators of human rights abuses.

■ In August, a civilian court convicted retired General Rito Alejo del Rio to 26 years in prison for the murder of a peasant farmer by paramilitaries. The court found that Rito Alejo del Río did not participate directly in this and the many other killings committed in the area under his command, but maintained close links with paramilitaries, allowing them to commit abuses with impunity.

The vast majority of those responsible for human rights abuses continued to evade justice. Those involved in human rights-related criminal cases, such as lawyers and witnesses, were threatened and killed.

■ On 10 October, a man aimed a gun at Alfamir Castillo, the mother of a man killed by soldiers in 2009 in Valle del Cauca Department, and threatened to kill her and her lawyers, Jorge Molano and Germán Romero. The attack took place days before a court hearing into the involvement of four army officers in the case; seven soldiers were already serving long prison terms for the killing.

Two laws threatened to exacerbate impunity. In June, Congress approved the "legal framework for peace", which could allow human rights abusers to evade justice. In December, Congress approved a reform to the Constitution which will give the military greater control over criminal investigations implicating members of the security forces in human rights violations and could see many cases of human rights violations transferred to the military justice system, contrary to international human rights standards. In October, 11 UN Special Rapporteurs and Independent Experts criticized the reform.

Human rights defenders

Despite the government's public condemnation of attacks against them, human rights defenders continued to suffer attacks, threats, judicial persecution and the theft of sensitive case information. In 2012, at least 40 human rights defenders and community leaders and 20 trade union members were killed.

■ On 28 February, the Black Eagles Capital Bloc paramilitaries sent death threats to several human rights NGOs, including women's organizations and those working on land restitution issues, accusing them of "brainwashing the displaced, acting as if they were Human Rights Defenders", and told them to "stop making trouble over the issue of land restitution".

Women human rights defenders were targeted, principally by paramilitary groups. Some were raped in order to punish and silence them.

■ On 29 January, Cleiner María Almanza Blanco, a community leader working with displaced women, was forced into a taxi by a group of unidentified men. They took her to an undisclosed location where they interrogated her about people she knew and worked with. They kicked her and slammed her against the taxi. One of the men then raped her. In 2010 the Inter-American Commission on Human Rights had ordered the authorities to provide protection measures for Cleiner María Almanza and 13 other women leaders at risk; four of the 14 women had been raped.

C

Violence against women and girls

All parties to the conflict subjected women to sexual violence, including rape, and other forms of gender-based violence.

■ On 18 May, an Indigenous woman was raped by an army soldier at the side of a road in Putumayo Department. The army unit to which the soldier belonged was reportedly only 100m away at the time.

■ On 16 March, eight heavily-armed masked men wearing civilian clothes and thought to be paramilitaries, entered an Afro-descendent community in Tumaco, Nariño Department. They threatened and beat residents, raped two women and sexually abused a 16-year-old girl.

Very few of the perpetrators of such abuses were brought to justice. However, in a rare success, on 27 August sub-Lieutenant Raúl Muñoz Linares was sentenced to 60 years in prison for the rape and murder of 14-year-old Jenni Torres, as well as the murder of her brothers, aged nine and six, and the rape of another girl, in Tame, Arauca Department, in October 2010.

A bill "to guarantee access to justice for victims of sexual violence, especially sexual violence in the context of the armed conflict" was before Congress at the end of the year. If approved, it will, among other things, amend the Criminal Code to make certain forms of conflict-related sexual violence, such as forced nudity, abortion and pregnancy, specific criminal offences.

The Special Representative of the UN Secretary-General on Sexual Violence in Conflict visited Colombia in May. During the visit she stated that more needed to be done to ensure access to justice for survivors of conflict-related sexual violence.

US assistance

In 2012, the USA allocated some US$482 million in military and non-military assistance to Colombia, US$281 million of which was for the security forces. In September, around US$12 million in security assistance funds from 2011 was released after the US State Department determined that Colombia had made significant progress in improving human rights.

International scrutiny

The report on Colombia of the Office of the UN High Commissioner for Human rights (OHCHR), published in January, acknowledged that "[s]ignificant legislative and public policy initiatives were undertaken [and] human rights violations were condemned [by state authorities]", but that "these efforts have yet to achieve the desired results at the local level". The report also noted that a "significant number of human rights and international humanitarian law violations are still committed, primarily by illegal armed groups, but also allegedly by State agents" and that this was having "serious humanitarian consequences for civilians". According to the OHCHR, impunity remained "a structural problem".

Amnesty International visits/reports

🚌 Amnesty International delegates visited Colombia in January, March, April, June, October and November.

📄 Colombia: The Victims and Land Restitution Law – an Amnesty International analysis (AMR 23/018/2012)

📄 Colombia: Hidden from justice – impunity for conflict-related sexual violence, a follow-up report (AMR 23/031/2012)

CONGO (REPUBLIC OF)

REPUBLIC OF CONGO
Head of state and government: Denis Sassou-N'Guesso

Torture and other ill-treatment by members of the security forces were reported, in some cases leading to deaths. Three asylum-seekers from the Democratic Republic of the Congo (DRC) held without charge or trial since 2003 were released. Government critics were denied freedom of expression and detained for several months.

Background

On 4 March, as many as 300 people died, some 2,000 were injured and nearly 20,000 were made homeless by explosions caused by a fire in a munitions depot at the Congolese armoured regiment in the capital, Brazzaville. The government set up a commission of inquiry to investigate the cause and establish responsibility; more than 20 people were arrested at the end of March and were still held without trial at the end of the year. Those arrested, who included army Colonel Marcel Ntsourou, deputy secretary general of the National Security Council, were initially detained by the General Directorate for the Surveillance of the Territory (Direction générale de la surveillance du territoire, DGST) security service and subsequently transferred to Brazzaville central prison. The former Minister of Defence, Charles Zacharie Bowao, who had been dropped from the government during the September reshuffle, was subsequently charged with "clumsiness, carelessness, inattention and negligence which resulted in the events of 4 March and caused deaths, injuries and significant material damage". None of those accused in connection with the explosions had been brought to trial by the end of the year and the commission of inquiry had not published its findings.

Two rounds of National Assembly elections took place in July and August. They were won by the ruling Congolese Workers' Party (Parti congolais du travail, PCT). Opposition parties and several human rights groups claimed that less than 20% of the electorate had voted.

Torture and other ill-treatment

Members of the security forces committed torture and other ill-treatment. In some cases, the victims died from their injuries and the perpetrators were not brought to justice.

■ Delly Kasuki died on 26 May after he was severely beaten by members of the Group for the Repression of Banditry (Groupe de répression contre le banditisme, GRB), who left his body at the university hospital in Brazzaville without informing his family. A local human rights organization reported that Delly Kasuki had been beaten when he resisted what he believed was an unlawful arrest.

■ In July, two bodyguards for a government minister and National Assembly candidate of the ruling PCT severely beat François Batchelli whom they accused of supporting a rival candidate. The bodyguards also briefly detained Felix Wamba, a suspected supporter of an opposition candidate, and beat his wife and children.

Refugees and asylum-seekers

Three asylum-seekers from the DRC who had been detained without charge or trial since March 2003 were released. Médard Mabwaka Egbonde was

released in June while Germain Ndabamenya Etikilime was released in September. Bosch Ndala Umba was released in November. Médard Mabwaka Egbonde sought asylum in Sweden. The future of the other two men and that of Germain Ndabamenya's family remained uncertain as they continued to be denied asylum in the Republic of Congo or in a third country.

Thousands of refugees who had fled to the north of the Republic of Congo in 2009 returned to the DRC from May onwards.

Nearly 300 Congolese nationals whose refugee status had ceased were forcibly returned from Gabon. About 100 others reportedly returned voluntarily. Some of those who were forcibly returned claimed to have been ill-treated by the Gabonese authorities and to have lost their property.

C

Prisoners of conscience

Paul Marie Mpouele, a National Assembly candidate and Vice-President of the Congolese People's Party (Parti du peuple congolais, PPC), was arrested on 17 April after the authorities accused him of insulting the President and of threatening him with death. The accusation was related to a petition Paul Marie Mpuele had initiated calling for the resignation of President Sassou-N'Guesso in connection with the munitions explosions in March. He was first detained by the DGST before being transferred to Brazzaville central prison. He was granted provisional release in September; no formal charges had been brought against him by the end of the year. He was prevented from travelling abroad or carrying out any political activities.

■ Two lawyers representing Colonel Marcel Ntsourou and others arrested in connection with the March munitions explosions were arrested on 9 April. Ambroise Hervé Malonga and Gabriel Hombessa had tried to hold a press conference to protest against being denied access to their clients and were accused of endangering the security of the state by attempting to hold it at Marcel Ntsourou's home, situated in a military barracks. Ambroise Hervé Malonga was also accused of attempting to practise as a defence lawyer without a licence. Earlier, the lawyers had been prevented from holding the press conference at a hotel. Gabriel Hombessa was released in July and Ambroise Hervé Malonga in August.

CÔTE D'IVOIRE

REPUBLIC OF CÔTE D'IVOIRE
Head of state: Alassane Ouattara
Head of government: Daniel Kablan Duncan (replaced
Jeannot Kouadio-Ahoussou in November,
who replaced Guillaume Soro in March)

Throughout the year people were arbitrarily detained and tortured against a backdrop of continued insecurity and attacks by unidentified armed combatants. Many people were displaced as a result. Freedom of the press was under attack and newspapers banned. Legal proceedings at national and international levels were slow; many detainees remained in detention without trial. Impunity continued, notably for supporters of the authorities who committed international crimes during the 2011 post-election crisis. The dialogue and reconciliation process was stalled.

Background

Insecurity persisted throughout the year, with attacks launched by unidentified armed combatants against military targets. There were military and civilian casualties as well as ethnic and political tensions between security services and civilians. Attacks increased after June when seven peacekeepers with the UN Operation in Côte d'Ivoire (UNOCI) were killed along with 10 civilians in the south-west of the country by militias from Liberia. These attacks triggered new population displacements and led to waves of arrests. The authorities accused the Ivorian Popular Front (FPI), the party of former President Laurent Gbagbo, of orchestrating them and declared that they had foiled several attempted coups and plots to destabilize the government. The FPI denied these accusations.

As part of the process to reform the Republican Forces of Côte d'Ivoire (FRCI), initiated in December 2011, a military police force was created to end abuses committed by the army. In practice, however, the force arbitrarily detained and tortured real or supposed opponents. In addition, throughout the year elements of the armed forces as well as Dozos (state-sponsored militia) continued to arbitrarily detain and torture people with total impunity.

In a context of mutual distrust between the government of President Ouattara and the FPI, attempts to resume political dialogue failed. The FPI continued to condition its participation in political life on the release of its members arrested after the post-election crisis, including Laurent Gbagbo.

Members of ethnic groups (including Bétés and Guérés) who were generally accused of being supporters of former President Gbagbo were targeted on ethnic grounds, notably in the west of the country where Dozos reportedly prevented returning internally displaced people from accessing their land or imposed arbitrary payments.

Arbitrary detention

More than 200 people suspected of threatening state security, including members of the FPI, faced illegal detention, mostly in unrecognized places of detention. Many were still detained without trial by the end of the year while others were released after paying a ransom.

■ In March, 77 people were arrested on suspicion of attempting to destabilize state power. All were former members of the Defence and Security Forces (FDS, former regular army) and were held in an FRCI camp in Abidjan. They were released without charge after two months.

■ In August, an FPI member was detained in Abidjan by two men in plain clothes and accused of being a militiaman. He was released two days later after his parents paid a ransom.

Torture and deaths in custody

The FRCI regularly resorted to torture and other ill-treatment against people suspected of armed attacks and political plots. Suspects were sometimes held for long periods in unrecognized places of detention before being brought before a judge and transferred to prison.

■ In March, a member of the former regular armed forces, detained in an FRCI camp in Abidjan, was undressed, handcuffed to an iron bar, beaten and had molten plastic poured on his body.

■ In August, police staff sergeant Serge Hervé Kribié died on the day he was arrested while being subjected to electric shocks in the FRCI command post in San Pedro. His fate remained unknown to his family for three weeks.

C

Refugees and internally displaced people

In June, an estimated 13,000 people were displaced after violent incidents in villages situated between Taï and Nigré along the border with Liberia. By the end of the year, some 160,000 Ivorians remained displaced, including an estimated 80,000 internally displaced people and nearly 60,000 refugees in Liberia. Armed attacks against civilians and military personnel provoked protection concerns as well as continued inter-communal mistrust and fresh displacements, mainly in the west of the country.

Human rights violations and abuses in the west

Insecurity remained persistent in the west of the country. Members of ethnic groups, including Guérés, who were perceived to have been supporters of Laurent Gbagbo, were targeted by FRCI and Dozos and were victims of extrajudicial killings, beatings, torture, unlawful arrests and enforced disappearances.

In July, members of the Dioula community, with the active involvement of Dozo fighters and FRCI soldiers, attacked a UNOCI-guarded displaced persons' camp at Nahibly, outside Duékoué, which was home to approximately 4,500 people. The attack was reportedly launched in retaliation for alleged crimes by camp-dwellers, including the killing of four people in Duékoué. At least 13 displaced people were killed. Many were severely injured, including being tortured with drops of molten plastic and beaten. Dozens were arbitrarily arrested, many of whom remained disappeared.

In October a mass grave was discovered in Duékoué containing bodies thought to be those of people who disappeared after the camp was attacked. An investigation was opened but had made little progress by the end of the year.

Freedom of expression

There were numerous violations of the right to freedom of expression.
■ In September, the National Press Council suspended for six days all the daily newspapers close to the opposition party FPI, stating that photographs and captions relating to former President Gbagbo and former ministers prolonged the post-election crisis.

Justice system

Eighteen months after the post-election crisis, only people associated with former President Gbagbo's government had been arrested. No members of the former Forces Nouvelles, nor any military officials or civilians responsible for serious human rights abuses supporting President Ouattara, had been brought to account.

Delays and shortcomings to the legal proceedings against relatives and aides of former President Gbagbo raised concerns that they may be held for a lengthy period without trial, or that they will be subject to trials which fail to meet international standards of fairness.

Between May and July, eight people were charged with genocide, including Simone Gbagbo, wife of former President Gbagbo.

On 20 December, the provisional release was announced of nine close aides of former President Gbagbo, mainly detained in the north of the country.

International justice

In February, the Pre-Trial Chamber of the International Criminal Court (ICC) authorized the Prosecutor to investigate other relevant crimes committed between September 2002 and 2010.

While both sides were accused of international crimes, the ICC investigations focused on alleged crimes committed by the administration of former President Gbagbo.

Investigations into former President Gbagbo, transferred to the ICC in November 2011, barely progressed. In November, the ICC issued an arrest warrant for the former first lady, Simone Gbagbo, for alleged crimes against humanity, including murder, rape, other forms of sexual violence, other inhumane acts, and persecution committed during the post-election crisis.

Steps towards ratification of the Rome Statute were undertaken. In December, Parliament adopted a bill to amend the Constitution, thereby removing all domestic legal barriers to ratification. A week later, Parliament adopted a bill authorizing ratification, which remained to be enacted.

Impunity

The government repeatedly stated its willingness to try those responsible for crimes committed during the post-election crisis. In August, a national commission of inquiry, set up to investigate the violence committed during the post-election crisis, submitted its report and concluded that both sides had killed hundreds of people. However, by the end of the year no judicial proceedings were known to have been instigated against alleged perpetrators.

Dialogue, Truth and Reconciliation Commission

Created in July 2011, the Dialogue, Truth and Reconciliation Commission faced organizational and financial difficulties and was called to "review and accelerate its activities" by UNOCI in May. In June, it publicly denounced illegal arrests, but public calls for reconciliation and dialogue were not followed by concrete developments.

Corporate accountability

Six years after the dumping of toxic waste that affected tens of thousands of people in the Abidjan area, many victims had yet to receive adequate compensation. At the end of the year, the authorities had still not taken measures to ensure that all of the registered individuals whose health was impacted were able to access the state compensation scheme, which had been suspended. An investigation into the misappropriation, in 2010, of part of the compensation paid by the oil trading company, Trafigura, to victims who had taken the company to court in the UK, did not make progress by the end of the year. Although the Minister of African Integration was dismissed by the President in May over his alleged role in misappropriation of the funds, no further action appears to have been taken by the authorities to recover the missing money or progress investigations into those involved.

Amnesty International visits/reports

The toxic truth: About a company called Trafigura, a ship called the Probo Koala, and the dumping of toxic waste in Côte d'Ivoire (AFR 31/002/2012)

Côte d'Ivoire: Time to put an end to the cycle of reprisals and revenge (PRE 01/513/2012)

CROATIA

REPUBLIC OF CROATIA
Head of state: Ivo Josipović
Head of government: Zoran Milanović

Despite some progress in prosecuting crimes under international law committed during the 1991-1995 war, the measures taken to address impunity remained inadequate. Many crimes allegedly committed by members of the Croatian Army and police forces against Croatian Serbs and other minorities remained uninvestigated. Discrimination against Roma, Croatian Serbs and LGBTI people continued.

Crimes under international law

The European Commission reported in October that further arrests, indictments and court rulings related to crimes under international law were being pursued in the implementation of Croatia's 2011 Strategy for the Investigation and Prosecution of War Crimes. Additional cases were transferred to the four Special War Crimes Chambers in Osijek, Rijeka, Split and Zagreb.

However, the Commission reiterated that tackling impunity for past crimes remained a major challenge, and that the government needed to take measures to facilitate the attendance of witnesses at trials, especially in cases transferred to the Special War Crimes Chambers.

Impunity for war crimes was exacerbated by the use of the 1993 Basic Criminal Code in the prosecution of crimes committed during the 1991-1995 war, although it failed to meet international standards. It did not include crimes against humanity and most crimes of sexual violence, while superior and command responsibility for crimes under international law was also not recognized. Those gaps led to impunity.

Some progress was made in providing witness support, but witness protection measures continued to be inadequate. Those responsible for intimidation of witnesses were not brought to justice. Twelve years after it began, the investigation into the killing of the witness Milan Levar continued to make no progress.

The authorities failed to provide victims and their families access to reparation.

C

At the end of the year, 490 incidents giving rise to allegations of war crimes registered in Croatia since the end of the war had resulted in the opening of 1,090 criminal cases. Alleged perpetrators were identified in 316 incidents, resulting in 849 criminal cases. However, out of the total number of registered cases only 112 cases (10%) were completed before the domestic courts. In 174 war crime incidents, resulting in 241 criminal cases, the alleged perpetrators were still unidentified.

■ Tomislav Merčep, former Assistant Minister of the Interior and the commander of the Ministry's special reserve unit, who was indicted in 2011 and had been under arrest since 2010, was released in July. He had been charged in relation to the killing and enforced disappearance of 43 Croatian Serb civilians in the area of Zagreb and Pakračka poljana.

■ Allegations against the Deputy Speaker of the Croatian Parliament, Vladimir Šeks, for his command responsibility for crimes committed in Eastern Slavonija in 1991, were not investigated, despite publicly available information about his alleged role. The evidence included several witness testimonies in criminal proceedings related to crimes committed in Eastern Slavonija, orders from the then President of the country as well as statements in court by Vladimir Šeks himself.

■ Former Croatian Army general, Davor Domazet-Lošo, continued to evade prosecution. He had been named in the May 2008 judgement in the case against Rahim Ademi and Mirko Norac as having an effective command responsibility for the crimes committed in 1993 in Medak Pocket. The judgement had acquitted Rahim Ademi of responsibility for the crimes committed in Medak Pocket because it was ruled that Davor Domazet-Lošo held effective command responsibility.

International justice

Several cases concerning Croatia were pending before the International Criminal Tribunal of the Former Yugoslavia (the Tribunal).

The trial of Jovica Stanišić and Franko Simatović, accused of war crimes and crimes against humanity, continued.

Following his arrest in Serbia and transfer to the Tribunal in 2011, the trial of Goran Hadžić, President of the self-proclaimed Republic of Serbian Krajina, accused of crimes against humanity and war crimes, commenced in October.

The appeal procedure on the 2011 judgement on Momčilo Perišić started in October and had not concluded by the end of the year. The Tribunal had sentenced him to 27 years' imprisonment for war crimes and crimes against humanity. He was convicted on the basis of individual criminal responsibility in BiH, and on the basis of superior criminal responsibility in Croatia, the latter in relation to the shelling of Zagreb.

In November, the Appeals Chamber of the Tribunal acquitted two generals, Ante Gotovina and Mladen Markač. The Appeals Chamber reversed their convictions for crimes against humanity and war crimes, for which they had received sentences of 24 and 18 years. The verdict resonated strongly in region, prompting a surge in nationalistic rhetoric in both Croatia and Serbia. While the two generals were welcomed back to Croatia by government officials, human rights defenders in the region reiterated the importance of holding perpetrators accountable for the crimes committed against Serb civilians between 1991 and 1995.

Discrimination

Roma continued to face discrimination in access to economic and social rights, including education, employment and housing. Measures undertaken by the authorities remained insufficient. The authorities failed to implement the European Court of Human Rights' ruling to end segregation of Romani children in schools.

Croatian Serbs continued to face discrimination, mainly in relation to housing and employment.

Hate crimes

Legal protection against homophobic and transphobic hate crimes was improved; amendments to the Criminal Code adopted in 2012 included gender identity as a ground for prosecution of hate crimes. However, with no specific guidelines for police, physical attacks against LGBTI people were sometimes classified as minor offences, while alleged hate motives were often not investigated.

Amnesty International visits/reports

🚍 Amnesty International delegates visited Croatia in February, March and June.

▤ The right to know: Families still left in the dark in the Balkans (EUR 05/001/2012)

▤ Inadequate protection: Homophobic and transphobic hate crimes in Croatia (EUR 64/001/2012)

⬚ Protection of LGBT people must go beyond the Pride (EUR 64/004/2012)

⬚ Medak Pocket arrests: Senior officials must be investigated (PRE01/119/2012)

CUBA

REPUBLIC OF CUBA
Head of state and government: Raúl Castro Ruz

Repression of independent journalists, opposition leaders and human rights activists increased. There were reports of an average of 400 short-term arrests each month and activists travelling from the provinces to Havana were frequently detained. Prisoners of conscience continued to be sentenced on trumped-up charges or held in pre-trial detention.

Rights to freedom of expression, association, movement and assembly

Peaceful demonstrators, independent journalists and human rights activists were routinely detained for exercising their rights to freedom of expression, association and assembly. Many were detained and others were subjected to acts of repudiation by government supporters.

■ In March, local human rights activists faced a wave of arrests and local organizations reported 1,137 arbitrary detentions before and after the visit of Pope Benedict XVI.

The authorities adopted a range of measures to prevent activists reporting on human rights including surrounding the homes of activists and disconnecting phones. Organizations whose activities had been tolerated by the authorities in the past, such as the Cuban Commission on Human Rights and National Reconciliation, were targeted. Independent journalists reporting on dissidents' activities were detained.

The government continued to exert control over all media, while access to information on the internet remained challenging due to technical limitations and restrictions on content.

■ In July, Oswaldo Payá Sardiñas, one of Cuba's most respected human rights and pro-democracy campaigners, died in a car accident in Granma Province. Several journalists and bloggers covering the hearing into the accident were detained for several hours.

■ Roberto de Jesús Guerra Pérez, founder of the independent news agency Let's Talk Press (Hablemos Press), was forced into a car in September, and reportedly beaten as he was driven to a police station. Before being released, he was told that he had become the "number one dissident journalist" and would be imprisoned if he continued his activities.

A number of measures were used to stop or penalize activities by political opponents. Many attempting to attend meetings or demonstrations were detained or prevented from leaving their homes. Political opponents, independent journalists and human rights activists were routinely denied visas to travel abroad.

■ For the 19th time since May 2008, Yoani Sánchez, an opposition blogger, was denied an exit visa. She had planned to attend the screening in Brazil of a documentary on blogging and censorship in which she featured.

■ In September, around 50 members of the Ladies in White organization were detained on their way to Havana to attend a public demonstration. Most were immediately sent back to their home provinces and then released; 19 were held incommunicado for several days.

In October, the government announced changes to the Migration Law that facilitate travel abroad, including the removal of mandatory exit visas. However, a series of requirements – over which the government would exercise discretion – could continue to restrict freedom to leave the country. The amendments were due to become effective in January 2013.

Prisoners of conscience

Seven new prisoners of conscience were adopted by Amnesty International during the year; three were released without charge.

■ Antonio Michel Lima Cruz was released in October after completing his two-year sentence. He had been convicted of "insulting symbols of the homeland" and "public disorder" for singing anti-government songs. His brother, Marcos Máiquel, who received a longer sentence for the same offences, remained in prison at the end of the year.

■ Ivonne Malleza Galano and Ignacio Martínez Montejo were released in January, along with Isabel

Haydee Álvarez, who was detained after calling for their release. They were held for 52 days without charge after taking part in a demonstration in November 2011. On their release, officials threatened them with "harsh sentences" if they continued dissident activities.

■ Yasmín Conyedo Riverón, a journalist and representative of Ladies in White in Santa Clara province, and her husband, Yusmani Rafael Álvarez Esmori, were released on bail in April after nearly three months in prison. They faced charges of using violence or intimidation against a state official, who later withdrew the accusation.

Arbitrary detention

Short-term arbitrary detention continued and reports of short-term incommunicado detentions were frequent.

■ In February, former prisoner of conscience José Daniel Ferrer García was detained and held incommunicado for three days. While detained, he was threatened with imprisonment if he continued dissident activities through the Patriotic Union of Cuba. In April, he was detained again on charges of "public disorder" and released 27 days later on condition that he give up political activism.

■ Ladies in White Niurka Luque Álvarez and Sonia Garro Alfonso, and Sonia's husband Ramón Alejandro Muñoz González, were detained without charge in March. Niurka Luque Álvarez was released in October. Sonia Garro Alfonso and her husband remained in detention at the end of the year, but had not been formally charged.

■ Andrés Carrión Álvarez was arrested for shouting "freedom" and "down with communism" at a mass celebrated by Pope Benedict XVI. He was released after 16 days in prison. He was detained for five hours three days later and charged with another count of "public disorder". He was released on condition that he report to the police once a week, and that he did not leave his home municipality without prior authorization or associate with government critics.

The US embargo against Cuba

In September, the USA renewed the Trading with the Enemy Act, which imposes financial and economic sanctions on Cuba and prohibits US citizens from travelling to and engaging in economic activities with the island. In November, the UN General Assembly adopted, for the 21st consecutive year, a resolution calling on the USA to lift the unilateral embargo.

The WHO, UNICEF and UNFPA and other UN agencies reported on the negative impact of the embargo on the health and wellbeing of Cubans and in particular on marginalized groups. In 2012, Cuba's health care authority and UN agencies did not have access to medical equipment, medicines and laboratory materials produced under US patents.

Amnesty International visits/reports

🚫 The Cuban authorities have not granted Amnesty International access to the country since 1990.

📄 Routine repression: Political short-term detentions and harassment in Cuba (AMR 25/007/2012)

📄 Cuba: Freedom of assembly and expression limited by government policies (AMR 25/027/2012)

CYPRUS

REPUBLIC OF CYPRUS
Head of state and government: **Demetris Christofias**

Irregular migrants were detained for prolonged periods with no alternative measures being considered. There were allegations of police ill-treatment of peaceful activists.

Background

Negotiations between Greek Cypriot and Turkish Cypriot leaders regarding the reunification of the island did not progress.

Refugees, asylum-seekers and migrants

Irregular migrants, rejected asylum-seekers and certain categories of asylum-seekers were detained for prolonged periods. Detention appeared routine with no alternative measures being considered.

Irregular migrants and asylum-seekers continued to be held in poor conditions in unsuitable facilities, such as short-stay police cells and two wings of Nicosia Central Prison. The opening of the purpose-built immigration detention facility in Menogia, with a capacity of 276 people, was pushed back to 2013.

Several individuals held for immigration purposes continued to be detained although their deportation could not be enforced. In several cases, Syrian nationals were held in immigration detention for several months, despite the authorities' policy to suspend any returns to Syria during the internal armed conflict in the country. As a result, their detention appeared arbitrary, unnecessary and unlawful.

■ In November, the Cyprus Supreme Court ordered the release of Majid Eazadi, a rejected asylum-seeker from Iran detained for 14 months under immigration powers, as there was no realistic prospect for his deportation. Majid Eazadi had been repeatedly detained for the purpose of deportation for almost three years between 2008 and 2011. The Commissioner for Administration (Ombudsperson) had written a number of times to the Ministry of Interior raising concerns over the lawfulness of his detention.

In some cases, Supreme Court judgements ordering the release of individuals as their prolonged detention was unlawful, were not respected in practice. Upon their release, those individuals were immediately re-detained on the same grounds as before.

The authorities reportedly refused to examine subsequent asylum applications from Syrian nationals who wished to have their claims re-examined in view of the dramatic change in the situation in Syria.

Police and security forces

On 7 April, Cypriot police, including the anti-terrorist unit, raided a building in the buffer zone that was occupied by a multi-communal peace movement and arrested 28 activists, including minors. Many allegations were made regarding police ill-treatment of several activists during the raid. A lawyer who was present reported that the raid was unlawful since no arrest warrant was provided. The authorities denied having used excessive force.

Human rights defenders

In July, the executive director of KISA, a migrant and refugee NGO, was acquitted of criminal charges of "rioting and participating in an illegal assembly". The charges related to events at the anti-racism Rainbow Festival in Larnaca in 2010, where participants were reportedly attacked by members of an anti-migrant demonstration and clashes ensued. Two Turkish Cypriot musicians, reportedly attacked and seriously injured allegedly by anti-migrant protesters, sued the authorities at the end of the year for their failure to arrest and prosecute those responsible for the attack.

Enforced disappearances

During the course of the year, the Committee of Missing Persons in Cyprus had exhumed the remains of 43 people, bringing the total number of exhumations since 2006 to 857. By the end of the year the remains of 336 missing individuals (269 Greek Cypriots and 67 Turkish Cypriots) had been identified and restored to their families. However, no perpetrator was identified or prosecuted in either Cyprus or Turkey by the end of the year.

Amnesty International visits/reports

Amnesty International delegates visited Cyprus in June and October.

Punishment without a crime: Detention of irregular migrants and asylum-seekers in Cyprus (EUR 17/001/2012)

CZECH REPUBLIC

CZECH REPUBLIC

Head of state:	**Václav Klaus**
Head of government:	**Petr Nečas**

Intergovernmental bodies, NGOs and human rights experts voiced strong criticism of the government's failure to take effective measures to address segregation of Romani pupils in education. Roma continued to be forcibly evicted.

Discrimination – Roma

Intimidation and violent attacks against Roma continued. The European Roma Rights Centre reported arson attacks on the homes of Romani families, anti-Roma rallies and other attacks.

Education

The Minister of Education, Josef Dobeš – in the past heavily criticized by NGOs for stalling efforts to end Roma segregation in schools – resigned in March and was replaced by Petr Fiala in May. The new Minister made a commitment to end discrimination of Romani children in access to education.

In October, the Czech Republic's human rights record was assessed under the UN Universal Periodic

Review. The Czech Republic was urged to eliminate continued segregation of Romani children at school and fully implement the National Plan of Action for Inclusive Education.

The Council of Europe Commissioner for Human Rights, Nils Muižnieks, stated in November that "practical schools" (formerly "special schools") perpetuate Roma segregation, inequality and racism. He called for such schools to be phased out and replaced by mainstream schools prepared to host, and provide support to, all pupils, irrespective of their ethnic origin.

In December, the Council of Europe Committee of Ministers expressed concerns that, five years after the decision of the European Court of Human Rights in the case of *D.H. and Others v. the Czech Republic*, there had been little progress in addressing the causes of discrimination against Roma in schools. The Committee, however, acknowledged the government's renewed commitment to end Roma segregation in education.

Housing

■ More than 300 Romani residents of Přednádraží Street in Ostrava were threatened with forced eviction in August, after receiving an eviction notice which left them 24 hours to vacate their houses voluntarily. Most of the residents eventually left the area and moved to temporary accommodation they were offered in hostels despite concerns raised by NGOs over affordability and overcrowding. In response to this, both the government and the Mayor of Ostrava declared that it was not their responsibility to resolve these problems.

■ In October, the High Court in Olomouc held that Ostrava municipality had not discriminated against Romani applicants for permanent housing when it imposed additional administrative requirements on them.

■ In November, Ústí nad Labem municipality evicted 36 inhabitants from a building in Předlice, a predominantly Romani neighbourhood. The municipality argued that the building was uninhabitable due to structural hazards. Residents and local activists alleged that the eviction was carried out without adequate consultation and that the municipality had failed to provide adequate alternative housing. The evicted Roma were moved temporarily to a local gymnasium and eventually transferred to unaffordable and unsuitable workers' hostels. The inhabitants also experienced difficulties accessing schools and other municipal services. Those remaining in Předlice were concerned that further forced evictions would follow.

Enforced sterilization of Romani women

■ In October, in the course of the UN Universal Periodic Review, the Czech Republic was again asked to investigate cases of sterilization without consent of Romani women and to ensure adequate compensation and reparation were provided.

Migrants' rights

NGOs continued to criticize the detention of asylum-seekers and the absence of effective legal remedies against this practice.

■ Criminal investigations into allegations of fraud, trafficking and blackmailing of foreign migrant workers in the forestry industry continued. Lawyers representing affected workers issued several complaints against decisions by the police to close investigations of individual cases. Lawyers also expressed concern that the length of proceedings was resulting in the loss of essential evidence.

■ In October, the European Court of Human Rights held in the case *Buishvili v. the Czech Republic* that the Czech authorities violated the right of a Georgian asylum-seeker to challenge his detention in judicial proceedings. The man had been transferred to the Czech Republic from the Netherlands under the Dublin II Regulation. On the basis of the Ministry of Interior's decision not to grant him entry to the country, he was held at the reception centre at Prague airport. He successfully argued that he had been prevented from starting judicial proceedings for his release, as a court could quash the Ministry's decision but not order a release.

Amnesty International visits/reports

🚗 Amnesty International delegates visited the Czech Republic in June and July.

▤ *Five more years of injustice: Segregated education for Roma in Czech Republic* (EUR 71/006/2012)

▤ Czech Republic: Joint NGO Submission – *D.H. and Others v the Czech Republic* (EUR 71/009/2012)

▤ Czech Republic: Comments to the consolidated action plan for the execution of the judgment of the European Court of Human Rights in the case of *D.H. and Others v. the Czech Republic* (EUR 71/010/2012)

DEMOCRATIC REPUBLIC OF THE CONGO

DEMOCRATIC REPUBLIC OF THE CONGO
Head of state: Joseph Kabila
Head of government: Augustin Matata Ponyo Mapon
                             (replaced Louis Koyagialo in May,
                             who replaced Adolphe Muzito in March)

The already precarious security situation in eastern Democratic Republic of the Congo (DRC) deteriorated gravely due to the proliferation of armed groups, including the newly formed March 23 group, easy access to ammunition and weapons and violations by the Congolese armed forces. Both armed groups and government security forces threatened, harassed and arbitrarily arrested human rights defenders, journalists and members of the political opposition.

Background

On 28 April, newly re-elected President Joseph Kabila appointed a new government after months of disputed election results.

The national army, Forces Armées de la République Démocratique du Congo (FARDC), continued a reconfiguration process, which involved, in parts, the integration of armed groups into the army. This restructuring was unco-ordinated and ultimately opened the door for armed groups to take control of areas vacated by FARDC.

In April 2012, FARDC defectors in North and South Kivu formed the March 23 (M23) armed group, following a call to mutiny by General Bosco Ntaganda, who is under indictment by the International Criminal Court for crimes against humanity and war crimes. The M23 claimed to be fighting for the Congolese government to fully respect the 23 March 2009 peace agreement.

Clashes between FARDC and armed groups heightened insecurity and thousands were forced to flee their homes. Violent clashes between FARDC soldiers and the M23 took place between April and September and again in November when the North

Kivu capital Goma fell under M23 control for 11 days. Other armed groups were allegedly also involved and widespread human rights abuses were committed by all parties.

Attacks by armed groups against the civilian population increased.

The peacekeeping force MONUSCO (UN Organization Stabilization Mission in the DRC) took various measures to address security gaps and increased its presence in areas abandoned by the FARDC, but its already overstretched resources greatly limited its ability to provide adequate protection to civilians.

In 2012, the UN Group of Experts on the Democratic Republic of the Congo, Amnesty International and several international NGOs documented Rwandan support to the M23, including by facilitating and supporting recruitment for the M23 in Rwanda and through the supply of weapons and ammunition.

Following the renewed fighting between the M23 and FARDC in November, and the M23's temporary takeover of Goma, negotiations between countries in the Region started on 9 December under the aegis of the International Conference for the Great Lakes Region.

Abuses by armed groups

The redeployment of FARDC troops to fight the M23 in eastern DRC created security vacuums in other localities. This allowed various armed groups, such as the Raia Mutomboki, Nyatura, Forces Démocratiques de Libération du Rwanda (FDLR), Burundian Forces Nationales de Libération, Mayi Mayi Sheka, and Alliance des Patriotes pour un Congo Libre et Souverain, to commit serious human rights abuses as they expanded their military operations into those areas.

Abuses included unlawful killings, summary executions, forced recruitment of children, rape and sexual violence, large-scale looting and destruction of property and were characterized by extreme violence, sometimes ethnically motivated. The situation was fuelled by easy access to weapons and ammunition.
■ On the night of 13 May, in Bunyakiri, Kalehe territory, South Kivu province, at least 20 civilians were unlawfully killed and others wounded in an attack reportedly carried out by the FDLR, which took place a few kilometres from a MONUSCO base.

Other armed groups have continued to be active in the north east, including the Lord's Resistance Army

(LRA), the Mayi Mayi Lumumba and the Allied Democratic Forces/National Army for the Liberation of Uganda (ADF/NALU).

Violence against women and girls

Women and girls bore the horrific cost of intensified hostilities and were widely subjected to rape and other forms of sexual violence committed both by the FARDC and armed groups. Women and girls at particular risk were those in villages targeted for looting and intimidation operations by armed groups and the national army, as well as those living in camps for displaced people, who often had to walk long distances to reach their fields.

■ Between April and May, M23 combatants reportedly raped several dozen girls and women in the Jomba area in Rutshuru territory in North Kivu, where the M23 established its base. Most of those attacked had been displaced by the conflict.

Sexual violence was more pervasive where the national army lived alongside the population.

■ In late November, the UN reported that the FARDC were responsible for at least 126 cases of rape within a few days in Minova where the national army had retreated after the fall of Goma on 20 November.

Elsewhere in the country, members of the national police and other security forces continued to commit acts of rape and sexual violence.

Rape survivors were stigmatized by their communities, and did not receive adequate support or assistance.

Child soldiers

Children were recruited by both armed groups and the FARDC. Many were subjected to sexual violence and cruel and inhuman treatment while being used as fighters, carriers, cooks, guides, spies and messengers.

■ In March and April, in advance of the creation of the M23 armed group, children were abducted and forcibly recruited by defecting FARDC soldiers, particularly in Masisi territory in North Kivu.

On 4 October, the DRC government signed an Action Plan, adopted in the framework of Security Council Resolutions 1612 (2005) and 1882 (2009), to end the recruitment of children. The agreement outlined specific measures for the release and reintegration of children associated with the government security forces and the prevention of further recruitment.

MONUSCO continued to carry out Demobilization, Disarmament, Repatriation, Resettlement and Reintegration of FDLR soldiers, which included child soldiers.

Internally displaced people

Due in part to the escalating conflict in eastern DRC since April, the number of internally displaced people increased this year to more than 2.4 million, which is the highest number of internally displaced people since 2009. By 1 November, some 1.6 million people were internally displaced within North and South Kivu alone. Many of those internally displaced were civilians fleeing forced recruitment by armed groups.

■ In July, thousands of people, mostly women, children and the elderly, were displaced when the M23 fought the national army and took control of the town of Bunagana in Rutshuru territory.

Torture and other ill-treatment

Torture and other ill-treatment was endemic throughout the country, and often took place during unlawful arrests and detention by state security services.

Death penalty

Military courts continued to sentence individuals, including civilians, to death. No executions were reported.

■ On 30 May, a military court in Uvira sentenced two soldiers to death in their absence, and several other officers to life in prison, for participating in the call to mutiny by General Bosco Ntaganda in April.

Impunity

Impunity continued to fuel further human rights abuses. Efforts by judicial authorities to increase the capacity of the courts to deal with cases, including cases involving human rights abuses, had only limited success; many older cases did not progress. The Ministry of Justice's initiatives in 2011 to address impunity for past and current crimes under international law were stalled and victims continued to be denied access to truth, justice and reparations. Court rulings were not implemented and key cases, such as the Walikale and the Bushani and Kalambahiro mass rapes of 2010 and 2011, progressed no further.

Although the Ministry of Justice and Human Rights asked the civil and military judicial authorities in February to open investigations into allegations of electoral violence, there was little evidence of any progress in the investigations during the year.

Unfair trials

Lack of independence of courts, violations of the rights of defendants, unavailability of legal aid, and corruption were some of the factors hindering fair trials.

The fundamentally flawed Congolese military justice system maintained exclusive jurisdiction over the crimes of genocide, crimes against humanity and war crimes – including in cases with civilian defendants.

Prison conditions

The prison system continued to be severely under-funded, failing to address decaying facilities, overpopulation and extremely poor hygiene conditions. Dozens of inmates died in prisons or hospitals as a consequence of malnutrition and a lack of appropriate medical care. Insecurity for detainees was increased by a failure to effectively separate women from men, pre-trial detainees from convicted prisoners, and members of the military from civilians.

Human rights defenders

The security situation for human rights defenders in the east deteriorated throughout the year. Defenders faced increasing intimidation and were often subjected to arbitrary arrests or death threats by state security forces, the M23, and unidentified armed men, severely hindering their work.

From July, when the M23 took control of Rutshuru town in North Kivu, human rights defenders had to close their offices. Many fled after they received repeated death threats through text messages, anonymous phone calls, and visits at night by armed men. Similarly, at the end of November when the M23 took temporary control of Goma, many human rights defenders based in the town fled for safety.

On 6 December, the National Assembly adopted a law establishing the National Commission on Human Rights. The Commission, if created, would seek to help authorities meet their human rights obligations.

Arbitrary arrests and detentions

Arbitrary arrests and detentions continued to be systemic throughout the country. Security services, in particular the national police, the intelligence services, the national army and the migration police, carried out arbitrary arrests and, frequently, extorted money and other items of value from civilians during law enforcement operations or at checkpoints. In the western provinces in particular, security forces carried out arbitrary arrests for private interests, or to obtain illegal payments.

Political opposition activists were subjected to arbitrary arrests during the post-electoral period. An opposition leader was arrested in February by security services and allegedly tortured and otherwise ill-treated before being released a few days later.

■ Political opponent Eugène Diomi Ndongala went missing on 27 June on his way to sign a coalition charter with other political parties. He was released 100 days later, having been detained incommunicado by the intelligence services (Agence nationale de renseignements) in Kinshasa without access to his family, lawyer or a doctor, despite a chronic medical condition.

Freedom of expression

Freedom of expression was significantly curtailed, particularly in the post-electoral period and following increasing control of the east by M23. The main targets were political opponents and journalists who were threatened or arbitrarily arrested. TV, radio and newspaper outlets were subjected to arbitrary suspension of their operations by the authorities, as well as arson attacks and other damage to their premises by unidentified actors.

■ On 30 November, the Superior Audiovisual and Communication Council suspended Radio Okapi's broadcast in Kinshasa without notification following a radio show featuring an interview with an M23 spokesperson.

International justice

On 10 July, the International Criminal Court sentenced Thomas Lubanga Dyilo, the alleged founder and president of the Union of the Congolese Patriots and commander in chief of its armed wing, the FPLC, to 14 years in prison. On 14 March, he had been convicted of the war crimes of conscripting and enlisting children under the age of 15 and using them to participate actively in hostilities in Ituri district.

On 13 July, the ICC issued an arrest warrant for Sylvestre Mudacumura, alleged commander of the armed branch of the FDLR, for nine counts of war crimes allegedly committed between January 2009 and September 2010 in eastern DRC.

A second arrest warrant was issued in July for Bosco Ntaganda for three counts of crimes against humanity as well as four counts of war crimes. The Congolese authorities refused to arrest and surrender Bosco Ntaganda prior to his defection from the Congolese army in April.

On 18 December, the ICC acquitted Mathieu Ngudjolo Chui, the alleged former leader of the Nationalist Integration Front of crimes that were perpetrated in Bogoro village of Ituri district in February 2003.

Amnesty International visits/reports

🚐 Amnesty International delegates visited the DRC in February, May and September.

📄 Democratic Republic of Congo: The Congolese government must arrest and surrender Bosco Ntaganda to the ICC (AFR 62/004/2012)

📄 "If you resist, we'll shoot you": The Democratic Republic of the Congo and the case for an effective Arms Trade Treaty (AFR 62/007/2012)

📄 Petition containing 102,105 signatures delivered by Amnesty International to the Minister of Justice and Human Rights (AFR 62/008/2012)

📄 The Human Rights Council must act for better protection of civilians and an end to threats and intimidation against human rights defenders, journalists and political opponents (AFR 62/011/2012)

📄 Democratic Republic of Congo: Letter to the five permanent members of the Security Council (AFR 62/015/2012)

📄 Democratic Republic of Congo: ICC acquits Congolese armed group leader (AFR 62/017/2012)

📄 Canada: Court decision in Kilwa Massacre case denies right to remedy for victims of corporate human rights abuses (AMR 20/002/2012)

📄 DRC urged to stop violence as it plays host to Francophonie Summit in Kinshasa, 10 October 2012

📄 DRC must investigate assassination attempt on activist Dr Denis Mukwege, 26 October 2012

📄 DRC: Civilian protection urged as tens of thousands flee escalation in fighting, 19 November 2012

DENMARK

KINGDOM OF DENMARK
Head of state: Queen Margrethe II
Head of government: Helle Thorning-Schmidt

A European Parliament report recommended that Denmark conduct an independent investigation into its involvement in the US-led rendition programme. A suspension of the transfer of detainees to the Afghan intelligence service by Danish armed forces was lifted despite the real risk of torture and other ill-treatment faced by those transferred. Immigration detention practices in relation to vulnerable people remained a cause for concern.

Torture and other ill-treatment

In April, the government established a commission to examine Denmark's involvement in the Iraq war, including claims that the army transferred detainees to the Iraqi authorities despite allegedly knowing that they would be at risk of torture or other ill-treatment. In October, it emerged that Danish soldiers were in possession of video footage apparently showing detainee mistreatment by Iraqi soldiers.

■ According to reports in December, 11 Iraqis were effectively prevented from bringing a court case against Denmark for allegedly transferring them to the Iraqi authorities despite knowing they would be at risk. The men had been denied legal aid and were required to pay a deposit of 40,000 kroner each as security before the case could proceed, an amount none of them could afford.

In October, the suspension of transfers of detainees by Danish armed forces to the Afghan intelligence service, the National Directorate of Security (NDS), was lifted despite the real risk of torture and other ill-treatment that those held by the NDS faced. As a result, on 20 October and 23 November, Danish armed forces in Afghanistan transferred Afghan detainees to the NDS facility in Lashkar Gah.

Counter-terror and security

In September, a European Parliament report recommended that Denmark conduct an independent investigation into its alleged complicity in the CIA's rendition programme. A study commissioned by the government and conducted by the Danish Institute of International Studies, published in May, involved a paper review of previously collected documents, which did not amount to a human rights compliant investigation.

Also in September, an expert committee presented a draft bill providing for independent oversight of the collection and storage of data on private individuals and organizations by the Danish Security and Intelligence Service. However, concerns were raised that the bill did not establish a properly independent and effective control mechanism. Nor did it contain substantive provisions on the passing of such information to foreign intelligence services.

Police and security forces

In August, the director of the Independent Police Complaints Authority stated that a considerable number of complaints against the police had to be closed without further action being taken because it was not possible to identify the officers involved. As a result, several politicians called for police officers to wear identity numbers on their uniform – a suggestion opposed by heads of police.

Violence against women and girls

In November, the Standing Committee on Criminal Law issued its report on sexual offences, which contained several proposals for legislative reform. These included the criminalization of sexual abuse by a spouse, where the victim is in a "helpless state"; and to end the possibility of reduced or rescinded criminal punishments if the perpetrator and the victim marry each other or continue to be married after a rape.

Refugees and asylum-seekers

Vulnerable people – including victims of torture, persons with a mental illness and unaccompanied minors – continued to be detained for immigration control purposes.

There were no forcible returns to Syria during the year. The Danish Immigration Services granted protection status to Syrian asylum-seekers in about 88% of cases. However, the remaining asylum-seekers from Syria – around 180 cases – were denied asylum and the possibility to work or study in Denmark.

Some asylum-seekers from countries such as Uganda, who were at risk of persecution at home due to their sexual orientation, were denied asylum based on arguments that they should "hide" their sexuality.

■ In June, the Supreme Court ruled in the case of Elias Karkavandi, an Iranian citizen who was denied asylum, that some of the requirements placed on him under the so called "tolerated stay" regime – having to remain at Sandholm Asylum Centre and report regularly to the police – were disproportionate and violated his right to freedom of movement.

DOMINICAN REPUBLIC

DOMINICAN REPUBLIC
Head of state and government: **Danilo Medina Sánchez**
(replaced Leonel Antonio Fernández Reyna in August)

The number of unlawful killings by police remained high. People of Haitian descent continued to be denied identity documents. Violence against women and girls remained a major concern. There were concerns that proposed reforms to the Penal Code could have a negative impact on women's rights and freedom of expression.

Background

Danilo Medina of the Party for the Dominican Liberation was elected President in May and took office in August.

A law on fiscal reform approved in November sparked a wave of demonstrations across the country, some of which were violently repressed by the police.

For the 11th consecutive year, the authorities failed to appoint a Human Rights Ombudsman.

On 23 February, the UN Convention against Torture came into force in the Dominican Republic.

In March, the UN Human Rights Committee considered the Dominican Republic's fifth periodic report and made several recommendations on issues including reducing human rights violations by the police; protecting Haitian migrants and Dominicans of Haitian descent from discrimination; and combating gender-based violence.

Police and security forces

The number of killings committed by the police fell by 18% compared with 2011, but remained high. Evidence suggested that many of these killings may have been unlawful.

■ Yefri Felizor was killed by police on 31 October during a police operation in the neighbourhood of La Mina in the city of Santiago. According to eyewitnesses, the officers searched him and then ordered him to run. When he started running, police officers fatally shot him. Nobody had been charged with the killing by the end of the year.

Several people were killed by the police in the context of demonstrations. In many of these incidents unnecessary or excessive force appeared to have been used.

■ In June, three men and a pregnant woman were killed in Salcedo during a demonstration sparked by the lack of progress in the investigation into the killing of a sportsman on 12 May 2012, allegedly by police. In October, the Prosecutor General said the investigation into the June killings was continuing.

In November, the President appointed a commission to propose legislative and policy measures for a comprehensive reform of the police.

Impunity

Many alleged abuses by the police remained unpunished, despite compelling evidence.

■ The authorities failed to clarify the enforced disappearance of Gabriel Sandi Alistar and Juan Almonte Herrera. The men were last seen in police custody in July and September 2009 respectively. Their whereabouts remained unknown at the end of 2012.

In February, the Inter-American Court of Human Rights established state responsibility for the enforced disappearance of journalist Narciso González Medina in 1994. In October, the Court found the state responsible for the killing of seven Haitian migrants by members of the armed forces in 2000.

Discrimination – Haitian migrants and Dominico-Haitians

Several courts ordered the Dominican Electoral Board to issue identity documents to hundreds of Dominicans of Haitian descent who had been denied their right to documents. However, by the end of the year, the Central Electoral Board had failed to implement the decision of the courts.

In July, local human rights organizations reported that people who had brought cases against the Dominican Electoral Board had been threatened and intimidated when Board personnel visited their communities to question them about the migration status of their parents.

Migrants' rights

Mass deportations of Haitian migrants continued. In many cases, expulsions appeared to be arbitrary.

On 25 May the Director of Migrations issued a directive instructing the Minister of Education not to accept undocumented foreign children in schools. The directive was withdrawn in June following criticism.

Violence against women and girls

According to the Office of the Prosecutor General, the number of women and girls killed by partners or former partners fell by 19% compared with 2011.

Women's rights organizations expressed concern that proposed changes to the Penal Code represented a backward step in combating violence against women and girls. For example, it did not include the crime of gender-based violence and reduced the penalties for certain forms of violence against women and girls.

Sexual and reproductive rights

The total ban on abortion remained in place. Proposed changes to the Penal Code would allow for an exception to the ban when the life of the woman is at risk. However, women's rights organizations considered the formulation to be too vague.

■ In August, Rosaura, a 16-year-old girl with leukaemia, died of complications caused by a miscarriage. She had been prevented from having a therapeutic abortion – as recommended by various health professionals – because it was against the law. Chemotherapy was also delayed as doctors were concerned it would harm the foetus.

Freedom of expression – journalists

The Dominican National Union of Press Workers reported that scores of journalists and other media workers were harassed or physically attacked. In most cases the perpetrators were not brought to justice.

There were concerns that proposed reforms to the Penal Code included penalties of up to three years' imprisonment for criticizing elected representatives or government-appointed officials.

D

Housing rights – forced evictions

According to local NGOs, several forced evictions were carried out and police used force unlawfully on several occasions.

Amnesty International visits/reports

🚗 Amnesty International delegates visited the Dominican Republic in November/December.

📁 Dominican Republic: Submission to the UN Human Rights Committee (AMR 27/001/2012)

📁 Dominican Republic: Open letter from Amnesty International to Dominican presidential candidates for the May 2012 elections (AMR 27/005/2012)

📁 Towards a successful reform? Proposals for an organic law to help bring about comprehensive reform of the National Police in the Dominican Republic (AMR 27/016/2012)

ECUADOR

REPUBLIC OF ECUADOR
Head of state and government: **Rafael Vicente Correa Delgado**

Indigenous and community leaders faced spurious criminal charges aimed at restricting their freedom of assembly. The rights of Indigenous Peoples to consultation and to free, prior and informed consent were not fulfilled.

Background

Mass demonstrations and blockades led by Indigenous organizations took place against government proposals on the use of natural resources and to demand the right to consultation.

In August, Ecuador granted diplomatic asylum to Wikileaks founder Julian Assange. At the end of the year, he remained in the Ecuadorian embassy in the UK where he had sought asylum after the UK Supreme Court dismissed his appeal against extradition to Sweden to answer allegations of sexual assault. Ecuador granted him diplomatic asylum on the basis that, if extradited to Sweden, he could be extradited to the USA where he could face an unfair trial, cruel, inhuman and degrading treatment, life imprisonment and the death penalty.

In October, an Ecuadorian court issued an order that froze approximately US$200 million of the assets of the oil company Chevron in Ecuador in order to implement an earlier ruling awarding US$18.2 billion to Amazon Indigenous communities for environmental damage. Earlier that month, Chevron had lost an appeal before the US Supreme Court to stop the plaintiffs from trying to collect the damages awarded. In November, a judge in Argentina embargoed Chevron's assets in that country to carry out the Ecuadorian court's ruling.

In September, Ecuador accepted most recommendations made under the UN Universal Periodic Review. These included ensuring the right to peaceful assembly and protest of community activists and Indigenous leaders; undertaking a review of existing and proposed legislation relating to freedom of expression; and decriminalizing defamation. However, it rejected a recommendation to ensure the right of Indigenous Peoples to free, prior and informed consent.

Freedom of association

Indigenous and *campesino* leaders were subjected to unfounded charges of terrorism, sabotage and homicide; criminal prosecutions; arbitrary arrests; and strict bail conditions in an attempt to discourage them from voicing their opposition to government laws and policies. In most cases, judges dismissed the charges as baseless. However, by the end of the year, three Indigenous and *campesino* leaders were still involved in court proceedings and subject to bail restrictions and three others were convicted and given short prison sentences.

■ In August, Carlos Pérez, leader of the Communal Water Systems of Azuay; Federico Guzmán, President of the Victoria del Portete Parish Council; and Efraín Arpi, leader of the Tarqui Parish, were given reduced sentences of eight days' imprisonment for blocking a road during a protest in Azuay province against proposed legislation. The men claimed the legislation would affect their community's access to water and was not adequately consulted. Federico Guzmán and Efraín Arpi had stated that they did not directly participate in the protest. Carlos Pérez admitted that he did, but that traffic had been allowed to flow every 30 minutes and emergency vehicles were allowed to pass. By the end of the year a warrant for their arrest had not yet been issued.

Indigenous Peoples' rights

In July the Inter-American Court of Human Rights confirmed that Ecuador had not consulted the Sarayaku Indigenous community in Pastaza province regarding an oil project to be carried out in their territory. It ordered the state to remove or inactivate explosives buried on Sarayaku territory; consult the Sarayaku regarding future development projects that might affect them; and take steps to make the right to consultation a reality for all Indigenous Peoples, among other measures.

In November bids for oil exploration in the Amazon region went out to public tender amid concerns that Indigenous communities that might be affected had not been consulted.

In a report published in August, the CERD Committee raised concerns at the absence of a regulated and systematic process for consultation with Indigenous Peoples on issues that affect them, including the extraction of natural resources.

Freedom of expression

There were concerns that laws dealing with the crime of insult were being used against journalists in violation of the right to freedom of expression and could deter other critics of government authorities from speaking out.

■ In February, the National Court confirmed a sentence of three years' imprisonment and US$40 million in damages against three owners of *El Universo* and a journalist working for the newspaper. They had been convicted of slander for an editorial in which they described the President as a "dictator" and accused him of giving the order to open fire on a hospital during the police protests of September 2010. The President later granted a pardon to all four men.

Amnesty International visits/reports

▤ "So that no one can demand anything": Criminalizing the right to protest in Ecuador? (AMR 28/002/2012)

EGYPT

ARAB REPUBLIC OF EGYPT

Head of state:	Mohamed Morsi (replaced Mohamed Hussein Tantawi in June)
Head of government:	Hisham Qandeel (replaced Kamal Ganzouri in August)

Protests against military rule resulted in the killing of at least 28 protesters by security forces in Cairo and Suez. Riot police and the army used excessive force to disperse protesters, who later alleged that they were tortured or otherwise ill-treated in custody. Protests, sometimes violent, by opponents and supporters of the President took place in November and December. Unfair trials by Emergency Supreme State Security Courts continued and security forces continued to act above the law. Former President Hosni Mubarak and the former Minister of Interior were sentenced to life imprisonment for killings of protesters during the 2011 uprising; many other suspected perpetrators were acquitted. No members of the Supreme Council of the Armed Forces (SCAF) were held to account for violations committed during their rule. President Mohamed Morsi established a committee to investigate violations committed between January 2011 and June 2012. He issued pardons for some civilians tried by military courts and a general amnesty for offences by protesters during demonstrations against military rule. Discrimination against religious minorities persisted. Journalists and activists were prosecuted for "insulting the President" and blasphemy. Women faced discrimination in law and practice as well as widespread sexual harassment. Thousands of families continued to live in "unsafe areas" in informal settlements (slums), while thousands more faced threats of forced eviction. Migrants were reportedly killed by security forces while attempting to cross into Israel or were exploited by traffickers in the Sinai Peninsula. At least 91 people were sentenced to death. It was not known whether there were any executions.

Background

A newly elected parliament met for the first time on 23 January. In March, parliament appointed a 100-

E

member Constituent Assembly to draft Egypt's new Constitution. The Constituent Assembly was dominated by Islamist parties and criticized for including only six women and six Coptic Christians. It was suspended by an administrative court on 10 April following a legal challenge. With the expiry of the 31-year state of emergency in May, the authorities tried to preserve some exceptional powers; on 13 June the Ministry of Justice gave military and intelligence officers powers to arrest, but an administrative court quickly overturned the move. Parliament approved a new Constituent Assembly in June, which faced fresh lawsuits and was increasingly boycotted by opposition political parties, civil society and the Coptic Christian Church. On 16 June, the SCAF dissolved parliament, following a Supreme Constitutional Court ruling that the elections had been unconstitutional. On 17 June, days before the result of the presidential elections, the SCAF widely expanded its own powers and limited those of the incoming administration. On 12 August, newly elected President Morsi announced that he had overturned the SCAF's new powers, and that SCAF leader Mohamed Tantawi was to retire. The announcement followed an attack by an armed group in the Sinai Peninsula which killed 16 soldiers. The authorities subsequently launched a security crackdown in the area.

On 22 November, President Morsi decreed that the courts could not challenge his decisions nor hear any lawsuit against the Constituent Assembly. President Morsi also issued a repressive new law to "protect the Revolution", replaced the Public Prosecutor, and urged new investigations and prosecutions in cases of deaths of protesters. The Constituent Assembly finalized the draft Constitution on 30 November.

The decree and draft Constitution triggered nationwide protests and a judges' strike, as well as incidents of violence between supporters and opponents of the President. On 5-6 December, at least 10 people were killed in clashes outside the Presidential Palace in Cairo. In response to the unrest, President Morsi partially lifted his decree on 8 December. The new Constitution was subsequently adopted in a national referendum in late December.

Torture and other ill-treatment

No legal or policy reforms were implemented to eradicate torture under either the SCAF or President Morsi's administration. The People's Assembly discussed harsher penalties for torture but did not introduce them before its dissolution. Torture and other ill-treatment continued and security forces acted with impunity. One NGO recorded 88 cases of torture or other ill-treatment by police during President Morsi's first 100 days in power. Protesters arrested by riot police or the military were subjected to severe beatings and electric shocks in custody, including in Tora Prison, south of Cairo, where detainees also suffered overcrowding, inadequate clothing and lack of medical care. Some male protesters said they were abducted and taken to undisclosed locations, where they were given electric shocks and sexually abused to make them give information on their involvement in protests.

■ George Ramzi Nakhla was arrested in Cairo on 6 February. He said riot police tied his arms and legs to the back of an armoured vehicle and slowly dragged him along the road while others beat him with batons. He was beaten again at the Ministry of Interior and given electric shocks. He received no medical treatment for a broken arm and was forced to squat with 13 other men for several hours. At Tora Prison, he was beaten with electric cables and verbally abused. Following a three-day hunger strike, he was released on 25 March.

■ Abdel Haleem Hnesh was arrested by military forces on 4 May at a protest in Abbaseya, Cairo. He said troops severely beat him with 2m-long sticks and electric batons, and then took him with some 40 others to military area S28 in Cairo. He was presented to military prosecutors, and then transferred to Tora Prison where he was beaten on arrival with hoses and sticks. He was released five days later.

Unfair trials

The new Constitution allowed for military trials of civilians, which are inherently unfair. The People's Assembly amended the Military Justice Code in April 2012, stripping the President of his authority to refer civilians to military court. However, it did not amend articles giving military courts jurisdiction to try civilians. In July, President Morsi established a committee to review cases of civilians tried by military courts as well as others held by the Ministry of Interior, and "revolutionaries" imprisoned by the ordinary judiciary. In July and August, President Morsi pardoned some 700 people based on the committee's recommendations, and in October decreed a general amnesty for offences committed while "supporting the revolution" in 2011 and 2012. However, the decree failed to provide fair trials for some 1,100 civilians imprisoned by military courts for other criminal offences.

Although the state of emergency expired at the end of May, some cases continued to be tried by emergency courts, including terrorism-related offences and protest and communal violence cases.

■ On 4 May the army arrested Mahmoud Mohamed Amin among some 300 protesters demonstrating against military rule in Abbaseya, Cairo. They were referred to military prosecution and trials, on charges such as "attacking army members" and "disrupting public order". On 20 May, Mahmoud Mohamed Amin and other detainees went on hunger strike to protest against their trial by military courts. He was released on 19 June pending trial, but charges against him were dropped under the presidential amnesty in October.

Excessive use of force

Protests in early 2012 were mainly against military rule. Following President Morsi's election, demonstrations were held by his supporters and opponents. Security forces were largely absent, especially during large Tahrir Square protests, but in some instances they clashed with protesters. No reform of the police was initiated and the authorities employed tactics reminiscent of the Mubarak era, with security forces using excessive force against protesters. Riot police used excessive and unnecessary force, including firearms and US-made tear gas.

■ Security forces used lethal force without prior warning to disperse protesters, killing 16 protesters between 2 and 6 February in Cairo and Suez. The protests were in reaction to the killing of some 70 Al-Ahly football supporters by men in plain clothes during a match in Port Said, witnessed by security forces that did not prevent the violence.

■ Between 28 April and 4 May, at least 12 people were killed by men in plain clothes during a sit-in in Abbaseya Square, Cairo, in protest at the presidential election process. Security forces did not intervene, suggesting that the men acted at the army's command or with their acquiescence.

■ On 20 November, teenage protester Gaber Salah Gaber was reportedly shot dead by security forces near the Ministry of the Interior in Cairo.

Impunity

In a historic step towards combating impunity, in June, former President Mubarak and former Minister of Interior Habib El Adly were found responsible for the killing and injury of protesters during the 2011 uprising and sentenced to life imprisonment. However, six senior security officials were acquitted. The prosecution argued that the lack of evidence against them was due to a lack of co-operation from General Intelligence and the Ministry of Interior.

Most police officers put on trial in relation to killings of protesters during the 2011 uprising were acquitted. Courts generally ruled that police used justified lethal force, or that evidence was insufficient. Truth and justice remained elusive for hundreds of victims of the uprising and their families.

In October, all defendants were acquitted in the "Battle of the Camels" trial in relation to clashes between pro- and anti-Mubarak protesters in Tahrir Square in February 2011. Subsequently, members of the Public Prosecution suggested that the case would be reopened.

No army members were brought to justice in relation to killings or torture during the Mohamed Mahmoud Street protests and Cabinet Offices protests in November and December 2011. Civilian investigative judges instead referred protesters to stand trial for alleged violence. Those accused in the Mohamed Mahmoud Street protests were amnestied, but the Cabinet Offices trial continued. Only one riot police officer stood trial for abuses committed during the Mohamed Mahmoud Street protests. His trial continued at the end of the year.

In September, a military court sentenced two army soldiers to two years' imprisonment each, and a third soldier to three years' imprisonment, for "involuntary homicide" for driving their armoured vehicle into 14 Coptic protesters in October 2011 in Maspero, Cairo. Investigations by civilian judges into the killings of 13 others failed to identify perpetrators. No SCAF members faced justice for the killings of protesters during their 17-month rule.

In July, President Morsi set up a fact-finding committee of officials, civil society activists and victims' families to identify the perpetrators of the killing and injury of protesters during the 2011 uprising and the SCAF's rule.

No measures were taken to provide justice, truth or reparation to victims of serious human rights

E

violations, including torture, carried out under President Mubarak's 30-year rule.

Freedoms of expression and association

There were ongoing criminal investigations and charges for blasphemy and insulting public officials. New constitutional provisions restricted freedom of expression, prohibiting insults against individuals or religious prophets. Draft legislation restricted freedom of association and imposed repressive rules on registration and foreign funding for NGOs.

■ Prisoner of conscience Maikel Nabil Sanad was released on 24 January as part of a wider pardon by the SCAF. A blogger, he had been imprisoned in April 2011 following an unfair trial by a military court for criticizing the army and objecting to military service.

■ In August, *El-Dostor* newspaper editor Islam Affifi was tried for publishing false information "insulting the President". The trial was ongoing at the end of the year.

■ In October, television personality Tawfiq Okasha was fined and sentenced to four months' imprisonment for "insulting the President". He remained free pending appeal.

■ Prisoner of conscience Alber Saber Ayad was arrested on 13 September after people surrounded his home accusing him of promoting the controversial film *Innocence of Muslims*. In December he was sentenced to three years' imprisonment for "defamation of religion" on the basis of his videos and internet posts, but bailed pending appeal.

■ In February, the trial began of 43 staff members of five international organizations for allegedly accepting foreign funding without government permission and operating illegally. Most were tried in their absence and the trial continued at the end of the year.

Women's rights

The new Constitution prohibited discrimination between Egyptian citizens, but did not explicitly prohibit discrimination against women, referring instead to their duties as homemakers. Women were marginalized in the new political institutions. They occupied only 12 seats out of 508 in the People's Assembly, before its dissolution. Only seven women were included in the second Constituent Assembly. Women were largely excluded from the Egyptian Cabinet appointed by President Morsi and none were appointed to the role of governor. Women also continued to face exclusion from serving in the judiciary. Discriminatory laws and practices relating to marriage, divorce, child custody and inheritance were not addressed.

Several women were reported to have been sexually harassed or assaulted during mass protests including in Tahrir Square. In June, a march in Cairo against sexual harassment was attacked by men who sexually harassed and assaulted the participants. In September, a man shot dead a woman in the street in Asyut, reportedly after she resisted his sexual harassment. After the Eid holiday in October the authorities announced they had received over 1,000 complaints of sexual harassment. No members of the security forces were held to account for sexual or gender-based violence against women detainees following anti-SCAF protests in 2011.

■ In March, a military court acquitted an army doctor in relation to forced "virginity testing" of women protesters in March 2011.

Discrimination

The new Constitution did not explicitly prohibit discrimination on the basis of race, potentially affecting minorities such as Nubians.

The Constitution guaranteed freedom of religion but limited it to religions officially recognized as "heavenly", potentially affecting Baha'is and Shi'a Muslims. The Constitution provided for separate personal status laws for Christians and Jews, as well as the right to regulate their religious affairs and leadership, but not for other religious minorities.

Egyptian law made it difficult for Coptic Christians to build or repair churches as it required hard-to-obtain official authorization. Some church-building works were obstructed by neighbouring Muslims, sometimes causing communal violence. In such cases, security forces generally failed to protect Copts from attacks.

■ At the end of January, three Coptic families from Sharbat village, Alexandria, were forcibly evicted from their homes by Muslims who suspected a Coptic man of possessing "indecent" images of a Muslim woman. Crowds attacked Copts' homes and businesses. Village "reconciliation meetings" decided that the Coptic man and his extended family, as well as five neighbouring Coptic families, should leave the village and have their possessions sold on their behalf. The police did not intervene to protect the Copts from the attacks or forced eviction. Following a visit by a parliamentary delegation, only the five Coptic families unconnected to the original dispute were able to return.

Housing rights – forced eviction

The Constitution upheld the right to adequate housing, but did not explicitly prohibit forced evictions. Guarantees against forced eviction remained absent in Egypt's laws and policies.

The government's Informal Settlements Development Facility (ISDF) estimated that some 11,500 homes, mainly in Cairo, were located in "unsafe areas" and posed an imminent threat to life, requiring immediate clearance. The ISDF also marked a further 120,000 homes in "unsafe areas" for clearance before 2017. The ISDF reportedly considered the options of upgrading slums and providing alternative housing near existing dwellings.

Housing Ministry officials said the Cairo 2050 plan had been reviewed and some projects which would have involved mass evictions had been dropped. A new urban Egypt 2052 master plan was under development, but communities in informal settlements were not consulted.

■ In August, police clashed with residents of Ramlet Bulaq informal settlement, central Cairo, after a policeman allegedly killed a resident. Police then raided Ramlet Bulaq several times, arresting men and forcing many male community members to flee the area. Residents said the police threatened to continue such intimidation until they cleared the area. Ramlet Bulaq is planned for demolition.

Refugees and migrants

Egyptian security forces continued to shoot foreign migrants, refugees and asylum-seekers who sought to cross Egypt's Sinai border into Israel, killing at least eight people. Human traffickers reportedly extorted and abused refugees, asylum-seekers and migrants crossing the Sinai Peninsula into Israel.

Death penalty

At least 91 people were sentenced to death, including after unfair trials by emergency courts. It was not known whether there were any executions.

■ In September, an emergency court sentenced to death 14 men, including eight in their absence, in relation to an attack which led to the killing of six people. They were also convicted of belonging to a Jihadist group.

Amnesty International visits/reports

🚗 Amnesty International delegates visited Egypt several times in 2012 to conduct research.

📄 Brutality unpunished and unchecked: Egypt's military kill and torture protesters with impunity (MDE 12/017/2012)

📄 Agents of repression: Egypt's police and the case for reform (MDE 12/029/2012)

📄 Egypt: New President must restore rule of law, govern for all (PRE01/316/2012)

📄 Egypt's new Constitution limits fundamental freedoms and ignores the rights of women (PRE01/590/2012)

EL SALVADOR

REPUBLIC OF EL SALVADOR
Head of state and government: **Carlos Mauricio Funes Cartagena**

Impunity for human rights violations committed during the armed conflict (1980-1992) persisted. A crisis gripped the judicial system as members of congress were accused of attempting to interfere in the selection and appointment of judges. Violations of sexual and reproductive rights remained a concern.

Background

Violent crime continued to dominate the political agenda, although the government reported an overall fall in the murder rate.

Impunity

Impunity for past human rights violations continued to be a concern.

■ In January, in accordance with a 2010 ruling by the Inter-American Commission on Human Rights, the President apologized on behalf of the state for the massacre of over 700 men, women and children in El Mozote and surrounding hamlets in Morazán province. The victims had been tortured and killed by the armed forces over a three-day period in 1981. In December, the Inter-American Court of Human Rights set down its final decision on the massacre, ordering the state to conduct investigations, and to hold those responsible to account. The ruling also called on the state to ensure the 1993 Amnesty Law was not an obstacle to the prosecution of war criminals; to continue compiling a list of victims; to conduct exhumations; and to ensure reparations for the relatives.

■ In August, survivors and relatives of victims marked 30 years of impunity for the 1982 El Calabozo massacre in which more than 200 women, men and children were killed by the armed forces. In a public event in November, representatives of the relatives and survivors handed in over 5,000 signatures urging the government to take action and respond to the demands of victims and their relatives for truth, justice and reparation.

Sexual and reproductive rights

Abortion in all circumstances remained a criminal offence.

■ Mery (not her real name) a 27-year-old woman, sought a clandestine medically induced abortion when she was eight weeks pregnant. When she sought medical assistance after taking the medication, some medical staff at the hospital reported her to the police. Although Mery was in a state of extreme distress and still undergoing treatment, she was handcuffed to a stretcher and kept under police guard. In August Mery was convicted and sentenced to two years in prison for an induced abortion. Just a few days into serving her sentence, Mery attempted suicide and was transferred from the prison to a psychiatric hospital where she was kept under guard. At the end of the year, she was awaiting the results of her appeal.

International justice

At a hearing in a US court in September, Inocente Orlando Montano, former Salvadoran Vice-Minister for Public Security and a former military commander, faced charges of lying to the US immigration authorities in order to stay in the USA. If found guilty, this could pave the way for Inocente Orlando Montano's extradition to Spain to face charges for his alleged role in the killing of six Jesuit priests, their housekeeper and her 16-year-old daughter in 1989 in El Salvador.

Justice system

In April, members of Congress made statements apparently indicating that the rules governing the appointment of judges would be bypassed, particularly in relation to two members of the

Constitutional section of the Supreme Court. Concerns were raised that the attempts to bypass the appointments procedure would facilitate the appointment of judges on the basis of their political affiliation rather than their professional capabilities. In November, the UN Special Rapporteur on the independence of judges and lawyers visited the country to assess the situation. At the end of her visit she reminded the authorities of the state's obligations to respect the independence of the judiciary and to refrain from any interference in the judiciary. She also recommended a review of the appointments procedure. No such review had been carried out by the end of the year.

EQUATORIAL GUINEA

REPUBLIC OF EQUATORIAL GUINEA
Head of state: **Teodoro Obiang Nguema Mbasogo**
Head of government: **Teodoro Obiang Nguema Mbasogo**
                                (replaced Ignacio Milán Tang in May)

The amended Constitution which increased the power of the President was promulgated in February. A transitional government was appointed pending elections in 2013. There were reports of unlawful killings by soldiers. Human rights defenders as well as political activists and government critics were harassed, arbitrarily arrested and detained. Some detainees were subjected to torture. A prisoner of conscience and at least 20 other political prisoners were released in a presidential pardon. Freedom of expression and of the press continued to be restricted.

Background

The amended Constitution, which was approved by referendum in November 2011, was promulgated in February. In accordance with the new Constitution and pending elections in early 2013, a caretaker government was appointed in May which included 12 members of President Obiang Nguema's family. Although not provided for by the Constitution, the

President appointed his eldest son, Teodoro "Teodorín" Nguema Obiang, as second Vice-President.

In March, investigating judges in France sought an international warrant for the arrest of "Teodorín" Nguema Obiang in the context of an investigation into embezzlement of public funds and money laundering. In August, French police confiscated his residence in Paris alleging that it was bought with cash embezzled from Equatorial Guinea. In September the government of Equatorial Guinea asked the International Court of Justice to rule that France should drop an investigation of the country's President and his son, cancel an arrest warrant against the son, and return seized property. In October the Malabo Investigating Court issued an arrest order against the director of the French branch of the NGO Transparency International, accusing him of libel and defamation, and extortion of the Equatorial Guinea state and illicit amassing of wealth.

Human rights defenders

Human rights defenders were harassed and arrested in relation to their work, as well as their peaceful political activities.

■ Human rights defender Wenceslao Mansogo Alo, a medical doctor and leading member of the opposition political party Convergence for Social Democracy (CPDS), was arrested without a warrant at Bata Central Police Station, on the mainland, on 9 February. He had voluntarily made a statement regarding the death of a woman during surgery in his private clinic on 1 February. The deceased's family had accused him of mutilating the body, although two reports of post-mortem examinations confirmed that the body was intact and the woman had died of a heart attack. The Minister of Health asserted that the heart attack had been caused by maladministration of the anaesthesia. Despite lack of evidence and without accusing or charging him, the investigating judge ordered the detention of Wenceslao Mansogo. Various courts rejected the appeals by his lawyers against his arrest and detention. In May he was convicted of professional negligence and sentenced to three years' imprisonment, as well as payment of compensation. He was released in June following a presidential pardon. An appeal to the Supreme Court against the conviction and sentence was heard in November but no verdict had been delivered by the end of the year.

Arbitrary arrests and detentions

There were arbitrary arrests and detentions of suspected opponents, including for not attending the August celebrations of the anniversary of President Obiang taking power. Most were released without charge after a few days or weeks. Several were tortured or otherwise ill-treated.

■ Florentino Manguire Eneme, a former business associate of President Obiang's eldest son, "Teodorín" Nguema Obiang, was arrested in Bata Central police station on 11 August, when he responded to a telephone summons. He was accused of providing documents related to "Teodorín" Nguema's businesses to third parties. Two days later he was transferred to Malabo and held in the central police station until his release uncharged on 23 August.

■ Police arrested Agustín Esono Nsogo at his home in Bata on 17 October at 11pm, without a warrant. He was held incommunicado at Black Beach prison for at least a week, and was tortured on three occasions, apparently to force him to confess to a plot to destabilize the country. His detention was not legalized until one month after his arrest, well beyond the 72 hours prescribed by national law. He was not charged with any offence by the year's end.

Some 10 people, including relatives and friends of Agustín Esono Nsogo, were subsequently arrested in Bata. At least three were transferred to Black Beach prison in Malabo and were released without charge on 30 October, together with Agustín Esono Nsogo's lawyer, Fabián Nsue, who had been arrested without a warrant on 22 October in Black Beach prison, where he had gone to see a client arrested a week earlier.

Enforced disappearance

Antonio Lebán, a member of the Army Special Forces, was arrested in Bata soon after 17 October and was not seen or heard from since. His arrest appeared to be linked to that of Agustín Esono Nsogo.

Extrajudicial executions

Soldiers and police reportedly carried out extrajudicial executions.

■ Blas Engó was shot, reportedly at close range, by a soldier outside the prison in Bata as he tried to escape together with 46 others during the night of 14 May.

■ In May, a military officer in Bata shot dead Oumar Koné, a Malian national, for refusing to pay a bribe at a routine road block.

Freedom of expression – journalists

The press remained under state control and criticism was not allowed. In mid-October, a programme on national radio was stopped and suspended indefinitely as it broadcast an interview with a woman representative of 18 families who had been forcibly evicted from their homes in Bata. The woman had criticized the president of the Supreme Court for alleged personal involvement in the dispute.

Prisoners of conscience

A prisoner of conscience and 20 other prisoners who may have been prisoners of conscience were released in a presidential pardon in June.

ERITREA

ERITREA
Head of state and government: **Isaias Afewerki**

National service conscription was compulsory and frequently extended indefinitely. Military training for children remained compulsory. Conscripts were used as forced labour. Thousands of prisoners of conscience and political prisoners continued to be arbitrarily detained in appalling conditions. Torture and other ill-treatment were common. No opposition parties, independent media or civil society organizations were permitted. Only four religions were sanctioned by the state; all others were banned and their followers arrested and detained. Eritreans continued to flee the country in large numbers.

Background

The humanitarian situation in the country was reported to be serious and the economy remained stagnant. However, the mining sector continued to develop, with foreign governments and private companies interested in Eritrea's significant deposits of gold, potash and copper, despite a risk of complicity in human rights violations through the use of forced labour at mining sites.

The Ethiopian army conducted military incursions into Eritrea twice in March, announcing successful attacks on camps where they claimed Ethiopian rebel

groups trained. Ethiopia blamed Eritrea for backing a rebel group that attacked a group of European tourists in Ethiopia in January (see Ethiopia entry). The group which claimed responsibility for the incident said it had no camps in Eritrea.

In July, the UN Human Rights Council appointed a Special Rapporteur on Eritrea, in response to "the continued widespread and systematic violations of human rights… by the Eritrean authorities." The Eritrean government dismissed the appointment as politically motivated.

In July, the UN Monitoring Group on Somalia and Eritrea reported that Eritrea's support for al-Shabab in Somalia had declined, but that Eritrea continued to harbour armed opposition groups from neighbouring countries, especially Ethiopia. The report also found that Eritrean officials were involved in trafficking of weapons and human beings.

Around the middle of the year, reports indicated that the government was distributing guns to the civilian population, for unknown reasons.

Prisoners of conscience and political prisoners

Thousands of prisoners of conscience and political prisoners remained in arbitrary detention in appalling conditions. They included politicians, journalists and religious practitioners. They also included people caught trying to evade national service, flee the country or move around the country without a permit. Some prisoners of conscience had been detained without charge for over a decade.

High profile prisoners were not permitted visitors and in most cases their families did not know their location or health status. The government continued to refuse to confirm or deny reports that a number of prisoners had died in detention.

■ It was reported that three journalists – Dawit Habtemichael, Mattewos Habteab and Sahle Tsegazab – all arbitrarily detained since their arrest in 2001, had died in detention in recent years. The government did not confirm these reports.

Freedom of religion or belief

Only members of permitted faiths – the Eritrean Orthodox, Roman Catholic and Lutheran Churches, and Islam – were allowed to practice. Members of banned faiths continued to be arrested, arbitrarily detained and ill-treated.

■ In April, 10 Jehovah's Witnesses were arrested in Keren, in connection with their attendance at a funeral. At the end of the year, 56 Jehovah's Witnesses were reported to be imprisoned for practising their faith.

Torture and other ill-treatment

Torture and other ill-treatment of prisoners were widespread. Prisoners were beaten, tied in painful positions and left in extreme weather conditions, and held in solitary confinement for long periods. Conditions in detention amounted to cruel, inhuman or degrading treatment. Many detainees were held in metal shipping containers or underground cells, often in desert locations, where they were exposed to extremes of heat and cold. Detainees received inadequate food and water. They were frequently denied – or provided with only inadequate – medical care.

■ Journalist Yirgalem Fisseha Mebrahtu, arrested in February 2009, was reportedly admitted to hospital in January, under permanent guard and with no visitors permitted. Her family was not told why she had been admitted.

■ Petros Solomon, a former Foreign Minister and one of the G15 group – 11 high-profile politicians detained arbitrarily since 2001 – was reportedly hospitalized in July due to a serious illness. However, adequate medical care was unavailable in Eritrea. His fate remained unknown.

A number of deaths in custody were reported.

■ In August, Yohannes Haile, a Jehovah's Witness detained since September 2008, reportedly died at Me'eter prison from the effects of extreme heat after being confined underground since October 2011. Three others detained with him were reportedly in critical condition. Their fate remained unknown.

Military conscription

National service remained compulsory for all adult men and women. All schoolchildren were required to complete their final year of secondary education at Sawa military training camp, a policy which affected children as young as 15. At Sawa, children suffered poor conditions and harsh punishments for infractions.

The initial national service period of 18 months was frequently extended indefinitely, on minimal salaries that were inadequate to meet families' essential needs. Conscripts continued to be used widely as forced labour in state projects, including agricultural production, or in private companies owned by military or ruling party elites. They faced harsh penalties for evasion, including arbitrary detention and ill-treatment.

Refugees and asylum-seekers

Thousands of Eritreans fled the country during the year, mainly to evade indefinite national service. A "shoot to kill" policy remained in place for those caught attempting to cross into Ethiopia. People caught crossing into Sudan were arbitrarily detained and severely beaten. Family members of those who fled successfully were forced to pay fines or risk imprisonment.

Eritrean asylum-seekers forcibly returned faced a serious risk of arbitrary detention and torture. Despite this, several countries including Egypt, Sudan, Sweden, Ukraine and the UK, planned or carried out forced returns to Eritrea.

■ On 24 July, Sudan forcibly returned nine asylum-seekers and one refugee to Eritrea. They had been convicted of unlawful entry by a Sudanese court.

Trafficking in human beings

The July report of the UN Somalia and Eritrea Monitoring Group stated that Eritrean officials, including senior military officials, presided over weapons smuggling and people trafficking through criminal networks in Sudan and the Sinai, Egypt. According to the report, the scale of activity suggested the complicity of the Eritrean government.

E

ESTONIA

REPUBLIC OF ESTONIA
Head of state: **Toomas Hendrik Ilves**
Head of government: **Andrus Ansip**

About 100,000 people, most of them Russian speakers, remained stateless, limiting their political rights. National human rights institutions did not comply with international standards. Conditions of reception for asylum-seekers and refugees were inadequate.

Discrimination – ethnic minorities

About 100,000 people (approximately 7% of the population) remained stateless. The large majority of these were Russian speakers. Children born of stateless parents continued to be denied automatic citizenship, although a simplified naturalization procedure was available to them. Stateless people continued to be denied political rights. They were reportedly disproportionately affected by poverty and unemployment. Language requirements appeared to be one of the main obstacles for Russian speakers to access citizenship and other rights.

Legal, constitutional or institutional developments

The Chancellor of Justice – acting as Ombudsman and national preventive mechanism under the Optional Protocol to the UN Convention against Torture – failed to meet the requirements of the Paris Principles for independent national human rights institutions.

The definition of torture and the penalties provided for that crime in the Criminal Code remained inconsistent with the requirements of the Convention against Torture.

Refugees and asylum-seekers

Reception conditions for the small number of asylum-seekers arriving in the country each year remained inadequate. The provision of interpreters was insufficient, which reportedly hampered the filing of applications and communications in general between asylum-seekers and the authorities.

There were insufficient measures to ensure social and economic integration of refugees.

ETHIOPIA

FEDERAL DEMOCRATIC REPUBLIC OF ETHIOPIA

Head of state:	**Girma Wolde-Giorgis**
Head of government:	**Hailemariam Desalegn** (replaced Meles Zenawi in August)

The state stifled freedom of expression, severely restricting the activities of the independent media, political opposition parties and human rights organizations. Dissent was not tolerated in any sphere. The authorities imprisoned actual and perceived opponents of the government. Peaceful protests were suppressed. Arbitrary arrests and detention were common, and torture and other ill-treatment in detention centres were rife. Forced evictions were reported on a vast scale around the country.

Background

In August, the authorities announced the death of Prime Minister Zenawi, who had ruled Ethiopia for 21 years. Hailemariam Desalegn was appointed as his successor, and three deputy prime ministers were appointed to include representation of all ethnic-based parties in the ruling coalition.

The government continued to offer large tracts of land for lease to foreign investors. Often this coincided with the "villagization" programme of resettling hundreds of thousands of people. Both actions were frequently accompanied by numerous allegations of large-scale forced evictions.

Skirmishes continued to take place between the Ethiopian army and armed rebel groups in several parts of the country – including the Somali, Oromia and Afar regions.

Ethiopian forces continued to conduct military operations in Somalia. There were reports of extrajudicial executions, arbitrary detention, and torture and other ill-treatment carried out by Ethiopian troops and militias allied to the Somali government.

In March, Ethiopian forces made two incursions into Eritrea, later reporting that they had attacked camps where they claimed Ethiopian rebel groups trained (see Eritrea entry). Ethiopia blamed Eritrea for backing a rebel group that attacked European tourists in the Afar region in January.

E

Freedom of expression

A number of journalists and political opposition members were sentenced to lengthy prison terms on terrorism charges for calling for reform, criticizing the government, or for links with peaceful protest movements. Much of the evidence used against these individuals consisted of examples of them exercising their rights to freedom of expression and association.

The trials were marred by serious irregularities, including a failure to investigate allegations of torture; denial of, or restrictions on, access to legal counsel; and use of confessions extracted under coercion as admissible evidence.

■ In January, journalists Reyot Alemu, Woubshet Taye and Elias Kifle, opposition party leader Zerihun Gebre-Egziabher, and former opposition supporter Hirut Kifle, were convicted of terrorism offences.

■ In June, journalist Eskinder Nega, opposition leader Andualem Arage, and other dissidents, were given prison sentences ranging from eight years to life in prison on terrorism charges.

■ In December, opposition leaders Bekele Gerba and Olbana Lelisa were sentenced to eight and 13 years' imprisonment respectively, for "provocation of crimes against the state".

Between July and November, hundreds of Muslims were arrested during a series of protests against alleged government restrictions on freedom of religion, across the country. While many of those arrested were subsequently released, large numbers remained in detention at the end of the year, including key figures of the protest movement. The government made significant efforts to quash the movement and stifle reporting on the protests.

■ In October, 29 leading figures of the protest movement, including members of a committee appointed by the community to represent their grievances to the government, and at least one journalist, were charged under the Anti-Terrorism Proclamation.

■ In both May and October, Voice of America correspondents were temporarily detained and interrogated over interviews they had conducted with protesters.

The few remaining vestiges of the independent media were subjected to even further restrictions.

■ In April, Temesgen Desalegn, the editor of *Feteh*, one of the last remaining independent publications, was fined for contempt of court for "biased coverage" of the trial of Eskinder Nega and others. *Feteh* had published statements from some of the defendants. In August, he was charged with criminal offences for articles he had written or published that were deemed critical of the government, or that called for peaceful protests against government repression. He was released after a few days' detention and the charges were dropped.

In May, the authorities issued a directive requiring printing houses to remove any content which could be defined as "illegal" by the government from any publications they printed. The unduly broad provisions of the Anti-Terrorism Proclamation meant that much legitimate content could be deemed illegal.

■ In July, an edition of *Feteh* was impounded after state authorities objected to one cover story on the Muslim protests and another speculating about the Prime Minister's health. Subsequently, state-run printer Berhanena Selam refused to print *Feteh* or *Finote Netsanet*, the publication of the largest opposition party, Unity for Democracy and Justice. In November, the party announced that the government had imposed a total ban on *Finote Netsanet*.

A large number of news, politics and human rights websites were blocked.

In July, Parliament passed the Telecom Fraud Offences Proclamation, which obstructs the provision and use of various internet and telecommunications technologies.

Human rights defenders

The Charities and Societies Proclamation, along with related directives, continued to significantly restrict the work of human rights defenders, particularly by denying them access to essential funding.

■ In October, the Supreme Court upheld a decision to freeze around US$1 million in assets of the country's two leading human rights organizations: the Human Rights Council and the Ethiopian Women Lawyers Association. The accounts had been frozen in 2009 after the law was passed.

■ In August, the Human Rights Council, the country's oldest human rights NGO, was denied permission for proposed national fundraising activities by the government's Charities and Societies Agency.

It was reported that the Agency began enforcing a provision in the law requiring NGO work to be overseen by a relevant government body, severely compromising the independence of NGOs.

E

Torture and other ill-treatment

Torture and other ill-treatment of prisoners were widespread, particularly during interrogation in pre-trial police detention. Typically, prisoners might be punched, slapped, beaten with sticks and other objects, handcuffed and suspended from the wall or ceiling, denied sleep and left in solitary confinement for long periods. Electrocution, mock-drowning and hanging weights from genitalia were reported in some cases. Many prisoners were forced to sign confessions. Prisoners were used to mete out physical punishment against other prisoners.

Allegations of torture made by detainees, including in court, were not investigated.

Prison conditions were harsh. Food and water were scarce and sanitation was very poor. Medical treatment was inadequate, and was sometimes withheld from prisoners. Deaths in detention were reported.

■ In February, jailed opposition leader, Andualem Arage, was severely beaten by a fellow prisoner who had been moved into his cell a few days earlier. Later in the year, another opposition leader, Olbana Lelisa was reportedly subjected to the same treatment.

■ In September, two Swedish journalists, sentenced in 2011 to 11 years' imprisonment on terrorism charges, were pardoned. After their release, the two men reported that they were forced to incriminate themselves and had been subjected to mock execution before they were allowed access to their embassy or a lawyer.

Arbitrary arrests and detentions

The authorities arrested members of political opposition parties, and other perceived or actual political opponents. Arbitrary detention was widespread.

According to relatives, some people disappeared after arrest. The authorities targeted families of suspects, detaining and interrogating them. The use of unofficial places of detention was reported.

■ In January the All Ethiopian Unity Party called for the release of 112 party members who, the party reported, were arrested in the Southern Nations, Nationalities and Peoples (SNNP) region during one week in January.

Hundreds of Oromos were arrested, accused of supporting the Oromo Liberation Front.

■ In September, over 100 people were reportedly arrested during the Oromo festival of Irreechaa.

Large numbers of civilians were reportedly arrested and arbitrarily detained in the Somali region on suspicion of supporting the Ogaden National Liberation Front (ONLF).

■ The authorities continued to arbitrarily detain UN employee, Yusuf Mohammed, in Jijiga. His detention, since 2010, was reportedly an attempt to get his brother, who was suspected of links with the ONLF, to return from exile.

Between June and August, a large number of ethnic Sidama were arrested in the SNNP region. This was reportedly in response to further calls for separate regional statehood for the Sidama. A number of arrests took place in August around the celebration of Fichee, the Sidama New Year. Many of those arrested were detained briefly, then released. But a number of leading community figures remained in detention and were charged with crimes against the state.

There were reports of people being arrested for taking part in peaceful protests and publicly opposing certain "development projects".

Excessive use of force

In several incidents, the police were accused of using excessive force when responding to the Muslim protest movement. Two incidents in Addis Ababa in July ended in violence, and allegations included police firing live ammunition and beating protesters in the street and in detention, resulting in many injuries. In at least two other protest-related incidents elsewhere in the country, police fired live ammunition, killing and injuring several people. None of these incidents was investigated.

■ In April, the police reportedly shot dead at least four people in Asasa, Oromia region. Reports from witnesses and the government conflicted.

■ In October, police fired on local residents in Gerba town, Amhara region, killing at least three people and injuring others. The authorities said protesters started the violence; the protesters reported that police fired live ammunition at unarmed people.

Security forces were alleged to have carried out extrajudicial executions in the Gambella, Afar and Somali regions.

Conflict in the Somali region

In September, the government and the ONLF briefly entered into peace talks with a view to ending the two-decade long conflict in the Somali region. However, the talks stalled in October.

The army, and its proxy militia, the Liyu police, faced repeated allegations of human rights violations, including arbitrary detention, extrajudicial executions, and rape. Torture and other ill-treatment of detainees were widely reported. None of the allegations was investigated and access to the region remained severely restricted.

■ In June, UN employee Abdirahman Sheikh Hassan was found guilty of terrorism offences over alleged links to the ONLF, and sentenced to seven years and eight months' imprisonment. He was arrested in July 2011 after negotiating with the ONLF over the release of two abducted UN World Food Programme workers.

Forced evictions

"Villagization", a programme involving the resettlement of hundreds of thousands of people, took place in the Gambella, Benishangul-Gumuz, Somali, Afar and SNNP regions. The programme, ostensibly to increase access to basic services, was meant to be voluntary. However, there were reports that many of the removals constituted forced evictions.

. Large-scale population displacement, sometimes accompanied by allegations of forced evictions, was reported in relation to the leasing of huge areas of land to foreign investors and dam building projects.

Construction continued on large dam projects which were marred by serious concerns about lack of consultation, displacement of local populations without adequate safeguards in place, and negative environmental impacts.

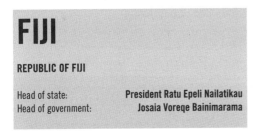

FIJI

REPUBLIC OF FIJI

Head of state:	**President Ratu Epeli Nailatikau**
Head of government:	**Josaia Voreqe Bainimarama**

People's rights to freedom of expression, association and peaceful assembly continued to be restricted under military rule. Political leaders and human rights defenders were arrested and charged with serious offences, in some cases leading to imprisonment. Concerns remained about the rule of law and independence of the judiciary.

Background

In July, a process for reviewing the Constitution was established by decree. Under the process, participants in the 2006 coup were given full immunity from prosecution. The Constitutional Commission, established in April 2012, and others expressed concern about the review process. Despite earlier public consultations, the process was amended in November to prevent public consultation on a draft Constitution before it could go before the Constituent Assembly.

Freedoms of expression, association and assembly

In January, the Public Order (Amendment) Decree replaced the Public Emergency Regulations, but retained similar restrictions on freedoms of expression and peaceful assembly. A number of decrees passed since 2009 have been used to stifle government critics, prevent peaceful protests and disperse meetings.

■ In May, police revoked a permit to march for the International Day against Homophobia and Transphobia on the day of the march.

■ On 11 July, police arrested and detained overnight a Fiji Labour Party official, Vyas Deo Sharma, and 14 male supporters for meeting at a private dwelling.

Former political leaders and human rights advocates were prosecuted in cases which appeared to be politically motivated, undermining freedom of expression.

■ In July, the Citizens' Constitutional Forum was charged with contempt of court for an article published in its newsletter in April entitled "Fiji: Rule of Law Lost".

■ In August, deposed Prime Minister Laisenia Qarase was sentenced to 12 months in prison on what were believed to be politically motivated charges of corruption.

Government remained critical of external institutions reviewing human rights in Fiji.

■ In September, an International Labour Organization delegation was expelled from Fiji.

Torture and other ill-treatment

Police and security forces faced allegations of torture and other ill-treatment, including beating, threatening and intimidating people, particularly government critics.

■ In September, five men who escaped from prison were recaptured by security forces and were reportedly

F

tortured. All five were hospitalized as a result of their injuries and one had his leg amputated.

Justice system and lack of accountability

The rule of law and access to justice were undermined by an absence of judicial review of government decisions and security of tenure for judges. Impunity prevailed in cases of past human rights violations.
■ In July, Felix Anthony of the Fiji Trades Union Congress issued a formal complaint, after he was assaulted by officers in February 2011. Police refused to investigate his complaint against Prime Minister and Military Commander Josaia Voreqe Bainimarama.
■ In January, the UK Law Society Charity released a report claiming that there is "no rule of law" in Fiji and that "the independence of the judiciary cannot be relied upon".

FINLAND

REPUBLIC OF FINLAND
Head of state: Sauli Niinistö (replaced Tarja Halonen
                                                    in March)
Head of government: Jyrki Katainen

Asylum-seekers faced detention in unsuitable facilities. An investigation began into Finland's involvement in the US-led rendition programme. Conscientious objectors to military service were imprisoned.

Migrants and asylum-seekers

At least 1,300 migrants and asylum-seekers were detained during the year. Over 65% were detained in police facilities with people facing criminal charges (contrary to international standards), without access to services, such as rehabilitation for victims of torture and education. An unaccompanied minor was held in the Metsälä Detention Centre for three months in the same facilities as adults and without access to education.

The asylum process still did not provide for an in-country suspensive right of appeal, increasing the risk of people being returned to countries where they might risk torture or other ill-treatment.
■ In August, a Chechen asylum-seeker was forcibly

returned to Russia while his appeal was pending before the Supreme Administrative Court. An hour later, the UN Committee against Torture granted interim measures preventing his return, but the authorities removed him anyway.

Violence against women and girls

In September, the Council of Europe Commissioner for Human Rights reported that violence against women continued to be a serious problem. Women and girls remained inadequately protected from rape and other forms of sexual violence. Rape continued to be categorized according to the degree of violence used or threatened by the perpetrator, and few cases reached court or concluded in a guilty verdict.

Counter-terror and security

The Parliamentary Ombudsman of Finland started an investigation into the state's complicity in the CIA rendition programme. The Ombudsman has the power to review classified information and to lay charges against any state actor who may have committed crimes in the course of official duties. In November, the Ombudsman sent detailed written requests for information to 15 government agencies.

International justice

On 30 April, the Helsinki Court of Appeals confirmed the conviction of François Bazaramba for crimes of genocide committed in Rwanda in 1994. On 22 October the Supreme Court dismissed François Bazaramba's application for leave to appeal.

Excessive use of force

■ On 26 May, a 30-year-old man died in custody at Vantaa police station, after police officers had used an electro-stun device on him. The incident was being investigated to assess whether his death was directly caused by the device.
■ In August, police in Miehikkälä used an electro-stun device against a 14-year-old boy, injuring his arm. An investigation into the incident was dropped by the state prosecutor.

Prisoners of conscience

Conscientious objectors to military service continued to be imprisoned for refusing to perform the alternative civilian service, as it remains punitive and discriminatory in length.

Amnesty International visits/reports

▨ Finland: Limited inquiries into rendition programme fail to meet obligation of investigation under international human rights law (EUR 20/001/2012)

FRANCE

FRENCH REPUBLIC
Head of state: François Hollande (replaced Nicolas Sarkozy in May)
Head of government: Jean-Marc Ayrault (replaced François Fillon in May)

Investigations into allegations of deaths in custody, torture and other ill-treatment by police remained ineffective and inadequate. Thousands of Roma were left homeless after being forcibly evicted from informal settlements. The fast-track procedure for the assessment of asylum applications continued to fall short of international standards.

Deaths in custody

Concerns about the promptness, effectiveness and independence of investigations into cases of deaths in police custody remained. Investigations into four long-standing cases of death in custody were closed.

■ On 26 September, the examining magistrate concluded in the case of Abou Bakari Tandia that there was "no evidence to hold a police officer responsible in the process leading to the death of the victim". Abou Bakari Tandia fell into a coma during the night of 5 to 6 December 2004, when he was being held in the police station of Courbevoie, and died on 24 January 2005. The police officer who performed the restraint technique believed to have put Abou Bakari Tandia into the coma was still in post at another police station at the end of the year. An appeal hearing was pending.

■ On 15 October, in the case of Ali Ziri, a 69-year-old Algerian man who died two days after being held in custody in the Argenteuil police station in June 2009, the judge of Pontoise concluded that "no acts of voluntary violence which may have directly or indirectly caused the death of Ali Ziri" were found. However, an autopsy of April 2011 had confirmed that Ali Ziri died as a result of the restraint techniques he was subjected to and repeated vomiting while held in custody. The

police officers involved in the arrest and transportation of Ali Ziri and his friend Arezki Kerfali had never been questioned by the judge. An appeal hearing was pending.

■ Also on 15 October, the case of Mahamadou Maréga, an irregular migrant from Mali who died on 30 November 2010 after being shot twice by an electro-stun device during his violent arrest in Colombes, was closed by the examining magistrate . On 4 May, the Defender of Rights demanded disciplinary proceedings against the law enforcement officials involved, who he considered to have made disproportionate use of their stun devices. An appeal hearing was pending.

■ In December, the case of Mohamed Boukrourou, who died in a police van on 12 November 2009, was dismissed. An appeal of that decision remained pending. At the end of the year, the four police officers involved in his arrest in Valentigney were reportedly still in office and had not faced disciplinary proceedings.

Investigations proceeded in other cases.

■ On 24 February, three of the seven policemen involved in the death of Abdelhakim Ajimi during his arrest on 9 May 2008 were given suspended custodial sentences of six, 18 and 24 months respectively by the Grasse Criminal Court. Amnesty International expressed concern that these sentences did not match the gravity of the offence committed. The three policemen appealed the decision. Four others implicated in the incident were acquitted.

■ Little progress was made in the investigation of Lamine Dieng's death during his arrest on 17 June 2007 in Paris. Lamine Dieng had been restrained by police officers on the street and then in a police vehicle, where he lost consciousness and died of mechanical asphyxia.

Torture and other ill-treatment

The Criminal Code continued to lack a definition of torture in line with international standards. There was a lack of prompt, independent, impartial and effective investigations into allegations of ill-treatment by law enforcement officials. On 19 April, the European Committee for the Prevention of Torture called for "zero tolerance" of police ill-treatment and for limiting the use of electro-stun devices.

Discrimination

Ethnic and religious minorities, as well as LGBTI people, continued to experience discrimination.

In December, the Minister of the Interior presented a new draft code of ethics for security forces which, for the first time, regulated identity checks and body searches. In September, he had opposed the idea of officially registering all identity checks in order to combat racial profiling. Several human rights organizations continued to document identity checks based on ethnic profiling.

A law aimed at prohibiting the concealment of the face remained in force. Such laws indirectly discriminate against Muslim women freely choosing to wear full face veils. In January the Senate adopted a bill aimed at prohibiting employees in private childcare facilities from wearing religious and cultural symbols and dress. A circular issued by the former Ministry of Education in 2011 remained in force, which already banned women wearing such forms of dress from taking part in school outings.

In August, a law on sexual harassment introduced "sexual identity" as a prohibited ground in anti-hate crime law and in legislation aimed at combating discrimination in the workplace.

On 5 October, the Constitutional Council revoked several provisions of a 1969 law on Travellers. It removed the requirement to be registered in a municipality for three years to be able to vote and to carry and periodically renew a "circulation notebook" for Travellers without a regular income. However, those with a regular income were still obliged to carry a new "circulation booklet"; all Travellers still had to register with municipal authorities; and they were not allowed to constitute more than 3% of the town's population.

On 7 November, the Council of Ministers adopted a bill on same-sex marriage, which was due to be examined by the National Assembly from January 2013.

Forced evictions

Camps and makeshift homes inhabited by Roma continued to be dismantled in forced evictions throughout the year. According to NGO estimates, 9,040 Roma were forcibly evicted throughout France in the first three quarters of 2012.

On 26 August, the government issued an interministerial circular containing discretionary guidelines for Prefects on how to plan and carry out evictions and support the people targeted by them. However, international safeguards against forced evictions continued to be flouted at a local level when implementing expulsion orders.

Refugees, asylum-seekers and migrants

The fast-track procedure for asylum-seekers remained in place, although it did not adequately protect their fundamental rights, and they continued to be denied a suspensive right of appeal before the National Asylum Court.

On 26 March, the Council of State quashed the April 2011 decision of the French Office for the Protection of Refugees and Stateless Persons (OFPRA) to add Albania and Kosovo to the list of safe countries of origin for asylum-seekers. On 3 October, the Council of State condemned OFPRA's lack of individual assessment in reviewing the applications of asylum-seekers whose fingerprints seemed to be voluntarily modified.

On 7 July, the government issued a circular which recommended that families of irregular migrants with children be placed under strict house arrest rather than in detention centres.

On 11 July, the UN Committee on Torture stopped the expulsion of a Somali woman detained in a "waiting zone" at Roissy Charles de Gaulle airport. Her asylum claim and appeal had been rejected within a week, although UNHCR, the Refugee Agency, opposes deportation to certain parts of Somalia.

In December, Parliament adopted a law amending the Code of Entry and Stay of Foreigners and the Asylum Law, which abolishes the so-called "solidarity offence". Under the law, supporting the irregular stay of a foreigner is no longer punishable with a fine or imprisonment, so long as the person providing the support receives no direct or indirect compensation.

Legal, constitutional or institutional developments

In December, France signed the Optional Protocol to the ICESCR.

Amnesty International visits/reports

🚗 Amnesty International delegates visited France in February, May, June, August, September and November.

📋 Choice and prejudice: Discrimination against Muslims in Europe (EUR 01/001/2012)

📋 The European Committee for the Prevention of Torture calls for "zero tolerance" of ill-treatment (EUR 21/005/2012)

📋 Chased away: Forced evictions of Roma in the Ile-de-France (EUR 21/012/2012)

GAMBIA

REPUBLIC OF THE GAMBIA
Head of state and government: **Yahya Jammeh**

For the first time in nearly 30 years the death penalty was carried out, as nine death row inmates were executed without prior notification. The inmates had not exhausted all of their appeals. The authorities also repressed dissent through harassment and intimidation. Security forces routinely made arbitrary arrests and subjected people to arbitrary detention. Prison conditions were appalling.

Death penalty

In August, nine death row prisoners – seven Gambian men, one Senegalese man and one Senegalese woman – were executed by firing squad, a week after President Jammeh had announced plans to carry out all existing death sentences. No prior notification was given to the individual prisoners, their families, their lawyers or the Senegalese authorities. The authorities did not confirm the executions – which caused an international outcry – until several days afterwards. Three of those executed, Malang Sonko, Tabara Samba and Buba Yarboe, were killed without exhaustion of their legal appeals, in violation of international fair trial standards. Another executed man, Dawda Bojang, had been sentenced in 2007 to life imprisonment for murder. When he appealed his conviction at the High Court in 2010, his sentence was changed to death. He had not exhausted his appeal to the Supreme Court when he was executed. The Constitution states that all those sentenced to death must be guaranteed the right of appeal to the Supreme Court.

In September, the President announced a moratorium on executions conditional on the crime rate, thus making the lives of those on death row dependent on external factors.

In October, the Supreme Court upheld the convictions for treason of seven men sentenced to death in June 2010 for plotting to overthrow the government. International observers were barred from the courtroom.

At the end of the year at least 36 people remained on death row.

Arbitrary arrests and detentions

The National Intelligence Agency (NIA) and police routinely carried out arbitrary arrests. Individuals were often held without charge and beyond the 72-hour time limit within which a suspect must be brought before a court, in violation of the Constitution.

■ In April, 18 men and two women who were or were perceived to be lesbian, gay, bisexual or transgender, were arrested during a raid on a nightclub. They were charged with attempting to commit "unnatural acts" and "conspiracy to commit felony". The charges were dropped for lack of evidence in August.

■ In October, the media and family members reported that former government Minister Mambury Njie was arrested and detained by the NIA. His detention exceeded the maximum 72 hours and his family was not informed of the reason for arrest. He was released on bail a few days later and re-arrested in December, after reporting to the police in line with his bail conditions. He was taken to court and charged with economic crimes and abuse of office, with no further details, before being remanded in custody at Mile II Prison. In court, Mambury Njie did not have legal representation and he was not informed of his right to a lawyer. He remained in detention at the end of the year. It was reported in the media that while serving as Minister of Foreign Affairs in August, Mambury Njie was opposed to orders to execute death row inmates.

Repression of dissent

■ In January, the former Minister of Information and Communication, Dr Amadou Scattred Janneh, was sentenced to life imprisonment with hard labour after being convicted of treason. Modou Keita, Ebrima Jallow and Michael Uche Thomas were each sentenced to three years with hard labour for sedition. The four were arrested in June 2011 for being in possession of T-shirts which featured the slogan "End Dictatorship Now". Michael Uche Thomas died in prison in July due to illness and reported lack of medical care. In September, Dr Janneh was granted presidential pardon and expelled from the country. A month later, Modou Keita was also released. Ebrima Jallow remained in prison.

■ In September, two journalists, Baboucarr Ceesay and Abubacarr Saidykhan, were arbitrarily arrested after applying to the police for a permit to demonstrate peacefully against the August executions of nine death row inmates. Both men were arbitrarily detained,

G

charged with sedition and released on bail. In October, the charges were dropped on the orders of the President. A few days later the journalists received death threats, which the police said they would investigate, but no progress had been made by the end of the year.

Freedom of expression

In January, an independent radio station, Teranga FM, was closed down without explanation. In August, a few months after its reopening, Teranga FM was ordered to shut down again by NIA officers. The station had previously been briefly closed in 2011.

In September, plain-clothed men, suspected to be NIA officers, entered the offices of *The Standard* and *Daily News* newspapers and ordered them to suspend their activities. No court order or document was issued and the editors were not given any explanation. The papers remained closed at the end of the year.

The same month a BBC journalist, a French national, was held for more than five hours at Banjul airport. He was told to leave the country within 48 hours without any explanation and despite the fact that he had obtained previous authorization to report from the Gambia. He had come to report on the August executions.

Enforced disappearances

In May the Inspector General of Police stated that, according to information received by Interpol, Ebrima Manneh, a journalist who disappeared while in police custody in 2006, had been seen in the USA. This information was not confirmed by Interpol and Ebrima Manneh remained listed as a missing person on Interpol's website. The reported sighting was strongly denied by his family.

■ On 3 December, two NIA officers arrested Imam Baba Leigh, a prominent Muslim cleric and human rights activist. Imam Leigh publicly condemned the execution of nine inmates at Mile II prison in August when he called the executions "un-Islamic" and urged the government to return the bodies to the families for proper burial. Subsequently, Imam Leigh was not brought before a court, his detention was not acknowledged by the NIA, and his family and lawyer remained unaware of his fate and whereabouts. As such, he was subjected to enforced disappearance and was at risk of torture and other ill-treatment. At the end

of the year, Amnesty International believed he was held by state agents and considered him a prisoner of conscience.

Prison conditions

Poor sanitation, illness, lack of medical care, overcrowding, extreme heat and malnutrition plagued Gambia's prisons. External monitors were not allowed access. Lack of equipment such as fire extinguishers put prisoners' safety at risk.

Prisoners on death row were not allowed visits by family or friends. Food in prisons was of poor quality but only remand prisoners were allowed food from outside. Rehabilitation programmes were non-existent.

In October, it was reported that four inmates had died from illness, including two death row prisoners, Abba Hydara and Guinea-Bissau national Sulayman Ceesay; further information was not available. According to sources, inmate Amadou Faal, known as Njagga, was severely beaten in October by a prison officer. He suffered the loss of his eye but was denied medical care for several days. The prison officer was not disciplined or charged.

Amnesty International visits/reports

⊟ The Gambia must release four activists jailed for distributing anti-government T-shirts (AFR 27/001/2012)

⊟ Gambia: Statement for 52nd Ordinary Session of the African Commission on Human and Peoples' Rights (AFR 27/011/2012)

⊟ Gambia: Two Gambian journalists receive death threats (AFR 27/012/2012)

⊟ Gambia: Government must stop intimidation and harassment of human rights defenders, journalists, lawyers and government critics (AFR 27/015/2012)

GEORGIA

GEORGIA
Head of state: **Mikheil Saakashvili**
Head of government: **Bidzina Ivanishvili (replaced Vano Merabishvili in October, who replaced Nikoloz Gilauri in July)**

Parliamentary elections in October marked the first peaceful democratic transfer of power in Georgia's post-Soviet period. However, there were numerous violations of the right to freedom of expression before and after the election.

Background

In October, the Georgian Dream coalition, united around billionaire Bidzina Ivanishvili, won the general election, ending nine years of dominance by President Saakashvili's United National Movement (UNM). The months leading up to the elections were accompanied by reports of harassment of Georgian Dream activists and supporters. Following the election, scores of high-ranking officials and UNM party members were questioned and arrested. They included a former Minister of Defence and of the Interior, the Chief of the General Staff and the Vice-Mayor of Tbilisi, on charges such as possession of illegal drugs and weapons, abuse of office, illegal detention and torture. The arrests prompted international criticism and requests to the new government to avoid the selective targeting of political rivals.

Freedom of association

In the run-up to the elections, there were reports of harassment, intimidation, obstruction and unfair punishment of opposition members and supporters. Fines against Georgian Dream coalition supporters, organizations and individuals associated with them were often imposed unfairly. Attacks on opposition supporters were reported. They ranged from threats to physical beatings and violent assaults against opposition supporters and increased each month as the election approached.

Scores of public and private sector employees were dismissed allegedly for supporting or being related to the leaders of the opposition parties. Schoolteachers in the regions appear to have been specifically targeted. In most cases the dismissals were decided after the individuals or their relatives made declarations about their political affiliations.

■ On 7 March, four teachers – Venera Ivanishvili, Nana Ivanishvili, Marina Nadiradze and Lela Khurtsilava – were dismissed from a secondary school in Samtredia in the Imereti region. Their contracts were terminated but no grounds were given for the dismissals. The teachers believed they were dismissed for signing a petition for the restoration of Bidzina Ivanishvili and his wife's citizenship in February.

■ In March, a large number of opposition party members and presumed sympathizers were summoned for questioning by the State Audit Agency empowered to investigate political party funding. The widespread summoning and questioning lasted several weeks; it was often carried out in an intimidating fashion and in violation of due process. Approximately 370 citizens were summoned and 295 people questioned in different, mainly rural, parts of Georgia.

■ Mamuka Kardava, the leader of the Khobi Branch of the Georgian Dream coalition, was attacked and beaten by four unidentified men on 20 May. Despite evidence that the marks on his back were likely to have been caused by a beating, the initial investigation was opened against Mamuka Kardava himself for violations of traffic safety rules. On 29 May, a formal investigation into allegations of assault was opened, but by the end of the year no progress was reported.

■ On 27 June, Ioseb Elkanashvili, a member of the Georgian Dream coalition in Gori, was attacked and beaten by five unidentified men, one of whom allegedly wore a police uniform. The case remained under investigation at the end of the year.

Freedom of expression – journalists

Journalists from pro-opposition media outlets were attacked on several occasions while covering campaign meetings and events. Pro-government journalists also reported attacks and verbal abuse. Investigations were initiated and several individuals, including a local government representative, were charged with administrative offences.

■ In Mereti in the Shida Qartli region, on 26 June journalists from Info 9, Channel 9 and Trialeti reported being physically and verbally assaulted when covering a meeting of the opposition with residents.

■ On 12 July, 10 reporters were injured and hospitalized following a clash between opposition

G

leaders and pro-government supporters in Karaleti village in the Shida Qartli region. The injured journalists were from national as well as local news agencies such as Trialeti, and Shida Qartli Information Centre. Saba Tsitsikashvili, one of the injured journalists, said that he recognized staff from the local municipal authority among his attackers.

Freedom of assembly

Freedom of assembly remained largely unrestricted, with representatives from both the UNM and the Georgian Dream coalition holding large-scale peaceful rallies in the capital Tbilisi as well as in the regions before the elections. However, a handful of incidents of violence and disruption were reported at smaller meetings, mostly in the regions.

■ In May, city authorities in Kutaisi used water cannon to prevent opposition activists from holding a peaceful candle vigil to mark the city day celebration.

■ On 26 June, a fistfight broke out before a meeting of the Georgian Dream coalition with local people in Mereti, preventing it from starting. As a result of the fight, several people, including a number of journalists, sustained injuries and two coalition supporters were taken to hospital for treatment. A video of the event allegedly showed several public employees involved in the incident.

Discrimination

Members of the majority Orthodox Christian religion clashed with minority religious groups in rural villages. Police intervened, and Muslim worshippers were able to conduct their prayers. However, the authorities failed to condemn the religious violence in unequivocal terms.

■ On 26 October, the majority Christian population of Nigvziani village, in the Lanchxuti region, threatened the Muslim population with expulsion and physical violence, demanding that they stop religious gatherings and group prayers.

■ On 30 November, in the village of Tsintskaro, in the Qvemo Qartli region, the majority Christian population threatened and verbally abused Muslim religious followers, demanding that they stop their group prayers and the construction of a mosque.

Lesbian, gay, bisexual, transgender and intersex people

In Tbilisi, Orthodox Christians attacked LGBTI individuals.

■ On 3 May, a peaceful march in central Tbilisi marking the International Day against Homophobia and Transphobia came under attack when a group of Orthodox Christians and members of the "Orthodox Parents' Union" began insulting and threatening protesters from IDENTOBA, a Georgian LGBTI rights organization. Police intervened after a scuffle broke out between the two groups. Five people were detained and were released shortly afterwards.

Amnesty International visits/reports

🚗 Amnesty International delegates visited Georgia in June, September and November.

📖 Georgia: A lot to contest – Rights abuses in the run-up to Georgia's 2012 Parliamentary Election (EUR 56/005/2012)

GERMANY

FEDERAL REPUBLIC OF GERMANY
Head of state: Joachim Gauck (replaced Christian Wulff in March)
Head of government: Angela Merkel

The authorities failed to establish an independent police complaints body and ensure that all police officers on duty wore identity badges. The National Agency for the Prevention of Torture remained severely under-resourced. The authorities continued to return Roma, Ashkali and Egyptians to Kosovo, and to return asylum-seekers to Hungary despite risks of human rights violations there. The authorities refused to rule out seeking diplomatic assurances to facilitate the return of individuals to countries where they were at risk of torture or other ill-treatment.

Torture and other ill-treatment

The authorities continued to fail to address obstacles preventing effective investigation of allegations of ill-treatment by police. No federal state established an independent police complaints body to investigate allegations of serious human rights violations by police. Except for the federal states of Berlin and Brandenburg, police officers remained under no legal obligation to wear identity badges. Police officers in

Brandenburg were due to start wearing identification badges in January 2013.

The National Agency for the Prevention of Torture, Germany's national preventive mechanism under the Optional Protocol to the UN Convention against Torture, remained severely under-resourced and unable to fulfil its functions, including regular visits to detention sites. Its chairperson and another member resigned in August over the lack of resources.

■ Investigations continued into excessive use of force by police during a demonstration in Stuttgart in September 2010. In October, the Stuttgart local court found one police officer guilty of physical assault, for hitting a protester with a baton, and issued him with an eight-month suspended prison sentence.

■ On 10 October, the Frankfurt Higher Regional Court confirmed the Frankfurt Regional Court judgement of 4 August 2011, which had awarded moral damages worth €3,000 to Markus Gäfgen. He was threatened by two police officers with intolerable pain in 2002 as he was apprehended on suspicion of kidnapping an 11-year-old boy. The first instance court had qualified the threat as "inhuman treatment" under the European Convention on Human Rights.

■ On 13 December, Magdeburg regional court convicted a police officer of negligent homicide for the death of asylum-seeker Oury Jalloh, who burned to death in a cell in Dessau police station in 2005. Despite lengthy legal proceedings, the circumstances of Oury Jalloh's death and the degree of police involvement in it were still not clarified.

Refugees and asylum-seekers

In September and October, 195 refugees from Shousha, Tunisia, and 105 Iraqi refugees who lived in Turkey, arrived on the basis of a new resettlement programme established in December 2011. They were meant to remain in Germany permanently but were not granted the same legal status as refugees under the UN Refugee Convention and were excluded from certain rights, especially relating to family reunification.

On 14 December, the Federal Ministry of Interior prolonged the suspension of asylum-seeker transfers to Greece under the Dublin Regulation (see Greece entry) until 12 January 2014.

Asylum-seekers were transferred to Hungary despite the risks they faced there (see Hungary entry). These included a risk of removal to unsafe third countries due to inadequate procedures in accessing international protection. Asylum-seekers returned from Germany to Hungary after having transited through Serbia were at the risk of *refoulement* until November, when Hungary stopped considering Serbia as a "safe third country". Serbia had not granted refugee status to anyone in the last five years.

Several federal states continued to forcibly return Roma, Ashkali and Egyptians to Kosovo despite cumulative forms of discrimination they faced on return. In April, Baden-Württemberg issued a decree requiring individual risk assessments before forcibly returning Roma, Ashkali and Egyptians to Kosovo.

On 18 July, the Federal Constitutional Court ruled that benefits available to asylum-seekers were insufficient to enable them to live in dignity and that this constituted a breach of the right to a dignified minimum existence, as enshrined in Article 1 of the German Constitution. The Court ordered the legislature to immediately enact new provisions as part of the Asylum Seekers Benefits Act.

Counter-terror and security

In September, the EU Parliament called on Germany and other EU member states to disclose all necessary information on all suspect planes associated with the CIA's rendition and secret detention programmes, and to effectively investigate the roles of those states in the CIA operations.

The government again failed to disclose whether it was still requesting "diplomatic assurances" to return individuals suspected of involvement in terrorism-related activities to states where they would face a real risk of torture or other ill-treatment. Regulatory rules governing the Residence Act continued to allow the use of "diplomatic assurances".

International justice

The first trial based on the German Code of Crimes under International Law of June 2002 against Rwandan citizens Ignace Murwanashyaka and Straton Musoni continued at Stuttgart Higher Regional Court. The accused were indicted on 26 charges of crimes against humanity and 39 war crimes charges for crimes committed in the Democratic Republic of the Congo between January 2008 and November 2009.

Germany did not codify enforced disappearance as a criminal offence, as required by the International Convention against enforced disappearance.

G

Discrimination

On 29 October, the Higher Administrative Court of Rheinland-Pfalz ruled that federal police officers had violated the constitutional principle of non-discrimination by subjecting a person to an identity check solely on base of his skin colour.

Amnesty International visits/reports

📰 Germany: Legal provisions and political practices put persons at risk of human rights violations (EUR 23/002/2012)

📰 Submission to the European Commission against Racism and Intolerance on Germany (EUR 23/003/2012)

GHANA

REPUBLIC OF GHANA
Head of state and government: **John Dramani Mahama**
                              (replaced John Evans Atta Mills in December)

Over 1,000 people were forcibly evicted from their homes in the capital, Accra. Thousands more remained at risk of forced eviction. Violence continued against people suspected of same-sex relationships, who still had little or no legal protection. There were no executions. The death penalty was still on the statute books, despite the government having accepted recommendations to abolish it. The criminal justice system remained slow.

Background

President John Atta Mills died in July. His deputy, John Dramani Mahama, was immediately sworn in as President. General elections were held in December 2012 and John Dramani Mahama was declared the winner. In June, the government published its White Paper in response to the Constitutional Review Commission's (CRC) final report. The government did not publish the final report itself. By the end of the year, the Freedom of Information bill had not become law.

Justice system

Court procedures were long and slow. Access to legal aid was limited or non-existent and some prisoners spent years waiting to be tried. Prisons were overcrowded and failed to provide inmates with basic services, including medical care. In March, 200 prisoners were transferred to the maximum security Ankaful prison in an attempt to address overcrowding.

Death penalty

Twenty-seven men were sentenced to death. At the year's end, 166 people were on death row, including four women. No executions were carried out. In June, the government accepted the CRC's recommendation to abolish the death penalty. However, the death penalty remained on the statute books at the end of 2012.

Housing rights

In January 2012, the Accra Metropolitan Authority demolished around 500 houses and structures along Accra's railway line. One estimate suggested that over 1,500 people were left homeless. They were only given three days' notice to leave their communities, and were offered no compensation or alternative accommodation. Thousands more continued to be at risk of forced eviction.

Violence against women and girls

Violence against women and girls remained rife, with nearly 10,000 cases reported to the Ghana police Domestic Violence Support Unit in 2012. Violence against women was thought to be under-reported, and not adequately addressed by the authorities.

Rights of lesbian, gay, bisexual, transgender and intersex people

Sexual activity between consenting adults of the same sex remained a crime under Ghana's Criminal Code. Violence against people suspected of same-sex relationships continued. In March 2012, young people in Accra's James Town community disrupted a planned wedding ceremony between two women, and assaulted them and their guests. The women were later arrested and detained at the James Town Police station for "engaging in illegal practice". They were released after their relatives intervened.

The CRC's final report recommended that the country's Supreme Court should rule on whether Ghana should legalise same-sex acts. The government "took note" of the recommendation.

Refugees and asylum-seekers

In June, the Ghana Refugee Board announced plans to close the Buduburam refugee camp in Accra. It said an estimated 11,000 Liberian and Sierra Leonean refugees were being registered for repatriation to their respective countries.

Amnesty International visits/reports

Amnesty International visited Ghana in April.

'Prisoners are bottom of the pile': The human rights of inmates in Ghana (AFR 28/002/2012)

Ghana: Human rights shortcomings in law and in practice – Submission to the UN Universal Periodic Review (AFR 28/003/2012)

GREECE

HELLENIC REPUBLIC
Head of state: Karolos Papoulias
Head of government: Antonis Samaras (replaced Panagiotis Pikrammenos in June, who replaced Loukas Papademos in May)

Allegations of human rights abuses by police, including torture and excessive use of force continued throughout the year. Migrants and asylum-seekers faced impediments in registering their asylum applications and were often detained in substandard conditions. Hate crime on the basis of race and ethnicity escalated dramatically.

Background

The economy was in crisis, and unemployment reached 26.8% in October. Further austerity measures were voted by Parliament in February and November, amid protests in Athens and other cities. In May, the European Committee on Social Rights found that austerity legislation relating to public sector workers violated various provisions of the European Social Charter.

Golden Dawn, a far right-wing party with an aggressive anti-migrant rhetoric, won 18 seats in the June parliamentary elections.

Excessive use of force

Allegations of the police using excessive force during demonstrations persisted.

■ In April, several journalists and photographers were attacked by riot police during protests held in Athens in memory of a 77-year-old retired pharmacist, who committed suicide. Marios Lolos, a photojournalist, suffered a serious skull fracture when a riot police officer beat him on the back of his head with a baton. No individual was arrested or charged for the attack.
■ On 5 August, riot police made excessive use of chemical irritants and reportedly fired rubber bullets and other impact rounds directly at peaceful protesters opposing gold mining operations in the Halkidiki region.

Torture and other ill-treatment

Allegations of torture and other ill-treatment against individuals including members of vulnerable groups such as migrants and asylum-seekers held in immigration detention persisted. Systemic problems leading to impunity remained, including the authorities' frequent failure to conduct prompt, thorough and impartial investigations and to ensure the right to effective remedy. In January, the European Court of Human Rights held that the rape with a truncheon of an irregular migrant by a coastguard in May 2001 amounted to torture (*Zontul v. Greece*). In August, the UN Human Rights Committee found that Greece failed to investigate the complaint of ill-treatment and discrimination by the police of a Greek Romani man in 1999 (*Katsaris v. Greece*).
■ In March, a Mixed Jury Appeal Court in Athens acquitted two police officers of causing bodily harm under the provision against torture in the Criminal Code to two refugees at the Aghios Panteleimon police station, Athens, in December 2004. The officers had been found guilty at first instance.
■ In October, serious allegations of torture of 15 anti-fascist protesters by police at the General Police Directorate in Athens on 30 September came to light. Supporters of the protesters, arrested on 1 October, also alleged that they were subjected to treatment amounting to torture at the Directorate. The authorities denied the allegations, but an investigating judge requested that the Public Prosecutor bring criminal charges against the police officers involved in the human rights violations of the protesters.

Refugees, asylum-seekers and migrants

Despite reported improvements at the appeal level of asylum determination procedures, Greece made little progress towards establishing a fair and effective

G

system. At the end of the year, the new Asylum Service had not yet started to process asylum applications, due to serious recruitment problems. The impediments faced by asylum-seekers when attempting to register applications persisted. For example, at the Attika Aliens' Police Directorate in Athens, only around 20 applications were registered by the authorities each week.

Individuals trying to enter Greece from Turkey across the River Evros reported that they had been pushed back to Turkey by the Greek authorities. A 10.5km fence along the land border with Turkey in the Evros region was completed in December. Concern remained that the fence would prevent people seeking international protection from reaching safety, and that it would lead them to attempt unsafe crossings.

Asylum-seekers and irregular migrants, including unaccompanied children, were routinely detained and for long periods. In April, a new legislative provision was introduced allowing for the detention of irregular migrants and asylum-seekers on grounds such as suspicion of carrying infectious diseases such as HIV. The police crackdown on migrants that started in August raised concerns about discrimination against people because of their perceived ethnicity and that it would fuel xenophobia.

In October, an amendment to the legislation on asylum determination procedures allowed for police to extend the maximum three- or six-month period that an asylum-seeker can be held by a further 12 months. Substandard detention conditions in various immigration detention centres and police stations where asylum-seekers and irregular migrants were held continued. Conditions at the Elliniko detention facilities in Athens were inhuman and degrading. Between August and the end of the year, many asylum-seekers and irregular migrants, including many Syrian nationals fleeing the conflict there, were reported to be held in very poor conditions in police stations or were left without shelter.

Discrimination
Hate crime
The number of racially motivated attacks escalated dramatically during the year. In October, the Racist Violence Recording Network reported that more than half of the 87 recorded incidents were connected with extremist right-wing groups that had acted in an organized and planned manner. A presidential decree providing for specialized police units in Athens and Thessaloniki to investigate racially motivated crime was signed in December. However, the decree fell short of providing protection for victims with no papers from arrest and deportation for the duration of criminal proceedings.

■ In August, a series of violent attacks was reported against migrants and asylum-seekers and unofficial places of worship in Athens and other cities. On 13 August, an Iraqi national was fatally stabbed. A criminal investigation was ordered but no perpetrator was identified.

■ On 24 September, an Athens court postponed the trial for the seventh time of three Greek nationals including a parliamentary candidate of Golden Dawn. They were accused of beating three Afghani asylum-seekers and stabbing one of them in 2011. It was one of the very few cases of racially motivated violence brought to trial.

■ In October, Parliament lifted the immunity of two Golden Dawn MPs linked with two attacks against market stalls belonging to migrants in the cities of Rafina and Messolongi on 9 September. In November, charges were brought against the MP linked with the incident in Messolongi.

■ On 3 November, migrants and asylum-seekers and their shops and houses in the neighbourhood of Aghios Panteleimon, Athens, were attacked, reportedly by extreme right-wing groups.

People with HIV
In May, the authorities arrested and reportedly forcibly tested for HIV over 100 alleged sex-workers. Serious concerns were expressed over the stigmatization of 29 of the arrested after their personal details including their HIV status and photographs were published by police and charges were brought against them for intentionally causing serious bodily harm. At the end of the year, 12 of them remained in prison, awaiting trial.

Roma
According to the NGO Greek Helsinki Monitor, Romani children continued to be segregated or excluded from education while Romani families were evicted or threatened with eviction from their settlements without alternative and adequate accommodation being provided.

■ In December, the European Court of Human Rights found that the Greek authorities' failure to integrate Romani children in Aspropyrgos into ordinary education amounted to discrimination (*Sampani and others v. Greece*). This was the second time that Greece was found to have violated the European Convention on Human Rights by segregating Romani children in primary education in Aspropyrgos.

Lesbian, gay, bisexual, transgender and intersex people

In November, LGBTI activists reported that incidents of homophobic violence had escalated in Athens. Victims reported that their attackers were members of extreme right-wing groups allegedly including individuals belonging to the Golden Dawn party.

Conscientious objectors

Repeated prosecutions of conscientious objectors continued.

■ In February, the Athens Military Court convicted 49-year-old Avraam Pouliasis, one of the first conscientious objectors in Greece, to six months' imprisonment, suspended for three years. Avraam Pouliasis was no longer obliged under the law to serve his military service as he was over 45.

Prison conditions

During the year, the European Court of Human Rights found Greece in breach of the European Convention on Human Rights in three cases, due to poor detention conditions in the prisons of Ioannina, Korydallos and at the detention facility of Thessaloniki Police Headquarters.

Freedom of expression

Freedom of expression was threatened on several occasions.

■ In November, Kostas Vaxevanis, a journalist and magazine editor, was put on trial in Athens for breach of privacy, after he published the names of 2,000 Greeks alleged to have private bank accounts in Switzerland and called for investigations into possible tax evasion. He was acquitted after a day's hearing. The Prosecutor's Office of the Athens First Instance Courts appealed, and Kostas Vaxevanis was referred for trial before the Athens Misdemeanours Court.

■ In October, members of extreme Christian groups and the far-right party Golden Dawn, including some MPs, tried to prevent the premiere of the play *Corpus Christi*, by verbally abusing and threatening the actors and members of the audience. In November, the people who had staged the play were charged with blasphemy.

Amnesty International visits/reports

🚍 Amnesty International delegates visited the country in January, July and October.

📄 Police violence in Greece: Not just 'isolated incidents' (EUR 25/005/2012)

📄 Greece: The end of the road for refugees, asylum-seekers and migrants (EUR 25/011/2012)

GUATEMALA

REPUBLIC OF GUATEMALA
Head of state and government: **Otto Pérez Molina (replaced Álvaro Colom in January)**

Large-scale mining and hydroelectric projects continued to be imposed on rural communities without prior consultation and regardless of the risks to human rights. Some cases of human rights violations committed during the internal armed conflict (1960-1996) progressed, but the army refused to co-operate in any meaningful way with such efforts. Human rights defenders were attacked and threatened because of their work.

Background

The public security situation remained a concern. Rival drug-trafficking organizations and street gangs contributed to high levels of violent crime; 4,614 men and 560 women were killed during the year.

In April, Guatemala became a state party to the Rome Statute of the International Criminal Court. Also in April, the UN Human Rights Committee urged the government not to undermine efforts to prosecute those responsible for crimes against humanity committed during the 1960-1996 internal armed conflict after President Molina denied that genocide had ever occurred during the conflict.

In October, the UN Human Rights Council urged Guatemala to abolish the death penalty, increase promotion of women's rights, improve prison conditions, protect human rights defenders and guarantee effective consultation of Indigenous Peoples in relation to development proposals in their territory.

G

Corporate accountability

The lack of consultation prior to the installation of mining, hydroelectric and other projects in rural areas led to increased tension. Despite repeated calls for Guatemala to observe its international obligations, the authorities failed to ensure meaningful consultation with affected communities, while international companies failed to observe international standards on business and human rights.

■ In May, one person was killed and another injured in Santa Cruz Barillas, Huehuetenango Department, allegedly by security guards working for the hydroelectric company Hidro Santa Cruz, a subsidiary of Spanish company Hidralia Energía. The killing led to protests and further clashes, including the occupation of the local army base and the imposition of martial law. The community argued they had not been consulted prior to the installation of the hydroelectric project.

■ Local activists in Santa Rosa Department opposed to the activities of silver mining company Minera San Rafael, a subsidiary of Canadian company Tahoe Resources Inc, were the subject of spurious criminal complaints that appeared to be aimed at curtailing their activism. In October, the municipal council of San Rafael las Flores announced that due to legal challenges and irregularities in the process it would not hold a Municipal Consultation of Residents in relation to the mine's activities.

Impunity

Some former junior officers and soldiers were convicted for their involvement in the 1982 massacres in Plan de Sánchez and Dos Erres in which more than 500 people were killed in total. However, the army failed to provide any meaningful information for ongoing investigations and efforts to locate victims of enforced disappearance. In May the government closed down the Peace Archives, where some documents relating to the conflict had been previously deposited.

The former head of state, retired General Efraín Ríos Montt, appeared in court in January charged with genocide and crimes against humanity. He was accused of bearing command responsibility for hundreds of massacres and a "scorched earth" policy targeting Indigenous Peoples while he was the de facto head of state (March 1982-August 1983). Proceedings were continuing at the end of the year.

In October the Inter-American Court of Human Rights held the state responsible for a series of massacres in Río Negro, Baja Verapaz department, between March 1980 and May 1982.

Indigenous Peoples' rights

Discrimination against Indigenous Peoples meant they were disproportionately represented among those living in poverty.

Indigenous Peoples' organizations organized protests to demand consultation prior to the installation of mining and hydroelectric projects in rural communities.

Eight protesters from the Maya K'che' Indigenous community were killed during a protest against rising electricity costs and proposed constitutional amendments in October in the town of Totonicapán, Totonicapán Department. One army officer and eight soldiers were charged in connection with their deaths.

Human rights defenders

At least 305 attacks against human rights defenders were reported during 2012. In March, the UN High Commissioner for Human Rights called on the government to adopt and implement effective protection measures for human rights defenders.

■ In June, anti-mining activist Yolanda Oquelí was seriously wounded on her way home from a protest against the presence of the El Tambor gold mine in the municipalities of San José del Golfo and San Pedro Ayampuc.

■ Luis Ovidio Ortíz Cajas, leader of the National Trade Union of Health Workers and a campaigner against corruption in the health service, was shot dead in March. No one had been brought to justice for the killing by the end of the year.

Death penalty

One prisoner remained on death row. No new death sentences were handed down during the year. There were no executions.

GUINEA

REPUBLIC OF GUINEA
Head of state: **Alpha Condé**
Head of government: **Mohamed Saïd Fofana**

Legislative elections due to be held in 2012 were postponed until 2013. Human rights violations committed by the security forces included excessive use of force and extrajudicial killings, as well as torture and other ill-treatment. Freedom of assembly and expression remained tightly restricted. An independent journalist was subjected to intimidation and beatings.

Background

The National Transitional Council (Conseil national de la transition, CNT), created by the Ouagadougou agreements of January 2010, had still not transferred power to an elected National Assembly by the end of the year. In April, President Condé postponed legislative elections, scheduled for July, citing the need to ensure that they were transparent and democratic. The opposition questioned the impartiality and transparency of the National Independent Electoral Commission (Commission électorale nationale indépendante, CENI). In October, the CENI was reshuffled; elections were set for July 2013.

Excessive use of force and extrajudicial executions

Protest marches organized by the opposition including the Union of Guinean Democratic Forces (Union des forces démocratiques de Guinée, UFDG) were repressed by security forces throughout the year. At least eight people were killed by security forces.

In May, protests organized by the UFDG demanding free and transparent legislative elections continued in Conakry. Several people were injured, including one man who was reportedly shot in the back by security forces.

In early August the premises of a Brazilian mining company were vandalized following a strike by workers living in the neighbourhood, including the village of Zogota, 900 km from Conakry. Later the same day, security forces went to Zogota and shot dead at least five people. Others were arrested and were beaten and tortured.

In September, following unrest in the Koloma neighbourhood of Conakry, security forces opened fire in disproportionate retaliation. Mamadou Alpha Barry was shot dead and more than 40 people were injured.

Trials – attack on presidential residence

The trial began in February of 48 people suspected of attacking President Condé's residence in July 2011. In March, 17 people were cleared of all charges and were released. In July, the public prosecutor appealed against the decision of the Conakry court. In November, the Conakry Court of Appeal reversed the decision to drop charges against 15 of the defendants and sent them before a military court and the court of assizes. Some prisoners were tortured and otherwise ill-treated at the time of their arrest.

Torture and other ill-treatment

Allegations of torture and other ill-treatment by security forces continued.

■ In February, three men suspected of armed robbery were arrested and tortured at the police station in Bambeto, Conakry. One was tortured with electricity, and another was beaten for four hours with his hands tied behind his back, a method known as the "chinoise". After refusing to confess, he was stripped naked and kicked as well as beaten with rifle-butts in front of his family. Both were sent to the Escadron Mobile No 2 in Hamdallaye where they were burned with cigarettes and held in the "brochette" position (handcuffed and suspended in a squatting position, with a piece of wood placed between the knees). The third arrested man was considered missing for a week before his body was found in the mortuary of Donka Hospital. He had died reportedly as a result of torture.

Freedom of expression – journalists

Restrictions of freedom of expression and of the press, as well as the targeting of certain journalists, remained causes for concern.

In February, Kounkou Mara, a journalist for the private Guinean press group Lynx-La Lance, was beaten by gendarmes while on her way to an event organized by the Central Bank of the Republic of Guinea in Conakry (BCRG). She was briefly hospitalized. The heads of the Lynx-La Lance press group did not press charges for fear of reprisals. None of the gendarmes had been brought to justice by the end of the year.

In August, the authorities in the southeastern N'Zerekore region closed the private radio station Liberté FM, reportedly to prevent it from reporting on protests planned for the next day.

Impunity

The inquiry into the massacre in the Grand Stade de Conakry in 28 September 2009, begun in February 2010, made some progress.

In February and again in September, several people, including officials, were charged in Conakry for human rights violations and for their suspected role in the massacre. Among these were Colonel Moussa Tiegboro Camara, who continued to hold a government position, and Colonel Abdoulaye Chérif Diaby, Health Minister in 2009.

In April and May, four people filed two separate complaints before a court in Conakry regarding torture that took place in 2011 and 2012. These concerned two instances in which gendarmes used torture to exhort confessions during a robbery investigation. Seven gendarmes were implicated and had not been brought to trial by the end of the year. One of the victims died from the injuries and another was seriously injured.

Death penalty

At least two people were sentenced to death.

GUINEA-BISSAU

REPUBLIC OF GUINEA-BISSAU
Head of state: **Manuel Serifo Nhamadjo (replaced Raimundo Pereira in May, who replaced Malam Bacai Sanhá in January)**
Head of government: **Rui Duarte de Barros (replaced Carlos Gomes Júnior in May)**

The political situation deteriorated sharply following the death in January of President Malam Bacai Sanhá, culminating in a coup in April. It deteriorated further following a reported attack on a military barracks in October, which exacerbated the already fragile human rights and humanitarian situation. The armed forces committed numerous human rights violations with impunity, including arbitrary arrest and detention, beatings and extrajudicial executions. Freedoms of assembly, expression and the press were severely curbed. The killings of political and security figures since 2009 remained unpunished.

Background

In January, President Malam Bacai Sanhá died after a long illness. Presidential elections held in March were won by former Prime Minister Carlos Gomes Júnior. As he fell just short of an outright majority, a second round was scheduled for late April. Ten days before the second round of the elections, the military staged a coup, took control of the capital, Bissau, and arrested the former Prime Minister and Interim President. Both were released from military custody two weeks later and sent into exile.

Repressive measures were imposed to stifle criticism of the self-styled Military Command that had taken control. All demonstrations were banned and soldiers used force to disperse peaceful spontaneous demonstrations. The military claimed their action was prompted by the presence of Angolan troops in the country under a bilateral agreement to assist with the training and reform of the security sector. In early May the Military Command and its civilian allies reached an agreement with ECOWAS for a one-year transition and the deployment of ECOWAS troops to Bissau. Two weeks later, a transitional President and government were appointed, which was not recognized by the international community.

In October the authorities claimed that a group of soldiers and civilians had launched an attack on a military base in the outskirts of Bissau and that six attackers were killed. They accused the former Prime Minister of involvement. Military personnel committed serious human rights violations in the search for the alleged perpetrators of the attack.

Freedom of expression – journalists

Private radio stations were shut down at the time of the military coup and remained off the air for two days. They were allowed to resume broadcasting under severe censorship and at least one radio station decided to remain closed. Journalists were also impeded from carrying out their work and were harassed or arrested. The correspondent of Portugal's state broadcaster, Radio Televisão Portuguesa, was expelled in October for his critical reporting of the government and military authorities.

Unlawful killings and extrajudicial executions

There were reports suggesting that the six people allegedly killed during the attack on the military base in October, four civilians and two military officers, had been extrajudicially executed. Soldiers also reportedly extrajudicially executed five people in Bolama, Bijagos Islands, whom they accused of being accomplices of Pansau Ntchama, the alleged leader of the October attack. Others were unlawfully killed for their links with deposed government figures.

Luis Ocante da Silva, a close friend of the former Chief of Staff of the Armed Forces, José Zamora Induta, died as a result of beatings by soldiers. On 6 November he was taken from his home by a group of soldiers, beaten and taken to an undisclosed location. Two days later soldiers took his body to the morgue in the central hospital. His family were allowed to see only his face and were not allowed to take the body for burial.

No investigations were carried out into these killings or other human rights violations by the military. Impunity also persisted for political killings since 2009.

Torture and other ill-treatment

Following the coup in April, soldiers searching for deposed government officials beat their families, friends and employees and vandalized their homes. Most ministers went into hiding, where they remained for several months; a few fled the country. Members of civil society groups were also targeted. Some, including several members of the Human Rights League, received threats against their lives and took refuge in embassies.

The day after the October attack on the military base, soldiers arrested and beat Iancuba Indjai, president of the opposition Party of Solidarity and Labour and spokesperson of the Anti-Coup National Front, a grouping of political parties and civil society groups who opposed the April coup. Iancuba Indjai was abandoned by the roadside some 50 km from Bissau. Local residents found him seriously injured and alerted his family. He was subsequently taken to a hospital abroad.

Later the same day, soldiers went to the Bissau office of Silvestre Alves, a lawyer and president of the Democratic Movement party; they beat him and took him away. He was later found unconscious by a road 40km from the city by local people who took him to a hospital. He was taken abroad for medical treatment.

Amnesty International visits/reports

Guinea-Bissau: Amnesty International's concerns following the coup in April 2012 (AFR 30/001/2012)

GUYANA

REPUBLIC OF GUYANA
Head of state and government: **Donald Ramotar**

Alleged unlawful killings by police continued to be reported. At least five people were sentenced to death; no executions were carried out.

Background

Following commitments made during Guyana's Universal Periodic Review at the UN Human Rights Council in 2010, the government announced in August that it would launch public consultations on issues including the abolition of the death penalty and the decriminalization of consensual adult same-sex relations. Consultations on the death penalty and sexual orientation had not begun by the end of the year.

Police and security forces

On 18 July, three people were alleged to have been shot dead by riot police in the town of Linden during protests against rising electricity prices. A further 17 people required treatment for gunshot and pellet wounds. Protesters had reportedly hurled bottles and rocks at the security forces who had used tear gas against them. A five-person Commission of Inquiry into the incident was established and was due to issue its findings in February 2013.

On 11 September, 17-year-old Shaquille Grant was fatally shot and another man was injured by the police in the village of Agricola. Local residents refuted the official version that police were responding to reports of robbery and had been fired upon. Three police officers were charged with murder in October; one was awaiting trial at the end of the year while the other two remained at large.

Violence against women and girls

In July, the CEDAW Committee highlighted the high prevalence and under-reporting of violence against women. Among its recommendations were the full implementation of the Sexual Offences Act; mandatory training for judicial officials; strengthening the capacity of shelters and crisis centres; raising public awareness; improved collection of statistical data on domestic and sexual violence; and improved access to legal aid services.

In August, the High Court ruled that "paper committals" – hearings to decide whether there is enough evidence to send a case to trial – in cases of sexual offences were unconstitutional as the accused were given no opportunity to defend themselves at that stage. There were concerns that the ruling would have a negative impact on the already very low conviction rates for sexual offences.

Rights of lesbian, gay, bisexual, transgender and intersex people

A report issued in March by the University of the West Indies examined the social impact of laws affecting LGBTI people. The report found that the majority of those interviewed were reluctant to report crimes against them as they feared charges would be brought against them because of their sexual orientation.

Right to health – HIV/AIDS

In May the National AIDS Committee, an independent advocacy body, criticized the government's failure to decriminalize same-sex relations; the slow progress in reducing stigma against people living with HIV/AIDS; the failure to explore links between sexual violence and the spread of HIV among women and girls; and the lack of focus on Indigenous people as a group at particular risk.

Death penalty

At least five people were sentenced to death. Thirty people remained on death row at the end of the year. In June, four death-row inmates had their sentences commuted to life imprisonment on the grounds that the length of time they had spent under sentence of death – ranging from 16 to 24 years – constituted cruel and inhuman treatment.

HAITI

REPUBLIC OF HAITI
Head of state: Michel Joseph Martelly
Head of government: Laurent Lamothe
(replaced Garry Conille in May)

More than 320,000 people made homeless by the January 2010 earthquake remained displaced during 2012. Thousands of internally displaced people were forcibly evicted by local authorities and private landowners. Women reporting gender-based violence received little redress. No steps were taken to address impunity for past human rights abuses.

Background

Increasing political tensions between Parliament and the presidency led to the resignation in February of Prime Minister Garry Conille after four months in office. The President's choice of Prime Minister, Laurent Lamothe, took office in May. In the last quarter of the year, there were demonstrations in several parts of the country against the government's apparent failure to respond to socio-economic problems. Protesters demanded the resignation of President Martelly.

In August, President Martelly established the Permanent Electoral Council. Only six of the nine members were appointed as Parliament could not reach consensus on its three representatives. Three appointments by the High Council of the Judiciary were contested for failing to respect selection procedures and in October the High Council appointed three new representatives. The creation of a Permanent Electoral Council, a key institution in organizing local and general elections, had been pending since the adoption of the Constitution in 1987.

In October, the UN Security Council renewed the mandate of the UN Stabilization Mission in Haiti (MINUSTAH) for a ninth year and recommended the gradual reduction of its military and police component. There was growing public discontent with MINUSTAH, particularly because a UN Nepalese battalion was alleged to be responsible for the outbreak of cholera in Haiti and because MINUSTAH soldiers were alleged to be involved in a number of cases of sexual violence.

Tropical storms Isaac and Sandy, which lashed Haiti respectively in late August and late October, exacerbated the cholera outbreak, intensified food insecurity and increased the number of homeless families. The storms affected more than 15,000 households living in makeshift camps for internally displaced people.

The post-quake humanitarian situation in Haiti remained a source of concern in several areas as regards protection, shelter, health care, water and sanitation. The cholera outbreak, which killed around 900 people during the year, compounded the situation, while lack of funding hindered the humanitarian response. Post-quake recovery efforts continued at a slow pace due in part to political instability, weak public institutions and delays in the disbursement of funds pledged by the international community. As of September, only US$2.79 billion of the US$5.53 billion pledged had been disbursed.

A law ratifying the ICESCR was adopted in May. However, by the end of the year, the President had not promulgated the law.

Internally displaced people

More than 320,000 people made homeless by the January 2010 earthquake were still living in makeshift camps at the end of 2012. The government, assisted by the International Organization for Migration and its partners, continued implementing return and relocation programmes for internally displaced people living in those camps most at risk due to natural hazards. Throughout 2012, around 134,000 families were helped to move out of the camps by rent subsidies or offers of temporary shelter.

Living conditions in the camps remained dire. Sanitation in some camps improved, but there were concerns about water quality and its connection to an increase of reported cases of cholera during the rainy and hurricane season (April to November).

Housing rights – forced evictions

Forced evictions of internally displaced people continued in Port-au-Prince and other quake-affected areas. Thousands of people were made homeless again when their makeshift shelters were destroyed during forced evictions. These were carried out without due process, adequate notice or consultation. Those who lost their homes were not offered alternative housing. Coercion, harassment and violence accompanied the forced evictions.

Evictions contributed to the overall decrease in the number of people living in makeshift camps and to the closure of numerous camps. Between January and June, more than 30 camps were closed following forced evictions, affecting more than 2,140 people. More than 75,000 people were under constant threat of forced eviction.

■ In May, municipal officials accompanied by armed members of the municipal Street Control Brigade and national police forcibly evicted 131 families from Camp Mozayik in Port-au-Prince. Former camp residents said that officials demolished their houses and destroyed their belongings. None received alternative accommodation or adequate notice.

■ In July, the authorities tried to forcibly evict 142 families belonging to a community set up in the 1980s in Parc La Visite, a nature reserve in the South-East department. According to eyewitnesses, 30 police officers and 20 armed civilians arrived to carry out the eviction. Members of the community threw stones at the police when they started to destroy homes. Officers then opened fire, killing four men. The authorities denied any involvement and no investigation had been carried out into the shootings by the end of the year.

The government presented the first ever draft National Housing Policy in April. Among the concerns were the lack of a human rights perspective and the failure to address the issue of forced evictions.

Violence against women and girls

Women and girls continued to face gender-based violence. According to reports from women's rights organizations, women living in camps for internally displaced people remained at particular risk of gender-based violence and sexual exploitation. Driven by poverty, women and girls continued to be involved in transactional sex to ensure their livelihoods. Haiti's police and justice system made some progress in responding to gender-based violence, but offered women few opportunities for justice and reparation.

H

Impunity

Those responsible for serious human rights violations, including enforced disappearance, torture, rape and extrajudicial executions, over the past four decades continued to evade justice.

In January, an investigating judge dismissed complaints of crimes against humanity filed by 22 victims against former President Jean-Claude Duvalier. He concluded that Jean-Claude Duvalier should be tried only for corruption and misappropriation of public funds. In his report, and contrary to Haiti's obligations under international law, the judge stated that Haiti's courts were not competent to investigate and prosecute crimes against humanity. An appeal by victims and their relatives was pending at the end of the year.

Justice system

In July, the High Council of the Judiciary was finally established. However, its functioning was hampered by internal divisions which resulted in the temporary withdrawal of two members, including the representative for the human rights sector. The Council is a key institution for the reform and independence of the justice system. One of the main roles of the Council is to confirm the appointment of new judges. However, according to local human rights organizations, judges continued to be appointed without the agreement of the Council.

On 28 September, the Chief Prosecutor of Port-au-Prince, Jean Renel Sénatus, was dismissed. Interviewed on a local radio station, he said he was removed from office because he refused to implement a ministerial order to arrest 36 political opponents, including human rights lawyer Mario Joseph and anti-corruption lawyers Newton St-Juste and André Michel. In October, Lucman Delille became the eighth Chief Prosecutor of Port-au-Prince to be appointed since President Martelly took office.

The authorities failed to take effective steps to address the problem of prolonged pre-trial detention.

Amnesty International visits/reports

🚌 Amnesty International delegates visited Haiti in May and July 2012.

HONDURAS

REPUBLIC OF HONDURAS
Head of state and government: Porfirio Lobo Sosa

Human rights defenders continued to be threatened, attacked and killed. Prison conditions remained a concern following the deaths of 360 prisoners in a fire at Comayagua Prison. There were fears that legislation might be introduced criminalizing access to contraception. The independence of the judiciary came under the spotlight after the sacking of members of the Supreme Court.

Background

Levels of violent crime remained high and continued to dominate the political agenda. Attempts were made by the government to purge the police in response to allegations of abuses and corruption, such as police involvement and complicity in killings, such as those of two university students in 2011.

Human rights defenders

Human rights defenders continued to be subjected to intimidation, physical attack and were even killed because of their work.

Campesino community leaders and human rights defenders involved in representing *campesino* communities in the context of the continuing land disputes in Bajo Aguán were subjected to threats and attacks.

■ In September, human rights lawyer Antonio Trejo Cabrera died after being shot five times by gunmen in the capital, Tegucigalpa. Antonio Trejo had been representing three peasant co-operatives and had helped farmers to regain legal rights to land. He had been scheduled to travel to the USA to take part in hearings at the Inter-American Commission on Human Rights about the ongoing land dispute. He reported receiving death threats during the year. By the end of 2012 no one had been held to account for his killing.

The government failed to undertake effective measures to prevent and punish human rights violations against defenders. In February, the UN Special Rapporteur on the situation of human rights defenders expressed concern at the absence of a programme of specialized protection for human rights defenders. In November, the Vice-Minister of Justice and Human Rights announced the development of a draft bill that would establish protection measures for human rights defenders, media workers and those working in the justice system. The draft bill had not been finalized by the end of the year.

■ Bertha Oliva and Nohemí Pérez of the Committee of Relatives of the Detained and Disappeared in Honduras (Comité de Familiares de Detenidos Desaparecidos en Honduras, COFADEH) received verbal threats in March and April.

■ In February, Dina Meza, also a COFADEH worker, received text and telephone threats, including one which said, "We'll burn your pussy with lime until you scream and the whole squad will enjoy it... CAM". The name of the group (CAM, Comando Álvarez Martinez) refers to a general in the Honduran armed forces (1982-1984) who has been linked by human rights groups to paramilitary death squads at a time of grave human rights abuses.

Sexual and reproductive rights

In February, the Supreme Court of Justice ruled that it was constitutional to ban the emergency contraceptive pill, despite serious concerns that banning it would breach international and national legal obligations to protect the human rights of women and girls. Should the National Congress decide to enforce the Supreme Court ruling, Honduras would become the first country in the world to criminalize a contraceptive method.

Prison conditions

More than 360 prisoners were killed and scores seriously injured in a prison fire in Comayagua Prison. The authorities accepted responsibility for the deaths, and made commitments to carry out far-reaching reforms to the prison system and alleviate the dire conditions, as well as addressing the circumstances that led to the fire.

The establishment of the National Monitoring Mechanism for the Prevention of Torture, required under the Optional Protocol to the UN Convention against Torture, was a positive step. However, there were concerns that the necessary resources and personnel had not been put in place to ensure the Mechanism's effectiveness.

In December, the Law on the Prison System was passed. However, overcrowding and poor prison conditions persisted, putting those in detention at heightened risk of abuses.

Justice system

In December, the National Congress voted to remove four of the five Supreme Court judges who comprise the Constitutional Section of the Supreme Court. The judges had earlier set down a judgement that blocked a law proposed by Congress intended to facilitate a clean-up of the police force. The judges found some aspects of the law to be unconstitutional. The controversial dismissal of the judges was criticized by the Inter-American Commission on Human Rights, which urged the government to respect and guarantee the independence of the judiciary.

Amnesty International visits/reports

Honduras: Public letter to the Honduran government: No more killings, attacks or threats against journalists and human rights defenders (AMR 37/009/2012)

HUNGARY

HUNGARY
Head of state: János Áder (replaced Pál Schmitt in May)
Head of government: Viktor Orbán

A new Constitution entered into force with concerns over its possibly discriminatory impact. Roma were subjected to harassment and intimidation by far-right groups on numerous occasions. Despite amendments, legislation continued to impose political control on the media.

Background

In January, a new Constitution came into force. It had been criticized for its potential to restrict human rights, notably the right to be protected from discrimination and the right to an effective remedy.

In November, the Court of Justice of the European Union held that Hungary breached EU law by lowering the retirement age for judges and prosecutors.

Discrimination

The new Constitution restricted the legal definition of a family to a union between a man and woman, raising concerns over discrimination against same-sex couples. In December, the Constitutional Court annulled the provision.

In July, a new Criminal Code was adopted which extended the definition of hate-motivated assaults to those committed on the grounds of sexual orientation, gender identity and disability. NGOs welcomed the change, but expressed concerns over how the new provisions would be implemented without effective guidelines for police and prosecution services on the investigation of such crimes.

Roma

Despite some commitments from the government to prevent intimidation, Roma continued to be subjected to racist abuse and violent assaults. The trial of the suspects accused of attacks against Roma in 2008 and 2009 (during which six people, including a child, were killed) was delayed. One of the defence lawyers resigned in October after it was revealed that he was the son of one of the judges involved in the case.

■ In March, a parliamentary Committee reported on the "vigilante" activities in the village of Gyöngyöspata in March 2011. However, the report failed to refer to the slow and inadequate response of the authorities to the intimidation, harassment and threat of violence suffered by the Roma in Gyöngyöspata, when the village was "patrolled" by three vigilante groups for almost a month.

■ On 5 August, the far-right party Jobbik and a number of vigilante groups held a march in the village of Devecser. Pieces of concrete and other missiles were reportedly thrown at the houses of Roma. Police officers allegedly failed to intervene to stop the attacks. Following these events, the government made a commitment not to tolerate and to prevent any kind of intimidation of ethnic and other minorities.

■ Vigilante groups reportedly intimidated Romani residents in the village of Cegléd on 18 August. People mostly dressed in black uniforms gathered in small groups in Romani neighbourhoods, chanted anti-Roma slogans and made death threats. The police advised the Romani families to return to their houses and did not intervene. The vigilantes remained in the town for two days. The NGOs alleged that the police addressed the incidents as public disorder and not as an "assault against a member of a community".

■ Several thousand Jobbik supporters marched through a Romani neighbourhood in the town of Miskolc on 17 October. They were reportedly chanting anti-Roma slogans. Hundreds of Roma held a peaceful counter-demonstration. NGOs acknowledged that the police acted with due diligence to protect the Romani inhabitants from attacks.

Justice system

In January, the law on the Constitutional Court entered into force. Human rights organizations, including Eötvös Károly Institute, the Hungarian Civil Liberties Union and the Hungarian Helsinki Committee, warned that the law introduced unreasonable obstacles – including mandatory legal representation – which would make access for citizens complaining of human rights violations to the Constitutional Court more difficult. The law also removed the provision for collective complaints.

Freedom of expression

In May, Parliament amended the media legislation, addressing some of the shortcomings identified by the Constitutional Court in December 2011. In particular, the amendments restricted the control of the authorities over the content of the print and internet media, and strengthened the protection of journalistic sources. However, the Council of Europe voiced concerns that some negative provisions, such as the obligation for printed and online media to be registered or face heavy fines, still persisted. Critics warned that media legislation continued to expose the media to political control.

■ In September Hungary's national news service, MTI, sued a journalist for defamation following his accusation that it was using taxpayers' money to misinform the public. The move was criticized by the OSCE Representative on Freedom of the Media as likely to have an intimidating effect on independent critical journalists.

Refugees, asylum-seekers and migrants

UNHCR, the UN Refugee Agency, criticized Hungary's treatment of asylum-seekers, reporting that conditions in reception centres and the increased use of administrative detention of asylum-seekers fell short of international and EU standards. Asylum-seekers returned to Hungary under the Dublin Regulation were usually issued with expulsion orders and detained, irrespective of their wish to seek asylum.

Rights of lesbian, gay, bisexual, transgender and intersex people

More than 3,000 participants attended the Pride march in Budapest on 12 July. In April, the Chief of the Budapest Police decided to ban it on the grounds that it would disrupt traffic flows. The ban was quashed by the Budapest Metropolitan Court a few days later. According to the organizers, the police provided adequate protection for the march.

Amnesty International visits/reports

- An Amnesty International delegate visited Hungary in July.
- Hungary: Report into vigilante activities in Gyöngyöspata fails to address discrimination (EUR 27/001/2012)
- New Hungarian Criminal Code: A missed opportunity to do more on hate crimes (EUR 27/003/2012)

INDIA

REPUBLIC OF INDIA
Head of state: **Pranab Kumar Mukherjee (replaced Pratibha Patil in July)**
Head of government: **Manmohan Singh**

Torture and other ill-treatment, extrajudicial executions, deaths in custody and arbitrary detentions persisted. Victims of human rights violations and abuses were frustrated in their quest for justice largely due to ineffective institutions and a lack of political will. The first execution in India since 2004 took place in November. At least 78 people were sentenced to death. The authorities persistently failed to curb violence against women and girls, and a high-profile rape case in December spurred countrywide protests for legal and other reforms. At least 340 people, including civilians, were killed in clashes between armed Maoists and security forces. Accountability for crimes under international law remained outside the scope of ongoing peace initiatives in Nagaland and Assam. At least 65 people were killed in intra-ethnic and communal clashes in Assam leading to the temporary displacement of 400,000 people. Adivasi (Indigenous), fishing and other marginalized communities continued to protest against forced eviction from their land and habitats, while official investigations progressed into the allocation of land for corporate mining. Defenders of human rights were threatened and harassed by state and non-state actors; some were sentenced to long-term imprisonment. The government attempted to censor websites and stifle dissent expressed through social media, prompting protests against internet restrictions.

Background

The government faced allegations of corruption over its failure to ensure inclusive growth, within the context of a global recession which severely affected India's economy. Poor and already marginalized communities, estimated at 30% to 50% of the population, were hit hard by price rises.

Government talks with neighbouring Pakistan continued, including on Kashmir. In March, India supported UN Human Rights Council Resolution 19/2, urging Sri Lanka to address alleged violations of international law, but was reluctant to speak out on other human rights concerns. The Special Rapporteur on extrajudicial, summary or arbitrary executions visited India in March. India's human rights record was assessed under the UN Universal Periodic Review in May; the state did not accept recommendations to facilitate a visit by the UN Special Rapporteur on torture and by the Working Group on Arbitrary Detention, or to hold its security forces to account for human rights violations. Parliament amended the Unlawful Activities (Prevention) Act on financing terrorism but failed to bring it in line with international human rights standards.

Violence between security forces, militia and Maoists

Clashes between armed Maoists and security forces continued in eastern and central India. Both sides routinely targeted civilians, and killings, arson and abductions spread to Gadchiroli district in Maharashtra state, where Maoists killed 19 civilians including eight serving and former local government members.

In Chhattisgarh, the number of people killed since 2005, including members of the security forces and armed Maoists, rose to 3,200. Some 25,000 people remained displaced – 5,000 in camps and 20,000 dispersed in neighbouring Andhra Pradesh and

I

Orissa. Hundreds of members of the state-sponsored Salwa Judum militia continued to be integrated into a 6,000-strong auxiliary police force, despite concerns over their involvement in human rights violations.

■ In March and April, Maoists abducted two Italian tourists in Orissa, releasing them in exchange for six Maoists captured by security forces. Maoists released an Orissa legislator after 33 days.

■ In April and May, Maoists shot dead two security guards and abducted the head of Sukma district administration in Chhattisgarh. They released him after 13 days, when the state authorities promised to consider the release of 300 Maoist suspects on bail.

■ In June, central paramilitary forces in Chhattisgarh claimed to have killed 17 Maoists in "combat", but human rights activists discovered the victims to be local unarmed Adivasis, including three teenagers. A judicial inquiry into the killings commenced five months later.

Corporate accountability

In August, the Indian Supreme Court ordered that toxic waste lying in and around the Union Carbide factory in Bhopal should be disposed of within six months by the central and state governments. It also ordered better medical surveillance, monitoring and referral systems to improve health care for victims. The Court ruled that the state government should provide clean water to people living in the vicinity of the factory.

UK-based Vedanta Resources continued to fail to provide remedies to Indigenous and other local communities for the impact of its alumina refinery project in Lanjigarh and failed to consult on plans to undertake mining in a joint venture with the Orissa Mining Corporation (OMC) in the Niyamgiri Hills. The OMC's challenge to the central government's refusal to grant forest clearance for the mining project was pending before the Supreme Court.

■ Adivasis in the Mahan and Chhatrasal areas of Madhya Pradesh state and the Saranda area of Jharkand state, protested against moves to divert land to mining projects which flouted their claims to the land under the Forest Rights Act.

Death penalty

On 21 November, India resumed executions after an eight-year hiatus by hanging Ajmal Kasab, a Pakistani national, for his involvement in the 2008 Mumbai terror attacks. During the year, courts sentenced at least 78 people to death, raising the number of prisoners on death row to over 400. Ten death sentences were commuted by presidential order. Five other prisoners challenging the President's rejection of their mercy petitions awaited the Supreme Court's verdict.

In July, 14 former judges appealed to the President to commute the death sentences of 13 prisoners, which the judges claimed had been wrongly upheld by the Supreme Court. In November, the Supreme Court called for a review of the sentencing principles given the inconsistent application of the death penalty. The Supreme Court ruled against the mandatory application of the death penalty for the use of prohibited firearms resulting in death. In December, India voted against UN General Assembly resolution 67/176 calling for a worldwide moratorium on executions with a view to abolishing the death penalty.

Violence against women and girls

The authorities failed to curb high levels of sexual and other violence against women and girls, even as reports of such incidents increased.

■ In December, 11 men were convicted for the sexual assault of a woman in Guwahati city, Assam.

■ Five men and one boy were arrested in December for the gang-rape and subsequent death of a young woman in Delhi. The assault prompted countrywide protests calling for a review of laws addressing violence against women.

Impunity

Impunity for human rights violations remained pervasive, with no repeal of the Armed Forces Special Powers Act or the Disturbed Areas Act. Both Acts grant excessive powers to security forces in specified areas, and provide them with de facto impunity for alleged crimes. Protests against these laws were held in Jammu and Kashmir and the north-east, with concerns expressed by the UN Special Rapporteur on extrajudicial, summary or arbitrary executions during his visit to India in March, and by the UN Human Rights Council in September. Suspected perpetrators of enforced disappearances and extrajudicial executions in Assam (in 1998 and 2001), Manipur, Nagaland, Punjab (during 1984-1994) and other states, remained at large.

■ In January, the Supreme Court ordered new investigations into 22 alleged extrajudicial executions in Gujarat, mostly of Muslim youth, during 2003-2006.

In April, the National Human Rights Commission (NHRC) closed its inquiry into alleged unlawful killings and mass cremations by police during the Punjab conflict, without recommending criminal investigations. It awarded 279.4 million Indian rupees (US$5.78 million) in compensation to the families of 1,513 of the 2,097 dead. The findings of a Central Bureau of Investigation probe into the killings remained unpublished.

During 2007-2012, the NHRC distributed cash compensation to the families of 191 out of 1,671 people killed in the country, after determining they had been extrajudicially executed. Criminal investigations into the majority of such killings failed to make serious progress.

Jammu and Kashmir

Widespread impunity prevailed for violations of international law in Kashmir, including unlawful killings, extrajudicial executions, torture and the enforced disappearance of thousands of people since 1989. The majority of cases of more than 100 youths shot dead by the police and other security forces during protests in the summer of 2010 were not fully investigated.

In May, the Supreme Court allowed eight members of the armed forces, suspected of involvement in the extrajudicial executions of five villagers from Pathribal in 2000, to effectively sidestep civilian courts. Instead, they faced trial in military courts, later boycotted by the victims' relatives.

In July, the Jammu and Kashmir High Court cited the Pathribal verdict when ruling on a similar case, relating to the 2010 Machil extrajudicial executions of three villagers.

In August, the state authorities rejected the state Human Rights Commission's recommendation to use modern forensic techniques to identify bodies in more than 2,700 unmarked graves in north Kashmir.

In December, a report by two Srinagar-based human rights organizations on 214 cases of enforced disappearance, torture, extrajudicial executions and other violations since 1989, alleged that the authorities were unwilling to investigate serious charges against 470 security personnel and 30 state-sponsored militia members.

Limited amendments to the Public Safety Act (PSA) in April after calls for its repeal, failed to bring it in line with India's international human rights obligations.

Administrative detentions under the PSA continued with political leaders and separatist activists held without charge or trial.

In December, the authorities acknowledged that 219 people were detained under the PSA, including 120 foreign nationals, and seven whose detention orders had already been quashed by the courts. Teenagers Mushtaq Saleem Beigh, Mohammed Mubarak Bhat and Danish Farooq were released from administrative detention.

Proposed amendments to the state's juvenile justice law, raising the age of majority from 16 to 18, remained pending before the legislative assembly.

Communal and ethnic violence

In July and August, 75 villagers were killed in clashes between Bodo and Muslim communities in Assam. A total of 400,000 people were temporarily displaced across 270 camps. Involvement of armed groups exacerbated tensions and violence. The authorities were criticized for their inadequate response.

Ten years after the 2002 Gujarat violence in which 2,000 people, mostly Muslims, were killed, the majority of victims and their families had not secured justice. At least 78 suspects were convicted, including former Minister Maya Kodnani, and some 90 acquitted, in three of the cases being monitored by the Supreme Court.

In February, a special team set up by the Supreme Court to investigate 10 Gujarat cases found no evidence to prosecute Chief Minister Narendra Modi and 62 other senior politicians and officials. Zakia Jaffri, who had accused the Chief Minister and others of failing to save the life of her husband Ehsan Jaffri and 68 others, petitioned the Court, questioning the basis for the team's conclusions.

Members of Dalit communities continued to face discrimination and attacks. Special laws to prosecute suspected perpetrators were rarely used.

In November, 268 Dalit houses in Natham Colony, Tamil Nadu, were looted and damaged by caste Hindus enraged by the suicide of a man whose daughter had married a Dalit.

Excessive use of force

On several occasions, police used unnecessary or excessive force to quell protests, and authorities failed to conduct prompt, impartial and effective inquiries into most incidents.

■ In March and April, at least 10 people were injured when police used excessive force to evict slum-dwellers from Nonadonga area, Kolkata, in a bid to acquire land for urban infrastructure projects.

■ In September, one protester was killed by police and more than 60 others were injured when police cleared a demonstration against the Kudankulam nuclear power plant in Tamil Nadu.

■ In November, one person was killed and five others were injured by police during protests over the amount of compensation for land in Loba village, West Bengal, acquired for a private coal mine.

Sedition laws

Protests grew against archaic sedition laws used to imprison peaceful demonstrators.

■ Over 50 peaceful protesters against the Kudankulam nuclear power plant, including Dr Udayakumar and Pushparayan, were charged with sedition and "waging war against the state".

■ In August, social activists Seema Azad and Vishwa Vijay, were released on bail by the Allahabad High Court while appealing against their conviction on sedition charges for collaborating with armed Maoists.

Human rights defenders

People defending the rights of marginalized communities continued to be targeted by state and non-state actors – as highlighted by the UN Special Rapporteur on human rights defenders in February.

■ In July, environmental activist Ramesh Agrawal, who had sought to expose environmental and Adivasi rights violations linked to mining projects, was shot and injured in Raigarh district, Chhattisgarh.

■ In September, the Supreme Court rejected the bail petition of prisoner of conscience and Adivasi leader Kartam Joga, jailed since September 2010.

■ In September, the Supreme Court agreed to consider the medical report of Adivasi schoolteacher Soni Sori, after she complained of torture, including sexual violence, by the Chhattisgarh police while she was in their custody in October 2011.

■ In October, Adivasi rights activist Dayamani Barla was imprisoned for two months for a 2008 incident, amid allegations that she was being targeted by Jharkhand authorities for protesting against the forced eviction of farmers at Nagri.

Freedom of expression

The authorities used overbroad and imprecise laws to arrest at least seven people for posting online comments criticizing the government.

■ In April, Kolkata police arrested academic Ambikesh Mahapatra for posting a cartoon criticizing West Bengal Chief Minister Mamata Banerjee.

■ In September, Mumbai police arrested Aseem Trivedi for publishing a series of cartoons parodying India's national symbols as part of an anti-corruption protest.

■ In October, Puducherry police arrested Ravi Srinivasan for tweeting about allegations of corruption involving the Union Finance Minister's son.

■ In November, Mumbai police arrested two women, Shaheen Dhada and Renu Srinivasan, for posting Facebook comments questioning a public protest called for by supporters of a recently deceased senior political figure.

Amnesty International visits/reports

🗐 Human rights defenders in India need effective protection: Amnesty International's written statement to the 19th session of the UN Human Rights Council (ASA 20/005/2012)

🗐 India: Vedanta's perspective uncovered – policies cannot mask practices in Orissa (ASA 20/029/2012)

🗐 Amnesty International urges India to promptly ratify the Convention against Torture and invite the Special Rapporteur on torture to visit India (ASA 20/034/2012)

🗐 India: Still a "lawless law" – detentions under the Jammu and Kashmir Public Safety Act (ASA 20/035/2012)

INDONESIA

REPUBLIC OF INDONESIA
Head of state and government: **Susilo Bambang Yudhoyono**

Security forces faced persistent allegations of human rights violations, including torture and other ill-treatment and excessive use of force and firearms. At least 76 prisoners of conscience remained behind bars. Intimidation and attacks against religious minorities were rife. Discriminatory laws, policies and practices prevented women and girls from

exercising their rights, in particular, sexual and reproductive rights. No progress was made in bringing perpetrators of past human rights violations to justice. No executions were reported.

Background

In May, Indonesia's human rights record was assessed under the UN Universal Periodic Review. The government rejected key recommendations to review specific laws and decrees which restrict the rights to freedom of expression and thought, conscience and religion. In July, Indonesia reported to the CEDAW Committee. In November, Indonesia adopted the ASEAN Human Rights Declaration, despite serious concerns that it fell short of international standards.

Indonesia's legislative framework remained inadequate to deal with allegations of torture and other ill-treatment. Caning continued to be used as a form of judicial punishment in Aceh province for Shari'a offences. At least 45 people were caned during the year for gambling, and being alone with someone of the opposite sex who was not a marriage partner or relative (*khalwat*).

Police and security forces

Police were repeatedly accused of human rights violations, including excessive use of force and firearms, and torture and other ill-treatment. Internal and external police accountability mechanisms failed to adequately deal with cases of abuses committed by police, and investigations into human rights violations were rare.

■ In March, 17 men from East Nusa Tenggara province were arbitrarily arrested for the murder of a policeman. They were allegedly stripped, handcuffed and beaten in detention for 12 days by the West Sabu sub-district police. Some suffered stab wounds and broken bones. Some were reportedly forced by police to drink their own urine. They were released without charge at the end of June due to lack of evidence.

Indonesian security forces, including police and military personnel, were accused of human rights violations in Papua. Torture and other ill-treatment, excessive use of force and firearms and possible unlawful killings were reported. In most cases, the perpetrators were not brought to justice and victims did not receive reparations.

■ In June, Mako Tabuni, a Papuan political activist and deputy chair of the pro-independence National Committee for West Papua, was shot dead by police officers in Waena, near Jayapura, Papua province. Police alleged he was resisting arrest. There was no impartial or independent investigation into the killing.

■ Also in June, soldiers attacked a village in Wamena, Papua province, in retaliation for the death and injury of two of their personnel. They reportedly opened fire arbitrarily, stabbed dozens of people with bayonets – resulting in one death – and burned a number of houses, buildings and vehicles.

■ In August, police and military personnel in Yapen island, Papua province, forcibly dispersed a peaceful demonstration commemorating the International Day of the World's Indigenous Peoples. Security forces fired their guns into the air and arbitrarily arrested at least six protesters. Some were reportedly beaten during their arrest.

■ Also in August, police personnel from the Jayawijaya District in Papua province arbitrarily arrested and allegedly slapped, punched and kicked five men in an attempt to force them to confess to a murder. No investigation into the abuse was carried out.

Freedom of expression

The authorities continued to use repressive legislation to criminalize peaceful political activists. At least 70 people from the regions of Papua and Maluku were in prison for peacefully expressing their views.

■ In March, five Papuan political activists charged with "rebellion" under Article 106 of the Indonesian Criminal Code were imprisoned for three years for their involvement in the Third Papuan Peoples' Congress, a peaceful gathering in Abepura in October 2011.

■ In July, Malukan prisoner of conscience Johan Teterissa, who is serving a 15-year prison sentence, was kicked and beaten with electric cables following his transfer from Madiun prison to Batu prison on Nusakambangan island, Central Java. He did not receive medical attention following the beating.

Human rights defenders and journalists repeatedly faced intimidation and attacks because of their work. International observers, including NGOs and journalists, continued to be denied free and unimpeded access to the Papua region.

■ In May, Tantowi Anwari, an activist from the Association of Journalists for Diversity, was beaten and kicked by members of the hardline Islamic Defenders

Front in Bekasi, West Java. Tantowi filed a police report, but there was no progress on his case by the end of the year.

■ In September, Papuan human rights lawyer Olga Hamadi was threatened after investigating allegations of police torture and other ill-treatment in a murder case in Wamena, Papua province. There was no investigation into the threats, and fears for her safety remained.

Freedom of religion and belief

The authorities used incitement and blasphemy provisions to criminalize freedom of religion, as well as freedoms of expression, thought and conscience. At least six prisoners of conscience remained behind bars on incitement and blasphemy charges.

■ In June, Alexander Aan, an atheist, was sentenced to two and a half years' imprisonment and fined 100 million rupiah (US$10,600) for incitement after he posted statements and pictures which some people construed as insulting to Islam and the Prophet Mohamed.

■ In July, Tajul Muluk, a Shi'a Muslim religious leader from East Java, was sentenced to two years' imprisonment for blasphemy under Article 156(a) of the Indonesian Criminal Code by the Sampang District Court. Local human rights groups and legal experts raised fair trial concerns. In September, his sentence was increased to four years on appeal.

Religious minorities – including Ahmadis, Shi'as and Christians – faced ongoing discrimination, intimidation and attacks. In many cases the authorities failed to adequately protect them or bring the perpetrators to justice.

■ In August, one person was killed and dozens were injured when a mob attacked a Shi'a community in Sampang, East Java. According to the National Human Rights Commission (Komnas HAM) the police did not take adequate steps to prevent the attack or protect the community.

■ At least 34 families from an Ahmadiyya community in West Nusa Tenggara province, who were attacked by a mob and displaced in 2006 because of their beliefs, continued to live in temporary shelter in Mataram, Lombok city. No one had been prosecuted for the attack.

■ The authorities refused to enforce decisions by the Indonesian Supreme Court in 2010 and 2011 to reopen the Taman Yasmin Indonesian Christian Church in Bogor and the Filadelfia Batak Christian Protestant Church in Bekasi city. The churches had been sealed off by local authorities in 2010. Both congregations remained at risk of harassment and intimidation by hardline groups for continuing to worship just outside their buildings.

Women's rights

Women and girls faced ongoing barriers to exercising their sexual and reproductive rights. In July, the CEDAW Committee recommended that the government promote understanding of sexual and reproductive health and rights, including among unmarried women and women domestic workers. The Committee also recommended that women be given access to contraception without having to obtain their husband's consent.

A 2010 government regulation permitting "female circumcision" remained in effect, in violation of Indonesia's obligations under international human rights law. The CEDAW Committee called on the government to withdraw the regulation and adopt legislation to criminalize the practice.

For a third successive year, Parliament failed to debate and enact a domestic workers law, leaving domestic workers, the vast majority of whom are women and girls, vulnerable to economic exploitation and the denial of their rights to fair conditions of work, health and education. Although Indonesia ratified the 1990 International Convention on the Protection of the Rights of All Migrant Workers and Members of Their Families in May, a lack of adequate legal protection in the country exposed migrant domestic workers, mostly women and girls, to trafficking, forced labour practices and other human rights abuses in Indonesia and overseas.

Impunity

There was little progress in delivering justice, truth and reparation for past human rights violations, including in Aceh, Papua and Timor-Leste (formerly East Timor). Survivors of sexual violence had yet to receive adequate medical, psychological, sexual and reproductive, and mental health services or treatment. In September, the Indonesian government announced at the UN Human Rights Council that they were finalizing a new law on a Truth and Reconciliation Commission; however, no progress was reported. A multi-agency team set up by the

President in 2011 to devise a plan to resolve past human rights violations had yet to announce any concrete plans.

■ In July, Komnas HAM submitted its report to the Attorney General on possible crimes against humanity committed against members of the Indonesian Communist Party (PKI) and suspected communist sympathizers in the context of the 1965 failed coup. The Commission called on the Attorney General to initiate an official investigation, to bring the perpetrators to justice in a Human Rights Court and to establish a truth and reconciliation commission. No progress was reported.

■ In September, the Acehnese provincial parliament announced a delay to setting up an Aceh truth and reconciliation commission. This left victims and their families without an official mechanism to establish the truth about the violations they suffered during the conflict or to establish the fate or whereabouts of their loved ones who were killed or had disappeared.

■ The President failed to act on Parliament's recommendations in 2009 to bring to justice those involved in the enforced disappearance of 13 pro-democracy activists in 1997 and 1998, to conduct an immediate search for activists who had disappeared, and provide rehabilitation and compensation to their families.

■ The government failed to implement recommendations made by the bilateral Indonesia-Timor-Leste Commission of Truth and Friendship, in particular to establish a commission for disappeared persons tasked with identifying the whereabouts of all Timor-Leste children who were separated from their parents and notifying their families.

Death penalty

For a fourth successive year no executions were reported. However, at least 12 death sentences were handed down during the year and at least 130 people remained under sentence of death. In a positive move in October, it was reported that the Supreme Court had commuted the death sentence of a drug trafficker in August 2011, citing the death penalty as a violation of human rights and the Constitution. Also in October, it was announced that the President had commuted 19 death sentences between 2004 and 2011.

Amnesty International visits/reports

🚗 Amnesty International delegates visited Indonesia in April, May and October.

📄 Stalled reforms: Impunity, discrimination and security force violations in Indonesia – Amnesty International Submission to the UN Universal Periodic Review, May-June 2012 (ASA 21/003/2012)

📄 Excessive force: Impunity for police violence in Indonesia (ASA 21/010/2012)

📄 Indonesia: Briefing to the UN Committee on the Elimination of Discrimination against Women (ASA 21/022/2012)

IRAN

ISLAMIC REPUBLIC OF IRAN
Head of state: Ayatollah Sayed 'Ali Khamenei
               (Leader of the Islamic Republic of Iran)
Head of government: Mahmoud Ahmadinejad (President)

The authorities maintained severe restrictions on freedoms of expression, association and assembly. Dissidents and human rights defenders, including minority rights and women's rights activists, were arbitrarily arrested, detained incommunicado, imprisoned after unfair trials and banned from travelling abroad. There were scores of prisoners of conscience and political prisoners. Torture and other ill-treatment were common and committed with impunity. Women, religious and ethnic minorities, and members of the LGBTI community were subject to discrimination in law and practice. The cruel judicial punishments of flogging and amputation continued to be used. Official sources acknowledged 314 executions, but a total of 544 were recorded. The true figure may be considerably higher.

Background

Iran's nuclear programme continued to cause international tension. The UN, EU and some governments, including the USA, maintained and in some cases imposed additional sanctions, including travel bans on suspected human rights violators. Food insecurity and economic hardship grew.

Thousands of prospective candidates for parliamentary election in March were disqualified.

Also in March, the mandate of the UN Special Rapporteur investigating human rights in Iran was renewed for one year. Both he and the UN Secretary-General issued reports identifying widespread human rights violations, including failure to adhere to the rule of law and impunity.

Amendments to the Penal Code passed by parliament in February continued to allow cruel, inhuman and degrading punishment, and punishments not based on codified law, and provided impunity in some circumstances for rape. They neither prohibited the death penalty for juvenile offenders nor executions by stoning. The amended Penal Code was not in force at the end of the year.

In December, the UN General Assembly passed a resolution urging the government to improve human rights in Iran.

Freedoms of expression, association and assembly

The authorities maintained tight restrictions on freedoms of expression, association and assembly. They took steps to create a controlled, national internet, routinely monitored telephone calls, blocked websites, jammed foreign broadcasts and took harsh action against those who spoke out. Media workers and bloggers were harassed and detained. Student activists and members of minority groups were imprisoned or harassed, with some barred from higher education. Scores of prisoners of conscience arrested in previous years remained in prison and more were sentenced to prison terms in 2012.

■ Shiva Nazar Ahari, a journalist, human rights activist and member of the Committee of Human Rights Reporters, began serving a four-year prison term in September. In October, she and eight other women prisoners of conscience went on hunger strike in protest at their alleged abuse by guards at Tehran's Evin Prison.

■ Abbas Khosravi Farsani, a student at Esfahan University, was arrested on 21 June for criticizing the authorities in a book and his blog, and forced to "confess" to charges including "acting against national security by publishing lies and causing public unease", "insulting the Supreme Leader" and "membership of an opposition group with links to Israel". He was released after 20 days but prevented from continuing his university studies. He was awaiting trial at the end of the year.

Dozens of independent trade unionists remained imprisoned for their peaceful trade union activities.

■ Reza Shahabi, treasurer of a bus workers' union detained since 2010, learned in February that he had been sentenced to six years' imprisonment for "gathering and colluding" against "state security" and

"spreading propaganda against the system". He was reported to be in poor health following torture and denial of prompt medical care.

Arbitrary arrests and detentions

Government critics and opponents were arbitrarily arrested and detained by security forces. They were held incommunicado for long periods and denied medical care. Many were tortured or otherwise ill-treated. Tens were sentenced to prison terms after unfair trials.

Dozens of peaceful government critics detained in connection with mass protests in 2009-2011 remained in prison or under house arrest throughout the year. Many were prisoners of conscience.

■ Opposition leaders Mehdi Karroubi and Mir Hossein Mousavi and the latter's wife Zahra Rahnavard remained under house arrest imposed without a warrant in February 2011.

■ Mansoureh Behkish, a member of the human rights NGO Mothers of Laleh Park, was sentenced on appeal in July to six months in prison after being convicted of threatening national security "by establishing the Mourning Mothers group" and "spreading propaganda against the system". She also received a 42-month suspended prison term. She remained free at the end of the year.

■ Blogger Hossein Ronaghi Maleki was among dozens of relief workers and human rights activists arrested at a camp for earthquake victims in East Azerbaijan province in August. A former prisoner of conscience serving a 15-year prison term imposed in 2010, he had been released on medical grounds seven weeks earlier, after paying a substantial bail. He said he was tortured after his rearrest at a Ministry of Intelligence facility in Tabriz. He was released in November.

Human rights defenders

Human rights defenders, including lawyers, trade unionists, minority rights activists and women's rights activists, continued to face harassment, arbitrary arrest and detention, and imprisonment after unfair trials. Many, including some sentenced after unfair trials in previous years, were prisoners of conscience. The authorities persistently harassed activists' families.

■ Mohammad Sadiq Kabudvand, a journalist and founder of the Human Rights Organization of Kurdistan, continued serving a 10-and-a-half-year prison term because of his journalism and human rights activities. He went on hunger strike in May and July to protest against the authorities' refusal to allow him access to his gravely ill son, causing his own health to deteriorate. He was denied appropriate medical treatment.

■ Nasrin Sotoudeh, a lawyer who formerly represented Nobel Peace Laureate Shirin Ebadi, continued serving a six-year prison term imposed in 2011 for "spreading propaganda against the system" and "membership of an illegal group aiming to harm national security". A prisoner of conscience since 2010, she ended a 49-day hunger strike in December when the authorities agreed to lift restrictions against her 13-year-old daughter.

■ Lawyers Mohammad Ali Dadkhah, Abdolfattah Soltani and Mohammad Seyfzadeh, co-founders of the Centre for Human Rights Defenders (CHRD), which was forcibly closed at the end of 2008, were held as prisoners of conscience at the end of the year. The CHRD's Executive Chair Narges Mohammadi was granted temporary medical leave from prison in July. In November, Abdolfattah Soltani's wife received a suspended sentence of one year and was banned from leaving Iran for five years in connection with a human rights award received by her husband.

Unfair trials

Political and other suspects continued to face grossly unfair trials before Revolutionary and Criminal Courts. They often faced vaguely worded charges that did not amount to recognizably criminal offences and were convicted, sometimes in the absence of defence lawyers, on the basis of "confessions" or other information allegedly obtained under torture. Courts accepted such "confessions" as evidence without investigating how they were obtained.

■ Mohammad Ali Amouri and four other members of the Ahwazi Arab minority were sentenced to death in July on vague capital charges, including "enmity against God and corruption on earth". They had already been in custody for up to a year because of their activism on behalf of the Ahwazi Arab community. At least four were reported to have been tortured and denied access to a lawyer. An appeal had not been heard by the end of the year.

Torture and other ill-treatment

The security forces continued to torture and otherwise ill-treat detainees with impunity. Commonly reported methods included beatings, mock execution, threats, confinement in small spaces and denial of adequate medical treatment.

■ Saeed Sedeghi, a shop worker sentenced to death for drug offences, was tortured in Evin Prison after his scheduled execution was postponed following international protests. He was hanged on 22 October.

At least eight deaths in custody may have resulted from torture, but none were independently investigated.

■ Sattar Beheshti, a blogger, died in the custody of the Cyber Police in November after lodging a complaint that he had been tortured. Contradictory statements by officials called into question the impartiality of a judicial investigation. His family were pressured by security forces to keep silent.

Discrimination against women

Women faced discrimination in law and practice in relation to marriage and divorce, inheritance, child custody, nationality and international travel. Women breaching a mandatory dress code faced expulsion from university. Some higher education centres introduced gender segregation, or restricted or barred women from studying certain subjects.

A Family Protection Bill that would increase discrimination remained under discussion. The draft Penal Code failed to address existing discrimination, maintaining, for example, that a woman's testimony holds half the value of that of a man.

■ Bahareh Hedayat, Mahsa Amrabadi and seven other women held at Evin Prison went on hunger strike in October to protest against humiliating body searches and the removal of personal possessions by guards. Subsequently, 33 women political prisoners signed an open letter calling body cavity searches a form of sexual abuse and demanding an apology from prison officials and an undertaking that they would not be subjected to further abuses.

Rights of lesbian, gay, bisexual, transgender and intersex people

LGBTI people continued to face discrimination in law and practice.

Discrimination – ethnic minorities

Members of ethnic minorities, including Ahwazi Arabs, Azerbaijanis, Baluch, Kurds and Turkmen, were discriminated against in law and practice, being denied access to employment, education and other economic, social and cultural rights on an equivalent basis with other Iranians. The use of minority languages in government offices and for teaching in schools remained prohibited. Activists campaigning for the rights of minorities faced official threats, arrest and imprisonment.

■ Jabbar Yabbari and at least 24 other Ahwazi Arabs were arrested in April during demonstrations commemorating a 2005 demonstration against discrimination.

The authorities failed to adequately protect Afghan refugees from attack and forced some to leave Iran. In Esfahan, local authorities banned Afghan nationals from entering a city park.

Azerbaijani activists criticized the Iranian authorities' response to the 11 August earthquake in Qaradagh, East Azerbaijan, calling it slow and inadequate, and accused them of downplaying the destruction caused and the number of lives lost while detaining some of those helping with relief efforts. In September, 16 minority activists received six-month suspended prison sentences for security-related convictions in connection with their relief work.

Freedom of religion or belief

The authorities discriminated against non-Shi'a minorities, including other Muslim communities, dissident Shi'a clerics, members of Sufi religious orders and the Ahl-e Haq faith, and certain other religious minorities and philosophical associations, including converts from Islam to Christianity. Persecution of Baha'is intensified; Baha'is were publicly demonized by officials and state-controlled media.

■ Dissident Muslim cleric Sayed Hossein Kazemeyni Boroujerdi continued to serve an 11-year sentence handed down in 2007. The authorities summoned 10 of his followers for questioning in April, May and December, though none was known to have been charged.

■ In August, the authorities arrested at least 19 Sunni Muslims in Khuzestan province and 13 in West Azerbaijan, apparently on account of their beliefs. Eight others were arrested in Kordestan in October. It is not known whether any were charged or faced further questioning.

■ Pastor Yousef Naderkhani, arrested in 2009, was sentenced to death after a court convicted him of apostasy in 2010. The Supreme Court upheld the sentence but his conviction was overturned when the case was referred for guidance to the Supreme Leader. He was released in September, having served a three-year prison term for evangelizing Muslims.

■ At least 177 Baha'is – who were denied the right to practise their faith – were detained for their beliefs. Seven community leaders arrested in 2009 continued to serve 20-year sentences imposed for "espionage for Israel" and "insulting religious sanctities".

Cruel, inhuman or degrading punishments

Sentences of flogging and amputation continued to be imposed and carried out.

■ Siamak Ghaderi, a journalist and blogger, and 13 other political prisoners were reported to have been flogged in August in Evin Prison. He had been sentenced to four years in prison and 60 lashes for allegedly "insulting the President" and "spreading lies" in part for posting interviews with LGBTI individuals on his blog in 2007.

Death penalty

Hundreds of people were sentenced to death. Official sources acknowledged 314 executions. Credible unofficial sources suggested that at least 230 other executions were also carried out, many of them in secret, totalling 544. The true figure may have been far higher, exceeding 600.

Of those executions officially acknowledged, 71% were for drugs-related offences and followed unfair trials. Many were from poor and marginalized communities, including Afghan nationals. The death penalty remained applicable in cases of murder, rape, deployment of firearms during a crime, spying, apostasy, extra-marital relations and same-sex relations.

There were at least 63 public executions. No executions by stoning were known to have occurred but at least 10 people remained under sentence of death by stoning.

■ Allahverdi Ahmadpourazer, a Sunni Muslim belonging to the Azerbaijani minority, was executed for alleged drugs offences in May. His trial may have been unfair.

■ Amir Hekmati, a dual Iranian-US national, was sentenced to death in January after being convicted of espionage. His alleged "confession" was broadcast on state television. In March the Supreme Court overturned the sentence. He remained in prison awaiting a retrial.

■ The family of Hamid Ghassemi-Shall, a dual Canadian-Iranian national, was told in April that his execution was imminent, though he remained on death row at the end of the year. He was held in solitary confinement for 18 months without access to a lawyer and sentenced to death in December 2008 after an unfair trial in which he was accused of "enmity against God", "espionage" and "co-operation with an illegal opposition group".

■ Three members of the Kurdish minority were executed on 20 September in Oroumieh's Central Prison for their political activities.

■ The authorities suspended the death sentence imposed on Canadian resident Saeed Malekpour for "insulting and desecrating Islam" after software he had devised for uploading photographs online was used by others, without his knowledge, to post pornographic images. Saeed Malekpour had been held since his October 2008 arrest; his torture allegations have never been investigated.

Amnesty International visits/reports

🚗 Amnesty International has not been permitted to visit Iran to undertake human rights research since 1979. The authorities rarely responded to communications from the organization.

📰 "We are ordered to crush you": Expanding repression of dissent in Iran (MDE 13/002/2012)

IRAQ

REPUBLIC OF IRAQ
Head of state: Jalal Talabani
Head of government: Nuri al-Maliki

Thousands of people were detained; hundreds were sentenced to death or prison terms, many after unfair trials and on terrorism-related charges. Torture and other ill-treatment of detainees remained rife and were committed with impunity. Hundreds of prisoners were on death row. At least 129 people were executed, including at least three women. Armed groups opposed to the government continued to commit gross human rights abuses, killing

hundreds of civilians in suicide and other bomb attacks. Harassment, intimidation and violence against journalists and media workers continued to be reported. Over 67,000 refugees from Syria sought safety in Iraq.

Background

The political stalemate in parliament continued to stifle the legislative progress, preventing, among other things, the adoption of an amnesty law. Political tensions were exacerbated by the arrest of scores of people associated with Vice-President Tareq al-Hashemi, who fled from Baghdad after he was accused of organizing death squads. In December 2011 Iraqi television broadcast "confessions" by detainees reported to have worked for him as bodyguards, who said they had been paid by the Vice-President to commit killings. The Vice-President evaded capture but was charged, tried and sentenced to death in his absence in September, together with his son-in-law, Ahmad Qahtan, in connection with the murder of a woman lawyer and government official. They received further death sentences in their absence in November and December following further trials.

Relations between the Baghdad authorities and the Kurdistan Regional Government (KRG) remained fraught due to differences over the distribution of oil revenues and the continuing dispute over internal boundaries.

Young people, particularly those seen locally as nonconformists, were subject to a campaign of intimidation after flyers and signs targeting them appeared in the Baghdad neighbourhoods of Sadr City, al-Hababiya and Hay al-'Amal in February. Those targeted included youths suspected of homosexual conduct and those seen as pursuing an alternative lifestyle because of their distinctive hairstyles, clothes or musical tastes.

In March, the League of Arab States held its summit meeting in Baghdad for the first time since the overthrow of Saddam Hussein in 2003. Prior to the meeting, the security forces carried out mass arrests in Baghdad, apparently as a "preventive" measure.

In April, parliament approved the establishment of an Independent High Commission for Human Rights.

In December, tens of thousands of mostly Sunni Iraqis began holding peaceful daily anti-government protests against the abuse of detainees. The unrest was triggered by the detention of several bodyguards of Finance Minister Rafi'e al-Issawi, a senior Sunni political leader, and by allegations of sexual and other abuse of women detainees. Parliamentary committees delegated to examine these allegations reached conflicting conclusions.

Abuses by armed groups

Armed groups opposed to the government continued to commit gross human rights abuses, including indiscriminate killings of civilians.

■ On 5 January, at least 55 civilians, including Shi'a pilgrims making their way to Karbala, were killed and dozens injured in suicide bombings and other attacks. The attacks targeted predominantly Shi'a districts in Baghdad, including Sadr City and Khadimiya, and a police checkpoint near al-Nassirya where pilgrims were waiting to travel south.

■ At least 100 people, both civilians and members of the security forces, were killed on 23 July in a wave of bomb attacks and shootings in Baghdad and other cities, including Kirkuk and Taji.

■ At least 81 people, including many civilians, were killed on 9 September in a wave of co-ordinated bomb attacks in Baghdad, Baquba, Samarra, Basra and other cities.

Torture and other ill-treatment

Torture and other ill-treatment were common and widespread in prisons and detention centres, particularly those controlled by the Ministries of the Interior and Defence, and were committed with impunity. Methods included suspension by the limbs for long periods, beatings with cables and hosepipes, the infliction of electric shocks, breaking of limbs, partial asphyxiation with plastic bags, and sexual abuse including threats of rape. Torture was used to extract information from detainees and "confessions" that could be used as evidence against them at trial.

■ Nabhan 'Adel Hamid, Mu'ad Muhammad 'Abed, 'Amer Ahmad Kassar and Shakir Mahmoud 'Anad were arrested in Ramadi and Fallujah at the end of March/early April. They were reported to have been tortured while held incommunicado for several weeks at the Directorate of Counter-Crime in Ramadi. Their "confessions" were then broadcast on local television. When brought to trial, they told the Anbar Criminal Court that they had been forced under torture to

"confess" to assisting in murder. Witness testimony of fellow detainees supported their torture allegations. A medical examination of one defendant recorded burns and injuries consistent with torture. Despite this, all four men were sentenced to death on 3 December. No independent investigation into their torture allegations was known to have been held.

Deaths in custody

Several detainees died in custody in circumstances suggesting that torture or other ill-treatment caused or contributed to their deaths.

■ 'Amer Sarbut Zaidan al-Battawi, a former bodyguard of Vice-President al-Hashemi, died in detention in March. His family alleged that marks on his body had been caused by torture. Authorities denied that his death was caused by torture and announced further investigations.

■ Samir Naji 'Awda al-Bilawi, a pharmacist, and his 13-year-old son, Mundhir, were detained by security forces at a vehicle checkpoint in Ramadi in September. Three days later, his family learned that Samir Naji 'Awda al-Bilawi had died in custody. Images they released to Iraqi media showed injuries to his head and both hands. Following his release, Mundhir said he and his father had been assaulted at a police station then taken to the Directorate of Counter-Crime in Ramadi and tortured, including with electric shocks. He said he was ordered to tell an investigating judge that his father was connected to a terrorist organization. Lawyers for the family were allowed to read but not copy an official autopsy report that reportedly said Samir Naji 'Awda al-Bilawi's death was due to torture, including electric shocks. No action was known to have been taken against those responsible by the end of the year.

Counter-terror and security

The authorities arrested and detained hundreds of people on terrorism charges for their alleged participation in bomb and other attacks on security forces and civilians. Many alleged that they were tortured or otherwise ill-treated in pre-trial detention and were convicted and sentenced after unfair trials. In some cases, the authorities allowed Iraqi television stations to broadcast footage of detainees making self-incriminating statements before they were brought to trial, gravely prejudicing their right to a fair trial. Some were subsequently sentenced to death. The Ministry of Interior paraded detainees before press conferences at which they "confessed". The

Ministry also regularly uploaded detainees' "confessions" on its YouTube channel.

■ In late May, the Ministry of Interior paraded at least 16 detainees accused of belonging to an armed group linked to al-Qa'ida at a press conference and gave television stations recordings of some of them making self-incriminating statements. At the press conference, one of the detainees, Baghdad Provincial Council member Laith Mustafa al-Dulaimi, protested and shouted out that he and others had been abused.

■ Ramzi Shihab Ahmad, a 70-year-old with joint Iraqi and British nationality, was sentenced to 15 years' imprisonment on 20 June by the Resafa Criminal Court for helping to fund terrorist groups and issuing religious fatwas. The court accepted his "confession" made in pre-trial detention as evidence, despite strong indications that it was obtained through torture.

Death penalty

As in previous years, many, possibly hundreds, of people were sentenced to death, swelling the number of prisoners on death row. Most were convicted on terrorism-related charges. Ramadi's Tasfirat Prison held 33 prisoners sentenced to death during the first half of the year, 27 of whom had been convicted on terrorism charges. Trials consistently failed to meet international standards of fairness; many defendants alleged that they were tortured during interrogation in pre-trial detention and forced to "confess".

■ Muhammad Hussain and Sohail Akram, two associates of Vice-President al-Hashemi, were sentenced to death in October after the Central Criminal Court convicted them of murdering security officers.

At least 129 prisoners were executed, more than in any year since executions resumed in 2005. The authorities sometimes carried out multiple executions; 34 prisoners were executed in one day in January and 21 prisoners, including three women, were executed in one day in August. In September at least 18 women were reported to be on death row in a prison in the al-Kadhemiya district of Baghdad.

■ 'Abid Hamid Mahmoud, formerly Saddam Hussein's presidential secretary and bodyguard, was executed in June. He was sentenced to death in October 2010 by the Supreme Iraqi Criminal Tribunal.

Refugees and asylum-seekers

The process of gradually relocating some 3,200 Iranian political exiles from Camp New Iraq (formerly "Camp Ashraf") to Hurriya Transit Center ("Camp Liberty"), north-east of Baghdad, began in February and was nearly completed at the end of the year. They were long-term residents of Iraq and most were members or supporters of the People's Mojahedin Organization of Iran. They accused Iraqi security forces of attacking some of them while they were being relocated and criticized living conditions at Camp Liberty. In July, UNHCR, the UN refugee agency, publicly urged the international community to offer resettlement places or other forms of humanitarian admission to the residents of Camp Liberty.

The worsening conflict in neighbouring Syria impacted heavily on Iraq. Over 67,000 refugees from Syria crossed into Iraq, mostly after 18 July, and mostly entering the Kurdistan Region. Thousands of Iraqi refugees returned from Syria. In October, the Iraqi authorities violated international law by closing al-Qaem border crossing to refugees fleeing Syria, except in emergency cases. Following an earlier closure in August, restricted access had been allowed.

Kurdistan region of Iraq

Tension between the KRG and the central government in Baghdad remained high. In June, Kurdistan's parliament adopted a general amnesty law applicable to the Kurdistan region. The amnesty law excluded prisoners convicted of "honour" killings, rape, terrorism and drug trafficking crimes.

The KRG authorities continued to target some who spoke out against official corruption or expressed dissent. Incidents of torture or other ill-treatment continued to be reported.

■ Hussein Hama Ali Tawfiq, a businessman, was arrested on 27 March. He was taken to General Security (Asayish) in Suleimaniya where he was reportedly blindfolded, punched and beaten with an object while his hands were cuffed diagonally across his back. He was told to testify against others in a corruption case but refused. He was then charged with bribery and remained in detention until his acquittal in November. No investigations into his torture allegations were known to have been conducted.

Amnesty International visits/reports

🚌 Amnesty International delegates visited Iraq in September.

📄 Iraqi women held without charge (MDE 14/003/2012)

📖 Iraqi men detained incommunicado (MDE 14/005/2012)

📖 Iraq: Amnesty International condemns killings of civilians and calls for investigation (MDE 14/009/2012)

📖 Iraq must halt executions (MDE 14/011/2012)

IRELAND

REPUBLIC OF IRELAND
Head of state: **Michael D. Higgins**
Head of government: **Enda Kenny**

Conditions in a young offender institution were heavily criticized. Calls were renewed to regulate access to legal abortion. Legislation criminalizing female genital mutilation was enacted.

Prison conditions

In August, a new system for the investigation of serious complaints from prisoners by external investigators with an appeal to the Inspector of Prisons and Places of Detention, was announced. The government promised its eventual extension to other less serious complaints. However, this reform remained short of the independent complaints mechanism recommended by the UN Committee against Torture in 2011.

A report by the Inspector of Prisons on St Patrick's Institution for Young Offenders, published in October, described ill-treatment, intimidation and harsh punishment of the young men and boys detained there. It also identified inadequate provision of education and health care. Following the report, the government announced reforms within the facility – including improved training for prison officers – and the investigation of some staff. Earlier in the year, the placement of 16-year-olds in St Patrick's ended, although there remained concerns that 17-year-olds would continue to be placed there until a new children's detention facility becomes available in 2014.

Right to health

The government began a review of conformity with international human rights standards of the 2001 Mental Health Act. The Act primarily governs the circumstances in which a person may be involuntarily admitted to, detained and treated in a hospital.

In October, a 31-year-old woman died in hospital of septicaemia in circumstances where it was alleged that she was denied a potentially life-saving abortion. Her case highlighted the lack of clarity in legislation and regulations regarding women's right to access abortion where their life is at risk.

Violence against women and girls

At the end of the year, the government had still not established an independent investigation into allegations of ill-treatment of women and girls placed in religious-run institutions, known as the Magdalene Laundries, as recommended by the UN Committee against Torture. An inter-departmental committee established by the government in 2011 to "clarify any State interaction with the Magdalene Laundries" had also not issued its report.

In April, the Criminal Justice (Female Genital Mutilation) Act was enacted, criminalizing female genital mutilation (FGM). It also criminalized the removal of a girl from the country to undergo FGM, and provides protection for victims during legal proceedings.

Police and security forces

In October, the Oireachtas (parliament) approved an extension to the Smithwick Tribunal by a further nine months to end-July 2013. The Tribunal was examining allegations that members of An Garda Síochána (the police) colluded in the 1989 Provisional Irish Republican Army killing of two Royal Ulster Constabulary police officers in Northern Ireland.

Legal, constitutional or institutional developments

Ireland signed the Optional Protocol to the International Covenant on Economic, Social and Cultural Rights in March.

A government-appointed Constitutional Convention was established in July to examine elements of the Irish Constitution (Bunreacht na hÉireann), including in the areas of marriage equality for same-sex couples, women's equality and blasphemy. The Convention did not expressly include an examination of the Constitution's incorporation of human rights, and of economic, social and cultural rights.

In November, the Constitution was amended to provide some improved protections for children's rights.

Amnesty International visits/reports

📄 Ireland: Amnesty International welcomes the commitments to respect economic, social and cultural rights and to sign the Council of Europe Convention on Violence against Women and Domestic Violence (EUR 29/001/2012)

📄 Ireland's candidacy for election to the Human Rights Council elections: Open letter (EUR 29/002/2012)

📄 Ireland: Follow-up procedure to the forty-sixth session of the UN Committee against Torture (EUR 29/003/2012)

📄 Ireland: Abortion issue must be clarified by Irish government (PRE01/564/2012)

ISRAEL AND THE OCCUPIED PALESTINIAN TERRITORIES

STATE OF ISRAEL
Head of state: **Shimon Peres**
Head of government: **Benjamin Netanyahu**

The Israeli authorities held more than 4,500 Palestinian prisoners, including 178 administrative detainees at the end of the year, after a temporary decrease in numbers following Palestinian and international protests. Torture and other ill-treatment of detainees during arrest and interrogation was reported. Israel's military blockade of the Gaza Strip continued to severely affect Gaza's 1.6 million residents. In November, Israel launched an eight-day military campaign against Palestinian armed groups who fired rockets indiscriminately from Gaza into Israel; more than 160 Palestinians as well as six Israelis were killed, including many civilians. Both sides violated international humanitarian law in the conflict. The Israeli authorities continued to restrict the movement of Palestinians in the West Bank,

including East Jerusalem, construct the fence/wall, and expand illegal Israeli settlements while failing to protect Palestinians and their property from settler violence. They also continued to demolish Palestinian homes and carry out forced evictions. The Israeli military continued to use excessive force against protesters in the Occupied Palestinian Territories (OPT); in addition to 100 civilians killed during the November conflict in Gaza, Israeli forces killed at least 35 civilians in the OPT during the year. Palestinian citizens of Israel faced discrimination in housing and residency rights, and continued home demolitions, particularly in the Negev/Naqab region. Thousands of people seeking international protection were detained administratively under a new law implemented in June. Israeli forces responsible for the killing and injuring of Palestinian civilians and torture and other ill-treatment of detainees continued to evade accountability.

Background

Negotiations between Israel and the Palestinian Authority (PA) did not resume. Relations worsened after Palestine was recognized as a non-member observer state by the UN General Assembly in November. In response, Israel announced settlement expansion plans and withheld customs payments due to the PA. In March, Israel withdrew its co-operation with the UN Human Rights Council after the Council established a fact-finding committee to "investigate the implications" of Israeli settlements on Palestinians in the OPT.

In July, a government-appointed committee concluded that Israeli settlements in the occupied West Bank did not violate international law, despite the weight of international legal findings to the contrary, and recommended that the government formalize unauthorized settler outposts. For the first time in seven years, 14 new outposts and settlements were established, with support from the Israeli authorities.

Periodically throughout the year, Israeli military forces carried out air strikes on Gaza while Palestinian armed groups launched rocket attacks on Israel. Israel continued to fire live ammunition to enforce the land and sea "exclusion zones" inside Gaza's perimeter and territorial waters, killing at least six civilians and injuring others. Israeli leaders publicly advocated bombing Iranian nuclear sites.

One Israeli civilian was killed by militants from Egypt in June.

Freedom of movement – Gaza blockade and West Bank restrictions

The myriad restrictions imposed by the Israeli authorities on the movement of Palestinians amounted to collective punishment of the population of Gaza and the West Bank, in violation of international law. Over 500 Israeli checkpoints and barriers in the West Bank, as well as the fence/wall, restricted Palestinians' movement, particularly in East Jerusalem, part of Hebron, the Jordan Valley and areas near settlements. Palestinians were required to obtain permits from the Israeli authorities while Israelis, including settlers, enjoyed free movement in these areas. There were continued reports of harassment and abuse of Palestinians at checkpoints by Israeli personnel. Movement restrictions also impeded Palestinians' access to medical care, water and farmland.

As Israel's military blockade of the Gaza Strip entered its sixth year, its impact on basic infrastructure, including water, sanitation and power supplies continued to be severe. Israel continued to severely limit exports from and imports to Gaza, stifling its economy and driving the perilous underground smuggling trade from Egypt, which continued to claim the lives of those using the tunnels. More people were able to travel through the Rafah border crossing with Egypt than during previous years, despite continuing restrictions, but permits for travel to the West Bank remained rare and difficult to obtain, even for patients requiring urgent medical treatment. In September, Israel's High Court of Justice affirmed this policy of separating Gaza from the West Bank, rejecting a petition by Gazan women seeking to study at West Bank universities.

Forced evictions and demolitions

In more than 60% of the West Bank, known as Area C, the Israeli army continued to control planning, zoning and security and regularly demolished Palestinian homes. Some 604 structures, a third of them homes, and including 36 water cisterns, were destroyed, resulting in the forced eviction of some 870 Palestinians from their homes and affecting at least 1600 others. Israeli settlers continued to attack Palestinian residents and their property with virtual

impunity. Palestinian citizens of Israel, particularly those living in officially "unrecognized villages" in the Negev region, were regularly subjected to home demolitions by the Israel Land Administration (ILA) and municipal bodies.

■ In the West Bank, the army demolished homes, water cisterns and animal pens repeatedly in Umm al-Kheir and other villages in the southern Hebron hills, while villages such as al-'Aqaba, Khirbet Tana, Humsa and Hadidiya were threatened with complete demolition.

■ The ILA demolished tents and other structures in al-'Araqib, an "unrecognized" village in the Negev, 13 times during 2012, following dozens of previous demolitions since July 2010.

Impunity

The authorities again failed to independently investigate killings of Palestinian civilians by Israeli soldiers in the West Bank and Gaza or to prosecute those responsible. Impunity continued for war crimes committed by Israeli forces during Operation "Cast Lead" in 2008-2009, and there were no indications that independent investigations would be conducted into violations committed during the November 2012 Gaza-Israel conflict. Police investigations into Israeli settler violence against Palestinians rarely led to prosecutions.

■ In May, the military authorities closed their investigation into the killing of 21 members of the Samouni family, including young children, during Operation "Cast Lead". The family was sheltering in a house into which Israeli soldiers had ordered them to move, when they were killed, apparently by shelling. The authorities ruled that the deaths did not result from negligence by Israeli troops.

■ In August, a soldier who shot dead two Palestinian women holding a white flag during Operation "Cast Lead" received a 45-day prison sentence for "illegal use of a weapon" as the result of a plea bargain.

■ On 28 August, a court in Haifa absolved the Israeli authorities of responsibility for the death of US activist Rachel Corrie, who was run over and killed in 2003 while protesting against home demolitions in Rafah, Gaza.

Operation "Pillar of Defense"

Israeli forces launched a major military operation on Gaza on 14 November, beginning with an airstrike that killed the leader of the military wing of Hamas.

In the following eight days, before a ceasefire on 21 November was reached with Egyptian mediation, more than 160 Palestinians, including more than 30 children and some 70 other civilians, and six Israelis, including four civilians, were killed. Both sides committed war crimes and other violations of international humanitarian law. The Israeli air force carried out bomb and missile strikes on residential areas, including strikes that were disproportionate and caused heavy civilian casualties. Other strikes damaged or destroyed civilian property, media facilities, government buildings and police stations. In most cases, Israel did not present evidence that these specific sites had been used for military purposes. The Israeli navy shelled populated coastal areas with artillery in indiscriminate attacks. The military wing of Hamas and other Palestinian armed groups fired rockets and other weapons into Israel, killing civilians and damaging civilian property.

■ On 18 November, 10 members of the al-Dalu family, including four children under the age of eight, a teenage girl, and four women, and two of their neighbours were killed when their home was struck in an Israeli air strike on Gaza City. Israeli military spokespersons stated variously that the strike was an accident, or was intended to hit a militant, but gave different names for the target, without providing evidence to support their claims.

■ On 19 November, five-year-old Mohammed Abu Zur and two of his aunts were killed, and dozens wounded, when their neighbour's house was targeted in an Israeli air strike.

Detention without trial

More than 320 Palestinians from the OPT were held without charge or trial in administrative detention during the year, but their numbers decreased substantially following a mass hunger strike (see under 'Prison conditions' below). Several Palestinians released in a 2011 prisoner exchange were re-arrested on the orders of a military committee and held for extended periods without being charged or having their previous sentences formally reinvoked.

■ West Bank resident Hana Shalabi was transferred to Gaza, probably against her will, for at least three years in April following a 43-day hunger strike against her administrative detention, which began in February 2012.

Prison conditions

On 17 April, some 2,000 Palestinian prisoners and detainees went on hunger strike to protest against their conditions, including the use of solitary confinement, detention without charge or trial and the denial of family visits. They ended their hunger strike on 14 May following an Egyptian-brokered deal with the Israeli authorities, according to which the Israeli authorities agreed to end the solitary confinement of 19 prisoners and lift a ban on family visits to prisoners from Gaza. Two Palestinian prisoners were still held in long-term isolation at the end of 2012, and short-term isolation continued to be used as punishment.

■ Hassan Shuka, an administrative detainee held without charge or trial since 17 September 2010, was permitted to receive family visits only from his sisters, aged 14 and eight, at Ketziot prison in southern Israel; other family members were barred from entering Israel.

Torture and other ill-treatment

Palestinian detainees reported being tortured and otherwise ill-treated during interrogation by the Israel Security Agency (ISA), including being subjected to painful shackling or binding of the limbs, immobilization in stress positions, sleep deprivation, threats and verbal abuse. Detainees were denied access to lawyers while under interrogation for days and occasionally weeks. Detainees on prolonged hunger strikes were repeatedly denied access to independent doctors and ill-treated by Israel Prison Service (IPS) staff.

The authorities failed to independently investigate allegations of torture of detainees by the ISA, fuelling a climate of impunity. Investigations were the responsibility of the Interrogee Complaints Comptroller, an ISA employee, despite a November 2010 decision by the Attorney General to place the Comptroller under the Ministry of Justice. A law exempting the Israeli police and ISA from recording interrogations of "security" detainees, almost all of whom are Palestinian, was extended, helping to perpetuate impunity for torture and other ill-treatment. Despite the filing of more than 700 complaints relating to 2001-2012, only one criminal investigation had been opened by the end of 2012.

■ Samer al-Barq went on hunger strike three times from April 2012, in protest against his administrative detention since July 2010 and harsh conditions at a prison medical centre in Ramleh. He was denied

I

specialized medical care and ill-treated by prison guards, who beat and verbally abused him.

■ Gazan engineer Dirar Abu Sisi, who was forcibly transferred from Ukraine to Israel in February 2011, entered his second year in solitary confinement without family visits at Shikma Prison, near Ashkelon. He was reportedly in ill health and had been denied adequate medical treatment. His lawyer and family alleged that he had been coerced, under torture, into "confessing" that he had designed rockets for use by the military wing of Hamas.

Freedoms of expression and assembly

Israeli soldiers opened fire with live ammunition on Palestinian protesters on numerous occasions in areas inside Gaza's perimeter and routinely used excessive force against demonstrators in the West Bank, killing at least four. As local human rights groups documented, Israeli soldiers also fired tear gas canisters directly at peaceful protesters, causing serious injuries. The authorities also used excessive force against demonstrations inside Israel.

■ Mahmoud Zaqout was killed and scores of protesters were injured on 30 March when Israeli soldiers fired live ammunition at "Land Day" demonstrators near the Erez Crossing in Gaza and used excessive force against several demonstrations in the West Bank, including East Jerusalem.

■ Security forces arrested over 100 people and used excessive force to disperse hundreds of Israeli protesters who gathered in Tel Aviv on 22 and 23 June to call for lower housing costs and better health and education.

■ In October, activist Bassem Tamimi was imprisoned for the second time during 2012 for his involvement in non-violent protests against Israeli settlements. In an unfair trial in November he received a four-month sentence.

Conscientious objectors

At least six Israeli citizens were sent to jail for refusing to serve in the army on grounds of conscience. One, Natan Blanc, continued to be held at the end of the year.

■ Noam Gur was arrested on 17 April for refusing to carry out military service. She served two 10-day prison sentences in April and May.

Refugees and asylum-seekers

People seeking international protection continued to be denied access to fair refugee-determination procedures and faced arrest and detention. Thousands of asylum-seekers were imprisoned under the Anti-Infiltration Law, which was passed in January and implemented from June. In violation of international refugee law, the law empowered the authorities to automatically detain asylum-seekers alongside others crossing irregularly into Israel, for a minimum of three years and allowed indefinite detention in some cases. At the end of the year, the authorities were expanding detention capacity in the Negev desert to hold more than 11,000 people, and at least 2,400 asylum-seekers were detained, many in tents.

■ Hundreds of asylum-seekers were deported to South Sudan without being permitted access to fair, consistent and transparent individual asylum procedures.

Amnesty International visits/reports

🚗 Amnesty International delegates visited Israel and the OPT in June/July and November/December.

📄 Israel and the Occupied Palestinian Territories: Stop the transfer– Israel about to expel Bedouin to expand settlements (MDE 15/001/2012)

📄 Israel and the Occupied Palestinian Territories: Starved of justice – Palestinians detained without trial by Israel (MDE 15/026/2012)

📄 Israel/OPT: Letter to UN Committee against Torture regarding adoption of list of issues by the Committee (MDE 15/029/2012)

📄 Israel/OPT: International pressure mounts over Gaza blockade (MDE 15/033/2012)

📄 Israel: Amnesty International urges government to respect the right to freedom of peaceful assembly (MDE 15/037/2012)

ITALY

REPUBLIC OF ITALY
Head of state: Giorgio Napolitano
Head of government: Mario Monti

Roma continued to be discriminated against, ethnically segregated in camps, forcibly evicted and left homeless. The authorities regularly failed to protect the rights of refugees, asylum-seekers and migrants. Attempts to introduce the crime of torture and establish an independent national human rights institution failed again. No systemic measures were taken to prevent human rights violations by police and ensure accountability. Violence against women, including killings, remained widespread.

Discrimination
Roma

The government failed to address adequately the ongoing human rights violations of Roma, especially in access to adequate housing. Several hundred Roma were forcibly evicted with many being left homeless. Authorized or "tolerated" camps continued to be closed without adequate legal safeguards and procedures. The authorities failed to improve the very poor living conditions in most authorized camps. Conditions in informal camps were even harsher, with little access to water, sanitation and energy. Local authorities continued to exclude many Roma from social housing, preferring instead to perpetuate policies of ethnic segregation of Roma in camps.

The National Strategy for the Inclusion of Roma presented in February remained largely unimplemented. The UN CERD Committee in March and the Council of Europe Commissioner for Human Rights in September reiterated their criticisms of the authorities' failures to ensure the rights of Roma. The government failed to provide reparations to Roma whose rights were violated during the state of emergency declared in 2008 in relation to "nomad" settlements in five Italian regions, which remained in force until November 2011, when it was declared unlawful by the Council of State. Instead, the government appealed against the Council of State ruling in February, alleging that the court went beyond its powers of scrutiny. The case was pending before Italy's Supreme Court at the end of the year. In May, the Council of State declared that – pending the Court's decision – certain activities initiated during the emergency could be completed.

■ The Rome authorities continued to implement their "Nomad Plan", which resulted in several forced evictions of informal, "tolerated" and authorized camps and the resettlement of many Roma in segregated authorized camps. The residents of Tor de' Cenci camp were forcibly evicted in two operations on 25 July and 28 September, without adequate prior consultation and despite the opposition of NGOs, the Catholic Church and the national government. In June, the municipal authorities opened a new segregated camp in an isolated location at La Barbuta, near Ciampino airport. NGOs started legal proceedings in March before Rome's civil tribunal, to have the housing of Roma at La Barbuta ruled as discriminatory. About 200 residents from Tor de' Cenci camp were transferred to La Barbuta.

■ Racist threats, intimidation and incitement to violence against Roma took place in May in the town of Pescara, following the killing of a football supporter reportedly by a Romani man. Romani families reported being afraid to go out and take children to school. Soon after the beginning of the unrest, the Mayor of Pescara made discriminatory remarks against Roma, mentioning the need to review their access to social housing.

Rights of lesbian, gay, bisexual , transgender and intersex people

The Supreme Court confirmed that same-sex couples had a right to family life including, in certain circumstances, to treatment consistent with that of married opposite-sex couples. However, it also ruled that a marriage contracted abroad by same-sex couples had no standing in the Italian legal system.

Refugees, asylum-seekers and migrants

Many refugees and asylum-seekers, including minors, continued to face economic hardship and destitution, prompting some courts in EU countries to halt their returns to Italy under the Dublin Regulation. The authorities frequently failed to address their needs and protect their rights.

Conditions in detention centres for irregular migrants fell well below international standards. Legal safeguards for the return of irregular migrants to their countries of origin were reportedly breached on many

I

occasions. Migrant workers were often exploited and vulnerable to abuses, while their access to justice remained inadequate. Italy's migration policies failed to respect the rights of migrants to work, to just and favourable working conditions and to justice. In September, the Council of Europe Commissioner for Human Rights criticized the treatment of refugees, asylum-seekers and migrants, including the lack of integration measures for refugees and their destitution, the degrading detention conditions of irregular migrants and the risk of human rights abuses arising from agreements with countries such as Libya, Egypt and Tunisia.

■ In February, the European Court of Human Rights ruled that Italy had violated international human rights obligations to not return individuals to countries where they could be at risk of abuses, by pushing back African migrants and asylum-seekers on the high seas. In the case of *Hirsi Jamaa and Others v. Italy*, the Court considered the plight of 24 people from Somalia and Eritrea, among more than 200 people intercepted at sea by Italian authorities in 2009 and forced to return to Libya. In September, the Council of Europe opened proceedings to examine how Italy had progressed in executing the judgement.

On 3 April, Italy signed a new agreement with Libya on migration control. The Italian authorities sought support from Libya to stem migration flows, but ignored the fact that migrants, refugees and asylum-seekers continued to risk serious human rights abuses there. Libya committed to strengthen its border controls to prevent departures of migrants from its territory, with Italy providing training and equipment to enhance border surveillance. Effective human rights safeguards were absent. The agreement gave no consideration to the needs of migrants for international protection.

Counter-terror and security

On 19 September, the Supreme Court confirmed the convictions on appeal of 22 CIA agents, a US military official, and two Italian secret services operatives for the kidnapping in Milan in February 2003 of Usama Mostafa Hassan Nasr (known as Abu Omar), who was subsequently transferred to Egypt by the CIA where he was allegedly tortured. The US nationals were all tried in their absence. The Supreme Court also ordered the retrial of two top-level officials of the Italian intelligence agency and of three other high-

ranking officials for their involvement in the abduction. The charges against them had been dismissed by the Milan Court of Appeal in December 2010 due to government claims that key evidence should not be disclosed as a matter of "state secrecy". The Milan Court of Appeal was asked to reconsider the scope and limits of "state secrecy", and how this would apply in the retrial.

Also in September, the EU Parliament called on Italy and other EU member states to disclose all necessary information on all suspect planes associated with the CIA rendition and secret detention programmes; to effectively investigate governments' roles in the CIA operations; and to respect the right to freedom of information and respond appropriately to requests for access to information.

Torture and other ill-treatment

In October, Parliament approved the ratification of the Optional Protocol to the UN Convention against Torture, but failed to introduce the crime of torture into the criminal code, as the Convention requires. No systemic measures were taken to prevent human rights violations by police, or to ensure accountability for them. Conditions of detention and the treatment of detainees in many prisons and other detention centres were inhumane and violated detainees' rights, including to health. In April, the Senate published a report on the state of prisons and migrants' detention centres, documenting grave overcrowding and failures to uphold respect for human dignity and other international obligations.

Genoa G8 trials

On 5 July, the Supreme Court confirmed all 25 convictions issued on appeal against high-ranking officials and police officers responsible for the torture and other ill-treatment of demonstrators on 21 July 2001. Senior officials were convicted for falsifying arrest documents, and sentences ranged from five years to three years and eight months of imprisonment. However, due to a law designed to cut inmate numbers, which allows for a three-year reduction in sentences, nobody was imprisoned, although all were suspended from duty for five years. Convictions issued on appeal for grievous bodily harm against nine officers lapsed, as the statute of limitation came into effect prior to the conclusion of the appeal to the Supreme Court, which also meant they would not be suspended from duty. All the convicted officers, including those whose crimes were covered by the statute of limitations, were due to undergo disciplinary proceedings.

Unlawful killings

Shortcomings in the investigations of a number of deaths in custody resulted in a lack of accountability for police and prison officers. There were concerns that municipal police forces were assigned firearms without adequate safeguards and were using them in a manner not consistent with international law.

■ On 13 February, Marcelo Valentino Gómez Cortés, a 28-year-old Chilean national, unarmed, was shot and killed by an officer of the Milan municipal police. In October, the officer was found guilty at first instance of homicide and sentenced to 10 years' imprisonment. The officer appealed against the verdict. He had been assigned to desk duties after the incident and his firearm licence was revoked.

■ In March, a prison officer was found guilty of failure to assist Aldo Bianzino, who died in Perugia prison in 2007 two days after his arrest, and of falsifying documents. The officer received a suspended 18-month custodial sentence. The trial revealed failures in the original investigation into the death. The family continued to campaign for the reopening of the case.

■ In April, a first-instance judge acquitted a doctor accused of manslaughter for prescribing the wrong medical treatment to Giuseppe Uva, who died shortly after being stopped by police in 2008 in Varese. The judge ordered a new investigation focusing on the period between when Giuseppe Uva was stopped by police and his arrival at the hospital. Forensic examinations carried out in December 2011 had revealed that the victim could have been raped and ill-treated.

Violence against women and girls

Violence against women remained widespread, with approximately 122 killings reported in 2012. The UN Special Rapporteur on violence against women noted in June that, notwithstanding improvements in legislation and policy, killings had not decreased. Her recommendations included: an independent national human rights institution with a section dedicated to women's rights; a law on violence against women; and the amendment of the crime of irregular migration to ensure access to justice for migrant women in irregular situations.

Legal, constitutional or institutional developments

In December parliament passed overdue legislation required to comply with the Rome Statute of the International Criminal Court, which Italy ratified in 1999. Measures were introduced to regulate judicial co-operation with the International Criminal Court.

Also in December, a parliamentary committee examining a bill aimed at creating a national human rights institution concluded that, due to imminent parliamentary elections, it was impossible to pass the bill in the current session. The bill had already been through a lengthy parliamentary debate in the higher chamber. International bodies, including the UN High Commissioner for Human Rights, had criticized Italy on many occasions for its failure to establish a national human rights institution compliant with international standards.

Amnesty International visits/reports

🚌 Amnesty International delegates visited Italy in March, April, June, September, November and December.

▦ S.O.S. Europe: Human rights and migration control (EUR 01/013/2012)

▦ Italy: Briefing to the UN Committee on the Elimination of Racial Discrimination: 80th session (EUR 30/001/2012)

▦ On the edge: Roma, forced evictions and segregation in Italy (EUR 30/010/2012)

▦ Exploited labour: Migrant workers in Italy's agricultural sector (EUR 30/020/2012)

J

JAMAICA

JAMAICA
Head of state: **Queen Elizabeth II, represented by Patrick Linton Allen**
Head of government: **Portia Simpson Miller**

High levels of gang-related murders and killings by police persisted in inner-city communities. There was no significant progress in the investigation into alleged human rights violations during the 2010 state of emergency. Attacks and harassment of LGBTI people were reported to be increasing. No death sentences were passed and there were no executions.

Background

A new government took office in January. In her inaugural speech, the Prime Minister pledged to initiate the process for Jamaica to become a Republic.

In July, the government tabled three bills in the House of Representatives aimed at replacing the Judicial Committee of the Privy Council with the Caribbean Court of Justice as Jamaica's final court of appeal. However, the debate in parliament stalled after the Opposition argued that such a change required a referendum.

High levels of gang violence, mainly in marginalized inner-city communities, remained a concern; 1,087 killings were reported during the year. Several incidents of mob attacks were reported. In April, the first part of a new National Security Policy was published.

Police and security forces

The number of people killed by police fell in 2012 as compared with 2011, but remained worryingly high. Several people were killed in controversial circumstances.

Following public outrage at the killings of 21 people by police in just six days at the beginning of March, the Minister of National Security announced that a review of the policy on police use of force would be undertaken and that the government would hold "the Commissioner of Police and the High Command accountable for a reduction in the level of Police fatal shootings". However, by the end of the year no information had been made available about how this would be implemented.

In July, three soldiers were charged with the murder of Keith Clarke in his home during the first week of the 2010 state of emergency. In spite of repeated promises, the Public Defender failed to submit a report to Parliament with the findings of his investigation into allegations of human rights violations, including unlawful killings, during the state of emergency. The government stated that the decision on whether to appoint an independent commission of inquiry about what happened would depend on the results of the Public Defender's investigation.

In its report to Parliament in June, the Independent Commission of Investigations into abuses by the security forces (INDECOM) identified collusion among members of the security forces, wearing masks and balaclavas during operations, and delays in obtaining forensic evidence as major challenges in the investigations. Following several judicial challenges brought by the police against INDECOM, a review of the legislation was initiated with the aim of clarifying INDECOM's powers and mandate.

In October, the Minister of National Security announced that the government intended to dismantle the committee overseeing the implementation of police reform. Civil society organizations criticized this decision.

Justice system

Significant delays in the delivery of justice continued to be reported. Problems highlighted included the authorities' failure to deal with witness absenteeism and the unavailability of citizens for jury service. Parliament continued debating the Committal Proceedings Bill, which seeks to reduce delays by abolishing preliminary enquiries.

Children's rights

According to local human rights organizations, boys continued to be detained in police lockups, often with adults. No plan was made to open a separate remand centre for girls. In September, the Youth Minister said that a submission to Cabinet would be prepared within a month with recommendations for child offenders remanded by the court or awaiting court appearance to be held in separate facilities from those housing adults. No information that this had been done was available at the end of the year.

Violence against women and girls

Sexual violence against women and girls remained a concern. On 27 September, following a meeting with several government and civil society representatives, the Office of the Prime Minister promised a plan of action to address violence against women.

In July, the CEDAW Committee recommended, among other things, strengthening the capacity of the Bureau of Women's Affairs, collecting and compiling comprehensive data on violence against women, and strengthening victim assistance and support programmes.

Rights of lesbian, gay, bisexual, transgender and intersex people

LGBTI organizations reported an increase in attacks, harassment and threats. Many such attacks were not fully and promptly investigated.

During the electoral campaign in December 2011, Portia Simpson Miller stated that no one should be discriminated against because of their sexual orientation. However, once elected, the government took no steps to remove discriminatory laws.

A second petition was filed with the Inter-American Commission on Human Rights challenging articles in the Offences Against the Person Act (commonly known as the "buggery" law) on the grounds that they are unconstitutional and promote homophobia.

Death penalty

No death sentences were handed down. There were seven people on death row at the end of the year.

Amnesty International visits/reports

- Jamaica: One more year without justice (AMR 38/002/2012)
- Jamaica must tackle shocking wave of police killings (PRE01/123/2012)

JAPAN

JAPAN
Head of government: Shinzo Abe (replaced
                     Yoshihiko Noda in December)

Police abuse and irregularities in police interrogations took place in Japan's criminal justice system. The authorities continued to reject calls for justice for the survivors of Japan's military sexual slavery system. Japan resumed executions after a 20-month hiatus. The number of people being granted refugee status remained extremely low.

Background

The Liberal Democratic Party headed by Shinzo Abe won parliamentary elections on 16 December. Although a state party to the Rome Statute of the International Criminal Court since 2007, Japan had still not implemented its obligations under this treaty.

About 160,000 people continued to live in temporary housing or outside Fukushima prefecture, as a result of the 2011 earthquake in the Tohoku area of eastern Japan. In October, Greenpeace stated that several government radiation-monitoring posts in the area were under-reporting radiation levels, including by monitoring decontaminated spots. Protests against restarting nuclear power plants attracted tens of thousands of people and ran for several months throughout the country.

Justice system

The *daiyo kangoku* system, which allows police to detain suspects for up to 23 days, continued to facilitate torture and other ill-treatment to extract confessions during interrogation. The Special Committee of the Legislative Council under the Ministry of Justice continued to discuss potential reforms to the criminal justice system.

■ Govinda Prasad Mainali, a Nepalese national, was acquitted of murder on 7 November after spending 15 years in prison. He was ill-treated and denied access to a lawyer while being held under the *daiyo kangoku* system. In July 2011, the prosecution handed over evidence that subsequently proved him innocent.

Violence against women and girls

When Japan's human rights record was assessed under the UN Universal Periodic Review in October, government officials claimed compensation for former "comfort women" had already been resolved under the San Francisco Peace Treaty, bilateral agreements and treaties. On 4 November, then opposition leader Shinzo Abe was among signatories to a US newspaper advertisement which denied that the Japanese Imperial Army forced women into military sexual slavery during World War II.

Death penalty

Seven people were executed in Japan, including the first woman to be executed in over 15 years. There were 133 people on death row. The working group established within the Ministry of Justice by former Minister Keiko Chiba in July 2010 to study capital punishment was disbanded in March by Minister of Justice Toshio Ogawa without providing any clear recommendations.

■ Junya Hattori was executed on 3 August. The Shizuoka District Court sentenced him to life imprisonment but the Tokyo High Court sentenced him to death after the prosecution appealed. The Supreme Court upheld his death sentence in February 2008.

Asylum-seekers and refugees

Asylum applications increased to over 2000, up from 1,867 last year, but the numbers granted refugee status remained low. The majority of applicants were from Myanmar. Japan's 2010 pilot project to resettle 30 refugees from Myanmar who were processed in Thailand was extended in March for a further two years. No one was accepted under the system this year after three families withdrew their application.

JORDAN

HASHEMITE KINGDOM OF JORDAN
Head of state: King Abdullah II bin al-Hussein
Head of government: Abdullah Ensour (replaced Fayez Tarawneh in October, who replaced Awn al-Khasawneh in May)

The security forces used excessive force and arrested hundreds of peaceful and other demonstrators calling for reform. The authorities maintained tight restrictions on freedoms of expression, association and assembly, and imposed new restrictions on electronic media. There were reports of torture and other ill-treatment of detainees. Unfair trials continued before the State Security Court (SSC). Hundreds, possibly thousands, of criminal suspects were detained indefinitely without charge or trial. Women faced discrimination and violence; at least ten were reported to be victims of "honour" killings. Migrant domestic workers were exploited and abused. There were reports that some refugees were forcibly returned to Syria. At least 16 people were sentenced to death; there were no executions.

Background

Demonstrations continued throughout the year against the slow pace of political reform and economic conditions, including cuts in government fuel subsidies. Protests in November became violent; one man was killed in Irbid in November in disputed circumstances and two police officers died of gunshot wounds sustained during disturbances in Karak and Amman. The King sought to assuage dissent by appointing new prime ministers in May and again in October when he dissolved parliament. Elections were set for January 2013 under an Elections Law approved by royal decree in July; opposition members argued that pro-government candidates retained an unfair advantage.

Thousands of refugees entered Jordan to escape the conflict in Syria, adding to the pressure on resources.

In November, a UK court prevented the UK government from deporting Abu Qatada to Jordan, ruling that he could not be guaranteed a fair trial there (see United Kingdom entry).

Freedoms of expression, association and assembly

The security forces detained hundreds of peaceful and other protesters calling for political and other reform; many were beaten on arrest or in detention. In September, the government amended the Press and Publications Law to tighten restrictions on electronic media, creating powers to close or block websites.

■ Six members of the pro-reform Free Tafileh Movement were arrested in March and held for over a month accused of "insulting the King" and other offences relating to a violent protest in Tafileh in which they were apparently uninvolved. One, Majdi Qableen, was reported to have been blindfolded, chained by his feet and beaten during interrogation by General Intelligence Department (GID) officers. At least two others were also beaten in custody. They were released without charge in April.

■ Ola Saif, was arrested in November at a peaceful protest in Amman against economic policy. She says she was beaten in the Central Amman Public Security Directorate and denied access to a lawyer or relatives. She was charged with trying to overthrow the political system and released on 5 December.

Torture and other ill-treatment

There were reports of torture and other ill-treatment of security suspects and people detained, some incommunicado for prolonged periods, following pro-reform protests.

■ Eleven men arrested on 21 October for allegedly planning violent attacks in Amman were held by the

GID in Amman in almost continuous incommunicado detention without access to lawyers or family for more than two months. Most of them claimed to have "confessed" under torture.

■ Rami al-Sehwal was reportedly stripped naked, tied and beaten over two days by police and GID officers who sought to "teach" him and 12 other men "a lesson" after they were detained at a peaceful protest in Amman on 30 March. All 13 were released without charge.

Unfair trials

The SSC continued to prosecute civilians for security offences in trials that fell short of international standards of fairness. Hundreds of people including nine children faced charges under Penal Code articles criminalizing peaceful dissent and were referred to the SSC for trial.

■ 'Uday Abu 'Isa was sentenced to two years' imprisonment by the SSC in January for burning a picture of the King at a demonstration. A prisoner of conscience, he was held for seven weeks before being released under a royal pardon. He said police had beaten him after his arrest.

Detention without trial

Hundreds, possibly thousands, of people continued to be detained without charge or trial for long periods under the 1954 Law on Crime Prevention, which empowers provincial governors to order the indefinite detention without charge of anyone they suspect of having committed a crime or deem a "danger to society".

Discrimination and violence against women

Women were discriminated against in law and practice, and were inadequately protected against gender-based violence. At least ten women were reported to have been killed by male relatives, victims of so-called "honour" crimes.

The UN CEDAW Committee and the UN Special Rapporteur on violence against women urged the government to amend the Citizenship and Nationality Law to enable Jordanian women to pass on their nationality to their children and spouses on an equal basis with Jordanian men, and to lift reservations to Articles 9 and 16 of CEDAW relating to nationality and to discrimination in family relations. In November, the

Prime Minister said the government would address these reservations.

Migrants' rights – domestic workers

There were reports of migrant domestic workers, mostly women, being confined to their employers' homes, denied pay, having their passports seized or being physically, psychologically or sexually abused by their employers.

In March, the UN CERD Committee urged the government to ensure full labour rights for all employees including migrant domestic workers, regardless of nationality or ethnicity.

Refugees and asylum-seekers

Thousands of people fleeing the conflict in Syria sought refuge in Jordan. UNHCR, the UN refugee agency, said in December that 163,088 refugees from Syria had registered or were waiting to register with them; the total number of refugees was believed to be higher. There were reports that some Syrian and Palestinian refugees were forcibly returned to Syria. On 31 August, Jordan's Foreign Minister said some 200 Syrians had been removed from al-Za'atari refugee camp and returned to the border area between Jordan and Syria after "rioting" and inciting violence.

Death penalty

At least 16 people were sentenced to death; at least five death sentences were commuted. There were no executions; the last execution was in 2006.

Amnesty International visits/reports

🚌 Amnesty International visited Jordan in February and July to carry out human rights research relating to Syria.

▨ Jordan: Decision to release two government critics welcomed as a positive first step (MDE 16/001/2012)

▨ Jordan: Six pro-reform activists under investigation for "insulting" the King must be released (MDE 16/002/2012)

▨ Jordan: Arbitrary arrests, torture and other ill-treatment and lack of adequate medical care of detained protesters (MDE 16/003/2012)

▨ Jordan: Arrest of 20 pro-reform activists heralds crackdown on freedom of expression (PRE01/489/2012)

KAZAKHSTAN

REPUBLIC OF KAZAKHSTAN
Head of state: **Nursultan Nazarbaev**
Head of government: **Serik Akhmetov (replaced**
Karim Massimov in September 2012)

A criminal investigation into the use of lethal force by security officials during the mass unrest in Zhanaozen in December 2011 resulted in charges being brought against five individual officers. Alleged organizers and participants were put on trial in March. Most of those charged with organizing and participating in the violence claimed that they were tortured to force their confessions. The leader of an unregistered opposition party received a long prison sentence for his alleged involvement in the Zhanaozen violence after an unfair trial. Independent media outlets were branded as "extremist" and closed down. Extraditions continued of individuals at risk of torture and other ill-treatment upon return to the countries requesting their return.

Excessive use of force

In January 2012, following an investigation into the lethal use of force by security forces, five senior security officers were charged with abuse of office in relation to the use of force in Zhanaozen. However, the number of deaths and serious injuries from gunshot wounds indicated that many more security officers had used firearms. The trial followed the events on 16 December 2011, where celebrations of the 20th anniversary of Kazakhstan's independence in the south-western city of Zhanaozen were marred by violent clashes between protesters and police. At least 15 people were killed and more than 100 seriously injured. Reportedly, security forces had no specific training in using non-violent and proportionate methods of crowd control while policing protest demonstrations and strikes, despite months of being confronted by striking and protesting oil industry workers and their families and supporters in 2011.

In response to calls for further investigations into all cases of deaths and injuries, including those not recorded officially, in order to establish the true number of fatalities and casualties and bring all those

responsible to justice, the General Prosecutor's Office asserted in October that all available evidence had been thoroughly investigated by the Regional Department of Internal Affairs and that there was no need to bring further criminal charges against other security officers.

■ Five senior security officers from Mangistau Region and Zhanaozen city were charged in late January with abuse of office in relation to the use of firearms. According to the General Prosecutor's Office, some of them had been identified using video footage. They were sentenced to between five and seven years in prison in May. Several police officers testifying at the trial as witnesses confirmed that they had used firearms to shoot directly at protesters. However, no charges were brought against them.

Torture and other ill-treatment

Most of the 37 defendants, put on trial in March in the regional capital Aktau for organizing or participating in the violence in Zhanaozen, alleged that they were tortured or otherwise ill-treated in detention by security forces in order to extract confessions, and recanted their confessions in court. The torture methods described by the defendants were consistent with the allegations made by many of the released detainees in December 2011, namely that they were taken to unofficial places of detention or underground detention facilities at police stations, stripped naked, made to lie or crouch on a cold concrete floor, doused with cold water, beaten and kicked by security officers, often to the point of losing consciousness. They would then be doused with cold water again and beaten at regular intervals in cycles lasting for hours. Ten of the witnesses for the prosecution withdrew their testimonies against the defendants during the trial proceedings and complained that they had been tortured or otherwise ill-treated into giving evidence implicating the defendants.

Some of the defendants identified police and security officers who had subjected them to torture and other ill-treatment. The police and security officers, accused by the defendants and their lawyers of opening fire at the demonstrators and ill-treating them in detention, testified in court as victims or witnesses, some of them anonymously. All police and security officers pleaded self-defence. When asked who had given the order to open fire, some of the officers stated that they had not received any orders to open fire but neither had they received any orders not to open fire. The General Prosecutor's Office reviewed the allegations of torture at the request of the presiding judge but rejected the claims. Seven of the defendants were sentenced to up to seven years in prison.

■ Roza Tuletaeva, a labour activist who had been one of the main contact points for media and international organizations during the strike by oil industry workers in 2011, stated in court that during interrogations she was suspended by her hair, that security officers threatened to harm her 14-year-old daughter, that they put a plastic bag over her head to suffocate her and that they sexually humiliated and assaulted her. She said that she was too ashamed to describe the sexual torture she was subjected to in the courtroom as her family and friends were present. She was sentenced to seven years in prison for "inciting social discord".

Unfair trials

In addition to the 37 individuals who were detained in Zhanaozen in December 2011 and stood trial in March 2012, security forces detained three political opposition activists based in Almaty in January, and a prominent theatre director and a youth activist in June, and charged them with "inciting social discord" and "destabilizing the situation in the region" in relation to the Zhanaozen events. All but two were released conditionally after several weeks in National Security Service (NSS) detention when they agreed to sign confessions, admitting that they had travelled to Zhanaozen to support the striking oil industry workers.

Prejudicial statements made in state-owned media outlets by high-ranking officials against all those charged in relation to Zhanaozen, as well as numerous procedural violations, such as restrictions on legal access and family visits, precluded them from receiving a fair trial. Lawyers acting for the activists in NSS detention were forced to sign non-disclosure statements, barring them from divulging any information relating to the criminal investigation into their clients' cases.

■ On 23 January, NSS officers arrested Vladimir Kozlov, the leader of the unregistered opposition Alga party, at his Almaty home on charges of "inciting social discord". They also searched his home, the Alga party office in Almaty, and the homes of several other party members. Vladimir Kozlov had gone to Zhanaozen in January as part of an independent public monitoring group to investigate the allegations of torture and other ill-treatment in police custody and then had briefed the European Parliament on his findings. He was detained in the NSS facilities in Aktau, with restricted access to his lawyers and family. On 8 October, he was convicted of "inciting social discord" and of attempting to overthrow the constitutional order by Aktau City Court, sentenced to seven-and-a-half years in prison and the court ordered the confiscation of his property. He was a prisoner of conscience. Independent monitors allowed into the trial reported that there was no presumption of innocence and that the evidence used against Vladimir Kozlov did not conclusively prove his guilt. In its verdict, the court also labelled several opposition media outlets that had covered the 2011 strikes and the investigations into the Zhanaozen violence, as "political extremists" that incited "social hatred". On 19 November, the Appeals Court in Aktau upheld the verdict.

■ In March, prisoner of conscience Natalia Sokolova, the former legal representative for the striking Kazmunaigas workers in Zhanaozen, was unexpectedly released from prison after the General Prosecutor's Office lodged a complaint against her sentence with the Supreme Court. She had been sentenced to six years in prison by Aktau City Court in August 2011 for "inciting social discord".

Freedom of expression

New provisions in the security law which came into force in January penalized individuals and/or organizations for "influenc[ing] public and individual consciousness" through the distribution of "distorted" and "unreliable" information "to the detriment of national security". There were fears that the authorities were intent on using national security legislation to curtail freedom of speech and of the media.

■ On 21 November, the Almaty city Prosecutor filed a complaint seeking to close down almost all remaining independent and opposition media – some of which had been named in Vladimir Kozlov's verdict. He accused them of being "extremist", inciting social discord and threatening national security. The complaint covered approximately 40 print, online and broadcast media outlets. It also called for the Alga party and the social movement Khalyk Maydany, both unregistered, to be classified as "extremist". On the

K

same day a court in Almaty ordered the immediate suspension of all Alga activities and other courts ordered the majority of the targeted media outlets to stop publication, distribution and broadcasting.

Refugees and asylum-seekers

In defiance of a decision of the UN Committee against Torture and in contravention of its obligations under international human rights and refugee law, Kazakhstan continued to detain individuals with a view to extraditing them to countries, such as Uzbekistan, where they would risk facing torture or other ill-treatment.

In June, the Committee decided that by extraditing 28 Uzbek men, including asylum-seekers to Uzbekistan, Kazakhstan was in violation of the UN Convention against Torture.

■ Sobir Nosirov, an Uzbekistani man, was held for 12 months for extradition purposes, and then released in July 2012 without charge. He had left Uzbekistan with his family to work in Russia in 2005 and was granted legal temporary residence and work permits. In July 2011 he was unexpectedly detained at the border with Kazakhstan, due to an arrest warrant issued by Uzbekistan for his alleged participation in the violent unrest in Andizhan in May 2005. He was held incommunicado for several days in Uralsk. Despite clear evidence that charges outlined in the extradition request did not stand up to scrutiny, the court did not release him from detention. He was released without an official explanation on 24 July 2012 and escorted by security forces to the Russian border.

Amnesty International visits/reports

🚌 Amnesty International delegates visited Kazakhstan in December.

📱 Kazakhstan: Progress and nature of official investigations called into question 100 days after violent clashes between police and protesters in Zhanaozen (EUR 57/001/2012)

KENYA

REPUBLIC OF KENYA
Head of state and government: Mwai Kibaki

Freedom of assembly and expression were attacked. Impunity persisted for both past and current human rights violations, including unlawful killings. Somali refugees and asylum-seekers were targets of xenophobic violence, and faced arbitrary arrest by the police. There were a number of grenade and bomb attacks in border towns in North-Eastern Province and in Nairobi.

Background

The implementation of constitutional reforms continued throughout the year, with Parliament passing more than 27 Bills. However, the Commission for the Implementation of the Constitution (CIC) criticized some of the Bills as not in line with the Constitution. The implementation of some laws that had been passed by Parliament, including the National Police Service Act, was delayed.

The country's security situation was affected by episodes of violence across the country, including in North-Eastern Province, Coastal Province and the cities of Kisumu and Nairobi.

Impunity – post-election violence

No steps were taken to bring people responsible for crimes and human rights violations, including possible crimes against humanity, allegedly committed during the post-election violence of 2007-2008, to justice, despite the government saying several times that investigations were continuing.

In February, the Director of Public Prosecutions established a taskforce to deal with the prosecution of 5,000 pending cases. It was the third time a taskforce had been created to look into the caseload. In August, the taskforce revealed that most of the evidence was not of a sufficient standard for trial.

The UN Human Rights Committee, in its Concluding Observations issued in July following consideration of Kenya's record in implementing the International Covenant on Civil and Political Rights, expressed concern at the lack of investigations and prosecution of those responsible for the violence.

Human rights violations by police

Amnesty International continued to receive reports of a range of human rights violations by the police including excessive use of force, arbitrary arrests and cases of ill-treatment of people in police detention. There were also numerous reports that the police targeted members of particular communities, in particular people of Somali origin, across the country.

Impunity for human rights violations committed by the police continued. The implementation of key laws setting the framework for police reform was seriously delayed. The Independent Policing Oversight Authority (IPOA) began work in June. It was mandated to investigate complaints and disciplinary or criminal offences committed by any member of the National Police Service. However, there were concerns that the budget allocated to IPOA was not sufficient for it to carry out its mandate.

■ In October, police arrested Mombasa Republican Council (MRC) leader Omar Mwamnuadzi, as well as more than 40 other people believed to be members of the MRC. During their arrest, two people were killed and several others injured by the police, including Omar Mwamnuadzi who was beaten. The group was charged with a range of offences, including belonging to an unlawful group, incitement and possession of firearms. Their cases were pending at the end of the year.

■ In October, police fired rubber bullets into a crowd demonstrating outside a police station about insecurity in Mathare, an informal settlement in Nairobi. Three protesters were arrested and charged with incitement to violence. Seven activists, including an Amnesty International staff member and two volunteers, who had attempted to meet with the police to discuss the protest, were arbitrarily detained, held overnight at Pangani police station in incommunicado detention and beaten. They were charged with incitement to violence, obstructing an officer while on duty and disorderly behaviour. The case was pending at the end of the year.

In November and December, hundreds of ethnic Somali people were arbitrarily or discriminatorily detained by the police and other security forces, particularly in the Eastleigh area of Nairobi, following grenade or other bomb attacks. The attacks were thought to be linked to Al Shabaab, an Islamist armed group operating in Somalia but which has allegedly carried out some operations in Kenya. However, there is also a pattern of discrimination against Somalis in Kenya because of the perceived burden on the country as it hosts a large number of Somali refugees (see Refugees and asylum-seekers sub-section). Over the course of three days in December, up to 300 people were reported to have been arrested, including Somali refugees and asylum-seekers as well as Kenyan Somalis. Most were subsequently released without charge. However, many of those detained alleged that security forces had ill-treated them during arrest or detention and had extorted, or attempted to extort, money from them. The wave of arrests and lack of charges gives rise to serious concerns that the response of the authorities was rooted in discrimination against Somalis.

■ In October, Shem Kwega, an Orange Democratic Movement politician, was killed in Kisumu city by unknown people. His death led to a public demonstration, which turned violent, with stones being thrown at police. In responding to the protest the police used live ammunition and four people were reported to have been fatally shot. A number of people also died when a container in which they took shelter caught fire. Witnesses said that the fire started when police fired tear gas into the container.

Communal violence

Conflict between the Pokomo and Orma communities over water and pasture land intensified in Tana River County. It is believed that some 200 people had been killed in such clashes by the end of the year, and approximately 30,000 displaced.

Despite the deployment of more than 2,000 police officers to the Tana Delta in September, the clashes persisted, raising serious concerns about the security forces' response to the situation and their ability to protect the human rights of people in Tana. Residents claimed that they repeatedly attempted to raise their concerns about the escalating situation with the police and security forces before August, but they were not taken seriously.

The Kenyan authorities created a Commission of Inquiry to investigate these killings and allegations that the police failed to respond appropriately, but it had yet to report by the end of the year.

International justice

In January, Pre-Trial Chamber II of the International Criminal Court (ICC) decided to proceed to trial in cases against William Ruto, Joshua arap Sang, Uhuru Kenyatta and Francis Muthaura for crimes against humanity allegedly committed during post election violence in Kenya in 2007-2008. Uhuru Kenyatta, currently the Deputy Prime Minister, and William Ruto, a former government minister had declared they would be candidates in Kenya's 2013 elections. The Kenyan government appeared to try to undermine the ICC's jurisdiction over the four cases. The East African Legislative Assembly (EALA) passed a resolution in April urging the East African Community Council of Ministers to request the transfer of the ICC cases to the East African Court of Justice (EACJ). However, the East African court does not have jurisdiction over crimes under international law. In July, the ICC announced that the trials would commence in April 2013.

Refugees and asylum-seekers

By the end of 2012 Kenya was hosting in excess of 600,000 refugees and asylum-seekers, the vast majority of whom were from Somalia. Most were living at the Dadaab refugee camps. The process for registration of new arrivals in Dadaab remained suspended, as did the transportation of asylum-seekers from the border to Dadaab – which meant people had to walk about 100km to seek asylum. Police continued to abuse refugees in the Dadaab camps. In May, Kenyan police arbitrarily arrested, detained, and beat refugees after an attack on a police vehicle in the camps. Police were purportedly searching for explosives.

Senior government officials repeatedly threatened to close the Dadaab refugee camps and forcibly return all residents to southern Somalia throughout the year, describing Dadaab as a "security threat" and claiming that areas of southern Somalia were safe. Amnesty International and other human rights groups disputed this (see Somalia entry).

In addition to those living in refugee camps in Kenya, some 55,000 refugees and asylum-seekers were registered with UNHCR in Nairobi and other urban centres.

In December, the Kenyan government announced that all refugees and asylum-seekers in urban areas should be relocated to refugee camps. UNHCR expressed serious concern and called on the government not to implement the policy.

Internally displaced people

The Internally Displaced Persons Act was passed by Parliament in October. The Act requires the government and others to protect people against factors which could cause them to become displaced, and requires the government to put in place structures to assist those who become internally displaced.

Housing rights – forced evictions

■ On 28 January, police forcibly evicted scores of people in Mukuru Kwa N'jenga in the east of Nairobi from their homes. Three people died in the process. One woman was electrocuted by a live power cable that fell during the eviction and another woman was killed by a stray bullet. The third person, a child, was killed during a stampede by anti-eviction demonstrators fleeing from police.

■ In August, people from 70 homes were forcibly evicted from Kiamaiko informal settlement in Nairobi, in spite of an ongoing court case to settle ownership of the land.

■ Deep Sea community in Nairobi remained at risk of forced eviction to make way for a road development project by the Kenya Road Authority (KURA). While KURA was developing a relocation plan for affected residents, community members said that they had not been adequately consulted about the plan and that it did not accurately reflect the number of people due to be affected by the eviction.

A Private Member's Bill providing guidelines for evictions and prohibiting forced evictions was tabled in Parliament in October. However, the Bill was not debated by the end of the year. In October, the Ministry of Lands appointed a new taskforce to review a similar Bill which the Ministry had drafted in 2011 but which had not been tabled in Parliament.

Death penalty

No executions were carried out in the country, but at least 21 death sentences were imposed throughout the year. The Kenya Defence Forces Act, passed in 2012, allowed for members of Kenya's Defence Forces being sentenced to death for a range of offences, including treachery, spying, aiding the enemy, assisting the enemy with intelligence information and unlawfully advocating for a change of government.

Amnesty International visits/reports

🚌 Amnesty International visited Kenya in January, October and December.

📄 Kenya: Submission to the Human Rights Committee, July 2012 (AFR 32/002/2012)

KOREA
(DEMOCRATIC PEOPLE'S REPUBLIC OF)

DEMOCRATIC PEOPLE'S REPUBLIC OF KOREA	
Head of state:	Kim Jong-un
Head of government:	Choe Yong-rim

Systematic human rights violations remained widespread. The food crisis persisted, with chronic and widespread malnutrition still a public health concern. Millions faced continued food insecurity and remained dependent on food aid. Despite reports that one political prison camp had closed, tens of thousands remained detained in such camps where they were subjected to sustained violations of their human rights, including extrajudicial executions, forced labour and torture and other ill-treatment. There were reports of executions, including of those purged in the leadership transition. Severe restrictions on the rights to freedom of expression, association, opinion and assembly persisted. The media remained under strict control.

Background

Kim Jong-un, North Korea's Supreme Leader following the death of his father in 2011 was elected to the newly created position of First Secretary of the Workers' Party of Korea on 11 April and promoted to Marshal of the Korean People's Army in July. The Democratic People's Republic of Korea (North Korea) successfully launched an Unha-3 rocket on 12 December, sending a satellite into space, after a number of failed attempts.

State media announced a prisoner amnesty in January, due to begin 1 February, marking the anniversary of the birth of the late North Korean leader Kim Jong-il; however, no information about the releases was made public.

In July, floods resulted in severe damage to housing, infrastructure and public buildings. According to government figures, at least 212,200 people were left homeless and 169 people were killed.

Food crisis

Despite reports that harvests had improved for a second year, food insecurity remained widespread. In November, the UN's Food and Agriculture Organization and World Food Programme Crop and Food Security Mission report stated that although household food consumption had improved, "serious gaps remained between recommended and actual nutrient intake. The predominant share of the population remains food insecure". Chronic malnutrition continued to plague most people, with several reportedly dying of starvation.

Arbitrary arrests and detentions

Hundreds of thousands remained arbitrarily detained, or held for indeterminate periods without charge or trial in political prison camps and other detention facilities. Detainees faced systematic and sustained violations of their human rights, including extrajudicial executions and long hours of forced hard labour with no rest days. Torture and other ill-treatment appeared to be widespread in prison camps. Many detainees died due to forced labour in perilous conditions, including inadequate access to food or medical care.

In October, there were reports that Political Prison Camp 22 in Hoeryong, North Hamkyung province, had been closed. It was not clear when the prison camp closed and where the prisoners, estimated at between 20,000 and 50,000, had been transferred. The camp, one of five of its kind, was a total control zone where inmates were held for life, without reprieve. Many of those held in political prison camps had not committed any crime, but were related to those deemed hostile to the regime and were held as a form of collective punishment.

■ In response to a query from the UN Working Group on Arbitrary Detention, the government stated in April that Shin Sook-ja, last known to have been held with her two daughters in Political Prisoner Camp 15 at Yodok, had died of complications linked to hepatitis. They also claimed that her daughters did not want any contact with their father Oh Kil-nam, now based in the Republic of Korea. This information could not be verified and it was not clear when Shin Sook-ja died or

K

where. The fate and whereabouts of her two daughters remained unknown.

■ In December, North Korea announced that it had detained Kenneth Bae, a US national of Korean origin, on charges of committing "hostile acts against the Republic". Kenneth Bae ran a travel company that specialized in taking tourists and prospective investors to North Korea. He had entered the country on 3 November and was reportedly detained after security officials found he had a computer hard disk that they believed contained delicate information about the country.

Enforced disappearances

The authorities continued to refuse to acknowledge cases where North Korean agents carried out abductions on foreign soil of people from countries including Japan, Lebanon, the Republic of Korea and Thailand.

■ In July, Fujita Takashi attended a meeting of the UN's Working Group on Enforced or Involuntary Disappearances where he raised the case of his brother Susumu, feared abducted by North Korea from Japan in February 1976.

Freedom of expression

The authorities continued to impose severe restrictions on freedoms of expression, opinion and assembly. Strict media controls were believed to have been imposed to prevent challenges to the government during its period of transition. There appeared to be no independent civil society organizations or independent political parties.

Freedom of movement

The authorities reportedly further tightened controls along the border with China and threatened individuals crossing it without permission with severe punishment on their return.

■ In February, 31 people who left North Korea without permission were detained by Chinese authorities. According to news reports, in March, China forcibly returned some members of this group back to North Korea where they risked detention, torture and other ill-treatment, forced labour and death.

Death penalty

Executions of political opponents were reported, but this information could not be verified.

■ According to unconfirmed reports received in October, Army Minister Kim Chol was executed in early 2012 for drunkenness and inappropriate behaviour during the mourning period of former leader Kim Jong-il.

International scrutiny

In October, the UN High Commissioner for Human Rights stated that the "use of political prison camps, frequent public executions and severe food shortages, coupled with the extreme difficulty of gaining access, make DPRK [North Korea] singularly problematic." For the first time, both the UN Human Rights Council and the Third Committee of the UN General Assembly passed resolutions without a vote in March and November respectively. Both expressed serious concerns at continuing reports of systematic, widespread and grave violations of civil, political, economic, social and cultural rights in North Korea.

KOREA
(REPUBLIC OF)

REPUBLIC OF KOREA
Head of state: Lee Myung-bak
Head of government: Kim Hwang-sik

The National Security Law (NSL) was increasingly and arbitrarily used to curtail freedoms of association and expression. This extended to the internet, where online debate on the Democratic People's Republic of Korea (North Korea) was tightly controlled. Media workers took industrial action in protest against the state's denial of their right to freedom of expression. Workers' rights remained under threat, as long-term labour disputes went unresolved. Migrant workers continued to face discrimination and labour exploitation. There were no executions.

Background

In December, Park Geun-hye was elected as the first woman President of the Republic of Korea (South Korea), due to take office in February 2013. In April, elections to the National Assembly saw the Saenuri Party win 152 of 300 seats, while the main opposition

Democratic United Party took 127 seats. In August, Hyun Byung-chul was reappointed as Chairperson of the National Human Rights Commission of Korea, without proper consultation with relevant stakeholders, raising questions about its independence and credibility. In October, South Korea's human rights record was assessed under the UN Universal Periodic Review.

Freedom of expression

Law enforcement authorities used vaguely worded clauses of the NSL to detain for questioning and/or charge 41 people. NSL provisions continued to be used to control online debate on North Korea.

■ On 22 February, an appeal court sentenced Kim Myeong-soo to six months in prison suspended for two years, after prosecutors appealed against a not guilty verdict issued in May 2011. Kim Myeong-soo appealed to the Supreme Court against his latest conviction.

■ On 21 November, Park Jeong-geun was sentenced to 10 months in prison suspended for two years for violating the NSL. He had been under investigation since September 2011, when he satirically re-tweeted messages from a banned North Korean website. Although the judgement acknowledged that some of his posts were parody, it stated that overall, his acts were tantamount to "supporting and joining forces with an anti-state entity".

In some cases, people were denied entry to South Korea in an effort to silence them.

■ In April and October, six staff members from Greenpeace were denied entry at Incheon International Airport. In December, Greenpeace filed a legal challenge against the government over what it called "attempts to prevent anti-nuclear criticism".

Journalists and media workers

Demanding editorial independence, staff at Munhwa Broadcasting Corporation (MBC) went on strike in January followed by staff at the Korea Broadcasting System (KBS), the news-only cable-channel YTN, and the news agency Yonhap. Workers at KBS and Yonhap ended their strike in June, but the strike at MBC, the longest in its history, continued until July.

Conscientious objectors

At least 750 conscientious objectors remained in prison as of December.

■ In April, human rights activist Yoo Yun-jong was sentenced to 18 months' imprisonment for refusing military conscription.

Freedom of assembly

Protests against the construction of a naval base in Gangjeong village, Jeju island, continued, with many residents and activists facing civil suits and criminal charges. Between July 2009 and August 2012, police arrested 586 demonstrators. Since October, when all-day construction commenced, at least six demonstrators were hospitalized after police tried to forcibly remove them at night. In May, a joint letter written by three UN Special Rapporteurs to the South Korean government expressed serious concerns, citing reports of harassment, intimidation and ill-treatment of peaceful protesters.

Workers' rights

Long-term labour disputes remained unresolved. The authorities continued to impose criminal sanctions, increasingly taking out lawsuits and claiming extensive damages against striking workers and unions.

■ On 20 September, the National Assembly's environment and labour committee conducted a hearing on the long-running Ssangyong Motors' labour dispute in which around 2,600 workers had lost their jobs. In November, three members of the Ssangyong workers' union began a protest from 9m up an electricity pylon near the Ssangyong Motors' plant in Pyongtaek.

■ In July, some 200 employees of the private security company Contactus reportedly threw sharp iron projectiles at and clubbed approximately 150 workers, injuring 34 people. Police did not intervene to protect them. The workers had been holding a sit-in protest at a factory owned by auto parts manufacturer SJM at the Banwol Industrial Complex in Ansan.

Migrants' rights

Undocumented migrant workers continued to be arrested and deported, following crackdowns against them.

■ In November, Suweto, an Indonesian national and undocumented migrant worker, died in hospital from injuries following a fall as he attempted to escape a night-time raid conducted by immigration officials.

In August, the UN Committee for the Elimination of Racial Discrimination expressed concern that in South Korea "migrant workers are subject to discrimination, exploitation and lower or unpaid wages."

K

Death penalty

People continued to be sentenced to death; there were no executions. As of December, at least 60 people were under sentence of death. Three bills calling for abolition of the death penalty lapsed following the end of the National Assembly's term. South Korea's last executions took place in December 1997.

Amnesty International visits/reports

🚗 An Amnesty International delegate visited South Korea in April, June and November.

KUWAIT

STATE OF KUWAIT
Head of state: al-Shaikh Sabah al-Ahmad al-Jaber al-Sabah
Head of government: al-Shaikh Jaber al-Mubarak al-Hamad
al-Sabah

Riot police used excessive force against peaceful demonstrators as part of a crackdown on freedoms of expression and assembly. Thousands of stateless Bidun continued to be denied Kuwaiti nationality and thus access to health care, education and employment on the same basis as citizens. Women continued to face discrimination in law and practice. Migrant domestic workers were exploited and abused by their employers. At least one person who died in custody may have been tortured or otherwise ill-treated. Nine death sentences were passed, four of which were commuted. No executions were reported.

Freedoms of expression, association and assembly

The authorities increased restrictions on freedoms of assembly and expression, including by prosecuting some social media users. Riot police used excessive force, tear gas and stun grenades against peaceful demonstrations by government opponents and Bidun.

In the run-up to the 1 December parliamentary elections, a series of demonstrations called "March of Dignity" was organized by government opponents, in part to protest against proposed amendments to the parliamentary election law.

Following a large gathering in October, the authorities invoked a 1979 law banning gatherings of more than 20 people. While some demonstrations were allowed to take place, others, including one on 27 December, were forcibly dispersed.

Former parliamentarians, activists and children were among those arrested during demonstrations. Most were released within a few days; some faced charges.

A proposal to amend the law on blasphemy to make "insulting God, his prophets and his messengers" a capital offence was vetoed by the Amir.

■ Prisoner of conscience Hamad al-Naqi, a member of the Shi'a Muslim minority, was arrested in April and sentenced in June to 10 years in prison with hard labour. He was convicted of posting Twitter messages criticizing the leaders of Saudi Arabia and Bahrain, and for "insulting" Islam. His appeal was ongoing at the end of the year.

■ Musallam al-Barrak, an opposition leader and former MP, was arrested on 29 October and charged with "undermining the status of the Amir" for statements he made during a demonstration on 15 October. He was released on bail on 1 November. His trial was ongoing at the end of the year and he faced up to five years' imprisonment if convicted.

Torture and other ill-treatment

Legislation halving the maximum period of police custody without a court order from four days to two was enacted in July.

Reports suggested that torture or other ill-treatment may have been a factor in the death of Nawaf al-Azmi, one of five reported cases of deaths in custody.

■ On 24 December, an Appeal Court upheld the sentences, including two life sentences, of police officers involved in the death in custody of Mohammad Ghazzai al-Maimuni al-Mutairi in 2011. Two other officers were fined; all were dismissed from the police.

Discrimination – Bidun

More than 100,000 stateless Bidun, long-term residents of Kuwait, continued to be denied nationality. Hundreds held regular, peaceful demonstrations. Security forces occasionally forcibly dispersed these demonstrations, arbitrarily arresting dozens. Over 150 Bidun demonstrators faced trial.

On 18 October, the Prime Minister told Amnesty International that the government would extend Kuwaiti nationality to 34,000 Bidun and resolve the remaining cases within five years.

K

In February, the CERD Committee recommended that the Kuwaiti authorities issue civil documents to all people in Kuwait and give the Bidun access to adequate social services, education, housing, employment, property and business registration rights, among other things.

Women's rights

Women continued to face discrimination in law and practice. In September, the Supreme Judicial Council announced that women could apply for various posts in the Public Prosecution and judiciary. This followed lawsuits brought against the Ministry of Justice by women law graduates in 2011, after the Ministry advertised certain jobs as open to men only.

Migrant workers

Migrant domestic workers remained unprotected by Kuwait's labour laws and continued to face exploitation and abuse by employers. The labour sponsorship (kafala) system did not adequately protect migrant workers, and non-Kuwaitis were prohibited from forming collective bodies.

The CERD Committee recommended that Kuwait adopt specific labour legislation to protect foreign and domestic workers and guarantee their rights according to international standards, including the ILO conventions to which Kuwait is a party.

Death penalty

Nine death sentences were passed, four of which were commuted. Others were upheld by the Appeals Court. Three other death sentences imposed in 2011 on two Iranians and a Kuwaiti for "espionage for Iran" were reduced to life imprisonment on appeal. Three people facing execution for murder were pardoned by their victims' relatives. No executions were reported.

Amnesty International visits/reports

🚍 Amnesty International delegates visited Kuwait in May. In October, Amnesty International's Secretary General met the Prime Minister, former parliamentarians, opposition activists, members of the Bidun community and human rights activists in Kuwait.

📑 Kuwait: Joint open letter to His Highness the Amir of Kuwait regarding the Bidun (MDE 17/004/2012)

KYRGYZSTAN

KYRGYZ REPUBLIC
Head of state: Almaz Atambaev
Head of government: Zhantoro Satibaldiev (replaced Omurbek Babanov in September)

Torture and other ill-treatment remained pervasive throughout the country and law enforcement and judicial authorities failed to act on such allegations. The authorities continued to fail to impartially and effectively investigate the June 2010 violence and its aftermath and provide justice for the thousands of victims of serious crimes and human rights violations, including crimes against humanity. Ethnic Uzbeks continued to be targeted disproportionately for detention and prosecution in relation to the June 2010 violence.

Torture and other ill-treatment

Torture and other ill-treatment persisted, despite the development of a comprehensive national programme on combating torture, based on the recommendations of the UN Special Rapporteur on torture, and the adoption of a law on the establishment of a National Centre for the Prevention of torture and other ill-treatment.

The Special Rapporteur reported in February that incidents of torture and other ill-treatment to extract confessions "remained widespread". He further observed, "that, in practice, there is no clear procedure in place prescribing the measures to be taken by courts should evidence appear to have been obtained through torture or ill-treatment. Furthermore, in practice, there appears to be no instruction to the courts with regard to implementing that rule or ordering an immediate, impartial and effective investigation if the rule is violated."

He noted that in contrast to the actions taken and statements made by the current and former Presidents and the Prosecutor General, he had not heard of any instructions "communicated by the responsible officials of the Ministry of the Interior [Ministry of Internal Affairs] to condemn torture and ill-treatment or to declare unambiguously that torture and ill-treatment by police officers would not be tolerated".

K

■ Anna Ageeva, a pregnant 18-year-old woman, was detained by police officers in Bishkek on 11 September on suspicion of murder and held incommunicado for three days in Sverdlovsk District police station. During this time, she alleged that police officers dragged her by her hair, handcuffed her to a radiator and kicked and punched her in the stomach and kidneys to force her to confess to the murder of another young woman. A lawyer from the NGO Kylym Shamy submitted a complaint about the torture to the Sverdlovsk District Prosecutor. Three other suspects, including 17-year-old Aidiana Toktasunova, also detained in relation to the same murder, similarly complained to the District Prosecutor's Office that police officers had tortured them to extract confessions. The Ministry of Internal Affairs dismissed the torture allegations as "absurd" and stated that their investigations had found no evidence of any wrong-doing by police officers. The District Prosecutor's Office opened a criminal investigation into the allegations in October.

■ In November, the human rights organization Spravedlivost (Justice) wrote to the Prosecutor General requesting that she personally supervise an investigation into allegations that eight detainees in the centre for temporary detention (IVS) in Jalal-Abad had been ill-treated by over a dozen police officers. Spravedlivost had visited the IVS after being alerted to the violations by relatives of some of the detainees.

The detainees reported that police officers beat them in the face, skull and body. They stripped the detainees naked and forced them to run. The regional Ombudsman visited the IVS two days after Spravedlivost and met with all 42 detainees at the facility, 37 of whom confirmed that they had been ill-treated. In turn she asked the Regional Prosecutor's Office to investigate these allegations. The Ministry of Internal Affairs also conducted an internal investigation, but claimed to have found no evidence of any ill-treatment.

While arbitrary arrests of mainly ethnic Uzbeks appeared to have become less frequent in 2012, reports persisted of serious human rights violations committed against Uzbeks in relation to ongoing investigations into the June 2010 violence and its aftermath, including torture and other ill-treatment in detention, forced confessions and unfair trials. In his February report, the Special Rapporteur on torture expressed his concerns that "serious human rights violations committed in the context of [these] investigations have continued unabated in recent months".

Unfair trials

The Special Rapporteur on torture stated that he had heard "testimonies, according to which, in trials relating to the violence of June 2010, judges and prosecutors repeatedly failed to act on information of torture or ill-treatment supplied by defendants or their lawyers". He cited the 20 December 2011 Supreme Court decision to turn down Azimzhan Askarov's appeal and to confirm his life sentence as an "example of the highest judicial body's failure to act on allegations of torture and ill-treatment". The government accused the Special Rapporteur of being one-sided and stated that the Prosecutor General's Office had conducted a thorough investigation into all the allegations of torture and forced confessions of Azimzhan Askarov and his co-defendants and had found no compelling evidence to substantiate these claims.

■ Azimzhan Askarov, prominent human rights defender and prisoner of conscience, remained in solitary confinement at the end of the year. According to the October report by Physicians for Human Rights (PHR), his medical condition had markedly deteriorated including his eyesight, his nervous system and his breathing, but he did not receive the necessary medical care, which constituted a form of ill-treatment. Following an examination in January, PHR experts concluded that Azimzhan Askarov showed clinical evidence of traumatic brain injury as a result of torture. In November, his lawyer submitted a complaint to the UN Human Rights Committee.

Impunity

Despite initiatives taken by the authorities in the last two years – often in the face of considerable internal opposition – they failed to fairly and effectively investigate the June 2010 violence and its aftermath in the cities of Osh and Jalal-Abad and provide justice for the thousands of victims of the serious crimes and human rights violations, including crimes against humanity.

. The Osh City Prosecutor stated in April that out of 105 cases which had gone to trial in relation to the June 2010 violence, only two resulted in acquittals. Only one of those cases involved an ethnic Uzbek, Farrukh Gapirov, the son of human rights defender Ravshan Gapirov. He was released after the appeal court found his conviction had been based on his confession which had been obtained under torture.

K

However, no criminal investigation against the police officers responsible for his torture was initiated.

By contrast, the first – and, to date, the only – known conviction of ethnic Kyrgyz for the murder of ethnic Uzbeks in the course of the June 2010 violence was overturned.

■ In May, the Jalal-Abad Regional Court quashed the convictions of four ethnic Kyrgyz men charged with the murder of two Uzbeks during the June 2010 violence. Two of them had been sentenced to 25 and 20 years in prison respectively in November 2010. Both had alleged that they had been tortured in detention. The others had received suspended sentences of three years. The first appeal court reversed the convictions of the four men, sent the case for additional investigation and released them on bail. Three of the defendants were fully acquitted and the one sentenced to 25 years by the court of first instance was granted a conditional release.

Despite official directives from the Prosecutor General's Office to investigate every single report of torture, prosecutors regularly failed to investigate such allegations thoroughly and impartially, or to bring anyone identified as responsible to justice. The Special Rapporteur found that "[t]he efforts made by the interim Government to investigate and punish the abuses that resulted from the events of June 2010 have proved to be largely ineffective".

■ In March, the trial of four police officers charged with torture of Usmonzhon Kholmirzaev, which had led to his death in August 2011, was returned to Jalal-Abad. The presiding judge at Jalal-Abad Regional Court called for further investigations and released two of the accused police officers on bail. Before the trial had started, in September 2011, relatives and supporters of the accused police officers held public protests, which were sometimes violent. They intimidated witnesses for the prosecution, the family and lawyer of Usmonzhon Kholmirzaev outside the court and inside the courtroom, and put pressure on the judge to find the accused not guilty. The trial was moved to Chui Region, 500km away, for security reasons. Nevertheless, key witnesses were threatened with violence and some changed their testimony in favour of the accused. Several felt compelled to leave the country fearing for their family's safety. By the end of the year, the Jalal-Abad Regional Prosecutor had not started investigations into the actions of the relatives and supporters of the accused, despite complaints by the

widow of Usmonzhon Kholmirzaev and her lawyers. On 26 December, the Regional Court indefinitely postponed the trial after three of the defence lawyers failed to show at the scheduled hearing.

Amnesty International visits/reports

🚗 Amnesty International delegates visited Kyrgyzstan in April, May, September and December.

📓 Kyrgyzstan: Dereliction of duty (EUR 58/001/2012)

LAOS

LAO PEOPLE'S DEMOCRATIC REPUBLIC
Head of state: **Choummaly Sayasone**
Head of government: **Thongsing Thammavong**

Restrictions on freedom of expression, association and assembly continued. Three prisoners of conscience and two Hmong political prisoners remained imprisoned. Harassment of Christians in several provinces was reported. Concerns increased over land disputes caused by development projects affecting livelihoods.

Background

In February, the UN Committee on the Elimination of Racial Discrimination expressed concern about the lack of international access given to Hmong involuntarily returned from Thailand. In September, Laos ratified the UN Convention against Torture. In November, Laos adopted the ASEAN Human Rights Declaration, despite serious concerns that it fell short of international standards. The death penalty remained mandatory for some drug offences; no official statistics were made public. Harassment of Christians in provincial areas continued, with confiscation of property, closing of churches, short-term detention and forced recanting.

Freedom of expression

Freedom of expression remained tightly controlled with media and others conforming to state policies and self-censorship. In January, the Ministry of Information, Culture and Tourism ordered the radio call-in programme *Talk of the News* to be taken off air.

L

The programme was popular with callers complaining about land grabs and corruption.

■ Prisoners of conscience Thongpaseuth Keuakoun, Bouavanh Chanhmanivong and Seng-Aloun Phengphanh remained in prison, despite the authorities' claims in September 2011 that two of them would be released. They had been imprisoned since October 1999 for trying to hold a peaceful protest.

■ Ethnic Hmong Thao Moua and Pa Fue Khang had nine months deducted from their 12- and 15-year sentences respectively. They were arrested in 2003 for helping two foreign journalists gather information about Hmong groups hiding in the jungle.

Land disputes

Amid concerns over a rise in land disputes, in June the authorities announced a four-year moratorium on new mining investments and concessions for rubber plantations due to environmental and social concerns. Large-scale development projects intruding on villagers' land affected livelihoods, with lack of adequate compensation reported.

■ In June, eight villagers were arrested for petitioning the authorities over a land dispute with a Vietnamese company granted a rubber concession in 2006 which affected Ban Yeup village, Thateng district in Sekong province. All were released within a few days, except for one man who was held for around two weeks and reportedly ill-treated before being freed.

Enforced disappearances

On 15 December, Sombath Somphone, a respected member of Lao civil society well known for his work promoting education and sustainable development, was taken away in a truck by unknown persons after being stopped by police in the capital, Vientiane. He helped to organize the Asia-Europe People's Forum in Vientiane in October.

LATVIA

REPUBLIC OF LATVIA
Head of state: Andris Berzins
Head of government: Valdis Dombrovskis

Victims of hate crimes based on gender, disability or sexual orientation were not protected under the law. Asylum-seekers lacked adequate access to status determination procedures. The complete abolition of the death penalty entered into force. Over 300,000 people remained stateless.

Discrimination

Hate crime legislation did not protect lesbian, gay, bisexual, transgender and intersex people, disabled people, or victims of gender-based hate crimes. Criminal law punished incitement to hatred based solely on racial, ethnic or religious motives. Only racist motives were regarded as aggravating circumstances.

In June, the fourth annual Baltic Pride march took place in Riga with over 600 participants and in a climate of co-operation with police. Members of parliament and the Minister of Foreign Affairs attended the event.

Over 300,000 people – about one-sixth of the population, mostly of Russian origin – remained stateless according to UNHCR, the UN refugee agency, although the authorities regarded them as "non-citizens" with greater protection and access to rights than stateless people under the 1954 Convention Relating to the Status of Stateless Persons and the 1961 Convention on the Reduction of Statelessness. They were excluded from political rights.

Refugees and asylum-seekers

Asylum-seekers often encountered difficulties in accessing their right to seek international protection. Potential asylum-seekers were given insufficient information on arrival, which in some cases led to their detention as irregular migrants. A lack of translators also hampered access to status determination procedures.

International scrutiny

The European Commission against Racism and Intolerance published its fourth report on Latvia in February. The Commission's recommendations included: the closure of any remaining special classes for Roma children and their integration into mainstream classes; the automatic granting of citizenship to children born of "non-citizen" parents after Latvia's independence in 1991; and the reconsideration of the policy on state language to ensure that an obligation to use it applies only in clear cases of legitimate public interest.

Death penalty

Legislative amendments implementing the abolition of the death penalty in all circumstances entered into force on 1 January, followed by the ratification of Protocol 13 to the European Convention on Human Rights.

LEBANON

LEBANESE REPUBLIC
Head of state: Michel Suleiman
Head of government: Najib Mikati

Reports of torture and other ill-treatment continued, including forced, abusive physical examinations of detainees. Discrimination against Palestinian refugees continued, impeding their access to education, health, employment and adequate housing. Migrant workers faced abuse from employers and sometimes security forces. Some refugees and asylum-seekers, including those fleeing violence in neighbouring Syria, were arbitrarily detained. At least 170,000 refugees from Syria sought safety in Lebanon during the year. Women were discriminated against in law and practice. The Special Tribunal for Lebanon (STL) announced a trial date in 2013 but the Lebanese authorities again failed to address the fate of the long-term missing and disappeared. Civilians were sentenced to death or to prison terms after unfair trials before military courts. At least nine death sentences were imposed; there were no executions.

Background

Tension rose among Lebanon's diverse faith communities, amid fears that the conflict in Syria would spill over into Lebanon. There was a large influx of refugees from Syria. Sporadic violent clashes along the Syria-Lebanon border caused deaths and injuries among civilians. Repeated armed clashes occurred in and around Tripoli between pro-Syrian government Alawite Muslims and Sunni Muslims supportive of Syrian opposition forces. Armed clashes also occurred in Sidon in August and November. Protests broke out in Beirut and elsewhere, notably following the 19 October assassination of the head of intelligence within Lebanon's Internal Security Forces, who was killed by a car bomb in Beirut. Dozens of people, including children, were killed in the violence and hundreds were wounded. At least 20 Syrians and other foreign nationals were kidnapped and held for up to one month in August and September by armed members of the Meqdad clan to pressure a Syrian armed group to release one of their relatives. In December, a draft National Action Plan for human rights in Lebanon was launched in Parliament, but had not been endorsed at the end of the year.

Torture and other ill-treatment

There were new reports of torture and other ill-treatment of detained security and criminal suspects. In at least one case, an individual suspected on security grounds was reported to have been apprehended, beaten and threatened by armed non-state agents and then handed over to Military Intelligence for further interrogation, during which he was subjected to additional assaults.

In an effort to address torture and other abuses, the government, with assistance from the UN Office of the High Commissioner for Human Rights, launched in January a code of conduct for the Internal Security Forces. However, the government again failed to establish an independent monitoring body to visit prisons and detention centres, in breach of its international obligations. It was therefore difficult to establish whether the code of conduct brought about any improvements.

Unfair trials

Civilians accused of spying for Israel or other security-related offences continued to be unfairly tried before military courts, which lacked independence and impartiality. Military courts generally failed to investigate allegations by defendants that they were tortured in pre-trial detention to force them to "confess".

Freedom of expression

Journalists and other media workers were attacked and harassed by security forces and non-state actors for their real or perceived political views.

■ In June, at least three men threw burning material into the entrance of Al-Jadeed television station following the broadcast of a controversial interview with a Salafist cleric.

The Special Tribunal for Lebanon

The Netherlands-based STL announced that the trial of four men it indicted in 2011 for alleged involvement in the assassination of former Prime Minister Rafic Hariri in 2005 and other crimes, would begin in March 2013. It was expected that the accused would be tried in their absence.

Impunity – enforced disappearances and abductions

The fate of thousands who were abducted, detained or went missing during and after Lebanon's 1975-1990 civil war, including many said to have been taken to Syria, mostly remained unresolved. A draft decree proposed by the Minister of Justice to establish an Independent National Commission to investigate the fate of the disappeared and missing was widely criticized and had not been enacted by the end of the year. The release of Yacoub Chamoun from a Syrian prison almost 27 years after he went missing gave hope to families of the disappeared that some of their loved ones may still be alive.

Women's rights

Women continued to face discrimination in law and practice. A draft law to allow Lebanese women married to foreign nationals to pass on their nationality to their children, as Lebanese men can do, was discussed by the Cabinet, although not enacted. Parliament continued to discuss a draft law against domestic violence.

Refugees, asylum-seekers and migrants

Thousands of Palestinian refugees, long-term residents in Lebanon, continued to be excluded by law from working in certain professions and accessing other rights available to Lebanese citizens.

Tens of thousands of refugees from Syria fled across the border to Lebanon, increasing pressure on Lebanon's housing, education, health and other resources. UNHCR, the UN refugee agency, was aware of over 170,000 refugees from Syria in Lebanon by the end of the year, although the true figure was likely to be much higher. Most were in northern Lebanon and the Bekaa valley area. Palestinian refugees fleeing Syria faced discriminatory entry requirements imposed by the Lebanese authorities. Lebanon had not ratified the 1951 UN Convention relating to the Status of Refugees or its 1967 Protocol.

Some refugees, asylum-seekers and migrant workers said they were ill-treated by the security forces, in particular during arrest and detention, which in some cases were carried out arbitrarily or during raids in their neighbourhoods or work places. They included around 70 mostly Syrian, Egyptian and Sudanese migrant workers who alleged that they were beaten by soldiers in October during a raid on Beirut's Geitawi district.

Women foreign nationals employed as domestic workers under the official sponsorship scheme remained vulnerable to abuse by employers.

■ UN human rights experts called for an investigation into the suicide in March of an Ethiopian woman after the alleged owner of her employment agency was filmed dragging her and forcing her into his car to prevent her entering the Ethiopian Consulate in Beirut.

Rights of lesbian, gay, bisexual, transgender and intersex people

LGBTI people faced discrimination and abuse.

■ In July, 36 men arrested at a film show were forcibly subjected to rectal examinations to determine whether they had engaged in anal sex. Following this, the national medical association advised all doctors to refuse to participate in such abusive examinations or they would face disciplinary measures.

Death penalty

At least nine death sentences were imposed; no executions had been carried out since 2004. The proposed National Human Rights Action Plan suggested substituting life imprisonment for the death penalty in all relevant Lebanese laws.

- At least five men were sentenced to death for spying for Israel.
- In April, a military judge requested the death penalty for 26 men after charging them with abducting and detaining a group of Estonian nationals in 2011. The trial was continuing at the end of the year.

Amnesty International visits/reports

Amnesty International delegates visited Lebanon in May, August/September and November/December to conduct human rights research, including into the situation in Syria.

LIBERIA

REPUBLIC OF LIBERIA
Head of state and government: **Ellen Johnson Sirleaf**

The justice system continued to be inefficient. Access to prisons was restricted and discrimination continued against women and LGBTI people. Forty-one people were extradited to Côte d'Ivoire without due process.

Background

Former Liberian President Charles Taylor was found guilty by the Special Court of Sierra Leone, and sentenced to 50 years in prison for crimes committed in Sierra Leone. The Liberian people have yet to see anyone prosecuted for human rights violations committed during the armed conflict in their own country, however.

Impunity

Most of the 2009 recommendations of the Liberian Truth and Reconciliation Commission (TRC) were yet to be implemented. These included establishing a criminal tribunal for prosecuting crimes under international law, as well as other legal and institutional reforms, and recommendations relating to accountability, and reparations.

Death penalty

Despite acceding, in 2005, to the Second Optional Protocol to the ICCPR, which commits the country to work towards abolition of the death penalty, death sentences continued to be handed down in 2012, although no executions took place. The death penalty was retained for armed robbery, terrorism and hijacking offences resulting in death.

Justice system

The justice system remained inefficient, under-resourced and corrupt. Court processes were slow resulting in detainees being kept in lengthy pre-trial detention. Approximately 80% of the prison population was awaiting trial. By the end of the year, public defenders were operating in each county, but civil society organizations reported it was still a challenge to find free legal representation.

Prison conditions

Throughout the year, medical care improved slightly with the Ministry of Health and Social Welfare providing regular medical care, although drugs and supplies were still in short supply.

Poor security and harsh conditions contributed to at least a dozen prison breakouts across the country. Sources indicate the authorities responded by cutting time for fresh air and exercise. In January, a ground-breaking ceremony was held for construction of a new central prison in Montserrado County, which was expected to reduce overcrowding and provide improved facilities, but little progress had been made by the end of the year. Many expressed concern that a new prison would not solve the underlying issues that result in high numbers of pre-trial detainees.

Following a 2011 Amnesty International report on prison conditions, the government restricted the access of national and international organizations to prisons and prison data.

By the end of the year, the government had failed to make public a report by the UN Subcommittee on the Prevention of Torture, following a 2011 visit to inspect places of detention.

Refugees and asylum-seekers

In June, 41 people, arrested in 2011 and accused of attempting to cross into Côte d'Ivoire from Liberia with weapons, were extradited to Côte d'Ivoire at the request of the Ivorian government despite the expressed fears of UN agencies, human rights organizations and others that the individuals would be at risk of torture or other ill-treatment, unfair trial or

L

other human rights abuse. The customary international legal principle of *non-refoulement* was also violated during the extradition process, as was the right to due process of many of the accused. During court proceedings related to the extradition many individuals did not have interpreters, and an appeal against their extradition as well as a habeas petition were pending at the time of their extradition. At least 11 were registered refugees. Others who claimed to be seeking asylum were not allowed to access asylum proceedings and the UN refugee agency, UNHCR, lawyers and others were not allowed access to these people to verify their identities or their potential claims to asylum.

In December, another extradition request was made for eight nationals of Côte d'Ivoire – seven adult men and one child. They were accused by the Ivorian government of having launched an attack that resulted in the death of seven UN peacekeepers and one Ivorian soldier in June 2012. They were also charged in Liberia with various offences including murder, rape, and being mercenaries. There are serious concerns about the lack of evidence in both cases. If extradited, they could be at risk of torture or other ill-treatment, unfair trial, arbitrary detention, enforced disappearance or extra-legal, arbitrary or summary execution.

Violence against women and girls

Domestic violence was still not a crime, and remained rife, as did rape and other forms of sexual violence against women and girls, including harmful traditional practices, such as female genital mutilation and early marriage.

Rights of lesbian, gay, bisexual, transgender and intersex people

Against a backdrop of widespread homophobia in the Liberian general public and the media, two laws aiming to further criminalize same-sex sexual conduct were introduced into the legislature and led to further discrimination. In July, the Senate voted unanimously to pass an amendment to the Domestic Relations Law of Liberia which seeks to make same-sex marriage a second-degree felony. At the end of the year a vote by the House of Representatives was pending. A second bill seeking to amend the New Penal Code, criminalizing the "promotion" of homosexuality and imposing long sentences for entering into a

consensual same-sex relationship, was awaiting a vote by the House of Representatives at the end of the year, before proceeding to the Senate. The ambiguity of the "promotion" clause in the House of Representatives bill has the potential for criminalizing the work of human rights defenders.

A number of LGBTI people reported incidences of discrimination, harassment and threats based on their sexuality. Many of them also reported that the introduction of these bills, perpetuating the stigma of same-sex relationships, made them increasingly concerned for their safety and frightened to seek government services such as health, security, welfare.

Amnesty International visits/reports

🚍 Amnesty International delegates visited Liberia in September/October.

📕 Liberian police must take immediate action to protect journalist (AFR 34/001/2012)

LIBYA

LIBYA

Head of state: Mohammed Magarief (replaced Mostafa Abdeljalil in August)
Head of government: Ali Zeidan (replaced Abdurrahim al-Keib in November)

Armed militias continued to commit serious human rights abuses with impunity, including arbitrary arrests, arbitrary detention, torture and unlawful killings. Thousands of people suspected of formerly supporting or fighting for Mu'ammar al-Gaddafi's government, overthrown in 2011, remained detained without charge or trial and with no means of remedy. Most were beaten or otherwise ill-treated in custody; tens died after torture. Tens of thousands of people who were forced to leave their homes in areas perceived to have supported Mu'ammar al-Gaddafi in 2011 remained internally displaced and were at risk of revenge attacks and other abuses. Undocumented foreign nationals faced arbitrary arrest, indefinite detention, exploitation and torture or other ill-treatment. Sporadic armed confrontations between militias across the country caused hundreds of deaths; the victims included children and other civilians not involved in the fighting. Impunity remained entrenched, both for gross human rights violations committed in the past and for ongoing human rights abuses by armed militias. Women continued to face discrimination in law and practice. The death penalty remained in force; there were no executions.

Background

On 7 July, Libyans elected a 200-member General National Congress (GNC), tasked with passing legislation, preparing the next parliamentary elections, appointing a government, and possibly overseeing the process of drafting the country's first Constitution in over 40 years. The National Transitional Council (NTC), which was established on 2 March 2011 and led the opposition to Mu'ammar al-Gaddafi, officially handed over power to the GNC on 8 August 2012.

Successive governments failed to rein in hundreds of armed militias that filled the security vacuum following the demise of al-Gaddafi's government in 2011. Many militias continued to act above the law, refusing to disarm or join the police or army. Efforts to integrate former anti-Gaddafi fighters into the Supreme Security Committee (SSC) of the Ministry of the Interior, for example, were devoid of any systematic vetting to weed out perpetrators of torture or other crimes under international law, potentially fuelling further abuses.

At the Human Rights Council (HRC) in March, the UN Commission of Inquiry on Libya reported that both pro- and anti-Gaddafi forces had committed war crimes, crimes against humanity and human rights abuses during the 2011 conflict and that armed militias had committed serious human rights abuses, including arbitrary detention and torture after the hostilities ended. Nevertheless, the Libyan government rejected the inclusion of human rights monitoring and any reference to continuing violations in an HRC resolution on "Assistance to Libya in the field of human rights".

Armed militias destroyed Sufi religious sites including in Tripoli and Zliten in August; no one was known to have been arrested or prosecuted for these attacks. Bomb and other attacks, particularly in Benghazi, targeted government buildings, including courthouses and police stations, as well as diplomatic missions and international organizations.

On 11 September, US Ambassador J. Christopher Stevens and three other US nationals were killed in an attack on the US diplomatic post in Benghazi. The Libyan government condemned the attack and announced arrests but no one was brought to justice by the end of the year.

Arbitrary arrests and detentions

In May, the NTC passed Law 38 on Procedures relating to the Transitional Period, giving the Ministries for the Interior and Defence no more than 60 days to refer cases of detainees held by armed militias to civilian or military prosecutors. Despite this, thousands of people alleged to have supported or fought for al-Gaddafi's government remained in the custody of militias and semi-official security bodies. Although over 30 prisons were officially transferred to the Department of the Judicial Police, and in December the Ministry of Justice devised a strategy to resume effective control of prisons, militiamen continued working as guards or administrators in many prisons. Most detainees held in connection with the 2011 armed conflict had not been charged or tried by the end of 2012. Some were denied family visits; very few had access to lawyers.

Armed militias continued to seize or abduct individuals they suspected of having supported or fought for al-Gaddafi's government, taking them from their homes, workplaces, streets or checkpoints. Many were immediately beaten and had their homes looted and damaged. Members of communities deemed to have supported Mu'ammar al-Gaddafi, notably Tawarghas, were especially vulnerable. Detainees were frequently moved from one makeshift place of detention to another before being transferred to official or semi-official prisons or detention centres, at which point relatives could discover their whereabouts. The fate and whereabouts of some individuals abducted by militias remained unknown.

■ Bashir Abdallah Badaoui, the former head of the Tripoli Criminal Investigations Department, and his son Hossam Bashir Abdallah, aged 19, were abducted by armed militiamen on 13 April near their Tripoli home. Hossam Bashir Abdallah was released after five days, but his father's whereabouts remained unknown despite his family's efforts to find him.

Torture and other ill-treatment

Torture and other ill-treatment remained widespread, particularly in detention facilities controlled by militias, and were used to punish detainees and extract "confessions". Detainees were especially vulnerable during arrest, in their first days of detention and during interrogation. Many signed "confessions" under torture or duress. Article 2 of Law 38 of 2012 gave legal weight to interrogation records of armed militias, at the discretion of judges.

Many detainees were subjected to sustained beatings with hoses, rifle butts, electric cables, water pipes or belts, often while suspended in contorted positions. Some were tortured with electric shocks, burned with cigarettes or heated metal, scalded with boiling water, threatened with murder or rape and subjected to mock execution. Tens of detainees died in the custody of militias, the SSC and in official prisons in circumstances suggesting that torture contributed to or caused their deaths.

■ Tawarghan former police officer, Tarek Milad Youssef al-Rifa'i, died on 19 August after being taken from Wehda Prison to the SSC in Misratah for questioning. He had been seized from his Tripoli home in October 2011 by armed militiamen from Misratah. His relatives found his bruised body at a Misratah morgue; a forensic report indicated that his death was caused by beatings. His family lodged a complaint with the authorities but no proper investigation into his death was begun.

■ The family of Ahmed Ali Juma' found his body at a Tripoli morgue several days after he was summoned for questioning by the Abu Salim Military Council in July. A forensic report identified "multiple bruises on the body, on the head, on the torso and the limbs and genitals" and concluded that he was "beaten to death". No one was held to account for his death.

Armed confrontations

Sporadic clashes between armed militias resulted in deaths and injuries to bystanders and residents as well as fighters. Such confrontations were widespread, occurring at Kufra in February, April and June, at Sabha in March, in the Nafousa/Western Mountain area in June, at Barak al-Shat in September, and in Bani Walid in October. Militia fighters fired weapons such as Grad rockets, mortars and anti-aircraft machine guns in residential areas, causing casualties and damaging or destroying property. In June, armed militias were reported to have used white phosphorus in Sgeiga despite the threat this posed to residents.

Following weeks of siege and an armed assault on Bani Walid by the army and militias that ended on 24

October, officials said 22 people had been killed, although the true total was believed to be higher. The dead included residents of Bani Walid who were not involved in the fighting, including children. For example, nine-year-old Mohamed Mustafa Mohamed Fathallah died from shrapnel injuries sustained when his home was shelled on 10 October. On 30 October, then Defence Minister Ossama Jweili claimed that the army was not in control of the situation and alleged widespread abuses by militias.

The authorities appointed fact-finding committees to investigate some armed clashes, but by the end of the year none of their results were made public, no perpetrators were brought to justice and no victims had received reparation.

Refugees, asylum-seekers and migrants

Despite guarantees contained in Libya's Constitutional Declaration, promulgated in August 2011, to recognize the right to seek and enjoy asylum, the government failed to ratify the UN Refugee Convention, sign a memorandum of understanding with UNHCR, the UN refugee agency, or adopt asylum legislation.

Armed militias and police continued to arbitrarily detain undocumented foreign nationals, including individuals in need of international protection, for alleged migration-related "offences", such as entering the country "irregularly". At the end of the year, thousands were detained indefinitely, pending deportation, in overcrowded and unhygienic conditions in detention centres. They had no means of challenging the legality of their detention or their treatment and conditions. Suspected irregular migrants faced habitual verbal abuse, beatings and other ill-treatment, in some cases amounting to torture, in detention. At least two foreign nationals died in custody at the hands of militias.

■ On 13 September, a group of Nigerian women held at the Tweisha detention centre in Tripoli received sustained beatings with hoses and other objects by around 11 men in plain clothes. Some women were given electric shocks. The authorities took no action against the men responsible.

Internally displaced people

The authorities took no real steps to facilitate the safe return to their homes of entire communities forcibly displaced during the 2011 conflict, including

L

residents of Tawargha, Mashashiya, Gawalish and other areas perceived to have supported Mu'ammar al-Gaddafi. Armed militias wrought further destruction in these areas to render them uninhabitable and arbitrarily detained and abused people from these communities, especially Tawarghas.

■ Four men from Tawargha were arrested at Tripoli airport on 6 May when they arrived on a flight from Benghazi. A relative accompanying them was told that they would be quickly released but they were still detained without trial at Misratah at the end of the year.

Some 58,000 people were reported to be internally displaced at the end of the year; thousands were accommodated in poorly resourced camps in Tripoli and Benghazi.

Impunity

The authorities vowed to investigate gross human rights violations committed under Mu'ammar al-Gaddafi's government and initiated investigations into a number of former high-level officials and alleged al-Gaddafi loyalists, but took no steps to investigate ongoing violations by armed militias or bring those responsible to justice.

In May, the NTC passed Law 17 to establish a Fact-Finding and Reconciliation Commission. It was unclear whether the Commission's mandate covered only crimes committed by the former government or included those committed by others. No effective investigations were known to have been carried out by the Commission by the end of the year.

Law 35 on Amnesty, approved by the NTC in May, failed to comply with Libya's obligation under international law to investigate alleged crimes against humanity, war crimes, enforced disappearances and extrajudicial executions, and prosecute alleged perpetrators.

Law 38 of 2012 provided blanket immunity to militiamen for acts deemed to have been committed with the aim of "protecting the 17 February Revolution".

No meaningful investigations were carried out by the authorities into alleged war crimes and serious human rights abuses, including torture and unlawful killings, committed by armed militias during and following the armed conflict. No official findings were disclosed in relation to the apparent extrajudicial executions of Mu'ammar al-Gaddafi, his son Mu'tassim, and other alleged al-Gaddafi loyalists and soldiers after their capture in 2011.

The Libyan authorities refused to hand over Saif al-Islam al-Gaddafi and Abdallah al-Senussi, extradited from Mauritania to Libya on 5 September, to the International Criminal Court (ICC) to face charges on two counts of crimes against humanity. In June, four ICC staff were detained for over three weeks by militias in Zintan who accused them of violating national security. At the end of the year, the ICC Pre-Trial Chamber had yet to rule on an admissibility challenge filed by the Libyan government on 1 May to try Saif al-Islam al-Gaddafi under Libyan rather than ICC jurisdiction.

Freedoms of expression and assembly

The number of media outlets and civil society groups mushroomed. Critics of armed militias, including Libyan and foreign journalists, faced threats, intimidation, harassment and detention, leading to self-censorship.

■ On 25 August, Nabil Shebani, director of al-Assema TV station, was questioned for several hours by the SSC in Tripoli about al-Assema's coverage of the destruction of Sufi religious sites in Tripoli. He was released without charge.

■ On 19 July, British freelance journalist Sharron Ward was detained by armed militia members in Tripoli after filming at the Janzour Naval Academy Camp, where internally displaced Tawargha residents were sheltering. She was re-arrested on 21 July and forced to leave the country on 24 July. Some of her equipment was seized.

In June, the Supreme Court ruled that Law 37 of 2012, which criminalized the "glorification of al-Gaddafi" and placed undue restrictions on freedom of expression, was unconstitutional.

In November, the GNC passed Law 65 of 2012 regulating demonstrations, which placed undue restrictions on the right to peaceful assembly.

Women's rights

Women continued to face discrimination in law and practice.

Two women were appointed in the interim government of Ali Zeidan. Thirty-three women were elected to the 200-member GNC, 32 from party lists and one independent candidate from Bani Walid. During the power handover ceremony to the GNC on 8 August, a female presenter was forced to leave the stage for not wearing a veil.

L

In February, small protests in Tripoli and Benghazi calling for equality and condemning sexual harassment and violence against women were publicly criticized by powerful militia leaders and others. Several of the organizers received threats and discontinued their public activism.

Justice system

The justice system remained virtually paralysed and unable to process the thousands of pending cases, as police stations and court complexes remained closed in parts of the country. Some hearings into high profile cases, such as that against Abuzeid Dorda, former head of intelligence body the External Security Agency, were initiated and adjourned, amid concerns over respect for fair trial guarantees.

Prosecutors, criminal investigators, members of the judicial police and lawyers defending people accused of having fought for or supported Mu'ammar al-Gaddafi faced intimidation, threats and violence from armed militias.

■ In August 2012, a poster appeared around Misratah, naming and denouncing 34 lawyers representing alleged al-Gaddafi loyalists. It accused the lawyers of "seeking to obtain money and secure the release of dregs [as al-Gaddafi loyalists are commonly referred to] at the expense of the blood of martyrs, the injured, and the missing". The poster was removed after protests by the Lawyer's Syndicate and others but some of the 34 lawyers received anonymous threats.

No steps were taken to reform the judiciary and implement a systematic vetting mechanism to remove judges involved in unfair trials, arbitrary detention and other human rights abuses during the al-Gaddafi era.

Death penalty

The death penalty remained in force for a wide range of crimes. At least five people were sentenced to death in their absence in November. No executions were carried out in 2012.

Unlawful killings

Dozens of security officials, including from the former al-Gaddafi government, were shot dead or were targeted with explosive devices in eastern Libya, particularly in Benghazi and Derna, in apparently politically motivated killings. No meaningful investigations were known to have been carried out.

■ On 30 October, Khaled al-Safi al-Adli, a member of al-Gaddafi's Revolutionary Committee, was shot dead in Derna by unidentified assailants.

NATO

No findings were made public concerning civilian casualties resulting from NATO's air campaign against al-Gaddafi forces in 2011. NATO maintained that the issue of victim reparations was the responsibility of the Libyan authorities.

Amnesty International visits/reports

🚗 Amnesty International delegates visited Libya in January/February, May/June and August/September.

📖 Libya: The forgotten victims of NATO strikes (MDE 19/003/2012)

📖 Libya: Rule of law or rule of militias? (MDE 19/012/2012)

📖 Libya: 10 steps for human rights: Amnesty International's human rights manifesto for Libya (MDE 19/017/2012)

📖 "We are foreigners, we have no rights." The plight of refugees, asylum-seekers and migrants in Libya (MDE 19/020/2012)

LITHUANIA

REPUBLIC OF LITHUANIA
Head of state: Dalia Grybauskaitė
Head of government: Algirdas Butkevičius (replaced Andrius Kubilius in December)

A lack of accountability persisted over complicity in US-led rendition and secret detention programmes. Lesbian, gay, bisexual, transgender and intersex people continued to be discriminated against, including in their rights to freedom of expression and assembly.

Counter-terror and security

The authorities failed to re-open the investigation into Lithuanian involvement in CIA rendition and secret detention programmes, despite the emergence of new lines of inquiry and flight data presented by NGOs. They also failed to bring to justice any individuals responsible for human rights violations that may have occurred on Lithuanian territory, including torture and enforced disappearance.

In April, European Parliament delegates visited the country and concluded that Lithuania had not conducted an independent, impartial, thorough and effective investigation into its involvement in the CIA programmes: a European Parliament report adopted in September called on Lithuania to conduct a human rights compliant investigation into its complicity.

Discrimination – lesbian, gay, bisexual, transgender and intersex people

Discriminatory legislative provisions and other provisions which could be implemented in a discriminatory manner against people based on their sexual orientation remained in force. In particular, this affected the rights of lesbian, gay, bisexual, transgender and intersex people and others advocating on their behalf to freedom of expression and assembly. Further discriminatory provisions were proposed.

■ In June, the latest attempt to amend the Code of Administrative Offences with the aim of prohibiting the promotion of homosexuality in public places was voted down in the parliament.

A constitutional amendment aimed at restricting the definition of "family" as comprising a married man and woman, and which could lead to discrimination on grounds of marital status and sexual orientation, was being examined by parliament.

International scrutiny

On 16 March, the UN Human Rights Council adopted the outcome of the Universal Periodic Review on Lithuania. Lithuania accepted recommendations to protect people from discrimination based on sexual orientation; and to investigate further the human rights implications of counter-terrorism measures, including secret detention programmes. However, at the end of the year, discriminatory legislation remained in force and no further action had been taken by the authorities on these recommendations.

In July, the UN Human Rights Committee urged Lithuania to ensure that its legislation is not interpreted and applied discriminatorily against people based on their sexual orientation or gender identity, and to guarantee that they enjoy all their human rights, including the rights to freedom of expression and assembly. The Committee further urged Lithuania to continue investigations into alleged human rights violations resulting from counter-terrorism measures and to bring those responsible to justice.

Amnesty International visits/reports

▤ Europe: "What is new on the alleged CIA illegal detention and transfers of prisoners in Europe?" (EUR 01/006/2012)

▤ Lithuania: Amnesty International urges the reopening of the criminal investigation into Lithuania's involvement in the US-led rendition and secret detention program (EUR 53/001/2012)

MACEDONIA

THE FORMER YUGOSLAV REPUBLIC OF MACEDONIA
Head of state: Gjorge Ivanov
Head of government: Nikola Gruevski

Relations between the Macedonian and ethnic Albanian populations deteriorated. Relatives of missing persons abducted in 2001 were denied access to justice. Conditions in places of detention fell short of minimum standards.

Background

The European Commission again recommended in October that negotiations on EU accession should commence, but the EU Council of Ministers deferred the talks, due in part to the continuing dispute with Greece over the country's name.

Relations between Macedonians and ethnic Albanians deteriorated further. In February, an off-duty Macedonian policeman shot dead two ethnic Albanians in Gostivar. Several reportedly ethnically motivated attacks took place in March, in Tetovo and Skopje. In May, 20 ethnic Albanians were arrested in raids after the killing of five Macedonian men at Smilkovci lake, outside Skopje. Five men were charged with murder and terrorism. Thousands of Albanians protested against the arrests and the authorities' depiction of them as terrorists.

In August, the ruling VMRO-DPMNE party (Internal Macedonian Revolutionary Organization – Democratic Party for Macedonian National Unity) proposed a draft law to provide reparations to Macedonian military and police forces (or their relatives) that fought and suffered losses in the 2001 armed conflict. In October, the bill was derailed in parliament by the coalition party, the Albanian Democratic Union for Integration, because it did not provide for the

M

National Liberation Army (NLA) combatants, an armed group which had fought the government forces.

Crimes under international law

In October, the Constitutional Court rejected an appeal by relatives of Macedonians allegedly abducted by the NLA in 2001 against the legality of an interpretation of the 2002 Amnesty Law, adopted by parliament in July 2011. Following the 2011 interpretation of the Amnesty Law the Prosecutor annulled four war crimes cases including the charges relating to the abductions, which had been returned to Macedonia for prosecution by the International Criminal Tribunal for the former Yugoslavia.

Torture and other ill-treatment

Allegations of torture and other ill-treatment by police officials continued, including of two men detained after the Smilkovci lake murder. In May, the Ombudsperson, as the National Protection Mechanism, reported that conditions in police stations in 2011 were below minimum standards – especially for juveniles – and detainees rarely had access to a lawyer or doctor. Juveniles were held in solitary confinement in inhuman and "utterly degrading" conditions. In December, the European Committee for the Prevention of Torture reported that the authorities had made little progress in implementing previous recommendations, particularly in Idrizovo Prison, where ill-treatment by staff, inter-prisoner intimidation/violence and "totally unsatisfactory conditions" for prisoners persisted.

Unlawful killings

In January, Igor Spasov, a member of a special police unit, was convicted and sentenced to 14 years' imprisonment for the murder of Martin Neskoski, during a July 2011 election rally.

Freedom of expression

A draft law to decriminalize defamation was agreed with the Journalists' Association. Other journalists and media workers criticized proposed new penalties, which they feared would cause media self-censorship. The law envisaged penalties of up to €2,000 per author, and further fines of €10,000 for editors-in-charge and €15,000 for media company owners.

Discrimination

The government failed to amend the 2010 Anti-Discrimination Law to include protection for LGBTI people. Homophobic remarks made in October by the Minister of Labour and Social Affairs were followed by an attack on the NGO-run LGBTI Support Centre.

Roma

Macedonia held the Presidency of the Decade of Roma Inclusion until July, but provided inadequate resources for implementation of its own National Action Plan and the National Strategy for the Advancement of Romani Women and Girls.

Refugees, asylum-seekers and migrants

According to UNHCR, the UN refugee agency, 1,087 mainly Kosovo Roma and Ashkali refugees remained in Macedonia. Without a durable solution, 30 voluntarily returned to Kosovo, and 14 to Serbia.

Under pressure from the EU, the government limited the right to leave the country. Border officials most often targeted Roma and ethnic Albanians, whose passports were marked to prevent them leaving again. Between January and October, 8,115 Macedonian citizens applied for asylum in the EU; fewer than 1% were provided with protection. Austria and Switzerland imposed an accelerated asylum process on Macedonian citizens.

Within Macedonia, 638 people applied for asylum; none was granted it.

Counter-terror and security

In December, the European Court of Human Rights held unanimously that Macedonia was responsible for the violations suffered by Khaled el-Masri, a German resident who was apprehended in 2003 by the Macedonian authorities, held incommunicado in Macedonia for 23 days, and subsequently transferred to the custody of US authorities and flown to Afghanistan. The Court ruled that Macedonia was liable for Khaled el-Masri's unlawful detention, enforced disappearance, torture and other ill-treatment, for his transfer out of Macedonia to locations where he suffered other serious human rights violations, and for the failure to carry out an effective investigation. It was the first time the Court had ruled on the case of a victim of the US-led rendition programme.

MADAGASCAR

REPUBLIC OF MADAGASCAR
Head of state: **Andry Nirina Rajoelina**
Head of government: **Jean Omer Beriziky**

Serious human rights violations, including hundreds of unlawful killings by the security forces, as well as illegal arrests and detention, continued to take place with almost total impunity. Political leaders, journalists, pastors and lawyers, as well as others critical of the authorities, were intimidated and some jailed following unfair trials.

Background
The political and social situation remained tense and security volatile in some parts of the country, especially the south. Some important provisions of the "Roadmap for Ending the Crisis in Madagascar", signed in September 2011 by the majority of Malagasy political actors under the mediation of the Southern African Development Community, were not implemented. These included the termination of politically motivated legal proceedings; the protection and promotion of human rights and respect for fundamental freedoms; and return of political exiles. Members of the international community and the government confirmed that the presidential election would take place in May 2013. In mid-April 2012, an amnesty law covering January 2002 to 31 December 2009 was voted into law by both chambers of the "parliament".

In September, Madagascar signed both the Second Optional Protocol to the ICCPR, aiming at the abolition of the death penalty, and the Optional Protocol to the UN Convention on the Rights of the Child.

Following Amnesty International's press release of 20 November highlighting serious human rights violations committed by security forces in the south and calling for an independent investigation, the Prime Minister decided to set up a commission of inquiry, to be led by the UN. Preparations for the inquiry were taking place at the end of the year.

Unlawful killings
There were widespread state killings of civilians over cattle theft, and a failure to protect hundreds from communal violence and mass murder, especially in the southern region of Anosy. Witnesses told Amnesty International that those unable to flee their homes were burned alive when security forces indiscriminately set fire to villages as part of the "Tandroka" military operation launched in September.

■ In September, security forces allegedly killed at least 11 people, including a six-year-old girl, and burned 95 homes in Elonty district. During the attacks, crops were destroyed and at least one school was razed to the ground. Officials said that only cannabis farms were destroyed by their forces.

■ Security forces extrajudicially executed suspected cattle thieves ("dahalo"), including one physically disabled person, in Numbi village in September. The parents and wife of a high-profile suspect were extrajudicially executed in Mahaly district in October.

■ At least 250 people were killed during the year around the southern town of Fort-Dauphin, in what the authorities described as communal clashes sparked by cattle thefts. Amnesty International feared the number could be far higher. Witnesses reported that neighbours had informed the authorities about an imminent attack on one village, in which at least 86 people were hacked to death by machetes, but the authorities had done nothing to prevent it.

Impunity
Security officials and members of armed groups responsible for serious human rights violations, including unlawful killings, continued to act with impunity.

■ A complaint into the death of prosecutor Michel Rahavana remained under investigation a year later. He was killed in December 2011 by a group of police officers attempting to release a colleague who had been arrested by the prosecutor in connection with a theft. The minister in charge of the police, the Minister of Internal Security, who was in the town at the time of the death, was allegedly informed that the attack was about to happen but failed to prevent it. The Minister of Justice announced at the end of 2011 that an investigation would be conducted.

■ No official investigation was opened into the killing of taxi driver Hajaharimananirainy Zenon, known as Bota, despite assurances from the Minister of Justice. Bota's family lodged a formal complaint on 30 August 2011 following his arrest, torture and killing by members of the Intervention Police Force (FIP) on 17 July 2011 in the 67ha neighbourhood of Antananarivo.

M

Freedom of expression – journalists

Several media outlets, including Radio Fahazavana, remained closed. At least five other radio stations were closed in February. The authorities continued to use the judiciary to intimidate and harass journalists.

■ On 13 November, Radio Free FM journalists Lalatiana Rakotondrazafy and Fidèle Razara Pierre each received a three months' suspended sentence and a fine of ariary 1 million (around US$500) by an Antananarivo tribunal. The two had been released on 3 May after being detained for 24 hours. In June, the authorities prevented them from leaving the country. They were convicted of defamation and spreading false news after a complaint by Ravatomanga Mamy, a businessman and official adviser to the President. Fearing for their safety, the two journalists, along with a technician from the radio station, had previously spent more than two months in the compound of the South African embassy in Antananarivo from 1 August.

■ On 8 and 9 November, four newspaper journalists – Zo Rakotoseheno, director of *Midi Madagasikara*; Rocco Rasoanaivo, director of *La Nation* and president of the journalists' trade union, Syndicat des journalistes malgaches; and Fidy Robson and Herivonjy Rajaonah, director and chief editor respectively of *Gazetiko* – appeared before the gendarmerie in Betongolo, Antananarivo. Ravatomanga Mamy, a businessman and official adviser to the President, had lodged a complaint against the journalists after the newspapers published extracts of a statement by a local chief accusing the businessman of links to trafficking in rosewood. The journalists were sent to the prosecutor's office on 12 November. They were not detained but their case was still under investigation at the end of the year.

Amnesty International visits/reports

🚌 An Amnesty International delegate visited Madagascar in November.
📓 Madagascar must end mass killings and investigate security forces (PRE01/570/212)

MALAWI

REPUBLIC OF MALAWI
Head of state and government: Joyce Banda (replaced Bingu wa Mutharika in April)

Harassment and intimidation of government critics continued in the early part of the year. Following the swearing in of President Joyce Banda in April, the environment for civil and political rights rapidly improved. Commissions of enquiry into the deaths of 20 people during the July 2011 nationwide demonstrations and into the death of a student activist presented their findings. Several laws which threatened internationally guaranteed human rights were repealed.

Background

Following the sudden death of President Bingu wa Mutharika on 5 April, the then Vice-President Joyce Banda was sworn into office.

In May, President Banda asked the AU to withdraw an invitation to Sudan's President al-Bashir, who has a warrant of arrest outstanding against him issued by the International Criminal Court, to an AU summit scheduled in the capital, Lilongwe, between 9 and 16 June. The AU rejected the request. Malawi subsequently declined to host the summit which was postponed and relocated to Addis Ababa, Ethiopia. President Banda did not attend.

In recognition of reforms made by President Banda, several major donors resumed previously suspended aid, including the EU, the International Monetary Fund and the World Bank.

Legal developments

Several laws, which were enacted amid widespread criticism under President Mutharika, were repealed in May. They included Section 46 of the Penal Code which had allowed the Minister of Information arbitrary power to prohibit a publication "if the minister has reasonable grounds to believe that the publication or importation of any publication would be contrary to the public interest".

Human rights defenders

On 13 February, Ralph Kasambara, a lawyer representing human rights activists and other dissenting voices, was arrested in Blantyre with his five security guards. The arrests followed an incident at his office in which Ralph Kasambara and his security team allegedly assaulted a group of men who were believed to have been sent to petrol bomb the premises. The previous day, Ralph Kasambara had been quoted in newspapers criticizing President Mutharika's governance. Ralph Kasambara and the security team were detained and charged with kidnapping and unlawful wounding before being transferred to Chichiri Prison. On 15 February, he was released and rearrested the same day. On 17 February, the High Court granted an injunction for his immediate release. He had still not been released when, on 17 February, he was transferred to hospital for medical treatment. He was granted police bail and released from police custody on 21 February. The case was not brought to court.

Institutional developments

On 10 July the report of the commission of enquiry into the July 2011 demonstrations which resulted in 20 deaths was made public. It found that police had used excessive force and that the live ammunition had caused deaths and injuries which could have been avoided. The President requested advice from the Attorney General on whether the findings constituted grounds for criminal prosecutions.

In April a commission of enquiry into the death of student activist Robert Chasowa, whose body was found on 24 September 2011, was appointed by President Banda. It found that the student had been unlawfully killed and that police had deliberately attempted to suppress the truth about the cause of death. Ten people were arrested and charged in connection with the death and granted bail by the High Court.

Rights of lesbian, gay, bisexual, transgender and intersex people

President Banda announced on 18 May that an urgent repeal of laws infringing human rights, including those criminalizing homosexuality, would be undertaken. While several legal reforms were made, laws criminalizing homosexuality remained in place.

MALAYSIA

MALAYSIA
Head of state: King Abdul Halim Mu'adzam Shah
Head of government: Najib Tun Razak

Colonial-era laws which had allowed for arbitrary detention and restricted freedom of expression were replaced with new legislation which nonetheless failed to meet international human rights standards. Peaceful protesters calling for electoral reform encountered police abuses and mass arrests. At least 14 people continued to be detained without trial under the Internal Security Act.

Background

Prime Minister Najib Tun Razak's coalition and the parliamentary opposition prepared for elections, which the Prime Minister was required to call by March 2013. Opposition leader Anwar Ibrahim, who faced imprisonment and a five-year ban from office on politically motivated charges of sodomy, was acquitted in January 2012.

Freedom of expression

The government announced in July that it would repeal the 1948 Sedition Act, which had been used to quash dissent, but the proposed National Harmony Act contained new restrictions on freedom of expression. Under Section 114A of the Evidence Act, an amendment which came into force in July, people who operated internet hosting services or websites open to public contributors (such as online forums) became liable for any offending content published through these services.

■ In May, the authorities banned Canadian author Irshad Manji's book *Allah, Liberty and Love* as "prejudicial to morality and public order". Nik Raina Nik Abdul Aziz, the manager of a Borders shop stocking the book, faced two years in prison after being charged under Shari'a law with distributing a book offensive to Islam.

Freedom of assembly

The state harassed civil society organizations critical of the authorities. Although the Peaceful Assembly Act 2012 removed requirements for police permits for

M

public assemblies, it allowed for them to be banned as "street protests".

■ In May, three opposition leaders, including Anwar Ibrahim, were charged with breaching the Peaceful Assembly Act for their involvement in the Bersih rally on the grounds that it was an alleged "street protest".

■ Government agencies pursued a campaign of harassment and intimidation against Suara Rakyat Malaysia (Suaram), a human rights group which had successfully petitioned for a French judicial review. The group had alleged that the French naval defence company DCNS had paid bribes to Malaysian officials to obtain a contract for two submarines.

■ In March, the High Court dismissed the appeal of the rights coalition Seksualiti Merdeka. The group had called for a judicial review of a 2012 police ban on their annual sexuality rights festival, which had taken place without interference since 2008.

Excessive use of force

Police used excessive force against peaceful protesters. The authorities rejected renewed calls to set up the Independent Police Complaints and Misconduct Commission (IPCMC), as recommended by the 2005 Royal Commission on Policing.

■ At the Bersih 3.0 march on 28 April, police in Kuala Lumpur fired tear gas and water cannon at tens of thousands of peaceful protesters calling for electoral reforms. Police beat peaceful protesters and arrested at least 471 participants.

■ In October, Home Affairs Minister Hishammuddin Hussein told Parliament that police had shot dead 298 suspected criminals between 2007 and August 2012, including 151 Indonesian nationals.

Arbitrary arrests and detentions

The government repealed the Internal Security Act (ISA), which allowed for indefinite detention without charge or trial, and replaced it with the new Security Offences (Special Measures) Act in July. Under it, the police were allowed to detain suspects incommunicado for 48 hours, and for up to 28 days without charge or judicial review.

■ As of November, at least 14 detainees, all foreign nationals, were held under the ISA until their detention orders expired, despite repeal of this law.

Refugees and migrants

Refugees were subjected to systematic detention, and migrant workers faced labour abuses. In June, Indonesia ended a two-year ban on sending migrant domestic workers to Malaysia, following abuses against domestic workers there.

■ On 12 February, Malaysia violated the international prohibition against *refoulement* by forcibly returning blogger Hamza Kashgari to Saudi Arabia, where he faced the possibility of a death sentence on criminal charges of apostasy for his tweets about the Prophet Mohamed.

■ Nigerian student Onochie Martins Nwankwo was beaten to death on 30 March by members of Ikatan Relawan Rakyat (RELA), a civilian para-police force mandated to enforce immigration controls. On 20 April, Parliament passed the Malaysia Volunteers Corps Bill 2012, which stripped RELA members of the power to make arrests and carry firearms.

Death penalty

At least 860 prisoners were on death row at the end of February, according to the Prisons Department. The authorities did not disclose the number of executions carried out in 2012.

■ In October, Law Minister Nazri Aziz announced that the government would consider replacing the mandatory death penalty with prison sentences, but only for drug offences and under certain circumstances.

Amnesty International visits/reports

📓 Malaysia: End harassment of anti-corruption campaigners (ASA 28/002/2012)

📓 Malaysia should broaden its proposal to scrap the death penalty (ASA 28/003/2012)

📓 Malaysia: Anwar case shows why sodomy law must be scrapped (PRE01/009/2012)

MALDIVES

REPUBLIC OF MALDIVES
Head of state and government: **Mohamed Waheed (replaced Mohamed Nasheed in February)**

The controversial resignation of the President in early February was followed by months of protest and political repression across the archipelago. Security forces used excessive force – including truncheons and pepper-spraying people in the eyes – to suppress demonstrations that were largely peaceful. Supporters of the former President's Maldivian Democratic Party (MDP) were targeted for attack in February. Detainees were subjected to torture and other ill-treatment. Weaknesses in the justice system perpetuated impunity for human rights violations.

Background

Months of party rivalry and unrest, followed by a police mutiny, preceded President Nasheed's resignation on 7 February. In a speech to his supporters the next day, Mohamed Nasheed stated that he had been forced to resign at gun point.

From 7 February, police used targeted violence against supporters of Mohamed Nasheed's MDP for several days, plunging the country into a human rights crisis. Although MDP protests were largely peaceful, police attacks on supporters in Malé on 8 February prompted a violent response in the southernmost city, Addu, the same day.

A Commission of National Inquiry formed by President Waheed in February concluded in August that Mohamed Nasheed had resigned voluntarily, echoing a statement made by President Waheed shortly after the resignation. The Commission noted "allegations of police brutality and acts of intimidation" and called for "investigations to proceed and to be brought to public knowledge with perpetrators held to account".

Excessive use of force

Throughout the year, security forces frequently attacked peaceful demonstrators, including MPs, journalists and bystanders, in the capital Malé or in Addu, both MDP strongholds. Officers clubbed them, kicked them and pepper-sprayed them directly in the eyes. Around the time of Mohamed Nasheed's resignation, from 7 to 9 February, police targeted senior MDP members for attack and tracked down and assaulted injured protesters in hospitals.

■ On 7 February, security forces attacked MP Ahmed Esa, beating him particularly on the head with metal rods and batons.

■ On 29 May, Mana Haleem, whose husband was a former minister in Mohamed Nasheed's cabinet, was on her way home when police stopped her. She had been walking through Majeedee Magu Street where an opposition rally was taking place. Police repeatedly beat her with truncheons on the arms, back and hips before taking her into custody.

Torture and other ill-treatment

Detainees were tortured upon arrest and on their way to police centres. Beatings, pepper-spraying the eyes and mouth, denial of drinking water and, in Addu, incarceration in dog cages, were all common methods used.

Human rights defenders

Campaigners or supporters of religious tolerance were attacked, and police or judicial authorities failed to bring the perpetrators to justice.

■ On 5 June, unidentified men slashed the throat of Ismail "Hilath" Rasheed. Ismail Rasheed, who survived the attack, was previously assaulted in December 2011 for advocating religious freedom during a small rally in Malé.

■ On 2 October, MP Afrasheem Ali was knifed to death outside his home in Malé. He was widely respected as a Muslim scholar who advocated the right to hold diverse religious views within Islam.

Lack of accountability

Serious failings in the justice system entrenched impunity. These included the absence of codified laws capable of providing justice equally to all and the appointment of judges who lacked formal training in law without serious scrutiny of their legal qualifications. Throughout the year, authorities were accused of political bias for fast-tracking the prosecution of opposition supporters accused of criminal behaviour during rallies while failing to prosecute police and others suspected of committing human rights abuses during the same protests.

M

Death penalty

At least two people were sentenced to death, but none was executed. However, the Chief Justice and the Minister of Home Affairs issued statements, implying that executions could not be ruled out under the law. Media reports that the government was drafting a bill to secure implementation of death sentences also raised concern about the possible resumption of executions after nearly six decades.

MALI

REPUBLIC OF MALI

Interim head of state: **Dioncounda Traoré (replaced Amadou Toumani Touré in April)**

Interim head of government: **Diango Cissoko (replaced Cheick Modibo Diarra in December, who replaced Mariam Kaïdama Cissé Sidibé in April)**

The armed conflict in the north of the country and the military coup that ensued led to very serious human rights violations committed by the security forces, including extrajudicial executions, enforced disappearances and torture. Armed groups in the north committed abuses including sexual violence, deliberate and arbitrary killings and corporal punishments. Both sides recruited child soldiers.

Background

In January, Tuareg and Islamist armed groups launched an uprising which triggered in March a military coup in the capital, Bamako, which overthrew the democratically elected President, Amadou Toumani Touré. This resulted in the de facto partition of the country in April. Despite the appointment in April of an interim Head of State and Prime Minister, the military coup leaders, under Captain Amadou Haya Sanogo, remained politically influential.

The conflict in the north resulted in military and civilian casualties and led to the mass displacement of more than 400,000 people, who found refuge in the south of Mali, or in neighbouring Algeria, Burkina Faso, Mauritania and Niger.

From April, the north was under total control of several armed groups including the Tuareg's Azawad National Liberation Movement (Mouvement national de liberation de l'Azawad, MNLA) and three Islamist groups: Ansar Eddin, the Movement for Unity and Jihad in West Africa (MUJAO) and al-Qa'ida in the Islamic Maghreb (AQIM).

In July, the government referred the crisis situation in the country to the International Criminal Court (ICC) on the basis that national authorities were unable to investigate and prosecute these crimes. In July and August, the ICC sent a preliminary investigation to determine whether an investigation should be opened. The results were not known by the end of the year.

In October, African leaders from ECOWAS decided to draw up a plan for military intervention to retake control of the north with the endorsement of the UN and several other governments, including France and the USA.

In December, the UN Security Council authorized an African-led force to use "all necessary measures" to take back northern Mali from armed groups.

Violations by government forces

In its fight against the MNLA, the army launched several indiscriminate attacks against civilian targets in the Kidal region.

■ In February, an army helicopter targeted the Kel Essouck camp near Kidal, injuring at least 12 people and killing a four-year-old girl, Fata Walette Ahmedou, who was fatally hit by a shell.

Torture and other ill-treatment, and extrajudicial executions

People suspected of being supporters of armed groups or targeted because they were Tuareg, were victims of torture and other ill-treatment or extrajudicial executions by security forces.

■ In January, soldiers arrested two Tuaregs accused of providing petrol to armed groups in Ménaka. They were beaten with rifle butts.

■ In April, soldiers arrested three unarmed men, including two Tuaregs and another man, all unarmed, accused of spying for the MNLA in Sévaré. They were beaten with rifle butts before being extrajudicially executed.

■ In September, the military arrested 16 Malian and Mauritanian nationals in Diabaly before extrajudicially executing them on suspicion of being supporters of Islamist armed groups. The 16 were members of a movement of Muslim preachers, the Dawa, who had come from Mauritania to attend an annual meeting of their movement in Bamako. An inquiry was set up but by the end of the year the results had not been made public.

Arbitrary arrests and detentions

People suspected of being supporters of the MNLA were arrested and detained without charge.

■ In February, four people, including the President and Vice-President of the Azawad Women's Assembly, both women, were arrested in the Kidal region and transferred to Bamako. They were all released in April in exchange for 13 people whom the MNLA were holding.

Abuses by the military junta
Extrajudicial executions, enforced disappearances and torture

In May, after an attempted counter-coup, soldiers and police officers loyal to former President Touré were tortured and extrajudicially killed or were victims of enforced disappearance. Two soldiers were stabbed to death at Kati military camp near Bamako by army personnel loyal to the junta. More than 20 others were victims of enforced disappearance after being abducted from their cells. They remained unaccounted for at the end of the year. Some of the soldiers and police officers were subjected to sexual abuse and held in harsh conditions during their interrogation and detention.

Arbitrary detention

The military junta arrested and arbitrarily detained political opponents who protested against their coup.

■ In March, the junta arrested several politicians, including the Minister of Foreign Affairs, Soumeylou Boubèye Maïga, and the Minister of Territorial Administration, Kafougouna Koné. They were detained, some for 20 days, without charge at Kati military camp.

■ In April, several opponents of the military junta, including former Prime Minister Modibo Sidibé and former Minister of Finance Soumaila Cissé, were arrested and taken to Kati military camp. They were released without charge within two days.

Freedom of the press

From March, the military junta targeted journalists to prevent them from reporting news.

■ In March, five journalists were arrested in Bamako by soldiers and taken to Kati military camp before being released a few days later. Another journalist, Omar Ouahmane, a French national working for the radio station France culture, was arrested, ill-treated and received death threats by soldiers loyal to the military junta.

■ In June, a privately owned TV station, Africable TV, was censored as it was about to broadcast an interview with an MNLA official.

Abuses by armed groups
Arbitrary killings and torture

Armed groups committed serious infringements of international humanitarian law by torturing and executing Malian soldiers taken prisoner.

■ In January, Malian soldiers taken prisoner during an ambush at Tilemci were tied up and beaten with rifle butts.

■ In January, dozens of Malian soldiers were shot and others had their throats slit by members of Ansar Eddin after being taken prisoner in Aguelhoc.

Violence against women and girls

During and after the seizing of the north by armed groups, a number of women and young girls were raped, sometimes gang-raped, by members of these groups. Most of the women were abducted at home or in the street and taken to a military camp.

■ At the end of March and beginning of April, several women were assaulted and raped in Gao as they were getting food supplies at the Office of Food Security (OPAM).

■ In April in Ménaka, women belonging to the Bambara ethnic group were reportedly targeted and raped by MNLA members.

■ In late July and early August, six women were attacked in Gossi by several members of an armed group on motorcycles. The women were robbed and three were captured and raped.

Corporal punishment

Islamist armed groups inflicted corporal punishment and deliberate and arbitrary killings on people who refused to comply with the new rules and behaviours they imposed according to their interpretation of Islamic law.

■ In June, members of the MUJAO flogged people smoking in Bourem.

■ In July, a man in Timbuktu was accused of drinking alcohol and was given 40 strokes of the cane by members of Ansar Eddin.

■ In July, members of Ansar Eddin in Aguelhoc publicly stoned to death an unmarried couple who had had a child.

M

A number of people accused of theft or robberies had limbs amputated following sham trials.

■ In August, a Tuareg livestock farmer accused of stealing cattle had his right hand amputated.

■ In September, five people accused of robbery each had their right foot and left hand amputated.

Child soldiers

Parties on both sides of the conflict recruited child soldiers.

In the government-controlled area of the country, self-defence militias recruited and trained children with the support of the authorities ahead of a planned offensive to regain control of the north.

Children were also recruited by the armed groups that took control of the north of the country. They were often posted at checkpoints to search passers-by.

Right to education and culture

The right to education in the north was undermined by AQIM who forbade the teaching of French in schools and the mixing of boys and girls.

■ In March, all schools and libraries in Kidal were burned and looted apart from two *madrasas* (Islamic schools).

The right to culture was undermined as armed Islamist groups destroyed historic mausoleums. They claimed it was to put an end to the cult of saints.

■ In May, AQIM members, supported by Ansar Eddin, began a series of destructions by desecrating the mausoleum of Muslim saint Sidi (Mahmoud Ben) Amar in Timbuktu.

Acts of terrorism and abductions

At the end of the year, 14 hostages were being held by armed groups, including AQIM, in the north.

■ Seven Algerian nationals, including the Algerian Consul in Gao, were kidnapped in April by members of MUJAO. Three of them were released in July.

■ In July, three people, two Spanish and one Italian, kidnapped by members of MUJAO in Algeria in October 2011, were released near Gao, reportedly in exchange for the release of three Islamists in neighbouring countries.

■ On 20 November, Gilberto Rodriguez Leal, a French national, was kidnapped in western Mali. His abduction was claimed by MUJAO.

Death penalty

Bamako's Court of Assizes sentenced 10 people to death during the year. Four were convicted of criminal association, robbery, conspiracy and illegal possession of firearms, and two were convicted of complicity in murder.

Amnesty International visits/reports

🚌 Amnesty International delegates visited Mali in April, July and August/September.

📖 Mali: Five months of crisis – armed rebellion and military coup (AFR 37/001/2012)

📖 Mali: "We haven't seen our cellmates since." Enforced disappearances and torture of soldiers and police officers opposed to the junta (AFR 37/004/2012)

📖 Mali: Civilians bear the brunt of the conflict (AFR 37/007/2012)

MALTA

REPUBLIC OF MALTA
Head of state: George Abela
Head of government: Lawrence Gonzi

Detention for up to 18 months remained mandatory for asylum-seekers and irregular migrants, and safeguards to challenge it were inadequate. Legal protection against hate crimes was extended to LGBTI people.

Refugees, migrants and asylum-seekers

The number of people who arrived by sea increased by 28% (from 1,577 to 2,023) on the previous year. The government continued to automatically detain undocumented migrants, often for up to 18 months, in breach of Malta's international human rights obligations. Unaccompanied children whose age was in question were also reportedly detained. Age determination procedures continued to be inadequate and lengthy.

Appeal procedures to challenge the length and legitimacy of detention and to challenge decisions to reject asylum claims did not meet international human rights standards. Migrants remained exposed to the risk of arbitrary detention.

Conditions in detention centres remained poor and were exacerbated by overcrowding, with hundreds

M

experiencing lack of privacy, insufficient access to sanitary and washing facilities, and poor recreation and leisure facilities. There were consistent and credible reports that being detained in such conditions was adversely affecting the mental health of migrants. Conditions in open centres for refugees and migrants released from detention also remained inadequate.

■ On 30 June, Mamadou Kamara, a 32-year-old migrant from Mali, died in custody. He had attempted to escape from Safi Barracks detention centre, and was allegedly severely ill-treated when recaptured. Two officers were charged with his murder and a third with perverting the course of justice. On 2 July, the Prime Minister appointed a judge to lead an independent inquiry into whether the individuals involved in Mamadou Kamara's death had been negligent, had disregarded procedures or abused their powers. It was also to investigate whether the recommendations made by the inquiry into the death of Infeanyi Nwokoye in 2011 had been implemented.

■ The judicial investigation into the death of Infeanyi Nwokoye in April 2011 continued. Infeanyi Nwokoye, a Nigerian migrant, had died in hospital after being recaptured following an escape attempt from Safi Barracks detention centre. He had been living in Malta since 2006. His request for asylum had been rejected, and he was returned to the detention centre after documents needed for his deportation had been finalized. A government inquiry to examine the circumstances of Infeanyi Nwokoye's death had published a summary of recommendations in October 2011.

Rights of lesbian, gay, bisexual, transgender and intersex people

In June, the Criminal Code was amended to add sexual orientation and gender identity to the list of circumstances which would increase the punishment for certain crimes.

Also in June, the definition of discrimination in the Equality for Men and Women Act was extended to include discrimination based on sexual orientation and gender identity. The mandate of the national equality body, the National Commission for the Promotion of Equality, which monitors the implementation of equality legislation, was extended accordingly.

Amnesty International visits/reports

S.O.S. Europe: Human rights and migration control (EUR 01/013/2012)

MAURITANIA

ISLAMIC REPUBLIC OF MAURITANIA
Head of state: **General Mohamed Ould Abdel Aziz**
Head of government: **Moulaye Ould Mohamed Laghdaf**

The authorities severely restricted freedom of expression, assembly and association. Protesters marched throughout the year, demanding the departure of President Mohamed Ould Abdel Aziz. The authorities continued to threaten anti-slavery activists. Former Libyan intelligence chief Abdullah al-Senussi was arrested and extradited to Libya, where he could face the death penalty. At least six people were sentenced to death.

Background

President Aziz was shot by soldiers from an army unit in October. The authorities declared it a mistake. The President was transferred to France for medical treatment as coup rumours started circulating. Several demonstrations in November challenged the political and legal vacuum resulting from the President's absence.

In October, Mauritania ratified the International Convention against enforced disappearance, and the Optional Protocol to the UN Convention against Torture.

Enforced disappearances

The authorities failed to disclose the whereabouts of 14 prisoners sentenced for terrorism-related offences and abducted from the central prison in the capital, Nouakchott, in May 2011. They included Mohamed Ould Chabarnou, Sidi Ould Sidina, Maarouf Ould Heiba, Khadim Ould Semane, Mohamed Ould Abdou, Abderrahmane Ould Areda and Mohamed Ould Chbih. The authorities maintained that their transfer to a secret location was a temporary measure for security reasons.

M

Freedom of expression

At least 36 people were arrested following peaceful demonstrations.

■ In February, peaceful demonstrations organized by University of Nouakchott students were violently repressed. More than 30 students were arrested. Some were released after a few days, while others were detained for more than a week without charge or trial.

Prisoners of conscience and political prisoners

■ In April, 11 members of an anti-slavery organization, Initiative pour la Résurgence du Mouvement Abolitionniste en Mauritanie (IRA-Mauritanie) were arrested, including Biram Ould Dah Ould Abeid, Yacoub Diarra, Ahmed Hamdy Ould Hamat Fall, Abidine Ould Salem, El Id Ould Lemlih, Oubeid Ould Imijine and Boumediene Ould Bata. The men had protested against Islamic scholars' writings, considered by IRA-Mauritanie to justify slavery. The men were charged with threatening state security, affronts to common decency and administration of an unauthorized organization. IRA-Mauritanie's president was also charged with apostasy. All were provisionally released in September after four months in detention. Their trial had not taken place by the end of the year.

■ Lemine Ould Dadde, former Commissioner for Human Rights, was provisionally released in December.

Counter-terror and security

At least 17 men were tried and imprisoned or sentenced to death for terrorism-related offences. Some trials did not comply with international fair trial standards.

■ At least three detainees convicted on terrorism-related charges, including Assad Abdel Khader Mohamed Ali, remained in detention despite being due for release. They were finally released after delays of four, 10 and 12 months.

Torture and other ill-treatment

Torture and other ill-treatment continued to be widely reported in detention centres, including in Ksar and Tevragh-Zeina police stations and in Nouakchott women's prison.

■ A student detained at Ksar police station following the February student demonstrations had his hands and feet tied together with a rope, and was beaten and stamped on during interrogation.

■ Two women detained at the women's prison reported being severely beaten when they were arrested in 2010, and during interrogation at a police station.

No investigations were opened into allegations of torture and ill-treatment in police custody and during interrogation.

Extradition

In March, former Libyan intelligence chief Abdullah al-Senussi was arrested as he arrived from Morocco. In July, the authorities stated that he had entered the country illegally and that they were considering different options for his extradition, including a request by the International Criminal Court (ICC). The ICC had issued an arrest warrant for alleged crimes against humanity in Libya. Mauritania's authorities finally extradited him to Libya in September, where he could face the death penalty.

Death penalty

At least six people were sentenced to death during the year.

■ In April, at least three people, Mohamed Saleck Ould Cheikh, Youssouf Galissa and Mohamed Lemine Ould Mballé, were sentenced to death. They were charged with attempting to commit a terrorist offence and being members of a terrorist group.

■ Mohamed Abdellahi Ould Ahmednah Ould Mohamed Salem's 2011 death sentence was confirmed in April after a Nouakchott Criminal Court appeal hearing. He was accused of being a member of al-Qa'ida in the Islamic Maghreb and of responsibility for the muder of a US national.

Slavery

■ Four IRA-Mauritanie activists were arrested on 11 January and detained for four days after they complained about a slavery case in Ayoun, a town in southern Mauritania. They were accused of attempting to resist law enforcement and to provoke a rebellion.

Migrants' rights

Migrants – mostly from Sub-Saharan Africa, in particular Mali, Guinea and Senegal – continued to be arbitrarily arrested and detained on suspicion of trying to reach Europe. At least 4,000 migrants were arrested and sent to either Mali or Senegal.

■ In April, armed security forces arrested between 400 and 800 migrants, mostly from West Africa, in

Nouadhibou. They were held for days in immigration detention centres in Nouadhibou and Nouakchott, and most were sent back to Mali and Senegal. They had no opportunity to challenge the legality of their detention or their collective expulsion.

Amnesty International visits/reports

🚗 Amnesty International delegates visited Mauritania in June and July.

📄 Mauritania: Activists held in unknown location (AFR 38/002/2012)

📄 Mauritania: The families of 14 prisoners subjected to enforced disappearance for over a year have the right to know their relatives' whereabouts (AFR 38/008/2012)

📄 Mauritania: Amnesty International calls on Mauritania to live up to their obligations after the ratification of two key international instruments (AFR 38/009/2012)

📄 Former Libyan intelligence chief must be sent to the ICC (PRE01/145/2012)

MEXICO

UNITED MEXICAN STATES
Head of state and government: **Enrique Peña Nieto**
(replaced Felipe Calderón Hinojosa in December)

President Calderón's government continued to ignore evidence of widespread human rights violations, such as arbitrary detentions, torture, enforced disappearances and extrajudicial killings, committed by security and police forces. During his six-year presidency, which ended in December 2012, more than 60,000 people were killed and 150,000 displaced as a result of drug-related violence. Drug cartels and other criminal gangs were responsible for the vast majority of killings and abductions, but often operated in collusion with public officials. The criminal justice system remained gravely flawed with 98% of all crimes going unpunished. Indigenous Peoples were at particular risk of unfair criminal justice proceedings. Migrants in transit were victims of attacks, including abduction, rape and people trafficking. Several journalists and human rights activists were killed, attacked or threatened. A protection mechanism for human rights defenders and journalists was established in law. Violence against women and girls

was widespread. Impunity for grave human rights violations committed during the 1960s, 1970s and 1980s persisted. The National Supreme Court (Suprema Corte de Justicia de la Nación, SCJN) incorporated human rights obligations into groundbreaking rulings, including restrictions on military jurisdiction. The new government of President Enrique Peña Nieto signed a pact with other political parties, which included some human rights commitments, and made promises to combat continuing high levels of poverty.

Background

In June, Enrique Peña Nieto of the Institutional Revolutionary Party (Partido Prevolucionario Institucional, PRI) was elected President and took office in December. The PRI also gained several state governorships and increased its representation in the Federal Congress. The acrimonious election campaign witnessed the emergence of a youth social protest movement, Iam132# (YoSoy132#), critical of the electoral process and the PRI candidate.

Insecurity and violence arising from President Calderón's militarized response to organized crime dominated political debate. In May, a drug cartel was allegedly responsible for leaving 49 dismembered bodies in Cadereyta, Nuevo León state; the identities of the dead had not been established by the end of the year. The Movement for Peace with Justice and Dignity continued to call for an end to violence and for all those responsible to be held to account. President Calderón's government vetoed the General Law on Victims. The Law, which the Movement for Peace with Justice and Dignity had promoted and which Congress approved, strengthened the rights of victims of the violence, including the right to reparation. In December, the new government of President Enrique Peña announced that the veto on the law was withdrawn.

In August, despite the failure of Mexican authorities to meet human rights conditions set by the US Congress as part of the Merida Initiative – a regional security co-operation agreement – the US State Department recommended that Congress release the 15% of funds subject to the conditions.

UN thematic committees on racial discrimination, discrimination against women and torture reviewed Mexico's compliance with treaty obligations and issued recommendations during the year. Mexico took

M

some steps to comply with Inter-American Court of Human Rights judgements on the cases of Rosendo Radilla, Inés Fernández, Valentina Rosendo, Rodolfo Montiel and Teodoro Cabrera. However, victims continued to demand full compliance.

Public security

Members of the army, navy and the federal, state and municipal police were responsible for widespread and grave human rights violations in the context of anti-crime operations and when operating in collusion with criminal gangs. The government consistently refused to acknowledge the scale and seriousness of the abuses or the lack of credibility of official investigations. Impunity was widespread, leaving victims with little or no redress.

The National Human Rights Commission (Comisión Nacional de Derechos Humanos, CNDH) received 1,921 complaints against the armed forces and 802 against the Federal Police. Twenty-one recommendations were issued against the army and navy and nine against the Federal Police during the year. There was no publicly available information on police prosecuted and convicted for human rights violations. Only eight military personnel were convicted in the military justice system during the year.

Arbitrary detention and torture and other ill-treatment

There was widespread use of arbitrary detention, torture and ill-treatment to obtain information and confessions from suspects under interrogation. The CNDH reported receiving 1,662 complaints of torture and ill-treatment during the year. There were no reported convictions for torture during the year.

Pre-charge judicial detention (*arraigo*) continued to be used routinely by federal and state prosecutors to hold suspects for up to 80 days pending investigation. *Arraigo* detention seriously undermined the rights of detainees, whose access to lawyers, family and medical attention was severely restricted, creating a climate in which reports of torture and ill-treatment were routine. In November, the UN Committee against Torture called for the abolition of *arraigo*. However, only the states of Chiapas, Oaxaca and Yucatán eliminated its use.

■ On 18 January, three brothers – Juan Antonio, Jesús Iván and 14-year-old Luis Adrián Figueroa Gómez – were picked up by judicial police in Ciudad Juárez, Chihuahua state. They were reportedly beaten, threatened and given electric shocks to force them to confess to extortion of local businesses. Their statements were video recorded and filed as evidence. However, signs of torture were ignored by officials, when the three were remanded in custody. They filed a complaint of torture, but by the end of the year there was no information about any investigation into their allegations.

■ On 1 December, violent protests in Mexico City against the inauguration of the new President resulted in 97 detentions. The majority of those detained were released in the following days. The Federal District Human Rights Commission documented instances of ill-treatment and torture as well as arbitrary detentions. On 27 December the remaining 14 detainees were released on bail. There was no information available on the investigation into alleged abuses committed by police.

Excessive use of force and extrajudicial executions

The CNDH recorded at least 25 killings of bystanders in armed encounters between criminal gangs and the security forces. Failure to conduct full investigations of the vast majority of killings prevented identification of many victims, clarification of circumstances of the killings, and the prosecution of perpetrators.

■ On 3 February, an Indigenous man, Carmen Puerta Carrillo, was shot and killed as he drove by a military base in the community of Baborigame, municipality of Guadalupe y Calvo, Chihuahua state. Eyewitnesses reported that soldiers opened fire without warning or provocation. Relatives were reportedly warned by military officials not to pursue the legal complaint.

■ The CNDH issued a damning report in March on the killing of two student teachers from Ayotzinapa rural teacher training college in Guerrero state during protests in December 2011 and the torture and ill-treatment of other students. The report implicated federal and state officials in the abuses. Three state officials were in prison, but many others were not brought to justice during the year. In May, Vidulfo Rosales, a human rights lawyer working on the case, received a death threat.

Enforced disappearances

In December, a leaked report from the Federal Attorney General's Office indicated that there had been at least 25,000 reports of abductions, disappearances and missing persons throughout the country during President Calderón's administration. Criminal gangs were responsible for the majority of abductions, but public officials were also implicated in some cases. The CNDH was investigating 2,126 cases of reported enforced disappearances.

The fate of victims remained unknown in most instances. The authorities were frequently reluctant to investigate cases, particularly enforced disappearances, leaving relatives to conduct their own enquiries – often at grave risk of reprisals from the perpetrators – to establish the fate of their loved ones. In some states, relatives of victims were treated with contempt as officials made unfounded allegations about the presumed criminal associations of victims. In the states of Coahuila and Nuevo León, victims and human rights organizations obtained commitments from local officials to review cases and institute rapid search and investigation responses to reports of disappearances. Commitments by federal government to establish a nationwide database on the disappeared remained unfulfilled.

According to the CNDH, there were at least 15,921 unidentified bodies and more than 1,400 remains had been exhumed from clandestine mass graves. In March, the UN Working Group on Enforced or Involuntary Disappearances published a report highlighting alarming levels of enforced disappearance and impunity in Mexico.

In November in Nuevo León state, legislation was approved criminalizing enforced disappearance. In virtually all other states and at federal level, enforced disappearance was not criminalized in accordance with international human rights standards. The new government made commitments to rectify this.

■ In May, Moisés Orozco Medina was reportedly detained by members of the municipal police in Uruapan Municipality, Michoacán state. The authorities denied any knowledge of his detention and his fate had not been clarified by the end of the year. His brother and father had been abducted by armed men in 2009 and 2008; their fate remained unknown and the state authorities had failed to provide information on the investigation into the cases by the end of the year.

Migrants' rights

Migrants in transit continued to face abduction, murder and forced recruitment into criminal gangs. Migrant women and children were at particular risk of abuses. Public officials were often suspected of colluding with criminal gangs and committing other abuses against migrants, such as extortion and arbitrary detention.

Despite government commitments to combat all abuses against migrants, measures remained ineffective and state governments failed to prevent and punish crimes against migrants. In November, the implementing code of the new Migration Law came into force. In October, mothers of disappeared Central American migrants toured Mexico in search of their relatives. A database of missing migrants had still not been established by the end of the year and the identification of remains believed to be of migrants did not progress. Those defending migrants' rights continued to face threats in reprisal for their work.

■ In July, the migrants' shelter in Lechería, Mexico state, was closed after repeated threats by criminal gangs against migrants and shelter workers. State authorities failed to ensure effective protection and some local residents protested against the presence of the shelter. Migrants and human rights defenders continued to face threats and insecurity in Huehuetoca, where alternative temporary shelters were opened.

■ In October, eyewitnesses reported that at least 40 migrants were kidnapped from a freight train in Medias Aguas, Veracruz state. An official investigation failed to establish the fate of the migrants and denied that the abduction had taken place.

Human rights defenders and journalists

Human rights defenders and journalists continued to face attacks and threats as a result of their work. At least six journalists were killed. The Special Federal Prosecutor's Office for Crimes against Journalists failed to make progress in most cases of murdered journalists. The vast majority of investigations into attacks and threats against human rights defenders also remained unresolved. A law establishing a protection mechanism for human rights defenders and journalists was promoted by civil society and approved by Congress in April. The new government made commitments to establish the mechanism and prioritize protection of human rights defenders and journalists.

In April and May, four journalists were killed in Veracruz state: Regina Martínez, correspondent for the investigative magazine *Proceso*; and local photojournalists Gabriel Huge, Guillermo Luna and Esteban Rodríguez. Those responsible had not been brought to justice by the end of the year despite state and federal level investigations.

■ In February, Lucila Bettina Cruz was arbitrarily arrested in Santa María Xadani, Oaxaca state, as she left a meeting with members of the Federal Electricity Commission. She was charged with illegally detaining public officials, but was later released on bail. She had been participating in peaceful protests by local Indigenous Peoples whose lands were affected by wind-farm construction.

Indigenous Peoples' rights

Indigenous Peoples in different regions of the country continued to suffer high levels of exclusion and discrimination, with limited access to many essential services. They were often denied their right to free, prior and informed consent on development and resources projects affecting their traditional lands. The criminal justice system routinely denied Indigenous people fair trial guarantees and effective redress.

One area of progress was the review of emblematic cases by the SCJN.

■ In October, the SCJN overturned the conviction and ordered the release of Hugo Sánchez Ramírez, a young Indigenous taxi driver from Mexico state, who had been wrongly imprisoned for a kidnapping in 2007 after state police and prosecutors fabricated evidence against him.

■ In November, the SCJN overturned the convictions of José Ramón Aniceto Gómez and Pascual Agustín Cruz and ordered their release. The two Indigenous human rights defenders and prisoners of conscience from Alta, Puebla state, had been falsely accused of stealing a car in 2009 and were denied a fair trial. They had been convicted in July 2010 on fabricated criminal charges in reprisal for extending water access in their community.

■ Alberto Patishtan, an Indigenous man convicted for killing seven policemen in Chiapas state in 2000, remained in prison pending the outcome of his legal petition to the SCJN against his conviction. Amnesty International raised with the SCJN its concerns that he had been denied the right to a fair trial leading to an unsafe conviction.

■ The Wixárika continued to campaign for an end to mining concessions in their ancestral pilgrimage sites in the Wirikuta, San Luis Potosí state. The government promised to create a biodiversity park to protect part of the land, but by the end of the year the Wixárika had not been adequately consulted on the project.

Discrimination and violence against women and girls

Violence against women and girls, including beatings, rape, abduction and murder, was widespread in many states. Legislation to prevent and punish violence was not enforced effectively and the training of officials on dealing appropriately with gender-based crimes was not adequately monitored to ensure compliance. Despite commitments to improve investigation of gender-based violence, new police investigation protocols were not introduced during the year and perpetrators usually evaded justice. Protection orders remained inoperative in many states and victims faced continued threats. The government's public security policy and high levels of criminal violence reportedly led some authorities to pay less attention to gender-based violence. Some states introduced the crime of "feminicide" (gender-based killing of women), but much state level legislation continued to be inconsistent with international human rights obligations.

■ In the first three months of 2012, at least 13 bodies of young women and girls were discovered in the Valle de Juárez district outside Ciudad Juárez. Seven bodies were reportedly identified as those of girls aged between 15 and 17 who had been abducted in central Ciudad Juárez.

Military jurisdiction

In August, the SCJN reviewed a series of cases to establish the limits of the military justice system. This followed four Inter-American Court of Human Rights' judgements on the issue and constitutional human rights reforms in June 2011 establishing the obligation to apply international human rights treaties. The SCJN ruled that cases in which military personnel are implicated in ordinary crimes, including human rights violations, not specifically related to military discipline must be dealt with in the civilian federal justice system. In the case of Bonfilio Rubio Villegas, an Indigenous teacher killed by the army at a roadblock in Guerrero state in 2009, the Court established relatives' right to challenge military jurisdiction. By the end of the year, the SCJN had not established the jurisprudence to direct the decisions of lower courts in similar cases and uncertainty remained about the application of military jurisdiction.

In April, proposed reforms to the Code of Military Justice to exclude human rights violations were blocked. By the end of the year, the new Congress had not taken up legislative proposals to bring the Code into line with the Inter-American Court or SCJN judgements. The federal government failed to issue instructions to prosecutors to ensure that all preliminary investigations were conducted solely by civilian authorities.

Amnesty International visits/reports

🚗 Amnesty International delegates visited Mexico in March and November.

📄 Mexico: Documentation of the case of José Ramón Aniceto Gómez and Pascual Agustín Cruz – prisoners of conscience (AMR 41/035/2012)

📄 México: Carta abierta a la y los candidatos a la Presidencia de la República (AMR 41/038/2012)

📄 Mexico: Briefing to the UN Committee on the Elimination of Discrimination against Women (AMR 41/041/2012)

📄 Known abusers, but victims ignored: Torture and ill-treatment in Mexico (AMR 41/063/2012)

MOLDOVA

REPUBLIC OF MOLDOVA
Head of state: **Nicolae Timofti (replaced Marian Lupu in March)**
Head of government: **Vladimir Filat**

There were reports of torture and other ill-treatment committed by the police with impunity. The state failed to protect people from discrimination on the grounds of sexual orientation and state of health.

Torture and other ill-treatment

In spite of changes to the law, impunity for torture and other ill-treatment continued. Of 128 complaints received by the Prosecutor General's Office in connection with incidents following demonstrations in April 2009, only 43 had reached the courts and only three police officers had been convicted by the end of 2012. In all three cases the officers received suspended sentences.

Parliament passed amendments to the Criminal and Criminal Procedural Codes in November to bring Moldova closer to its obligation to eradicate torture. The maximum sentence for torture was increased from 10 to 15 years, the statute of limitations for torture was abolished, and those convicted of torture were no longer eligible for amnesties or suspended sentences. Other procedural changes required police to record the state of health of detainees upon arrival at the place of detention and provide them with written confirmation of the reasons for the arrest.

■ On 8 May, the Supreme Court rejected an appeal by Eugen Fedoruc against his detention in Chişinău Psychiatric Hospital, and in July his detention was extended for a further six months. Eugen Fedoruc was first held by the police on 2 April 2011 in connection with a series of murders. He alleged that he was tortured when he was held in Chişinău General Police Directorate from 16 April to 17 June 2011. He said he had been suspended with his hands and legs bound together and given electric shocks to force him to confess. He was then transferred to Chişinău Psychiatric Hospital for 10 days for psychiatric assessment, and remained in detention until December. Eugen Fedoruc had been previously treated as an outpatient for schizophrenia, but his doctor said in June 2012 that he was calm and presented no threat to the public, and that there was no reason for him to be held as an inpatient. The torture allegations were not investigated.

Cruel, inhuman or degrading punishments

On 24 May, Parliament approved a new law to introduce compulsory chemical castration as a punishment for violent child abusers, despite a veto by the President in April.

Discrimination

In May, Parliament passed a Law on Ensuring Equality, due to come into effect on 1 January 2013. However, provisions fell short of international standards by omitting sexual orientation, gender identity and state of health from the list of forbidden grounds of discrimination. Discrimination against some individuals and groups continued.

■ In February, I.H., a 48-year-old HIV-positive woman, with severe deterioration of a hip joint (osteonecrosis), was refused a hip replacement operation on the grounds that she was HIV-positive. On 21 November 2011, the Deputy Director of the Traumatology and Orthopaedics Hospital in Chişinău told her that such

M

surgery could not be performed on HIV-positive patients. The NGO the Institute for Human Rights and the UN Development Programme human rights representative both intervened, pointing out that hip replacement operations were regularly carried out on HIV-positive patients throughout the world and that such surgery did not result in complications if the immune system before the operation was healthy. The hospital refused to carry out the operation.

■ In March, in the run-up to the passage of the Law on Ensuring Equality, several local councils across the country adopted discriminatory measures against different groups in their communities. Bans on "aggressive propaganda of non-traditional sexual orientation" targeted LGBTI individuals, and Muslims were discriminated against through bans on public Muslim worship. Only one council repealed its decision upon intervention by the Ombudsperson.

■ On 12 June, the European Court of Human Rights ruled that the banning of an LGBTI demonstration in May 2005 had violated the right to freedom of assembly as well as the right not to be discriminated against, and ordered the Moldovan government to pay the organizers, GenderDoc-M, €11,000 within three months.

Amnesty International visits/reports

🚐 An Amnesty International delegate visited Moldova in April and September.

📋 Unfinished business: combating torture and ill-treatment in Moldova (EUR 59/001/2012)

📋 Towards equality: discrimination in Moldova (EUR 59/006/2012)

MONGOLIA

MONGOLIA

Head of state:	Tsakhia Elbegdorj
Head of government:	Norov Altankhuyag (replaced Batbold Sukhbaatar in August)

Mongolia took one step closer to abolishing the death penalty by acceding to the Second Optional Protocol to the ICCPR. Trials of high-profile individuals, including political figures, failed to meet international standards of fairness. Lack of due process led to forced evictions in *ger* districts in Ulaanbaatar.

Background

Parliamentary elections were held on 28 June. The majority Democratic Party formed a coalition government with the Justice Coalition and the Civil Will Green Party.

Death penalty

There were no executions. In March, Mongolia became a party to the Second Optional Protocol to the ICCPR, aiming at the abolition of the death penalty.

Unfair trials

Lawyers and government officials reported that unfair trials were common, particularly those involving officials or political figures. Lawyers were given little time and access to case files prior to going to court. Defendants' right to confidential communication with a lawyer of their own choice was restricted.

■ Former President N. Enkhbayar was convicted in August on corruption charges along with two other former officials and one civilian. He was refused bail on the basis of insufficient evidence in May, prompting Amnesty International to raise concerns that he had effectively been arbitrarily detained. He was released shortly afterwards. According to his lawyers, officials undermined N. Enkhbayar's right to confidential access to legal counsel. They restricted his lawyers' access to case documents and gave them very little time to prepare before the first court hearing.

Forced evictions

Families were evicted from their homes without prior consultation and other appropriate legal protections. In some cases, families were coerced or threatened by representatives of the local authorities and private construction companies. Some families fell prey to deals between local authorities and private developers, and were expected to pay for whatever alternative housing was offered.

■ After being notified verbally in 2010 that their area had been slated for development, families in 7th micro-district of Ulaanbaatar were not formally consulted and access to the plans remained restricted.

International justice

Mongolia, a state party to the Rome Statute of the International Criminal Court since 2002, had still not implemented its obligations under this treaty. Likewise, the ratification of the International

Convention against enforced disappearance, signed in 2007, remained pending.

MONTENEGRO

MONTENEGRO
Head of state: Filip Vujanović
Head of government: Milo Djukanović (replaced Igor Luksić in December)

Verdicts in war crimes cases were inconsistent with international law. Independent journalists continued to face intimidation and attacks.

Background

Demonstrations against the government's economic and social policies continued throughout the year.

Negotiations on Montenegro's accession to the EU began in June, focusing on the rule of law, including combatting organized crime and high-level corruption.

After October elections, the longstanding ruling Democratic Party of Socialists was only able to form a coalition government with ethnic minority party support. Former President Milo Djukanović became Prime Minister for the sixth time.

Crimes under international law

Prosecution of crimes under international law continued. In some cases proceedings were not fully in line with international standards, and verdicts were inconsistent with international law.

■ In January, following a retrial, four former members of the Yugoslav People's Army were convicted and each sentenced to up to four years' imprisonment for war crimes against Croatian prisoners of war and civilians at Morinj camp. The sentences were less than the statutory minimum. Appeals were allowed in July.

■ In April, the prosecution appeal against the acquittal in 2011 of army reservists and police officials charged with inhuman treatment of Bosniaks in Bukovica in 1992 was dismissed. The court found that at the time of the offence, the defendants' actions "did not constitute a criminal act in the eyes of the law", although inhuman treatment was defined as a crime against humanity

in the 2003 Criminal Code which ought, under established principles of international law, to have been applied retroactively.

■ The retrial of four members of the Yugoslav Army (which succeeded the Yugoslav People's Army) indicted for the murder of six Kosovo Albanians in Kaludjeruski Laz in 1999 started in September.

■ In November, nine former police officials were again acquitted of war crimes in a retrial for the enforced disappearance of more than 79 Bosnian refugees in May 1992, on the basis that although they had unlawfully detained the Bosniaks, the defendants were not parties to the international armed conflict in Bosnia and Herzegovina.

Freedom of expression

Prime Minister Igor Luksić publicly criticized NGOs and media opposed to the government. Independent journalists also faced intimidation and threats from private actors.

■ In March, Olivera Lakić – a journalist for the independent newspaper *Vijesti* – was hospitalized after being beaten outside her home. Her reporting on alleged industrial fraud had resulted in the opening of criminal investigations.

■ In April, the Supreme State Prosecutor replied to a 2010 request by the NGO Human Rights Action, for information on investigations into 12 unresolved human rights violations, including the murders of journalists and other politically motivated killings. The partial information supplied revealed little progress in investigations.

Discrimination

Discrimination against LGBTI people continued.

■ In September three gay men, including an actor and the director of a video against homophobia, were violently attacked by members of a Podgorica football supporters' organization. Despite requests for police protection, actor Todor Vujosević was attacked again in October.

Refugees and migrants

Around 3,200 Kosovo Roma and Ashkali refugees remained in Montenegro. In July, 800 of them were made homeless after a fire at the Konik collective centre, where they had lived since 1999. The refugees protested when they were provided with tents; in November they were inadequately housed in metal containers. Long-term plans for permanent housing to replace the collective centre were delayed.

Montenegro remained a transit route for irregular migrants: of 1,531 new asylum applicants, one was granted asylum and one other subsidiary protection.

Amnesty International visits/reports

📰 Montenegro: Submission to the UN Universal Periodic Review (EUR 66/004/2012)

MOROCCO/ WESTERN SAHARA

KINGDOM OF MOROCCO
Head of state: **King Mohamed VI**
Head of government: **Abdelilah Benkirane**

The authorities restricted freedom of expression and prosecuted critics of the monarchy and state institutions as well as Sahrawi advocates of self-determination. The security forces used excessive force against demonstrators. People suspected of terrorism or other security offences were at risk of torture and other ill-treatment and unfair trials. Migrants, refugees and asylum-seekers were subject to attacks. Women and girls were discriminated against in law and practice. At least seven people were sentenced to death; there were no executions.

Background

The UN Security Council extended the mandate of the UN Mission for the Referendum in Western Sahara (MINURSO) for a further year in April, again without including any human rights monitoring component.

Morocco's human rights record was assessed under the UN Universal Periodic Review in May. The government subsequently agreed to criminalize enforced disappearances under the Criminal Code and enact a domestic violence law, but declined UN recommendations calling for a legal moratorium on executions and improved procedures for the registration of civil society organizations.

The UN Special Rapporteur on torture visited Morocco and Western Sahara in September.

Freedoms of expression, association and assembly

The authorities continued to clamp down on journalists and others who criticized the monarchy or state institutions. The security forces used excessive force to disperse demonstrations.

■ Abdelsamad Haydour, a student, was fined and sentenced to three years' imprisonment in February for "insulting the King" in an online video.

■ Rap singer Mouad Belghouat had his one-year prison sentence, imposed for insulting the police, confirmed by the Casablanca Court of Appeal in July. He was charged after a video featuring one of his songs was posted on the internet. He was imprisoned in March and remained in prison at the end of the year.

■ Tarek Rouchdi and five other activists in the 20 February Movement, which advocates political reform, were sentenced to prison terms of up to 10 months in September. They were convicted on charges such as insults and violence against public officials. Dozens of activists in the 20 February Movement were reported to be detained at the end of the year.

In August, police used excessive force against people demonstrating outside parliament in Rabat against an annual event marking the King's accession to the throne. A journalist reporting the event was also abused. In November, police used excessive force to prevent a planned demonstration outside parliament called by the 20 February Movement.

Repression of dissent – Sahrawi activists

The authorities continued to target Sahrawi human rights defenders and advocates of self-determination for Western Sahara, and used excessive force to quell or prevent demonstrations in Western Sahara. They also continued to block the legal registration of Sahrawi civil society organizations.

■ Police were reported to have injured dozens of people who demonstrated in Laayoune on 13 January in support of 23 Sahrawi prisoners. The 23 prisoners were held awaiting trial in connection with violence at Gdim Izik protest camp near Laayoune in November 2010. They were held in Sale prison, near Rabat, far from their homes. Many said they had been tortured or otherwise ill-treated in detention. Thirteen people, including 11 members of the security forces, were killed in the clashes that began at Gdim Izik and then spread to Laayoune.

- The Sahraoui Association for the Victims of Grave Human Rights Violations Committed by the Moroccan State (ASVDH) continued to be denied legal recognition despite a 2006 ruling that an administrative decision rejecting its registration was unlawful. The government rejected a recommendation from the UN Universal Periodic Review to allow the legal registration of NGOs advocating Sahrawi self-determination.

Torture and other ill-treatment
Torture and other ill-treatment continued to be reported, with detainees held for interrogation by the Department of State Surveillance (DST) particularly at risk. Following his visit in September, the UN Special Rapporteur on torture observed that torture tended to be more prevalent when the authorities perceived state security to be under threat. He noted that torture allegations rarely resulted in prosecutions of alleged perpetrators.

In October, the National Human Rights Council reported that prison staff continued to commit abuses against prisoners and that investigations were rare.

Counter-terror and security
People suspected of terrorism or other security-related crimes were at risk of torture or other ill-treatment and unfair trials.
- Ali Aarrass, who was convicted of belonging to a terrorist organization in November 2011, had his 15-year prison sentence reduced to 12 years by the Sale Court of Appeal. A further appeal to the Court of Cassation was pending at the end of the year. He had been extradited from Spain to Morocco in December 2010 contrary to interim measures issued by the UN Human Rights Committee due to a risk of torture and other ill-treatment in Morocco. He was reported to have been made to "confess" under torture.
- In August, the UN Working Group on Arbitrary Detention declared the detention of Mohamed Hajib, a Moroccan/German national, to be arbitrary, and urged the Moroccan authorities to release him. He was convicted of terrorism offences in 2010 on the basis of a confession allegedly obtained under torture while he was held in pre-trial detention and denied access to a lawyer. Mohamed Hajib received a 10-year prison sentence, reduced to five years in January. He was still held at the end of the year. The authorities did not investigate his torture allegations.

Transitional justice
The authorities again failed to implement recommendations made by the Equity and Reconciliation Commission in November 2005, including ratification of the Rome Statute of the International Criminal Court, or to ensure justice for those who suffered serious human rights violations between 1956 and 1999.

Refugees, asylum-seekers and migrants
Migrants, refugees and asylum-seekers were at risk of attack and ill-treatment. In September, the UN Special Rapporteur on torture reported a rise in "severe beatings, sexual violence, and other forms of ill-treatment" against undocumented migrants, and urged the authorities to investigate and prevent such "violence against sub-Saharan migrants".

Women's rights
Women and girls faced sexual violence and discrimination in both law and practice. In November, the government began the process to enable Morocco to become party to the Optional Protocol to CEDAW. However, it continued to qualify its obligation under CEDAW to eliminate discrimination against women with the condition that this should not conflict with Shari'a law. The government rejected a recommendation under the UN Universal Periodic Review to revise the Family Code to give women the same inheritance rights as men. It remained possible for men to escape punishment for rape by marrying their victim.

Polisario camps
The Polisario Front again failed to take any steps to hold to account those responsible for human rights abuses committed in camps under its control in the 1970s and 1980s.

Death penalty
At least seven people were sentenced to death. No executions have been carried out since 1993.

M

MOZAMBIQUE

REPUBLIC OF MOZAMBIQUE
Head of state: Armando Emílio Guebuza
Head of government: Alberto Vaquina (replaced Aires
                      Bonifácio Baptista Ali in October)

People were subject to arbitrary arrest and detention
by police, and prolonged detention without trial.
Excessive use of force by police was reported.
Appalling conditions in prisons led to riots.

Background

On 8 March a shoot-out between police in Nampula
city and about 300 members of the opposition
Mozambique National Resistance (Resistência
Nacional Moçambicana, Renamo) resulted in the
deaths of a police officer and a Renamo member, and
injuries to several others, both police and Renamo.
Police had raided the Renamo headquarters where the
men had set up camp since December 2011, apparently
awaiting orders from the party leader, Afonso
Dhlakama, to stage anti-government protests. At the
end of October Afonso Dhlakama moved with about
800 men to the Renamo former base in Gorongosa,
Sofala province, threatening to return to war unless
the government agreed to meet them. In November a
government commission was set up to begin dialogue
with Renamo. In December, four Renamo members
were convicted and sentenced to nine months and 11
days' imprisonment in connection with the March
shoot-out. They were released immediately as they
had spent that time in pre-trial detention.

On 11 May parliament elected former Minister of
Justice, José Abudo, as the first Justice Ombudsman.
On 5 September, 11 commissioners of the new
National Human Rights Commission were sworn in.

In September President Guebuza was re-elected
Frelimo president at the party's 10th congress.

Police and security forces

Between February and November, over 20 Asian
businessmen and family members were kidnapped in
the capital Maputo and held for ransom. The Asian
business community alleged that the police were
involved in the kidnappings. In September individuals
suspected of involvement were arrested and released,

apparently due to lack of evidence. Others were
arrested in November; no further information was
available by the end of the year.

In April the Commander General of Police acted in
defiance of a court decision and reportedly stated that
he was not bound by the decision of the judiciary with
regard to police discipline.

■ In March, five police officers in Nacala, Nampula
province, including the Nacala Police Commander,
were arrested in connection with the alleged illegal
storage of arms. A judge ordered their conditional
release pending investigation, but they were re-arrested
and detained by police before again being released
after intervention by lawyers. The Commander General
of Police stated that police had acted in accordance
with the Police Disciplinary Regulation of 1987 and
were not bound by the decision of the court. In
September the Constitutional Council determined that
the provision of the Regulation which the Commander
General had relied on had already been revoked.

Arbitrary arrests and detentions

Police carried out arbitrary arrests and detentions,
a number of which were politically motivated. Some
detainees were released without charge. None
appeared to have received compensation and no
police officers appeared to have been held criminally
responsible.

■ Police arrested members of the War Veterans
Forum, including its spokesperson, Jossías Alfredo
Matsena, who was arrested on three separate
occasions. On 10 January he was arrested and
released without charge after a few hours. On 19
January he was again arrested, and charged with fraud
and threats against a Frelimo district representative. He
was tried for fraud and acquitted in March; the charges
relating to the alleged threats were dropped in June. On
14 February he was arrested without a warrant while on
his way to the offices of the Mozambique Human Rights
League. He was held in Machava police station in
Maputo province for some hours and transferred to the
1st Police station in Inhambane for two days before
being taken to the Inhambane maximum security
prison. He was charged with concealment of arms and
incitement to violence and held for four months before
being released pending trial.

■ On 18 April, 38 members of the opposition
Democratic Movement of Mozambique (Movimento
Democrático de Moçambique, MDM) were arrested

during mayoral by-elections in the province of Inhambane. They were initially released without charge, but in August were accused of illegal campaigning at polling stations. The detainees said they were distributing food and water for the MDM polling station monitors. On 5 October they were convicted of alleged electoral offences and sentenced to two months' imprisonment without the option of a fine. Seven were tried in their absence.

Excessive use of force and unlawful killings

In July the Maputo Administrative Court ordered the state to pay 500,000 meticais (about US$17,000) in compensation to the mother of an 11-year-old boy who was killed by a stray bullet fired by police during violent demonstrations in Maputo in September 2010. No officer was held accountable. There were further cases of excessive use of force by the police during the year.

■ In July police shot and killed a 19-year-old man, known only as António, in the city of Nampula. António and a friend were reported to have driven a car into a police vehicle parked outside the 2nd police station in Nampula and failed to stop. Police pursued them and fired, hitting António, who died later. Police authorities told Amnesty International delegates in November that an investigation was being carried out. No further information was available at the end of the year.

■ In August, the district Police Commander in Ilha de Moçambique, Nampula province, beat a pregnant woman, resulting in her hospitalization. Police authorities said that the Commander had beaten her in his personal capacity during a private dispute. They stated that a disciplinary procedure had been instituted and that an investigation was being carried out. No further information was available at the end of the year.

Detention without trial

In at least three prisons in Maputo and two in Nampula, hundreds of people were held without trial, some without charge, for longer than the time legally allowed. Thousands of people remained similarly detained throughout the country.

■ On 16 February a joint delegation of Amnesty International and the Mozambique Human Rights League found José Capitine Cossa (also known as Zeca Capetinho Cossa) detained without charge or trial in Machava Maximum Security prison. He had been held for over 12 years; the authorities claimed they did not know why he was there. In September the Attorney General informed Amnesty International that José Capitine Cossa had been released on 4 September as his detention had been irregular and that an investigation was being carried out. By the end of the year no one had been held responsible and José Capitine Cossa had not received compensation for unlawful arrest and detention.

Prison conditions

Prisoners in Nampula Central Prison and Beira Central Prison rioted in March and September respectively in protest against overcrowding, poor food and health conditions. The Rapid Intervention Force used excessive force during the riots at Nampula Central Prison, which was condemned by the Minister of Justice. Conditions at Nampula Central Prison were harsh, with extreme overcrowding, insanitary conditions, nutritionally inadequate food and poor medical facilities. Similar conditions were recorded in other prisons.

Amnesty International visits/reports

Amnesty International delegates visited Mozambique in February and November.

Locking up my rights: arbitrary arrest, detention and treatment of detainees in Mozambique (AFR 41/001/2012)

M

MYANMAR

REPUBLIC OF THE UNION OF MYANMAR
Head of state and government: **Thein Sein**

Amid ongoing political, legal and economic reforms, the authorities released hundreds of prisoners of conscience; however, many remained behind bars. Security forces and other state agents continued to commit human rights violations, including unlawful killings, excessive use of force, arbitrary arrests, torture and other ill-treatment, and unlawful confiscation or destruction of property and livelihoods. Impunity for past crimes, including crimes against humanity, persisted.

Background

In April, Myanmar held by-elections, which international observers determined to be largely free and fair. The opposition party, the National League for Democracy (NLD), won 43 of the 44 seats it contested and were allowed to take their seats in parliament.

In August, former prisoner of conscience Daw Aung San Suu Kyi was appointed as chairperson to the newly created parliamentary Committee for Rule of Law and Tranquility. In September, the National Human Rights Commission was accepted as a member of the South East Asia National Human Rights Institutions Forum, and in November it was admitted as an associate member of the Asia Pacific Forum, but concerns remained about its ability to act as an independent human rights monitor.

In November, Myanmar adopted the ASEAN Human Rights Declaration, despite serious concerns that it fell short of international standards. Also in November, President Thein Sein authorized the ICRC to resume prison visits, and announced that the government planned to develop an inter-governmental mechanism to review prisoner cases.

The EU and Australia, Canada, Switzerland and the USA suspended most sanctions against Myanmar in the first half of the year, but arms embargoes remained in place.

Internal armed conflict

The government signed ceasefire or initial peace agreements with the political wings of some eight ethnic opposition groups, including the Arakan Liberation Party, Karen National Union, Shan State Army North and Shan State Army South. However, occasional clashes continued to be reported in eastern Myanmar. The armed conflict in the Kachin and northern Shan states intensified, with the armed forces using air strikes to target outposts of the Kachin Independence Army (KIA) at the end of the year. The current conflict started after the Myanmar army broke its ceasefire with the KIA in June 2011. Attempts at talks between the government and the KIA did not yield positive results during the year. An ILO Action Plan on under-age military recruitment and the Joint Action Plan on children in armed conflict under UN Security Council Resolution 1612 were signed in June, and the authorities publicly released 42 child soldiers in September.

Villagers in areas of armed conflict, in particular in the Kachin and northern Shan states, continued to be subjected to a range of human rights abuses, including arbitrary arrest, unlawful killings, sexual violence, torture, enforced disappearances and destruction of livelihood.

■ In January, lawyers acting on behalf of the family of disappeared Kachin woman Sumlut Roi Ja lodged a case with the Supreme Court in Nay Pyi Taw. Sumlut Roi Ja disappeared after reportedly being detained by the armed forces in October 2011. Her husband, who claimed that he witnessed her abduction, was not allowed to give evidence. In March, the Supreme Court dismissed the case citing a lack of evidence.

■ In June, the army arrested four Kachin men who were tending cattle, for suspected ties with the Kachin Independence Organization (KIO) and the KIA. Credible reports stated that the men were tortured.

■ On 1 July, soldiers arrested 27 Kachin villagers for their alleged association with the KIA. Most of the men were quickly released, but Galau Bawm Yaw remained in detention. On 22 July, his body was discovered reportedly bearing signs of torture.

Internally displaced people

The number of people displaced by the ongoing conflict in Kachin state reached more than 75,000 by the end of the year. Many of those displaced were living in makeshift camps in KIA-controlled areas close to the Chinese border, and suffered from inadequate access to food, medical care and proper sanitation facilities. Humanitarian organizations were unable to provide sustained assistance to KIA- and KIO-controlled areas due to government restrictions.

More than 400,000 people continued to be displaced in eastern Myanmar. Another 115,000 Rohingya and non-Rohingya Muslims remained displaced in Rakhine state due to communal violence and abuses. Humanitarian agencies faced obstacles in assisting those outside official camps for the internally displaced, particularly in late October and early November. Camps were overcrowded and insanitary.

Communal violence

In early June, violent clashes erupted between Rakhine Buddhist and Rohingya and other Muslim communities, following the alleged rape and murder of a Buddhist Rakhine woman by three Muslim men on 28 May in Rakhine state, and the subsequent killing of 10 Muslim men in a revenge attack. The President declared a state of emergency on 10 June. Sporadic violence continued in July and August, and intense communal violence broke out again between 21 and 30 October when other Muslim communities such as the ethnic Kaman were also targeted. Official figures indicated that around 160 people died. The actual figure may be considerably higher.

A government-appointed commission was set up on 17 August to investigate the cause of the violence in Rakhine state. The commission was composed of a range of stakeholders, including former political prisoners and six Muslim representatives, but lacked a representative from the Rohingya community. Two of the Muslim representatives were relieved of their duties in November. The commission had not released its final report at the end of the year.

Land disputes

Protests against land grabbing and evictions erupted during the year. A parliamentary committee was established to investigate land disputes. The committee was reported to have looked into several hundred cases in the last quarter of the year – out of a reported 4,000 reports of land seizures submitted to it – and was due to present its findings to parliament in early 2013.

■ In the early hours of 29 November, police forcibly dispersed peaceful protesters who were camped at the Letpadaung copper mine in Monywa township, Sagaing region, causing severe injuries to some of the protesters, including monks. Protesters had been objecting to the expansion of the mine, associated land confiscation, and the reported environmental impact already caused by the mine. In December, Daw Aung San Suu Kyi was appointed as the chair of a commission to investigate the expansion of the mine and the crackdown on protesters.

The Farmland Law and the Vacant, Fallow and Virgin Lands Management Law, both enacted in 2012, fail to provide adequate protection for farmers from having their land requisitioned by the authorities.

In March, the Ward or Village Tract Administration Act was amended to criminalize forced labour. In July, the government approved an action plan to end all forms of forced labour by 2015. Nevertheless, the practice continued, particularly in ethnic areas.

Freedom of assembly

In July, the government enacted the 2011 law on the Right to Peaceful Assembly and Peaceful Procession (Peaceful Assembly and Procession law). The law required protesters to apply at least five days in advance for permission to demonstrate, and stipulated that: "The application should not be denied unless the security of the State, rule of law, public tranquility and the existing laws protecting the public are to be breached."

Some who organized or took part in peaceful demonstrations without permits were charged under section 18 of the law, and faced up to one year in prison for each township entered without a permit.
■ Several people were charged under the Peaceful Assembly and Procession law for organizing a peace march without a permit in September. The marchers passed through multiple townships and were facing charges in each.
■ In December, at least six activists were charged under section 18 of the Peaceful Assembly and Procession law for demonstrating without a permit on 1 December in Yangon. They were expressing concern about the violent crackdown in November on protesters at the Monywa mine, Sagaing region.

Freedom of expression

On 20 August, the Ministry of Information announced the end of all pre-publication censorship procedures, and on the same day issued a strict set of publishing guidelines prohibiting, among other things, negative criticism of state policies. The Ministry still required articles to be submitted to the Press Scrutiny and Registration Division after publication.

In early August, the government created the Myanmar Core Press Council to serve as an interim body to monitor and address media issues until the new media law was enacted. There was strong opposition to its lack of independence, composition, and authority by journalists. A new interim Press Council was established in mid-September; more than half of its members were journalists.

Arbitrary arrests and detentions

Hundreds of people, including children, were arbitrarily detained, held in incommunicado detention, and subjected to cruel, inhuman and degrading treatment in places of detention without access to appropriate or adequate medical care.

M

There continued to be some reports of torture and other ill-treatment, occasionally leading to death in custody.

■ Prisoner of conscience Dr Tun Aung remained behind bars. He was a medical doctor and chairman of the Islamic Religious Affairs Council in Maungdaw, Rakhine state. On 11 June, he was arrested for provoking communal riots in Maungdaw, and sentenced to 11 years' imprisonment in the second half of the year. He was believed to have been persecuted for his role as a Muslim community leader in Maungdaw.

■ Myo Myint Swe died in a police station in Yangon in July after he was accused of involvement in a murder. His body showed signs of torture.

Prisoner amnesties

The authorities released more than 8,500 prisoners, including hundreds of prisoners of conscience. Most were granted conditional releases under section 401 of the Code of Criminal Procedure, violation of which could lead to re-imprisonment for the remainder of their sentence.

Death penalty

In early January, the President commuted the death sentences of all prisoners on death row to life imprisonment; however, at least 17 individuals received death sentences during the year.

Impunity

The National Human Rights Commission did not have the authority to receive and investigate complaints of human rights violations which had taken place prior to its formation on 5 September 2011. There was no comprehensive and independent mechanism to investigate possible war crimes and crimes against humanity, leaving victims and their relatives with inadequate access to measures of truth, justice and reparations. Many of those involved in grave human rights violations had not been brought to justice.

Amnesty International visits/reports

🚌 Amnesty International delegates visited Myanmar in May, November and December.

📄 Revisiting human rights in Myanmar (ASA 16/003/2012)

📄 Myanmar: Meet immediate humanitarian needs and address systemic discrimination (ASA 16/008/2012)

📄 Myanmar: Open letter to the Minister of Home Affairs (ASA 16/016/2012)

NAMIBIA

REPUBLIC OF NAMIBIA
Head of state and government: **Hifikepunye Pohamba**

The long-running treason trial of Caprivi detainees continued, with most of the men having spent more than 12 years in custody. Members of the ruling South West Africa People's Organization (SWAPO) continued to enjoy impunity for abuses against their political opponents. Ethnic minorities faced marginalization and exclusion from decision-making processes.

Caprivi detainees' trial

The last of the 379 witnesses in the Caprivi high treason trial gave testimony and the prosecution closed its case in the High Court on 7 February. The 111 men remaining on trial faced a total of 278 charges, including high treason, nine counts of murder and 240 charges of attempted murder in connection with an alleged conspiracy to secede the Caprivi region from Namibia between January 1992 and December 2002. After the closure of the prosecution's case, one of the suspects, Rodwell Kasika Mukendwa, who was arrested on 26 August 1999, was acquitted on 10 August 2012.

Amnesty International considered that many of the Caprivi detainees were possible prisoners of conscience because they were arrested solely on the basis of their actual or perceived political views, ethnicity or membership of certain organizations. The group was being tried under what is known as the "common purpose" doctrine, which essentially relieves the prosecution of having to prove beyond a reasonable doubt that each participant committed conduct which contributed causally to the ultimate unlawful consequence. The doctrine shifts the burden of proof from the prosecution to the defendants and undermines the right to presumption of innocence.

Freedoms of association and assembly

The rights to freedom of peaceful assembly and of association were violated by the Namibian police and members of SWAPO.

■ In October, seven teachers were arrested in Oshakati for demonstrating against poor working conditions.

They were among some 300 teachers who went on strike demanding fair salaries and better working conditions as part of nationwide industrial action by the profession.

Prison conditions

Most prisons and detention centres remained overcrowded, with some holding more than twice the intended number. Windhoek Central Prison, which was designed to hold 912 inmates, contained approximately 2,000 inmates and pre-trial detainees. Similar conditions prevailed in Ondangwa, Swakopmund, Oshakati and Otjiwarango towns.

Violence against women and girls

Gender-based violence remained a serious concern. Many women were killed by their partners in domestic disputes.

■ On 1 February, Fransina Ndinelago Amuteka died after being stabbed and having her throat slit by her boyfriend at Ondukutu village near Ondangwa.
■ On 15 February, Melody Monde Mbololwa died after her boyfriend stabbed her nine times at Mavuluma Extension Two at Katima Mulilo in Caprivi region.
■ On 19 July, Letitia Ndeshuulilwe Nghilongwa, a student, was shot dead by her boyfriend at Omulamba location in Omusati town.
■ On 20 September, Tangi Nanguka Martin of Epuku village in Ohangwena region was killed by her husband.

Discrimination

In September, the UN Special Rapporteur on the rights of indigenous peoples visited Namibia, highlighting the continued marginalization of the country's minorities. Children of the San and Ovahimba peoples, and other ethnic minorities, face numerous barriers preventing them from accessing education. This is particularly the case in Opuwo among the Ovahimba children, who are forced to cut their hair and to not wear traditional dress to attend public schools.

NEPAL

FEDERAL DEMOCRATIC REPUBLIC OF NEPAL
Head of state: Ram Baran Yadav
Head of government: Baburam Bhattarai

Impunity was further entrenched as the government promoted alleged perpetrators of human rights violations to senior public positions, withdrew criminal cases against them and attempted to establish a transitional justice mechanism with the power to recommend amnesties for crimes under international law. Debates on federalism led to political violence in several parts of the country. Arbitrary detention, torture and extrajudicial executions were reported throughout the year.

Background

The Constituent Assembly was dissolved on 27 May before completing a new Constitution, as political parties failed to reach a consensus on several key issues despite four years of negotiations. Confrontational political rhetoric around the model of federalism to be adopted and demands for greater autonomy for ethnic minorities and Indigenous Peoples increased, leading to violent clashes and divisions between and within political parties. In October, the government announced that it had completed the process of integrating former Maoist combatants into the Nepal Army as agreed under the Comprehensive Peace Agreement and Interim Constitution of 2007. The government passed a law in January increasing state control over the work of the National Human Rights Commission.

Transitional justice

On 28 August, the Council of Ministers proposed an ordinance to establish a Commission of Inquiry on Disappeared Persons, Truth and Reconciliation, sidelining plans for two separate commissions to cover these issues. The new Commission would have power to recommend amnesties for serious human rights violations but no mandate to recommend prosecutions for alleged crimes, ignoring Nepal's legal obligations to prosecute crimes under international law. The UN Office of the High Commissioner for Human Rights released a report in October on violations of international human rights law and humanitarian law committed during Nepal's armed conflict, together with an archive of approximately 30,000 supporting documents and cases.

Impunity

Efforts to ensure accountability for human rights violations and victims' rights to justice, truth and reparation were seriously undermined by the government's promotion of individuals alleged to have committed human rights violations to senior public positions.

■ Kuber Singh Rana, the subject of ongoing criminal investigations into the 2003 enforced disappearance and extrajudicial execution of five students in Dhanusha district, was promoted to the rank of Inspector General of Police in September.

■ The promotion of Raju Basnet, a colonel suspected of involvement in war crimes, to the rank of Brigadier General in October was widely condemned by human rights activists and put on hold following a stay order issued by the Supreme Court in the same month.

The government continued to request the withdrawal of criminal cases against individuals affiliated with political parties, as part of a commitment under the Comprehensive Peace Agreement and subsequent agreements to withdraw cases of a "political" nature. No clear definition of a "political case" was provided, and many cases recommended for withdrawal involved murder, abduction and other serious crimes.

Migrant workers' rights

Recruitment agencies continued to traffic migrant workers for exploitation and forced labour and to charge fees above government-imposed limits, compelling workers to take large loans at high interest rates. Recruiters deceived many migrants on terms and conditions of work. Recruitment agencies that violated Nepalese law were rarely punished. Redress and compensation mechanisms were poorly promoted, centralized and difficult to access.

■ In August, the government banned women under the age of 30 from migrating for domestic work to Kuwait, Qatar, Saudi Arabia and the United Arab Emirates due to complaints of sexual and other physical abuse in those countries. The bans potentially increased risks to women now forced to seek work through informal routes. Two successive Labour Ministers were forced out of office by the Prime Minister

for alleged corruption. Despite this, recruitment agencies remained above the law with few losing their licences for illegal practices.

Torture and other ill-treatment

Despite acceding to the UN Convention against Torture in 1991, Nepal had not defined torture as a crime under national law. In April, the Council of Ministers announced plans for a bill to criminalize torture, but this had not been completed by the time the Constituent Assembly was dissolved. In July, the UN Human Rights Committee reminded Nepal of its obligation to enact a law defining and criminalizing torture, and to repeal all laws granting impunity to alleged perpetrators of torture and enforced disappearance. Torture and other ill-treatment of men, women and children in police custody remained widespread. The UN Committee against Torture concluded in its annual report that torture in Nepal was habitual, widespread and deliberate, and was ultimately practised systematically.

Abuses in the Terai region

Lack of accountability for past violations and a long-standing culture of impunity meant that, although the activities of armed groups operating in the Terai region were reportedly on the decline, violations and abuses by the Nepal Armed Police Force, Nepal Police and armed groups continued to be reported. Abuses included arbitrary detention, torture and extrajudicial executions. High levels of insecurity and fear of reprisals represented a significant obstacle to access to justice for victims and human rights defenders in the region.

Discrimination

Discrimination on the basis of caste, ethnicity, religion, gender, economic situation and disability persisted. In October, Bhim Bahadur, a Dalit from Dailekh district, was reportedly hospitalized with serious injuries after he was attacked with a sickle for touching the main door of a house belonging to a member of a dominant caste. Dalit and poor women and girls from rural areas faced discrimination in accessing justice, education and health care.

Maternal health

Poverty, gender discrimination, malnutrition, lack of skilled birth attendants and emergency obstetric care, and workload during pregnancy and the postnatal period all contributed to Nepal's high incidence of uterine prolapse. An estimated 600,000 women in Nepal were suffering from the condition, of which 200,000 needed immediate surgery. The government organized surgical camps to treat uterine prolapse, but many women remained unaware of them. Nepal had not invested sufficiently in preventive interventions, alternatives to surgery or-follow-up care. According to reports, 24,498 women underwent surgery for prolapse between 2008 and 2011; however, the health condition of these women was largely unknown.

NETHERLANDS

KINGDOM OF THE NETHERLANDS
Head of state: **Queen Beatrix**
Head of government: **Mark Rutte**

The newly elected coalition government proposed criminalizing unlawful residency and instituting a partial ban on the wearing of full face veils. Immigration detention continued to be used excessively.

Legal, constitutional or institutional developments

In September, the government confirmed its intention to develop a national human rights action plan in response to a recommendation during the Universal Periodic Review in May.

In October, the newly established national human rights institution began its work.

Refugees, asylum-seekers and migrants

Immigration detention continued to be used excessively, despite the introduction of pilot alternative schemes for particular categories of migrants and asylum-seekers. Conditions in immigration detention centres largely mirrored those in criminal detention facilities.

The transparency of the Commission for Comprehensive Supervision of Return (Commissie Integraal Toezicht Terugkeer, CITT), the body overseeing forced removals and one of the national preventative mechanisms under the Optional Protocol to the UN Convention against Torture, remained limited. Annual reports published by the CITT do not include specific data on the use of force in individual removal proceedings.

In October, the new coalition government proposed criminalizing unlawful residency, leading to concerns over further marginalization and increased vulnerability of undocumented migrants.

Discrimination

In October, the coalition government proposed adopting measures to combat discrimination on the basis of sexual orientation and ratifying the Convention on the Rights of Persons with Disabilities.

However, it also proposed a partial ban on the wearing of full face veils by women on public transport and in health centres, schools and government buildings. This raised concerns that the prohibition would violate the freedoms of expression and religion of women who choose to wear the burqa or niqab as an expression of their identity or beliefs.

Ongoing concerns of discriminatory practices by law enforcement officials, including ethnic profiling, remained.

International justice

In April, the Dutch Supreme Court delivered a judgement on whether the UN Protection Force (UNPROFOR) could be held responsible for deaths of Bosnian Muslims during the 1995 Srebrenica genocide. The Court ruled that the UN held immunity from prosecution before national courts. The families of the victims appealed the decision to the European Court of Human Rights.

N

Amnesty International visits/reports

Europe: Choice and prejudice – discrimination against Muslims in Europe (EUR 01/001/2012)

Netherlands: Amnesty International urges implementation of recommendations on immigration detention, discrimination and developing a national human rights action plan (EUR 35/001/2012

NEW ZEALAND

NEW ZEALAND
Head of state: Queen Elizabeth II, represented by
Jerry Mateparae
Head of government: John Key

The rights of asylum-seekers were at risk of being undermined by a new bill. Levels of child poverty continued to be high, disproportionately affecting Māori (Indigenous People) and Pacific Island peoples. Violence against women remained widespread, but the authorities failed to collect sufficient data on how such violence affected women, especially those from minority groups.

Legal, constitutional or institutional developments

A government-sponsored review of the country's constitutional arrangements continued. The review was mandated to consider a range of constitutional issues, including whether there should be a written Constitution. By October 2012, the Constitutional Review Panel had met with 56 organizations; however, open public consultations had yet to occur by the end of the year.

In May, the UN Committee on Economic, Social and Cultural Rights expressed concern that such rights had yet to be incorporated into the Bill of Rights Act 1990. It also highlighted New Zealand's failure to sufficiently protect Indigenous Peoples' rights to their lands, territories, waters, maritime areas and other resources.

Children's rights

Child poverty remained high. An August study by the Ministry of Social Development identified up to 270,000 children as living in poverty, about 47% of whom were from Māori or Pacific Island peoples.

Women's rights

In July, the CEDAW Committee considered New Zealand's periodic report and expressed concern at persistently high and increasing levels of violence against women. The Committee criticized New Zealand's failure to collect sufficient statistical data on violence against women, especially against Māori women, migrant women and women with disabilities.

Rights of lesbian, gay, bisexual, transgender and intersex people

In August, the Marriage (Equality) Amendment Bill passed the first of three readings, with 80 votes for and 40 against. The bill sought to clarify the definition of marriage as contained in the 1955 Marriage Act. The new bill would allow marriage between two people regardless of their sex, sexual orientation or gender identity. The bill remained pending.

Refugees and asylum-seekers

In April, the Immigration Amendment (Mass Arrivals) Bill was introduced to Parliament. The new bill allowed for indefinite detention of asylum-seekers arriving by boat in groups of more than 10 people, as well as limitations on family reunification and access to judicial review. The bill gave the authorities new powers to suspend the processing of asylum claims. The bill had not been passed by the end of the year.

NICARAGUA

REPUBLIC OF NICARAGUA
Head of state and government: Daniel Ortega Saavedra

All forms of abortion remained criminalized. A new law on violence against women came into effect; most victims of rape and sexual violence were girls aged 17 and under.

Background

Three people died and dozens were wounded in the wake of municipal elections in November. Tensions had been heightened in the run-up to the elections by allegations of fraud and irregularities against the ruling Sandinista National Liberation Front (Frente Sandinista de Liberación Nacional, FSLN) and smaller parties allegedly allied to the FSLN, which continued to be reported on election day itself.

Arbitrary detention, torture and other ill-treatment

A fortnight after the municipal elections, continuing fraud allegations prompted clashes between supporters of the opposition Constitutional Liberal Party (Partido Liberal Constitucionalista, PLC) and supporters of the governing FSLN in Nueva Guinea, in the South Atlantic Autonomous Region.

Human rights organizations reported that PLC supporters were arrested by the police and ill-treated in custody. Detainees reported being beaten, and women and girl detainees said that they were forced to remove their clothes in front of male officers, who humiliated them and threatened them with sexual violence.

Violence against women and girls

During the first six months of 2012, the Police Unit for Women and Children received 1,862 reports of sexual violence. Children aged 14 or under accounted for 1,048 of the victims and 80% of all victims were aged 17 or younger. Although the statistics did not reveal the gender of victims, previous government statistics have shown that women and girls make up the majority of victims of sexual violence.

■ In October, the police in Matagalpa, in the north of Nicaragua, were instructed to execute an arrest warrant against a teacher accused of sexually abusing a 14-year-old pupil. However, the arrest warrant was not executed, allegedly due to a lack of space in the prison system and lack of police capacity; the teacher reportedly fled the city. At the end of the year, the accused remained at large.

The Integral Law Against Violence Against Women (Law 779) came into effect in June. While the law represented a positive step, lack of resources assigned to ensure its implementation remained a concern.

Sexual and reproductive rights

All forms of abortion remained illegal.

The Inter-American Commission on Human Rights Rapporteur on the Rights of Women visited Nicaragua in May and urged the government to repeal the total abortion ban and to examine the link between gender-based violence and sexual and reproductive rights.

In July, the Ministry of Health announced that over the decade 2000-2009, the number of births to girls aged between 10 and 14 had increased by 47.9%. Sexual intercourse with a child under the age of 14 is classed as statutory rape under Nicaraguan law.

On 28 September, human rights groups and women's organizations protested against the government's refusal to repeal the total abortion ban, and at the Supreme Court of Justice's continuing failure to rule on a 2007 petition challenging the constitutionality of the total ban.

NIGER

REPUBLIC OF NIGER
Head of state: Mahamadou Issoufou
Head of government: Brigi Rafini

People accused of belonging to terrorist groups were ill-treated in detention. Several aid workers and their driver were abducted and held for three weeks by an armed group.

Background

There were clashes between government forces and armed groups based in Mali and Nigeria. In the north, the army strengthened the security system to oppose elements of armed groups involved in hostage-taking, drug trafficking and armed banditry.

As a result of the crisis following the March 2012 military coup in Mali, at least 50,000 people sought refuge in camps in Niger. They had very limited access to basic necessities and health care.

Torture and other ill-treatment

Several people, including nationals of Nigeria, accused of being members of al-Qa'ida in the Islamic Maghreb (AQIM) or of Boko Haram, a Nigerian Islamist armed group, and suspected of terrorist activities, were ill-treated during arrest or shortly afterwards in an attempt to extract confessions.

■ In April, Moustapha Madou Abba Kiari was arrested in Difa, near the border with Nigeria, and punched and kicked. He was accused of being a member of Boko Haram and charged with terrorism offences.

Abuses by armed groups

Several people, including foreign nationals, were abducted by armed groups.

■ In October, five aid workers – four Niger nationals and a Chad national – and their driver, a Niger citizen, were kidnapped in Dakoro by armed men and held for three weeks. The Chadian hostage was shot and wounded during his capture and died shortly afterwards.

International justice

In May, the authorities expressed their readiness to examine the Libyan authorities' request to hand over several high-ranking Libyan officials from the government of former President Mu'ammar al-Gaddafi, who had sought refuge in Niger.

■ In February, under an Interpol operation, Saadi al-Gaddafi, son of the Libyan former leader, was put under house arrest in Niamey, the capital, after he appeared on Arab television and threatened Libya with an imminent uprising. He was still subject to restrictions to his movements and communications at the end of the year.

Amnesty International visits/reports

🚌 Amnesty International delegates visited Malian refugee sites in Niger in April.

NIGERIA

FEDERAL REPUBLIC OF NIGERIA
Head of state and government: **Goodluck Jonathan**

The situation of violence and insecurity for Nigerians intensified, with at least 1,000 people killed in attacks by Islamist armed group Boko Haram in central and northern Nigeria. Police and other soldiers carried out unlawful and summary killings with impunity. Thousands of people were forcibly evicted from their homes in different parts of the country. Unlawful detention and arbitrary arrests were commonplace.

Background

In January, the Nigeria Labour Congress, other trade unions and civil rights organizations declared a nationwide strike action in protest against proposals to remove fuel subsidies. The mostly peaceful protests began on 2 January and involved tens of thousands of people across many states. In several cases, police fired at protesters, and at least three people were killed and 25 injured across Kaduna, Kano and Lagos states. In January, one police officer was reportedly arrested and detained in relation to the use of force but no further action was known to have been taken against the officer by the end of the year.

On 20 January, at least 186 people were killed in Kano City when members of Boko Haram attacked security forces at eight different locations. The bombings were followed by an exchange of gunfire between Boko Haram and security forces lasting several hours. Among those killed were police officers, their relatives and residents living nearby. A journalist with the news station Channels, Enenche Akogwu, was also shot dead.

In the same month, President Jonathan declared a state of emergency in 15 Local Government Areas across four states, which elapsed after six months.

Renewed tensions emerged in the Niger Delta when some former members of the armed group MEND (Movement for the Emancipation of the Niger Delta) claimed they were not receiving their monthly "amnesty" stipends – part of an agreement with the government. The group also said it was dissatisfied with the operation of programmes set up to reintegrate militants into society.

Between August and October, the country's worst flooding in decades killed more than 300 people and displaced a million more, across 15 states.

Boko Haram
Boko Haram attacks

More than 1,000 people were killed in attacks by Islamist armed group Boko Haram, which claimed responsibility for bombings and gun attacks across northern and central Nigeria. The group attacked police stations, military barracks, churches, school buildings and newspaper offices and killed Muslim and Christian clerics and worshippers, politicians and journalists, as well as police and soldiers. In November, the Office of the Prosecutor of the International Criminal Court announced there was a reasonable basis to believe Boko Haram had been committing crimes against humanity since July 2009.

■ In April, at least 20 people were killed in Kaduna city on Easter Sunday as a suicide car bomb exploded near two churches.

■ On 26 April, Boko Haram bombed the offices of the Nigerian newspaper *Thisday* in Abuja and a building housing three newspapers in Kaduna. At least seven people died. On 1 May, Boko Haram issued a warning to 11 national and international media houses.

■ On 17 June, Boko Haram bombed three church services in Kaduna, killing at least 21 people. Revenge attacks between Christians and Muslims resulted in the death of at least 70 more people.

Responses by the police and security forces

Nigeria's security forces perpetrated serious human rights violations in their response to Boko Haram – including enforced disappearance, extrajudicial executions, house burning and unlawful detention.

Scores of people were unlawfully killed by the Joint Task Force (JTF) – army, police and other security forces – set up to deal with the violence, or police; others were subjected to enforced disappearance from police or JTF custody.

People in at least five communities in Maiduguri had their houses burned down by the JTF, often following raids and arrests in the areas and in some cases seemingly as a punitive measure.

Hundreds of people accused of having links to Boko Haram were arbitrarily detained by the JTF. Many were detained incommunicado for lengthy periods without charge or trial, without being brought before any judicial authority, and without access to lawyers. Hundreds of people were detained without charge or trial at Giwa Barracks, 21 Armoured Brigade, Maiduguri, in harsh conditions that may amount to inhuman and degrading treatment.

Independent and impartial investigations were rarely carried out into allegations of human rights violations by the security forces and, when they were, the findings were not made public.

■ On 9 March, Ali Mohammed Sadiq, Ahmed Yunusa, Auwalu Mohammed and two others – all staff or customers at a petrol station at Rijiyar Zaki, Kano State – were shot and killed when the JTF opened fire following an attack on a nearby police station. Ali Mohammed Sadiq was shot five times, including once in the head. No investigation was conducted and no officer was known to have been held responsible for the killings. The JTF Commander in Borno made a public apology on radio to the families of the victims.

■ A court order issued on 4 January for the production of Goni Ali, who was arrested by members of the JTF at his home in Maiduguri on 16 October 2011 and taken to Giwa Barracks and who had not been seen since, was ignored by the JTF. By the end of the year his family still had no information about his whereabouts.

■ On 1 May, following a killing by a suspected member of Boko Haram in Kawar Maila, JTF soldiers made women and children living nearby leave their homes before setting approximately 33 houses on fire. An Islamiyya school attended by local children was also burned down by the JTF. The building was unoccupied at the time.

Unlawful killings

Unlawful killings were carried out by the police across Nigeria. In March 2012, the Chairman of the National Human Rights Commission (NHRC) Governing Council said an estimated 2,500 detainees were summarily killed by the police every year.

■ On 8 April, Blessing Monday, a 16-year-old boy living on the streets around the Abali Park Flyover in Port Harcourt, was shot and killed by police officers from Mile 1 Police Station who suspected he had stolen a bag. The police later discovered that Blessing Monday had not stolen the bag.

■ On 24 May, Goodluck Agbaribote, a former resident of the demolished Abonnema Wharf in Port Harcourt, was killed by officers from the Special Anti-Robbery Squad (SARS) while he was bathing in a communal well. The police claimed he was an armed robber.

■ In November, the Nigerian Police Force eventually told a High Court in Port Harcourt that Chika Ibeku, who had "disappeared" in 2009 following his arrest and detention by the police, was in fact killed by the police in a "shootout". The family, through a local NGO, filed a lawsuit requesting the autopsy report.

Torture and other ill-treatment

Torture and other cruel, inhuman and degrading treatment of criminal suspects and detainees, perpetrated by the security forces, remained widespread.

■ On 9 January, Alexander Nworgu was arrested in Owerri, Imo State, and taken to the police anti-kidnapping unit in Rivers State. He claims that, while in custody, he was regularly beaten with a machete and suspended from the ceiling by his feet every other day. After spending more than a month in police detention he was remanded in prison on 15 February before eventually being released on bail on 6 July. The charges against him were changed to theft while he was in police detention.

Justice system

Widespread corruption and disregard for due process and the rule of law continued to blight Nigeria's criminal justice system. Many people were arbitrarily arrested and detained for months without charge. Police continued to ask people to pay money for their release from detention. Many detainees were kept on remand in prison for lengthy periods and in harsh conditions. Court processes remained slow and largely distrusted. According to the Executive Secretary of the NHRC, over 70% of people in detention were awaiting either trial or sentencing. Court orders were often ignored by police and security forces.

■ On 30 April, Patrick Okoroafor was released from prison after 17 years. He had been unfairly sentenced to death for robbery, at the age of 14, after an unfair trial.

Children's rights

Twelve states failed to enact the federal Child Rights Act into law. The country's remand homes remained overcrowded and under-resourced. Police continued to detain children in police cells with adults.

Communal violence

Inter-communal violence continued in the Middle Belt region of Nigeria and claimed the lives of more than 100 people.

■ In March, renewed clashes over land between ethnic groups in Benue State displaced up to 15,000 people.

■ More than 60 people were reportedly killed between 6 and 7 July in clashes between Fulani herdsmen and villagers in Riyom, Barkin Ladi and other Local Government Areas in Plateau State. On 8 July, mourners, including Senator Gyang Dantong and Majority Leader of the Plateau House of Assembly, Gyang Fulani, who were attending the funeral of some of those killed, were attacked by unidentified gunmen. On 10 July, clashes continued between Christians and Muslims in nine different communities in Plateau State, leaving about 50 people dead.

Death penalty

In September, the High Court of Lagos State declared the mandatory imposition of the death penalty to be unconstitutional, in a case brought in 2008 by the Legal Resources Consortium (LRC), assisted by Nigerian NGO LEDAP (The Legal Defence and Assistance Project).

But the death penalty remained mandatory in Nigeria's penal laws for a wide range of crimes. There were approximately 1,002 inmates on death row by the end of 2012 including people who were juveniles at the time of the crime. Many were sentenced after blatantly unfair trials or after spending more than a decade in prison. The Federal Government said in 2012 that the moratorium on the death penalty in place the previous year was "voluntary". Courts continued to pass death sentences.

■ In October, the Governor of Edo State signed the death warrants of two death-row inmates in Benin Central Prison in Benin City, Edo State, despite an ongoing appeal. The executions were still pending at the end of the year.

■ On 13 July, Olatunji Olaide was released from the Kirikiri Prison in Lagos after spending 23 years on death row for car robbery. The Court of Appeal declared him innocent on 5 June, and acquitted him.

Forced evictions

Forced evictions and illegal demolitions continued across Nigeria. The homes of tens of thousands of people in four different communities in Port Harcourt, Lagos and Abuja were demolished in 2012. Hundreds of thousands remained at risk as state governments continued to issue threats of mass demolitions.

■ In July, between 10,000 and 20,000 people were forcibly evicted from their homes in Abonnema Wharf in Port Harcourt, when the settlement was demolished without adequate notice or consultation, or compensation or provision of alternative housing. Residents had to sleep in cars, with friends or by the side of the road. Hundreds remained homeless.

■ On 16 July, dozens of houses and structures were demolished in Makoko settlement in Lagos, with more than 2,000 people displaced with no alternative accommodation or adequate compensation, according to Nigerian NGO SERAC (Social and Economic Rights Action Centre). One person was killed when police opened fire at a peaceful protest against the demolitions. The officer was reportedly arrested.

■ On 16 August, Mpape settlement in Abuja was partly demolished without adequate notice or consultation, despite an ongoing High Court case to prevent the demolitions. Mpape is one of 19 communities to be demolished as part of the "Abuja Master Plan". NGOs estimated that one million people could be made homeless if the plan goes ahead.

Freedom of expression

Intimidation of and attacks against human rights defenders continued.

■ On 26 January, human rights defender and labour leader Osmond Ugwu was granted bail by the Enugu State High Court. Osmond Ugwu had been arrested on 24 October 2011 by a heavily armed group of soldiers, police officers, and members of the State Security Service (SSS) at a peaceful trade union prayer session in Enugu after campaigning for the implementation of the Minimum Wage Act. He was subsequently charged with conspiracy to murder.

■ On 6 September, a journalist for the *Leadership* newspaper was beaten by soldiers and his equipment confiscated for covering a demolition exercise in Anambra State.

■ On 24 December, Musa Mohamed Awwal and Aliyu Saleh, two journalists working for the Hausa language newspaper, *Al-Mizan*, were arrested in Kaduna State and detained for one week by officers from the SSS.

Women's rights

Nigeria continued to have one of the highest maternal mortality ratios in the world. According to the World Health Organization, 14% of all maternal deaths worldwide happen in Nigeria.

Violence against women and girls, including rape, sexual assault and domestic abuse, remained serious problems.

Rights of lesbian, gay, bisexual, transgender and intersex people

Human rights abuses continued against people suspected of having same-sex relationships or non-conventional gender identity. The Same Sex Marriage (Prohibition) Bill, approved by the Senate in December 2011, passed its second reading in the House of Representatives on 13 November. The Bill imposes a 14-year prison sentence on anyone who "[enters] into a same sex marriage contract or civil union". The Bill, if passed into law, would criminalize freedom of speech, association, and assembly.

Oil pollution in the Niger Delta

Oil pollution and environmental damage continued to wreak havoc on people's lives and livelihoods in the Niger Delta. Environmental laws and regulations were poorly enforced. Recommendations on the clean-up of the Ogoniland region of the Niger Delta, made by the UN

Environment Programme in a major study published in 2011, were not implemented by the end of 2012.

■ On and around 21 June, an oil spill was discovered in the Bodo community in the Niger Delta. The leak was only stopped on 30 June. The pipeline was the responsibility of Shell. An investigation into the cause of the spill was delayed and had not completed by the end of the year, nor had the spill been cleaned.

On 11 October, a court case instituted against the oil company Shell by a group of farmers from the Niger Delta began at The Hague in the Netherlands.

On 14 December, a landmark judgement by ECOWAS found the Nigerian government had failed to prevent oil company operations from damaging human rights, and required the government to enforce adequate regulation of oil operations.

Amnesty International visits/reports

🚗 Amnesty International delegates visited Nigeria seven times between February and November.

📄 Nigeria: Forced eviction of Abonnema Wharf waterfront – "Pack and go!" (AFR 44/034/2012)

📄 Nigeria: Another Bodo oil spill – another flawed oil spill investigation in the Niger Delta (AFR 44/037/2012)

📄 Nigeria: Oil spill investigations in the Niger Delta – Amnesty International memorandum (AFR 44/042/2012)

📄 Nigeria: Trapped in the cycle of violence (AFR 44/043/2012)

NORWAY

KINGDOM OF NORWAY
Head of state: **King Harald V**
Head of government: **Jens Stoltenberg**

Concerns about reception conditions for children seeking asylum continued. Protection and access to justice for survivors of rape and sexual violence remained inadequate.

Refugees, asylum-seekers and migrants

On 8 June, the government published proposals to address the needs of unaccompanied asylum-seeking children and children of asylum-seekers. NGOs criticized the proposals for over-emphasizing returns and for not focusing sufficiently on the rights of the child.

By December, 85 unaccompanied asylum-seeking children reportedly disappeared from asylum reception centres. NGOs expressed fears that some of the children were victims of trafficking and called for responsibility for unaccompanied children to be transferred from the immigration authorities to Child Welfare.

International justice

On 25 September, the prosecution of a 47-year-old Rwandan national for participation in the 1994 genocide in Rwanda began before the Oslo District Court.

On 10 October, the Ministry of Justice and Public Security decided that a Rwandan national could be extradited from Norway to Rwanda to face charges of participation in the 1994 genocide in Rwanda.

Violence against women and girls

Women remained inadequately protected against violence in law and practice. Statistics on reported rape and sexual assault were not regularly updated.

In March, the CEDAW Committee expressed concern at the prevalence of violence against women in Norway, the high level of acquittals and lenient sentences imposed on perpetrators. The Committee also expressed concern about the definition of rape contained in the General Penal Code which maintains the requirement of the use of threat or force. In November, the Committee against Torture reiterated many of the same concerns.

Discrimination

In February, the European Commission against Racism and Intolerance stated that Norwegian authorities had failed to implement its 2009 recommendations to address racial profiling in stop and search operations carried out by police, customs and immigration officials.

Legal, constitutional or institutional developments

In October, the Norwegian Centre for Human Rights was downgraded from its status as a national human rights institution for failing to comply fully with the UN Paris Principles. Parliament considered proposals for a stronger Human Rights Commission in November.

OMAN

SULTANATE OF OMAN
Head of state and government: **Sultan Qaboos bin Said Al Said**

Over 30 human rights activists and government critics became prisoners of conscience after they were arrested, charged with using social media to insult the Sultan or committing other security-related offences, and sentenced to up to 18 months in prison.

Background

There was sporadic labour unrest. Brief strikes were held by oil industry employees and workers building Muscat's new international airport. Those on strike included both Omani and expatriate workers.

The authorities proposed to enhance judicial independence by removing the Minister of Justice from the Supreme Judicial Council. However, the Council continued to be chaired by the Sultan.

Freedoms of expression and assembly

The authorities restricted freedom of expression and took action against more than 35 government critics, including human rights activists and bloggers, who they accused of offences including insulting the Sultan on social media networks.

■ On 31 May, police detained lawyer Yaqoub al-Kharousi along with two members of the newly formed Omani Group for Human Rights – Habeeba al-Hina'i and Ismail al-Muqbali – at the Fohoud oil field where workers had gone on strike several days earlier. Their mobile phones were seized and they were held incommunicado for five days. Yaqoub al-Kharousi and Habeeba al-Hina'i were released on bail but Ismail al-Muqbali remained in detention. On 9 September, he was sentenced to 18 months' imprisonment and fined.

■ Between 2 and 8 June, four people were arrested, including writer Hamoud al-Rashidi and poet Hamad al-Kharous. On 11 June, a further 22 people were detained while holding a peaceful protest calling for the release of the four detainees. One of those detained on 11 June was Basma al-Kiyumi, a leading lawyer, who had previously been detained during protests in May 2011. Following the arrests, the Public Prosecution declared its intention to clamp down on those who, it said, "prejudice national security and public interests" by engaging in "libel, spreading rumours [and] provoking sit-ins and strikes" using online media.

One detainee, Saeed al-Hashimi, was reported to have needed hospital treatment after going on hunger strike to protest against his imprisonment.

At least 32 of those detained were prosecuted and, between 9 July and 9 September, fined and sentenced to prison terms of up to 18 months. They were convicted on charges such as insulting the Sultan, publishing defamatory information on the internet, undermining the state, inciting or engaging in protests and obstructing traffic. A number were released on bail pending appeals.

■ On 5 and 12 December, the appeal court in Muscat upheld sentences of between six months and one year against 28 activists, including Nabhan al-Hanashi, for insulting the Sultan, publishing defamatory information on the internet and inciting or engaging in protests.

Women's rights
Women and girls continued to face severe discrimination in law and practice, particularly in relation to personal status, employment and their subordination to male guardians.

Death penalty
No information was released about the imposition of the death penalty. No executions were reported. In December, Oman rejected a UN General Assembly resolution calling for a moratorium on the death penalty. In previous years it had abstained on this vote.

Amnesty International visits/reports
- Protesters and writers detained in Oman (MDE 20/001/2012)
- Peaceful activists face prison in Oman (MDE 20/002/2012)
- Oman: Further information – another 20 activists sentenced to prison (MDE 20/003/2012)
- Oman: Further information – more activists face prison in Oman (MDE 20/004/2012)
- Oman: Further information – six activists' appeals rejected (MDE 20/005/2012)
- Oman must end assault on freedoms of expression and assembly (MDE 20/006/2012)

PAKISTAN

ISLAMIC REPUBLIC OF PAKISTAN
Head of state: Asif Ali Zardari
Head of government: Raja Pervaiz Ashraf (replaced Yousuf Raza Gilani in June)

The Pakistani Taliban's assassination attempt on a teenage human rights activist in October underscored the serious risks faced by human rights defenders and journalists in the country. Religious minorities suffered persecution and attacks, with targeted killings by armed groups and religious leaders inciting violence against them. The Armed Forces and armed groups continued to perpetrate abuses in the tribal areas and Balochistan province, including enforced disappearances, abductions, torture and unlawful killings. The courts successfully compelled the authorities to bring a handful of victims of enforced disappearance before them, but failed to bring perpetrators to justice in fair trials. In November, the military authorities carried out Pakistan's first execution since 2008. Attacks on health workers had a significant impact on access to medical services in remote and strife-torn regions of the country. Parliament passed laws, in February and March respectively, on the establishment of separate national commissions on the status of women and on human rights.

Background
Pakistan faced several political crises as the military, courts and elected government clashed over a range of issues, including corruption investigations. On 19 June, the Supreme Court forced then Prime Minister Gilani to resign after finding him in contempt of court, underlining the increasing power of the judiciary. In a landmark decision on 23 September, the Supreme Court ruled that members of the transgender community are entitled to the same rights under the Pakistan Constitution as other citizens. Hundreds of prisoners were transferred between India and Pakistan as part of a wider agreement on consular relations signed in May, signalling improved relations between the two countries. An undisclosed number of civilians, including children, were killed or injured as a result of

P

"targeted killings" carried out by unmanned US drones in the tribal areas (see USA entry). By the end of the year, relations had improved between Pakistan and the USA, its chief foreign ally.

Pakistan began its two-year membership of the UN Security Council in January. A number of UN human rights experts visited the country for the first time in 13 years: the Special Rapporteur on the independence of judges and lawyers in May, the High Commissioner for Human Rights in June, and the Working Group on Enforced or Involuntary Disappearances in September. Pakistan's human rights record was assessed under the UN Universal Periodic Review in October; states raised a range of human rights issues including reform of the blasphemy laws, progress towards abolishing the death penalty, and ending enforced disappearances. Pakistan was elected to the UN Human Rights Council for the third time on 12 November.

Violations by security forces

Security forces continued to act with impunity and were accused of widespread human rights violations, including arbitrary arrests, enforced disappearances, torture, deaths in custody and extrajudicial executions targeting political activists, journalists, and suspected members of armed groups. In the northwest tribal areas, the armed forces exploited new and old security laws to provide cover for these violations beyond the reach of the courts.

■ After an alleged plot to murder human rights lawyer Asma Jahangir was exposed in June, the authorities provided extra security but appeared unable or unwilling to investigate claims that military authorities "at the highest levels" had authorized the plot.

Unlawful killings

Hundreds of unlawful killings, including extrajudicial executions and deaths in custody, were widely reported. They were most common in the northwest tribal areas, and Balochistan and Sindh provinces.

■ On several occasions during the year, the Peshawar High Court ordered investigations into the more than 100 bodies found dumped across Peshawar, capital of Khyber Pakhtunkhwa province.

■ Muzaffar Bhutto, leader of an ethnic Sindhi political party, was found dead on 22 May in Bukhari village near Hyderabad, Sindh, after he was abducted by men in plain clothes accompanied by police 15 months earlier. His body reportedly bore torture marks and

bullet wounds but no one was brought to justice for his abduction or killing.

Enforced disappearances

The Supreme Court was granted unprecedented access to some victims of enforced disappearances, including seven surviving members of the "Adiala 11" in February, and several others from Balochistan throughout the year. The Chief Justice threatened to order the arrest of law enforcement personnel for failing to provide a legal basis for arrests and detentions in Balochistan, and the Peshawar High Court continued to pressure the authorities to provide details of all individuals held in security detention in the northwest tribal areas. However, reports of enforced disappearances continued across the country, especially in Balochistan province and the north-west tribal areas; no serving or retired security personnel were brought to justice for their alleged involvement in these or other violations.

The UN Working Group on Enforced or Involuntary Disappearances made its first ever visit to the country in September, but key officials refused to meet them, including the head of the Commission of Inquiry on Enforced Disappearances, Chief Justices of the Supreme Court and most High Courts, and senior security and military representatives.

■ The body of Baloch Republican Party leader Sangat Sana was found dumped on the outskirts of Turbat, Balochistan, on 13 February. More than two years earlier, he was seen being taken by several men in plain clothes at a police roadblock at the Bolan Pass on the Quetta-Sindh highway.

Abuses by armed groups

The Pakistani Taliban, Lashkar-e-Jhangvi, the Balochistan Liberation Army and other armed groups targeted security forces and civilians, including members of religious minorities, aid workers, activists and journalists. They carried out indiscriminate attacks using improvised explosive devices and suicide bombs.

■ The Pakistani Taliban announced a ban on health workers in the tribal areas until the USA ceased its programme of "targeted killing" there. An ICRC nurse was killed in April. Nine mostly women health workers administering polio vaccinations were killed in co-ordinated attacks in Peshawar, Nowshera and Charsadda in the north-west, and the southern city of Karachi over three days in December.

- Lashkar-e-Jhangvi claimed responsibility for the execution-style killing of at least 14 people during an attack on a bus carrying Shi'a Muslim pilgrims from Quetta to Iran on 28 June. The group was responsible for at least eight attacks across Pakistan, which claimed 49 lives.
- Senior Awami National Party politician Bashir Ahmed Bilour and eight others were killed in a Pakistani Taliban suicide bombing in Peshawar on 22 December as they left a political rally.

Freedom of expression

Journalists remained under serious threat from state security forces, armed opposition and other groups, particularly in Balochistan and Sindh provinces, and the north-west tribal areas. At least eight journalists were killed during the year. Several journalists claimed to have been threatened for reporting on the military, political parties or armed groups.

- Journalist Mukarram Aatif was shot dead during evening prayers in a mosque in Charsadda city on 17 January. He had earlier resettled there from his native Mohmand Tribal Agency following death threats over his reporting from the Pakistani Taliban, which claimed responsibility for the killing.
- On 19 May, the bullet-riddled body of Express News television correspondent Razzaq Gul was found dumped on the outskirts of Turbat, Balochistan. He had been kidnapped the previous day. The authorities failed to bring the perpetrators to justice.
- Senior broadcaster Hamid Mir escaped an assassination attempt in November when a bomb under his car failed to detonate. The Pakistani Taliban claimed responsibility for the attempt.

The government occasionally blocked websites, including YouTube and Facebook, without explanation or for content deemed offensive to religious sentiments. The courts threatened to bring criminal proceedings against journalists under contempt of court laws for reports criticizing the judiciary.

Discrimination – religious minorities

Ahmadis, Hindus and Christians remained at serious risk of violence and intimidation on the basis of their religious beliefs. There were at least 79 attacks on Shi'a Muslims – the most for any religious group in the country. Religious minorities were disproportionately represented in incidents where private individuals sought to invoke Pakistan's vaguely formulated blasphemy laws.

- The northern region of Gilgit-Baltistan experienced unprecedented sectarian violence, with the authorities largely failing to bring the perpetrators of over 70 killings to justice following clashes between Sunni and Shi'a Muslims in April.
- On 4 July, a mob lynched a homeless man held at a police station, then burned his body for allegedly burning a Qur'an in Channigoth town, Punjab province.
- On 20 November, the Islamabad High Court acquitted Rimsha Masih, a Christian girl charged with blasphemy by police in August under public pressure for allegedly burning pages of the Qur'an. In September, the cleric who had accused her was in turn charged under the same laws for allegedly fabricating evidence against her. Her release was a rare instance of a speedy court acquittal in which the blasphemy charge against her was publicly criticized by the court.
- The authorities allowed religious groups to prevent Ahmadis from entering places of worship. The graves of over 100 Ahmadis were vandalized in a Lahore cemetery on 3 December.
- The state failed to protect the Shi'a Hazara community in Balochistan from armed group attacks despite a heavy military presence in the province, resulting in at least 84 deaths in the year.

Violence against women and girls

Women and girls and those campaigning for their rights continued to face discrimination and violence in the home and in public. Human rights groups documented thousands of cases of violence against women and girls across the country with a majority from the most populous province of Punjab. Cases included murders, rapes and incidents of domestic violence. This was likely only a fraction of all incidents given limited reporting of these abuses.

- In May, local tribal elders reportedly ordered the killing of four women for singing and clapping, allegedly in the company of two men, at a wedding in Kohistan district, Khyber Pakhtunkhwa province. The Supreme Court ordered an investigation into the incident in June and concluded that the women were probably alive. However, the Supreme Court's investigation appeared to be significantly flawed.
- On 4 July, women's human rights activist Fareeda Afridi was killed in a drive-by shooting as she left her home in Peshawar for work in the Khyber Tribal Agency. Local civil society groups said she had been

P

targeted for promoting the human rights of women. The authorities failed to bring the perpetrators to justice.

■ The Pakistani Taliban claimed responsibility for attempting to assassinate 15-year-old Malala Yousafzai on 9 October. They vowed to continue to target her for promoting education for women and girls. In response, a new law was signed by the President on 20 December, guaranteeing free and compulsory education to boys and girls between the ages of five and 16.

Death penalty

More than 8,300 people remained on death row, some for 20 to 30 years, and 242 were sentenced to death during the year. In November, military authorities executed Muhammad Hussain for killing a superior officer and two others in Okara district, Punjab province, after appeals for clemency from the Army Chief and President were rejected. It was the first death sentence carried out in Pakistan since 2008. The government distanced itself from the decision to proceed with the execution, as it had been carried out by the military authorities, but activists were concerned it risked opening the door to a resumption of executions.

In July, the government began consultations on a draft parliamentary bill to commute all death sentences to life imprisonment.

Amnesty International visits/reports

🚗 Amnesty International delegates visited Pakistan in February/March, July/August and December. Amnesty International consultants maintained a continuous presence in the country.

📖 Pakistan: Human rights and justice – the key to lasting security: Amnesty International submission to the UN Universal Periodic Review (ASA 33/003/2012)

📖 Open Letter: Pakistan must resolve the crisis of enforced disappearances (ASA 33/012/2012)

📖 "The hands of cruelty": Abuses by Armed Forces and Taliban in Pakistan's tribal areas (ASA 33/019/2012)

PALESTINIAN AUTHORITY

PALESTINIAN AUTHORITY
Head of Palestinian Authority: **Mahmoud Abbas**
Head of government: **Salam Fayyad**

Arbitrary arrests and detentions by both the Palestinian Authority (PA) in the West Bank and the Hamas de facto administration in the Gaza Strip continued, particularly of their respective political opponents. In both areas, security forces tortured and otherwise ill-treated detainees with impunity. Four detainees died in custody in suspicious circumstances; two in Gaza and two in the West Bank. Palestinian armed groups in Gaza continued to commit war crimes by firing indiscriminate rockets into Israel, especially during an eight-day armed conflict with Israel during November. During that conflict, Hamas' armed wing summarily killed seven men accused of "collaborating" with Israel. Both the PA and Hamas arbitrarily restricted the rights to freedom of expression, assembly and association, and their security forces used excessive force against demonstrators. Women in both areas continued to face violence and discrimination; at least six women were reportedly killed in "honour" killings. In Gaza, at least five people were sentenced to death and six people were executed. One man was sentenced to death in the West Bank; there were no executions there. The 1.6 million residents of the Gaza Strip continued to suffer severe deprivation due to Israel's ongoing military blockade and the sanctions imposed on Hamas by other states; however, conditions eased in comparison to previous years.

Background

On 29 November, the UN General Assembly granted Palestine non-member observer state status. The West Bank, including East Jerusalem, and the Gaza Strip remained under Israeli occupation, and two separate Palestinian authorities operated with limited powers – the Fatah-led PA government in the West Bank and the Hamas de facto administration in Gaza.

Efforts to reconcile Fatah and Hamas and form a unified Palestinian government continued with Egyptian and Qatari mediation.

The PA held local elections in the West Bank in October but political parties associated with Hamas and Islamic Jihad did not participate; the Hamas authorities in Gaza prevented the registration of voters there. The judiciary in the West Bank briefly suspended work in October in protest against alleged government interference.

Israel maintained its military blockade of Gaza, in force since 2007, controlling its land and sea borders and airspace. The blockade continued to impact severely on Gaza's civilians, including children, the elderly and sick, although more people were able to travel through the Rafah crossing between Gaza and Egypt than during previous years. Around 20 Palestinians were killed in accidents while using tunnels to smuggle goods between Egypt and Gaza.

In the West Bank, Israel maintained extensive restrictions on the movement of Palestinians and continued to develop and extend Israeli settlements built on Palestinian land in breach of international law.

Israeli forces carried out aerial and artillery attacks on the Gaza Strip periodically throughout the year and during an eight-day military campaign in November, killing many civilians and destroying homes and other civilian property. Palestinian armed groups periodically fired indiscriminate rockets into Israel from Gaza, and fired over 1,500 rockets during the November conflict.

Abuses by armed groups

Both before and during the November conflict, Palestinian armed groups associated with Hamas, Fatah, Islamic Jihad, the Popular Front for the Liberation of Palestine and Salafi-affiliated groups committed war crimes by firing indiscriminate rockets and mortars into Israel. Some fell short in Gaza, killing at least two Palestinians. Others struck homes and other buildings in Israel, killing four Israeli civilians during the November conflict, injuring scores and damaging civilian property. Those responsible were not held to account by the Hamas authorities.

■ Two-year-old Hadeel Ahmad Haddad was killed and her eight-year-old cousin was severely injured when a rocket fired by a Palestinian armed group hit their home in al-Zeitoun neighbourhood in Gaza City on 19 June.

■ On 15 November, three Israeli civilians, Mirah Scharf, Itzik Amsalem and Aharon Smadja, were killed and other civilians were injured when an indiscriminate rocket fired by a Palestinian armed group in Gaza hit their house in Kiryat Malachi.

Arbitrary arrests and detentions

In the West Bank, PA security forces arbitrarily arrested and detained hundreds of people, including members of Fatah; most were denied due legal process. Hundreds of Hamas supporters were detained, mostly for up to two days, when President Abbas visited the UN in September. In Gaza, Hamas security forces arbitrarily arrested and detained hundreds of suspected Fatah supporters, usually holding them without access to lawyers. Detainees were frequently beaten and otherwise ill-treated with impunity by both PA and Hamas security forces.

The Independent Commission for Human Rights (ICHR), a PA-established monitoring body, said it received complaints of more than 685 arbitrary arrests in the West Bank and more than 470 in Gaza in 2012.

Prison conditions

In the West Bank, the PA denied the ICHR access to detention centres run by Preventive Security, while inmates went on hunger strikes to protest against harsh conditions and continued detention despite court orders for their release. In Gaza, Hamas allowed the ICHR to resume visiting detention centres run by Internal Security in October for the first time in five years.

Torture and other ill-treatment

Detainees were tortured or otherwise ill-treated with impunity, particularly by the Police Criminal Investigation Department and Preventive Security in the West Bank, and by police and Internal Security in Gaza. The ICHR reported receiving 142 allegations of torture or other ill-treatment in the West Bank and 129 in Gaza. Methods alleged included beatings, suspension by the wrists or ankles, and enforced standing or sitting in painful positions for long periods.

■ Mohammad Said al-Zaqzouq died in suspicious circumstances in Gaza while held at Khan Younis police station in October. An investigation was announced but no results were reported by the end of the year.

■ Tareq Khriesheh said he was made to stand for more than eight hours with one hand tied to a wall and beaten while being interrogated by Criminal Investigations Department officers in Ramallah in January.

P

Justice system

PA security forces continued to detain people without charge or trial for prolonged periods and to delay or fail to implement court orders for release. PA military courts continued to try civilians whose prosecutions began before a January 2011 decision to cease sending civilians to military courts. In Gaza, Hamas held detainees without charge or trial and tried civilians before military courts.

In both the West Bank and Gaza, civilian and military prosecutors failed to act impartially or to prevent the police and security services arresting people without warrants, abusing people and bringing politically motivated charges against them.

■ A court ordered the release of Abd al-Fatah al-Hassan in 2010 but he continued to be held throughout 2012 by Preventive Security in Ramallah. He had been sentenced to 12 years' imprisonment by a military court in September 2009. In October, the Palestinian Constitutional Court refused to rule on an appeal filed by his lawyer for his release.

■ Isma'il Abd al-Rahman was taken from his home in Gaza City by Internal Security officials in September, detained without charge or trial and denied access to a lawyer. He was released in December.

Freedoms of expression, association and assembly

Both the PA and Hamas maintained tight restrictions on freedoms of expression, association and assembly, harassing and prosecuting journalists, bloggers and other critics. In both the West Bank and Gaza, security forces used excessive force against demonstrators, scores of whom were arbitrarily arrested and detained.

■ Journalist Mohammad Qunayta was detained and ill-treated after Internal Security officers arrested him at his house in Gaza in June. He was released on bail in August.

■ PA police in uniform and plain clothes used excessive force against demonstrators and journalists in Ramallah on 30 June and 1 July. Dozens of protesters were injured and others were detained. Journalist Mohammad Jaradat was tortured in police detention; he was held down and beaten all over his body with a baton.

■ Hamas authorities prevented women from demonstrating on 2 October in Gaza to call for Palestinian unity. Police briefly detained five women.

Human rights defenders

Human rights defenders were harassed by the PA and Hamas authorities and their supporters, and in some cases attacked.

■ Mahmoud Abu Rahma, a director at Al Mezan Center for Human Rights, was stabbed and wounded in January by unidentified assailants in Gaza City after he published an article criticizing the Hamas administration.

Violence against women and girls

Women and girls continued to face discrimination in law and practice and to face gender-based violence, including murder, committed by male relatives. The defence of "preserving the family's honour" was suspended by a presidential decree as mitigating evidence in murder cases heard by courts in the West Bank. However, the police failed to protect women who complained of domestic violence and threats to their lives. In Gaza the excuse of "honour" continued to allow for very low sentencing – under 24 months – in rare cases of convictions.

■ Randa al-Mahareq, from Samu in the West Bank, sought the protection of the police and other authorities for months until her father and brother were arrested in July on charges of beating her. They were released four days later and killed her soon afterwards, apparently because they disapproved of her divorce.

■ A 22-year-old woman was shot and killed on 23 March in al-Nasser hospital in Khan Younis. Her uncle and brother were detained. Police said the crime was carried out in the name of "honour".

Summary killings

In November, seven men accused of "collaborating" with Israel who were in Internal Security custody in the Gaza Strip were taken by members of Hamas' military wing and summarily killed. The Hamas authorities pledged to investigate the killings but no action was known to have been taken against those responsible.

Impunity

The Hamas authorities failed to investigate allegations of war crimes and possible crimes against humanity committed by Hamas' forces and other Palestinian armed groups in Gaza during Israel's military Operation "Cast Lead" in 2008–2009 and during the eight-day conflict in November. Neither the PA nor

Hamas credibly investigated allegations of torture and other abuses by their security forces or held perpetrators to account.

Death penalty

In Gaza, military and criminal courts sentenced at least five people to death after convicting them of "collaboration with Israel" or other offences. Six people were executed. One man was sentenced to death in the West Bank; there were no executions there.

Amnesty International visits/reports

🚍 Amnesty International visited the West Bank and Gaza in June/July and Gaza in November/December.

📑 Palestinian Authority: Three men hanged; more facing execution (MDE 21/004/2012)

📑 Palestinian Authority: Deliver justice for victims of Ramallah police violence (4 July 2012)

PANAMA

REPUBLIC OF PANAMA
Head of state and government: Ricardo Martinelli

Several people were killed or injured during the year in the context of protests. The authorities failed to ensure effective investigations and to bring those responsible for deaths of protesters to account. There was some limited progress in setting up mechanisms for locating and identifying victims of past enforced disappearances.

Excessive use of force

Possible excessive use of force by the security forces remained a concern.

■ Two Indigenous people were killed and 40 people, including police officers, were wounded during protests by the Ngöbe-Buglé Indigenous People in January and February. The protests were sparked by proposed laws that would make it easier for companies to build hydroelectric projects on Ngöbe-Buglé land. Reports indicated that the police used tear gas in close proximity to medical centres and that those arrested

were denied access to legal representation. In February, the UN Special Rapporteur on the rights of indigenous peoples urged the government to open a dialogue with the Ngöbe-Buglé affected, to investigate the circumstances of the deaths and to ensure that those responsible were held to account.

■ Three people, including a nine-year-old boy, were reportedly killed during protests in October against the proposed sale of state-owned Free Trade Zones in the city of Colón. The police reported that several officers had been injured by gunshots and missiles thrown by some of the protesters.

Impunity

Efforts to ensure justice for victims of human rights violations during the military governments (1968-1989) made slow progress. In January, the government established a Special National Commission to assist in locating and identifying the remains of victims of enforced disappearance. A Truth Commission, which reported in 2002, estimated that 207 people had been forcibly disappeared and killed under the military governments.

Manuel Noriega, head of state from 1983 to 1989, who had been extradited from France in 2011, remained in custody throughout the year awaiting trial. He was charged with human rights violations, including extrajudicial executions.

PAPUA NEW GUINEA

P

INDEPENDENT STATE OF PAPUA NEW GUINEA
Head of state: Queen Elizabeth II, represented by
                        Governor General Michael Ogio
Head of government: Peter Charles Paire O'Neill (de facto
                        since August 2011, elected
                        in August 2012)

The government did little to address high rates of violence against women; sorcery-related killings remained common. Residents of informal settlements continued to live with the threat of arbitrary and violent eviction. Police accountability remained a serious concern, particularly in cases of forced eviction.

Background

A Supreme Court decision in May declared Peter O'Neill's government, supported by the majority of Parliament in August 2011, illegal. The ruling called for former Prime Minister Michael Somare to be reinstated. Peter O'Neill failed to comply with the Supreme Court's decision and two rival governments subsequently claimed to have control over the country. The Supreme Court judges who decided the case were arrested for treason, but these charges were later dropped. In August following elections, Prime Minister O'Neill formed a coalition government with former Prime Minister Somare.

Violence against women and girls

Violence against women and girls remained widespread. Domestic violence was common, and a culture of silence and impunity prevailed. Assaults in police custody were frequently reported.

■ In June, a police officer from Port Moresby was found guilty of two counts of rape of a woman in custody.

■ In August, a young girl with a disability was burned to death in election-related violence in the highlands. Concerns were also raised that women in some areas were prevented from freely expressing their vote at the ballot box.

Following a visit to the country in March, the UN Special Rapporteur on violence against women declared such violence "a pervasive phenomenon in Papua New Guinea", with incidents occurring at every level of society – "in the home, community and institutional settings". She identified polygamy as one factor contributing to violence in the family, and called on government to meet its responsibilities to protect women from violence, including addressing traditional practices that are harmful to women.

Sorcery-related killings

Reports of sorcery-related killings were common, with women generally more vulnerable to being targeted. The authorities did little to address the issue, with some exceptions.

■ In July, police arrested and charged eight women and 21 men with murdering and cannibalizing three women and four men in Madang province. The assailants had claimed the victims were sorcerers.

Forced evictions

People continued to be forcibly evicted from informal settlements for development projects or as an expedient to reducing crime in the area. The authorities often resorted to violence to quell resistance.

■ In May, armed police officers carried out a forced eviction at Paga Hill, one of Port Moresby's oldest settlements. A court injunction stopped the eviction after some homes had been demolished. Opposition leader, Dame Carol Kidu, was assaulted by police officers for opposing the forced evictions and weapons were fired to disperse a crowd.

PARAGUAY

REPUBLIC OF PARAGUAY
Head of state and government: Federico Franco
(replaced Fernando Lugo Méndez in June)

There were some advances in the fulfilment of the rights of Indigenous Peoples. However, some communities continued to be denied access to their traditional lands. There were a number of protests over land rights during the year. Concerns persisted over the lack of impartiality and independence of the judiciary.

Background

In June, former President Fernando Lugo was impeached following clashes in the eastern department of Canindeyú in which 11 *campesinos* (peasant farmers) and six police officers were killed.

In October, a Selection Committee was established to appoint members to the National Mechanism to Prevent Torture. However, members had not been appointed by the end of the year.

Legislation to prevent discrimination remained before Congress at the end of the year. The draft law, which would incorporate international standards into national law, had been under discussion since 2007. There were concerns that Congress might seek to exclude sexual orientation as a prohibited ground for discrimination.

A draft law to prevent, eradicate and punish violence against women was submitted to Congress in November, but had not been approved by the end of the year.

Indigenous Peoples' rights

Progress was made in resolving the land claims of some Indigenous communities, but other communities continued to be denied their traditional lands.

■ The Sawhoyamaxa continued to live in appalling conditions by the side of a main road because their traditional lands had not been returned to them, despite a ruling by the Inter-American Court of Human Rights in 2006 in their favour. In November, negotiations between the authorities and the landowner started again after the community organized protests and a roadblock. No agreement on the land had been reached by the end of the year.

■ In February, an agreement between the authorities and a landowner secured lands claimed by the Yakye Axa. At the end of the year the Yakye Axa were waiting to move onto the land. The community development fund that the Inter-American Court of Human Rights had requested be set up in its 2005 ruling had not been established by the end of the year.

■ In August, police tried to evict more than 30 families of an Ava Guaraní community in the Itakyry district. Community members stated that the police burned down a number of huts. The land on which the community had lived for some 70 years was claimed by a commercial company. However, the community argued that they had a legal title to the land.

Justice system

There were allegations that the justice system lacked impartiality and independence and that it was inadequately resourced. Delays in the administration of justice were reported.

Land disputes in the Curuguaty district, Canindeyú department, erupted into clashes between protesters and police in June. Seventeen people – 11 campesinos and six policemen – were killed. In December, 14 campesinos were charged with offences including illegal occupation of land and criminal association; 10 were also charged in connection with the killings of the six policemen. There were concerns at the lack of impartiality of investigations into the clashes, which reportedly focused solely on the actions of protesters. The judicial proceedings against the 14 campesinos were continuing at the end of the year.

Some of those detained in connection with the clashes went on hunger strike to protest their innocence. They stated that they were either not present during the clashes or were not involved.

There were allegations that some of those held in the context of the Curuguaty clashes were tortured. No investigation into these allegations was known to have been initiated by the end of the year.

Various occupations of the same land in Curuguaty had taken place in previous years and judicial processes to determine ownership of the land were continuing at the end of the year.

Human rights defenders

Four members of Iniciativa Amotocodie, an NGO working to protect the rights of uncontacted Ayoreo Indigenous Peoples living in the Paraguayan Chaco region, continued to face legal proceedings on charges including breach of trust.

Investigations into the organization started after they publicly declared their opposition to a scientific expedition called "Dry Chaco 2010" on the grounds that it could harm the rights of uncontacted Indigenous Peoples. The expedition was subsequently cancelled. During the two-year investigation, there had been several changes of prosecutor and hearings had been suspended on a number of occasions. In August, the prosecutor failed to substantiate the charges and requested a temporary suspension of proceedings, arguing that some information still needed to be gathered. The judge granted the prosecutor's request.

Amnesty International visits/reports

🚗 Amnesty International delegates visited Paraguay in November.

PERU

REPUBLIC OF PERU
Head of state and government: **Ollanta Humala Tasso**

Several protests related to mining led to clashes with security forces; protesters were killed and human rights defenders were arbitrarily detained and ill-treated. Progress was slow in human rights cases dating back to the internal armed conflict

(1980–2000). Lack of adequate consultation with Indigenous Peoples remained a concern.

Background

Mass demonstrations took place during the year to demand labour rights and in opposition to extractive industry projects.

At least 30 members of the security forces were killed and scores were injured in clashes with remnants of the armed opposition group, Shining Path. In February, Shining Path's leader, Florindo Eleuterio Flores Hala (known as "Comrade Artemio") was arrested.

In September, Peru ratified the International Convention against enforced disappearance. However, by the end of the year it had not recognized the competence of the Committee on Enforced Disappearances to deal with individual complaints.

Peru's human rights record was assessed under the UN Universal Periodic Review in November. It accepted most of the recommendations made. These included preventing the torture and ill-treatment of detainees and prisoners; guaranteeing justice and reparation for victims of human rights violations; adopting a national protocol for abortion and reviewing the decriminalization of abortion in cases of rape; and ensuring consultation with Indigenous Peoples on measures that may affect their rights and livelihood.

Police and security forces

Allegations of arbitrary detentions, torture and other ill-treatment, and excessive use of force by the security forces were reported during protests against extractive projects.

■ Six people, one of whom was 17 years old, were shot dead, allegedly by the security forces, during clashes in Espinar province, Cusco department, and in Celendín, Cajamarca department, in May and July respectively.
■ In September, Nemesio Poma Ascate was shot dead and scores of people were injured during a demonstration in Huaraz, Áncash department. Nemesio Poma Ascate and other Mareniyoc community members were protesting against a mining company for failing to provide the community with safe drinking water.

Human rights defenders

Human rights defenders were threatened, arbitrarily detained, and ill-treated.

■ In May, Jaime Cesar Borda Pari and Romualdo Tito Pinto, both members of the human rights organization Vicaria de Solidaridad de Sicuani, and community leader Sergio Huamani, were arrested outside a mining camp and accused of having ammunition in the car. They claimed that the bullets had been planted by the police during a car search at which none of them had been present. The three men and a local prosecutor had been assessing the situation of detainees following violent clashes during protests in the area. All three were released on bail after two days, but remained under investigation at the end of the year.
■ In June, police officers in Cajamarca department allegedly beat human rights defender Amparo Abanto, a lawyer for the local NGO Comprehensive Training for Sustainable Development Group (Grupo de Formación e Intervención para el Desarrollo Sostenible, GRUFIDES) and the National Human Rights Coordinating Body (Coordinadora Nacional de Derechos Humanos, CNDDHH), a national umbrella human rights organization; and Genoveva Gómez, a staff member at the Peruvian Ombudsman's Office. They had been trying to gain access to detainees during protests against a mining project. Communities feared the project could affect their right to water. At the end of the year an investigation into the allegations of ill-treatment was pending.
■ In July, police officers detained and ill-treated Marco Arana, also a member of GRUFIDES, as he protested against the same mining project. He was conditionally released a day later. He filed complaints of ill-treatment and torture. His appeal against a decision to archive his complaint was pending at the end of the year. Marco Arana was awaiting trial on charges of "disturbing the peace" and "resisting arrest" at the end of the year. An investigation into his complaints of abuse of authority remained open at the end of the year.

Indigenous Peoples' rights

In April, the Ministry of Culture published the Regulatory Framework on the Law on the Right of Indigenous Peoples to Prior Consultation. There were concerns about the legislation, including that the consultation process with Indigenous Peoples to create the law had been inadequate.

In August, the government announced the first consultation process under the new regulatory framework. This was intended to involve consultation with Achuar, Quechua and Kichwa Indigenous Peoples on an oil extraction project in Loreto in the north of Peru in 2013.

Impunity

Progress in ensuring truth, justice and reparation for the victims of past human rights violations remained slow and faced setbacks. The lack of full co-operation by the Ministry of Defence in providing relevant information remained a concern.

Legislation granting access to reparation for all victims of sexual violence was approved by Congress in May, but had not come into force by the end of the year. As a result, victims of sexual violence, other than rape, committed during the internal armed conflict continued to be denied reparation.

Sexual and reproductive rights

Women and girls faced obstacles in getting access to their sexual and reproductive rights. There was no access to emergency contraception in state health services and the authorities did not create long-overdue national guidelines to regulate access to therapeutic abortion.

In November, the UN Committee against Torture raised concerns at the criminalization of abortion in cases of rape, as well as at the 2009 Constitutional Court ruling prohibiting the state from distributing emergency contraception.

PHILIPPINES

REPUBLIC OF THE PHILIPPINES
Head of state and government: **Benigno S. Aquino III**

Human rights defenders and journalists were at risk of unlawful killings, and thousands of cases of grave human rights violations remained unresolved. Victims of human rights violations, including during martial law from 1972 to 1981, continued to be denied justice, truth and reparations. In April, the Philippines acceded to the Optional Protocol to the UN Convention against Torture, but had not yet established the required mechanism to monitor treatment of detainees. Access to reproductive health care remained restricted; a new Reproductive Health Law was enacted in December.

Background

In October, the government and the Moro Islamic Liberation Front signed a Framework Agreement, which laid the ground for a peaceful resolution to decades of armed conflict in Mindanao but did not address human rights comprehensively. In October, Congress enacted the Cybercrime Prevention Act, which allows for a person to be jailed for up to 12 years for posting online comments judged libellous. After a public outcry, the Supreme Court later suspended implementation of the law pending judicial review. In November, the Philippines adopted the ASEAN human rights declaration, despite serious concerns that it falls short of international standards.

Unlawful killings

More than a dozen political and anti-mining activists and members of their families, and at least six journalists, were unlawfully killed.

■ Gunmen on motorcycle shot dead Mindanao radio broadcasters Christopher Guarin in January, Rommel Palma and Aldion Layao in April, Nestor Libaton in May, and Cabanatuan radio broadcaster Julius Causo in November. In September, the body of journalist and politician Eddie Apostol was found in Maguindanao with gunshot wounds to his head.

■ In September, unidentified men fired at Subanen tribal leader and anti-mining activist Timuay Lucenio Manda, while he was taking his 11-year-old son, Jordan, to school. Timuay Manda was injured in the ambush; Jordan was killed. Two suspects were arrested.

■ In October, soldiers fired at the house of B'laan tribal leader and anti-mining activist Daguil Capion in Davao del Sur, killing his pregnant wife Juvy and their children Jordan, aged 13, and John, aged eight. The authorities announced that 13 soldiers would face court martial, but it remained unclear whether they would be prosecuted in a civilian court.

Three years after the Maguindanao massacre, where state-armed militias led by government officials killed 57 people, the police still failed to arrest half of the 197 suspects. As trials of alleged perpetrators continued, prospective state witnesses, witnesses and their families continued to face threats.

■ In February, Alijol Ampatuan, an undisclosed witness willing to identify members of the Civilian Volunteer Organisation involved in the massacre, was killed.

■ Also in February, Hernanie Decipulo, a policeman being considered as a state witness, reportedly committed suicide while in police custody.

P

- In May, the body of Esmail Amil Enog, who testified in court, had been found "chainsawed" to pieces.
- In June, police reported that three relatives of witnesses connected to the Maguindanao case had been killed since the massacre.

In October, the UN Human Rights Committee concluded that the government should enhance the effectiveness of the witness protection programme and "fully investigate cases of killings and suspected intimidation of witnesses to put an end to the climate of fear that plagues investigation and prosecution."

Torture and other ill-treatment

Three years after its promulgation, implementation of the Anti-Torture Act remained weak, with no perpetrator yet convicted of this crime. Torture victims, particularly criminal suspects, were reluctant to file complaints due to fear of reprisals and lengthy prosecution.
- The court case of Darius Evangelista, in which the act of torture and the identity of the perpetrators were caught on video in 2010, continued. Seven policemen were accused, but only two faced charges. The suspects were initially in police custody, but according to the Philippine Commission on Human Rights, they went missing in April 2012 and remained at large.

Enforced disappearances

Enforced disappearances of activists, suspected insurgents and suspected criminals continued to be reported.
- In January, after flying to Manila from Zamboanga City, farmers Najir Ahung, Rasbi Kasaran and Yusoph Mohammad were apprehended at the airport, allegedly by state forces, and were not seen since. The authorities refused to provide lawyers representing the missing men with closed-circuit video tapes or a list of security forces on duty at the airport at the time of their disappearance.

In October, Congress passed the Anti-Enforced or Involuntary Disappearance Bill, after more than two decades of lobbying from civil society. The bill, which criminalizes enforced disappearance and prescribes penalties up to life imprisonment, awaited the President's signature to bring it into force.

Impunity

Impunity for torture, enforced disappearances and unlawful killings continued despite the government's stated commitment to eradicate these crimes and bring perpetrators to justice. Court cases arising from human rights violations during martial law (1972-

1981) were dismissed or languished in court. In November, the President ordered the establishment of an interagency committee to investigate more recent cases of these grave crimes.
- In January, Raymond Manalo, a survivor of torture and enforced disappearance, was called to testify at the Office of the Ombudsman more than three years after he filed complaints against his captors for abducting, arbitrarily detaining and torturing him. He and several others were subjected to enforced disappearance and torture in 2006, allegedly by soldiers under the command of General Jovito Palparan, who had evaded arrest since 2011.

Right to health

In June, the government released the results of its 2011 Family Health Survey, which found that from 2006 to 2010 "maternal deaths" increased from 162 deaths to 221 deaths per 100,000 live births. Based on this data, the Health Secretary estimated that 11 women died every day from easily preventable complications arising from pregnancy and childbirth.

Following a decade of lobbying by civil society groups, the Reproductive Health Law was passed in December. The law introduced proactive funding for modern contraceptive methods by government, and mandatory health and sexuality education.

Amnesty International visits/reports
- Amnesty International delegates visited the Philippines in September.
- Philippines: Torturers evade justice on Aquino's watch (ASA 35/004/2012)
- Philippines: Amnesty International submission to the Human Rights Committee – 106th session (ASA 35/006/2012)
- Philippines: "Cybercrime" law threatens free speech and must be reviewed (ASA 35/008/2012)

POLAND

REPUBLIC OF POLAND
Head of state: Bronislaw Komorowski
Head of government: Donald Tusk

The investigation of Poland's involvement in US-led renditions and secret detentions progressed slowly. Public access to information in the case of al-Nashiri being considered by the European Court of Human Rights continued to be denied. Discussions about changes to the law on abortion continued while the European Court ruled that Poland had denied a teenage girl's right to a legal abortion.

Counter-terror and security

The criminal investigation, begun in 2008 into Poland's role in the CIA's rendition and secret detention programmes, was moved in February from the Warsaw Prosecutor's Office to Krakow, raising concerns about further delays and staff changes. The Warsaw Prosecutor's Office had previously granted victim status to Abd al-Rahim al-Nashiri and Zayn al-Abidin Muhammad Husayn (also known as Abu Zubaydah), both of whom remained in detention at Guantánamo Bay. The men alleged that between 2002 and 2003 they were illegally transferred to Poland, subjected to enforced disappearance, held in a secret CIA detention centre and tortured and otherwise ill-treated.

Polish media reported in March that the former head of the Polish Intelligence Agency, Zbigniew Siemiątkowski, and his deputy had been charged with crimes relating to the detention and ill-treatment of people held in secret by the CIA on Polish territory. Polish prosecutors refused to confirm or deny that such charges had been brought. The investigation continued to be conducted in secret and victims expressed concern about access to information and full participation in the proceedings.

The European Parliament adopted a report in September on alleged transportation and illegal detention of prisoners in European countries by the CIA. The report called on all EU member states alleged to have hosted secret CIA detention centres to comply with their legal obligation to conduct independent, impartial, thorough and effective investigations into their involvement in the CIA programmes. The Rapporteur on the report visited Poland in May to discuss Polish complicity in the programmes with the authorities.

In July, the European Court of Human Rights communicated the case of *al-Nashiri v. Poland* to the Polish authorities. In September, the government submitted its observations confidentially to the Court, which then instructed the al-Nashiri legal team to respond confidentially, so denying public access to information on the case.

Sexual and reproductive rights

In June, Poland's human rights record was assessed under the UN Universal Periodic Review. Poland was asked to improve access to reproductive health services, including lawful abortion. In October, parliament rejected a proposal to widen legal access to abortion, introduce comprehensive sex education and subsidize contraception.

■ In October, in the case of *P. and S. v. Poland*, the European Court of Human Rights held that Poland had violated a 14-year-old girl's right to a lawful abortion, following an alleged rape. Although legally entitled to terminate her pregnancy, she was hindered from timely access to abortion services. Workers in three hospitals, the police and private actors obstructed the girl's access to lawful health care and subjected her to harassment, humiliation and intimidation, including by detaining her in a juvenile centre. The European Court ruled that such treatment violated the prohibition of inhuman or degrading treatment and the rights to private life and to liberty.

Freedom of expression

Defamation continued to be a criminal offence.

■ In April, in the case *Kaperzyński v. Poland,* the European Court of Human Rights found that Polish authorities interfered with the right to freedom of expression of a journalist who had not published a local authority's reply to his article accusing them of environmental mismanagement. He was given a four-month suspended sentence of community service and banned from working as a journalist for two years. The European Court held that imposing a criminal sentence for a failure to publish a reply was disproportionate and discouraged free debate on issues of public interest.

■ In September, the editor of Antykomor.pl website was sentenced to 10 months' community service for publishing satirical materials about the President of Poland.

■ Also in September, the European Court of Human Rights found that Poland had violated the right to freedom of expression of a local councillor in the case *Lewandowska-Malec v. Poland*. The councillor had publicly expressed an opinion that the town's mayor was putting extra-legal pressure on the prosecution service in the case relating to alleged fraud by municipality officials in Świątniki Górne. Following a complaint by the mayor, the councillor was found guilty of defamation in 2006. The European Court held that imposing a criminal sentence – in this case a fine of 1,900 euros – was disproportionate.

P

Refugees and migrants

In October, Poland announced its plan to introduce a ban on detaining unaccompanied migrant children under 13 years of age. However, according to available statistics, most unaccompanied children in Poland were over 13 years old. In September, Poland rejected the full implementation of the recommendation of the UN Universal Periodic Review for a complete ban on placing migrant minors in detention facilities.

PORTUGAL

PORTUGUESE REPUBLIC
Head of state: **Aníbal António Cavaco Silva**
Head of government: **Pedro Manuel Mamede Passos Coelho**

There were reports of excessive use of force by police against demonstrators and Roma. Domestic violence remained a serious concern.

Torture and other ill-treatment

A criminal investigation into the use of a Taser against an inmate in Paços de Ferreira prison in 2010 did not progress despite the findings of an inquiry by the Audit and Inspection services of the General Directorate for prisons that two members of the Prison Security Intervention Group had used the weapon disproportionately. The outcome of disciplinary proceedings against the two prison officers remained pending at the end of the year.

■ The trial of three police officers accused of torturing Virgolino Borges in March 2000 while in police custody, which started in November 2011, made little progress.

Excessive use of force

In March, police reportedly used excessive force against peaceful demonstrators during anti-austerity protests. On 22 March, two journalists received medical treatment after allegedly being beaten by police at a demonstration in Lisbon.

■ In September, members of the Guarda Nacional Republicana reportedly used excessive force when attempting to arrest a man in a Romani community in Regalde, Vila Verde Municipality. At least nine Roma, including children, were allegedly beaten and physically and verbally abused by about 30 police officers; at least three needed medical treatment.

■ On 14 November, during a general strike, police reportedly charged peaceful demonstrators using batons. Some of those detained were reportedly not informed of the grounds for their detention and denied timely access to legal representation. The media reported 48 wounded.

Violence against women and girls

Domestic violence continued to be a serious concern. The Portuguese Association for Victim Support (APAV) and the Portuguese Ombudsman reported an increase in complaints by elderly victims of domestic violence. According to APAV, the total number of complaints by victims of domestic violence increased to 16,970 in 2012, compared with 15,724 in 2011. According to the NGO UMAR, deaths resulting from domestic violence were estimated at 36 as of September 2012, compared with 27 for the whole of 2011.

International scrutiny

On 31 October, the UN Human Rights Committee issued its concluding observations on the fourth periodic report on Portugal. Recommendations focused on the rights of people detained in police custody, prison conditions, domestic violence and discrimination against migrants and ethnic minorities, including Roma.

Following his visit to Portugal in May, the Council of Europe Commissioner for Human Rights expressed concerns over ongoing discrimination against Roma and the impact of the economic crisis and fiscal austerity measures on the rights of children and the elderly.

P

PUERTO RICO

COMMONWEALTH OF PUERTO RICO
Head of state: Barack H. Obama
Head of government: Luis G. Fortuño

Parts of a new penal code curtailed the right to protest. A Justice Department investigation into abuses by the Puerto Rico Police Department remained ongoing.

Freedom of expression

Civil liberties groups criticized a provision in an updated penal code as infringing the right to freedom of expression. The code, which came into force in July, includes a section criminalizing demonstrations that block public buildings and interfere with local government. The measures would outlaw protests such as those that had taken place in recent years at the University of Puerto Rico and at the Capitol (the building housing the legislative assembly). A legal challenge to the provision, filed by the American Civil Liberties Union in Puerto Rico, was pending at the end of the year.

Police and security forces

Negotiations to reform the Puerto Rico Police Department were ongoing, following a 2011 US Justice Department report on widespread, systematic abuses.

QATAR

STATE OF QATAR
Head of state: Shaikh Hamad bin Khalifa Al Thani
Head of government: Shaikh Hamad bin Jassim bin Jabr
                                              Al Thani

Freedom of expression continued to be curtailed. New cases of torture emerged. Women continued to face discrimination in law and practice, as well as violence. Foreign migrant workers, who comprised the majority of the workforce, were exploited, abused and inadequately protected under the law. At least one death sentence was imposed; no executions were reported.

Freedom of expression

The authorities maintained strict controls on freedom of expression, and moved to tighten these further with a new draft media law. If approved, this would require all publications to be approved by a government-appointed "competent authority" empowered to remove content or prevent printing.

■ The poet Mohammed al-Ajami, also known as Mohamed Ibn al-Dheeb, who was charged with "inciting to overthrow the ruling regime" and "insulting the Amir" was sentenced to life imprisonment by the Doha Criminal Court on 29 November. His poems criticized repression in the Gulf States. He was detained incommunicado following his arrest in November 2011 and appeared to be a prisoner of conscience. He appealed against his conviction.

Migrant workers' rights

Foreign migrant workers, who comprised more than 90% of Qatar's workforce, continued to be exploited and abused by employers despite protective provisions set out in the 2004 Labour Law and related decrees, which the authorities failed to adequately enforce. Workers' living conditions were often grossly inadequate and many workers said they were made to work excessive hours beyond the legal maximum or were paid far less than agreed when they were contracted.

Migrant domestic workers, mostly women, and certain other workers were specifically excluded from the 2004 Labour Law, exposing them to greater labour exploitation and abuse, including sexual abuse. The government had previously committed to enact legislation to address this problem but it had not done so by the end of the year.

The 2009 Sponsorship Law, which requires foreign workers to obtain a sponsor's permission to leave Qatar or change employer, was exploited by employers to prevent workers from complaining to the authorities or moving to a new job in the event of abuse. The sponsorship system increased the likelihood of workers being subjected to forced labour. In October the state news agency reported that the Cabinet would form a panel to study the sponsorship issue.

P.

Discrimination – denial of nationality

Some 100 people, mostly members of al-Murra tribe who were arbitrarily stripped of their Qatari nationality in previous years, continued to be denied access to employment, social security and health care due to their statelessness. They were not permitted to challenge the decision to revoke their nationality in the courts and were denied any means of remedy.

Torture and other ill-treatment

New cases of torture and other ill-treatment emerged.
■ Following their release, Abdullah al-Khawar and Salem al-Kawari alleged that while detained without charge or trial as security suspects in 2011, they were beaten, suspended by their limbs and made to remain standing for hours at a time, deprived of sleep, held in solitary confinement in tiny cells, and subjected to cold temperatures for long periods while interrogators sought to obtain "confessions" from them. The authorities took no steps to investigate their allegations or bring the perpetrators to justice.

In November, following its review of Qatar's implementation of the UN Convention against Torture, the UN Committee against Torture urged the government to ensure that the fundamental safeguards required by the Convention were applied in practice to all persons deprived of their liberty, including by ensuring that complaints of abuse were promptly and impartially examined and that detainees could challenge the legality of their detention or treatment.

Discrimination and violence against women

Women continued to face discrimination in law and practice and were inadequately protected against violence within the family. In particular, family law discriminated against women, making it much easier for men to seek divorce compared to women, and placing women at a severe economic disadvantage if they sought divorce or if their husbands left them.

Death penalty

At least one death sentence was imposed, on a Sri Lankan man convicted of murder; no executions were reported. Prisoners on death row included at least six men sentenced to death in 2001 for participating in a 1996 plot to overthrow the government.

Amnesty International visits/reports

🚌 Amnesty International delegates visited Qatar in October.
📄 Qatar: Briefing to the United Nations Committee against Torture (MDE 22/001/2012)
📄 Qatar should take steps to end use of torture and other ill-treatment (MDE 22/003/2012)

ROMANIA

REPUBLIC OF ROMANIA
Head of state: Traian Băsescu
Head of government: Victor Ponta (replaced Mihai Razvan Ungureanu in May, who replaced Emil Boc in February)

Police were alleged to have used arbitrary and disproportionate force during anti-austerity and anti-government demonstrations. Local authorities in the towns of Baia Mare and Piatra Neamț carried out large-scale forced evictions of Roma. The European Parliament called on Romanian authorities to open a new investigation into their involvement in the CIA-led rendition and secret detention programmes.

Background

The government fell twice in 2012. Following weeks of protests against austerity measures, the cabinet of Emil Boc (Democratic Liberal Party) resigned in February. In April, after another wave of protests, the cabinet of the Prime Minister Mihai Razvan Ungureanu lost a vote of no-confidence. The President appointed an interim Prime Minister, Victor Ponta (Social Democratic Party), whose party then won the majority of the seats in the December parliamentary elections.

In a vote on impeachment, the Romanian parliament suspended the President in July. The vote followed allegations made by the government that the President had breached the Constitution. The subsequent referendum on the suspension was invalid due to a low turnout and the President remained in office.

In July, the European Commission expressed serious concerns over respect for the rule of law and the independence of the judiciary in Romania.

R

Excessive use of force

Incidents of violence between demonstrators and the police during the anti-government protests in January gave rise to allegations of excessive use of force by police officers. Media reports and video footage showed police using excessive force against seemingly peaceful demonstrators who were not offering any resistance. The NGO APADOR-Helsinki Committee documented several cases of abuses by the police during the demonstrations. It concluded that some of the law enforcement officers' actions had been arbitrary and disproportionate. In February, the Ministry of Administration and Interior stated that four criminal complaints relating to the behaviour of police officers during the demonstrations were being investigated. No charges had been brought by the end of the year.

Discrimination – Roma

Right to education

In October, the Advisory Committee on the Framework Convention for the Protection of National Minorities of the Council of Europe stated that Roma children were still being placed in schools for children with disabilities, in separate schools or in separate classrooms.

Housing rights

Local authorities continued to forcibly evict and relocate Roma to inadequate and segregated housing.

■ About 76, mostly Romani, families, who had been forcibly evicted from the centre of the city of Cluj-Napoca in December 2010, continued to live in inadequate housing conditions on the outskirts of the city, close to the city's rubbish dump and a former chemical waste dump. In meetings with the evicted families, the local authorities made a commitment to start moving them from the area in 2013 as part of a project developed with the UN Development Programme. However, details of the planned relocation remained vague.

■ On 18 April the court of Cluj-Napoca rejected another request from the National Railway company to remove approximately 450 people, mainly Roma, living in the settlement in Cantonului Street, in the city of Cluj-Napoca thus preventing a possible forced eviction. Many of the residents had been moved to the area by the municipality since 2002.

■ In April, a Court of Appeal quashed the decision of the National Council for Combating Discrimination (NCCD) to fine the municipal authorities of Baia Mare for erecting a concrete wall separating blocks of houses inhabited by Roma from the rest of the residential area. The Court held that the wall was a proportionate response to the risk of traffic-related injury and that it did not ethnically segregate the Roma residents. The NCCD announced that it would appeal the decision.

■ In May and June, the municipality of Baia Mare forcibly evicted about 120 Romani families from the town's biggest settlement of Craica. The families were moved to three blocks belonging to the metallurgical factory CUPROM. The buildings were not adapted for residential use before the people were moved there. Whole families were allocated either one or two rooms. The rooms did not have heating or adequate insulation. The sanitation facilities were also limited.

■ In August, the municipality of Piatra Neamţ relocated about 500 Roma living in housing units on the margins of the town to completely segregated accommodation 2km away from the closest bus stop. The housing units had no electricity and the area lacked infrastructure such as street lights or an adequate access road.

Sexual and reproductive rights

In September, a legislative proposal was put before parliament to introduce mandatory counselling for pregnant women that would, among other things, result in additional expenses and possibly prolonged waiting periods for those seeking abortions.

Counter-terror and security

The European Parliament issued a report in September calling on all EU member states, including Romania, alleged to have hosted secret CIA detention centres, to comply with their absolute legal obligation to conduct an independent, impartial, thorough and effective investigation into their involvement in the rendition and secret detention programmes. The report called on the authorities to open a new investigation in light of the identification by former US officials of a secret detention site in the capital, Bucharest, and in light of evidence of rendition flights linking Romania with Poland and Lithuania, other states alleged to have hosted secret CIA sites.

■ In October, the European Court of Human Rights communicated the case of *al-Nashiri v. Romania* to the Romanian authorities. The case involved a Saudi national who alleged that he was imprisoned and tortured at a secret CIA detention centre in Romania prior to his eventual transfer to the US military base at Guantánamo Bay in Cuba.

R

Amnesty International visits/reports

🚌 Amnesty International delegates visited Romania in March, May, October and December.

📄 Europe: Policing demonstrations in the European Union (EUR 01/022/2012)

📄 Unsafe foundations: Secure the right to housing in Romania (EUR 39/002/2012)

📄 Romania: Forced eviction of Roma and alleged collusion in US-led rendition and secret detention programmes (EUR 39/012/2012)

RUSSIAN FEDERATION

RUSSIAN FEDERATION
Head of state: **Vladimir Putin (replaced Dmitry Medvedev in May)**
Head of government: **Dmitry Medvedev (replaced Vladimir Putin in May)**

Increasing peaceful political protest was met with repression. New laws restricting the rights to freedom of expression, assembly and association were introduced. Human rights defenders, journalists and lawyers continued to face harassment, while investigations into violent attacks were ineffective. Torture and other ill-treatment remained widespread, and were seldom effectively prosecuted. Trials did not meet international standards of fairness, and the number of apparently politically motivated decisions grew. Insecurity and volatility in the North Caucasus persisted, and security operations launched in response were marred by systematic human rights violations with near-total impunity for the perpetrators.

Background

Vladimir Putin's return as President, following widely criticized elections, led to a surge in popular protest and demands for greater civil and political freedoms, particularly around his inauguration in May. The result was increased restrictions. Protests were frequently banned and disrupted. New laws were adopted, often without public consultation and in the face of widespread criticism, which introduced harsh administrative and criminal penalties that could be used to target legitimate protest and political and civil society activities, and to restrict foreign funding for civic activism.

The Russian Federation responded belligerently to international criticism of its human rights record. A law on travel and other sanctions on officials allegedly responsible for the death of lawyer Sergei Magnitsky in custody in 2009 was passed in the USA and proposed in several other countries. The Russian authorities retaliated with reciprocal sanctions and by banning the adoption of Russian children by US citizens and prohibiting Russian NGOs from receiving funding from the USA.

Russia continued to enjoy economic growth, although this slowed with falling oil prices, the global economic downturn and the lack of structural reforms at home. Public protest decreased by the end of 2012, but so did public support for the political leadership, according to opinion polls.

Freedom of assembly

Peaceful protests across Russia, including gatherings of small groups of people who presented no public threat or inconvenience, were routinely dispersed by police, often with excessive force. The authorities regarded every such event, however peaceful and insignificant in number, as unlawful unless expressly sanctioned, although gatherings of pro-government or pro-Orthodox Church activists were often allowed to proceed uninterrupted even without authorization. There were frequent reports of police brutality towards peaceful protesters and journalists, but these were not effectively investigated.

■ On 6 May, the day before the inauguration of President Putin, a column of protesters moving along a permitted route to Bolotnaya Square in Moscow was halted by police, resulting in a stand-off and localized skirmishes. Subsequently, 19 protesters faced criminal charges in connection with events characterized by authorities as "mass riots"; one pleaded guilty and was sentenced to four-and-a-half years' imprisonment; the remainder were still awaiting trial at the end of the year. Several leading political activists were named as witnesses in the case and had their homes searched in operations that were widely broadcast by state-controlled television channels. Over 6 and 7 May, hundreds of peaceful individuals were arrested across Moscow, some merely for wearing white ribbons as a symbol of protest against electoral fraud.

R

The law governing public events was further amended in June. It expanded the list of violations, introduced new restrictions and increased sanctions.

Freedom of expression

The right to freedom of expression was increasingly restricted. Most media remained under effective state control, except for some outlets with limited circulation. Prime-time national television was regularly employed to smear government critics.

Libel was re-criminalized, eight months after its decriminalization. Changes to the Criminal Code expanded the definitions of treason and espionage and made them vaguer by including sharing information with, or providing miscellaneous assistance to, foreign states and organizations whose activity is "directed against security of the Russian Federation".

New legislation gave the government powers to blacklist and block websites publishing materials considered "extremist" or otherwise harmful to public health, morals or safety. By the end of the year, this legislation was already being used to shut down sites publishing content protected by the right to freedom of expression.

■ Maria Alekhina, Ekaterina Samutsevich and Nadezhda Tolokonnikova, members of the punk group Pussy Riot, were arrested in March after a brief and peaceful, albeit provocative, political performance in the Cathedral of Christ the Saviour in Moscow. They were convicted of "hooliganism motivated by religious hatred" in August and were each sentenced to two years in prison, although Ekaterina Samutsevich received a conditional sentence on appeal and was released on 10 October.

■ On 29 November a Moscow court declared video footage of the group's church performance "extremist", rendering its publication on the internet unlawful.

Discrimination

Discrimination on grounds such as race, ethnicity, gender, religion or political affiliation remained widespread. Discriminatory legislation targeting LGBTI individuals was introduced in several regions and proposed at the federal level. A law banning "propaganda of sodomy, lesbianism, bisexualism and transgenderness among minors" came into force in St Petersburg in April. Similar laws were also introduced in Bashkiria, Chukotka, Krasnodar,

Magadan, Novosibirsk and Samara regions, and tabled before the State Duma. A number of public LGBTI events were forbidden and participants dispersed by police.

Across Russia, LGBTI individuals and members of various minority groups continued to face attacks. Such attacks were not effectively investigated by the authorities, and the perpetrators often unidentified.

■ On 4 August, four men forcibly entered an LGBTI club in Tyumen and physically and verbally assaulted several customers. Police detained the attackers. When the victims came to the police station to file complaints, they were left in the same room with the perpetrators, who continued to threaten them and were later released without charge.

Human rights defenders

Reports of harassment of human rights defenders continued. In the North Caucasus and elsewhere, activists, journalists and lawyers representing victims of human rights violations continued to face physical threats, including from law enforcement officials.

Investigations into many past attacks, including the killing of Natalia Estemirova, made no ostensible progress.

New legislation introduced further administrative hurdles and a legal obligation for NGOs to register as "organizations performing the functions of foreign agents" (language evocative of espionage) if they received foreign funding and engaged in broadly defined "political activities". Failure to comply with these provisions might lead to heavy fines, and imprisonment for NGO leaders.

Public officials routinely sought to blacken the reputation of individual human rights defenders and specific NGOs, as well as the work of human rights NGOs in general.

■ In October, a senior Federal Security Service (FSB) official reportedly stated that the FSB had secured the closure of 20 NGOs in Ingushetia for their links with foreign intelligence services. He provided no information either on any specific case involving charges of espionage against an NGO in Ingushetia, or on which NGOs had supposedly been closed for this reason. However, he singled out the well-known Ingushetian human rights NGO, Mashr, as a "foreign agent" still in operation.

■ On 20 January, lawyer Omar Saidmagomedov and his cousin were shot dead in Makhachkala, Dagestan, by

R

security officials. The authorities reported the incident as a killing of two armed group members during a shoot-out. Omar Saidmagomedov's colleagues dismissed this report and demanded an investigation into allegations that he had been extrajudicially executed because of his professional activities. The investigator summoned the lawyer representing Omar Saidmagomedov's family for questioning as a witness, apparently with the aim of disqualifying him from acting as legal counsel in the case.

■ Elena Milashina, a journalist from the independent newspaper *Novaya Gazeta*, together with a friend, was assaulted by two men in the street in Moscow on 4 April, and received serious injuries. The investigator identified and charged two individuals who initially signed confessions but retracted them after their families hired independent lawyers. The investigator ignored protests by Elena Milashina that the two did not fit her friend's description of the men who assaulted her and that the real perpetrators had not been identified.

■ Igor Kalyapin, head of the NGO Committee Against Torture, was threatened with criminal proceedings in connection with his work on the case of Islam Umarpashaev, torture victim from Chechnya. On 7 July, Igor Kalyapin was summoned by a criminal investigator for questioning for allegedly disseminating confidential information. In September, journalists who had interviewed Igor Kalyapin and individuals who wrote letters to show their support were summoned for questioning.

Torture and other ill-treatment

Allegations of torture and other ill-treatment remained widely reported and effective investigations were rare. Law enforcement officials allegedly frequently circumvented the existing legal safeguards against torture through, among other things: the use of secret detention (particularly in the North Caucasus); the use of force supposedly to restrain violent detainees; investigators denying access to a lawyer of one's choice and favouring specific state-appointed lawyers who were known to ignore signs of torture.

In March, one torture case in Kazan was widely reported in the media after a man died of internal injuries in hospital. He claimed that he had been raped with a bottle at the police station. Several police officers were arrested and charged with abuse of power, and two were later sentenced to two and two-and-a-half years' imprisonment respectively. Many more allegations of torture by police in Kazan and elsewhere followed media reports of this case. In

response to an NGO initiative, the Head of the Investigative Committee decreed to create special departments to investigate crimes committed by law enforcement officials. However, the initiative was undermined by the failure to provide these departments with adequate staff resources.

■ On the night of 19 January, Issa Khashagulgov, held in a pre-trial detention centre in Vladikavkaz, North Ossetia, was allegedly taken to an undisclosed location and beaten and threatened with further violence for refusing to co-operate with the investigation against him. Reportedly, between 6 and 8 February he was transferred from the detention centre to a different location in North Ossetia for several hours each day when his lawyers tried to see him, and subjected to ill-treatment. Issa Khashagulgov, suspected of armed group membership, had earlier been repeatedly transferred between different detention facilities while his family and lawyers were denied information about his whereabouts, sometimes for several days. His complaints were not investigated.

■ Russian opposition activist Leonid Razvozzhayev went missing on 19 October in Kiev, Ukraine, outside the office of a partner organization to UNHCR, the UN refugee agency. On 22 October, the Investigative Committee in Moscow stated that he had voluntarily returned to the Russian Federation and handed himself in to the authorities. Leonid Razvozzhayev disavowed this statement via his lawyer, and alleged that he had been abducted and smuggled into the country, held at a secret location, ill-treated and forced to sign a statement implicating himself and other political activists in plotting mass disturbances in Russia on foreign orders. The Russian authorities dismissed his allegations and refused to investigate them.

Justice system

The need for judicial reform was widely acknowledged, including by senior officials. However, no effective steps were taken towards ensuring the independence of the judiciary. Reports of unfair trials were numerous and widespread. A range of court decisions, including those concerning extremism and economic and drug-related crimes, were affected by political considerations, and a growing number of convictions appeared politically motivated, including those of the Pussy Riot members (see above).

Allegations were frequently made of collusion between judges, prosecutors, investigators and other law enforcement officials resulting in unfair criminal convictions or disproportionate administrative penalties.

Lawyers across the country complained of procedural violations undermining their clients' right to a fair trial. These included denial of access to clients, detention of individuals as criminal suspects without promptly informing their lawyers and families, appointment of state-paid lawyers as defence counsel who are known to raise no objections about procedural violations and the use of ill-treatment.

■ Lawyer Rustam Matsev complained that on 31 May a senior police official at a pre-trial detention centre in Nalchik, Kabardino-Balkaria, demanded that he should "stop teaching his defendant to lie" and convince him to withdraw a complaint about abduction and ill-treatment by police. The officer allegedly told Rustam Matsev that lawyers "get blocked" in the same way as members of armed groups during their "elimination" in security operations. The authorities refused to investigate the lawyer's allegations.

■ On 27 October, dozens of protesters lined up 50m apart (a form of picketing which requires no prior authorization) in front of the central FSB headquarters in Moscow. Later, when several known political activists tried to leave, surrounded by reporters, they were detained by police. On 30 October and 4 December respectively, activists Alexey Navalny and Sergei Udaltsov were fined nearly US$1,000 each for organizing and participating in an unauthorized rally that violated public order. The judge hearing Alexey Navalny's case reportedly declined his defence lawyer's request to cross-examine the police officers who had detained him, and refused to admit video footage of the event as evidence.

North Caucasus

The region remained highly volatile. Human rights violations in the context of security operations remained widespread.

Armed groups continued to launch attacks against security forces, local officials and civilians. A double bomb attack on 3 May in Makhachkala, Dagestan, left 13 people dead (including eight police officers), and over 80 emergency and rescue workers were injured. On 28 August, an influential Dagestani Muslim cleric, Sheikh Said Afandi, and his five visitors were killed by a woman suicide bomber. Other attacks by armed groups took place across the North Caucasus.

Some republics sought to develop non-repressive responses to the threats posed by armed groups. Commissions for Adaptation were established in Dagestan and Ingushetia with the aim of encouraging the surrender and re-integration into society of former members of armed groups. The Dagestani authorities adopted a more tolerant attitude towards Salafi Muslims.

However, security operations continued to be conducted on a regular basis throughout the region. In the course of these, numerous human rights violations by law enforcement officials were reported, including enforced disappearances, unlawful detentions, torture and other ill-treatment, and extrajudicial executions.

The authorities systematically failed to conduct effective, impartial and prompt investigations into human rights violations by law enforcement officials, or to identify those responsible and bring them to justice. In some cases, criminal proceedings were initiated, but for the most part, the ensuing investigation either failed to establish the perpetrators or confirm involvement of officials in the relevant incidents, or concluded that there had been no violation by law enforcement officials. Only exceptional cases led to the prosecution of police officials for abuse of authority in connection with torture and other ill-treatment. Not a single case of enforced disappearance or alleged extrajudicial execution was resolved, and no perpetrators from any other law enforcement agency were brought to justice.

■ Rustam Aushev, a 23-year-old resident of Ingushetia, was last seen on 17 February at Mineralnye Vody railway station in the neighbouring Stavropol region. The next day, his relative spoke to staff at the station. They reported seeing a young man being detained by plain-clothes men and driven away in a Gazelle minivan, which was also captured on CCTV. A security guard had reportedly spoken to the minivan's driver asking it to be parked in the designated area, and was shown an FSB official's ID. Rustam Aushev's family reported these details to the authorities and demanded an investigation, but his fate and whereabouts were unknown at the end of the year.

■ In Ingushetia, the first ever trial of two former police officials concluded in Karabulak. Some charges related to the secret detention and torture of Zelimkhan Chitigov although the officials faced other charges as well. The announcement of the verdict was postponed repeatedly for almost three months, and on 7

November the judge sentenced one defendant to eight years' imprisonment, and fully acquitted the other, his former superior. Allegations of intimidation of victims and witnesses had persisted throughout the trial, during which both defendants remained at large. No other perpetrators were identified despite Zelimkhan Chitigov naming at least one other official by name and alleging that many others had been involved in the incessant bouts of torture during the three days he was kept in secret detention.

Amnesty International visits/reports

🚌 Amnesty International delegates visited the Russian Federation in May and June.

📄 Russian Federation: The circle of injustice – security operations and human rights violations in Ingushetia (EUR 46/012/2012)

📄 Russian Federation: Briefing to the UN Committee against Torture (EUR 46/040/2012)

RWANDA

REPUBLIC OF RWANDA
Head of state: **Paul Kagame**

The government continued to stifle legitimate freedom of expression and association. Cases of illegal detention and allegations of torture by Rwandan military intelligence were not investigated. Military support from Rwanda to the M23 armed group in the neighbouring Democratic Republic of the Congo (DRC) tarnished Rwanda's international image built on economic development and low levels of corruption. The international community's support for Rwanda wavered.

Background

A final report by the UN Group of Experts on the DRC, published in November 2012, contained evidence that Rwanda had breached the UN arms embargo by transferring arms, ammunition and military equipment to the M23. The report stated that Rwandan military officials were supporting the M23 by recruiting civilians in Rwanda and providing logistics, intelligence and political advice.

In an interim report addendum published in June, the Group of Experts had already named high-ranking Rwandan military officials – including the Minister of Defence – as having played a key role in providing this support. Rwanda published a detailed rebuttal, denying any support and criticizing the methodology and credibility of the sources used.

Major donors to Rwanda, including the USA, the EU, the UK, the Netherlands, Germany and Sweden, subsequently suspended or delayed part of their financial assistance.

In October, Rwanda was elected to hold a non-permanent seat on the UN Security Council for two years starting in 2013.

Community-based gacaca courts, set up to try genocide cases, completed their work in 2012 and were officially closed in June following several delays.

Impunity

The government failed to investigate and prosecute cases of illegal detention and allegations of torture by Rwandan military intelligence. In May and October, Amnesty International published evidence of illegal and incommunicado detention and enforced disappearances. The research included allegations of torture, including serious beatings, electric shocks and sensory deprivation used to force confessions during interrogations, mostly of civilians, in 2010 and 2011.

In May, the government categorically denied all allegations of illegal detentions and torture by Rwandan military intelligence before the UN Committee against Torture. In June, the Rwandan Minister of Justice acknowledged that illegal detentions had occurred, attributing them to operatives' "excessive zeal in the execution of a noble mission". On 7 October, the government issued a statement reaffirming that illegal detentions had taken place, but made no reference to investigations or prosecutions.

■ Sheikh Iddy Abassi, a Congolese religious leader, was abducted in Rwanda on 25 March 2010. He was a known supporter of Laurent Nkunda, a leader of the former Congolese armed group, the National Congress for the Defence of the People (CNDP). His family reported him missing to the local police and military the following day, 26 March. Mary Gahonzire, the Deputy Commissioner General of the Rwanda Correctional Service, told the UN Committee against Torture that investigations were ongoing, but that indications pointed to Sheikh Iddy Abassi being in the DRC.

Freedom of expression

There was almost no space for critical journalism in Rwanda. The aftermath of a 2010 clampdown on journalists and political opposition members left few independent voices in the country. Private media outlets remained closed. Efforts to improve media freedom through legislative reform, technical improvement and private sector investment, were undermined by the continued imprisonment of journalists for their legitimate work. Defamation remained a criminal offence.

Laws on 'genocide ideology' and 'sectarianism'

Vaguely worded laws on "genocide ideology" and "sectarianism" were misused to criminalize legitimate dissent and criticism of the government. A new draft "genocide ideology" law was before parliament.

Journalists

Several media-related laws were approved by parliament and pending promulgation at the year's end.
■ On 5 April, the Supreme Court reduced the prison sentences of Agnes Uwimana Nkusi, editor of the private Kinyarwanda tabloid newspaper *Umurabyo*, and her deputy editor, Saidati Mukakibibi, to four and three years respectively. In February 2011, the women were sentenced to 17 and seven years in prison respectively for publishing opinion pieces criticizing government policies and alleging corruption in the run-up to the 2010 presidential elections. The Supreme Court cleared Agnes Uwimana Nkusi of "genocide ideology" and "divisionism" charges but upheld a conviction for defamation. For both women, the sentence for threatening national security was reduced.

Unfair trial

Victoire Ingabire, President of the United Democratic Forces (FDU-Inkingi), was sentenced to eight years in prison on 30 October. She had returned to Rwanda in January 2010 after 16 years in exile. She had hoped to register FDU-Inkingi prior to the August 2010 presidential elections, before she was first arrested in April 2010.

Despite international scrutiny, the trial was marred by violations of due process. The court failed to test evidence brought by the prosecution. Confessions of two co-accused incriminating Victoire Ingabire were made after a prolonged period of detention in a military camp where Amnesty International has documented allegations of the use of torture to coerce confessions. A defence witness claimed he had been held in military detention with one of the co-accused and alleged that the individual's confession had been forced.

In the build-up to the trial, official statements were made by the Rwandan authorities which posed problems in relation to Victoire Ingabire's presumption of innocence. The freedom of expression charges lacked a clear legal basis and certain charges were based on pieces of imprecise and broad Rwandan legislation punishing "genocide ideology" and "discrimination and sectarianism". The accused was not treated fairly during the trial and was regularly interrupted and subject to hostility.

Freedom of association

Certain political parties had still not been able to register. Members of political opposition parties reported being harassed and intimidated, and some were imprisoned for exercising their right to freedom of association.
■ On 27 April, the Supreme Court upheld charges against Bernard Ntaganda, president of the Ideal Social Party (PS-Imberakuri). He is currently serving a four-year prison sentence after being found guilty on 11 February 2011 of "divisionism" for making public speeches criticizing government policies ahead of the 2010 elections, breaching state security and attempting to plan an "unauthorized demonstration".
■ Eight members of Victoire Ingabire's FDU-Inkingi party – predominantly teachers and students – were arrested in September, after holding a meeting where they reportedly discussed development and education issues. They were charged with inciting insurrection or trouble among the population and remanded in pre-trial detention. One was released before the end of the year.

International justice
International Criminal Tribunal for Rwanda

The International Criminal Tribunal for Rwanda (ICTR) Trial Chamber transferred its first case to Rwanda, that of former Pastor Jean Uwinkindi. Several other cases were also transferred in 2012. Two ICTR staff were assigned to monitor referral cases on a temporary basis, pending agreement on trial monitoring with the African Commission on Human and Peoples' Rights. They were required to file monthly reports through the Registry to the President of the ICTR, or the President of the Mechanism for International Criminal Tribunals, as appropriate.

R

Universal jurisdiction

Judicial proceedings against genocide suspects took place in Belgium, Finland, Germany and the Netherlands.

■ The European Court of Human Rights rejected Sylvère Ahorugeze's appeal against the Swedish government's decision to extradite him to Rwanda. He remained in Denmark at the year's end.

■ Charles Bandora's extradition to Rwanda was pending. His case had passed through all stages of Norway's criminal justice system. His final appeal was pending.

Impunity for war crimes and crimes against humanity

The authorities did not investigate or prosecute allegations of war crimes and crimes against humanity committed by the Rwandan army in Rwanda and also the DRC, as documented in the UN Mapping Report.

Refugees and asylum-seekers

The implementation of a cessation clause for Rwandan refugees, invoked on 31 December 2011 by UNHCR, the UN refugee agency, was delayed until June 2013. Under the clause, refugees who left Rwanda up to and including 1998 would lose their status, but should be interviewed to establish any individual grounds for continued fear of persecution in Rwanda.

Prisoners of conscience

■ Charles Ntakirutinka, a former Rwandan government minister and prisoner of conscience, was released on 1 March after serving a 10-year sentence following an unfair trial. He was arrested in April 2002 during a crackdown before the 2003 presidential elections, and convicted of "inciting civil disobedience" and "association with criminal elements".

Amnesty International visits/reports

🚗 Amnesty International delegates visited Rwanda in February, March and June. An Amnesty International observer monitored Victoire Ingabire's trial in March and April.

📄 Rwanda: Briefing to the UN Committee Against Torture (AFR 47/003/2012)

📄 Rwanda: Shrouded in secrecy – illegal detention and torture by military intelligence (AFR 47/004/2012)

📄 Rwanda urged to end clampdown on dissent as Charles Ntakirutinka released (PRE01/113/2012)

📄 Rwanda must investigate unlawful detention and torture by military intelligence (PRE01/464/2012)

📄 Rwanda: Ensure appeal after unfair Ingabire trial (PRE01/523/2012)

SAUDI ARABIA

KINGDOM OF SAUDI ARABIA
Head of state and government: King Abdullah bin Abdul Aziz
Al Saud

The authorities severely restricted freedoms of expression, association and assembly and clamped down on dissent. Government critics and political activists were detained without trial or sentenced after grossly unfair trials. Women were discriminated against in law and practice and inadequately protected against domestic and other violence. Migrant workers were exploited and abused. Sentences of flogging were imposed and carried out. Hundreds of people were on death row at the end of the year; at least 79 people were executed.

Background

In January, the head of the religious police said he would issue guidelines advising his forces that they are not empowered to arrest or interrogate Saudi Arabian citizens or to attend trials.

Prince Salman bin Abdul Aziz Al Saud became Crown Prince following the death of Prince Naif bin 'Abdul Aziz Al Saud in June.

Also in June, the semi-official National Society for Human Rights published its third report on human rights and urged the government to end discrimination; to strengthen the regulatory powers of the Shura Council; to require arresting and detaining authorities to comply with the Code of Criminal Procedure and to hold to account those who do not comply.

Repression of dissent

The authorities continued to clamp down on people calling for political and other reform as well as human rights defenders and activists. Some were detained without charge or trial; others faced prosecution on vague charges such as "disobeying the ruler".

■ Dr Abdullah bin Hamid bin Ali al-Hamid and Mohammad bin Fahad bin Muflih al-Qahtani, co-founders of the Saudi Civil and Political Rights Association (ACPRA), an unlicensed NGO, were charged with threatening state security, inciting disorder and undermining national unity, disobeying and breaking allegiance to the ruler, and questioning the integrity of officials. The charges appeared to arise from their involvement in setting up ACPRA, calling for protests, and criticizing the judiciary for accepting as evidence "confessions" allegedly made under torture or other duress. Their trial began in June but had not concluded by the end of the year.

■ Mohammed Saleh al-Bajady, another of ACPRA's co-founders, was sentenced to four years' imprisonment in April and banned from travelling abroad for five years. He was convicted of communicating with foreign bodies to "undermine security" and other offences, including harming the state's image through the media, calling for protests by detainees' families and possessing banned books. He went on hunger strike for five weeks to protest against his imprisonment.

■ Fadhel Maki al-Manasif, a human rights activist detained since October 2011, went on trial in April charged with sedition, "inciting public opinion against the state", "disrupting order by participating in marches" and other offences, apparently because of his human rights activism. His trial was ongoing at the end of the year.

■ Human rights defender and writer Mikhlif bin Daham al-Shammari went on trial before the Specialized Criminal Court in March. He faced an array of charges, including seeking to damage Saudi Arabia's reputation in the international media, communicating with suspect organizations and accusing state organs of corruption. He had been released on bail in February after a year and a half in detention. He was arrested after he publicly criticized alleged prejudice by Sunni religious scholars against the Shi'a minority and their beliefs. In April, the authorities banned him from leaving Saudi Arabia for 10 years. His trial was continuing at the end of the year.

■ Khaled al-Johani, the only man to reach the site of a planned demonstration in Riyadh to mark a "Day of Rage" on 11 March 2011, was released on 8 August and was believed to be no longer facing trial. His exact legal status was unclear. He was allowed out of prison for a two-day family visit in July.

Counter-terror and security
A draft anti-terrorism law was reported to have been amended by the Shura Council but it had not been enacted by the end of the year.

The authorities continued to hold in incommunicado detention suspected members and supporters of al-Qa'ida and Islamist groups. Thousands of security suspects arrested in previous years were believed to be held in virtual secrecy with no means to challenge their continuing imprisonment and without access to lawyers or doctors. Some were not permitted to see or communicate with their families. The authorities said hundreds were put on trial but provided no details, leading to concerns that such trials were secret and unfair.

There were several protests by family members of security detainees. On 23 September, scores of people, including women and children, gathered in the desert near al-Tarfiya prison in Qassim Province to call for the release of their detained relatives. They were surrounded by security forces and forced to remain without food or water until the following day, when a number of men among the protesters were arrested, beaten and detained.

In October, the authorities said that anyone who demonstrated would face prosecution and be "firmly dealt with" by members of the security forces. Despite this, relatives of security detainees held a protest outside the Saudi Arabian Human Rights Commission in Riyadh. The security forces cordoned off the area and arrested at least 22 women, eight children and more than 20 men when they refused to disperse. One man was beaten and one woman kicked by security officials. Most were released after they agreed to sign undertakings not to protest again; however, some 15 men continued to be detained.

Discrimination – Shi'a minority
There were protests in Eastern Province by members of the minority Shi'a community, who alleged long-term discrimination on account of their faith. The security forces were alleged to have used excessive force at times against the protesters. Some 10 protesters were reportedly shot dead and others injured by security forces, during or in connection with the Eastern Province protests. The authorities said the deaths and injuries occurred when security forces were confronted by people with firearms or Molotov cocktails, but such incidents were not independently investigated. Some 155 men and 20 children were believed to be held without charge in connection with the protests at the end of the year.

■ On 26 September, two men were killed and a third was fatally injured in unclarified circumstances when security forces raided a house in search of a man

S

wanted for allegedly "stirring up unrest". No official investigation into the deaths was known to have been held.

Several men were reportedly sentenced to flogging for participating in the Eastern Province protests and others banned from travelling abroad. Shi'a clerics who publicly advocated reform or criticized the government were detained and in some cases charged with disobeying the ruler and other offences.

■ Sheikh Nimr Baqir al Nimr, a frequent critic of discrimination against the Shi'a minority, was arrested on 8 July in al-Awwamiya in Eastern Province, apparently because of comments he allegedly made following the death of the Interior Minister Prince Naif bin 'Abdul Aziz Al Saud. He received a gunshot wound in disputed circumstances at the time of his arrest. The authorities said he was an "instigator of sedition" who was shot at a checkpoint as he and others resisted arrest and sought to flee; however, his family said he was alone and unarmed when detained. He was still detained without charge or trial at the end of the year.

■ Sheikh Tawfiq al-Amer, a Shi'a Muslim cleric and advocate of reform detained since August 2011, was charged with incitement against the authorities, slandering the Council of Senior Scholars and other offences in August. He was sentenced in December to three years' imprisonment followed by a five-year travel ban and a ban on giving sermons and speeches.

Torture and other ill-treatment

Torture and other ill-treatment of detainees and sentenced prisoners were reported to be common, widespread and generally committed with impunity. Reported methods included beating, suspension by the limbs and sleep deprivation. Those tortured reportedly included detained protesters, who were held incommunicado for days or weeks without charge or trial.

■ Detainees held at al-Hair prison reportedly told their families in August that they were assaulted by prison guards and feared for their lives.

Women's rights

Women continued to face discrimination in law and practice, and were inadequately protected against domestic and other gender-based violence.

For the first time, two Saudi Arabian women were permitted to participate in the Olympic Games, under conditions relating to the Islamic dress code and the presence of male guardians.

Women continued to be required by law to obtain the permission of a male guardian before getting married, travelling, undertaking paid employment or enrolling in higher education. Saudi Arabian women with foreign spouses, unlike their male counterparts, could not pass on their nationality to their children. Women continued to be prohibited from driving, although the "Women2Drive" campaign by local activists challenged the ban. Discriminatory rules relating to marriage and divorce appeared to cause some women to remain trapped in violent and abusive relationships.

Migrant workers' rights

Migrant workers, who comprised around a third of the population, were inadequately protected by labour laws and were vulnerable to exploitation and abuse by employers. Women domestic workers in particular were at risk of sexual violence and other abuses.

Cruel, inhuman or degrading punishments

The courts continued to impose sentences of flogging as a principal or additional punishment for many offences. At least five defendants were sentenced to flogging of 1,000 to 2,500 lashes. Flogging was carried out in prisons.

Death penalty

The courts continued to impose death sentences for a range of drugs and other offences. Several hundred prisoners were believed to be on death row; some for many years. At least 79 prisoners were executed, mostly in public. They included at least 52 Saudi Arabians and at least 27 foreign nationals, including at least one woman. Some prisoners were executed for non-violent offences.

■ Rizana Nafeek, a Sri Lankan domestic worker, remained on death row. She was convicted in 2007 of murdering her employer's baby when aged 17, at a trial in which she had no defence lawyer. She confessed during police questioning, possibly under duress, and later withdrew her confession.

■ Suliamon Olyfemi, a Nigerian national, remained on death row having been sentenced to death after an unfair trial in 2004.

■ Qassem bin Rida bin Salman al-Mahdi, Khaled bin Muhammad bin Issa al-Qudaihi and Ali Hassan Issa al-Buri, all Saudi Arabian nationals, appeared to be at risk of execution after exhausting all appeals against their convictions on drugs charges. They reportedly had no access to a lawyer while held in pre-trial detention following arrest in July 2004; at least one was reportedly coerced to "confess". Ali Hassan Issa al-Buri was initially sentenced to 20 years in prison and 4,000 lashes but was sentenced to death when the General Court in Qurayyat rejected a Court of Cassation ruling that the sentences on the other two should be commuted. All three death sentences were confirmed by the Supreme Judicial Council in 2007.

Amnesty International visits/reports

🚗 Amnesty International continued to be effectively barred from visiting Saudi Arabia to conduct human rights research.

📰 Saudi Arabia's 'Day of Rage': One year on (MDE 23/007/2012)

📰 Saudi Arabia: Dissident voices stifled in the Eastern Province (MDE 23/011/2012)

SENEGAL

REPUBLIC OF SENEGAL
Head of state: **Macky Sall (replaced Abdoulaye Wade in April)**
Head of government: **Abdoul Mbaye (replaced Souleymane Ndéné Ndiaye in April)**

The unrest which marked the pre-election period in January and February resulted in serious human rights violations, including excessive use of force leading to the death of several protesters; torture and other ill-treatment; and attacks on freedom of expression. In Casamance, in the south, clashes between the army and an armed group intensified at the beginning of the year leading to arrests and targeting of civilians. An agreement was signed between Senegal and the AU to establish a special court to try former Chadian President Hissène Habré.

Background

In January and February, security forces violently repressed opponents to the candidacy for a third term of the outgoing President Wade and used excessive force, leading to several casualties. Despite this unrest, new President Macky Sall was elected in March; the results were not challenged.

In October, representatives of the Senegalese government and members of the Democratic Forces of Casamance Movement (MFDC) met in Rome, Italy, under mediation undertaken by the Catholic community Sant'Egidio.

Excessive use of force

At least six people were killed by security forces during the pre-elections unrest.

■ In January, gendarmes (paramilitary police) used live ammunition against peaceful demonstrators in Podor. Two people were killed: Mamadou Sy and Bana Ndiaye, a woman aged around 60 who was not participating in the protest.

■ In January, Mamadou Diop was killed by a police vehicle during a peaceful demonstration at the Place de l'Obélisque in Dakar. An inquiry was opened but had not concluded by the end of the year.

Torture and other ill-treatment

Several people were tortured and otherwise ill-treated by security forces and at least two of them died in detention, reportedly as a result of torture.

■ In February, Ibrahima Fall was tortured and otherwise ill-treated after being arrested in Tivavouane while returning from a demonstration against President Wade's candidacy. He was tortured by gendarmes who hit him with batons, water hoses and electric cables.

■ In February, Ousseynou Seck died after being tortured in custody. All the police officers implicated were arrested and were awaiting trial at the end of the year.

■ In August, Kécouta Sidibé, a man who was deaf and mute, died reportedly as a result of torture in custody in Kédougou after he was arrested for consuming Indian hemp. In December, the Kaolack Appeal Court declared the deputy commander of the Kédougou gendarmerie guilty of murder and he was arrested. An investigation into the involvement of five other gendarmes was in progress at the end of the year.

Freedom of expression

Political activists and human rights defenders were assaulted and imprisoned for peacefully expressing their opposition to President Wade's candidacy.

■ In January, three journalists were beaten by the police. Two worked for the Senegalese daily Le Populaire, and one for the French news agency, Agence France Presse.

■ In February, security forces prevented members of the Y'en a marre (We are fed up) movement from organizing a sit-in at the Place de l'Obélisque in Dakar

S

and arrested several people. All were released shortly afterwards without charge.

Human rights violations and abuses in Casamance

Several civilians were arrested or targeted as tension escalated between the MFDC and the army.

■ In January, eight people were arrested by the security forces in the village of Affiniam (30km north of Ziguinchor, the main city of the region), reportedly as part of reprisals by the army a few hours after a Senegalese gendarme was killed and three others were injured in the area by alleged armed members of the MFDC. The eight were charged with undermining state security and released without trial in June.

■ In February and March, armed people claiming to be members of the MFDC assaulted and robbed civilians to dissuade them from voting in the Presidential election.

■ In December, eight hostages, including Senegalese soldiers, who had been held for more than a year by armed branches of the MFDC, were released in the Gambia.

International justice – Hissène Habré

In August, an agreement was signed between Senegal and the AU to establish a special court to try former Chadian President Hissène Habré. This court would have jurisdiction to try those responsible for crimes under international law committed in Chad between 1982 and 1990.

On 19 December, the National Assembly adopted a law establishing special chambers within the existing court structure. However, some key elements to the successful conduct of a fair trial had not been set up, such as a programme for protection of victims and witnesses, and an effective mutual legal assistance agreement with other countries, including France and Chad, where victims, witnesses, evidence and assets may be located.

Amnesty International visits/reports

🚗 Amnesty International delegates visited Senegal in February, March and June.

📰 Senegal: The human rights situation – brief overview in the run-up to the presidential election (AFR 49/001/2012)

📰 Senegal: An agenda for human rights – an opportunity not to be missed by the authorities elected in the March 2012 presidential election (AFR 49/004/2012)

SERBIA

REPUBLIC OF SERBIA, INCLUDING KOSOVO
Head of state: Tomislav Nikolić (replaced
        Boris Tadić in May)
Head of government: Ivica Dačić (replaced
        Mirko Cvetković in July)

Prosecutions of Ratko Mladić and Goran Hadžić began at the International Criminal Tribunal for the former Yugoslavia (Tribunal). In Belgrade more than 1,000 Roma were forcibly evicted in April. The Belgrade Pride was again banned in October. In Kosovo, impunity continued for crimes under international law perpetrated by the Kosova Liberation Army (KLA). Violence in the north, inter-ethnic attacks and discrimination against minorities continued.

Background

Following elections in May, a coalition government headed by the Serbian Progressive Party and Socialist Party of Serbia was formed in July, replacing the Democratic Party coalition government.

Both incoming President Nikolić and former President Tadić made statements that genocide had not taken place in Srebrenica.

In March, the European Council confirmed Serbia's candidacy for EU membership, but the European Commission in October recommended no date for opening negotiations, pending Serbia's "constructive participation" in talks on "normalization" of relationships with Kosovo. Talks between the respective Prime Ministers began in October.

International justice

Trials commenced in May and October respectively against former Bosnian Serb General Ratko Mladić and Croatian Serb leader Goran Hadžić, both arrested in Serbia and surrendered to the Tribunal in 2011. Serbian Radical Party leader Vojislav Šešelj, indicted for war crimes and crimes against humanity, was sentenced to two years' imprisonment for contempt of court in June.

Ramush Haradinaj, former Prime Minister of Kosovo and KLA commander, was acquitted at the Tribunal in November on charges of war crimes,

S

following a partial retrial. Along with Idriz Balaj and Lahi Brahimaj, who were also acquitted, he had been indicted for his individual and joint responsibility for a criminal enterprise to mistreat Serb, Roma, Egyptian and Kosovo-Albanian civilians perceived as collaborating with the Serbian authorities or not supporting the KLA. Charges included unlawful detention, ill-treatment, torture and murder.

In December a Swedish appeal court acquitted a former Serbian police officer convicted in January of war crimes in Ćuška/Qyshk in Kosovo in 1999.

Serbia

Crimes under international law

Proceedings continued at the Belgrade Special War Crimes Chamber. Some 37 Serbian defendants were convicted and sentenced in first instance war crimes trials, but only seven new indictments were issued. Some witnesses allegedly were threatened by officials charged with their protection.

At the end of the year, the Appeal Court considered an appeal against the conviction of nine members of the Gnjilane/Gjilan KLA group for war crimes, including the abduction of Serbs, murder and rape. Thirty-four of the victims were still listed as missing.

Following the acquittal of two Croatian generals by the Tribunal Appeals Chamber (see Croatia entry), the War Crimes Prosecutor requested that the Tribunal made available evidence from relevant case files for use in domestic investigations into alleged war crimes against the Serb population in Croatia during Operation Storm in 1995.

Discrimination – Roma

Forced evictions continued in Belgrade.
■ Around 1,000 Roma were forcibly evicted in April from the Belvil settlement by the Belgrade City authorities. Almost half were returned to southern Serbia; many were made homeless. Some Roma returned to Niš had no running water or adequate sanitation until mid-July. Those registered in Belgrade were sent to segregated container settlements on the city's outskirts where they could not find work. The European Commission agreed to fund solid housing for evicted Roma, but the city proposed that the housing be sited on isolated sites, creating racially segregated settlements. In November the Commissioner for Protection of Equality found that the Belgrade City authorities had discriminated against Roma by imposing rules and conditions in their contracts for the containers which were not applied to any other groups, and which resulted in the eviction of 11 families.

Legislative amendments adopted in September potentially reduced discrimination by assisting "legally invisible" people, predominantly Roma, to obtain birth certificates, enabling them to acquire identity documents.

Rights of lesbian, gay, bisexual, transgender and intersex people

In September, a gay man was beaten with a meat-hammer by youths in a homophobic attack in Belgrade. In October, the Prime Minister banned the Belgrade Pride for the second year running on the basis of unspecified security threats. In November, the Appeal Court revoked the conviction and ordered the retrial of Mladen Obradović, leader of the right-wing organization "Obraz", who had been sentenced in March to 10 months' imprisonment for inciting discrimination against the 2009 Belgrade Pride.

Refugees and migrants

The government took further measures to intensify border controls which denied people, predominantly Roma, the right to leave the country. Between January and October, 15,135 Serbian citizens, mostly Roma, claimed asylum in the EU. In October, six EU member states urged the European Council to consider measures to reduce their number. Austria and Switzerland introduced an accelerated determination procedure for Serbian asylum-seekers.

More than 1,700 individuals, including unaccompanied minors, sought asylum in Serbia. None was granted asylum in a process that failed to provide a fair assessment of individual protection needs. In September, more than 100 asylum-seekers camped outside the Bogovađa asylum centre in the absence of any other accommodation.

Kosovo

In January, the European Commission launched a visa liberalization dialogue with Kosovo. In September, the International Steering Group declared the end of Kosovo's supervised independence. The European Council in December called for progress on the rule of law, minority protection, freedom of expression and co-operation with EU-led Police and Justice mission (EULEX).

In June, the mandate of a downsized EULEX was extended to 2014. EULEX retained responsibility for the investigation and prosecution of crimes under international law, organized crime and corruption; and witness protection.

The situation in the north

Both EULEX and the Kosovo authorities continued to assert their authority in the three predominantly Serbian northern municipalities. Armed attacks by Serbs opposed to the Kosovo government's authority over the Serb majority municipalities took place in Mitrovica/Mitrovicë when the Kosovo government opened municipal offices in July.

At the border posts, established in 2011 by the Kosovo authorities and controlled by EULEX and the Kosovo Force (KFOR), there were almost daily violent incidents, as Kosovo Serbs continued to protest against the control of the border with Serbia. KFOR personnel and civilians, mostly Kosovo Serbs, were wounded, and at least one Kosovo Police officer was fatally injured, in the repeated clashes. Border crossings, negotiated between Kosovo and Serbia under the Integrated Border Management agreement, opened in December.

■ On the Serbian religious holiday of Vidovdan in June, the Kosovo Police removed Serbian flags and other insignia including T-shirts from Serbian men travelling across the border. Many Kosovo Police and at least four Serbs were reportedly injured in the ensuing violence. Sixteen children returning from Vidovdan celebrations were injured when their bus was attacked by ethnic Albanians in Pristina.

In December, a Serbian government proposal for autonomy for the north was dismissed by Prime Minister Thaçi.

Crimes under international law

EULEX recruited two additional prosecutors for the investigation and prosecution of war crimes. The 2011 Law on Witness Protection, which entered into force in September, was not implemented before the end of the year.

In May, the former Minister of Transport and KLA leader Fatmir Limaj and three others were acquitted of war crimes at Klečka/Kleçkë prison camp in 1999, including ordering the torture and killing of Kosovo Serb and Albanian civilians. Six other defendants were acquitted in March. In November, after the Supreme Court overturned the May verdict, ordering a retrial, EULEX arrested Fatmir Limaj and three other defendants. The Prime Minister immediately challenged EULEX's right to arrest them, but they remained in detention pending trial at the end of the year.

Two Kosovo Serbs suspected of raping Kosovo Albanian women in April 1999 were arrested in September, under the first indictment issued in Kosovo for war crimes of sexual violence.

Enforced disappearances and abductions

The Special Investigative Task Force established by the EU continued to investigate allegations that the KLA had abducted Serbs and subsequently transferred them to Albania, where they were tortured, murdered and some allegedly had their organs removed for trafficking.

In December the Human Rights Advisory Panel (HRAP), established to decide on alleged human rights violations by the UN Interim Administration Mission in Kosovo (UNMIK), considered three complaints, in which they decided that UNMIK had violated the right to life of Kosovo Serbs abducted following the 1999 armed conflict, by failing to conduct an effective investigation.

By September, the Department of Forensic Medicine had exhumed the remains of 20 individuals; 51bodies, (including 33 ethnic Albanians and 18 Kosovo Serbs), identified by DNA analysis, were returned to their families for burial. Exhumations concluded at Zhilivoda/Žilivoda mine, thought to contain remains of 25 Kosovo Serbs; however no bodies were found.

The Kosovo Government Commission for Missing Persons largely failed to implement the 2011 Law on Missing Persons. Relatives demanded the authorities address the issue of missing persons in talks with Serbia.

Excessive use of force

Kosovo Police used excessive force at demonstrations against government policy organized by the political movement Vetëvendosje in January and October.

Freedom of expression

Physical attacks on journalists continued. Journalists and government officials protested against the retention of restrictions on constitutional rights to freedom of expression in the revised Criminal Code, which criminalized defamation and provided for the imprisonment of journalists who refused to reveal their sources. In May, Kosovo President Atifete Jahjaga refused to approve the Code and returned it to the National Assembly; a law removing the articles was adopted in October.

In December, the launch of a magazine examining heterosexual and same-sex sexuality in Western Balkans was disrupted by a violent homophobic attack. The following day, the office of Libertas, an LGBTI NGO, was attacked.

Discrimination

Roma faced widespread and persistent discrimination. According to the OSCE, implementation of the Kosovo Action Plan on the Implementation of the Strategy for the Integration of Roma, Ashkali and Egyptian Communities was hampered by a lack of funding, co-ordination and relevant data.

In August, the HRAP declared partially admissible a complaint by 147 Roma, that UNMIK had violated their right to health by allowing them to remain in lead-contaminated camps for more than 10 years. The majority had been resettled, but children affected by lead-poisoning lacked adequate health care. The Roma had been denied compensation in a separate UN process.

Refugees and asylum-seekers

According to UNHCR, the UN refugee agency, 997 members of minority communities voluntarily returned to Kosovo; another 489 individuals were induced to return. Some 1,997 individuals were forcibly repatriated, mainly from the EU, including 680 from groups considered in need of international protection. Barriers to their sustainable return persisted. Municipalities lacked the political will, structures and financial resources to reintegrate returnees. Roma in particular received little assistance with reintegration and were unable to access civil registration, education, health, housing, employment and social welfare.

Just over 300 Serbs returned voluntarily to Kosovo. Violent and other attacks on returning Kosovo Serbs continued. In Klinë/Klina municipality, returnees received threatening letters; two houses recently reconstructed for Serb returnees were burned down.
■ In July, Ljiljana and Milovan Jevtić were shot dead in the village of Talinovc i Muhaxherëve/ Muhadzer Talinovac, to which they had returned in 2004. An investigation was opened.

Amnesty International visits/reports

🚌 Amnesty International delegates visited Serbia in April, June and November.

📓 Kosovo: Time for EULEX to prioritize war crimes (EUR 70/004/2012)

📓 After Belvil: Serbia needs new laws against forced eviction (EUR 70/015/2012)

SIERRA LEONE

REPUBLIC OF SIERRA LEONE

Head of state and government: Ernest Bai Koroma

The former President of Liberia, Charles Taylor, was convicted and sentenced for crimes committed in Sierra Leone during the 11-year armed conflict. The country held its third elections since the end of the conflict, which international observers declared were orderly and transparent. The police used unlawful force against unarmed citizens. The government moved closer to abolition of the death penalty. Agreements between the government and corporations were not transparent and communities affected by corporate activity were not properly consulted about the potential impacts.

Background

In April, the Special Court for Sierra Leone (SCSL), sitting in The Hague, found former Liberian President Charles Taylor individually responsible for planning and aiding and abetting war crimes and crimes against humanity during Sierra Leone's internal armed conflict. He was found guilty on all 11 counts of the indictment, including use of child soldiers, murder, rape and sexual slavery, and sentenced to 50 years in prison. In July, both the defence and the prosecution entered appeals; a decision was expected in 2013.

Due to an amnesty provision in the Lomé peace accord and the limited mandate of the SCSL, thousands of perpetrators of grave human rights violations during the conflict were never investigated or brought to justice. Tens of thousands of victims and their families were waiting for extensive reparations programmes to be fully implemented.

Sporadic clashes between supporters of the two main political parties occurred in the lead-up to the November general elections, but the process was peaceful overall. President Ernest Bai Koroma from the ruling All People's Congress (APC) was elected for a second term.

The Constitutional Review process was years overdue. The government promised to reinvigorate discussions after the 2012 elections. Two key pieces of legislation – the Freedom of Information Bill and

S

the Gender Equality Bill – were still pending in Parliament by the end of the year. No attempts were made to amend the Public Order Act of 1965, which allows for the imposition of restrictions on freedom of expression.

Death penalty

The government continued to move closer to total abolition of the death penalty, following the establishment of an official moratorium on executions in 2011. At the end of 2012, according to civil society organizations, no inmates remained on death row and no new death sentences were passed.

However, the death penalty was retained in law for treason and aggravated robbery, and was mandatory for murder.

Justice system

In May, the Legal Aid Act was passed but was not implemented by the end of the year. The justice system continued to suffer from lack of capacity and resources. Civil society organizations reported that many people could not make use of bail provisions as they were often asked to pay bribes, at the police station or court, before bail would be granted.

According to civil society organizations, imprisonment for debt, under fraudulent conversion and other charges, and loitering, were commonplace. Women attempting to make a living through trade or microfinance institutions were at risk of imprisonment for debt. A lack of legal expertise within the criminal justice system and corruption were found to be serious underlying problems. Without access to lawyers, many individuals remained in prison for extended periods.

Constant adjournments, indictment delays, missing case files and shortage of magistrates contributed to lengthy pre-trial detention and prison overcrowding.

Police and security forces

In January, it was leaked to the press that the Sierra Leone police had received a shipment, worth several million dollars, of arms which they had purchased, including small arms, ammunition and grenade launchers. The shipment, ahead of the November elections, alarmed national and international actors. Members of the UN Security Council visited the country in May and raised this issue with the government, who gave assurances that some of the

weapons were transferred to the armed forces.

■ In April, police killed an unarmed woman, Musu Conteh, and injured at least 11 others when workers at a mining company held a peaceful demonstration against poor working conditions and remuneration. The Human Rights Commission of Sierra Leone investigated the incident and released its findings in September which included recommendations for criminal investigations and prosecutions. The government initiated a Coroner's Inquest into the killing but the investigation had not concluded by the end of the year. No one was held to account.

■ In June, police shot and killed Alieu Sonkoh and Ishmael Kargbo-Sillah in Wellington. A third man was seriously injured. According to the families and community members who witnessed the incident, the unarmed men were part of a neighbourhood watch group who were in the area where police were looking for a vehicle. The President visited the community and set up a Coroner's Inquest, which closed in July. The results of the investigation had not been made public by the end of the year.

■ In June, a motorcyclist was shot and killed by police in Goderich when he failed to stop at a police checkpoint. One officer was arrested and charged with murder. The trial continued at the end of the year.

Civil society groups called for an effective independent oversight mechanism to investigate complaints and hold the police to account.

Right to health

The government made some progress towards ensuring that the Free Health Care Initiative (FHCI), launched in 2010, became a reality for pregnant women and girls, lactating women and girls, and children aged under five. In June, the government passed the National Pharmaceutical Procurement Unit Act to monitor and regulate the supply chain of drugs and medical equipment. Health staff continued to report problems in receiving essential supplies.

Challenges remained in implementing the FHCI. Health facilities continued to charge fees for health care services that were intended to be free. A toll-free line, set up to enable people to make complaints if they did not receive the care to which they were entitled, was set up but the process was subject to delays and inefficiencies.

The overall budget for the health sector was reduced from 11% to 7.4% in 2012, or just half of the

S

15% recommended by the Abuja Declaration on health funding.

Women's and girls' rights

In August, the Sexual Offences Act was passed but had not been enacted by the end of the year. Discriminatory provisions remained under Section 27(4)(d) of the Constitution, in relation to adoption, marriage, divorce, burial, devolution of property on death, or other interests of personal law.

The level of violence against women and girls remained high and harmful traditional practices, such as early marriage and female genital mutilation, continued.

Corporate accountability

Land use agreements between communities, corporations and the government greatly favoured multinational corporations over local communities. Tracts of land were given over by traditional chiefs to companies with little or no adequate consultation with affected communities. Land agreements were often not available in local languages or made accessible for non-literate people. Community members and civil society organizations that spoke out in favour of corporate accountability and transparency faced harassment and intimidation.

In April, farmers, civil society organizations and activists gathered in Freetown to demand a review of all recent land deals. They called on the government to institute measures to ensure that deals between communities and multinational corporations were fair and transparent.

Amnesty International visits/reports

🚗 Amnesty International delegates visited Sierra Leone in April/May and September.

📄 Sierra Leone: Briefing on the events in Bumbuna (AFR 51/004/2012)

📄 Seven-point human rights agenda for candidates in Sierra Leone's 2012 elections (AFR 51/005/2012)

📄 Taylor verdict sends message that no one is above the law (PRE01/226/2012)

SINGAPORE

REPUBLIC OF SINGAPORE
Head of state: Tony Tan Keng Yam
Head of government: Lee Hsien Loong

Singapore took steps to roll back the mandatory death penalty, but the media remained tightly controlled and dissidents continued to face political repression. Laws on arbitrary detention and judicial caning remained.

Death penalty

The government stated in July that it would review laws on the mandatory death penalty for murder and drug trafficking. In October, the government proposed amendments which would allow for discretionary sentencing in some drug trafficking cases, including where the suspect acted only as a courier or co-operated substantively with the Central Narcotics Bureau. Moreover, the Appellate Court would be required to review the legality of each death sentence before execution.

The government stated that executions were deferred during this review. There were at least 32 people on death row by the end of the year.

Torture and other ill-treatment

Judicial caning – a practice amounting to torture or other ill-treatment – continued as a punishment for a wide range of criminal offences.

Drug traffickers sentenced to life imprisonment instead of the mandatory death penalty would be liable to caning under proposed amendments to the Misuse of Drugs Act.

Freedoms of expression and assembly

Opposition activists, including former prisoners of conscience, continued to voice their opinions online, in books and in public meetings, but repression of political dissidents was widespread.

■ In May, Robert Amsterdam, a Canadian human rights lawyer representing the Singapore Democratic Party and its leader Dr Chee Soon Juan, was denied entry to Singapore, thereby infringing his client's right of access to his lawyer.

S

■ In July, the president of US Yale University's new campus in Singapore told the *Wall Street Journal*, a US newspaper, that students would not be allowed to organize political protests. Under the UN Guiding Principles on Business and Human Rights, this policy put the university's governing body, the Yale Corporation, at odds with its responsibility to avoid causing adverse impacts on human rights, including freedom of expression and assembly.

■ In September, former Prime Ministers Lee Kuan Yew and Goh Chok Tong accepted a settlement of US$30,000 from Singapore Democratic Party leader Dr Chee Soon Juan, allowing him to avoid bankruptcy and later, travel abroad and contest the next election. In August, for the first time in many years, his books were made available in local bookstores.

SLOVAKIA

SLOVAK REPUBLIC
Head of state: Ivan Gašparovič
Head of government: **Robert Fico (replaced Iveta Radičová in April)**

Discrimination against Roma persisted. The European Court of Human Rights held that a hospital had forcibly sterilized a Romani girl in violation of her human rights. Forced evictions of Roma were reported throughout the country.

Background

In September, the office of the Deputy Prime Minister for Human Rights and National Minorities was disestablished. Responsibility for human rights protection and the prevention of discrimination was entrusted instead to the Ministry of Foreign and European Affairs and the Ministry of Interior.

Discrimination – Roma

The government made little progress in eliminating systemic discrimination against Roma. In May, the UN Committee on Economic, Social and Cultural Rights (CESCR) criticized Slovakia's failure to take measures to combat discrimination against Roma in education, employment, health and housing.

Right to education

The CESCR concluded that segregation of Romani children in schools continued.

■ Some of the Romani children who had been placed in Roma-only classes in a primary school in Levoča were transferred back to mixed classes. However, the school continued to run Roma-only classes. The segregated classes were established in September 2011 as a result of pressure on the school from non-Roma parents.

■ In October, the Regional Court in Prešov in eastern Slovakia held on appeal that the primary school in the town of Šarišské Michaľany had violated anti-discrimination legislation by placing Romani children in separate classes.

Housing rights

The authorities continued to forcibly evict inhabitants of informal Romani settlements throughout Slovakia and failed to provide access to basic services.

■ In May, local authorities in the town of Vrútky demolished several unauthorized Romani homes built on municipal land. As a result, some people were made homeless. Some of the evicted children were reportedly taken away from their parents by social services and placed in a shelter.

■ On 22 October, the inhabitants of an informal settlement near Prešov were forcibly evicted and forced to demolish their own homes. Beforehand, the mayor had announced the eviction on his Facebook page, and left a message for the Government Plenipotentiary for Roma Communities, asking him to look after "his flock".

■ An informal Romani settlement of about 150 people in the city of Košice was demolished on 31 October. Reportedly, only four people accepted temporary accommodation. Residents said they had lived in the settlement for up to 12 years. The mayor of the city claimed that the demolition was carried out as a "cleanup of illegal landfill" as the houses of the Roma houses were in fact "constructed of garbage material".

Enforced sterilization of Romani women

The European Court issued two further judgements in cases of forced sterilizations of Romani girls and women in the early 2000s. It held that sterilizations without full and informed consent amounted to a violation of the women's right not to be subjected to inhuman or degrading treatment, as well as a violation of their right to respect for private and family life.

Following the judgements, the NGO Centre for Civil and Human Rights (Poradňa) criticized the government for failing to investigate all the alleged cases of enforced sterilizations and to apologize and offer compensation to all victims.

Torture and other ill-treatment

Slovakia was criticized for forcibly returning people to countries where they risked torture or other ill-treatment.

■ The European Court of Human Rights found in May that Slovakia had violated the rights of Mustafa Labsi, by disregarding an interim measure issued by the Court. Slovakia had forcibly returned Mustafa Labsi to Algeria in 2010, where he was at risk of ill-treatment and of the violation of his right to an effective remedy.

■ In June, the European Court of Human Rights issued interim measures against the extradition of Aslan Achmetovich Yandiev to the Russian Federation, where he was accused of being a member of an armed group. Aslan Yandiev alleged that before escaping, he had been tortured by the Russian police. In June, while his request for asylum in Slovakia was pending, the Slovak Supreme Court held that the Russian prosecutor's request for Aslan Yandiev's extradition was admissible. The European Court blocked the extradition on the basis that it would expose him to the risk of torture. In August, the Slovak Constitutional Court accepted the complaint against the extradition decision, stating that no extradition could be carried out while his asylum application was pending.

Rights of lesbian, gay, bisexual, transgender and intersex people

In October, the government established a new Committee for the rights of LGBTI people within its Council for Human Rights. The role of the Committee is to monitor the compliance of the Slovak authorities with the international human rights treaties.

Amnesty International visits/reports

🚌 Amnesty International delegates visited Slovakia in March, June and November.

📘 Slovakia: Briefing to the UN Committee on Economic, Social and Cultural Rights, 48th session, May 2012 (EUR 72/001/2012)

SLOVENIA

REPUBLIC OF SLOVENIA

Head of state: Borut Pahor (replaced Danilo Türk in December)
Head of government: Janez Janša (replaced Borut Pahor in February)

The authorities failed to restore the rights of people whose permanent residency status was unlawfully revoked in 1992. Discrimination against Roma continued.

Discrimination

The "erased"

Former permanent residents of Slovenia originating from other former Yugoslav republics, whose legal status was unlawfully revoked in 1992 (known as the "erased"), continued to be denied restoration of their rights. Past legislative initiatives failed to provide them with reparation for the violations of economic, social and cultural rights they suffered as a result, or to guarantee their access to these rights in future. The authorities also failed to present any new measures to fully restore their rights.

■ On 26 June, the Grand Chamber of the European Court of Human Rights ruled in the pilot case *Kuric v. Slovenia* that the "erasure" and its consequences constituted a violation of the applicants' rights to family and private life and to effective legal remedy. The Grand Chamber also found that the applicants had suffered discrimination in relation to these rights, and set a one-year deadline for the creation of a domestic compensation scheme for victims. By the end of the year, there was no indication that the authorities had made efforts to set up such a scheme.

Roma

The government again failed to put in place adequate mechanisms to monitor discriminatory practices against Roma, or to establish a legal and institutional framework to ensure effective remedies for victims of discrimination.

The majority of Roma living in isolated and segregated informal settlements in rural areas continued to be denied access to adequate housing, security of tenure and protection against forced evictions. Many also remained without access to

S

public services, including access to water for everyday needs, which often had to be sourced from polluted streams, and public taps at petrol stations and cemeteries.

■ In July, the national Ombudsperson issued a special report on the situation of Roma in the south-east of the country. The Ombudsperson called on the authorities to immediately ensure access to water and sanitation for Roma by amending the relevant legislation. During the process to formally adopt the recommendations, the parliament rephrased and considerably weakened some of them.

■ In September, the Governmental Commission for the Protection of the Roma Community concluded that the Roma Act should be amended. Initial discussions focused on the need to include measures to provide access to basic public services.

SOMALIA

SOMALI REPUBLIC

Head of state: Hassan Sheikh Mohamud (replaced Sheikh
                     Sharif Sheikh Ahmed in September)
Head of government: Abdi Farah Shirdon Saaid (replaced
                     Abdiweli Mohamed Ali in October)
Head of Somaliland Republic: Ahmed Mohamed Mahamoud
                     Silanyo

Armed conflict continued between pro-government forces, the African Union Mission in Somalia (AMISOM) and the Islamist armed group al-Shabab, in southern and central Somalia. Pro-government forces took control of a number of key towns from al-Shabab, including the port of Kismayo. Political transition ended the mandate of the Transitional Federal Government (TFG). A new parliament was selected in August, a new president was appointed in September and a new prime minister in October. Thousands of civilians were killed, injured or displaced by armed conflict and generalized violence. Aid agency access remained constrained by fighting, insecurity and restrictions imposed by parties to the conflict. Eighteen journalists were killed; others were attacked, harassed and forced into exile. Humanitarian and human rights workers

also remained targets for abuses. Armed groups continued to forcibly recruit people, including children, and to abduct, torture and unlawfully kill people. Serious human rights abuses, including war crimes, remained unpunished. In Somaliland, freedom of expression deteriorated, and one journalist was killed.

Background

The TFG and AMISOM remained in control of Somalia's capital, Mogadishu. Clashes with al-Shabab continued throughout the year, but there were fewer reported incidents and civilian casualties. Al-Shabab lost control of a number of key towns, including Baidoa, Afgoye, Merka and Kismayo, but remained in control of large parts of the countryside. Insecurity remained high. Civilians were at risk of indiscriminate fire, direct targeting and suicide attacks.

In July, Kenyan troops were formally incorporated into AMISOM, following their intervention in October 2011. International support for government security forces and allied militias continued, despite their lack of accountability for ongoing, serious human rights abuses.

In July, the UN Monitoring Group highlighted continuous violations of Somalia arms embargoes.

In February, the UN declared an end to famine in Somalia, but warned that a humanitarian crisis remained. By the end of 2012, 31% of the population remained in food crisis and required assistance.

In August, the TFG mandate ended. The 20 August deadline set for the TFG to hand over power to a new, more representative government was delayed several times. The parliament was selected in August and a new president appointed in September. A group of 135 elders was chosen to form a National Constituent Assembly (NCA), which would select 275 new MPs and approve Somalia's new Constitution. The NCA approved the Constitution on 1 August. While it did not amend the document, it made a number of recommendations for the new parliament to consider. The public referendum required to approve the Constitution had not taken place by the end of the year. A Technical Selection Committee (TSC) supported the NCA in vetting prospective MPs. Candidates were assessed according to a range of criteria, including consideration of whether they faced allegations of human rights abuses. The High Court overturned the TSC's decision to reject 16 nominated

MPs because they were alleged warlords. In September, parliament elected Hassan Sheikh Mohamud as President. He defeated the incumbent, Sheikh Sharif Sheikh Ahmed, in a run-off by 190-79 votes. In October, the President appointed Abdi Farah Shirdon Saaid as Prime Minister. Parliament approved his nominated Cabinet of Ministers in November. It included Somalia's first woman Minister of Foreign Affairs.

In January, the state of Khatumo was created, claiming to consist of Sool, Sanag and Ayn regions, and claiming affiliation with the Mogadishu-based government. These regions are subject to disputes over control between Somaliland and Puntland. Clashes between Somaliland armed forces and militias allied to Khatumo state displaced thousands of people.

Abuses by parties to the armed conflict
Indiscriminate attacks
Hundreds of civilians were killed or injured by indiscriminate attacks by all parties to the conflict. Mortar attacks decreased, but some reportedly caused civilian casualties. Shooting and in-fighting between different TFG units and militia, particularly in Mogadishu, killed and injured civilians. So did improvised explosive devices and grenades, increasingly set off by al-Shabab or their sympathizers. Al-Shabab claimed responsibility for suicide attacks that killed or injured hundreds of people. Air strikes – some conducted by Kenya – also killed or injured civilians in southern and central Somalia.
■ On 15 January, air strikes in Jilib killed at least seven people, including five children. No one claimed responsibility for the attack.
■ On 28 March, a mortar attack reportedly targeting pro-government militia landed in the Beerta Darawiishta camp for internally displaced people (IDPs) in Mogadishu, killing three people, including a three-year-old child. Eight others were reportedly seriously injured.
■ In April, suicide attacks in Mogadishu and Baidoa killed at least 22 people. At least 10 people, including the two presidents of Somalia's Olympic Committee and its Football Association, were killed in an attack on the capital's newly reopened National Theatre. In Baidoa, an attack close to a busy market killed at least 12 people and wounded more than 30, including 10 journalists.

Direct targeting of civilians
Civilians remained at risk of being directly targeted in attacks and killings in Mogadishu.
■ On 9 November, Malaaq Isaac Uus, one of the traditional elders responsible for selecting new MPs, was shot dead outside a mosque in Waberi district, Mogadishu.

Al-Shabab factions continued to torture and unlawfully kill people they accused of spying or not conforming to their own interpretation of Islamic law. They killed people in public, including by stoning, and carried out amputations and floggings. They also imposed restrictive behavioural codes on women and men.
■ Three men were reportedly shot and killed in public by al-Shabab members in Merka in July. They were accused of spying for the CIA and UK intelligence service MI6, and of being responsible for drone attacks.
■ A woman was abducted and beheaded in August near Baidoa. Days before, al-Shabab had reportedly threatened her to stop her selling tea to government forces in the area.

Extrajudicial executions, arbitrary detention, torture and ill-treatment were reportedly carried out in Baidoa and Beletweyne by militias allied to the government, often in response to ongoing insecurity and attacks by al-Shabab.
■ In August, a deaf man was reportedly shot dead by Ethiopian troops in Baidoa, after he failed to stop when they asked him to.

Child soldiers
Al-Shabab continued to forcibly recruit children before and during military operations. Most were sent to the front line. Militias affiliated to the government were also accused of continuing to recruit and use child soldiers.

In July, the TFG signed an action plan with the UN to end the recruitment and use of children in its own armed forces. Implementation of the plan had not started at the end of 2012, and children remained in their armed forces.

Freedom of expression
Somali journalists and media workers continued to be attacked, harassed and intimidated by parties to the conflict. At least 18 media workers were killed. In November, the President announced the creation of a taskforce to investigate the killings of journalists and

S

identify the perpetrators. However, no one was appointed to the taskforce and no one had been held accountable at the end of 2012. The Puntland authorities also continued to arbitrarily restrict media freedom.

■ On 28 January, Hassan Osman Abdi ("Fantastic"), director of the Shabelle Media Network, was shot by unknown gunmen. He reportedly died on his way to hospital.

■ On 20 September, three journalists – Abdirahman Yasin Ali, director of Radio Hamar; Abdisatar Daher Sabriye, head of news at Radio Mogadishu; and Liban Ali Nur, head of news for Somali National TV – were killed during a suicide attack on a popular restaurant in Mogadishu. At least 12 other people were killed and dozens injured, including four journalists.

■ On 27 September, the body of Abdirahman Mohamed, who worked for a sports website, was found beheaded close to a livestock market in Mogadishu.

■ On 4 March, Ali Ahmed Abdi, a journalist with Radio Galkayo, was shot dead by unidentified gunmen. Farhan Jemiis Abdulle, a reporter for Radio Daljir, was killed on his way home on 2 May 2012 by two unidentified gunmen. Both journalists were killed in the northern part of Galkayo town, controlled by the Puntland authorities.

■ The Puntland Minister of the Interior closed Radio Horseed in October, accusing it of spreading false news to destabilize Puntland. Horseed Media, owner of Radio Horseed, also had access to its website restricted in areas of Puntland.

Internally displaced people, refugees and asylum-seekers

Fighting, insecurity and acute malnutrition continued to displace hundreds of thousands of people. Almost 1.36 million Somalis were internally displaced in 2012, mostly in southern and central Somalia, according to UNHCR, the UN refugee agency.

IDP camps in Mogadishu continued to grow. There were regular reports of aid being diverted by government officials and camp managers, including from the UN Monitoring Group. Poor security also had an impact on service delivery to the camps. Reports of sexual violence against women and girls continued. IDPs were reportedly forcibly evicted from former government buildings to make way for rehabilitation projects, and from camps close to the airport for security reasons.

■ In February, at least 60,000 people fled from the Afgoye corridor, the road linking Mogadishu with Afgoye town, ahead of an anticipated government and AMISOM offensive to retake Afgoye from al-Shabab.

■ In September, over 10,000 people fled Kismayo ahead of an offensive that captured Kismayo port from al-Shabab.

There were over one million Somali refugees in the region, particularly in Ethiopia and Kenya. In November, Ethiopia's Dollo Ado refugee complex became the world's second largest, after Kenya's Dadaab complex – also for Somali refugees.

Restrictions on humanitarian aid

Humanitarian operations continued to be hampered by fighting, general insecurity and access restrictions.

■ In January, al-Shabab announced a ban on the ICRC from operating in areas under its control. It alleged that the ICRC had handed out unfit food and had accused al-Shabab of blocking aid. Al-Shabab announced a ban on Save the Children in March, accusing it of distributing expired food, corruption and failing to comply with al-Shabab's rules for aid agencies. On 8 October, al-Shabab announced via Twitter that it was banning Islamic Relief Worldwide.

■ In May, Ahmed Mohamed Noor, a humanitarian worker, was shot and killed by unidentified gunmen outside a mosque after leaving evening prayers in Mursil, close to Baidoa.

Death penalty

In Mogadishu, official government figures stated that four executions were carried out. However, there were indications that at least five executions were carried out. At least 51 death sentences were passed, following military court trials that lacked guarantees of fairness.

In Puntland, seven death sentences were reported and at least one execution was carried out.

Somaliland

Thousands of people were displaced by fighting in eastern Somalia between the Somaliland Army and militias affiliated to the newly created Khatumo state.

Freedom of expression was increasingly curtailed. Dozens of journalists were arbitrarily arrested and detained. Some reported being beaten in custody. One journalist was killed. A traditional elder was detained for four months for making statements criticizing the government.

■ Ahmed Saakin Farah Ilyas, a journalist for Universal TV, was shot dead by unknown gunmen on 25 October in Las Anod town.

■ Boqor Osman Mohamoud Buurmadow was arrested on 15 March in Hargeisa. He was charged on 24 April with "anti-national activity of a citizen abroad", "subversive or anti-national propaganda" and "continuing offence" for comments he made in the United Arab Emirates criticizing the President of Somaliland's visit to China. On 8 July he was convicted and sentenced to one year's imprisonment for "insulting a public official", but he was released on 18 July.

Amnesty International visits/reports

▨ Somaliland: Release prisoner of conscience (AFR 52/007/2012)

▨ Somalia: Protection of civilians and human rights are critical for stable future (PRE01/100/2012)

▨ Somalia: Attacks against journalists must stop (PRE01/112/2012)

▨ Somalia must end impunity for killing of media workers (PRE01/390/2012)

SOUTH AFRICA

REPUBLIC OF SOUTH AFRICA
Head of state and government: **Jacob G. Zuma**

Police use of excessive force against protesters, suspected extrajudicial executions and torture triggered national concern and some steps were taken towards accountability. Discrimination and targeted violence against asylum-seekers and refugees and barriers to accessing the asylum system increased. Progress was slow in addressing systematic hate-motivated violence based on victims' sexual orientation or gender identity. Despite continued expansion in access to treatment and care for people living with HIV, HIV-related infections remained the main cause of maternal deaths. Human rights defenders remained at risk of harassment and violence.

Background

President Zuma was re-elected as President of the African National Congress (ANC) in December. The leadership elections followed months of tension and incidents of violence between contending factions within the party. Apparent political interference, rivalries and corruption led to increased instability at senior levels within the police and crime intelligence, impacting on the integrity and efficiency of services.

Significant court rulings upheld human rights and protected the independence of the prosecution service.

There were widespread strikes in the mining and farming sectors and protests in poor urban communities over local government corruption, failures in education and other services and working conditions. In October, the government released national census data, which revealed continuing significant racial disparities in household incomes and rates of employment.

South Africa ratified the International Covenant on Economic, Social and Cultural Rights.

Deaths in custody and extrajudicial executions

In April, the Independent Police Investigative Directorate (IPID) Act became operational, making the police liable to criminal charges for failure to co-operate with its investigations. The IPID informed parliament that it had received 720 new cases for investigation of suspicious deaths in custody or in other policing contexts from April 2011 to March 2012.

■ Also in April, a Burundian asylum-seeker, Fistos Ndayishimiye, died while being interrogated by police at his home in KwaZulu-Natal province. Witnesses prevented by police from entering the house reported hearing him screaming for some time. He suffered multiple blunt force injuries to the head and body and severe internal injuries. An investigation was initiated by IPID but had not concluded by year's end.

■ In May, after numerous delays and obstructions, 12 police officers from the former Bellville South Organized Crime Unit were charged in court with the abduction and murder of Sidwell Mkwambi in 2009 and the abduction and alleged torture of Siyabulela Njova, who had been arrested with him. Sidwell Mkwambi's body showed multiple blunt force injuries to his head and body, which were inconsistent with the police account of how he died.

S

■ In June, members of the Cato Manor Organized Crime Unit appeared in Durban magistrate's court, facing a range of charges. After further arrests and court appearances, a total of 30 officers were facing trial at year's end on 116 counts, including racketeering, murder, assault with intent to cause grievous bodily harm and unlawful possession of firearms and ammunition. The offences covered a four-year period from 2008. All of the accused were released on bail pending trial. Families of victims expressed continued fear for their own safety. The arrests resulted from new investigations by the IPID and the police "Hawks" unit.

Excessive use of force

On 16 August, the policing authorities deployed units armed with assault rifles and live ammunition to crush a mine workers' strike at the LONMIN Marikana platinum mine in North West Province. Sixteen miners died at the scene and 14 others at another location where they had fled to escape police fire. There were indications that the majority had been shot while attempting to flee or surrender. Four other miners died later that day from their injuries. The striking miners had been involved in a wage dispute with LONMIN. The scale and visibility of the killings, as well as the growing unrest across the mining sector, caused a national crisis.

The National Commissioner of Police stated at a press conference on 17 August that the police actions were justified on the grounds of self-defence. Nevertheless, President Zuma ordered a judicial commission of inquiry into the circumstances of the deaths and those of 10 other people in the preceding week, including two LONMIN security guards and two police officers.

The start of the Commission, chaired by retired judge Ian Farlam, was delayed by the late issuing of regulations and critical problems affecting the Commission's integrity and accessibility; these included difficulties in securing support for the participation of the families of those killed and funding for legal representation to ensure witnesses were supported and measures taken for their protection. In October, Daluvuyo Bongo, a witness from the National Union of Mineworkers, was shot dead after assisting Commission officials; four witnesses assisting lawyers representing the Association of Mineworkers and Construction Union

and injured miners were allegedly hooded, assaulted and detained after leaving the Commission venue. The Legal Aid Board denied a request for funding to ensure representation for scores of miners injured by police on 16 August and others arrested and allegedly tortured in the aftermath of the shootings.

Before the Commission's closure in December, and its resumption in January, it began to hear evidence on the police actions on and prior to 16 August. Police evidence did not clarify why officers had advanced the operation to disarm and disperse the miners to a stage which relied on police units armed only with lethal force. In addition, a police witness tasked with investigating the scene of the 16 August shootings told the Commission that the scene had been altered; making it impossible for him and other investigators to link any of the deceased miners with weapons they were allegedly carrying before being shot.

■ In October, the South African Human Rights Commission issued a report criticizing the police for using excessive force, which led to the death of Andries Tatane during a community protest in Ficksburg in April 2011. He had been beaten with batons and shot with rubber bullets at close range despite posing no threat to the police or members of the public. In December, the trial of seven police officers charged with Andries Tatane's murder was postponed until March 2013.

Legal, constitutional or institutional developments

In November, the Parliamentary Portfolio Committee on Justice and Constitutional Development adopted amendments to the Prevention and Combating of Torture of Persons Bill for full parliamentary debate in 2013. This followed public hearings on the Bill in September. Legal, human rights and other civil society organizations, as well as Amnesty International, gave evidence and made recommendations to strengthen the draft legislation. While some were accepted, the provisions for reparations for victims of torture fell short of international standards.

In May, the High Court set aside as unlawful the decision by the authorities not to investigate allegations of torture by named perpetrators in Zimbabwe. The Southern African Litigation Centre and the Zimbabwe Exiles Forum brought the application in relation to South Africa's obligations under the Rome Statute of the International Criminal

Court. The High Court ordered the authorities to undertake the necessary investigations.

In July, the Constitutional Court rejected the government's appeal against an earlier High Court judgement, which had declared unlawful its attempts to transfer two Botswanan nationals to Botswana without prior assurances that the death penalty would not be applied. Amnesty International intervened as an *amicus curiae*, or friend of the court, in the Constitutional Court hearing.

Refugees and asylum-seekers

Far-reaching changes to the asylum system continued, with an increasing impact on non-discriminatory access to asylum determination procedures. Documents submitted by the government during court hearings indicated an intention to relocate services to the borders.

The partial or full closure of services at refugee reception offices in Port Elizabeth and Cape Town, as well as the closure of the Johannesburg office in 2011, had an increasing impact on asylum-seekers' and recognized refugees' ability to lodge applications, renew their temporary permits or extend refugee status documents. Testimonies by those affected, in particular the poorest and those with families, showed that they were at risk of fines, detention and direct or constructive *refoulement*.

Challenges to these practices, brought in the High Courts by refugee associations, service providers and human rights lawyers in Port Elizabeth and Cape Town, led to rulings against the Department of Home Affairs in February, May, July and August. Despite this, monitors observed that services continued to be denied at reception offices.

The ANC, at its National Policy Conference in June, adopted recommendations on immigration, including establishing "centres [camps] for asylum-seekers". In December, participants at the ANC's leadership election conference reportedly accepted the recommendations in a resolution on "peace and stability".

During the year, numerous incidents of looting and destruction of shops and displacement of recognized refugees, asylum-seekers and migrants were documented in most of the nine provinces. In one of the worst incidents, beginning in late June, large-scale property destruction occurred in Free State province with almost 700 mainly Ethiopian refugees and asylum-seekers displaced following the looting of their shops. In this and in many other incidents, the police response was slow and in some cases witnesses reported that police were complicit in the violence.

In Limpopo province, police forcibly closed at least 600 small businesses run by asylum-seekers and refugees, as part of operation "Hard Stick". The police raids took place without warning, were indiscriminate and also involved the seizure of trading stock. Some asylum-seekers and refugees were subjected to xenophobic verbal abuse, detention and charged or fined for running their businesses. The resulting loss of livelihood and homes increased their vulnerability to other abuses. In September, 30 displaced Ethiopians were forced to flee a house they had been sheltering in after it was petrol-bombed.

Unlawful, prolonged detentions of undocumented migrants as well as individuals in need of international protection remained a concern. In November, a court application by the South African Human Rights Commission and the NGO, People Against Suffering, Suppression, Oppression and Poverty, prompted the authorities to release 37 immigration detainees who had been held on average for 233 days without a court warrant.

Rights of lesbian, gay, bisexual, transgender and intersex people

Hate-motivated violence, in particular against lesbian women, continued to cause public concern and fear. Between June and November at least seven people, five of them lesbian women, were murdered in what appeared to be targeted attacks based on their sexual orientation or gender identity.

The government and civil society "Task Team", set up in 2011 to prevent further incidents, made slow progress. In September, South Africa's human rights record was assessed under the UN Universal Periodic Review; the government confirmed that a "policy framework on combating hate crime, hate speech and unfair discrimination" was at an "advanced stage of finalization".

In December, Justice Ministry officials publicly condemned hate crimes and gender-based violence as an assault on the right to life and human dignity and acknowledged the "dire need" for public education to combat prejudice based on sexual or gender identity.

Violence against women and children

High levels of sexual violence against women persisted, with police reporting 48,003 cases of rape from April 2011 to March 2012. In the same period, of the 64,514 recorded sexual offences, including rape, women were victims in 40.1% and children in 48.5% of cases. There were renewed calls for the revival of specialized sexual offences courts to address impunity for these crimes.

Women's rights, HIV and maternal health

Access to antiretroviral medication for people living with HIV continued to expand, with two million people on treatment by October. High levels of HIV-infection among pregnant women remained a concern, with KwaZulu-Natal province recording an infection rate of 37.4% among women attending antenatal clinics.

In August, a Ministry of Health-supported report on trends in maternal mortality noted that the deaths of 40.5% of the 4,867 women who died during pregnancy or within 42 days of delivery between 2008 and 2010 were due to non-pregnancy-related infections, in particular HIV. Delays in access to antenatal care and antiretroviral treatment were contributing factors.

Human rights defenders

Harassment of human rights defenders and improper pressure on institutions, including the Office of the Public Protector and senior prosecutors, continued.

■ In January, Ayanda Kota, chairperson of the Unemployed People's Movement, was assaulted by police and unlawfully detained at Grahamstown police station. He had gone to the police station voluntarily following a complaint made against him. Charges against him, including of resisting arrest, were later withdrawn.

■ In July, an environmental rights activist and survivor of torture, Kevin Kunene, was shot dead 10 days after he and three others lodged a complaint of corruption with the Public Protector against the KwaMbonambi Tribal Authority. No suspects had been brought to trial by the end of the year.

■ In October, Social Justice Coalition members Angy Peter and her partner Isaac Mbadu were arrested on a murder charge. Prior to their arrest, they had lodged a complaint against a senior police officer for corruption. Angy Peter was also assisting a judicial Commission of Inquiry, ordered by the Premier of the Western Cape,

into alleged service failures by police. They were released from remand custody before the end of the year but continued to experience harassment. In November, the National Commissioner of Police instituted legal proceedings to halt the inquiry.

Amnesty International visits/reports

🚍 Amnesty International delegates visited South Africa in February/March, May/June, August/September and October/November.

📄 Hidden from view: Community carers and HIV in rural South Africa [photo exhibition] (AFR 53/002/2012)

📄 Key human rights concerns in South Africa: Amnesty International's submission to the UN Universal Periodic Review, May-June 2012 (AFR 53/003/2012)

📄 South Africa: Amnesty International encouraged by initial steps to strengthen protections against torture but condemns continued use of excessive force by police and the failure to uphold refugee rights (AFR 53/005/2012)

📄 South Africa: Shop raids jeopardise safety of refugees (AFR 53/006/2012)

📄 South Africa: Police arrests are a positive step in the fight against impunity (PRE01/297/2012)

📄 Landmark ruling confirms South Africa cannot deport people at risk of death penalty (PRE01/369/2012)

📄 South Africa: Judge must oversee probe into mine protest deaths (PRE01/398/2012)

📄 South Africa: Marikana Inquiry must be enabled to operate effectively (PRE01/456/2012)

SOUTH SUDAN

REPUBLIC OF SOUTH SUDAN
Head of state and government: **Salva Kiir Mayardit**

South Sudan celebrated its first year of independence on 9 July. Post-independence agreements between South Sudan and Sudan on the sharing of oil, security arrangements, border demarcation, and the status of the disputed Abyei area, continued to be negotiated at the end of the year. The Sudan People's Liberation Army (SPLA, South Sudan's armed forces) and the South Sudan Police Service (SSPS) continued to commit human

rights violations with relative impunity. A large influx of refugees and returnees from Sudan continued, in addition to internal displacement.

Background

On 9 January, the President issued a decree appointing members to the National Constitutional Review Commission, mandated to draft a permanent Constitution. It began work in August following the signing into law of the National Elections Act on 6 July.

Implementation of post-independence agreements between South Sudan and Sudan remained outstanding at the end of the year. In February, South Sudan shut down its oil production due to disagreements with Sudan in relation to oil transit fees, resulting in a 98% loss of revenue to South Sudan. The AU Peace and Security Council adopted a road map on 24 April with implementation timelines to resolve outstanding issues. On 2 May the UN Security Council endorsed the roadmap through the adoption of resolution 2046, which called for both countries to reach an overall settlement on disputes within three months. Due to the continued shutdown of oil production, the National Legislative Assembly passed an austerity budget in July aimed at reducing expenditure by 34% for the fiscal year 2012/13. On 27 September, South Sudan and Sudan signed a number of economic, trade and security-related agreements in Addis Ababa, Ethiopia. The agreements allowed for the resumption of oil exports, the establishment of a demilitarized border zone and a cessation of all hostilities. An agreement was reached on the "four freedoms" principles which grant South Sudanese and Sudanese nationals the freedom to reside, move, acquire and dispose of property, and to undertake economic activity in both countries. Further negotiations to resolve the dispute over Abyei and to agree on the precise border between South Sudan and Sudan were required.

In March and April, the government launched a multi-pronged approach to address insecurity due to inter-communal violence which occurred in 2011 and early 2012 in Jonglei State. This included a state-wide civilian disarmament campaign, Operation Restore Peace, launched in March for an undefined period. In Pibor County, civilian disarmament was stalled in September due to attacks by a militia group led by David Yau Yau, who defected from the SPLA for a second time in April 2012.

An Investigation Committee into the Jonglei State Crisis, mandated to investigate those responsible for the inter-communal violence, was also established by the President in March. However, at the end of the year, committee members had not been sworn in and funding had not been provided to enable the committee to operate. In April, the Jonglei Peace Process was re-launched.

In March, the government signed an agreement with Peter Kuol Chol, leader of the armed opposition group the South Sudan Democratic Movement/Army, thus commencing a process to integrate 1,800 of the group's members into the SPLA.

In June, the President signed into force a Refugee Provisional Order, and in July South Sudan acceded to the 1949 Geneva Conventions and their Additional Protocols. However, South Sudan did not become a party to other key international human rights treaties, although the country is considered, under international law, to be bound by those treaties to which Sudan was a party at the time of South Sudan's independence. Critical gaps in national legislation undermined the protection of human rights, including the absence of an adequate legal framework to regulate the National Security Service.

In November, one of the human rights officers with the UN Mission in South Sudan (UNMISS) was ordered to leave the country, in breach of South Sudan's legal obligations under the UN Charter.

Armed conflict

In March, fighting between the SPLA and the Sudan Armed Forces (SAF) erupted around Heglig/Panthou, a disputed oil-producing area considered part of Sudan's Southern Kordofan State, but also claimed by South Sudan's Unity State. On 10 April, South Sudan captured and occupied Heglig/Panthou, and on 15 April fighting spread along the border between the two countries, at Kiir Adem in Northern Bahr El Ghazal. South Sudan ordered the unconditional withdrawal of SPLA troops from the Heglig/Panthou oil field on 20 April, in order to create an environment for talks with Sudan. Indiscriminate aerial bombardments, reportedly by the SAF, occurred in South Sudan's Unity and Northern Bahr El Ghazal states in April and May and in Northern Bahr El Ghazal State in November.

Inter-communal violence

In Jonglei State, a series of attacks, primarily between the two ethnic groups Lou Nuer and Murle, continued to occur. From 23 December 2011 to February 2012, the UN estimated that 888 people were killed. Over 170,000 were internally displaced between late December 2011 and April 2012, and women and children were abducted, property looted and large numbers of cattle were stolen. On 22 August clashes were reported in Pibor County between the SPLA and a militia group led by a former SPLA general, David Yau Yau. On 27 August, at least 24 soldiers were killed in an ambush, reportedly by the same militia group. Due to the threat of attacks by David Yau Yau's group, the SPLA sent additional troops and UNMISS sent additional peacekeepers to Pibor County. In August and September, two of three Médecins Sans Frontières clinics were looted, denying the population in Pibor County access to health care.

Intermittent cattle raids continued in the triangle between Lakes, Unity and Warrap states, across state borders. In late January and early February, fighting occurred on the border between Unity and Warrap states, reportedly due to the failure of government officials to follow through their undertaking to return cattle looted during an attack in September 2011. Over 70 people were reportedly killed during the attacks. In July, fighting between two Dinka sub-clans erupted in Lakes State, with 20 people killed and 20 injured. Further fighting in Lakes State occurred in November with a reported 12 people killed and 20 injured.

Freedom of expression

The operating environment for national and international media workers remained challenging. Security forces harassed national and international media workers, arbitrarily detained journalists and radio presenters, and confiscated equipment. Threats to shut down radio shows deemed critical of the government were also issued by the authorities, and South Sudan's only daily newspaper faced obstacles to its continued publication.

■ On 14 May, Ayak Dhieu Apar, a radio presenter in Rumbek, Lakes State, was arrested and held without charge for five days by the police for hosting a talk show asking "how could the public respect police?" on a state-owned radio station. Callers reportedly criticized the police for poor service delivery and disregard for the

rule of law. Ayak Dhieu Apar was released on bail, despite not being charged with an offence, and police threatened to take her to court for alleged "defamation and tarnishing the image of the police". In early June, Major-General Saed Abdulatif Chawul Lom, Police Commissioner for Lakes State and believed to be behind the arrest of Ayak Dhieu Apar, was removed from his post, reportedly due to his role in her arrest and detention.

■ On 30 May, Bonifacio Taban Kuich, a freelance journalist in Bentiu, Unity State, was arrested by the SPLA and detained in military barracks for six hours for writing an article in the online newspaper *Sudan Tribune*. He also reportedly received death threats from government officials. The article stated that over 500 women whose husbands had been members of the SPLA and had died in combat, had not received the full amount of compensation that they were entitled to from the government.

Lack of accountability

An investigation established in August 2011 into allegations against the former Director of Public Security and Criminal Investigations remained ongoing at the end of the year. The investigation was examining torture, corruption, the creation of illegal detention centres, and the enforced disappearance of John Louis Silvino, an architect at the Ministry of Housing who was last seen on 25 March 2011.

Violations perpetrated by the SPLA and the SSPS Auxiliary Force during the Jonglei state-wide civilian disarmament campaign Operation Restore Peace, launched in March, remained largely unaddressed by the government. These included extrajudicial executions; beating of men, women and children; simulated drowning; sexual violence against women; and looting in towns and villages. Seven arrests directly related to alleged violations during the civilian disarmament campaign were recorded. Of these seven, two soldiers were prosecuted by the end of the year.

Investigations into the abduction and ill-treatment of two civil society activists from the South Sudan Civil Society Alliance remained incomplete.

■ On 4 July, Deng Athuai Mawiir, chairperson of the Alliance, was kidnapped from his hotel in Juba. He was reportedly held and beaten for three days and interrogated about his work on corruption issues in South Sudan.

■ On 22 October, Ring Bulabuk was kidnapped and left in an abandoned graveyard in Juba. Prior to the abduction, he had received threats to stop working on a legal suit against an army general about land-grabbing in Juba.

Other instances of the lack of accountability by security forces were reported during the year.

■ On 9 December, security forces in Wau, Western Bahr El Ghazal State, shot and killed eight and wounded 20 people peacefully demonstrating about the death of a youth activist and the government's decision to move the headquarters of Wau County to Bagari. The Governor announced an immediate investigation but no investigation is known to have been carried out. Members of the security forces involved in the unlawful shootings were not brought to justice while dozens of alleged government opponents, including members of the Legislative Assembly, were detained.

Torture and other ill-treatment

Security forces including the SPLA, National Security Service (NSS) and SSPS harassed, arrested, tortured or otherwise ill-treated people, including UN and NGO staff. Attacks against East African workers in South Sudan also increased.

■ On 13 April, Tabitha Musangi, a Kenyan teacher at the John Garang International School, was shot dead by security forces because her taxi did not stop while guards were pulling down the national flag in Juba.

■ In August, Kenyan pharmacist Joseph Matu died after being tortured in police custody in Torit, Eastern Equatoria State, for allegedly not having a licence to operate.

■ On 31 October, a 17-year-old female student and a male teacher were shot and injured by security forces at Juba Day Secondary School, following protests at the school over the acquisition of school property by a private investor. Police and plain-clothes security personnel reportedly entered the school premises and fired live rounds of ammunition at the protesters. Students and teachers were arbitrarily arrested for participating in the demonstrations and released the same day.

Political prisoners

Members of armed opposition groups remained in detention without access to justice.

■ Armed opposition leader Gabriel Tanginye and his two deputies remained under house arrest in the capital, Juba, where they had been placed in April 2011 following fighting between his forces and the SPLA in Upper Nile and Jonglei. No charges were brought against them by the end of the year.

■ Peter Abdul Rahaman Sule, leader of the opposition group United Democratic Front, remained in detention without charge after more than a year. He was arrested in November 2011 in Western Equatoria State for allegedly recruiting young people.

Refugees and internally displaced people

South Sudanese who had lived in Sudan prior to South Sudan's independence continued to return, with over 120,000 South Sudanese estimated to have done so by the end of the year.

Refugees from Sudan's Southern Kordofan and Blue Nile states continued to flee to South Sudan due to an ongoing conflict between the SAF and the armed opposition group Sudan People's Liberation Movement-North (SPLM-N). From April to June, the number of refugees increased by over 50,000 people in Upper Nile and Unity states due to increased fighting and food shortages in the conflict-affected areas. There was a further influx of refugees from November, with the onset of the dry season. By the end of the year, over 180,000 Sudanese people had sought refuge in South Sudan.

Most of the 110,000 people who fled the disputed Abyei area in May 2011, after SAF overran the town, continued to be displaced in South Sudan and reliant on humanitarian assistance. Jonglei State was the hardest hit by seasonal flooding with over 259,000 people displaced.

Death penalty

More than 200 prisoners were on death row. At least two men were executed on 28 August in Juba Prison, and three men in Wau Prison on 6 September.

Amnesty International visits/reports

🚗 Amnesty International delegates visited South Sudan in March/April and August/September.

▨ "We can run away from bombs, but not from hunger": Sudan's refugees in South Sudan (AFR 65/001/2012)

▨ South Sudan: Overshadowed conflict – arms supplies fuel violations in Mayom County, Unity State (AFR 65/002/2012)

▨ South Sudan: Lethal disarmament – abuses related to civilian disarmament in Pibor County, Jonglei State (AFR 65/005/2012)

S

SPAIN

KINGDOM OF SPAIN
Head of state: King Juan Carlos I de Borbón
Head of government: Mariano Rajoy

There were continued reports of excessive use of force by police during demonstrations. Human rights bodies condemned Spain for the lack of adequate investigations into allegations of torture.

Background

Demonstrations continued throughout the year, calling for changes in the political system to allow for greater public participation in political affairs and to protest against austerity measures implemented to combat the financial and economic crisis.

In June, the UN Committee on Economic, Social and Cultural Rights recommended that Spain review reforms adopted in relation to the financial crisis to ensure that all austerity measures upheld economic, social and cultural rights and were temporary, proportionate and without prejudice to those rights. The Committee also recommended taking legislative measures to ensure that economic, social and cultural rights enjoy the same protections as civil and political rights.

No violent attacks by the armed Basque group Euskadi Ta Askatasuna (ETA) were reported during 2012, after the group announced the end of its armed struggle in October 2011.

In November, the Constitutional Tribunal ruled that same-sex marriage was consistent with the provisions of the Spanish Constitution, following the Popular Party's 2005 appeal against legislation permitting same-sex marriage.

Torture and other ill-treatment

Demonstrations took place throughout the year in different cities including Madrid, Barcelona and Valencia. There were frequent allegations of excessive use of force and of ill-treatment by law enforcement officials while dispersing crowds during the protests. In general, investigations into complaints were not thorough or effective; some were made impossible by the lack of identification tags on the uniforms of police alleged to have been involved.

■ In March, a Barcelona court closed the investigation on alleged excessive use of force by Mossos d'Esquadra police when dispersing demonstrators in Barcelona on 27 May 2011. The court found that the police action had been proportionate. However, on 29 October a higher court ordered the reopening of the case.

■ Also in March, a Madrid court issued a decision not to admit a complaint lodged in 2011 by Angela Jaramillo, as the policewoman responsible for hitting her could not be identified. Angela Jaramillo was among several people who, despite their peaceful conduct during a demonstration in Madrid on 4 August 2011, were repeatedly hit with batons by police and required medical treatment. Angela Jaramillo died in June 2012 after suffering a heart attack.

■ On 11 July, a freelance journalist, Paloma Aznar, was hit by a rubber bullet and injured on the hip while covering miners' demonstrations in Madrid. She was wearing her journalist tag with her camera round her neck. She reported that police were not wearing any visible identification and were shooting rubber bullets directly at the crowd after some demonstrators became violent. Video footage showed police using batons against people lying on the pavement and firing rubber bullets at close range.

■ On 25 September, during a demonstration in Madrid, unidentified police beat peaceful demonstrators with batons, fired rubber bullets at them, and threatened journalists covering the events – including inside Atocha train station. An internal investigation was reportedly opened on the police operation. Its results had not been made public at the end of the year.

Investigations into allegations of torture and other ill-treatment were often inadequate and recognized as such in decisions adopted by human rights bodies and courts during the year.

■ In April, two police officers charged with killing Osamuyia Akpitaye while he was being forcibly deported in June 2007 were convicted of the minor offence of negligence by a criminal court. No prison sentence was imposed.

■ In May, the UN Committee against Torture found that Spain had failed to adequately investigate allegations of torture in the case *Orkatz Gallastegi v. Spain*. Orkatz Gallastegi was convicted in 2005 on the basis of self-incriminating evidence allegedly extracted under duress while in incommunicado detention in 2002.

In July, the Constitutional Court declined to review the 2011 Supreme Court acquittal of four civil guards following their conviction in December 2010 by Guipúzcoa Criminal Court for torturing Igor Portu and Mattin Sarasola on 6 January 2008, while they were in police custody.

Counter-terror and security

Investigations of crimes committed by members of the armed group ETA continued.

Spain again failed to implement international human rights bodies' recommendations to abolish the use of incommunicado detention for people suspected of terrorism-related offences. The practice allows detainees to be held for up to 13 days, during which time they are denied access to a doctor or lawyer of their choice, cannot consult their state-appointed lawyer in private and cannot have their family informed of their whereabouts.

■ In December, the Spanish Supreme Court rejected an appeal from lawyers in the "Bush Six" case to prosecute in Spain six individuals alleged to be complicit in creating the legal framework that resulted in the torture of suspected terrorists at US-run detention facilities after the case had not progressed in US courts. Despite evidence to the contrary, the Court ruled that the USA was conducting investigations. The decision was expected to be appealed to the Constitutional Court.

Racism and discrimination

Muslims and other religious minorities continued to face obstacles in obtaining permits to open places of worship in some municipalities in Catalonia, following local moratoriums on new places of worship. Some local authorities, political parties and associations of neighbours continued to voice opposition to the establishment of Muslim prayer rooms.

Restrictions on wearing religious symbols and dress were maintained in some schools and continued to have a disproportionate impact on Muslim pupils.

■ On 25 January, a court in Madrid upheld the decision of a state-funded secondary school in Pozuelo de Alarcón, Madrid, to exclude a pupil from regular classes because she wore a headscarf.

■ On 21 May, the Head of Police issued a circular prohibiting the use of quotas and police raids for detaining foreign nationals with an irregular status. However, the measure failed to prohibit identity checks based on racial or ethnic characteristics. Local NGOs continued to report that police were targeting people from ethnic minorities when conducting such checks.

■ In July, the European Court of Humans Rights found that Spain had failed to conduct an effective investigation into allegations of police ill-treatment, and potential racist bias, in the case of a Nigerian, Beauty Solomon. She had reported being verbally abused and beaten by police officers in Palma de Mallorca in July 2005.

Violence against women

During 2012, 46 women were killed by their partners or former partners, according to the Ministry of Health, Social Policy and Equality. A survey carried out by the Spanish government estimated that more than 2 million women had suffered gender violence by partners or ex-partners at least once. Seven years after the introduction of the law against gender-based violence, women continued to lack access to effective remedies. Since 2005, when specialized tribunals on violence against women were set up, no assessment has been made of the obstacles to effective protection that women may face during judicial proceedings.

■ María (name withheld) survived sexual, psychological and physical violence by her partner, which resulted in her not being able to walk for six months. She continued to receive serious threats throughout the four years of the judicial investigation and after the trial. Although she reported her situation to the authorities, she received no protection and was forced to leave her home. Her ex-partner was acquitted. At the end of 2012, she was still receiving serious threats and living in hiding.

Refugees and migrants

In April, the adoption of Royal Decree-Law No. 16/2012 reformed the Aliens Act, limiting irregular migrants' access to public health services.

On 4 September, Spain collectively expelled 70 migrants from the Spanish islet Isla de Tierra to Morocco. None of them had access to an individual asylum procedure.

■ In August, the UN Working Group on Arbitrary Detention found Spain responsible for the arbitrary detention, discrimination and ill-treatment amounting to torture of a Moroccan citizen detained in an immigration detention centre in Madrid. Adnam el Hadj was stopped on the street for an identity check and

S

taken to the detention centre. There, five police officers allegedly hit him several times and made racist insults. The detention centre's medical department found multiple bruises on his body and recommended that he be taken to hospital. He was not taken to a hospital and no medical report was drawn up.

Crimes under international law

The definition of enforced disappearance as a crime against humanity in domestic legislation continued to fall short of obligations under international law, despite Spain's ratification of the International Convention against enforced disappearance.

■ On 27 February 2012, the Supreme Court acquitted former judge Baltasar Garzón of exceeding his authority. Baltasar Garzón was prosecuted, among other things, for violating the 1977 Amnesty Law by launching an investigation in 2008 into the enforced disappearances of 114,266 people between July 1936 and December 1951. Despite the acquittal, the Supreme Court concluded that Baltasar Garzón had wrongfully interpreted the law when considering the facts under investigation as crimes against humanity. According to the Court, the crimes were not defined as crimes against humanity within domestic law at the time they were committed. This judgement by the Supreme Court may rule out the possibility of investigating past crimes under international law in Spain.

Housing rights

The government implemented legislative reforms relating to the economic crisis without assessing their impact on vulnerable people's rights.

■ In Madrid, forced evictions continued to take place in Cañada Real, despite Law 2/2011 of 15 May 2011, which urged competent local authorities to consult affected residents and to strive towards reaching an agreement to avoid evictions. In the informal settlement of Puerta de Hierro, also in Madrid and inhabited by Roma, 300 people were evicted without being provided adequate alternative housing.

■ In June, the UN Committee on Economic, Social and Cultural Rights expressed concerns about continuing evictions being implemented in breach of international legal safeguards, including on genuine prior consultation, compensation and adequate alternative housing. The Committee recommended

the adoption of a legal framework setting out guidelines to be followed prior to evictions.

SRI LANKA

DEMOCRATIC SOCIALIST REPUBLIC OF SRI LANKA
Head of state and government: Mahinda Rajapaksa

Unlawful detentions, torture and enforced disappearances remained rife and went unpunished. Government officials and supporters harassed and threatened human rights defenders, journalists and members of the judiciary who spoke out about abuses of power or advocated human rights accountability. More than three years after the armed conflict between the Sri Lankan government and the Liberation Tigers of Tamil Eelam (LTTE) ended, impunity persisted for alleged war crimes and crimes against humanity. The government failed to implement recommendations aimed at accountability made by Sri Lanka's Lessons Learnt and Reconciliation Commission (LLRC) and the UN Human Rights Council. The authorities continued to rely on the Prevention of Terrorism Act to arrest and detain suspects for lengthy periods without charge or trial. Despite government claims, many people displaced by the armed conflict were not fully settled, including some whose land remained occupied by the Sri Lankan military.

Enforced disappearances

More than 20 alleged enforced disappearances were reported. Victims included political activists, business people and suspected criminals. Prominent cases from past years remained unresolved.

■ Armed men abducted Tamil businessman Ramasamy Prabaharan on 11 February, just two days before the Supreme Court was scheduled to hear his complaints against arbitrary arrest, detention and torture by police and seizure of his business in May 2009.

■ In April, Frontline Socialist Party activists Premakumar Gunaratnam and Dimuthu Attigala were abducted shortly before the launch of the new party; both were interrogated and eventually released.

S

Premakumar Gunaratnam, an Australian citizen, said he was tortured by his abductors, who he believed were linked to the government.

■ Investigations failed to progress into the cases of political activists Lalith Kumar Weeraraj and Kugan Muruganathan – both allegedly victims of enforced disappearance by the army in Jaffna in December 2011. The two had been planning a peaceful protest by families of the disappeared. The Court of Appeal repeatedly postponed the habeas corpus case filed by relatives of the missing men.

■ In June, former Attorney General Mohan Peiris was ordered to appear at a habeas corpus hearing into the disappearance of political cartoonist Prageeth Eknaligoda after he told the UN Committee against Torture in 2011 that Eknaligoda was living in a foreign country. At the hearing, Mohan Peiris admitted that he did not know Prageeth Eknaligoda's whereabouts and claimed he could not remember who said he was in exile.

Arbitrary arrests and detentions

The authorities continued to arrest people without warrants and detain them for extended periods without charge or trial. As of October, the authorities acknowledged holding almost 500 alleged former LTTE members without charge for what they termed "rehabilitation". Hundreds of other Tamil prisoners remained in administrative detention pending investigation into their suspected links with the LTTE; many had been detained for years. Surveillance and re-arrest of people released from rehabilitation continued.

Excessive use of force

■ In February Antony Warnakulasuriya was killed and three others were wounded when the Special Task Force (STF), a commando unit, fired live ammunition into a crowd of people from the fishing community who were protesting against fuel price increases outside the west coast town of Chilaw. Police reportedly blocked protesters from taking the injured to hospital by land, forcing them to go by boat.

Torture and other ill-treatment

Torture in police custody persisted. In at least five cases, victims died in custody after beatings or other ill-treatment by the police.

■ On 15 April, Chandrasiri Dassanayake, a witness in a human rights case filed with the Supreme Court against the Officer-in-Charge of Wadduwa Police Station, died in custody there. Police claimed they arrested him for cannabis possession and that he fell sick in his cell and was admitted to hospital. The victim's son reported seeing his father lying on the floor of the cell bleeding and said Chandrasiri Dassanayake told him he had been beaten by police. The death led to local protests and the Officer-in-Charge, a sergeant and two other police constables were transferred to other police stations, but no further action was taken.

■ Thirty Tamil prisoners were assaulted and two died of injuries inflicted by STF members who reportedly beat them in retaliation for a prison uprising in Vavuniya in June.

■ Twenty-seven inmates died in a clash between prisoners and STF members at Welikada prison on 9 November. Results of an official inquiry into allegations that some prisoners were extrajudicially executed were not made public.

Lack of accountability

The UN Human Rights Council adopted resolution 19/2 in March, calling on Sri Lanka to implement the LLRC's human rights recommendations and address accountability for alleged violations of international law. The government's Plan of Action on the LLRC recommendations, unveiled in July, failed to commit to new or independent investigations, and relied on the military and police – implicated in serious violations of human rights and humanitarian law – to police themselves. Sri Lanka's human rights record was assessed under the UN Universal Periodic Review in November; Sri Lanka maintained that it did not need independent investigations into alleged human rights violations and past crimes under international law despite concerns raised by UN members.

A report by the UN Secretary-General's Internal Review Panel on UN Action in Sri Lanka, released on 14 November, acknowledged the UN's failure to protect civilians during the country's armed conflict.

Human rights defenders

Government officials and state-owned media lashed out at human rights defenders who attended the UN Human Rights Council session in March, calling them traitors. The UN High Commissioner for Human

S

Rights and the President of the Human Rights Council denounced Sri Lanka's threats and called for an investigation. On 23 March, Sri Lanka's Public Relations Minister threatened physical harm against journalists and human rights defenders, and claimed responsibility for a violent attack in 2010 on a journalist who then went into exile. The Health Minister accused the Catholic organization Caritas of conspiring to undermine the government.

Freedom of expression – journalists

Journalists continued to come under pressure for their reporting.

■ On 5 July, Secretary of Defence Gotabaya Rajapaksa threatened *Sunday Leader* journalist Frederica Jansz with death when she attempted to interview him about an alleged abuse of power. In September, the newspaper's new owner fired her and she left the country.

■ Journalist Shantha Wijesooriya of the news website Lanka X News told police that assailants he believed to be members of the security forces attempted to abduct him on 5 July. A week earlier police had raided the office where he worked.

■ In September, journalist Nirmala Kannangara and a photographer were surrounded and threatened by army personnel when they tried to report on the relocation of displaced people from Manik Farm.

Justice system

On 7 October, armed assailants assaulted Manjula Thilakaratne, a senior high court judge and Secretary to Sri Lanka's Judicial Services Commission (JSC), and attempted to drag him from his car. On 18 September, he had issued a statement on behalf of the JSC complaining of attempts to interfere with the independence of the judiciary and particularly with the JSC through threats and intimidation.

In December, Parliament initiated impeachment proceedings against Chief Justice Shirani Bandaranayake. The UN Special Rapporteur on the independence of judges and lawyers criticized the impeachment process as "extremely politicized," and lacking due process and fair trial guarantees.

Internally displaced people

In late September, the authorities closed the vast Manik Farm displacement camp and announced that the last of more than 200,000 inhabitants had returned home. According to UNHCR, the UN refugee agency, tens of thousands of displaced people still could not go home or fully resettle elsewhere by the end of the year and depended on host families for shelter and assistance.

■ On 30 September, nearly 350 displaced people at Manik Farm boarded army buses expecting to return home to Keppapilavu village, but were relocated to a barren plot of land in Mullaitivu district because the army still occupied their land. Displaced people complained that the new camp had no infrastructure and inadequate drinking water. Other relocated villagers had similar experiences.

SUDAN

REPUBLIC OF THE SUDAN
Head of state and government: **Omar Hassan Ahmed al-Bashir**

Post-independence agreements on the sharing of oil, citizenship and border demarcation continued to be negotiated with South Sudan. Conflict continued in Darfur, Southern Kordofan and Blue Nile states. The National Security Service (NSS) and other government agents continued to commit human rights violations against perceived critics of the government for exercising their rights to freedom of expression, association and assembly.

Background

Tensions between South Sudan and Sudan mounted in relation to outstanding post-independence issues. The shutdown of oil production in South Sudan in February, due to disagreements with Sudan on oil transit fees, led to an escalation of conflict. Clashes between the two armies, including indiscriminate aerial bombardments by the Sudanese Armed Forces (SAF) on the border areas of Heglig/Panthou and Kiir Adem from late March to May and in November, led to the displacement of hundreds of people. In February, South Sudan and Sudan signed a "non-aggression" pact over their disputed border. The memorandum of understanding covered five principles, of which two clauses referred to "no cross-border

S

operations" and "no support of proxies". Despite the pact, border tensions persisted. On 24 April, the AU Peace and Security Council adopted a roadmap to resolve outstanding issues between the two countries, which the UN Security Council endorsed through resolution 2046, calling for both countries to reach a settlement on disputes within three months.

On 27 September, South Sudan and Sudan signed several agreements on trade, oil, security and citizenship issues in Addis Ababa, Ethiopia. However, at the end of the year implementation of these agreements remained pending, as did further agreements on the status of the disputed area of Abyei and the precise border between South Sudan and Sudan.

The armed conflict between the SAF and the armed opposition group Sudan People's Liberation Movement-North (SPLM-N) persisted in Southern Kordofan and Blue Nile. In April and May, a state of emergency was declared in a number of localities in states bordering South Sudan, including areas of Southern Kordofan, White Nile and Sennar states. In August, the government of Sudan and the SPLM-N signed two separate Memorandums of Understanding with the Tripartite group (UN, AU and the League of Arab States) to allow humanitarian access to conflict-affected populations in Southern Kordofan and Blue Nile states. However, no progress had been made in delivering humanitarian assistance to the populations in SPLM-N-controlled areas by the end of the year.

The majority of displaced people from Abyei remained in South Sudan, despite the presence of the UN Interim Security Force for Abyei (UNISFA) since June 2011. Notwithstanding the deployment of a Joint Military Observer Committee for Abyei in July, talks between Sudan and South Sudan over other administrative arrangements and broader political issues related to Abyei remained stalled. In November, the UN Security Council renewed UNISFA's mandate for a further six months under resolution 2075. While the mandate has included human rights monitoring since its inception, no progress was made in carrying this out.

On 19 September, President al-Bashir issued an invitation to NGOs and political parties to attend a consultative meeting on the Constitution. The text had already been drafted by the National Congress Party and there was reportedly no consultation on the draft prior to its publication. All of the main opposition parties refused to join the consultations.

Waves of protests broke out in January and June when students demonstrated against government policies and austerity measures; security agents responded with excessive force. Hundreds of activists were arrested and many faced torture and other ill-treatment before being released.

International justice

The government remained uncooperative with the International Criminal Court (ICC) regarding arrest warrants issued against President al-Bashir in 2009 and 2010, as well as against Ahmed Haroun, Governor of Southern Kordofan, and Ali Mohammed Ali Abdelrahman, a former Janjaweed militia leader, in 2007.

On 1 March, the ICC issued a warrant of arrest against Abdel Raheem Muhammad Hussein – the current Minister of National Defense – for 41 counts of crimes against humanity and war crimes allegedly committed in the context of the situation in Darfur.

Refugees and migrants

Eritrean asylum-seekers and refugees were forcibly returned, despite Sudan's obligations under international law not to return people to a situation where they would face a real risk of human rights violations.

■ Nine asylum-seekers and one refugee were convicted in July of unlawfully entering Sudan, and were subsequently forcibly deported to Eritrea.

■ On 11 October, a 24-year-old Eritrean man was forcibly returned to Eritrea following a decision by a court in Kassala. He was arrested after going to a police station to claim asylum.

Freedom of expression

The government severely curtailed freedom of expression, using new forms of censorship, such as confiscating entire newspaper print runs; preventing the publication of articles or opinion pieces; banning certain journalists from writing for newspapers; and harassing editors in order to influence their choice of news coverage.

In January and February, authorities suspended three newspapers using provisions contained in the 2010 National Security Act, which allow the NSS to ban any publication containing information considered a threat to national security. Print runs of the newspaper Al Midan were seized by the authorities five times in March alone. On 2 January,

S

three newspapers – *Alwan*, *Rai Al Shaab* and *Al Tayyar* – were shut down.

Journalists faced arrests, torture and other ill-treatment by members of the NSS and other security agents in Sudan. Many faced criminal charges and had their equipment confiscated, preventing them from carrying out their media work. More than 15 journalists remained banned from writing.

■ In April and May, Faisal Mohammed Saleh, a prominent columnist with several national newspapers, was repeatedly arrested and released, before being charged with "non-cooperation with a public agent". Faisal Mohammed Saleh was acquitted on 31 May, but continued to face criminal charges for his 2011 reporting on the alleged rape of an activist by NSS agents.

■ Najla Sid Ahmed, a Sudanese video-blogger covering human rights violations in Sudan through interviews with activists and victims of human rights abuses broadcast on YouTube, was continuously harassed by the NSS and forced to go into exile.

■ Jalila Khamis Koko, a teacher from the Nuba Mountains and a member of the SPLM-N, remained in detention following her arrest in March. She had provided humanitarian support to displaced people from Southern Kordofan, and appeared in a YouTube video denouncing the conditions in the Nuba Mountains. In December the NSS pressed charges against Jalila Khamis Koko on six criminal counts, five of which were under the category of crimes against the state, including two which carry the death penalty.

Freedom of association and assembly

Authorities continued to severely restrict freedom of assembly.

The government repressed a wave of demonstrations which began on 16 June in response to price increases and developed into a wider protest movement seeking broader political change. Demonstrations occurred in the capital, Khartoum, and other cities as well as in provincial towns. From June to August, security forces used batons, tear gas, rubber bullets and live ammunition against largely peaceful demonstrators, causing deaths and injuries. Some women were reportedly subjected to repeated "virginity tests", amounting to torture or other ill-treatment. Plain-clothed security officers, deployed in or near hospitals, arrested suspected demonstrators seeking treatment.

The NSS carried out a wave of arrests across civil society in reaction to the demonstrations, detaining hundreds of individuals, including protesters, but also lawyers, NGO staff, doctors, and members of youth organizations and political parties – regardless of their involvement in the protests. Many were detained without charge, or were tried summarily for rioting or disrupting public order and sentenced to fines or lashes. Others were held for up to two months and indicted on more serious charges – mostly terrorism – but not sentenced.

The NSS tortured or otherwise ill-treated many of those detained following the June demonstrations. NSS agents slapped, punched and kicked prisoners, and beat them with rubber hoses. Detainees were made to stand outside for hours in scorching heat, and to adopt stress positions. Many were denied food or water and access to basic hygiene facilities.

■ On 31 July, at least 10 people, predominantly high-school students, were killed when security services and paramilitary police opened fire during a demonstration against fuel prices and the cost of living in Nyala, Darfur.

■ On 6 and 7 December, four Darfuri students from Al Jazeera University in Wad Madani were found dead in a canal near the university. The four had been arrested by NSS officers following protests at the university. The bodies reportedly bore signs of beatings, suggesting torture or ill-treatment.

The Government of Sudan continued its harassment of members of opposition groups. In October and November, over 100 people suspected of being affiliated with the SPLM-N were arrested in or around Kadugli and Dilling in Southern Kordofan.

Death penalty

Death sentences continued to be handed down. At least two women were sentenced to death by stoning. In both cases, the women were deprived of legal representation, a clear violation of the right to a fair trial.

Death sentences were often passed after trials that blatantly violated the rights of the defence. The authorities continued to use delaying tactics to undermine the rights of defendants to appeal.

■ In May and July, two women, 23-year-old Layla Ibrahim Issa Jumul and 20-year-old Intisar Sharif Abdallah, were sentenced to death by stoning for adultery. In both cases, they were convicted solely on

S

the basis of their confession, which was obtained under duress. Both women were released on appeal.

■ Al-Tom Hamed Tutu, a JEM leader, remained on death row facing imminent threat of execution. He had been sentenced to death in 2011 after a flawed trial.

Armed conflict – Darfur

Grave human rights abuses continued throughout Darfur amid continued fighting between the government and armed opposition groups, and a breakdown of government control over government-affiliated militias. Attacks on civilians by pro-government militias, aerial bombings, and looting and destruction of property were widespread. The SAF continued to conduct aerial bombings in contravention of the UN ban on military flights in Darfur. Between July and November, the joint UN/AU Mission in Darfur (UNAMID) estimated that approximately 29,020 people were displaced by fighting. UNAMID reported that it continued to face hurdles in conducting its work due to restrictions by the government on the movement of, and delays in approval for, humanitarian assistance.

■ The village of Hashaba North and its surroundings were attacked by armed men between 26 September and 2 October. Over 250 casualties were reported.

■ On 2 October, four UNAMID peacekeepers were killed and eight wounded in an ambush in West Darfur near their base in El-Geneina.

■ On 17 October, an armed militia group attacked a UNAMID convoy on its way to Hashaba North to investigate reports of human rights atrocities being committed in the region. One UNAMID peacekeeper was killed and three others were wounded.

■ On the night of 31 December, aerial bombardments were reported in eastern Jebel Marra, killing five civilians and wounding two others in the village of Angero Rouka.

Rape and sexual violence by government-affiliated militia and government forces continued. There were numerous reports of armed men entering camps for internally displaced people at night to loot property and rape women and girls.

■ On 10 July pro-government militias entered the Hamidia camp in Zalingei town, central Darfur. They reportedly raped four women, injured four people, and kidnapped 20 others. One person who later escaped claimed that the group had been subjected to torture and other ill-treatment.

Armed conflict – Southern Kordofan and Blue Nile

Conflict between the SAF and the SPLM-N in Southern Kordofan and Blue Nile states, which erupted in June and September 2011, remained ongoing. From October, fighting intensified with indiscriminate attacks, including aerial bombardments, by the SAF, and mortar shelling by both parties in the Kadugli locality of Southern Kordofan, resulted in civilian deaths and injuries. Indiscriminate aerial bombardments by the SAF further led to the destruction of property and disrupted agriculture. Coupled with the denial of humanitarian access to SPLM-N-controlled areas, this resulted in over 200,000 people seeking refuge in South Sudan and Ethiopia.

Amnesty International visits/reports

▨ Sudan: No end to violence in Darfur. Arms supplies continue despite ongoing human rights violations (AFR 54/007/2012)

▨ Sudanese authorities must end the crackdown on demonstrators and activists (AFR 54/036/2012)

▨ "We can run away from bombs, but not from hunger": Sudan's refugees in South Sudan (AFR 65/001/2012)

SURINAME

REPUBLIC OF SURINAME
Head of state and government: **Desiré Delano Bouterse**

An amendment to the amnesty law prevented the trial of President Bouterse and 24 others accused of the extrajudicial killing of 15 political opponents in 1982.

Impunity

In April, the National Assembly approved an amendment to the 1992 amnesty law. This extended the period covered by the law from April 1980 to August 1992, thereby covering the torture and extrajudicial execution of 15 opponents of the then military government in December 1982. Twenty-five people, including President Desiré Delano "Dési" Bouterse, the country's military leader at the time,

S

were put on trial before a military court in November 2007 for the killings.

The amended law grants an amnesty to those who "have committed criminal offences and/or are suspected of having done so within the framework of the defence of the State and/or overthrow of the lawful authorities such as the events occurring during December 1982 and the Guerrilla War" in order to "promote national unity and the further uninterrupted development of the Republic of Suriname".

President Bouterse argued that the new amnesty law would help to reconcile the country. However, there were demonstrations in Paramaribo, the capital, in April and May against this initiative to grant immunity to President Bouterse and the other co-accused. International criticism of the law included statements by the Inter-American Commission on Human Rights that "laws that seek to leave serious human rights violations in impunity are incompatible with Inter-American human rights obligations". In April, following the approval of the law, the Netherlands withdrew their ambassador.

On 11 May, the military court adjourned the trial until the Constitutional Court could review the new amnesty law. This decision was confirmed by the Office of the Public Prosecutor on 12 December. However, this could result in a lengthy delay as, although the 1987 Constitution provides for the creation of a constitutional court, no such court had been established by the end of 2012.

In November, youth activist Sharona Lieuw On, Chair of Youth against Amnesty, filed a complaint after receiving a bullet through the post along with a letter warning her not to continue her protests against the amnesty law. She later withdrew her complaint as she feared for her safety.

Amnesty International visits/reports

🗐 Suriname: Amnesty law may end current trial (AMR 48/001/2012)

🗐 Suriname: Open Letter to the judiciary (AMR 48/003/2012)

SWAZILAND

KINGDOM OF SWAZILAND
Head of state: King Mswati III
Head of government: Barnabas Sibusiso Dlamini

The rights to freedom of expression, association and peaceful assembly continued to be violated, with arbitrary arrests and excessive force used to crush political protests. Torture and other ill-treatment remained a persistent concern. Some progress was made in the reform of laws which discriminated against women.

Background

The government's financial situation remained precarious despite increased revenue from the Southern African Customs Union. Its efforts to secure loans from various sources were not successful, partly due to its failure to implement fiscal reforms, and its unwillingness to accept conditions, including instituting political reforms. Pressure on public sector workers, including teachers, led to prolonged strikes. Political groupings and civil society organizations renewed calls for political transformation. The House of Assembly passed an unprecedented vote of no confidence in the government in October.

Legal, constitutional or institutional developments

There was continued pressure on the independence of the judiciary throughout the year, with consequences for access to justice.

In March, Swaziland's human rights record was assessed under the UN Universal Periodic Review (UPR). Swaziland reconfirmed its rejection of recommendations to allow political parties to participate in elections. Swaziland also confirmed that it intended to ratify the Optional Protocol to the UN Convention against Torture, but had not done so by the end of the year.

In May the African Commission on Human and Peoples' Rights adopted a resolution expressing alarm at the government's failure to implement the Commission's decision of 2002 and recommendations made in 2006 relating to the rights to freedom of expression, association and assembly.

S

It also expressed concern at the de-registration of the newly formed Trade Union Congress of Swaziland (TUCOSWA).

Freedom of expression

The rights to freedom of expression, association and peaceful assembly continued to be violated, with police using rubber bullets, tear gas and batons to break up demonstrations and gatherings viewed as illegal.

■ In March the High Court heard arguments that the summary contempt proceedings brought against Independent Publishers and the editor of *The Nation* violated their right to fair trial and to freedom of expression and opinion, and were accordingly unlawful and unconstitutional. The hearing had followed the publication of two articles calling on the judiciary to use the Constitution to better people's lives and raising concerns about the intentions of the then Acting Chief Justice. The criminal contempt case had been brought by the Attorney General, legal adviser to the head of state, although his office had no jurisdiction to prosecute. The Court had not issued a ruling by the end of the year.

■ On the eve of its participation in planned demonstrations in April, TUCOSWA was informed by the Attorney General that it was unlawfully registered, despite registration having been confirmed by the Acting Commissioner of Labour under the Industrial Relations Act. While TUCOSWA officials continued to challenge the legality of the de-registration, police disrupted their gatherings, confiscated banners displaying TUCOSWA insignia, conducted arbitrary arrests and threatened union officials and activists. At least one detained activist, lawyer Mary Pais da Silva, was assaulted in custody.

Torture and other ill-treatment and unfair trials

Torture and other ill-treatment remained a concern, with a High Court judge in April calling for a commission of inquiry into repeated allegations by accused in criminal trials that they had been subjected to torture, which included beatings and suffocation. Deaths under suspicious circumstances and the failure of the authorities to ensure independent investigation and accountability continued to cause concern. Police and members of the military were implicated in the reported incidents.

■ In February Maxwell Dlamini, President of the National Union of Students, and Musa Ngubeni, a political activist and former student activist leader, were released after 10 months in remand custody and placed under oppressive bail conditions.

■ On 12 March 43-year-old Lucky Montero was kicked and beaten in the head and body by soldiers at a border checkpoint. He died 12 days later in Mbabane Government Hospital from medical complications arising from his injuries.

■ In August the High Court found Amos Mbedze, a South African national, guilty of murder, in connection with the deaths in a car bomb explosion in 2008 of two men who were in the vehicle and with whom he was alleged to have conspired to undermine the security of the state. He was sentenced to 85 years' imprisonment. The incident, which had occurred near one of the King's palaces, led to the rapid promulgation of the Suppression of Terrorism Act. The murder conviction was not supported by any evidence heard during his trial.

Death penalty

In November, the Supreme Court of Appeal rejected David Simelane's appeal against his death sentence imposed in 2011 at the conclusion of his 10-year-long trial for the murder of 34 women. In the same month, Mciniseli Jomo Simelane was sentenced to death by the High Court for murder.

Women's rights

In March, at the UN Universal Periodic Review session, Swaziland accepted to amend "without delay" laws which discriminate against women.

In June the Deeds Registry (Amendment) Bill was passed by parliament. The Bill amended a provision in the original Act which prevented most women married under civil law from legally registering homes in their own name.

The Sexual Offences and Domestic Violence Bill had still not been tabled in the Senate by the end of the year, although it was passed by the lower house of parliament in October 2011.

In September The Children's Protection and Welfare Act was assented to by the King. The new law increased protection against forced marriage for girls and young women. The organization Swaziland Action Group Against Abuse publicly expressed alarm that a senior adviser to the King on traditional law and

S

custom announced an intention to seek a court review of the Act.

Amnesty International visits/reports

🚌 Amnesty International delegates visited Swaziland in March and November.

📄 Amnesty International urges Swaziland to take concrete and immediate measures to guarantee the independence and impartiality of the judiciary, and to amend laws which discriminate against women without delay (AFR 55/001/2012)

SWEDEN

KINGDOM OF SWEDEN
Head of state: King Carl XVI Gustaf
Head of government: Fredrik Reinfeldt

Ahmed Agiza, who had been subjected to rendition from Sweden to Egypt in 2001 and subsequently mistreated, was at last able to rejoin his family in Sweden. In July, the authorities suspended forced returns of Uighurs to China in light of the risk of persecution they faced there.

Torture and other ill-treatment

In December, Ahmed Agiza rejoined his family in Sweden after the authorities granted his application for a residence permit. Ahmed Agiza was detained with Mohammed al-Zari in Sweden in December 2001 and subjected to rendition from Sweden to Egypt on a CIA-leased plane. Both men were subsequently tortured and otherwise ill-treated while being held in Egypt. In 2008, the Swedish government awarded both men financial compensation for the human rights violations they suffered. Ahmed Agiza was released from prison in Cairo, Egypt, in 2011, having been held for over nine years after an unfair trial before a military court. Awarding Ahmed Agiza a residence permit contributed to ensuring that his right to redress for the human rights violations he has suffered is fulfilled. However, an effective, impartial, thorough and independent investigation into these violations remained outstanding.

Refugees, asylum-seekers and migrants

A number of Uighurs were forcibly returned to China between January and June, despite the real risk of persecution and other forms of serious harm they would face upon their return. However, in July, the Swedish Migration Board announced that in light of classified information it had recently received it would suspend all forced returns of Uighurs to China, including in cases where asylum claims had already been rejected.

Discrimination

In September, the European Commission against Racism and Intolerance published its country monitoring report on Sweden. The report raised concerns about, among other things, the continuing discrimination faced by Roma – notably in access to social rights; the proliferation of anti-semitic and Islamophobic comments, including by some members of Parliament; and that Jews and Muslims wearing visible signs of their faith had been targeted in "antisemitic and islamophobic incidents".

SWITZERLAND

SWISS CONFEDERATION
Head of state and government: Eveline Widmer-Schlumpf

Restrictive measures on access to asylum were adopted. Measures to limit the use of force during deportation were introduced.

Police and security forces

Allegations of ill-treatment by the police in the Canton of Geneva continued, including against minors, during or immediately after arrest. In October, the European Committee for the Prevention of Torture recommended introducing improved training and reinforcing existing safeguards to combat ill-treatment by police.

Prison conditions

The European Committee for the Prevention of Torture urged that any traumatic injuries detected by medical inspections in places of detention in the Canton of Geneva be reported to an independent body empowered to conduct investigations. Further recommendations to all cantons included establishing suitable care facilities for individuals suffering from mental illnesses.

Discrimination

Discrimination against ethnic and religious minorities and migrants continued in law and practice. Anti-discrimination legislation and redress mechanisms failed to meet international standards.

In March, the Council of Europe Commissioner for Human Rights expressed concern over certain "popular initiatives" which target and stigmatize migrant communities in breach of international human rights standards. The ban on minarets, the outcome of a popular initiative, remained in force during 2012.

In March, the Council of States rejected a motion approved by the National Council in 2011 which sought to introduce a law prohibiting full-face veils.

Refugees, asylum-seekers and migrants

In September, the right to claim asylum at Swiss embassies was suppressed. Parliament voted that conscientious objectors should no longer be granted refugee status, but a temporary residence permit instead.

In December, more than 10 restrictive measures were introduced into asylum law, such as excluding adult sons and daughters from family asylum and granting permanent residence to refugees only after 10 years and if they were deemed to have integrated successfully.

In March, the National Commission for the Prevention of Torture agreed to supervise the independent monitoring of forced deportations. Positive steps were taken to curb restraint measures during transportation to the airport, before and during boarding, and during the flight. In October, the Commission expressed concerns regarding the restrictive regime under which people detained for migration purposes were held.

In January, the criminal investigation into the death of Joseph Ndukaku Chiakwa, a Nigerian national who died at Zurich Airport during a mass deportation in March 2010, was closed. The appeal was still pending at the end of the year.

Corporate accountability

In December, the government agreed to deliver a national strategy to implement the UN Guiding Principles on Business and Human Rights, to be applied to transnational companies with headquarters in Switzerland.

Violence against women and girls

In June, legislative measures against forced marriage were introduced, enabling the annulment of any marriage concluded under duress. In September the government adopted a five-year programme to prevent forced marriages and domestic violence by reinforcing collaboration between schools, professionals and private consultation services.

In July, the Minister of Justice announced the creation of a national office for the protection of witnesses of human trafficking.

In October, the government adopted a National Action Plan on fighting human trafficking.

Legal, constitutional or institutional developments

In December the Federal Council initiated consultation towards the ratification of the International Convention against enforced disappearance, and agreed to ratify the UN Convention on the Rights of Persons with Disabilities.

Amnesty International visits/reports

Choice and prejudice: Discrimination against Muslims in Europe (EUR 01/001/2012)

S

SYRIA

SYRIAN ARAB REPUBLIC
Head of state: Bashar al-Assad
Head of government: Wa'el al-Halqi (replaced Omar
Ibrahim Ghalawanji in August, who
replaced Riyad Farid Hijab in August,
who replaced Adel Safar in June)

The internal armed conflict between government
forces and the opposition, composed of the Free
Syrian Army (FSA) and other armed opposition
groups, was marked by gross human rights abuses,
war crimes and crimes against humanity.
Government forces, which were responsible for the
vast majority of violations, carried out indiscriminate
attacks on residential areas using aircraft, artillery
shells, mortars, incendiary weapons and cluster
bombs. Together with their support militias, they
arrested thousands of people, including children,
subjecting many to enforced disappearance.
Torture and other ill-treatment of detainees were
commonplace; at least 550 were reported to have
died in custody, many after torture. Others were
extrajudicially executed. Security forces' snipers
continued to shoot peaceful anti-government
demonstrators and people attending public funerals.
Health workers treating the wounded were targeted.
A climate of impunity reigned both for past and
ongoing gross human rights violations. Armed groups
fighting against the government also committed
gross abuses, including war crimes. They tortured
and/or summarily killed government soldiers and
militia members after taking them prisoner and
carried out indiscriminate bombings that killed or
injured civilians. Hundreds of thousands of people
were forced to flee their homes; the UN estimated that
over 2 million people were internally displaced and
living under conditions of extreme hardship within
Syria, and that since the beginning of the conflict
almost 600,000 had fled as refugees to neighbouring
countries, where conditions were often harsh. It was
not possible to confirm whether any death sentences
were imposed or if executions were carried out.

Background

The internal armed conflict engulfed much of the
country, causing thousands of casualties among
the civilian population. Indiscriminate air strikes,
artillery and mortar attacks, bombings, extrajudicial
executions and summary killings, threats, abductions
and hostage-taking became commonplace.

In January, the Arab League suspended its mission
to monitor pledges by the Syrian government to
withdraw armed forces from cities, halt the violence
and release prisoners. Similarly, the UN Supervision
Mission in Syria, established in April to monitor and
support implementation of a plan by UN and Arab
League Joint Special Envoy Kofi Annan, ended on
19 August as armed violence continued. The Russian
Federation and China twice vetoed resolutions at the
UN Security Council aimed at addressing the situation
in Syria. Veteran Algerian diplomat Lakhdar Brahimi
replaced Kofi Annan in August but made no progress
towards obtaining an agreed political solution to the
conflict by the end of the year.

In February, the government held a referendum
on a new Constitution that ended the Ba'ath party's
long monopoly on power, but fell short of opposition
demands for sweeping political reforms.
Parliamentary elections were held 90 days later.

The government continued to attribute many
killings of protesters to shadowy "armed gangs"
and adopted a new anti-terrorism law in July. This
was used to detain and unfairly try political activists and
others on vague charges of committing "terrorist acts"
before a new Anti-Terrorism Court which began sitting
in September.

A bomb attack in the capital Damascus on 18 July,
for which the FSA claimed responsibility, killed the
Defence Minister and his deputy, the Assistant
Vice-President and the Head of the National Security
Bureau. Two days later, armed opposition groups
launched an offensive that spread the armed conflict
to Aleppo, Damascus and elsewhere.

In September, the UN Human Rights Council
extended the mandate of the Independent
International Commission of Inquiry established in
2011. The Commission reported in February and
August that government forces had committed crimes
against humanity, war crimes and serious human
rights abuses, while war crimes committed by
armed opposition forces did not reach the "gravity,
frequency and scale" of those committed by

government forces. The authorities continued to refuse both the Human Rights Council and the Commission entry to the country. They also restricted entry by international media and independent human rights organizations, although these gained access to various areas, including some controlled by armed opposition forces.

The government announced general amnesties in January and October, but it was unclear how many of those arbitrarily detained were released.

In November, various opposition groups united to form the National Coalition for Syrian Revolutionary and Opposition Forces, which was then increasingly recognized internationally as the sole, legitimate representative of the Syrian people.

The USA and the Arab League continued to impose sanctions on Syria, while repeatedly calling for President al-Assad to relinquish power. The EU expanded its targeted sanctions against Syrian officials.

Crimes under international law

Government forces and their associated militias committed war crimes while rampaging through cities, towns and villages perceived to be opposition strongholds in areas including Homs, Idlib, Hama, Damascus and Aleppo governorates. They carried out indiscriminate attacks that killed or injured thousands of civilians. Many of the deaths resulted from the government's improper use of imprecise battlefield weapons in densely populated civilian areas. In addition to dropping free-fall, unguided bombs from aircraft, security forces fired mortars, artillery, incendiary weapons and rockets in residential areas. They also used internationally banned weapons, including anti-personnel mines and cluster munitions, and systematically looted, destroyed and burned property and sometimes the bodies of those they killed.

■ Hassan and Rayan al-Bajri, aged 11 and eight, their mother Salha and father Naasan, were killed along with two of their neighbours when their home in Ma'arat al-No'man was hit by a mortar shell fired by government forces in July.

■ Twenty-two civilians were killed and many more injured when government air strikes hit the market in Kafr Anbel village on 28 August. Among the victims were Fathiya Fares Ali al-Sheikh, a mother of nine, and teenagers Mohamed and Jumaa al-Sweid.

Abuses by armed opposition groups

Armed groups fighting against the government, including some linked to the FSA, committed serious violations of international humanitarian law amounting to war crimes. The victims were mostly known or suspected members of government forces and militiamen whom they tortured or summarily killed after capture or after "trials" before unfair makeshift courts. They also targeted journalists working for pro-government media, and families of suspected members of government militias. Armed groups threatened and abducted civilians, sometimes demanding ransoms for their release and, in some cases, held individuals as hostages, including captured soldiers and Lebanese and Iranian nationals. They carried out suicide and other bomb attacks, and at times fired imprecise weapons such as artillery and mortars in densely populated neighbourhoods, used inherently indiscriminate weapons such as anti-personnel landmines, and prepared or stored munitions and explosives in residential buildings, endangering civilian occupants. Children were used militarily, mostly in support, not combat, roles. By the end of the year, armed opposition groups were reported to be increasingly threatening and attacking minority communities perceived to be pro-government.

■ Nine of 11 Shi'a Muslim Lebanese men taken as hostages by the armed group 'Asifat al-Shimal Brigade while travelling to Lebanon from Iran on 22 May were still being held at the end of the year.

■ On 31 July, following intense clashes, the armed group al-Tawhid Brigade captured 14 members of the Sunni Muslim pro-government al-Berri clan. Video footage showed the captured men being tortured before at least three of them, including a clan leader, Ali Zein al-'Abdeen al-Berri, were shot dead. The FSA's Head of Central Media condemned the killings and announced an investigation. No investigation was known to have been carried out.

Freedom of expression – attacks on journalists

All sides targeted journalists; Syrian government forces also targeted citizen journalists. At least 11 were killed in apparently targeted attacks, while others were detained or taken hostage. Other journalists died as a result of indiscriminate shelling or crossfire.

S

US journalist Marie Colvin and French photographer Remi Ochlik were killed when government forces shelled a building in Homs on 22 February. Journalists who survived alleged that the building was deliberately targeted because it was being used as a media centre. Rami al-Sayed, a Syrian citizen journalist reporting from Homs, died from shrapnel wounds from shelling on the same day.

■ Maya Nasser, a Syrian correspondent for the Iranian state-run Press TV, was shot dead, apparently by opposition snipers, while reporting on a bomb attack against the army headquarters in Damascus on 26 September. His colleague Hussein Mortada from the Iranian al-Alam news network was injured in the attack. Both men had previously received threats from opposition forces.

■ Ali Mahmoud Othman, an activist in the Homs media centre, was arrested at his home on 24 March. After an appearance on state television in April, his family had no further information from state officials concerning his whereabouts by the end of the year.

■ Mazen Darwish, head of the Syrian Centre for Media and Freedom of Expression (SCM), and four other SCM staff, Abd al-Rahman Hamada, Hussein Gharir, Mansour al-Omari and Hani al-Zitani, were detained incommunicado following their arrest by Air Force Intelligence officers on 16 February in Damascus and were still being held at the end of the year. Eleven other people arrested at the same time were released, although seven were later convicted by a military court of "possessing prohibited materials with the intent to disseminate them".

Extrajudicial executions by government forces and associated militias

Government forces and the militias operating alongside them summarily executed captured opposition fighters and civilians, sometimes in large numbers, during military incursions into areas perceived to be supportive of the opposition. Often the dead were found with their hands tied behind their backs, with multiple gunshot wounds to the upper body. Some were burned.

■ Government soldiers took three brothers – Yousef, Bilal and Talal Haj Hussein, all construction workers in their twenties – from their home in Sarmin, a suburb of Idlib, on 23 March. They summarily executed them in front of their mother and sisters, before setting their bodies on fire.

■ Scores of people, including many civilians not involved in fighting, were summarily executed during a military incursion into Houla village, near Homs, on 25 May. Despite government denials, the Independent International Commission of Inquiry concluded that "over 100 civilians, nearly half of whom were children" were killed there by government soldiers and associated militias.

Excessive use of force by government forces and associated militias

Government forces and militias routinely used lethal and other excessive force to quell peaceful protests calling for the "fall of the regime". Hundreds of people, including children and bystanders, who posed no threat to the security forces or others, were killed or wounded by government snipers during protests and public funerals of "martyrs". The authorities pressed some victims' families to sign statements blaming armed terrorist groups rather than the security forces for their relatives' deaths.

■ Mohammed Haffar, who owned a sweet shop in Aleppo, was shot dead on 17 May. He was standing outside his shop when government forces opened fire on a demonstration.

■ Mo'az Lababidi, a 16-year-old schoolboy, was among 10 people shot dead on 25 May by security forces and plain-clothes militias. He was killed outside an Aleppo police station while walking in the funeral procession of four demonstrators similarly shot dead earlier that day.

Targeting the wounded and health workers

Government forces and militias hunted down injured civilians and opposition fighters, some of whom were also ill-treated in state hospitals. Government forces also targeted makeshift medical centres set up by the opposition to assist the wounded, and the volunteer doctors, nurses and paramedics who worked in them.

■ The burned, mutilated bodies of students Basel Aslan, Mus'ab Barad and Hazem Batikh, who belonged to a medical network assisting injured protesters, were found in Aleppo on 24 June, a week after Air Force Intelligence officials detained them. Basel Aslan's hands were tied behind his back; he had been tortured and shot in the head.

■ Osama al-Habaly was reportedly arrested on 18 August by Syrian Military Intelligence at the Syrian-Lebanese border while returning home from receiving medical treatment in Lebanon. His family was told that he had been tortured, but they received no official information about his fate.

Repression of dissent

The government maintained tight controls on freedoms of expression, association and assembly. Government security forces and militiamen detained thousands of people during demonstrations, raids on homes and house-to-house searches during military clampdowns. Hundreds, possibly thousands, of people were held incommunicado in conditions that amounted to enforced disappearance, often in undisclosed and sometimes makeshift detention centres, where torture and other abuses were rife and committed with impunity. Those detained included political and human rights activists, journalists, bloggers, humanitarian workers and imams. Some were convicted and sentenced after unfair trials, including before military and special courts.

■ Prominent human rights lawyer Khalil Ma'touq and his friend Mohammed Thatha went missing on 2 October while travelling through security forces' checkpoints in Damascus. Their families were told that they were being held incommunicado at a State Security branch in Damascus.

■ Four women – Ru'a Ja'far, Rima Dali and sisters Kinda al-Za'our, and Lubna al-Za'our – were held for seven weeks after their arrest by security officials on 21 November while walking in a Damascus street dressed as brides and calling for an end to violence in Syria.

Torture and other ill-treatment

Torture and other ill-treatment of detainees, including children, were widespread and committed with impunity by government forces and associated militias seeking to extract information or "confessions" and to terrorize or punish suspected government opponents. Methods included severe beatings, suspension by the limbs, being suspended in a tyre, electric shocks and rape and other sexual abuse. Detainees were often held in very cramped, insanitary conditions and denied medical treatment or even abused by medical staff.

■ Salameh Kaileh, a Palestinian journalist with Jordanian nationality, was tortured by Air Force Intelligence officers after being arrested at his home in Damascus on 24 April, apparently because of a Facebook conversation and his possession of a left-wing publication. He was whipped on the soles of his feet and insulted. On 3 May he was moved to a military hospital, where he and others were beaten, insulted and denied access to toilets and medication. He was deported to Jordan on 14 May.

Some opposition armed groups also tortured and otherwise ill-treated members of the security forces or government supporters following capture.

Deaths in custody

At least 550 people, including children, were reported to have died in custody, most apparently as a result of torture or other ill-treatment. Many of those who died were suspected government opponents. Nobody was brought to justice for causing the deaths of detainees.

■ Brothers Ahmad and Yahia Ka'ake were arrested at an army checkpoint near Aleppo on 29 September. Days later, a relative located the body of Ahmad Ka'ake in a morgue; it had four bullet wounds. Yahia Ka'ake continued to be detained incommunicado.

Enforced disappearances

Government forces withheld information on the fate of hundreds, possibly thousands, of detainees held in connection with the conflict in conditions that amounted to enforced disappearance. The authorities also continued their failure to account for some 17,000 people who disappeared in Syrian custody since the late 1970s. They included hundreds of Palestinians and Lebanese nationals who were arrested in Syria or abducted from Lebanon by Syrian forces or by Lebanese and Palestinian militias. However, the release of Lebanese national Yacoub Chamoun almost 27 years after he went missing reinforced hopes among some families that their loved ones may still be alive.

■ Activist Zilal Ibrahim al-Salhani disappeared after security forces arrested her at her home in Aleppo on 28 July. Her fate was still unknown at the end of the year.

Impunity

The government took no steps to investigate the numerous allegations against their forces or to bring anyone to justice for alleged gross human rights violations, crimes against humanity or war crimes. The government maintained a regime of impunity, including legislation giving members of the security forces effective immunity for unlawful killings, torture, enforced disappearances and other human rights violations. Nor did the authorities take any steps to investigate and hold to account those responsible for gross violations committed in the past, including thousands of enforced disappearances and the killing of prisoners at Saydnaya prison in 2008 and Tadmur prison in June 1980. In February, the Independent International Commission of Inquiry gave the UN High Commissioner for Human Rights a sealed list of senior officials whom it said should be investigated for crimes against humanity.

Armed opposition groups also failed to respect international humanitarian law, including by failing to prevent war crimes such as torture and the summary killings of captives.

Refugees and internally displaced people

Government forces launched frequent, indiscriminate air strikes against opposition-controlled areas, prompting almost all residents of these areas to flee. Others, particularly those from minority groups, also fled their homes fearing attacks from armed opposition groups. Many camped in the countryside or sought refuge in caves; others went to live with relatives or left the country. Refugees from elsewhere resident in Syria, including Palestinian refugees, faced particular difficulties in accessing safety.

In December, the UN estimated that over 2 million people in Syria were internally displaced as a result of the conflict, requiring humanitarian assistance. UNHCR, the UN refugee agency, said almost 600,000 Syrians had been registered or were awaiting registration as refugees in Turkey, Jordan, Lebanon, Iraq and North Africa, although the total number of those who had fled Syria was believed to be higher. Neighbouring countries allowed thousands of refugees from Syria access to safety and assistance on their territories; however, in mid-August, Turkey and Iraq curtailed entry, in violation of international law. By the end of the year, thousands of people were living in camps beside the border with Turkey in dire conditions.

Death penalty

The death penalty remained in force. It was not possible to confirm whether any death sentences were imposed or if executions were carried out.

Amnesty International visits/reports

🚌 Amnesty International delegates undertook numerous visits to Syria and to neighbouring countries to carry out human rights research on Syria.

📄 "I wanted to die": Syria's torture survivors speak out (MDE 24/016/2012)

📄 Deadly reprisals: Deliberate killings and other abuses by Syria's armed forces (MDE 24/041/2012)

📄 All-out repression: Purging dissent in Aleppo, Syria (MDE 24/061/2012)

📄 Syria: Civilians bearing the brunt in the battle for Aleppo (MDE 24/073/2012)

📄 Syria: Indiscriminate attacks terrorize and displace civilians (MDE 24/078/2012)

TAIWAN

TAIWAN
Head of state: Ma Ying-jeou
Head of government: Chen Chun (replaced Wu Den-yih in February)

Taiwan carried out six executions. As of December, prosecution and defence lawyers were required to debate sentencing and related issues in death penalty cases before the Supreme Court. Indigenous people were caught in protracted land disputes and the authorities failed to protect their rights as the post-2009 typhoon reconstruction process continued. Media monopolies expanded further. A gender equality education curriculum was implemented after a year's delay.

Death penalty

Six men were executed – all in December; 55 prisoners were awaiting execution and had exhausted all appeals. From December, hearings of all death penalty cases at the Supreme Court were required to include oral arguments on sentencing and related issues by both prosecution and defence lawyers. The panel of judges would then also take into consideration the opinion of victims' families in determining the sentence.

■ On 31 August, after 21 years of litigation, the High Court reconfirmed a "not guilty verdict" and freed the "Hsichih Trio". Other death penalty cases similarly involving torture and forced confessions remained unresolved.

Justice system

In August, the Taipei District Prosecutor's Office again decided not to pursue charges against those responsible for airman Chiang Kuo-ching's wrongful execution in 1997.

Indigenous Peoples' rights

Guarantees in the Indigenous People's Basic Law were not implemented and disputes continued over relocation processes initiated after typhoon Morakot in 2009. Under the Regulation on Defining Special Areas, which allows authorities to designate land as unsafe for habitation, several Indigenous communities faced forced relocation and future land use restrictions.

Freedom of expression

Concentration of ownership of media outlets raised concerns about freedom of expression and editorial independence. In July, the National Communications Commission (NCC) conditionally approved Want Want China Times Group's acquisition of a major cable television channel and, in November, acquisition of newspaper giant Next Media. In December, the Taipei High Administrative Court ruled that the NCC had the executive power to revoke the Group's acquisition of another cable television channel because the channel had failed to meet the conditions set by the NCC.

Rights of lesbian, gay, bisexual, transgender and intersex people

A gender equality education curriculum was implemented after delays due to objections from conservative religious groups in 2011. However, three planned sets of resource manuals for elementary and high-school teachers including content on gender identity, sexual orientation and alternative families were not published.

TAJIKISTAN

REPUBLIC OF TAJIKISTAN
Head of state: Emomali Rahmon
Head of government: Ogil Ogilov

Torture and other ill-treatment remained widespread and impunity for perpetrators continued. There was no access to detention facilities for independent monitoring bodies. Freedom of expression was still under attack, despite some liberalization in the law.

Background

In July, clashes between government and armed groups took place in Khorog, Gorno-Badakhshan Autonomous Region (GBAO). In some of the most intense fighting since the end of the 1992-1997 civil war, unofficial reports said some 150 people including soldiers and civilians were killed during a government military operation launched against forces loyal to the deputy commander of the Ishkashim border unit, former opposition leader in the civil war Tolib Ayombekov.

Torture and other ill-treatment

In March, the government stated its intention to implement recommendations from the UN Human Rights Council's Universal Periodic Review, such as ensuring detainees access to legal and medical assistance when in custody. In April, the Criminal Code was amended to include torture as a criminal offence. In June, the Supreme Court provided guidelines for judges in cases of alleged or suspected torture or other ill-treatment; and the General Prosecutor's Office drafted recommendations for prosecutors on investigation of torture cases.

Despite these positive developments, reports of torture and other ill-treatment continued. The UN Special Rapporteur on torture and the UN Committee against Torture both published their findings. After his visit in May, the UN Special Rapporteur stated that torture and other ill-treatment "happens often... in a wide variety of settings".

In November, the UN Committee against Torture noted "numerous and consistent allegations ... of routine use of torture and ill-treatment of suspects, principally to extract confessions ... primarily during the first hours of interrogation in police custody as

T

well as in temporary and pre-trial detention facilities run by the State Committee of National Security (SCNS) and the Department for the Fight against Organized Crime."

Children, elderly people and witnesses in criminal cases reported instances of torture and other ill-treatment. Torture methods included the use of electric shocks, boiling water, suffocation, beatings, and burning with cigarettes. There were reports of rape and threats of rape in relation to female and male detainees, as well as psychological torture.

Most instances of torture and other ill-treatment occurred before the suspect was registered at a police station. Suspects were not informed of their rights (to see a lawyer, to notify family or to remain silent) until the detention was registered. This should happen within three hours of being taken to a police station, but in practice often happened much later. There were cases of incommunicado detention for several days or even weeks before registration.

■ Sherik Karamhudoev, head of the opposition group the Islamic Renaissance Party in Khorog, GBAO, disappeared on 24 July during the clashes. His whereabouts were only made known to his family on 8 August, and he was not allowed to see his defence lawyers for nearly two months. He was reportedly tortured while in the SCNS detention centre in Dushanbe. He was charged with organizing a criminal group and illegal possession of firearms.

Detainees were routinely interrogated without a lawyer and some lawyers were unable to see their clients for several days, despite legal provisions ensuring the right of detainees to see a lawyer from the time the detention is registered.

People accused of involvement in banned Islamic movements and Islamist groups or parties were usually detained by the Interior Ministry and the SCNS. They were at particular risk of torture and other ill-treatment and access to their defence lawyers was limited or denied. Their lawyers also had inadequate access to case materials against their clients.

There were reports of people being abducted by Tajikistani security forces outside their territory and being forcibly returned to Tajikistan. In several cases, the authorities based extradition requests for people they alleged to be members of banned Islamic groups or Islamist parties on unreliable or incomplete information. The individuals said they were tortured after their return.

■ In April, 27-year-old Savriddin Dzhurayev was sentenced to 26 years in prison after being convicted of plotting to overthrow constitutional order "in the period around 1992", when he was seven years old. He had fled to Russia in 2006 and his extradition was requested by Tajikistan in 2009. He was given temporary asylum status in Russia in August 2011. The European Court of Human Rights had instructed Russia not to extradite while it examined his case, but in October 2011 he was abducted in Moscow by unidentified men speaking Tajikistani and forcibly returned to Tajikistan. He told his lawyers he was subjected to ill-treatment in detention in Khujand and had been interrogated without a lawyer.

In November, the UN Committee against Torture urged Tajikistan to "cease the practice of abducting and forcibly returning individuals to Tajikistan from other States and subsequently holding them in incommunicado detention, and ensure that they are not subjected to acts of torture and ill-treatment".

Lack of accountability

A general climate of impunity persisted. Although – for the first time – a police inspector was found guilty of torture in the case of a 17-year-old boy in Khatlon region and sentenced to seven years' imprisonment in September, and a second officer was sentenced to one year for the crime of torture in December, in other cases, law enforcement officials sentenced for "exceeding official authority" were released early, under the 2011 Law on Amnesties. For example, in July, the Dushanbe Prosecutor's Office ruled to end the criminal investigations against two police officers allegedly responsible for the death in custody of Safarali Sangov in March 2011 and they were amnestied.

Despite the Criminal Procedural Code stating that evidence obtained through torture should be excluded from court, there were no cases in the year where judges implemented exclusionary measures.

Victims of torture and their relatives reported they were afraid to lodge complaints with Prosecutor's offices for fear of reprisals.

The authorities denied access to detention facilities for independent monitors, including the ICRC and local NGOs.

Judges at remand hearings regularly disregarded allegations of torture and other ill-treatment by detainees, referring detainees to the prosecutor to lodge a complaint.

During investigations into allegations of torture and other ill-treatment, victims and their families were not given regular updates or access to case materials. In May, the Constitutional Court upheld the General Prosecutor's decision to limit access for the victims of human rights violations to evidence against the alleged perpetrators.

Prosecutors' offices routinely did not disclose information about how the complaints were examined or the grounds for their rulings that there was no evidence of wrongdoing by officials. Delays by the prosecutor in demanding medical examinations on alleged victims of torture or other ill-treatment meant that physical traces had disappeared.

Deaths in custody

The authorities failed to protect the lives of people in custody. Deaths in custody were not investigated effectively and officials were rarely punished.

■ In September, 27-year-old Hamza Ikromzoda died in prison, allegedly after torture. In October, a forensic examination concluded that he had committed suicide. Former cellmates who alleged witnessing his death were reportedly subjected to torture and other ill-treatment in prisons in Dushanbe and Khujand.

Freedom of expression

On 2 August, the Criminal Code was amended to decriminalize libel, although penalties remained for insulting the President. However, there were continuing reports of government attempts to restrict the right to freedom of expression of human rights activists, lawyers, medical experts and journalists.

In October, Khujand city court ruled to shut down Amparo, a human rights organization monitoring abuses in the army, allegedly for administrative violations. Human rights activists believed the decision was politically motivated and that the charges against Amparo were unsubstantiated.

Violence against women

A law on the prevention of domestic violence was finally adopted in December, eight years after its first reading in Parliament.

Amnesty International visits/reports

🚍 Amnesty International delegates visited Tajikistan in June.

📄 Shattered lives: Torture and other ill-treatment in Tajikistan (EUR 60/004/2012)

📄 Tajikistan: Dissenting campaign groups should not be silenced (PRE01/579/2012)

TANZANIA

UNITED REPUBLIC OF TANZANIA
Head of state:	Jakaya Kikwete
Head of government:	Mizengo Peter Pinda
Head of Zanzibar government:	Ali Mohamed Shein

The authorities restricted the rights of freedom of expression and assembly. Violence against women continued and perpetrators were rarely held to account. Mtabila camp hosting some 37,000 Burundian refugees was closed.

Background

Tanzania embarked on a constitutional review process, after the 2011 Constitutional Review Act was amended in February. President Kikwete established the Constitutional Review Commission (CRC) in April, and in May commissioners were sworn in. The review process was due to be completed by October 2013.

Freedom of expression – media

Tanzania continued to regulate the media with laws incompatible with its Constitution and international law. The Newspaper Act and Penal Code were used to suppress media freedom, despite calls from journalists to review these laws.

■ In July, *Mwanahalisi*, a weekly tabloid, was banned amid allegations that it published seditious articles likely to incite violence and jeopardize peace after publishing a story on the abduction and beating of Dr Steven Ulimboka, Chairperson of the Special Committee of Doctors and leader of the doctors' strike. The newspaper remained banned at the end of the year.

■ In September David Mwangosi, a Channel Ten television journalist, was killed by police. He had been covering an event held by the opposition political party Chama Cha Demokrasia na Maendeleo (CHADEMA) in Nyololo village in the Iringa region, when police disrupted the event and dispersed CHADEMA supporters. One junior officer was charged with murder in relation to his death and was on remand at end of the year.

Freedom of assembly and excessive use of force

Tanzanian police and other security forces used excessive force to disperse protesters.

T

■ In August, riot police allegedly shot newspaper vendor Ally Nzona in the head as they dispersed a CHADEMA demonstration at a primary school in Morogoro. Ally Nzona, who was not participating in the demonstration, died from injuries he sustained.

In February, police arrested 16 human rights defenders, including 14 women, for holding an unlawful assembly. They were released the same day. The defenders were part of a group of around 200 activists taking part in a public demonstration in the capital, Dar-es-Salaam, calling for the government to resolve the doctors' dispute.

Violence against women and girls

Sexual and other forms of gender-based violence, particularly domestic violence, remained widespread. Older women were vulnerable to attack on the basis of allegations of witchcraft. Few perpetrators were brought to justice. The practice of female genital mutilation remained prevalent in some areas of the country.

Refugees and asylum-seekers

Following a meeting between the governments of Tanzania and Burundi and UNHCR, the UN refugee agency, the decision was made to close Mtabila camp – home to some 37,000 Burundian refugees – on 31 December. In July, the Ministry of Home Affairs declared that refugees in Mtabila camp would lose their refugee status when the camp closed.

In November, UNHCR reported that around 1,000 people per day were being assisted to voluntarily return to Burundi.

Death penalty

The courts continued to impose death sentences. No executions were carried out. A petition challenging the constitutionality of the death penalty filed by civil society in 2008 remained pending.

THAILAND

KINGDOM OF THAILAND
Head of state: King Bhumibol Adulyadej
Head of government: Yingluck Shinawatra

The armed conflict continued in the South as insurgents targeted civilians in violent attacks, while security forces enjoyed impunity for human rights violations. The Truth for Reconciliation Commission of Thailand issued its final report, placing responsibility for the 2010 political violence on both sides; however, accountability remained slow in coming. The government continued to use the lese-majesty law and the Computer Crimes Act to restrict freedom of expression. Asylum-seekers and refugees faced possible *refoulement* to their home countries.

Internal armed conflict

Civilians remained at risk of attacks that resulted in deaths and injuries in the southernmost provinces of Narathiwat, Pattani, Yala and parts of Songkhla. Government teachers and schools viewed as symbols of the state were targeted for attack, resulting in school closures during the latter part of the year. Insurgency leaders accused security forces of extrajudicial executions in Yala province. Impunity continued for most violations committed by security forces in the South.

■ On 29 January, government-sponsored paramilitary rangers shot at a group of nine ethnic Malay Muslim civilians travelling in a truck in Nong Chik district, Pattani province. Four of the travellers were killed and four others were injured in the shooting. The rangers claimed they shot the civilians, believing they had links with an insurgent group and were involved in an attack on the rangers' outpost. A Truth Commission set up to investigate the incident found that the civilians had no links to insurgent groups.

■ On 21 September, insurgents killed six people, including a local defence volunteer, and injured an estimated 50 after initially opening fire on a gold shop, then detonating a car bomb in a market in Sai Buri District, Pattani province.

■ On 30 October, Mahama Ma-ae, a Muslim religious schoolteacher who police suspected of having ties to an insurgency group, was shot dead in Yala province. On

14 November, Abdullateh Todir, a Yala imam who had been targeted in an attack in 2011 that resulted in the death of his daughter, was shot and killed. Insurgency leaders accused government security forces of these killings.

■ On 3-4 December, insurgents killed one teacher and injured another in two separate incidents in Narathiwat province. A school administrator and a teacher were also killed in a school attack in Pattani province on 11 December. Following these attacks, schools in Narathiwat, Pattani and Yala provinces closed for several days.

The 2005 Emergency Decree on Public Administration in State of Emergency remained in place throughout the year, with the government renewing its mandate every three months. The decree allows immunity from prosecution for officials who may have committed human rights violations – including torture.

Accountability for political violence

In September, the Truth for Reconciliation Commission released its final report on the violence surrounding the April-May 2010 anti-government protests in Bangkok, which resulted in 92 deaths. The report placed responsibility on government security forces, including the army, and the so-called "black shirts", a militant armed group embedded with the protesters and linked to the anti-government United Front for Democracy against Dictatorship (UDD), also known as the "red shirts". The report found that government forces had used weapons of war and live ammunition on protesters. It made extensive recommendations, including calling on the government to address abuses committed by all parties, through a fair and impartial justice system, and to provide "reparation and restoration to those affected by violent incidents".

In January, the government agreed to provide financial compensation to victims of the 2010 violence. In May, a National Reconciliation Bill that included an amnesty provision for those involved in the 2010 violence led to more protests. The Bill was put on hold in July. After a court found security forces responsible for the May 2010 killing of UDD protester Phan Khamkong, murder charges were lodged against former Prime Minister Abhisit Vejjajiva and his former deputy Suthep Thaugsuban in December. They were the first officials to be charged in

connection with the 2010 political violence. The trials of 24 UDD protest leaders charged with terrorism also started in December.

Freedom of expression

Freedom of expression continued to be curtailed, primarily through the lese-majesty law (Article 112 of the Criminal Code) and the 2007 Computer Crimes Act, which provide for heavy jail sentences for perceived insults to the monarchy. Efforts to challenge or amend the lese-majesty law in 2012 failed. In October, the Constitutional Court upheld Article 112 as constitutional and in November, Parliament dismissed a bill to amend the law.

■ In May, prisoner of conscience Amphon Tangnoppakul, aged in his sixties and known as "Uncle SMS", died of cancer while serving a 20-year prison term for lese-majesty. He was arrested in August 2010 and convicted in November 2011 for sending four SMS text messages deemed insulting to the monarchy. The court denied all eight requests for bail despite his poor health.

■ In May, Chiranuch Premchaiporn of the Prachatai online news site was sentenced to one year in prison under the Computer Crimes Act and fined 30,000 baht (US$979), reduced to a suspended sentence of eight months and a fine of 20,000 baht (US$653), for failing to promptly remove 10 comments deemed offensive to the monarchy which were posted by others on the Prachatai website between April and November 2008.

■ Magazine editor Somyot Prueksakasemsuk remained in detention throughout the year, facing up to 30 years' imprisonment after being charged under the lese-majesty law in April 2011 for publishing two articles in his magazine, *Voice of Taksin*. The court repeatedly denied his requests for bail.

Refugees and migrants

Asylum-seekers continued to face the risk of arrest and prolonged detention as well as forced return (*refoulement*) to countries where they would be at risk of persecution. Following discussions with the Myanmar government, Thailand's National Security Council indicated that the 146,900 Myanmar refugees living in Thailand could return to Myanmar within a year, despite continued instability in Myanmar's ethnic areas and the lack of protections to facilitate a safe, dignified and voluntary return process.

T

Documented and undocumented migrant workers were threatened with deportation in mid-December for failure to complete a national verification process.

Death penalty

There were no reported executions. Courts continued to hand down death sentences throughout the year. In August, the state commuted the sentences of at least 58 death row prisoners to life imprisonment.

TIMOR-LESTE

DEMOCRATIC REPUBLIC OF TIMOR-LESTE
Head of state: José Maria Vasconcelos (Taur
                              Matan Rua, replaced José Manuel
                              Ramos-Horta in May)
Head of government: Kay Rala Xanana Gusmão

Impunity persisted for crimes against humanity and gross human rights violations committed during the Indonesian occupation (1975-1999). Security forces were accused of human rights violations, including ill-treatment and excessive use of force. Women and girls faced high levels of domestic violence.

Background

Presidential and Parliamentary elections, held respectively in March-April and July, took place without incident. In December 2012, the UN Security Council ended the mandate of the UN Integrated Mission in Timor-Leste.

Police and security forces

Security forces faced allegations of ill-treatment and excessive use of force, sometimes leading to death. Accountability mechanisms for the police and military were weak. The UN Police presence ended in December.

Women's rights

Levels of domestic violence against women remained high. Although some cases were prosecuted in the courts, many resulted in suspended sentences. There were concerns about the lack of adequate protection for victims and witnesses.

Timor-Leste's maternal mortality ratio was one of the highest in the Asia-Pacific region.

Impunity

Little progress was made in addressing crimes against humanity and other human rights violations committed by Indonesian security forces and their auxiliaries from 1975-1999. The mandate of the Serious Crimes Investigation Team ended in December, having failed to complete around 60 investigations into outstanding cases of serious human rights violations committed in 1999.

■ In December, the Dili District Court imprisoned three former Besi Merah Putih militia members for crimes against humanity committed in the context of the 1999 independence referendum. Miguel Soares and Salvador de Jesus were sentenced to nine and 16 years respectively for murder, while Faustino de Carvalho was sentenced to six years for forcible transfer of a population and the illegal detention of women and children.

The Timorese authorities failed to implement recommendations of the Commission for Reception, Truth and Reconciliation and of the bilateral Indonesia-Timor-Leste Commission of Truth and Friendship. The recommendations included providing reparation to victims and their families, and taking effective measures to identify victims of enforced disappearance and children separated from their families.

■ In February, Parliament began debating two draft laws establishing a national reparations programme and a "Public Memory Institute". However, the debate was postponed for the third time since June 2010, and no date was set for its resumption.

Amnesty International visits/reports

🚘 Amnesty International delegates visited Timor-Leste in October and November.

▤ Timor-Leste: Remembering the past – recommendations to effectively establish the "National Reparations Programme" and "Public Memory Institute" (ASA 57/001/2012)

TOGO

TOGOLESE REPUBLIC
Head of state: **Faure Gnassingbé**
Head of government: **Kwesi Ahoomey-Zunu (replaced Gilbert Fossoun Houngbo in July)**

Demonstrations by political parties and students were dispersed by security forces using excessive force. Torture was used in order to extract confessions. Freedoms of expression, assembly and of the press were undermined by the authorities. The Truth, Justice and Reconciliation Commission (TJRC) published its first findings but by the end of the year no concrete measures had been taken to end impunity.

Background

Throughout the year, demonstrations in favour of political and economic changes were regularly organized, some of them resulting in clashes between protesters and security forces.

In January, the authorities tried to prevent publication of a report by the National Commission of Human Rights (CNDH). The report condemned torture by security forces and notably by the National Intelligence Agency against civilian and military personnel accused of plotting against the state, including Kpatcha Gnassingbé, half-brother of the President. Following national and international protests, the authorities accepted the findings of the CNDH and committed to implement its recommendations to fight against impunity. However, by the end of the year no concrete steps had been taken.

In May, the National Assembly adopted a law amending the Electoral Code. Several opposition parties accused the authorities of having "unilaterally" adopted the amendments and demanded their repeal. Changes were made to the legislation after protests, but some opposition parties still refused to restore dialogue and disagreed on the conditions for organizing legislative elections originally scheduled to be held before the end of 2012 and postponed until 2013.

Excessive use of force

The security forces regularly used excessive force to repress demonstrations organized by political parties.

■ In June, the security forces hunted down protesters in private homes as well as in a place of worship. They also threw tear gas into a classroom at a school in the Catholic mission of Amoutiévé in Lomé, the capital.

■ In July, police forces attacked the home of Jean-Pierre Fabre, Chairman of the National Alliance for Change (Alliance nationale pour le changement, ANC). They threw tear gas for several hours before entering by force to beat up those present and arrest some of them.

Torture and other ill-treatment

Torture in pre-trial detention was used to extract confessions or implicate defendants.

■ In April, four students, including three members of the National Union of Togolese Pupils and Students, were ill-treated during their arrest and detention in the civil prison of Kara, approximately 430km north of Lomé. They had been charged with "incitement to rebellion" for organizing a meeting to discuss the government's promises to allocate scholarships. They were released without trial one month later.

■ In August, Kossi Amétépé was arrested during an anti-government demonstration. He was beaten by members of the Rapid Intervention Force and detained in their camp in Lomé, where he was whipped with ropes and trampled upon.

Freedom of expression

The authorities curtailed freedom of expression and assembly by threatening human rights defenders and banning demonstrations. They claimed these measures were necessary to prevent risks to safety and to maintain public order.

■ In February, Koffi Kounté, President of the CNDH, received threats from the entourage of the Head of State after he refused to endorse a report known to have been falsified by the government. Fearing reprisals, Koffi Kounté took refuge in France.

■ In August, a citizenship education meeting organized by the Save Togo (CST) movement was banned in Kara. Leaders of the CST were assaulted and hunted down by security forces.

Security forces targeted journalists who were covering or filming anti-government marches.

■ In October, Justin Anani, a journalist affiliated to the International Federation of Journalists, was attacked by

T

security forces in Lomé while covering a protest march organized by the CST and other opposition groups.

Prison conditions

Conditions in many detention centres amounted to cruel, inhuman or degrading treatment due to overcrowding and lack of access to health care. The situation reportedly led to a number of deaths, including at least 19 prisoners at Lomé civil prison.
■ In May, Bertin Sama, charged with drug trafficking, died from a lung infection at Lomé civil prison. He had repeatedly sought care but was transferred to hospital only two days before he died.

Impunity

In April, the TJRC issued its first report after conducting interviews with victims and alleged perpetrators of political violence between 1958 and 2005. The President asked for forgiveness on behalf of the nation and the authorities committed to take appeasement actions and award compensation to victims. However, at the end of the year, no concrete action had been taken.

Amnesty International visits/reports

📓 Togo: The authorities censor a report denouncing torture (AFR 57/001/2012)

📓 Togo: Vague d'arrestations et répression de manifestants (AFR 57/004/2012)

TRINIDAD AND TOBAGO

REPUBLIC OF TRINIDAD AND TOBAGO
Head of state: George Maxwell Richards
Head of government: Kamla Persad-Bissessar

Reports of unlawful killings by police continued, some in circumstances suggesting that they may have been extrajudicial executions. Death sentences continued to be handed down.

Background

The murder rate remained high; 377 homicides were recorded during the year.

Legislation that allowed criminal proceedings for certain offences to be abandoned if more than 10 years had passed since the offence was committed was introduced in August and repealed in October following a public outcry at its application in high-profile corruption cases.

Police and security forces

There were continued reports of unlawful killings by police. Official claims that police had fired in self-defence were frequently challenged by eyewitnesses.
■ Atiba Duncan was fatally shot by police in April in the community of Mt D'or Road. Police officers claimed he had pointed a gun at them as they tried to arrest him. However, a forensic pathologist found that he had been shot in the back. Investigations were continuing at the end of the year.

In October the Police Complaints Authority called for a "quicker response time to the lengthy investigative process in matters of fatal police shootings". It also called for CCTV cameras to be placed in various key areas of police stations.

Justice system

A 2011 act to expedite the judicial process by eliminating preliminary inquiries was due to come into force in January 2013. However, there were concerns that the necessary infrastructure would not be in place to make the legislation operational.

Violence against women and girls

In November, the Trinidad and Tobago Police Service announced that 689 cases of sexual offences had been reported in the period between January and September. This represented an increase of more than 200 compared with the whole of 2011.

The draft National Policy on Gender and Development, under consideration since 2009, was reportedly before the Cabinet at the end of the year.

Rights of lesbian, gay, bisexual, transgender and intersex people

Advocates for LGBTI rights continued to lobby for the inclusion of discrimination on the grounds of sexual orientation in the Equal Opportunity Act. Same-sex relationships remained criminalized. Although these laws were not enforced, they contributed to creating a discriminatory environment.

Prison conditions

In several cases of ill-treatment, prison officers were successfully prosecuted through the civil courts. However, in the majority of cases there was no subsequent disciplinary action.

In March, the High Court ruled in the case of a prisoner beaten in Golden Grove Prison in December 2009, that "remarks made by the courts in several such matters appear to have been ignored, and there is every indication, from the repetition of like incidents, that the perpetrators face no consequences".

In July, in a separate case the High Court found that 302 assault and battery claims had been brought against state employees between September 2005 and May 2012. It called on the authorities to provide training for prison officers on the appropriate use of force.

Death penalty

At least five people were sentenced to death; there were no executions. In January the Prime Minister stated publicly that the government was committed to implementing the death penalty.

Amnesty International visits/reports

🚐 Amnesty International delegates visited Trinidad and Tobago in September/October.

TUNISIA

REPUBLIC OF TUNISIA
Head of state: Moncef Marzouki
Head of government: Hamadi Jebali

The authorities restricted freedom of expression and prosecuted several people using repressive laws enacted under the previous government. There were new reports of torture and other ill-treatment by police, who also used excessive force against demonstrators. Families of people killed and injured during the uprisings that ousted the former president in January 2011 continued to call for justice and reparations. Some former officials were tried and imprisoned. Women continued to face discrimination in both law and practice. Nine people were sentenced to death; no executions were carried out.

Background

The state of emergency imposed in January 2011 was renewed and remained in force throughout 2012.

The coalition government elected in October 2011 for one year remained in office throughout 2012. In October 2012, the government announced that new parliamentary and presidential elections would be held in June and July 2013. The National Constituent Assembly (NCA), tasked with drafting a new constitution, issued an initial draft in August but said that it could not meet its one-year deadline, which was then extended until February 2013. The initial draft was criticized on several human rights grounds, notably in relation to articles concerning the status of women, the right to life and the criminalization of expression deemed offensive to religion.

In August, a draft bill criminalizing acts considered offensive to "religion and the sacred" was submitted to the NCA by the Ennahda Islamist party, the majority party in the ruling coalition. The bill was still under consideration at the end of the year.

The authorities took steps apparently intended to reform the judiciary and promote judicial independence. The Minister of Justice dismissed 82 judges for alleged corruption in May, reinstating nine of them a month later, and in September the Supreme Council of the Judiciary (CSM) transferred, promoted or changed the functions of over 700 judges. However, divisions within the NCA prevented the adoption of a draft bill to replace the CSM with a Temporary Judiciary Council; the draft bill lacked adequate safeguards against the arbitrary dismissal or transfer of judges and would have given the executive authorities significant power over the proposed new judicial body. In September, the Minister of Justice appointed himself head of the CSM, a position previously held by former President Zine El 'Abidine Ben 'Ali.

There were continuing public protests and demonstrations by religious groups, people dissatisfied with the pace of reform and harsh living conditions, as well as activists advocating women's rights, media reform and greater freedom of expression. Some of the protests became violent and were met with force – sometimes excessive force – by the police. Nearly 300 protesters and bystanders were

T

reportedly injured during use of excessive force by the police in Siliana, a city south west of Tunis, during demonstrations on 27, 28 and 29 November calling for the departure of the governor of Siliana, economic development of the town and the release of 13 detainees arrested during protests in April 2011.

By contrast, the police were accused of failing to intervene in a timely manner on several occasions when artists, writers and others were violently attacked by groups of religious extremists, mostly alleged Salafists (Sunni Muslims who advocated a return to what they considered to be Islam's fundamental principles). Such attacks were mounted against alleged alcohol sellers as well as art exhibitions and cultural and other events. In September, the US embassy was attacked in relation to an anti-Islamist film posted on the internet.

Dozens of Salafists were reported to have been detained in the aftermath of these attacks. More than 50 of them went on hunger strike to protest against their arrest and detention conditions and two died in custody as a result in November. Most were reported to have ended their hunger strike by the end of the year. In October, after another Salafist was arrested, Salafists were reported to have attacked two police stations in Manouba, resulting in two deaths and injuries to several police officers.

Tunisia's human rights record was assessed under the UN Universal Periodic Review in May. The government accepted most of the UN recommendations but rejected those urging the decriminalization of defamation and same-sex relations, the repeal of laws that discriminated against women, and abolition of the death penalty.

The UN and African Union Special Rapporteurs on human rights defenders both visited Tunisia in September.

Transitional justice

The government created a Ministry for Human Rights and Transitional Justice in January to develop strategies for addressing past human rights violations and to guarantee the future protection of human rights. The following month, however, the new Minister publicly declared that homosexuality was not a human right but a "perversion".

In April, the Ministry of Justice established a Technical Committee composed of officials and civil society representatives to consult people throughout Tunisia on issues of truth, justice, reparation and reform. The Committee prepared a draft law proposing the creation of an independent Council of Truth and Dignity to oversee the process of transitional justice, which it submitted to the President and the NCA in October.

Following his November visit, the UN Special Rapporteur on the promotion of truth, justice, reparation and guarantees of non-recurrence expressed concern that Tunisia's transitional justice process was not comprehensive and was failing to give equal importance to each of the four elements of transitional justice.

The Fact-Finding Commission on Abuses Committed from 17 December 2010 until the End of its Mandate (known as the Bouderbala Commission) issued its report in May. This described the events during the uprisings which overthrew former President Ben 'Ali's government, and listed the names of those killed and injured. However, it failed to identify the individuals responsible for the use of lethal force and human rights violations.

The authorities provided financial compensation and medical care to those injured during the uprisings and to the families of those killed but were criticized for not taking into account the severity of victims' injuries and other factors, such as their loss of study or employment opportunities. Some families of people killed refused to accept compensation as they felt justice had not been done.

Several senior officials under former President Ben 'Ali were sentenced to long prison terms in connection with the killings of protesters during the December 2010-January 2011 uprisings. Some low- and middle-ranking former officials were convicted only of individual responsibility for shooting protesters, and were imprisoned.

■ Former Interior Minister Rafiq Haj Kacem was sentenced to 12 years' imprisonment in June for complicity in the murders of protesters in Kasserine, Thala, Kairouan and Tajerouine by a military tribunal at Kef. Four other former high-ranking officials in the Department of State Security were convicted and sentenced to prison terms of up to 10 years, and six former middle-ranking officials were sentenced to prison terms for murder.

■ Former President Ben 'Ali received a sentence of life imprisonment in July after the Tunis Military Tribunal convicted him in his absence over the killing and injuring of protesters in Greater Tunis. Thirty-nine former members of his security forces who were present in court were convicted and sentenced to prison terms of up to 20 years.

Both cases were referred to a military appeal tribunal and had not been resolved by the end of the year.

The process of bringing former officials to justice for crimes committed during the uprisings was questionable on several grounds, notably because trials were held before military tribunals rather than the civil courts. Also, victims, their families and lawyers criticized what they saw as a failure by the prosecuting authorities to conduct thorough investigations, and complained that they were subject to intimidation by those under investigation or accused, some of whom remained in positions of authority.

Torture and other ill-treatment

There were reports of torture and other ill-treatment by police. In August the Ministry of Human Rights and Transitional Justice said that, following a public consultation, it planned to establish a new independent national institution to combat torture. The proposed body would be empowered to visit places of detention and help draft new legislation, and would report annually and operate in line with international standards.

■ Abderraouf Khemmassi died on 8 September in police custody in Tunis, 11 days after his arrest for alleged theft. An autopsy attributed his death to a blow to the head and recorded other injuries. Four police officers were subsequently arrested and charged with causing his death.

Freedom of expression

Despite their stated commitment to respect freedom of expression, the authorities took action against journalists, artists, bloggers and critics using articles 121(3) and 226 of the Penal Code, which criminalize expression deemed to threaten public order, public morals or sacred values. In October, however, they said they would implement Decrees 115 and 116 of 2011 on the Press and Audiovisual Material.

■ Jabeur Mejri and Ghazi Beji were convicted of insulting Islam and Muslims under articles 121(3) and 226 of the Penal Code and article 86 of the Telecommunication Code in March, after they posted comments and images on the internet. Ghazi Beji fled the country and was sentenced in his absence. Both men were fined and sentenced to seven and a half years in prison, the maximum permitted. Their sentences were confirmed by the Monastir Court of Appeal on 20 June, following which the case was referred to the Court of Cassation, whose decision was still pending at the end of the year, at which time Jabeur Mejri was being held at Mehdia prison.

In June, Salafists attacked an art exhibition in Tunis, claiming that some of the artworks were offensive to Islam, sparking large protests in other cities. In September, protesters attacked the US embassy after a film deemed offensive to Islam was posted on the internet; four people were reported to have been killed in the violence and others injured.

■ Nadia Jelassi and Mohamed Ben Slima, artists associated with the art exhibition attacked by Salafists in June, were summoned to appear before an investigating magistrate on charges of attacking sacred values, offending public morals and disturbing public order. The case was ongoing at the end of the year.

■ Ayoub Massoudi was convicted in September of undermining the reputation of the army and defaming a civil servant. He received a suspended prison sentence of four months and was initially banned from travelling abroad. A presidential adviser, he had resigned and publicly criticized the extradition of former Libyan Prime Minister Al-Baghdadi Al-Mahmoudi from Tunisia to Libya in June, accusing the Minister of Defence and the head of the army of failing to inform the President of the planned extradition. He was tried under Article 98 of the Code of Military Justice and Article 128 of the Penal Code.

Women's rights

Women continued to face discrimination in both law and practice. The government rejected recommendations made under the UN Universal Periodic Review to repeal discriminatory laws relating to inheritance and child custody. The Penal Code continued to provide, among other discriminatory measures, that a man who rapes or abducts a female minor can escape punishment by marrying her.

■ A woman, aged 27, who accused two police officers of raping her while a third attempted to extort money from her fiancé, was herself charged with intentional indecent behaviour in September after the police said they found her and her fiancé in an "immoral position".

T

The couple were summoned to appear before an investigating judge. They filed charges against the three police officers, who were arrested and faced prosecution. The charges against the woman and her fiancé were later dropped.

Death penalty

The death penalty remained in force. Nine death sentences were reported to have been imposed. In September, the government rejected a recommendation made under the UN Universal Periodic Review calling for the abolition of the death penalty. However, the authorities maintained the moratorium on executions in place since 1991. According to the authorities there were 125 commutations and 179 people on death row at the end of the year.

Amnesty International visits/reports

🚌 Amnesty International delegates visited Tunisia in September.

📰 Tunisia: Submission for consideration by the National Constituent Assembly on the guarantee of civil, political, economic, social and cultural rights in the new constitution (MDE 30/004/2012)

📰 One step forward, two steps back? One year since Tunisia's landmark elections (MDE 30/010/2012)

TURKEY

REPUBLIC OF TURKEY
Head of state: **Abdullah Gül**
Head of government: **Recep Tayyip Erdoğan**

Freedom of expression remained restricted despite limited legislative reforms. The police used excessive force to break up peaceful demonstrations. Investigations and prosecutions into alleged human rights abuses by state officials were flawed. The pattern of unfair trials under anti-terrorism legislation persisted. Bomb attacks claimed the lives of civilians. No progress was made in recognizing the right to conscientious objection or in outlawing discrimination on grounds of sexual orientation or gender identity. The number of refugees from Syria seeking shelter in Turkey reached almost 150,000. Turkey adopted stronger legal protections to combat violence against women and girls but existing mechanisms were inadequately implemented in practice.

Background

Discussions regarding the adoption of a new Constitution continued throughout the year but with little evidence of consensus among the political parties or effective engagement with civil society.

In October, the Parliament passed a resolution authorizing military intervention in Syria for 12 months and another extending the existing authorization for intervention targeting the armed Kurdistan Workers' Party (PKK) in northern Iraq for another year. The vote followed a Syrian mortar landing in Akçakale, a border town in Turkey's Şanlıurfa province, killing five people.

Armed clashes between the armed forces and the PKK had also increased. The army claimed to have "rendered ineffective" 500 armed PKK members in September alone. In December the government announced that it had taken part in negotiations with the PKK.

Hundreds of prisoners across Turkey went on hunger strike in February and again in September to protest at the authorities' refusal to allow imprisoned PKK leader Abdullah Öcalan to receive visits from his lawyers, among other demands. The protests ended in April and November respectively, following calls to do so from Abdullah Öcalan.

In May, the Parliament passed the urban regeneration law, which removed procedural guarantees for residents affected by such projects and heightened concerns that they would result in forced evictions. In October, the Parliament passed trade union legislation that failed to uphold ILO standards, particularly with regard to the right to strike and the right to collective bargaining.

In September, more than 300 serving and retired military officers were convicted of planning "Sledgehammer", an alleged violent plot to overthrow the government. The verdict polarized opinion in Turkey between those seeing it as a victory against impunity for abuses by the military and others who alleged that the evidence used to secure the convictions had been fabricated.

Freedom of expression

Little progress was made in addressing the restrictions on freedom of expression in the media and more widely in civil society. Criminal prosecutions frequently targeted non-violent dissenting opinions, particularly on controversial political issues and criticism of public officials and institutions. Dissenting opinions related to issues of Kurdish rights and politics were foremost of those subjected to criminal prosecution.

In July, Parliament passed a series of reforms as part of the "Third Judicial Package", which abolished or amended several laws used to limit freedom of expression. The reforms did not amend the definitions of offences used to limit freedom of expression, including, notably, those contained in anti-terrorism legislation.

■ In February, conscientious objector and human rights defender Halil Savda was imprisoned for "alienating the public from military service" under Article 318 of the Penal Code. In April he was given a conditional release from his 100-day sentence. In September, he was fined and temporarily prevented from continuing on his "peace march" in the southern province of Osmaniye. In December, Halil Savda was acquitted in two separate cases brought under Article 318. Another conviction under Article 318 remained pending at the Supreme Court of Appeals.

■ In October, the trial of pianist Fazıl Say began. Prosecutors brought the case under Article 216 of the Penal Code for "publicly insulting religious values" in tweets he made mocking religious individuals and Islamic conceptions of heaven.

■ In March, journalists Ahmet Şık and Nedim Şener were released after 375 days of pre-trial detention. Their prosecution, with other journalists, for "committing a crime on behalf of a terrorist organization" under Article 220/6 of the Penal Code continued at the end of the year. They stood accused of assisting the media strategy of "Ergenekon", an alleged criminal network with links to the military and other state institutions, charged with plotting to overthrow the government.

■ Large-scale trials, targeting alleged membership of the PKK-linked Kurdistan Communities Union (KCK), continued throughout the year. The trial of 44 journalists accused of KCK membership began in September.

■ A separate prosecution of 193 people, including academics Ragıp Zarakolu and Büşra Ersanlı for membership of the KCK continued at the end of the year. The evidence against Ragıp Zarakolu and Büşra Ersanlı was based on their involvement in the Politics Academy of the pro-Kurdish Peace and Democracy Party (BDP), a recognized political party. They were released in April and July respectively pending the outcome of the trial.

Torture and other ill-treatment

Allegations of torture and other ill-treatment in official places of detention persisted. In June, the Parliament passed legislation to create an Ombudsman's Office and a separate national human rights institution. The national human rights institution lacked guarantees of independence. At the end of the year, it was unclear how or whether it would fulfil the obligations of the Optional Protocol to the UN Convention against Torture in providing independent monitoring of places of detention. Other independent mechanisms promised by the government, such as a police complaints procedure, were not established.

■ In March, boys held at Pozantı prison in the southern province of Adana were transferred, following allegations that prison officials had subjected them to abuse, including sexual abuse. An official investigation continued at the end of the year. The European Committee for the Prevention of Torture visited Pozantı prison in June but its report was not publicly available at the end of the year.

Excessive use of force

There were frequent allegations of excessive use of force by police during demonstrations, including beatings, throughout the year. Three deaths at demonstrations, allegedly as a result of excessive use of force, were reported.

■ In December, up to 50 students were injured following clashes with police on the campus of Ankara's Middle East Technical University. The clashes occurred following attempts by police to break up a peaceful protest that occurred during the Prime Minister's visit to the University. One student was hospitalized due to a suspected brain haemorrhage as a result of a police gas canister striking him in the head.

Impunity

Investigations and prosecutions of public officials for alleged human rights violations remained flawed with little prospect of those responsible being brought to justice. Convicted officials frequently received suspended sentences and remained in post.

■ In January, four people were convicted of participating in the 2007 murder of journalist and human rights defender Hrant Dink. They received sentences of up to 10 weeks (for possession of ammunition) to life imprisonment (for instigation of murder). The court ruled that the convicted men were not part of a wider organization and they were acquitted of "membership of an illegal organization". The culpability of state officials in the murder was still not fully investigated.

■ In July, Sedat Selim Ay, a police officer convicted of ill-treatment of detainees in 2004, was promoted to a senior post within Istanbul's Anti-Terrorism Branch.

■ No effective investigation was carried out into the December 2011 bombing by the armed forces of Uludere/Qileban, a district in Şırnak province on the Iraqi border. The armed forces claimed to have targeted armed PKK members, but instead killed 34 villagers. Prosecutors failed to conduct a prompt crime scene investigation or to interview witnesses to the attack.

■ In October, an Istanbul court convicted three prison officials of "causing death through torture" in the retrial of public officials following the 2008 death in custody of Engin Çeber. The retrial followed the overturning of the court's earlier judgement by the Supreme Court of Appeals on procedural grounds. The case remained pending at the Supreme Court of Appeals at the end of the year.

Unfair trials

Unfair trials persisted, particularly in respect of prosecutions under anti-terrorism legislation before Special Heavy Penal Courts. Extended pre-trial detention during protracted trials remained a problem notwithstanding legal changes introduced in July seeking to limit its use. Secret witness statements that could not be challenged were used in court and convictions continued to be issued in cases which lacked reliable and substantive evidence. Thousands of such cases brought under anti-terrorism laws related to alleged attendance at demonstrations. Many of those accused were university students. Reforms to the Special Heavy Penal Courts passed by the Parliament in July had not been implemented by the end of the year.

■ University student Cihan Kırmızıgül was released from prison in March following 25 months in pre-trial detention. In May, he was convicted of criminal damage and "committing a crime in the name of a terrorist organization". He was sentenced to 11 years and three months in prison. The conviction was based on his wearing of a traditional scarf that matched those

worn by people alleged to have taken part in a demonstration where Molotov cocktails were thrown. One police officer also identified him as having been at the scene, contradicting the statements of other officers. An appeal was pending at the end of the year.

Abuses by armed groups

Bomb attacks by unknown individuals or groups continued to kill civilians. The PKK kidnapped civilians in violation of the principles of international humanitarian law.

■ In August, an explosion close to a bus station in the south-eastern province of Gaziantep killed nine civilians and injured more than 60 others. The authorities blamed the PKK for the blast but the group denied responsibility.

■ In October, two civilians were killed when their car hit a landmine close to the Aşağı Torunoba Gendarmerie station in the province of Tunceli/Dersim.

■ In August, the PKK abducted Hüseyin Aygün, a parliamentarian representing Tunceli/Dersim. He was released unharmed after 48 hours.

Conscientious objectors

No reforms were introduced to recognize the right of conscientious objection or to prevent the repeated criminal prosecution of conscientious objectors for their refusal to perform military service. People publicly supporting the right to conscientious objection faced criminal prosecution.

■ In October, İnan Süver was released from prison on the grounds that time previously spent in pre-trial detention should be subtracted from his sentence. The execution of another sentence for refusing to perform military service remained pending at the end of the year.

■ The European Court of Human Rights issued a series of judgements against Turkey following its failure to recognize the right to conscientious objection. Government officials made contradictory statements about whether they would recognize the right.

■ In March, the UN Human Rights Committee found Turkey's failure to recognize the right to conscientious objection in the cases of Cenk Atasoy and Arda Sarkut had violated Article 18 of the ICCPR.

Refugees and asylum-seekers

Tens of thousands of people fleeing violence and persecution in Syria crossed the border to seek refuge in Turkey. Government figures cited by UNHCR, the UN refugee agency, showed that at the end of the year there were more than 148,000 refugees from Syria being accommodated in 14 camps, mostly in border provinces. While the camps were well resourced and organized, many were located close to the conflict zone in Syria and all remained closed to independent scrutiny. From the second half of August, Turkey partially closed its border with Syria in violation of international law. By the end of the year, thousands of displaced people were living in dire conditions in camps beside the border with Turkey.

The government failed to adopt promised legislation protecting the rights of refugees and asylum-seekers in Turkey. Problems remained regarding the implementation of existing regulations, in particular with regard to allowing asylum applications from places of detention, resulting in the return of individuals to places where they may be at risk of persecution.

Rights of lesbian, gay, bisexual, transgender and intersex people

The government rejected civil society calls to include sexual orientation and gender identity as prohibited discrimination grounds in the new Constitution. No progress was made in adopting comprehensive non-discrimination legislation. LGBTI rights groups continued to report suspected hate murders motivated by the victim's sexual orientation or gender identity, including the murders of five transgender women.

Violence against women and girls

In March, Turkey ratified the Council of Europe Convention on preventing and combating violence against women and domestic violence, and passed a law which strengthened protections and allowed for the direct application of the Convention. At the end of the year there were only 103 shelters for survivors of domestic violence, far below the number required by law.

In May, the Prime Minister announced forthcoming legislation on abortion which, if passed, would further restrict access to needed health care for women and girls and contravene their human rights. No proposals to change the law on abortion were introduced during the year, which was legalized in Turkey in 1983.

Amnesty International visits/reports

🚆 Amnesty International delegates visited Turkey in January, February, March, April, June, August, September, October and December including to monitor trials.

📃 Turkey: Uludere bombing investigation lacks credibility (EUR 44/001/2012)

📃 Turkey: Follow-up procedure to the forty-fifth session of the Committee against Torture (EUR 44/007/2012)

📃 Turkey: Turkish Prime Minister's staunch opposition to abortion undermines human rights (EUR 44/008/2012)

📃 Turkey: Ensure safety of Syrian refugees and access for national and international monitors (EUR 44/009/2012)

📃 Turkey: Time to recognize right to conscientious objection (EUR 44/010/2012)

📃 Turkey: Respect the rights of hunger strikers (EUR 44/020/2012)

📃 Turkey: Police actions against demonstrators must be investigated (EUR 44/025/2012)

TURKMENISTAN

TURKMENISTAN
Head of state and government: **Gurbanguly Berdimuhamedov**

A law on political parties was passed allowing for formal political opposition. However, opposition figures, journalists and human rights defenders continued to suffer harassment by the state. Torture and other ill-treatment remained widespread.

Background

In February, President Berdimuhamedov was re-elected with 97.4% of the vote. The OSCE did not send election monitors, citing limited political freedom in Turkmenistan.

In March, the UN Human Rights Committee concluded that although Turkmenistan showed a "new willingness" to improve its human rights record, a disparity between legislation and implementation persisted.

Turkmenistan remained closed to international scrutiny: despite a visit by the International Committee of the Red Cross, no independent international organizations were allowed to carry out monitoring. Turkmenistan failed to fully co-operate with UN human rights mechanisms.

T

On 9 October, the European Parliament's Subcommittee on Human Rights held hearings on human rights in Turkmenistan.

Rights to freedom of expression and association

Human rights defenders were unable to operate openly. Critical media reporting was rarely tolerated and journalists, human rights defenders and other activists continued to be subjected to harassment.

Several prisoners of conscience remained imprisoned for peacefully exercising their rights to freedom of expression. Annakurban Amanklychev and Sapardurdy Khadziev remained arbitrarily detained after being sentenced following unfair trials in August 2006 for their human rights work.

■ On 11 January, the Law on Political Parties was passed, legalizing the formation of political parties. On 21 August, the Party of Industrialists and Entrepreneurs was established, the first alternative to the ruling Turkmenistan Democratic Party permitted since 1991. However, human rights defenders and political opposition activists expressed doubts about the government's willingness to allow open political debate.

■ On 5 October, former government minister Geldimurat Nurmuhammedov was detained in Ashgabat and sent to a drug rehabilitation centre in Dashoguz for six months of treatment. He had no history of drug use. There were fears he would be subjected to forced medical treatment, possibly as punishment for his political activities and an interview with Radio Free Europe/Radio Liberty, where he criticized the government and called the ruling party "unlawful".

Torture and other ill-treatment

There were credible allegations of torture and other ill-treatment by security forces against people suspected of criminal offences. These included electric shocks, asphyxiation, rape, forcibly administering psychotropic drugs, deprivation of food and drink and exposure to extreme cold. Impunity for such abuses remained the norm and complaints by victims were rarely pursued.

■ On 4 August, the Foreign Ministry announced that amendments had been made to the Criminal Code criminalizing torture.

Prison conditions

Prison conditions fell short of international standards. Overcrowding, poor sanitation and poor nutrition were common and facilitated the spread of disease. Bribes were often required to obtain food and medicine.

Enforced disappearances and incommunicado detention

The whereabouts of dozens of people convicted in unfair trials in 2002 and 2003 for the alleged assassination attempt on then President Niyazov remained unknown. Relatives had heard nothing for over 10 years, and did not know if their loved ones were still alive. The authorities reportedly harassed and intimidated relatives of detainees who tried to lodge appeals.

Despite allegations by non-government sources that at least eight of those convicted had died in detention, the authorities failed to disclose any information or open investigations.

■ Tirkish Tyrmyev, former Commander of Border Troops of Turkmenistan, was sentenced to 10 years' imprisonment in 2002 for abuse of power. His relatives did not know his location but reported in March that he had been given an additional seven-year sentence as his release date approached, allegedly for a crime against a prison guard.

Freedom of movement

The *propiska* system of registering an individual's place of residence remained in place, restricting freedom of movement and impeding access to housing, employment and services.

UGANDA

REPUBLIC OF UGANDA
Head of state and government: **Yoweri Kaguta Museveni**

Restrictions on freedoms of expression and association continued. LGBTI people continued to face harassment. Police and other law enforcement officials continued to commit human rights violations, including torture, and perpetrators were not held to account.

U

Background

The government accepted recommendations on the rights to freedom of expression, assembly and non-discrimination in February during the assessment of the country's human rights record under the UN Universal Periodic Review in 2011.

The courts nullified constituency election results from 2011 which led to by-elections. Opposition parties subsequently won seven out of the nine seats contested.

Allegations of embezzlement within the Office of the Prime Minister led the UK, Sweden and Denmark to withhold aid money. Ministers charged in connection with allegations of embezzlement of public funds intended for the Commonwealth Heads of Government Meeting in 2007 were acquitted.

Freedom of expression

Journalists, opposition leaders and activists critical of the authorities continued to face intimidation, harassment, arbitrary arrest and trumped-up charges. At least 70 journalists reported physical attacks and arbitrary detention during the year.

■ Police harassed, beat and damaged equipment of journalists Isaac Kasamani and William Ntege while they filmed the arrest of Dr Kizza Besigye, leader of the Forum for Democratic Change (FDC), in September.

The government body regulating the mass media, the Ugandan Media Council (UMC), banned the staging of two plays in theatres. When one of them, *The River and the Mountain,* was informally staged in other areas in September, its co-producer, David Cecil, was arrested. He was charged with "disobeying an order by a public official" and released on bail. It was strongly suspected that the play was banned because the authorities believed it promoted homosexuality. Another play, *State of the Nation,* which was critical of the government's stance on corruption and poor governance issues, was banned in October. The producers subsequently staged the play twice and no further action was taken against them.

Freedom of assembly and association

The Attorney General declared the pressure group Activists for Change (A4C) an unlawful society and banned it in April. The group had resumed demonstrations which began in 2011 against the rising cost of living, corruption and poor governance, and which were violently suppressed by the police. The declaration was inconsistent with respect for the rights of freedom of assembly, speech and association.

In October, the authorities banned demonstrations ahead of Uganda's 50th anniversary of independence, and dispersed marches organized by the group For God and My Country (4GC) to demand investigations into the killings of protesters in 2011. Dr Kizza Besigye, leader of the FDC, was arbitrarily arrested twice and released without charge. Police justified the restrictions on the grounds that 4GC comprised many of the same people as the banned group A4C.

Government targeted advocacy NGOs and activists with dissenting views on oil governance, land, corruption and human rights for intimidation, harassment, surveillance and obstruction. Offices of some NGOs were reportedly broken into and equipment stolen and police searched and confiscated equipment of some NGOs.

Rights of lesbian, gay, bisexual, transgender and intersex people

The 2009 Anti-Homosexuality Bill was reintroduced before Parliament in February, but was not debated pending a report by the Parliamentary and Legal Affairs Committee. In October, the Speaker of Parliament stated that the Bill would "soon" be debated. If passed, it would further entrench discrimination against LGBTI people and lead to other human rights violations.

Restrictions on the right to freedom of association by LGBTI groups increased. In February the Minister of Ethics and Integrity forcibly closed a workshop for LGBTI activists in Entebbe, alleging that it was illegal. In June, police arbitrarily closed a workshop and briefly detained the organizers. The workshop, organized by the East and Horn of Africa Human Rights Defenders Project, was to teach human rights monitoring skills to LGBTI activists from Rwanda, Tanzania and Kenya, as well as Uganda. The Ministry of Internal Affairs threatened to deregister 38 NGOs, accusing them of promoting homosexuality.

International justice

In May, Caesar Aćellam Otto, a senior commander in the Lord's Resistance Army (LRA), was captured by government forces. The same month, the Minister of

U

Internal Affairs removed a provision in the Amnesty Act 2010 which had granted amnesty to LRA fighters. The law had previously shielded perpetrators of international crimes from prosecution and denied justice to victims.

The government began investigations into Caesar Acellam Otto, but by the end of the year no charges were preferred against him and his detention remained incommunicado. It was unclear whether he and others subsequently captured would be effectively prosecuted by the International Crimes Division of the High Court.

The International Criminal Court's arrest warrants issued in 2005 remained in force for LRA leader Joseph Kony and three LRA commanders. The men were still at large at the end of the year.

Refugees and migrants

The cessation of international protection for Rwandan refugees and asylum-seekers who fled before 1998 was postponed until June 2013. Uganda, Rwanda and UNHCR, the UN refugee agency, held tripartite discussions about implementing the cessation clause.

In March, the Constitutional Court heard a petition to determine whether refugees have the right to acquire Ugandan citizenship. The hearing was repeatedly postponed and remained pending, raising concerns that it might be difficult for Rwandan refugees who do not want to return to Rwanda to obtain alternative status, including citizenship.

Over 40,000 Congolese refugees fled into Uganda because of renewed fighting between the Congolese army and the armed group known as M23, and the general insecurity caused by various armed groups in the North Kivu province of the Democratic Republic of the Congo from April onwards.

Torture and other ill-treatment

The Anti-Torture Act, which came into force in 2012, prohibits, criminalizes and holds individuals responsible for acts of torture. It expands the definition of torture to include non-state actors and makes information obtained through torture inadmissible in court. If enforced, the Anti-Torture Act would address impunity, enable justice for the victims and reduce torture.

However, torture and other ill-treatment by police remained widespread. Despite investigations by the Uganda Human Rights Commission, no action was taken to hold law enforcement officials responsible for human rights violations to account, or to grant victims and their families an effective remedy.

Death penalty

Civilian and military courts continued to impose the death penalty for capital offences. There were no executions in 2012.

UKRAINE

UKRAINE
Head of state: Viktor Yanukovich
Head of government: Mykola Azarov

Torture and other ill-treatment remained widespread, and impunity for such acts continued. Failings in the criminal justice system led to lengthy periods of pre-trial detention, and a lack of safeguards for detainees. Refugees and asylum-seekers risked detention and forcible return to countries where they faced human rights violations. The rights of LGBTI individuals were at risk.

Torture and other ill-treatment

There were continuing reports of torture and other ill-treatment in police detention. In a report on a visit to Ukraine in 2011, published in November, the Council of Europe Committee for the Prevention of Torture stated that it had been "inundated with allegations from detained persons" who had been subjected to physical or psychological ill-treatment by police officers. Shevchenkivskiy police station in Kyiv was singled out as being particularly "problematic".

On 18 September, Parliament passed legislation allowing the Parliamentary Commissioner for Human Rights' Office to carry out the functions of a National Preventive Mechanism, in fulfilment of Ukraine's obligations under the Optional Protocol to the UN Convention against Torture.

■ Mikhail Belikov, a retired miner, was tortured by police officers from Petrovskiy District police station in Donetsk on 17 June. He was approached by three duty police officers in a park for drinking in public. He reported that he was beaten in the park and then taken

U

to the Petrovskiy District sub-police station, where a fourth duty police officer raped him with a police baton while three other policemen held him down. A more senior officer told him to forget what had happened, and asked him to pay 1,500 hryvna (€144) to be released. He agreed to pay and was released without charge. That night his condition worsened considerably. He was taken to hospital where doctors found that he had suffered serious internal injuries, and he would require a temporary colostomy. At the end of the year, three police officers were on trial for five separate incidents of beating and extortion, going back to 2009, including the torture of Mikhail Belikov. Two of the officers were charged with torture, under Article 127 of the Criminal Code.

Impunity

In October, members of the UN Human Rights Council's Universal Periodic Review of Ukraine's human rights situation recommended that Ukraine should create an independent body to investigate cases of torture and guarantee compensation to victims. Ukraine had not replied to this and the other 145 recommendations made to it by the Review before the end of the year. Victims of torture and other ill-treatment continued to experience difficulty in getting their complaints investigated. Punishments handed down by the courts often did not reflect the gravity of the crime.

■ On 5 January, police officer Serhiy Prikhodko received a five-year suspended sentence for abuse of office for causing the death of Ihor Indylo in police custody in Shevchenkivskiy police station in Kyiv in May 2010. A second police officer, Serhiy Kovalenko, had been amnestied in December 2011 on the basis that he had a young child. On 14 May, the Kyiv Appeal Court cancelled both the suspended sentence and the amnesty, and returned the case for further investigation. On 29 October the Kyiv Appeal Court again asked for additional investigation.

■ On 23 March, Ihor Zavadskiy, a celebrated accordion player, was detained in Kyiv and subjected to torture and other ill-treatment by police officers. He alleged that he was thrown to the ground outside his home and beaten by a group of plain-clothes police officers, who searched him, took his mobile phone, and searched his apartment without a warrant, and that he was then subjected to further torture and other ill-treatment at Shevchenkivskiy police station in Kyiv.

Three police officers beat him and one of them squeezed his testicles causing extreme pain. At one point he lost consciousness when he was thrown to the ground, hitting his head on the floor. Police officers insisted on interrogating him without a lawyer; he did not see a lawyer until 27 March. He was subsequently charged with "violent unnatural gratification of sexual desire" and "debauchery of minors". He lodged a complaint with the district prosecutor about the torture and other ill-treatment on 2 April. He was only informed on 3 July that a decision had been taken on 6 April not to start a criminal investigation into the torture allegations. The Shevchenkivskiy District Court overturned the prosecutor's decision on 31 July, and returned the case for additional investigation. At the end of the year there was no information about the progress of the investigation. The case against Ihor Zavadskiy was ongoing.

Refugees and asylum-seekers

Ukraine continued to breach its international human rights obligations under the UN Refugee Convention by complying with extradition requests even in cases where the individuals concerned were recognized refugees or asylum-seekers.

■ On 20 September, the Ukrainian authorities returned Ruslan Suleymanov to Uzbekistan, in violation of Ukraine's obligations under the UN Convention against Torture, and the UN Refugee Convention. He remained in pre-trial detention in Tashkent, the capital of Uzbekistan, at the end of the year. Ruslan Suleymanov had moved to Ukraine in November 2010, fearing an unfair trial, torture and other ill-treatment in Uzbekistan, after the construction company he worked for was targeted by rival business interests. He was detained in Ukraine on 25 February 2011, and in May 2011 the General Prosecutor's Office confirmed his extradition to Uzbekistan to stand trial for alleged economic crimes. Although his application for asylum in Ukraine was rejected, he had been recognized by UNHCR, the UN refugee agency, as a refugee, and they were actively seeking his resettlement.

■ On 19 October, Leonid Razvozzhayev, a Russian citizen and aide to Russian opposition MP Ilya Ponomaryov, was reportedly abducted by Russian law enforcement officers in Kyiv from outside the offices of the Hebrew Immigration Aid Society, where he had gone for legal assistance and advice in order to apply for asylum in Ukraine. On 22 October, Leonid

U

Razvozzhayev alleged that he was subjected to torture or other ill-treatment upon his return to Russia to force him to incriminate himself and other opposition activists in planning mass disorder. On 25 October, a spokesman for the Ministry of Internal Affairs confirmed that Leonid Razvozzhayev had been abducted "by law enforcement officers or law enforcement officers of another state". He stated that this was not a criminal matter, but "a matter of co-operation between law enforcement agencies, about which I know nothing."

In June, UNHCR, the UN refugee agency, noted that, despite the new 2011 Refugee Law, procedures and legislation still fell short of international standards. In particular, asylum-seekers, who are frequently undocumented, risked detention for up to 12 months for illegally staying in Ukrainian territory.

■ In January, 81 people detained in two migrant accommodation centres, the majority of whom were Somali nationals, declared a hunger strike to protest against their detention. They had been detained and sentenced to up to 12 months "for the purposes of deportation", following a police action to control "illegal immigration" at the end of December 2011. No Somali nationals had ever been returned from Ukraine, and forcible returns to Somalia would have been unlawful in all but exceptional circumstances. At least one detainee was registered with the UNHCR as an asylum-seeker, but many more had been unable to apply for asylum as the Regional Migration Services offices in many parts of Ukraine had not functioned for most of 2011. The detainees ended the hunger strike on 17 February, after the State Migration Service assured them that it would re-open its regional offices in Volyn district, in western Ukraine, and start accepting applications for refugee status and related protection. By November 2012, 53 of the detainees had been released.

Justice system

A new Criminal Procedural Code, with significant improvements on the previous one, was given Presidential assent on 14 May. It clarified that detention starts from the moment of apprehension by the police; that detainees have the right to a lawyer and to an independent medical expert from that moment; and clearly stated that pre-trial detention should only be applied in exceptional circumstances, in line with Council of Europe recommendations. It also provided for automatic review of the continuing justification for pre-trial detention at two-monthly intervals. Concerns remained that a lawyer was only mandatory in cases of especially grave crimes that entail a penalty of more than 10 years in prison, and that free legal aid was also only available in cases where a lawyer was mandatory.

■ On 27 February, Yuriy Lutsenko, former Minister of Internal Affairs and leader of the People's Self Defence opposition political party, was sentenced to four years' imprisonment and a fine of 643,982 hryvna (€61,621) for misappropriation of state property and abuse of office. Yuriy Lutsenko had been held in pre-trial detention since 26 December 2010. On 3 July the European Court of Human Rights found that Yuriy Lutsenko's pre-trial detention had violated his right to liberty, as well as having been ordered for political reasons in violation of the European Convention on Human Rights. On 17 August, he was found guilty additionally for professional negligence for ordering illegal surveillance of a driver while investigating the poisoning of former President Yushchenko. His sentence remained unchanged.

■ A new trial against former Prime Minister Yuliya Tymoshenko for tax evasion was due to start in April, but was postponed for health reasons. The new charges, which were made in October 2011, related to her activities as president of the energy trading company United Energy Systems of Ukraine (UESU) from 1995 to 1997. She continued to serve a seven-year sentence under politically motivated charges of abuse of office for signing a multi-million dollar energy contract with Russia in January 2009, while she was Prime Minister.

Rights of lesbian, gay, bisexual, transgender and intersex people

In October, Parliament passed the second reading of a draft law "On amendments to some legislative acts (to protect the right of children to a safe information environment)". The Law proposed to ban the production, importation or distribution of publications, film or video materials promoting homosexuality. If enacted, the law would severely restrict the right to freedom of expression of LGBTI individuals.

■ On 20 May, the Kyiv Pride march was called off just 30 minutes before it was due to begin after police warned that a large number of nationalist and religious protesters had threatened to interrupt the march. One of the organizers was beaten by a gang of youths and another was sprayed with mace.

International justice

On 24 October, the government stated that Ukraine remained committed to the idea of the establishment of an International Criminal Court. However, no steps were taken to make the necessary legislative changes to implement the Rome Statute of the International Criminal Court and the Agreement on Privileges and Immunities to which Ukraine acceded on 20 January 2000 and 29 January 2007 respectively.

Amnesty International visits/reports

🚍 Amnesty International delegates visited Ukraine in April, May, June, July, August and September.

📄 Ukraine: Euro 2012 jeopardised by criminal police force (EUR 50/005/2012)

📄 Ukraine: Proposed laws discriminate against LGBTI people and violate children's rights (EUR 50/008/2012)

📄 Ukraine: Authorities should not extradite refugees back to torture in Uzbekistan (EUR 50/010/2012)

📄 Ukraine: Leonid Razvozzhayev abduction must be investigated (PRE01/518/2012)

UNITED ARAB EMIRATES

UNITED ARAB EMIRATES
Head of state: Shaikh Khalifa bin Zayed Al Nahyan
Head of government: Shaikh Mohammed bin Rashid
                           Al Maktoum

More than 90 government critics, including human rights defenders, were in detention at the end of the year without charge or trial amid increasing restrictions on the rights to freedom of expression, association and assembly. At least two were prisoners of conscience. Seven of those detained were arbitrarily stripped of their nationality and one was then deported. At least six people faced charges for content they posted on social media. Women faced discrimination in law and practice. Foreign migrant workers continued to be exploited and abused. At least 21 death sentences were imposed; at least one person was executed.

Background

In February and June, the UN Working Group on Arbitrary Detention (WGAD) concluded that the arrests in 2011 of Abdelsalam Abdallah Salim, Akbar Omar and activist Ahmed Mansoor were arbitrary. The WGAD requested that the government provide reparations to the three men and ratify the ICCPR; the government had not fulfilled either request by the end of the year.

The UAE acceded to the UN Convention against Torture in July. It did not recognize the competency of the UN Committee against Torture to investigate allegations of torture. The government also made a declaration on the Convention, stating that in its view "pain and suffering arising from lawful sanctions" did not fall under the treaty's definition of torture.

Freedoms of expression, association and assembly

The authorities extended limitations on the exercise of freedoms of expression, association and assembly, intensifying the crackdown on peaceful dissent which began in 2011 and particularly targeting dissent in social media.

Syrian nationals who demonstrated outside the Syrian consulate in February faced questioning; around 50 were deported, although none to Syria.

Waves of arrests targeting government critics resulted in the detention without charge or trial of around 90 people linked to al-Islah (the Reform and Social Guidance Association), a UAE-based organization loosely modelled on Egypt's Muslim Brotherhood.

■ Sultan al-Qasimi was detained along with around nine others during a wave of arrests in March and April. He was still held without charge or trial at the end of the year. His arrest was in connection with his role in al-Islah.

■ In July, government allegations that a "foreign-based" group was threatening state security coincided with a second wave of arrests of over 50 individuals connected with al-Islah. Their families were not informed of their whereabouts and they were denied access to lawyers. One had been tried by the end of the year. Family members were threatened with arrest and one lawyer was subjected to a smear campaign in state media.

■ Dr Mohammad al-Roken, a lawyer and human rights defender, was arrested together with his son and son-in-law in July. Dr al-Roken had acted as defence lawyer

U

for some of the so-called "UAE 5" – prisoners of conscience sentenced to prison terms in 2011 after an unfair trial. He, his son and son-in-law remained in detention without charge or trial.

■ Ahmed Abdul Khaleq, one of the UAE 5, was one of seven people arbitrarily stripped of their UAE nationality. In July, the UAE authorities deported him to Thailand in contravention of international law.

■ Ahmed Mansoor, another of the UAE 5, was physically assaulted twice in apparently politically motivated attacks. No one was held to account.

■ Dr Ahmed al-Zaabi, a former judge, was sentenced to two six-month prison terms and fined in July by an Abu Dhabi court that convicted him on apparently politically motivated fraud charges.

In November, the federal government enacted a decree on cybercrime, which provided for the prosecution, fining or imprisonment of those using the internet to criticize government figures or to call for demonstrations or political reform.

Independent trade unions remained prohibited.

Arbitrary arrest, torture and other ill-treatment

An investigation into a death in custody resulted in one-month prison terms for five officials, while 13 others were acquitted of torture. A second case resulted in a finding of death by natural causes. Torture allegations made by two Syrian nationals and one US national were not known to have been investigated.

Most al-Islah detainees could not meet with family or legal representatives and in most cases their whereabouts remained unknown. They were permitted in rare cases to telephone their families.

Death penalty

At least 21 death sentences were imposed, mostly on people convicted of murder and drug trafficking. At least one person was executed.

In November, UAE abstained on a UN General Assembly resolution calling for a worldwide moratorium on executions.

Amnesty International visits/reports

📖 United Arab Emirates: Crackdown on fundamental freedoms contradicts human rights commitments – Amnesty International Submission to the UN Universal Periodic Review, July 2012 (MDE 25/009/2012)

UNITED KINGDOM

UNITED KINGDOM OF GREAT BRITAIN AND NORTHERN IRELAND
Head of state: Queen Elizabeth II
Head of government: David Cameron

Criminal investigations were announced in two alleged rendition cases. As a result of these new criminal investigations the Detainee Inquiry was closed early. Draft legislation was published which would allow the government to rely on secret evidence across the civil justice system in national security cases. A moratorium on the transfer of detainees to Afghan authorities was maintained.

Torture and other ill-treatment

On 12 January, the Metropolitan Police Service (MPS) and the Director of Public Prosecutions announced that, following an investigation, criminal charges would not be brought in two cases against UK intelligence officers alleged to be involved in the ill-treatment of detainees abroad. The first case related to involvement in the torture and other ill-treatment of Binyam Mohamed, the second to an unnamed individual held by US authorities at Bagram Air Base in Afghanistan in January 2002. However, the MPS stated that it had received other allegations, and was considering possible further criminal investigations.

Criminal investigations were announced, however, into UK involvement in the alleged rendition of Sami al Saadi and Abdel Hakim Belhaj to Libya in 2004 and their reported torture and ill-treatment. In December, Sami al Saadi and his family accepted a financial settlement from the government. A civil claim for damages brought by Abdel Hakim Belhaj against UK authorities remained pending at the end of the year.

On 18 January, the government announced that because of the new criminal investigations concerning alleged renditions to Libya, the Detainee Inquiry would conclude early. The Detainee Inquiry had been established in 2010 to examine allegations of UK involvement in human rights violations of individuals detained abroad in the context of counter-terrorism operations. However, it fell short of international human rights standards for effective, independent

U

and thorough investigations. On 27 June, the Detainee Inquiry provided the government with a report on its work to date, which remained unpublished at the end of year.

In September, a European Parliament report called on the UK and other states to disclose all necessary information on all suspect aeroplanes associated with the CIA rendition programme and their territory.

In October, the High Court rejected government attempts to strike out the claims of three Kenyan nationals who were tortured by British colonial authorities in Kenya during the 1950s. The Court ruled that despite the passage of time, the evidence was so extensive that a fair trial was still possible.

Counter-terror and security

The government continued to rely on unreliable and unenforceable diplomatic assurances when seeking to deport individuals alleged to pose a threat to national security to countries where they would be at risk of grave human rights violations, including torture.

■ In January, the European Court of Human Rights ruled in the case of Omar Othman (also known as Abu Qatada), a Jordanian national whose deportation the government was seeking on national security grounds. The Court found that, although Jordan's diplomatic assurances to the UK were sufficient to mitigate the risk of torture or other ill-treatment, Omar Othman might face on return, he would be at real risk of a "flagrant denial of justice" because of the use of testimony from other people who had been tortured. In November, the Special Immigration Appeals Commission ruled that the deportation could not go ahead because the risk of the admission of torture evidence at trial remained, despite the government's attempts to obtain further assurances. At the end of the year, the government was seeking to appeal against the ruling.

■ In April, the European Court of Human Rights ruled that five individuals facing extradition to the USA on terrorism-related charges would not be at risk of torture or other ill-treatment if they were convicted and imprisoned in a "supermax" prison in Florence, Colorado. All five men were extradited to the USA on 5 October.

Terrorist Prevention and Investigation Measures (TPIM) replaced the previous "control order regime" in January. Although narrower in scope than the previous control order regime, TPIM can restrict the liberty, movement and activities of people suspected

of terrorism-related activities, on the basis of secret material. As of 30 November 10 TPIM notices were in force.

Legal and policy developments

In May, the government published the Justice and Security Bill which provided for the expansion of "closed material procedures" to civil cases which the government claimed gave rise to national security concerns. These procedures allow the government to use secret evidence presented to the court behind closed doors and from which the claimant, her/his lawyer and the public are excluded. The Bill also contained provisions to end the ability of courts to order the disclosure of "sensitive" information, including information pertaining to alleged human rights violations, which would assist individuals in a case against a third party. NGOs, lawyers and the media raised serious concerns that the Bill contradicted principles of fairness and open justice and would hinder efforts by victims of human rights violations to secure disclosure of material related to those violations before the courts. The Bill contained some limited provisions to improve oversight of the intelligence services.

Civil society and NGOs raised concerns about the impact of the Legal Aid, Sentencing and Punishment of Offenders Act – which entered into force in May. They feared it might restrict access to justice, including for overseas victims of abuses by UK multinational companies.

In December, a Commission to determine whether a British Bill of Rights should be drafted to replace the Human Rights Act failed to reach a consensus in its report.

Armed forces

In July, 169 Iraqi citizens were granted permission to seek a judicial review in order to argue that the Iraq Historical Allegations Team – established to investigate allegations of torture and other ill-treatment of Iraqi citizens by UK armed forces – was still not sufficiently independent despite structural changes made by the government. Lawyers for the claimants argued that a public inquiry is necessary in order to properly investigate allegations of human rights violations by UK armed forces in Iraq.

On 29 November, the Ministry of Defence announced that it would maintain its moratorium on

U

the transfer of detainees to Afghan authorities for the foreseeable future in light of new information that detainees faced "serious mistreatment" in Afghanistan. The announcement came during High Court proceedings in the case of Serdar Mohammed, an Afghan national detained by UK forces in 2010 and subsequently handed over to the Afghan intelligence service. Serdar Mohammed alleged that he was tortured while in Afghan custody and then subjected to a flagrantly unfair trial.

■ In October, the Supreme Court upheld the writ of habeas corpus in the case of Yunus Rahmatullah. He was captured by UK forces in Iraq in February 2004 and handed over to US forces, which transferred him to Afghanistan where he was detained without charge. The Supreme Court stated that there was evidence that Yunus Rahmatullah's detention was unlawful under the Geneva Conventions and that the UK was obliged to request his return. However, the Supreme Court found that the USA's refusal to transfer Yunus Rahmatullah to UK custody was sufficient to demonstrate that the UK could not secure his release.

Police and security forces

In January, two men were convicted of the racist murder of Stephen Lawrence in 1993. In 1999, an inquiry into the case found that the police investigation had been flawed "by a combination of professional incompetence, institutional racism and a failure of leadership by senior officers".

In July, a police officer was found not guilty of manslaughter in the case of Ian Tomlinson who died during the G-20 demonstrations in London in April 2009. In an inquest in 2011, a jury had returned a verdict of unlawful killing, finding that Ian Tomlinson had died of internal bleeding after being struck with a baton and pushed to the ground by a police officer. In September, an MPS disciplinary panel ruled that the police officer's action constituted gross misconduct.

Northern Ireland

Incidents of paramilitary violence in Northern Ireland continued. On 1 November, David Black, a prison officer, was shot dead; dissident republicans claimed responsibility. A number of elected representatives and journalists experienced threats of or actual violence from loyalist paramilitary or anonymous sources. Public disorder during the year resulted in injuries to police officers and others.

In October, an inquiry established by the Northern Ireland Executive, into institutional child abuse during the period 1922-1995, commenced its work.

In November, Her Majesty's Inspectorate of Constabulary began a review of the work of the Historical Enquiries Team (HET), which was established to re-examine all deaths attributed to the conflict in Northern Ireland. The review will focus on whether HET investigations into cases involving the army are compliant with human rights and policing standards.

■ In December, the Police Service of Northern Ireland confirmed that a criminal investigation into the killing of 13 civil rights marchers by British soldiers on 30 January 1972, on a day known as Bloody Sunday, would begin in 2013.

■ In December, the High Court of Northern Ireland quashed a 2011 report by the Police Ombudsman for Northern Ireland into the killing of six men in a paramilitary attack on a bar in Loughinisland, County Down, in June 1994. A new Police Ombudsman took office in July and began reforms seeking to ensure the quality, thoroughness and independence of historical investigations into police misconduct.

■ In December, a review into the killing of solicitor Pat Finucane in 1989 identified that numerous and serious levels of state collusion had occurred in the killing, but found that there was no "overarching state conspiracy". The Prime Minister apologized to his family. The review however fell far short of being the independent, thorough and effective inquiry required and that the family had been promised.

Violence against women and girls

In May, the government announced a new initiative aimed at preventing sexual violence in conflict and post-conflict situations, stating that it would be a key focus of the UK G8 Presidency in 2013.

In June, the UK signed the Council of Europe's Convention preventing and combating violence against women and domestic violence.

In November, new laws in England and Wales were introduced to tackle stalking, making such behaviour a criminal offence in a bid to improve people's safety.

Refugees and asylum-seekers

In July, the Crown Prosecution Service announced that there was insufficient evidence to bring charges in connection with the death of Jimmy Mubenga in

2010. There were, however, witness statements available that he had been dangerously restrained and suggestions that there had been shortcomings in the security guards' training. Jimmy Mubenga, an Angolan national, had collapsed and died after being restrained by private security guards during an attempt to deport him to Angola.

In October, the authorities attempted to forcibly return a Syrian national back to Syria, contrary to the advice of UNHCR, the UN refugee agency. The removal was only halted following a High Court order. In December, the Upper Tribunal (Immigration and Asylum Chamber) issued a country guidance decision finding that, in the current context, no asylum-seekers should be forcibly returned to Syria in light of the risks that they would face.

Sri Lankan nationals were forcibly returned despite credible evidence of the real risk of torture and other grave human rights violations they would face on return.

Amnesty International visits/reports

🚍 Amnesty International delegates visited Northern Ireland in March, September and December and observed court proceedings in England throughout the year.

📄 UK: Detainee Inquiry closure presents an opportunity for real accountability (EUR 45/005/2012)

📄 United Kingdom: Submission to the Joint Committee on Human Rights – The Justice and Security Green Paper (EUR 45/006/2012)

📄 UK: Abu Qatada still at risk of torture and unfair trial (EUR 45/010/2012)

📄 Left in the dark: The use of secret evidence in the United Kingdom (EUR 45/014/2012)

📄 USA must respect rights of individuals extradited from the UK (AMR 51/086/2012)

📄 UK ordered to continue moratorium on detainee transfers in Afghanistan (ASA 11/020/2012)

📄 Libyan rendition case shows it's time for UK to come clean (PRE01/206/2012)

UNITED STATES OF AMERICA

UNITED STATES OF AMERICA
Head of state and government: **Barack H. Obama**

Forty-three men were executed during the year, and concerns about cruel prison conditions continued. Scores of detainees remained in indefinite military detention at Guantánamo. Pre-trial proceedings continued in six cases in which the administration was intending to seek the death penalty following trials by military commission. Use of lethal force in the counter-terrorism context continued to raise serious concerns, as did continuing reports of the use of excessive force in domestic law enforcement.

Counter-terror and security
Detentions at Guantánamo
At the end of 2012, nearly three years after President Obama's deadline for closure of the Guantánamo detention facility, 166 men were still held at the base, the vast majority without charge or criminal trial.

Four men were transferred from the base during the year, two of whom had been convicted by military commission. Two Uighur detainees, who had been held without charge or trial at the base since 2002, were transferred to El Salvador in April for resettlement there.

Adnan Farhan Abdul Latif, a Yemeni national who had repeatedly expressed his distress at his indefinite detention without charge or trial, died during the year, bringing to nine the number of detainees known to have died at Guantánamo since January 2002.

During the year, the US Supreme Court refused to review petitions from a number of Guantánamo detainees whose detentions had been upheld by the Court of Appeals. Among other things, the petitions had asked the Supreme Court to consider whether its 2008 *Boumediene v. Bush* ruling – that the detainees had the right to challenge the lawfulness of their detention in federal court – was being implemented in such a way as to deny the detainees the "meaningful" review promised.

Trials of Guantánamo detainees
In May, five Guantánamo detainees accused of leading involvement in the attacks in the USA of

U

11 September 2001 – Khalid Sheikh Mohammed, Walid bin Attash, Ramzi bin al-Shibh, 'Ali 'Abd al-'Aziz and Mustafa al Hawsawi – were arraigned for capital trial by military commission. The trials of the five men and that of 'Abd al-Rahim al-Nashiri, who had been arraigned for capital trial in 2011, had not begun by the end of 2012. Prior to their transfer to Guantánamo in 2006, the six men had been held incommunicado for up to four years in secret US custody, during which time at least two of them had been tortured.

In August, charges were sworn against Saudi Arabian national Ahmed Mohammed al Darbi. Arrested by civilian authorities in Azerbaijan in June 2002, he was transferred to US custody in August 2002 and to Guantánamo in March 2003. By the end of 2012, the charges against him had not been referred on for trial by military commission.

In February Pakistani national Majid Khan pleaded guilty to offences under the 2009 Military Commissions Act (MCA) before a military judge at Guantánamo. The terms of the pre-trial agreement would see him sentenced in or before February 2016 after having co-operated with the US authorities. Prior to being brought to Guantánamo in 2006, he had been held in secret US custody and allegedly tortured and otherwise ill-treated.

This brought to seven the number of people convicted by military commission at Guantánamo. Five had pleaded guilty in return for the possibility of early release from US custody. Two of the five were repatriated during 2012: Ibrahim al Qosi to Sudan in July, and Omar Khadr, who had been in US custody since the age of 15, to Canada in September.

In October, a US federal court overturned the 2008 conviction of Salim Hamdan for "material support for terrorism". The US Court of Appeals ruled that "material support for terrorism" was not a war crime in US law prior to the enactment of the MCA.

US detentions in Afghanistan

In June, a US District Court judge dismissed the habeas corpus petition brought on behalf of Zia-ur-Rahman, an Afghan national who had been taken into US military custody in Afghanistan in December 2008 and held without charge or trial ever since. The judge granted the US administration's motion that the court lacked subject-matter jurisdiction over the case.

On 9 September, under an agreement signed six months earlier, the Afghan authorities assumed control of detainee operations on the US airbase at Bagram. Although the Afghan authorities were reported to have taken custody of the approximately 3,000 Afghan nationals detained at Bagram as of 9 March, more than 600 detainees reported to have been taken to the base since that date apparently remained under US military jurisdiction, as did about 50 non-Afghan nationals (see Afghanistan entry).

In October, a US District Court judge dismissed the habeas corpus petitions of three non-Afghan nationals held in US custody at Bagram. According to the petitions, Amin al-Bakri was seized in 2002 in Thailand; Redha al-Najar was arrested in Pakistan in 2002; and Fadi al-Maqaleh's petition alleges that he was detained outside Afghanistan in 2003, but the US authorities asserted that he was in Afghanistan at the time. In May 2010, the US Court of Appeals had overturned a 2009 ruling by the District Court that the three detainees could file petitions to challenge the lawfulness of their detention. Lawyers for the detainees subsequently filed amended petitions in District Court, adding new information they claimed undermined the Court of Appeals' ruling. However, the District Court disagreed.

In November, a US District Court judge dismissed the habeas corpus petition of another detainee in US custody at Bagram. Amanatullah, a Pakistani national, had been held at the base for several years. He was one of two men taken into custody by UK forces in Iraq in February 2004, handed over to US custody, and transferred to Afghanistan. Both remained held without charge or trial in US custody in Bagram at the end of 2012.

Impunity

The absence of accountability for crimes under international law committed under the administration of President George W. Bush in relation to the CIA's programme of secret detention was further entrenched.

On 30 August, the US Attorney General announced the closure of criminal investigations into the death of two individuals in US custody outside the USA. He stated that no one would face criminal charges in relation to the deaths, believed to have occurred in Afghanistan in 2002 and Iraq in 2003. This followed the announcement in June 2011 that a "preliminary review" conducted into interrogations in the CIA programme was at an end and that, apart from in relation to the two deaths, further investigation was not warranted.

U

Use of lethal force

The USA's "targeted killing" of terrorism suspects, including in Pakistan, Somalia and Yemen, particularly through the use of unmanned aerial vehicles, continued during the year. Available information, limited by secrecy, indicated that US policy permitted extrajudicial executions in violation of international human rights law under the USA's theory of a "global war" against al-Qa'ida and associated groups.

Excessive use of force

At least 42 people across 20 states died after being struck by police Tasers, bringing the total number of such deaths since 2001 to 540. Tasers have been listed as a cause or contributory factor in more than 60 deaths. Most of those who died after being struck with a Taser were not armed and did not appear to pose a serious threat when the Taser was deployed.

In May the American Heart Association published a report which presented the first scientific, peer-reviewed evidence concluding that Tasers can cause cardiac arrest and death. The study analyzed information including autopsy reports, medical records and police data from eight cases in which individuals had lost consciousness after being shocked with a Taser X26 weapon.

■ On 20 June, 39-year-old Macadam Mason died outside his home in Thetford, Vermont, after being struck with a Taser deployed by a state trooper. In September the New Hampshire Medical Examiner's Office concluded that Macadam Mason had suffered "sudden cardiac arrest due to the conducted electrical weapon discharge".

In October, the Department of Homeland Security's Office of Inspector General reported that it was reviewing US Border Patrol policies on the use of lethal force. The review, which remained ongoing at the end of the year, followed a series of deadly shootings by Border Patrol agents along the US border with Mexico.

■ In October, 16-year-old José Antonio Elena Rodríguez died of gunshot wounds. The US authorities said that a Border Patrol agent from Nogales, Arizona, had opened fire after two individuals suspected of drug smuggling had fled across the border and begun throwing rocks. The case was under investigation by the Federal Bureau of Investigation (FBI) and Mexican officials at the end of the year.

■ In April, the US Department of Justice announced that no federal criminal or civil rights charges would be pursued regarding the death of Sergio Hernández Guereca, a 15-year-old shot in the head by a Border Patrol agent in 2010.

Prison conditions

Incarceration rates remained at historically high levels.

Thousands of prisoners across the USA remained in isolation in "super-maximum security" prisons. They were confined to cells for 22-24 hours a day, without adequate access to natural light, exercise or rehabilitation programmes. Conditions in such facilities violated international standards and in some cases amounted to cruel, inhuman or degrading treatment.

In October, five men were extradited from the UK to the USA to stand trial on terrorism-related charges after the European Court of Human Rights rejected their claim that they would face a real risk of torture or other cruel, inhuman or degrading treatment if imprisoned in the federal ADX "supermax prison" in Florence, Colorado. The US authorities denied an Amnesty International request to visit ADX prison.

Children's rights

In June, in *Miller v. Alabama*, the US Supreme Court outlawed mandatory life imprisonment without the possibility of parole for offenders who were under 18 years old at the time of the crime. The ruling came two years after the Court prohibited life imprisonment without parole for non-homicide crimes by under-18s.

In July, Terry Branstad, Governor of Iowa, responded to the *Miller v. Alabama* decision by commuting 38 life without parole sentences being served in Iowa by inmates convicted of first degree murder committed when they were under 18, to life imprisonment without the possibility of parole for 60 years. Any mitigating evidence that was not considered at the time of the trial due to the automatic imposition of the life without parole sentence, was again neglected in the Governor's blanket commutation.

Migrants' rights

In June, the US Supreme Court struck down key parts of an Arizona immigration law, including a provision that made it a state crime for irregular migrants to seek or hold a job. However, the Court upheld a section requiring state law enforcement officials to

U

check the immigration status of individuals they suspect of being in the country illegally, despite criticism from human rights groups that this would encourage "racial profiling"– that is, targeting individuals solely on account of their appearance or racial or ethnic origin. Following the ruling, federal courts upheld similar legislation in Alabama and Georgia.

The proliferation of state laws targeting migrants put them at increased risk of discrimination and impeded access to education and essential health care services.

Increased immigration enforcement along certain stretches of the US-Mexico border continued to push irregular migrants to use particularly dangerous routes through the US desert, resulting in hundreds of deaths. Increased collaboration between local law enforcement and immigration authorities put communities living along the US-Mexico border at risk of racial profiling by state and local law enforcement officials. Irregular migrants who were victims of crime, such as human trafficking and domestic violence, faced a range of barriers to justice.

Right to health

In June, the US Supreme Court upheld The Affordable Health Care Act, passed in 2010, which would expand health care coverage by 2014 to more than 30 million people in the USA who lack medical insurance. While a number of the law's provisions addressed barriers to obtaining quality maternal health care, such as preventing insurance companies from charging women more for health coverage, gaps and obstacles remained.

The Maternal Health Accountability Act remained before Congress at the end of the year.

Women's rights

Legislation outlawing the shackling of women prisoners at all stages of pregnancy was passed in California in October. This was the first such law in the USA.

In June, legislation came into effect in Virginia requiring women to undergo an ultrasound before having an abortion.

Congress failed to reauthorize the Violence Against Women Act, which includes provisions to address the high levels of violence against Indigenous women and to provide protection and services for survivors of domestic violence.

Reauthorization of the Trafficking Victims Protection Act, which would protect the thousands of individuals trafficked into the USA every year, remained stalled in Congress at the end of 2012.

Death penalty

Forty-three prisoners – all of them men – were executed in the USA during the year, all by lethal injection. Fifteen of the executions were carried out in Texas. By the end of 2012, Texas accounted for 492 of the 1,320 executions in the USA since 1976, when the US Supreme Court approved new capital laws.

In April, Connecticut became the 17th abolitionist state in the USA.

In November, the California electorate, by a vote of about 53% to 47%, rejected "Proposition 34", an initiative that would have abolished the state's death penalty and commuted over 700 death sentences to life imprisonment without the possibility of parole.

Amnesty International visits/reports

🚙 Amnesty International delegates observed military commission proceedings at Guantánamo during the year.

📗 USA: "Congress has made no such decision": Three branches of government, zero remedy for counter-terrorism abuses (AMR 51/008/2012)

📗 In hostile terrain: Human rights violations in immigration enforcement in the US southwest (AMR 51/018/2012)

📗 USA: Cruel isolation – Amnesty International's concerns about conditions in Arizona maximum security prisons (AMR 51/023/2012)

📗 USA: Another brick from the wall (AMR 51/028/2012)

📗 USA: Wrong court, wrong place, wrong punishment (AMR 51/032/2012)

📗 USA: Human rights betrayed – 20 years after US ratification of ICCPR, human rights principles sidelined by "global war" theory (AMR 51/041/2012)

📗 USA: "Targeted killing" policies violate the right to life (AMR 51/047/2012)

📗 USA: Deadly formula – An international perspective on the 40th anniversary of *Furman v. Georgia* (AMR 51/050/2012)

📗 USA: The edge of endurance – Prison conditions in California's Security Housing Units (AMR 51/060/2012)

📗 USA: One-way accountability – Guantánamo detainee pleads guilty; details of government crimes against him remain classified top secret (AMR 51/063/2012)

📗 USA: Texas – Still, doing its worst; 250th execution under current Governor imminent (AMR 51/092/2012)

📗 USA: Truth, justice and the American way? Details of crimes under international law still classified Top Secret (AMR 51/099/2012)

URUGUAY

EASTERN REPUBLIC OF URUGUAY
Head of state and government: José Alberto Mujica Cordano

Steps were taken to end impunity for crimes committed during the civil and military rule (1973-1985), including efforts to establish the identity of victims of enforced disappearance.

Background

Political debate centred around measures to combat crime and increase public security. In this context, the Electoral Court announced in September that enough signatures had been collected to hold a popular referendum to amend the Constitution and reduce the age at which juveniles can be tried as adults from 18 to 16.

In May, Parliament nominated members to the National Human Rights Institution, one of whose roles is to establish a national mechanism to prevent torture. At the end of the year this mechanism was still not functioning.

In December, Uruguay passed legislation to ratify the Optional Protocol to the ICESCR.

Impunity

In March, President Mujica publicly recognized the state's responsibility for the enforced disappearance of María Claudia García Iruretagoyena de Gelman and the abduction of her baby daughter, María Macarena Gelman García, in 1976. Public recognition was one of the measures called for in a 2011 ruling on the case by the Inter-American Court of Human Rights.

■ In March, the remains of Ricardo Blanco Valiente, who disappeared in 1978, were found in a military barracks outside Montevideo.

■ In September, forensic experts also identified the bodies of Luis Guillermo Vega, a Chilean national; and Horacio Abeledo and Roque Montenegro, both Argentine nationals. The three men had been abducted in 1976 in Argentina and their bodies were found the same year in Uruguay.

■ In March, a former police officer was charged with complicity in the killing of teacher and journalist Julio Castro in August 1977. Julio Castro had been abducted by the military and tortured while held in a clandestine detention centre. The judicial process was continuing at the end of the year.

■ In September, four Uruguayan marines serving as UN peacekeepers in Haiti were charged in Uruguay with "private violence" against a young man. However, no charges were brought in response to the victim's allegations of sexual assault. The trial was continuing at the end of the year.

Sexual and reproductive rights

In October, Congress passed legislation giving women access to legal abortion during the first 12 weeks of pregnancy. The law establishes a mandatory five-day reflection period and a review of cases by a panel of experts when voluntary abortion is requested. When pregnancy is a result of a rape, abortion is legal up to the 14th week of pregnancy and a judicial complaint must be filed. Women's and human rights groups welcomed the law as a step forward to stop unsafe abortions, but expressed concern that the new compulsory requirements could become obstacles to access to legal abortions. The law also decriminalizes abortions beyond the first trimester when the woman's health is at risk or when the foetus would not survive.

Prison conditions

In December, after a visit to Uruguay the UN Special Rapporteur on torture welcomed recent steps to improve prison conditions but drew attention to the persistent shortcomings including overcrowding and inadequate infrastructure.

Rights of lesbian, gay, bisexual, transgender and intersex people

At least five transsexual women were killed in 2012. In only one of the cases was the person responsible brought to justice.

U

UZBEKISTAN

REPUBLIC OF UZBEKISTAN
Head of state: **Islam Karimov**
Head of government: **Shavkat Mirzioiev**

Freedom of expression was curtailed as human rights defenders and journalists continued to be harassed, beaten, prosecuted and detained. Two human rights defenders were released early from prison on humanitarian grounds, but at least 10 others remained in prison, some in cruel, inhuman and degrading conditions. Concerns remained over the frequent use of torture and other ill-treatment to extract confessions, in particular from those suspected of links with banned religious groups.

Freedom of expression

Human rights defenders and journalists continued to face harassment and pressure from the authorities. They were routinely monitored by uniformed and plain-clothes security officers, summoned for questioning, placed under house arrest or prevented from taking part in peaceful demonstrations or from meeting with foreign diplomats. Several reported being beaten by law enforcement officers or by people suspected of working for the security services to prevent them from publicizing human rights violations or criticizing the authorities.

■ Prisoners of conscience and human rights defenders, Alisher Karamatov and Khabibulla Akpulatov, were freed in April and July after serving prison sentences of almost six and seven years respectively, on charges of "libel" and "extortion" after unfair trials in 2005 and 2006.

■ In May, the head of the Kashkadaria branch of the independent Human Rights Society of Uzbekistan, Gulshan Karaeva, was attacked by two women in a shop in the town of Karshi and her home was sprayed with graffiti, after she publicized her refusal of an offer by the National Security Service (SNB) to act as an informant. On 27 September, she was detained at the local police station where she was told she faced charges of "slander" and "insult", from the two women who had attacked her in May. The charges carried a sentence of up to four years' imprisonment. However, on 13 December she received a presidential amnesty

and criminal proceedings were stopped. Family members and colleagues of Gulshan Karaeva also faced harassment, insults and physical assaults. In July, her brother and sister-in-law were assaulted by two neighbours, who beat them and their nine-year-old daughter. The neighbours said that they were related to enemies of the people (referring to Gulshan Karaeva and her older brother Tulkin Karaev, a political refugee in Sweden). In August, Gulshan Karaeva's brother and sister-in-law were summoned to their local police station and threatened with criminal charges in relation to the assault.

Torture and other ill-treatment

Torture and other ill-treatment of detainees and prisoners by security forces and prison personnel continued to be routine. Scores of reports of torture and other ill-treatment emerged during the year, especially from men and women suspected or convicted of belonging to Islamic movements and Islamist groups and parties or other religious groups, banned in Uzbekistan. As in previous years, the authorities failed to conduct prompt, thorough, and impartial investigations into such reports and into complaints lodged with the Prosecutor General's Office.

■ In February, 12 Turkish businessmen were released from prison following a presidential amnesty in December 2011, and deported to Turkey. They were sentenced in 2011, with 42 other Turkish businessmen, to two to three years' imprisonment for various economic crimes including tax evasion. A documentary broadcast on state television showed some of the convicted businessmen allegedly confessing to committing economic crimes. It also claimed that the men had links to the banned "Nurchilar" Islamic movement. One of the men, Vahit Güneş, former general manager of the Turkuaz shopping centre in Tashkent, began legal action against the Uzbekistani authorities upon his return to Turkey. He alleged that he and others were tortured in SNB custody in order to force them to sign false confessions and that they had not been able to choose their own lawyers. He also alleged other detainees had been tortured in pre-trial detention, and that some had died as a result. Vahit Güneş received medical treatment for his injuries on his return to Turkey. He said another businessman, Hairetdin Öner, was still in hospital being treated for physical and psychological trauma two months after his release from prison.

In August, Jehovah's Witness Gulchehra Abdullaeva reported that she had been tortured at a police station in the town of Hazorasp, to make her confess to smuggling banned religious literature into Uzbekistan, a charge she denied. Police officers arbitrarily detained her in July after she returned from a trip to Kazakhstan. She said that they forced her to stand for hours without food or water, placed a gas mask over her head and cut off the air supply to suffocate her. She was made to sign a statement admitting to participating in proscribed religious activities and was then released. On 28 July she was convicted by the Hazorasp District Court of "teaching religious beliefs privately", and fined. Gulchehra Abdullaeva appealed against her sentence and lodged official complaints with the authorities but officials refused to respond or address her complaints.

Counter-terror and security

The authorities continued to seek the extradition of suspected members of Islamic movements and Islamist groups and parties banned in Uzbekistan in the name of security and the fight against terrorism. They also requested the extradition of political opponents, government critics and wealthy individuals out of favour with the regime. Many of these extradition requests were based on fabricated or unreliable evidence. The government offered diplomatic assurances to sending states to secure the returns, pledging free access to detention centres for independent monitors and diplomats. In practice, they did not honour these guarantees. Those forcibly returned to Uzbekistan faced incommunicado detention, torture and other ill-treatment and, after unfair trials, long prison sentences in cruel, inhuman and degrading conditions. The authorities were also accused of attempting assassinations of political opponents living abroad.

■ On 22 February, imam Obidkhon Nazarov, a refugee in Sweden since 2006, was shot in the head outside his home by an unidentified gunman. He remained in a coma. He was a popular dissident imam who had often publicly criticized the Uzbekistani authorities for their repression of independent Muslim groups. He had fled Uzbekistan in 2000, but in 2005 he was accused of being an organizer of the Andizhan protests and ensuing violence. The authorities had sought his extradition ever since and denounced him as a security threat to Uzbekistan. In the trial following his assassination attempt, the judge noted that he was most likely targeted for his political beliefs by a group from outside Sweden. The state prosecutor accused the authorities in Uzbekistan of having organized the assassination attempt. The lawyer representing Obidkhon Nazarov's family and many of his supporters blamed the Uzbekistani security services.

■ Ruslan Suleymanov was extradited from Ukraine to Uzbekistan on 20 September. He had moved to Ukraine in November 2010, fearing that he would be subjected to an unfair trial and to possible torture and other ill-treatment. He had been a manager in a private construction company in Uzbekistan which was targeted for takeover by business rivals in 2008. When the company refused to submit, it was raided by security services and company managers, including Ruslan Suleymanov, were investigated for economic crimes. He was detained in Ukraine in February 2011 following an extradition request from Uzbekistan. Although the UNHCR, the UN refugee agency, had recognized him as a refugee under its mandate in May and was seeking his resettlement, he was nevertheless extradited from Ukraine on 20 September, and in November his family reported that he was being held in pre-trial detention in Tashkent.

VENEZUELA

BOLIVARIAN REPUBLIC OF VENEZUELA
Head of state and government: **Hugo Chávez Frías**

Levels of violent crime, especially gun-related crime, remained high despite efforts to control the availability and use of firearms. Violence in prisons remained widespread and riots continued. The government initiated its withdrawal from the Inter-American Court of Human Rights.

Background

Venezuela's human rights record was assessed under the UN Universal Periodic Review, whose report was adopted in March. Venezuela had accepted several of the recommendations made, including those on human rights defenders. It made a commitment to support their activities and to publicly recognize their

V

role. However, it had rejected several recommendations, including to formulate a National Human Rights Plan and to issue standing invitations to regional and international human rights mechanisms and bodies.

In November, Venezuela became a member of the UN Human Rights Council, thereby making a commitment to co-operate with its Special Procedures and its universal system for the promotion and protection of human rights. By the end of 2012, Venezuela's ratification of several international human rights instruments and requests made by six Special Rapporteurs to visit the country remained pending.

Presidential elections took place in October. Election day was largely peaceful and approximately 81% of voters cast ballots, one of the highest levels of participation in Venezuelan history. Incumbent President Hugo Chávez was elected for a third six-year term.

Public security

Venezuela had one of the highest murder rates in Latin America due, among other factors, to the uncontrolled availability of firearms and ammunition. There also were concerns about the use of firearms by the police. According to a report from the National Police General Council, 80% of police institutions were using weapons that did not follow institutional guidelines. Lack of any other official and precise information on violence, especially around injury from firearms, remained a concern.

In 2012, the Presidential Commission for the Control of Arms, Munitions and Disarmament conducted research and consultations with the general public and initiated public campaigns to encourage people to voluntarily turn in their firearms. The government's new security initiative "Gran Misión a Toda Vida Venezuela" pledged to continue this work of disarmament, including through the creation of a national support system for the victims of gun violence.

In 2012, small arms were restricted in certain public areas and a new registration system was established to increase control over the existing firearms. People who owned small firearms were encouraged to register them, while new requests for licences to carry firearms were suspended for a year. At the end of 2012, a draft arms control law was before Congress.

Prison conditions

Violence in prisons was widespread. At least 591 people were killed in Venezuelan prisons during the year. Firearms, explosives, and other weapons continued to be routinely used in prison clashes.

■ In July, the announcement of a transfer of inmates from the Andean Region Penitentiary in Merida state to other prisons sparked a 20-day riot that left 17 people dead.

■ In August, an outbreak of violence resulted in 26 deaths and 43 people injured in Yare prison.

Human rights defenders

Government officials and the state-run media continued to make baseless accusations against human rights defenders in an attempt to delegitimize their work. Human rights defenders were also the targets of physical attacks; those responsible were not brought to justice.

■ In May, Marianela Sánchez Ortiz of the Venezuelan Observatory of Prisons (Observatorio Venezolano de Prisiones, OVP) was threatened. Her husband, Hernán Antonio Bolívar, was abducted at gunpoint and told to warn his wife to stop complaining about prison conditions and criticizing the government, or she and her family would face reprisals. Government officials also accused the OVP of falsifying information about prisons in order to receive money from US funders.

Impunity

■ In December, Jorge Antonio Barrios was assassinated in Aragua state. He was the ninth member of the Barrios family to be killed since 1998 in circumstances suggesting police involvement. The killings continued despite decisions since 2004 by the inter-American human rights system ordering Venezuela to ensure protection for the family and to bring those responsible to justice.

Independence of the judiciary

■ Judge María Lourdes Afiuni remained under house arrest throughout 2012. In September, unidentified gunmen drove past the building where she lives and opened fire, aiming towards her apartment. In November, she disclosed publicly that she had been raped while in jail. Judge Afiuni was detained in December 2009 and remained imprisoned for over a year. She was charged with offences including corruption, abuse of authority and association to commit a crime. She had ordered the conditional release of a banker who had been held in custody awaiting trial for more than two years, a decision within her remit and in line with Venezuelan law.

International scrutiny

In May, President Chávez, with the support of the National Assembly and the Supreme Court, announced plans to withdraw from the inter-American human rights system. In September, Venezuela officially removed itself as a signatory of the American Convention on Human Rights, thereby initiating its withdrawal from the Inter-American Court of Human Rights. As a result, victims of human rights violations will be barred from September 2013 from bringing complaints before the highest court in the Americas. However, Venezuela will remain a member of the OAS and so will be subject to monitoring by the Inter-American Commission on Human Rights.

Violence against women and girls

The Law on the Right of Women to Live Free of Violence continued to lack a regulatory framework that establishes guidelines on how the authorities should handle cases of violence against women.
■ Hearings were held in the case of Alexandra Hidalgo, who was raped and tortured by a group of men, among them her husband, in 2004. In October it was decided that her husband would stand trial for her kidnapping and rape.

Amnesty International visits/reports

🚌 Amnesty International delegates visited Venezuela in April.
📄 Carta abierta a los candidatos y las candidatas presidenciales de la República Bolivariana de Venezuela (AMR 53/006/2012)
📄 Bolivarian Republic of Venezuela's candidacy for election to the UN Human Rights Council: Open letter (AMR 53/008/2012)

VIET NAM

SOCIALIST REPUBLIC OF VIET NAM
Head of state: **Truong Tan Sang**
Head of government: **Nguyen Tan Dung**

Repression of government critics and activists worsened, with severe restrictions on freedom of expression, association and assembly. At least 25 peaceful dissidents, including bloggers and songwriters, were sentenced to long prison terms in 14 trials that failed to meet international standards. Members of ethnic and religious groups faced human rights violations. At least 86 people were sentenced to death, with more than 500 on death row.

Background

A political crisis arose over alleged mishandling of the economy, with high inflation and debt levels, and corruption scandals linked to state businesses. A secret "criticism" and "self-criticism" programme in the ruling Communist Party lasted for several months. The Prime Minister publicly apologized for economic mismanagement, but retained his position. Public consultations were announced on amending the 1992 Constitution, and on gay marriage. An escalation of the territorial conflict with China in the East Sea (also known as the South China Sea) resulted in anti-China demonstrations in Viet Nam. Reports of land disputes and violent forced evictions increased. Viet Nam announced it would run for a seat on the UN Human Rights Council in 2014-2016. In November, Viet Nam adopted the ASEAN Human Rights Declaration, despite serious concerns that it fell short of international standards.

Freedom of expression

Repression of dissent and attacks on the rights to freedom of expression and assembly continued. Short-term arrests of people taking part in peaceful demonstrations occurred, including in June, when 30 farmers were arrested after protesting for three days outside government buildings in Ha Noi about being forcibly evicted three years earlier.
■ In September, the Prime Minister called for greater controls on the internet and ordered legal action to be taken against three named blogs after they reported on the political crisis.

V

Vaguely worded provisions of the national security section of the 1999 Penal Code were used to criminalize peaceful political and social dissent. By the end of the year, dozens of peaceful political, social and religious activists were in pre-trial detention or had been imprisoned. They included Nguyen Phuong Uyen, a 20-year-old student arrested in October for distributing anti-government leaflets.

Prisoners of conscience

At least 27 prisoners of conscience (detained before 2012) remained held. They included Father Nguyen Van Ly, a Catholic priest serving an eight-year sentence for advocating human rights, freedom of speech and political change.

Bloggers

Long prison terms were handed down to bloggers in an apparent attempt to silence others. They were charged with "conducting propaganda" and aiming to "overthrow" the government. Dissidents were held in lengthy pre-trial detention, often incommunicado and sometimes beyond the period allowed under Vietnamese law. Reports of beatings during interrogation emerged. Trials failed to meet international standards of fairness, with no presumption of innocence, lack of effective defence, and no opportunity to call witnesses. Families of defendants were harassed by local security forces, prevented from attending trials and sometimes lost their work and education opportunities.

■ Well-known popular bloggers Nguyen Van Hai, known as Dieu Cay, "Justice and Truth" blogger Ta Phong Tan, and Phan Thanh Hai, known as AnhBaSaiGon, were tried in September for "conducting propaganda" against the state. They were sentenced to 12, 10 and four years' imprisonment respectively, with three to five years' house arrest on release. The trial lasted only a few hours, and their families were harassed and detained to prevent them from attending. Their trial was postponed three times, the last time because the mother of Ta Phong Tan died after setting herself on fire outside government offices in protest at her daughter's treatment. Phan Thanh Hai's sentence was reduced by one year on appeal in December.

■ Environmental activist and blogger Dinh Dang Dinh, was sentenced to six years' imprisonment in August after a three-hour trial. He was charged with "conducting propaganda" against the state for initiating a petition against bauxite mining in the Central Highlands. His wife reported that he was in poor health and had been beaten by prison officers.

Ethnic and religious minorities

Ethnic and religious minority groups perceived to oppose the government remained at risk of harassment, arrest and imprisonment. Those targeted included ethnic groups worshipping at unauthorized churches and others involved in protests over land confiscation by the authorities. A group of 14 Catholic bloggers and social activists arrested between July and December 2011 in Nghe An province remained in pre-trial detention.

■ In March, Nguyen Cong Chinh, a Mennonite pastor, was sentenced to 11 years' imprisonment for "undermining the national unity policy". He was accused of "inciting" ethnic minorities. He spoke out about harassment by local authorities and restrictions on religious freedom in the Central Highlands. In October, his wife claimed that she had not been allowed to visit him since his arrest in April 2011.

■ Twelve ethnic Hmong accused of involvement in major unrest in north-west Viet Nam in May 2011, were tried and sentenced to between two and seven years' imprisonment in March and December for "disrupting security" and aiming to "overthrow the government". No clear account of events was given and the authorities prevented access to the alleged area of unrest.

■ The Supreme Patriarch of the banned Unified Buddhist Church of Viet Nam, Thich Quang Do, aged 85, remained under house arrest. In July, he called for peaceful demonstrations against China's actions in the East Sea. Police surrounded the banned monasteries to prevent members from participating.

■ Three Catholic Youth members were tried in September and sentenced to between 30 and 42 months in prison for "conducting propaganda" against the state. They had participated in anti-China protests, and signed petitions against the trial of prominent dissident Cu Huy Ha Vu.

Death penalty

In November, an official stated that 508 prisoners were on death row, with around 100 ready to be executed. A delay in implementation of the use of lethal injection, due to an EU ban on export of the required drugs, resulted in no executions being carried out since July 2011. More than 86 people were sentenced to death, including two men for embezzlement.

YEMEN

REPUBLIC OF YEMEN
Head of state: Abd Rabbu Mansour Hadi (replaced
                        Ali Abdullah Saleh in February)
Head of government: Mohammed Salim Basindwa

The human rights situation improved during the transition that followed the 2011 uprising which ousted former President Saleh from power. However, there was an ongoing lack of information about the fate of those arrested or disappeared during 2011. Impunity for human rights violations committed during President Saleh's government was entrenched by a new immunity law, and most killings of protesters and other human rights violations committed in 2011 and 2012 were not investigated. Justice was also denied to victims of violations of human rights and international humanitarian law during armed conflicts in parts of the country. Over 20 people arbitrarily arrested during the 2011 uprising and subsequent protests remained in prison or were victims of enforced disappearance. Torture and other ill-treatment continued to be reported. In response to unrest in the South, security forces and groups linked to them used excessive force, killing at least a dozen people, and arbitrarily detained scores of people involved in protests or who supported secession of the South. Ansar al-Shari'a (Partisans of al-Shari'a), an armed group linked to al-Qa'ida in the Arabian Peninsula (AQAP) that controlled parts of Abyan governorate until June, committed human rights abuses, including summary killings and amputations. A government military offensive to drive Ansar al-Shari'a out of cities under its control was marked by violations of human rights and international humanitarian law on both sides, resulting in civilian deaths. Women and girls continued to face discrimination in law and practice, and domestic violence. Reports emerged of slavery in some parts of the country. The humanitarian situation reached crisis point. At least seven people were sentenced to death and at least 28 people were executed, including at least two juvenile offenders.

Background

On 25 February, former Vice-President Abd Rabbu Mansour Hadi was inaugurated as President following presidential elections in which he was the only candidate. The election was required by the power-transfer agreement brokered by the Gulf Cooperation Council and signed by former President Saleh on 23 November 2011. The new President, along with the "government of national reconciliation" formed in December 2011, were mandated to implement a two-year transition, during which they were to organize a national dialogue, hold a referendum on a new Constitution, reform the electoral system, restructure the military and security services, and take steps towards transitional justice. General elections in line with the new Constitution were to follow.

An outreach committee set up in May contacted different parties to join the national dialogue. On 14 July, a preparatory committee for the dialogue was formed and subsequently gave President Hadi a list of 20 recommendations to make the dialogue successful. These included an apology to people in the South and the northern Sa'dah province for past violations, and the release of all prisoners detained in connection with the Southern Movement, the Sa'dah conflict and events linked to the 2011 uprising. The recommendations were not implemented by the end of the year. In December, as part of the restructuring of the military, President Hadi announced that the head of the Republican Guards (a son of the former president), the Central Security's Chief of Staff (nephew of the former president), and the commander of the army's First Armoured Division would be removed from their posts.

Despite the stabilizing effects of the transition, there was continuing insecurity, including kidnappings. The killing of lawyer Hassan al-Dawlah in December prompted concerns that he may have been targeted for his work.

There was a deepening humanitarian crisis marked by acute shortages of food, water and other necessities, burgeoning unemployment and living costs, and cuts to power and oil supplies. International donors pledged over US$7 billion to help Yemen during its transition but international and Yemeni aid agencies called for more targeted emergency funding to avert the hunger crisis.

At least 28 people were charged in connection with an attack on the presidential palace on 3 June 2011,

Y

which wounded then President Saleh and killed and wounded others, but they had not been brought to trial by the end of the year. Several were reported to have been tortured or otherwise ill-treated.

Impunity

On 21 January, the government enacted an immunity law, Law No.1 of 2012, in accordance with the power-transfer agreement. The law granted former President Saleh and all those who were employed by his government immunity from criminal prosecution for "politically motivated acts" carried out in the course of their duties. Consequently, it prevented many victims of arbitrary detention, torture, extrajudicial execution, enforced disappearance and other violations carried out under President Saleh's long rule from obtaining justice, truth and reparation. As such, the immunity law breached Yemen's international legal obligations to investigate and prosecute crimes under international law and other human rights violations.

A draft Transitional Justice and National Reconciliation Law was under discussion. If enacted, it would provide some form of reparation to victims and survivors. However, the draft emphasized forgiveness as an element of reconciliation and did not provide justice for victims of past human rights violations.

It appeared that no judicial investigations were carried out into dozens of incidents in which protesters were killed or human rights were violated in the context of the 2011 unrest. Nor were there investigations into alleged violations of human rights and international humanitarian law committed during the internal armed conflicts in Ta'izz and other areas, such as the apparently indiscriminate and disproportionate attacks that killed civilians during fighting between government forces and armed supporters of Sadeq al-Ahmar, a tribal sheikh in Sana'a's al-Hasaba area in the second half of 2011.

However, a presidential decree issued on 22 September established a commission of inquiry into violations of human rights and international humanitarian law during the 2011 uprising, but it had not commenced at the end of the year.

Arbitrary arrests and detentions

Most of those held in connection with anti-government protests in 2011 were released in early 2012. Many had been held arbitrarily by different security forces, often in unregistered detention centres, for weeks or months without charge or trial. Some were reported to have been tortured or otherwise ill-treated. At least 20 people were believed to still be arbitrarily detained or to have disappeared in connection with the 2011 protests or after arrest in 2012.

■ Al-Nahari Mohammed Ali al-Nahari, aged around 13, was released without charge in July 2012. He disappeared in May 2011 after participating in protests in Sana'a and was believed to have been held secretly by National Security. He lost his hearing in one ear after being hit repeatedly in detention.

Protest camps remained in both Ta'izz and Sana'a, where the tent city in Change Square continued to be guarded by the army's First Armoured Division, which had supported the protests but also reportedly continued to carry out arrests and hold detainees without charge or trial.

Women's and girls' rights

Women and girls continued to face discrimination in both law and practice, notably in relation to marriage, divorce, child custody and inheritance, as well as high levels of domestic and other gender-specific violence.

Women became less visible in the protest camps after some were intimidated or beaten in 2011 by women apparently associated with the Islah party, a main opposition party, who objected to their joining in marches with men and protesting against the commander of the First Armoured Division.

Excessive use of force

The security forces continued to use excessive force against protesters, particularly in Aden and other southern cities, with impunity. Only two judicial investigations into killings of protesters during the 2011 uprising resulted in prosecutions.

■ In June, three men apparently connected with local authorities were sentenced to death in their absence in connection with a grenade attack on 17 February 2011 that killed one protester and wounded 15 others in Freedom Square, Ta'izz.

■ Charges were brought against 79 men in connection with the killing of dozens of protesters on 18 March 2011 in Sana'a. In June, the Attorney General said only 14 of the accused were in custody; others had been released on bail or were still at large. The trial before the Specialized Criminal Court was suspended while the judge sought clarification from the Supreme Court regarding the immunity law and amid questions over whether the real perpetrators were among those charged.

■ An official investigation which opened in 2011 into the killing of protesters in Freedom Square in Ta'izz on 29 May 2011 appeared to make no progress in 2012.

An administrative court ruled in November that the authorities were obliged to provide medical treatment to people injured in the 2011 protests or send them for treatment abroad, in line with a presidential decree issued in late 2011.

Repression of dissent – protests in southern Yemen

Security forces and pro-government supporters continued to use excessive, including lethal, force against protesters in Aden and other southern cities, killing at least a dozen people and wounding many others. They also arrested and briefly detained scores of people, mostly supporters of the Southern Movement, which advocates the secession of the South.

■ On 7 July, Central Security forces in armoured vehicles supported by snipers fired on a peaceful demonstration in Aden, killing four people and injuring 18. Security forces in three armoured vehicles opened fire as protesters reached a roundabout. Snipers then shot at fleeing protesters.

■ Student Abdul Raouf Hassan Zain al-Saqqaf, a Southern Movement activist, was detained with four others by security forces in Aden on 10 August. They were taken to a police station and beaten with rifle butts and a stick. The four others were released, but Abdul Raouf al-Saqqaf was transferred to the Central Prison in al-Mansura, where he was again beaten and held in solitary confinement in a tiny cockroach-infested cell without light or fresh air. He was released on 13 August, but was threatened with re-arrest. In November he was severely beaten by unidentified men apparently connected to the Islah party and later shot and wounded when masked gunmen attempted to abduct him.

Security forces raided hospitals to arrest injured protesters. Médecins Sans Frontières closed their hospital in Aden in October following repeated raids during which their staff were threatened by security forces.

■ On 27 September, two security guards employed by Médecins Sans Frontières were reported to have been beaten and threatened at gunpoint by unidentified men in Aden.

Armed conflict in Abyan

Ansar al-Shari'a continued to commit gross human rights abuses in the city of Ja'ar, Abyan governorate, which it took control of in February 2011, as well as in other cities in Shabwa governorate which it subsequently controlled. The armed group summarily executed and imposed cruel, inhuman and degrading punishments, including hand amputations, on those they accused of "crimes", and attempted to enforce discriminatory and repressive social and religious requirements using violence and threats of violence. They also abducted and harassed community activists.

The year saw continued fighting between government forces and Ansar al-Shari'a in which both sides violated international humanitarian law. Ansar al-Shari'a recklessly exposed civilians to harm by storing ammunition and explosives in crowded residential areas, launched attacks from the immediate vicinity of civilian homes, detained and ill-treated civilians, restricted access to medical care, and made extensive use of anti-personnel mines and booby traps. Government forces used air strikes, tanks, artillery and mortars, often in an indiscriminate or disproportionate manner, causing deaths and injuries among civilians, until they succeeded in driving Ansar al-Shari'a out of Abyan and the surrounding areas in late June. Government forces also obstructed access to medical treatment for the wounded and subjected suspected Ansar al-Shari'a fighters to enforced disappearance.

At the end of the year, Ansar al-Shari'a was continuing to carry out bomb and other attacks targeting government and security forces installations and officials.

Drone attacks

US forces used unmanned drones to attack suspected supporters of al-Qa'ida in Abyan province and elsewhere, apparently with the consent of the Yemeni government. Some civilians were reported to have been killed but it was unclear whether they died in US drone strikes or attacks by Yemeni forces, and no investigations were held.

Internally displaced people

Many of those forcibly displaced due to the armed conflict in Abyan and surrounding areas were able to return to their homes by the end of the year, despite the threat posed by anti-personnel mines and other ordnance left by Ansar al-Shari'a. However, tens of thousands of other people remained internally displaced, mostly in Aden.

Slavery

Reports emerged that generations of families had been held as slaves and continued to be enslaved in parts of the country. It appeared that the practice was able to continue due to a lack of state scrutiny.

Death penalty

At least seven people were sentenced to death and at least 28 people were executed. The real number was believed to be much higher. At least two juvenile offenders were executed for crimes allegedly committed when they were under 18. Hundreds of people were believed to be under sentence of death, including at least 25 alleged juvenile offenders.

■ Fuad Ahmed Ali Abdulla was executed in Ta'izz prison on 18 January; he was convicted of a murder committed in 2004 when he was under 18.

■ Hind al-Barati was executed in Sana'a Central Prison on 3 December; she was convicted of a murder committed when she was believed to have been 15.

Amnesty International visits/reports

🚍 Amnesty International delegates visited Yemen in June/July and December. They had not previously been allowed access to Yemen since January 2011.

📖 Yemen's immunity law: Breach of international obligations (MDE 31/007/2012)

📖 Conflict in Yemen: Abyan's darkest hour (MDE 31/010/2012)

📖 Yemen: Human rights agenda for change (MDE 31/012/2012)

ZIMBABWE

REPUBLIC OF ZIMBABWE
Head of state and government: **Robert Mugabe**

Mistrust between members of the Government of National Unity (GNU) continued to delay crucial reforms agreed under the 2008 Global Political Agreement between President Mugabe's ZANU-PF party and the two Movement for Democratic Change parties (MDC-T and MDC-N). Talk of an election in the second half of the year caused panic in rural areas affected by the 2008 election-related, state-sponsored violence. Police continued to suppress free expression, association and assembly throughout the year, through arbitrary arrest, unlawful detentions and politically motivated prosecutions.

Background

The GNU failed to finalize a new Constitution, which is crucial if the country is to hold violence-free elections in 2013. The second All Stakeholders Conference to review a draft was held in October, when ZANU-PF tried to reverse new elements that would restrict executive powers and strengthen the declaration of rights agreed during the inter-party negotiation process. The Southern Africa Development Community (SADC), represented by President Jacob Zuma of South Africa, achieved no meaningful reforms to guarantee non-violent elections, despite several visits to Zimbabwe by his facilitation team.

Remarks by senior leaders of the army, police and intelligence services stating their preferred election outcome fuelled fears that the security forces – which had been implicated in the 2008 election violence – would again try to influence the next election in favour of ZANU-PF. President Mugabe and Prime Minister Morgan Tsvangirai publicly spoke out against political violence; however, no concrete measures were taken to end partisan activities of the security forces.

Although incidents of mass political violence remained low, mainly because there were no major political events in the year, at least 300 people were injured as a result of politically motivated acts of torture or other violence.

Z

Freedoms of expression, association and assembly

Human rights defenders and political activists – other than ZANU-PF members – continued to operate under heavy restrictions. In urban areas, police were the main perpetrators, using the Public Order and Security Act to arbitrarily limit the rights to freedom of expression, association and peaceful assembly, including by blocking legitimate meetings and activities of human rights defenders and other political parties. In semi-urban and rural areas, local ZANU-PF activists continued to disrupt legitimate activities of their opponents with impunity. Some traditional leaders were also used by ZANU-PF to restrict access to rural areas. Incidents of uniformed soldiers assaulting people attending meetings organized by the two MDC parties were recorded.

■ An MDC-T (MDC-Tsvangirai) official, Cephas Magura, died in Mudzi district in May following clashes between MDC-T and ZANU-PF supporters at Chimukoko Business Centre. ZANU-PF supporters reportedly attacked people who were attending a police-sanctioned meeting of the MDC-T. Following the incident, seven ZANU-PF members, including a councillor in Mudzi, David Chimukoko, were arrested and charged with murder and public violence.

■ On 21 September, a group of soldiers in Mutoko district, Mashonaland East Province, disrupted a meeting led by Professor Welshman Ncube (MDC-N, the smaller of the two MDC parties), beating supporters.

■ In November, another group of soldiers in Zhombe district, Midlands Province, attacked MDC-T supporters attending a meeting at Samambwa Business Centre. Dozens of supporters were injured, including two men in their seventies who arrived at a Harare hospital with broken limbs and internal injuries.

■ Some of the 29 MDC-T members arrested in May 2011 in connection with the death of police officer Petros Mutedza, in Glen View, spent more than a year in custody. However, Cynthia Manjoro was granted bail in October after a state witness said that she had been arrested and detained to bait another suspect who was her friend. Solomon Madzore, the MDC-T's Youth Assembly president was also granted bail on 13 November together with another detainee, Taruvinga Magaya. It was widely believed that some of the suspects were arrested solely because they were known MDC-T activists living in Glen View. By the end of year only Last Maengahama, Tungamirai Madzokere, Rebecca Mafikeni, Yvonne Musarurwa and Simon Mapanzure remained in custody.

■ On 5 November, police in Harare raided the offices of the Counselling Services Unit (CSU), a registered medical clinic providing services to victims of organized violence and torture. Police initially arrived without a search warrant and threatened to force entry. After several hours they produced a warrant to recover "offensive and subversive material" which "defaces any house, building, wall, fence, lamp-post, gate or elevator", and illegally seized confidential patient medical records, a computer and documents not covered by the warrant. Five staff were arbitrarily arrested. Two were released the same day, but three others, Fidelis Mudimu, Zachariah Godi and Tafadzwa Geza, were illegally detained in police custody for four days, and on the third day they were illegally transferred more than 400km away to Bulawayo. The three men were released on bail on 8 November charged with "causing malicious damage to property", in contravention of Section 140 of the Criminal Law (Codification and Reform) Act. The charges against Fidelis Mudimu were later dropped after it was revealed that he was out of the country at the time of the alleged crime.

Arbitrary arrests and detentions

Throughout the year, activists from the activist organization Women of Zimbabwe Arise (WOZA) had their activities routinely disrupted by anti-riot police. Many were beaten and some sustained injuries. At least 200 arrests of WOZA members were recorded.

■ On 19 January, 17 activists were arrested in Bulawayo and taken to Donnington Police station where some were beaten and ill-treated. They were later transferred to Bulawayo Central Police station where the abuse continued, before being released without charge.

■ On 12 March, WOZA leaders Jennifer Williams and Magodonga Mahlangu, who were appearing in court on bail for trumped-up charges of kidnapping and theft, had their bail unjustly revoked by a Bulawayo Magistrate and were remanded in prison. The defence lawyers had asked for postponement of the case as Jennifer Williams was in poor health and had a doctor's letter substantiating her state of health. However, the prosecutor accused her of feigning illness.

Z

- On 27 June, 101 WOZA members were arrested in Bulawayo the morning after a peaceful march and detained for five hours, before being released without charge.

Section 33 of the Criminal Law (Codification and Reform) Act continued to be applied arbitrarily, with political activists and others being charged with "undermining the authority of or insulting the President". At least 12 people were arrested on these charges.

- In October, Elton Mangoma, the MDC-T Minister of Energy and Power Development in the GNU, was arrested and charged with "undermining the authority of or insulting the President" in connection with a statement he made in March at Manhenga Business Centre in Bindura, Mashonaland Central.

Torture and extrajudicial executions in police custody

At least eight people died in police custody under circumstances that suggest that they were tortured or summarily executed.

- On 19 March, three young men who had been taken into custody at Southerton Police station in Harare died in very suspicious circumstances. Tendai Dzigarwi and Rufaro Mahohoma had been arrested on 18 March in Harare's suburb of Kambuzuma by police from the Vehicle Theft Squad. They were arrested on suspicion of motor vehicle theft. A third man, Emmson Ngundu, was arrested on 19 March in Zvimba district. The police claimed the three men were killed during an attempted escape, but an independent post-mortem conducted on Tendai Dzigarwi concluded that he died from a gunshot wound to the head fired from 2-3cm. Eyewitness accounts of the wounds of the other two men point to the same conclusion.

- On 13 September, two days after his release, Harrison Manyati died at Harare Central Hospital from injuries sustained during torture while in detention at Makoni Police station in Chitungwiza. Harrison Manyati had been arbitrarily arrested and unlawfully detained on 7 September after he had gone to the police station to enquire about a friend arrested for housebreaking, theft and illegal entry. Police accused him of being an accomplice and he was detained for four days without being charged or taken to court. Police told family members that Harrison Manyati had committed no crime. When he was released he laid charges of assault against the police officers. According to an eyewitness,

Manyati was tortured during the first two days of his detention, and then detained for two days to allow the wounds to heal. An independent post-mortem report concluded that Manyati's death was a direct result of torture.

- Blessing Matanda was found dead in a police cell at Munyati Police Base station in Kwekwe on 4 October, the day he was taken into custody under unclear circumstances. Matanda told a relative who visited him that the arresting officers had threatened to "fix" him. Police claim Matanda shot himself, but offered no explanation as to how he had access to a gun. An independent pathologist cast doubt on the allegation of suicide.

Forced evictions

Seven years on, tens of thousands of people affected by the 2005 mass forced evictions Operation Murambatsvina still lived in settlements with no schools, health care, water, sanitation or roads. Despite public acknowledgement by authorities of the lack of schooling in particular, no measures were taken to ensure the thousands of affected children can access free primary education.

Rights of lesbian, gay, bisexual, transgender and intersex people

Hostility directed at non-gender-conforming individuals and discrimination against LGBTI people continued to be rife in the country. The media contributed to public prejudices against LGBTI individuals by publishing hostile comments about LGBTI people made by political leaders, particularly within the context of debate around the new Constitution. ZANU-PF and MDC-T accused each other of "harbouring" LGBTI people. Politicization of the debate on outlawing discrimination on the basis of sexual orientation or gender identity fuelled harassment and intimidation of LGBTI people by police.

- Forty-four members of the Gays and Lesbians of Zimbabwe (GALZ) organization were detained overnight at Harare Central Police station on 11 August when police raided their offices in Harare. The raid followed a meeting convened by GALZ to discuss Zimbabwe's draft Constitution and to launch a report on human rights violations perpetrated against its members. Following the detainees' release, police visited some of their homes and workplaces, risking exposing their sexual orientation and thereby putting them at increased risk of discrimination.

■ On 20 August, police raided the GALZ offices for a second time and seized computers and pamphlets. On 23 August, GALZ was charged with running an "unregistered" organization in contravention of Section 6(iii) of the Private Voluntary Organisation Act. For the first time in 20 years GALZ was forced to close its offices indefinitely for fear of further police raids.

Amnesty International visits/reports

🚌 Amnesty International delegates visited Zimbabwe in April, August and September/October.

📄 Zimbabwean authorities must stop abusing the law to curtail the work of human rights activists (AFR 46/001/2012)

📄 Zimbabwe: Brief to SADC on harassment and intimidation of NGO workers by police (AFR 46/016/2012)

📄 Zimbabwe: Members of the public at risk as police crack down on gang suspects (PRE01/434/2012)

Z

AMNESTY INTERNATIONAL REPORT 2013
PART THREE

13

AMNESTY INTERNATIONAL
SECTIONS

Algeria ❖ Amnesty International,
10, rue Mouloud ZADI (face au 113 rue Didouche Mourad),
Alger Centre, 16004 Alger
email: contact@amnestyalgerie.org
www.amnestyalgerie.org

Argentina ❖ Amnistía Internacional,
Cerrito 1050, 6° Piso, C1010AAV Buenos Aires
email: contacto@amnistia.org.ar
www.amnistia.org.ar

Australia ❖ Amnesty International,
Locked Bag 23, Broadway NSW 2007
email: nswaia@amnesty.org.au
www.amnesty.org.au

Austria ❖ Amnesty International,
Moeringgasse 10, A-1150 Vienna
email: info@amnesty.at
www.amnesty.at

Belgium ❖
Amnesty International **(Flemish-speaking)**,
Kerkstraat 156, 2060 Antwerpen
email: amnesty@aivl.be
www.aivl.be
Amnesty International **(francophone)**,
Rue Berckmans 9, 1060 Bruxelles
email: amnesty@amnesty.be
www.amnestyinternational.be

Bermuda ❖ Amnesty International,
PO Box HM 2136, Hamilton HM JX
email: director@amnestybermuda.org
www.amnestybermuda.org

Burkina Faso ❖ Amnesty International,
BP 11344, Ouagadougou 08
email: aiburkina@fasonet.bf
www.amnesty-bf.org

Canada ❖
Amnesty International **(English-speaking)**,
312 Laurier Avenue East, Ottawa, Ontario, K1N 1H9
email: info@amnesty.ca
www.amnesty.ca
Amnistie internationale **(francophone)**,
50 rue Ste-Catherine Ouest, bureau 500, Montréal,
Quebec, H2X 3V4
www.amnistie.ca

Chile ❖ Amnistía Internacional,
Oficina Nacional, Huelén 164 - Planta Baja,
750-0617 Providencia, Santiago
email: info@amnistia.cl
www.amnistia.cl

Colombia ❖ Amnistía Internacional,
On-line Action Platform
email: AIColombia.Online@amnesty.org

Côte d'Ivoire ❖ Amnesty International,
04 BP 895, Abidjan 04
email: amnesty.ci@aviso.ci

Czech Republic ❖ Amnesty International,
Provaznická 3, 110 00, Prague 1
email: amnesty@amnesty.cz
www.amnesty.cz

Denmark ❖ Amnesty International,
Gammeltorv 8, 5 - 1457 Copenhagen K.
email: amnesty@amnesty.dk
www.amnesty.dk

Faroe Islands ❖ Amnesty International,
Mannarættindarúmið Kongabrúgvin, Fo-100 Tórshavn
email: amnesty@amnesty.fo
www.amnesty.fo

Finland ❖ Amnesty International,
Hietaniemenkatu 7A, 00100 Helsinki
email: amnesty@amnesty.fi
www.amnesty.fi

France ❖ Amnesty International,
76 boulevard de la Villette, 75940 Paris, Cédex 19
email: info@amnesty.fr
www.amnesty.fr

Germany ❖ Amnesty International,
Zinnowitzer Strasse 8, 10115 Berlin
email: info@amnesty.de
www.amnesty.de

Ghana ❖ Amnesty International,
H/No. 347/7 Rolyat Castle Road, Opposite Havard College,
Kokomlemle, Accra
email: info@amnestyghana.org
www.amnestyghana.org

Greece ❖ Amnesty International,
Sina 30, 106 72 Athens
email: athens@amnesty.org.gr
www.amnesty.org.gr

Hong Kong ❖ Amnesty International,
3D Best-O-Best Commercial Centre, 32 Ferry Street, Kowloon
email: admin-hk@amnesty.org.hk
www.amnesty.org.hk

Iceland ❖ Amnesty International,
Þingholtsstræti 27, 101 Reykjavík
email: amnesty@amnesty.is
www.amnesty.is

Ireland ❖ Amnesty International,
Sean MacBride House, 48 Fleet Street, Dublin 2
email: info@amnesty.ie
www.amnesty.ie

Israel ❖ Amnesty International,
PO Box 14179, Tel Aviv 61141
email: info@amnesty.org.il
www.amnesty.org.il

Italy ❖ Amnesty International,
Via Giovanni Battista De Rossi 10, 00161 Roma
email: info@amnesty.it
www.amnesty.it

Japan ❖ Amnesty International,
7F Seika Bldg. 2-12-14 Kandaogawamachi, Chiyoda-ku,
Tokyo 101-0052
email: info@amnesty.or.jp
www.amnesty.or.jp

Korea (Republic of) ❖ Amnesty International,
Gwanghwamun P.O.Box 2045 Jongno-gu, 10-620 Seoul
email: info@amnesty.or.kr
www.amnesty.or.kr

Luxembourg ❖ Amnesty International,
23 rue des Etats-Unis, L-1019 Luxembourg
email: info@amnesty.lu
www.amnesty.lu

Mauritius ❖ Amnesty International,
BP 69, Rose-Hill
email: amnestymtius@erm.mu

Mexico ❖ Amnistía Internacional,
Tajín No. 389, Col. Narvarte, Del. Benito Juárez,
C.P. 03020 Mexico D.F.
email: info@amnistia.org.mx
www.amnistia.org.mx

Morocco ❖ Amnesty International,
281 avenue Mohamed V, Apt. 23, Escalier A, Rabat
email: amorocco@sections.amnesty.org
www.amnestymaroc.org

Nepal ❖ Amnesty International,
PO Box 135, Amnesty Marga, Basantanagar, Balaju,
Kathmandu
email: info@amnestynepal.org
www.amnestynepal.org

Netherlands ❖ Amnesty International,
Keizersgracht 177, 1016 DR Amsterdam
email: amnesty@amnesty.nl
www.amnesty.nl

New Zealand ❖ Amnesty International,
PO Box 5300, Wellesley Street, Auckland 1141
email: info@amnesty.org.nz
www.amnesty.org.nz

Norway ❖ Amnesty International,
Grensen 3, 0159 Oslo
email: info@amnesty.no
www.amnesty.no

Paraguay ❖ Amnistía Internacional,
Manuel Castillo 4987 esquina San Roque González,
Barrio Villa Morra, Asunción
email: ai-info@py.amnesty.org
www.amnesty.org.py

Peru ❖ Amnistía Internacional,
Enrique Palacios 735-A, Miraflores, Lima 18
email: amnistia@amnistia.org.pe
www.amnistia.org.pe

Philippines ❖ Amnesty International,
18-A Marunong Street, Barangay Central,
Quezon City 1100
email: section@amnesty.org.ph
www.amnesty.org.ph

Poland ❖ Amnesty International,
ul. Piękna 66a, lokal 2, I piętro, 00-672,
Warszawa
email: amnesty@amnesty.org.pl
www.amnesty.org.pl

Portugal ❖ Amnistia Internacional,
Av. Infante Santo, 42, 2°, 1350 - 179 Lisboa
email: aiportugal@amnistia-internacional.pt
www.amnistia-internacional.pt

Puerto Rico ❖ Amnistía Internacional,
Calle Robles 54, Suite 6, Río Piedras PR 00925
email: amnistiapr@amnestypr.org
www.amnistiapr.org

Senegal ❖ Amnesty International,
303/GRD Sacré-coeur II, Résidence Arame SIGA, BP 35269,
Dakar Colobane
email: asenegal@sections.amnesty.org
www.amnesty.sn

Sierra Leone ❖ Amnesty International,
42 William Street, Freetown
email: amnestysl@gmail.com

Slovenia ❖ Amnesty International,
Beethovnova 7, 1000 Ljubljana
email: amnesty@amnesty.si
www.amnesty.si

Spain ❖ Amnistía Internacional,
Fernando VI, 8, 1° izda, 28004 Madrid
email: info@es.amnesty.org
www.es.amnesty.org

Sweden ❖ Amnesty International,
PO Box 4719, 11692 Stockholm
email: info@amnesty.se
www.amnesty.se

Switzerland ❖ Amnesty International,
Speichergasse 33, CH-3011 Berne
email: info@amnesty.ch
www.amnesty.ch

Taiwan ❖ Amnesty International,
3F., No. 14, Lane 165, Sec. 1, Sinsheng S. Rd,
Da-an District, Taipei City 106
email: secretariat@amnesty.tw
www.amnesty.tw

Togo ❖ Amnesty International,
2322 avenue du RPT, Quartier Casablanca, BP 20013, Lomé
email: contact@amnesty.tg
www.amnesty.tg

Tunisia ❖ Amnesty International,
67 rue Oum Kalthoum, 3ème étage, escalier B, 1000 Tunis
email: admin-tn@amnesty.org

United Kingdom ❖ Amnesty International,
The Human Rights Action Centre, 17-25 New Inn Yard,
London EC2A 3EA
email: sct@amnesty.org.uk
www.amnesty.org.uk

United States of America ❖ Amnesty International,
5 Penn Plaza, 16th floor, New York, NY 10001
email: admin-us@aiusa.org
www.amnestyusa.org

Uruguay ❖ Amnistía Internacional,
San José 1140, piso 5, C.P. 11.100 Montevideo
email: oficina@amnistia.org.uy
www.amnistia.org.uy

Venezuela ❖ Amnistía Internacional,
Torre Phelps piso 17, oficina 17 A,
Av. La Salle, Plaza Venezuela, Los Caobos,
Caracas 1050
email: info@aiven.org
www.aiven.org

Zimbabwe ❖ Amnesty International,
56 Midlothean Avenue, Eastlea, Harare
email: amnestyinternational.zimbabwe@gmail.com

AMNESTY INTERNATIONAL
STRUCTURES

Hungary ❖ Amnesty International,
Rózsa u. 44, II/4, 1064 Budapest
email: info@amnesty.hu
www.amnesty.hu

Malaysia ❖ Amnesty International,
D-2-33A, 8 Avenue, Jalan Sungai Jernih, 8/1,
Section 8, 46050 Petaling Jaya, Selangor
email: aimalaysia@aimalaysia.org
www.aimalaysia.org

Mali ❖ Amnesty International,
Immeuble Soya Bathily, Route de l'aéroport,
24 rue Kalabancoura, BP E 3885, Bamako
email: amnesty.mali@ikatelnet.net

Moldova ❖ Amnesty International,
PO Box 209, MD-2012 Chişinău
email: info@amnesty.md
www.amnesty.md

Mongolia ❖ Amnesty International,
Sukhbaatar District, Baga Toirog 44,
Ulaanbaatar 210648
email: aimncc@magicnet.mn
www.amnesty.mn

Thailand ❖ Amnesty International,
90/24 Lat Phrao Soi 1, Jomphol, Chatuchak,
Bangkok 10900
email: info@amnesty.or.th
www.amnesty.or.th

Turkey ❖ Amnesty International,
Hamalbaşı Cd. No: 22 Dükkan 2-D2-D3-D4, 34425 Beyoğlu,
Istanbul
email: posta@amnesty.org.tr
www.amnesty.org.tr

AMNESTY INTERNATIONAL
NATIONAL ENTITIES

Benin ❖ Amnesty International,
01 BP 3536, Cotonou
email: info@aibenin.org
www.amnesty.bj

Brazil ❖ Amnesty International,
Praça São Salvador, 5-Casa, Laranjeiras 22.231-170,
Rio de Janeiro
email: contato@anistia.org.br
www.anistia.org.br

India ❖ Amnesty International,
1074/B-1, First Floor, 11th Main, HAL 2nd Stage, Indira Nagar,
Bangalore, Karnataka, 560 008
email: amnestyindia@amnesty.org
www.amnesty.org.in

Kenya ❖ Amnesty International,
Suite A3, Haven Court, Waiyaki Way, Westlands, P.O. Box 1527,
00606 Sarit Centre, Nairobi
email: amnestykenya@amnesty.org

Slovakia ❖ Amnesty International,
Karpatska 11, 811 05 Bratislava
email: amnesty@amnesty.sk
www.amnesty.sk

South Africa ❖ Amnesty International,
11th Floor Braamfontein Centre, 23 Jorrissen Street,
2017 Braamfontein, Johannesburg
email: info@amnesty.org.za
www.amnesty.org.za

Ukraine ❖ Amnesty International,
Olesya Honchara str, 37A, office 1, Kyev 01034
email: info@amnesty.org.ua
www.amnesty.org.ua

AMNESTY INTERNATIONAL
STRATEGIC PARTNERSHIPS

The Strategic Partnerships Project is part of the Growth Unit in Amnesty International. The project aims to grow human rights activism and impact in countries with no Amnesty International entities by establishing partnerships with local NGOs. It also aims to increase the visibility of Amnesty International and the strategic partner and create platforms for Amnesty International issues in the country. Amnesty International's Strategic Partnerships in 2012 were in Cambodia, Haiti, Indonesia, Kazakhstan, Kyrgyzstan, Tajikistan, Timor-Leste and Romania.

For more information on Strategic Partnerships, please contact: Strategic_Partnerships_Team@amnesty.org

AMNESTY INTERNATIONAL
INTERNATIONAL MEMBERSHIP

There are also International Members in several countries and territories around the world.

More information can be found online at:
www.amnesty.org/en/join
email: mobilization@amnesty.org

AMNESTY INTERNATIONAL
OFFICES

International Secretariat (IS)
Amnesty International,
Peter Benenson House, 1 Easton Street,
London WC1X 0DW,
United Kingdom
email: amnestyis@amnesty.org
www.amnesty.org

Amnesty International Language Resource Centre (AILRC)
Head office
Calle Valderribas, 13, 28007 Madrid, Spain
email: AILRC@amnesty.org
Arabic: www.amnesty.org/ar
Spanish: www.amnesty.org/es
Amnesty International Language Resource Centre – French (AILRC-FR)
Paris office
47 rue de Paradis - Bât C, 75010 Paris, France
www.amnesty.org/fr

IS New York – UN Representative Office
Amnesty International,
777 UN Plaza, 6th Floor, New York,
NY 10017, USA
email: aiunny@amnesty.org

IS Geneva – UN Representative Office
Amnesty International,
22 rue du Cendrier, 4ème étage,
CH-1201 Geneva, Switzerland
email: uaigv@amnesty.org

Amnesty International European Institutions Office
Rue de Trèves 35, Boîte 3,
B-1040 Brussels, Belgium
email: amnestyIntl@amnesty.eu
www.amnesty.eu

IS Beirut – Middle East and North Africa Regional Office
Amnesty International,
PO Box 13-5696,
Chouran Beirut 1102 - 2060, Lebanon
email: mena@amnesty.org
www.amnestymena.org

IS Dakar – Africa Human Rights Education Office
Amnesty International,
SICAP Sacré Coeur Pyrotechnie Extension,
Villa No. 22, BP 47582,
Dakar, Senegal
email: isdakaroffice@amnesty.org
www.africa-hre.org

IS Hong Kong – Asia Pacific Regional Office
Amnesty International,
16/F Siu On Centre, 188 Lockhart Rd, Wan Chai,
Hong Kong
email: admin-ap@amnesty.org

IS Johannesburg
Amnesty International,
Ground Floor, 3 on Glenhove, Melrose Estate,
Johannesburg, South Africa
email: adminjoburg@amnesty.org

IS Kampala – Africa Regional Office
Amnesty International,
Plot 20A Kawalya Kaggwa Close,
PO Box 23966,
Kampala, Uganda
email: ai-aro@amnesty.org

IS Moscow – Russia Office
Amnesty International,
PO Box 212,
Moscow 119019, Russian Federation
email: msk@amnesty.org
www.amnesty.org.ru

IS Paris – Research Office
Amnesty International,
76 boulevard de la Villette,
75940 Paris, Cédex 19, France
email: pro@amnesty.org

INDEX OF SELECTED TOPICS*

Mozambique 187; Panama 207; Portugal 214; Romania 217; Senegal 227; Serbia 230; South Africa 240; Sri Lanka 249; Syria 260; Tanzania 265-6; Togo 269; Turkey 275; United States of America 289; Yemen 298

extrajudicial executions
Bangladesh 35; Burundi 49; Equatorial Guinea 91; Guinea 111; Guinea-Bissau 113; India 120-1; Mali 172-3, 173; Mexico 178; South Africa 239-40; Syria 260; Zimbabwe 302

F

forced evictions
Angola 24; Cambodia 52; Chad 59; China 63; Dominican Republic 84; Egypt 89; Ethiopia 97; France 100; Haiti 115; Israel and the Occupied Palestinian Territories 134; Kenya 148; Mongolia 182; Nigeria 198; Papua New Guinea 208; Portugal 214; Zimbabwe 302

freedom of assembly and association
Algeria 21; Angola 23-4; Azerbaijan 29-30; Bahrain 34; Belarus 37-8; Cuba 74; Ecuador 84; Egypt 88; Fiji 97; Georgia 103, 104; Iran 126; Israel and the Occupied Palestinian Territories 136; Jordan 142; Korea (Republic of) 151; Kuwait 152; Libya 163; Malaysia 169-70; Morocco/Western Sahara 184; Myanmar 189; Namibia 190-1; Oman 200-1; Palestinian Authority 206; Russian Federation 218-9; Rwanda 223; Singapore 233-4; Sudan 252; Tanzania 265-6; Turkmenistan 278; Uganda 279; United Arab Emirates 283-4; Zimbabwe 301

freedom of expression (see also *repression of dissent*)
Afghanistan 18; Algeria 21; Angola 23-4; Armenia 26; Azerbaijan 29-30; Belarus 37; Benin 39; Bolivia 41; Burundi 50; Cambodia 51-2; Cameroon 54; Chad 58; Côte d'Ivoire 71; Cuba 74; Democratic Republic of the Congo 80; Dominican Republic 83; Ecuador 85; Egypt 88; Equatorial Guinea 92; Ethiopia 95; Fiji 97; Gambia 102; Georgia 103-4; Greece 109; Guinea-Bissau 112-3; Hungary 118; India 122; Indonesia 123-4; Iran 126; Israel and the Occupied Palestinian Territories 136; Jordan 142; Kazakhstan 145-6; Korea (Democratic People's Republic of) 150; Korea (Republic of) 151; Kuwait 152; Laos 155-6; Lebanon 158; Libya 163; Macedonia 166; Madagascar 168; Malawi 227; Malaysia 169; Mauritania 176; Montenegro 183; Morocco/Western Sahara 184; Myanmar 189; Nigeria 199; Oman 200-1; Pakistan 203; Palestinian Authority 206; Poland 213; Puerto Rico 215; Russian Federation 219; Rwanda 223; Senegal 227; Serbia 230-1; Singapore 233-4; Somalia 237-8; South Sudan 244; Sri Lanka 250; Sudan 251-2; Swaziland 255; Syria 259-60; Taiwan 263; Tajikistan 265; Tanzania 265; Thailand 267; Togo 269-70; Tunisia 273; Turkey 274-5; Turkmenistan 278; Uganda 279; United Arab Emirates 283-4; Uzbekistan 292; Viet Nam 295-6; Zimbabwe 301

freedom of movement
Israel and the Occupied Palestinian Territories 134; Korea (Democratic People's Republic of) 150; Turkmenistan 278

freedom of religion or belief
Eritrea 92-3; Indonesia 124; Iran 128

H

health (right to)
Burkina Faso 49; Guyana 114; Ireland 132; Nepal 192-3; Philippines 212; Sierra Leone 232-3; South Africa 242; United States of America 290

housing rights
Albania 21; Belgium 39; Brazil 46-7; Czech Republic 77; Ghana 106; Romania 217; Slovakia 234; Spain 248

human rights defenders
Algeria 21-2; Bahrain 33-4; Belarus 37; Brazil 46; Burundi 50; Cambodia 51-2; Cameroon 53; Chad 59; China 62; Colombia 67; Cyprus 76; Democratic Republic of the Congo 80; Equatorial Guinea 91; Ethiopia 95; Guatemala 110; Honduras 116-7; India 122; Iran 126; Malawi 168-9; Maldives 171; Mexico 179-80; Palestinian Authority 206; Paraguay 209; Peru 210; Russian Federation 219-20; South Africa 242; Sri Lanka 249-50; Venezuela 294

I

impunity
Algeria 22; Argentina 26; Bahrain 32-3; Bolivia 40; Brazil 44; Burkina Faso 49; Burundi 49; Chile 60; Colombia 67; Côte d'Ivoire 71-2; Democratic Republic of the Congo 79-80; Dominican Republic 83; Egypt 87-8; El Salvador 89-90; Guatemala 110; Guinea 112; Haiti 116; India 120-1; Indonesia 124-5; Israel and the Occupied Palestinian Territories 134; Kenya 146; Kyrgyzstan 154-5; Lebanon 158; Liberia 159; Libya 163; Madagascar 167; Myanmar 190; Nepal 192; Palestinian Authority 206-7; Panama 207; Peru 211; Philippines 212; Rwanda 222; Suriname 253; Syria 261-2; Timor-Leste 268; Togo 270; Turkey 275-6; Ukraine 281; United States of America 288; Uruguay 291; Venezuela 294; Yemen 298

Indigenous Peoples' rights
Argentina 25; Australia 27-8; Bangladesh 35-6; Bolivia 40; Canada 54-5; Chile 60-1; Colombia 65-6; Ecuador 85; Guatemala 110; Mexico 180; Paraguay 209; Peru 210-11; Taiwan 263

internal armed conflict
Colombia 65; Myanmar 188; Thailand 266-7

international justice
Austria 28; Bosnia and Herzegovina 42; Cambodia 52; Chad 59; Côte d'Ivoire 71; Croatia 73; Democratic Republic of the Congo 80-1; El Salvador 90; Finland 98; Germany 105; Kenya 147-8; Mongolia 182-3; Netherlands 193; Niger 196; Norway 200; Rwanda 223; Senegal 228; Serbia 228-9; Sudan 251; Uganda 279-80; Ukraine 283

international scrutiny
Colombia 68; Korea (Democratic People's Republic of) 150; Latvia 157; Lithuania 165; Portugal 214; Venezuela 295

J

justice system

Bolivia 40; Bosnia and Herzegovina 42; Burundi 50; China 61-2; Côte d'Ivoire 71; El Salvador 90; Fiji 98; Ghana 106; Haiti 116; Honduras 117; Hungary 118; Jamaica 140; Japan 141; Liberia 159; Libya 164; Nigeria 198; Palestinian Authority 206; Paraguay 209; Russian Federation 220-1; Sierra Leone 232; Sri Lanka 250; Taiwan 263; Trinidad and Tobago 270; Ukraine 282

L

land disputes

Laos 156; Myanmar 189

legal, constitutional or institutional developments

Belgium 39; Estonia 94; France 100; Ireland 132; Italy 139; Netherlands 193; New Zealand 194; Norway 200; South Africa 240-1; Swaziland 254-5; Switzerland 257

lesbian, gay, bisexual and transgender people (rights of)

Albania 20; Bahamas 31; Bosnia and Herzegovina 43; Bulgaria 48; Cameroon 54; Georgia 104; Ghana 106; Greece 109; Guyana 114; Hungary 119; Iran 127; Italy 137; Jamaica 141; Lebanon 158; Liberia 160; Lithuania 165; Malawi 169; Malta 175; New Zealand 194; Nigeria 199; Serbia 229; Slovakia 235; South Africa 241; Taiwan 263; Trinidad and Tobago 270; Turkey 277; Uganda 279; Ukraine 282; Uruguay 291; Zimbabwe 302

M

maternal health

Burkina Faso 49; Nepal 192; South Africa 242

migrants' rights (see also *refugees, internally displaced, asylum-seekers and migrants*)

Czech Republic 77; Dominican Republic 83; Jordan 143; Korea (Republic of) 151; Mauritania 176-7; Mexico 179; United States of America 289-90

P

police and security forces

Angola 23; Austria 28-9; Bahamas 31; Canada 55; Chile 60; Cyprus 76; Denmark 82; Dominican Republic 83; Guyana 113-4; Indonesia 123; Ireland 132; Jamaica 140; Mozambique 186; Peru 210; Puerto Rico 215; Sierra Leone 232; Switzerland 256; Timor-Leste 268; Trinidad and Tobago 270; United Kingdom 286

political prisoners

Eritrea 92; Mauritania 176; South Sudan 245

prison conditions

Argentina 26; Belgium 38; Benin 39; Burundi 50; Cameroon 54; Chad 58; Democratic Republic of the Congo 80; Gambia 102; Greece 109; Honduras 117; Ireland 132; Israel and the Occupied Palestinian Territories 135; Liberia 159; Mozambique 187; Namibia 191; Palestinian Authority 205; Switzerland 257;

Togo 270; Trinidad and Tobago 271; Turkmenistan 278; United States of America 289; Uruguay 291; Venezuela 294

prisoners of conscience

Angola 24; Azerbaijan 29; Bahrain 34; Belarus 36-7; Central African Republic 57; Congo (Republic of) 69; Cuba 74-5; Equatorial Guinea 92; Eritrea 92; Finland 98; Mauritania 176; Rwanda 224; Viet Nam 296

R

racism

Austria 29; Spain 247

refugees, internally displaced, asylum-seekers and migrants

Afghanistan 19; Australia 28; Austria 29; Bahamas 31; Belgium 39; Bulgaria 48; Canada 55; China 64; Congo (Republic of) 69; Côte d'Ivoire 71; Cyprus 75-6; Czech Republic 77; Democratic Republic of the Congo 79; Denmark 82; Dominican Republic 83; Egypt 89; Eritrea 93; Estonia 94; Finland 98; France 100; Germany 105; Ghana 107; Greece 107-8, 108; Haiti 115; Hungary 118; Iraq 131; Israel and the Occupied Palestinian Territories 136; Italy 137-8; Japan 142; Jordan 143; Kazakhstan 146; Kenya 148; Korea (Republic of) 151; Kuwait 153; Latvia 156; Lebanon 158; Liberia 159-60; Libya 162, 162-3; Macedonia 166; Malaysia 170; Malta 174-5; Mauritania 176-7; Mexico 179; Montenegro 183-4; Morocco/Western Sahara 185; Myanmar 188; Nepal 192; Netherlands 193; New Zealand 194; Norway 199-200; Poland 214; Qatar 215; Rwanda 224; Saudi Arabia 226; Serbia 229, 231; Somalia 238; South Africa 241; South Sudan 245; Spain 247-8; Sri Lanka 250; Sudan 251; Sweden 256; Switzerland 257; Syria 262; Tanzania 266; Thailand 267-8; Turkey 276-7; Uganda 280; Ukraine 281-2; United Kingdom 286-7; United States of America 289-90; Yemen 299

repression of dissent

Gambia 101-2; Morocco/Western Sahara 184-5; Saudi Arabia 224-5; Syria 261; Yemen 299

S

sexual and reproductive rights

Chile 61; Dominican Republic 83; El Salvador 90; Honduras 117; Nicaragua 195; Peru 211; Poland 213; Romania 217; Uruguay 291

T

torture and other ill-treatment

Albania 20; Argentina 26; Armenia 27; Austria 28; Azerbaijan 31; Bahrain 33; Bangladesh 35; Bulgaria 48; Burkina Faso 49; Congo (Republic of) 69; Côte d'Ivoire 70; Democratic Republic of the Congo 79; Denmark 81; Egypt 86; Eritrea 93; Ethiopia 96; Fiji 97-8; France 99; Germany 104-5; Greece 107; Guinea 111; Guinea-Bissau 113; Iran 127; Iraq 130; Israel and the Occupied Palestinian Territories 135-6; Italy 138-9; Jordan 142-3; Kazakhstan 144-5; Kuwait 152; Kyrgyzstan 153-4; Lebanon 157; Libya 161-2; Macedonia 166; Maldives 171; Mali 172-3; Mauritania 176; Mexico 178; Moldova 181; Morocco/Western Sahara 185; Nepal 192; Nicaragua 194-5; Niger 195; Nigeria 197;

Palestinian Authority 205; Philippines 212; Portugal 214; Qatar 216; Russian Federation 220; Saudi Arabia 226; Senegal 227; Singapore 233; Slovakia 235; South Sudan 245; Spain 246; Sri Lanka 249; Swaziland 255; Sweden 256; Syria 261; Tajikistan 263-5; Togo 269; Tunisia 273; Turkey 275; Turkmenistan 278; Uganda 280; Ukraine 280-1; United Arab Emirates 284; United Kingdom 284-5; Uzbekistan 292-3

trafficking in human beings
Eritrea 93

transitional justice
Morocco/Western Sahara 185; Nepal 191-2; Tunisia 272-3

U
unfair trials
Belgium 38; Democratic Republic of the Congo 80; Egypt 86-7; Iran 127; Jordan 143; Kyrgyzstan 145; Kyrgyzstan 154; Lebanon 157-8; Mongolia 182; Rwanda 223; Swaziland 255; Turkey 276

unlawful killings
Albania 20; Guinea-Bissau 113; Italy 139; Libya 164; Madagascar 167; Mozambique 187; Nigeria 197; Pakistan 202; Philippines 211-2

V
violence against women and girls
Afghanistan 18-9; Bahamas 32; Bangladesh 35; Central African Republic 57; Chad 59; Colombia 68; Democratic Republic of the Congo 79; Denmark 82; Dominican Republic 83; Finland 98; Ghana 106; Guyana 114; Haiti 115; India 120; Ireland 132; Italy 139; Jamaica 140; Japan 141; Jordan 143; Liberia 160; Mali 173-4; Mexico 180; Namibia 191; Nicaragua 195; Norway 200; Pakistan 203-4; Palestinian Authority 206; Papua New Guinea 208; Portugal 214; Qatar 216; South Africa 242; Spain 247; Switzerland 257; Tajikistan 265; Tanzania 266; Trinidad and Tobago 270; Turkey 277; United Kingdom 286; Venezuela 295

W
women's rights
Algeria 22; Argentina 25-6; Bolivia 41; Bosnia and Herzegovina 43; Brazil 47; Canada 55; Egypt 88; Indonesia 124; Kuwait 153; Lebanon 158; Libya 163; Morocco/Western Sahara 185; New Zealand 194; Nigeria 199; Oman 201; Saudi Arabia 226; South Africa 242; Swaziland 255-6; Timor-Leste 268; Tunisia 273-4; United States of America 290

workers' rights
Bangladesh 36; China 64; Korea (Republic of) 151; Nepal 192; Qatar 215; Saudi Arabia 226

* This is an index of topics based around the subheadings that appear in the A-Z country entries. It should be used by the reader only as a navigational tool, not as a statement of Amnesty International's human rights concerns in a particular country or territory.